Mate Threats and Defense
1000 Tactical Examples

Jakov Geller

Mate Threats and Defense – 1000 Tactical Examples
Author: Jakov Geller

Translated from the Russian by Alexei Zakharov
Edited by Vladimir Barsky
Typesetting by Andrei Elkov
Front cover artwork by Maxim Borisov
© LLC Elk and Ruby Publishing House, 2022

Follow us on Twitter: @ilan_ruby
www.elkandruby.com
ISBN 978-5-6047849-2-1

Contents

Introduction

Tactics are an integral part of any chess game. During the game, even the most ingenious strategic ideas may not lead to a win without the clear calculations of lines. Any tactical line, in turn, may also be divided into component parts, each of them consisting of one tactical pattern or a standard combination of several techniques. Chess players should have good knowledge of all tactical blows and standard combinations as well as a good sense of timing for such tactical blows. Further, they should strive to make a minimal number of mistakes during calculation.

This book studies those chess tactics called "mate threats"; it is a direct sequel to the book *1500 Forced Mates* that I published with Elk and Ruby in 2021. In my system for comprehensively studying chess tactics, the subject of mate threats comes second because it's a logical continuation of the study of the greatest tactical gain possible – checkmate of the enemy king. To solve the examples from this book, you don't need to possess a wealth of chess knowledge – it's enough to be able to give a forced checkmate. By studying the hundreds of combinations contained in this book, the reader will both learn to checkmate the king with the help of moves other than direct checks and hone one of the most difficult chess skills – the art of defense. He will also understand such important concepts as "threat" and "defending from threat", which are necessary for further tactical studies!

The book is divided into 28 chapters, with most of them focused on defense from mate threats. Nine defensive techniques are given their own chapters. At the beginning of every such chapter, there's a thorough theoretical explanation of the technique with several training examples and their solutions, and then a number of exercises for the reader to solve on their own. The defensive technique chapters are supplemented by "Combination" chapters, to consolidate and test the acquired knowledge. These chapters also feature theoretical basics of the combinations studied and several training examples with solutions, but to solve the exercises, the reader will need to combine several different defensive techniques he learned from previous chapters. With every new defensive technique studied, the combinations in subsequent chapters become increasingly diverse. The difficulty level of exercises in each chapter also gradually increases.

The remaining chapters focus on attacking – mate threats and combinations. They explain all the different elements of mating tactics, and the exercises will help hone the reader's acquired skills in combinations that mix various themes.

The final part makes this book useful even for highly-skilled chess players, because it's a universal test that checks the player's skills in executing mating combinations and finding the best defense against them, while also uncovering their weaknesses – such as defensive technique that constantly escapes attention or erroneous calculation of simple, but long lines. It contains 300 exercises split into three chapters with subheadings: Find the Mating Combination, Find the Best Defense Against the Mate Threat, and Find the Best Continuation. Even the strongest players will have to think hard to find the correct solutions in the last chapter!

All exercises from this book have been subject to a thorough computer check; every effort has been made to eliminate errors or alternative solutions. The defensive tactics especially stand out in this regard: in every exercise, one of the defensive moves will always be stronger than all the others.

In actual games, you don't as a rule look for a mate or a defense using a particular technique. For a strong player, it's usually enough to get an overwhelming position to win, while to defend against checkmate, he first and foremost tries to avoid hopeless positions. The same requirement is set for each example in this book. Rather than seeking a solution based on the studied technique, you should simply be seeking the strongest continuation! In every exercise, white creates mate threats against the black king or demonstrates an admirable defensive combination that stands out from the alternatives and enables him to win or draw.

Methodological Recommendations

The volume of available study material grows every year, and it becomes progressively harder to navigate the information streams of the modern world. All too often, to find truly useful and correctly selected material, you need to sift through dozens of poor-quality resources. We must also add that even a set of exercises that was considered optimal just a decade ago might already be obsolete and ineffective today. All the while, chess is getting progressively younger, and professional players have less and less time to learn. Thus, in my opinion, the quality of methodical literature is now paramount. One of the main goals of this work is to create an "ideal" tactical textbook for exercises on each specific subject. To that end, the following principles were followed in the book:

• A clearly arranged system setting the order of study of every subject;
• The opportunity to hone and check your skills with the studied material;
• A gradual increase in the level of difficulty of the exercises;

- There are no unsolvable exercises included;
- The number of alternative solutions is minimized.

The logically ordered system of tactical study in this book can become a foundation for working with younger players. I have used this system many times when working with my pupils, and it has proved its practical worth. In conjunction with carefully prepared examples, it turns the book into a universal textbook useful both for players and coaches. An experienced chess teacher will be able to supplement the presented exercises with more examples if needed, slowly building their own database for every chapter.

Tactical vision

Not all games can be won thanks to even a thorough study of core tactics. When you have limited time, there's no point in searching for a complicated winning line on every move, because often no such line exists. Thus, during the game the player must instinctively sense when to stop and calculate concrete lines. It's important to understand that none of the following conditions guarantees that the game will be won with an immediate tactic. Rather, it should prompt the player to ask whether he should search for a forced mate in the given position.

In the following cases, it might be useful to search for mate threats or a forced mate:

- The opposing king is targeted by a large number of your pieces;
- One of your long-range pieces (queen, rook, bishop) is X-raying the king;
- A battery of your pieces is directed towards the opposing king;
- The opposing king is exposed (fully or partially lacking pawn cover);
- There's a weak square (or squares) in immediate proximity to the opposing king;
- The opponent's back rank is poorly defended;
- The opposing king is blocked (has only a few possible moves);
- Most of the opposing pieces are positioned far away from their king.

Finally, it's important to understand that the list of conditions for carrying out other tactical blows would be quite different.

Mate Threats and Defense – a Schematic Representation

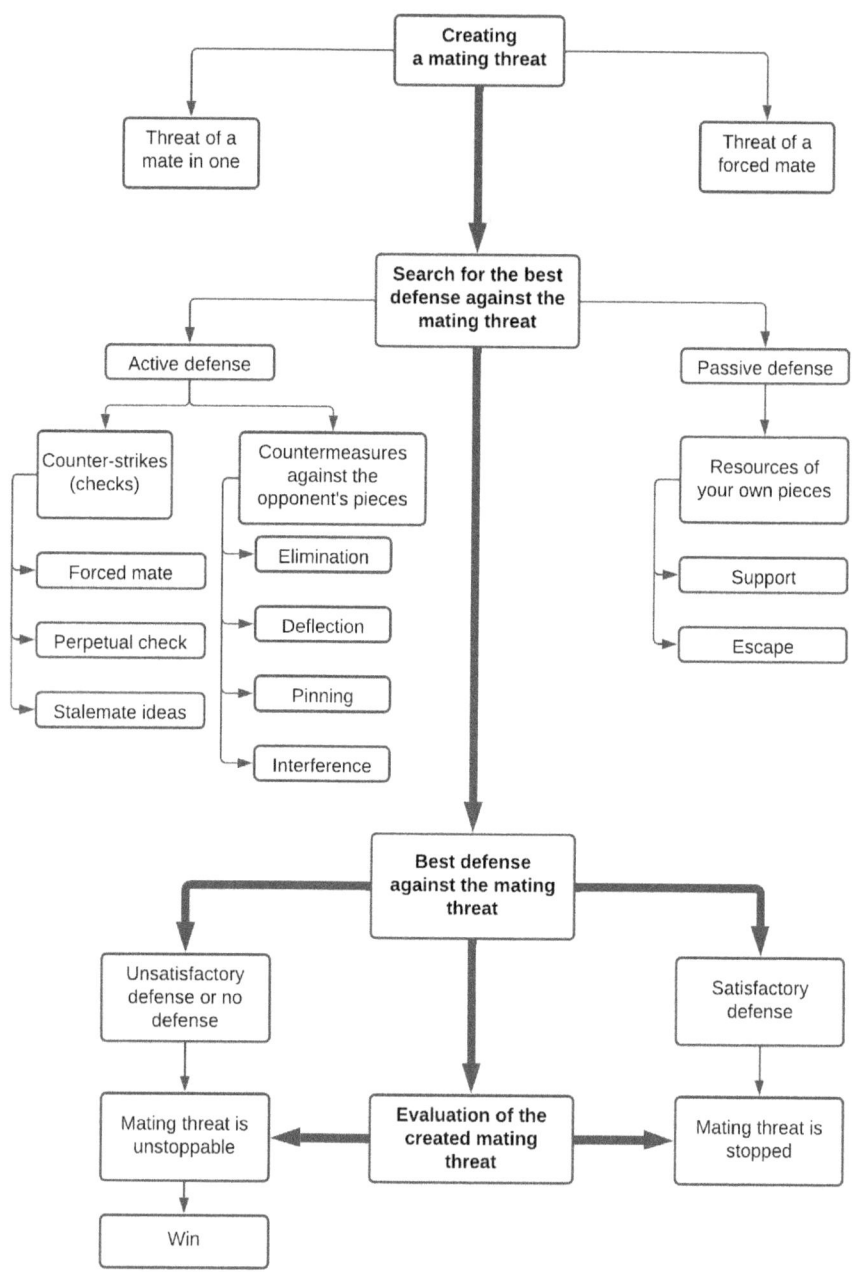

Part 1

Basic Concepts

There are several fundamental concepts of chess tactics, and if you don't understand them, it's virtually impossible to compete on the highest level. This book studies three of those concepts, looking at them from the point of view of a possible checkmate.

The first basic concept is called the "mate threat". Mate threats can technically be divided into the threat of mate in one and the threat of a forced mate (mate in several moves). In practice, such a split is unimportant, and both concepts are known as "mate threats".

The second basic concept is "defense against a mate threat" – all possible countermeasures against the threat of checkmate. The main goal of defense against a mate threat, rather than stopping the checkmate itself, is to ensure that you can continue the game. A strong chess player should be able to apply all nine existing defensive techniques against mate threats and know how to calculate them.

The third basic concept is "satisfactory defense". It's important both for creating mate threats and calculating defensive lines. Any defense against mate can be characterized in two ways, depending on the nature of the subsequent position: satisfactory (a defense that does not lead to a hopeless position) or unsatisfactory. If the opponent doesn't have a satisfactory defense, the creation of a mate threat becomes a valuable tactical blow! Otherwise, mate threats might give no benefits at all or even turn out to be harmful.

The ability to create mate threats and mating combinations and find the strongest defense against them is a very important part of every player's tactical mastery. Before studying the next parts of this textbook, it's recommended that you learn the basic concepts and check your knowledge by solving the exercises below. Most exercises in this part don't require complex calculations; their solutions are short and fairly simple, but the reader still has to understand the essence of the studied positions.

Chapter 1

THREAT OF A MATE IN ONE

In chess, a threat means the full readiness of one side to reach his goal. The turn to move, however, belongs to the second player, and he can, in theory, prevent the opponent from making the threatened move. In other words, he can defend against the threat. The threat may entail material gains or other beneficial factors, such as changing the pawn structure, improving a piece's position or much else. The most important purpose of a threat is checkmate – the most valuable tactical gain of all.

The concept of a threat of a mate in one, studied in this chapter, implies that one side is ready to checkmate the opponent's king in one move. In every upcoming example, white will have several ways to create a threat of mate in one to the black king. Only one of these moves will be winning, however, and other attempts to checkmate black can be repelled easily enough. To solve the exercises in this chapter, you need to find all the moves that create the threat of a mate in one, and then choose the strongest one. Please note that the move that creates a mate threat cannot be a check.

1

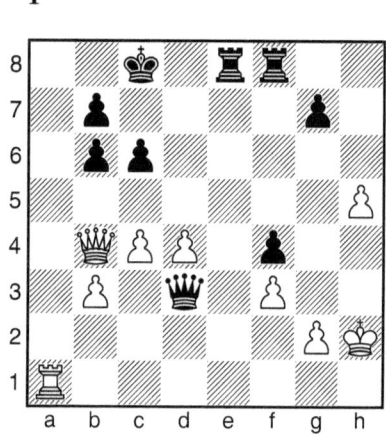

While searching for the moves that create a mate threat, you may see that it's much easier to checkmate the black king when it has very few possible moves. In this position, there are only two ways to create the threat of a mate in one: **1.♕d6!** and 1.♕e7?. In both cases, white threatens **2.♖a8#**, but while in the first case white immediately wins because any possible move by black is met with checkmate, in the second case, black can just capture the white queen, repelling the mate threat and winning easily.

This first example shows us that a mate threat is not a tactical combination in and of itself, because it does not necessarily lead to a mating finale. A mate threat just means that you are ready to deliver checkmate if it's your move, and it can lead to any result, depending on your opponent's defensive resources.

2

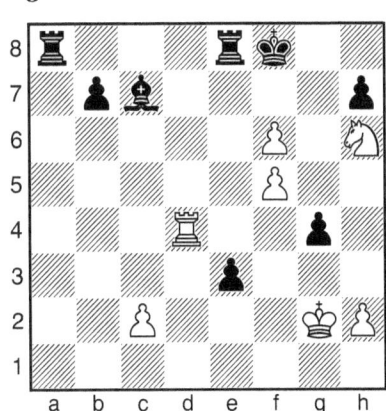

The black king has only one escape square. To create the threat of a mate in one, it's logical to try to gain control of this square, which can be done with 1.♖g8??, threatening 2.♖2g7#. However, it's easy for black to repel the threat: he can just capture the blundered piece. Another possible mate-in-one threat is 1.♗xf8?!, with the idea 2.♖xh6#, but this does not lead to a win either, since after 1...♖xf8, the best thing white can count on is 2.♖g7+ ♔h8 3.♖7g6! ♔h7, with a draw by repetition. Only the third mate threat is winning: **1.♗c1!**, and there is no way to prevent **2.♖xh6#.**

Notice the difference between 1.♗c1! and 1.♗xf8?! – it's not beneficial for white to win an exchange, because checkmate is a much more important tactical gain.

3

Here, the black king has no legal moves. In such situations, it's often said that the king is in a "mating net": white pieces cut off all escape routes for the black monarch.

To deliver checkmate, white only needs to prepare and execute a check to the king, which can be done with 1.♖d7?, threatening 2.♖f7#. Black, however, has a way to save the game in this case: he can play 1...♖e4! (or 1...♖e5), freeing up the e8 square for his king and allowing him to escape the mating net: 2.♖f7+ ♔e8 etc.

But white has a much stronger move **1.♖xg4!**, and now black has no defense against the threat **2.♖g8#.** Obviously, this is the strongest continuation.

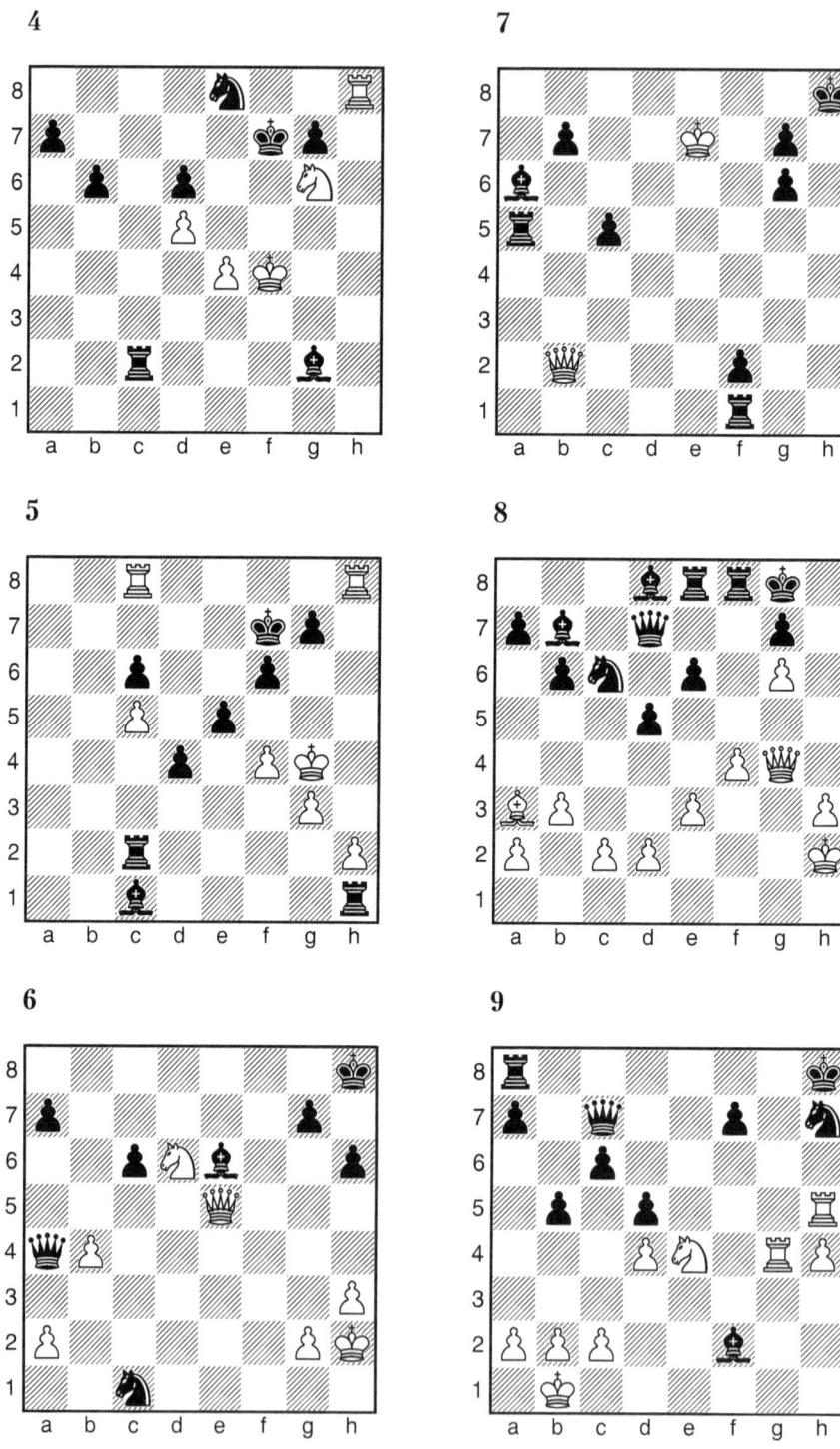

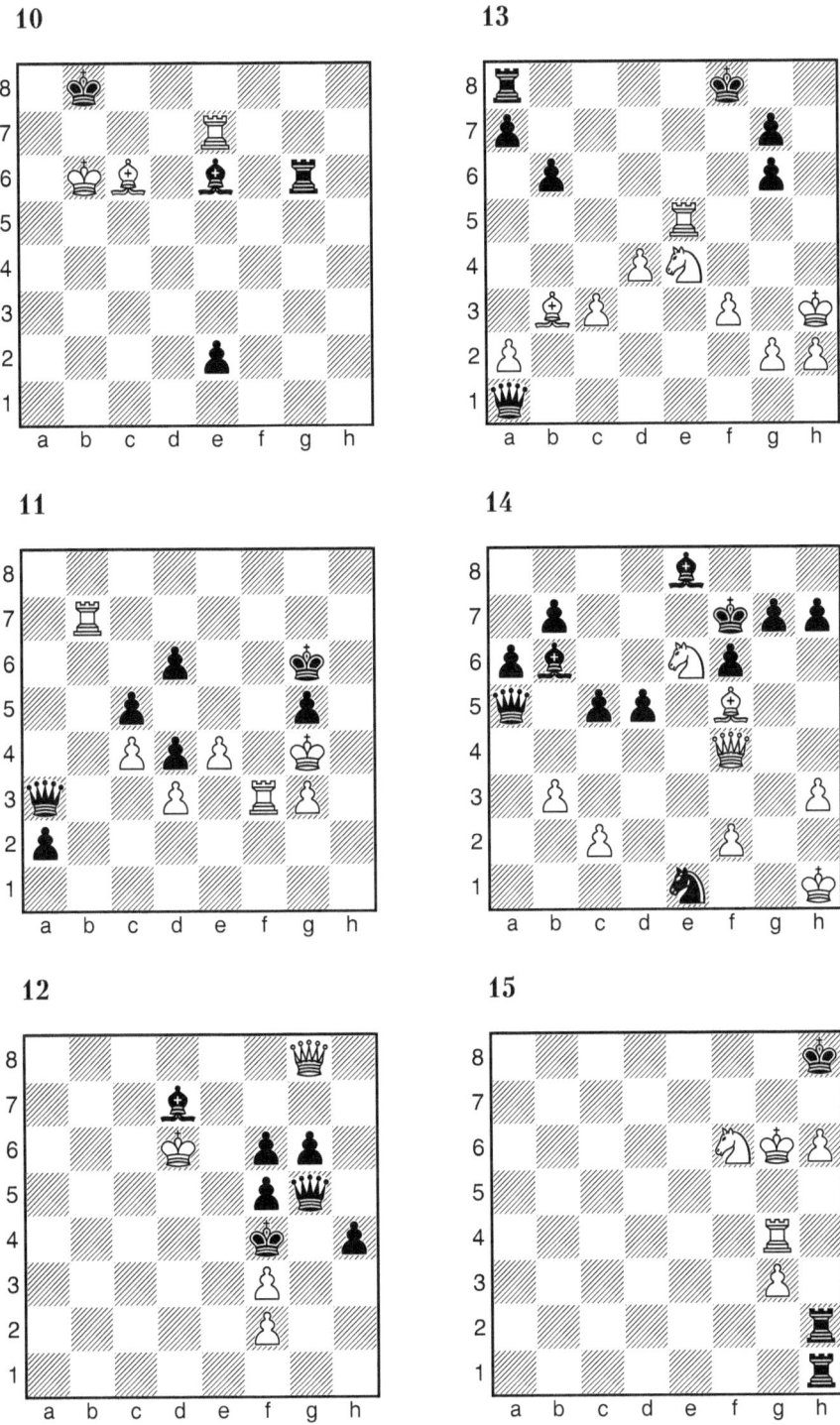

10

11

12

13

14

15

Chapter 2

THREAT OF A FORCED MATE

The threat of a forced mate is quite similar to the threat of a mate in one that we studied in the previous chapter. The only difference is the number of moves a player needs to checkmate his opponent's king. This number has no bearing on the game's final result, but we should point out that finding the threat of a forced mate (mate in several moves) can be much harder than spotting the mate-in-one threat. Readers who have thoroughly studied my book *1500 Forced Mates* will know well that even delivering a forced mate can be a challenge in itself, and creating the threat of a forced mate requires going at least one move deeper in the calculations. In practice, the distinction between threats of a mate in one move or in more moves does not exist, and they are lumped together under a single name, "mate threat".

In every exercise in this chapter, white can create the threat of a forced mate that black cannot defend against – any attempt to avoid white's planned mate in several moves will only result in an even faster mate.

16

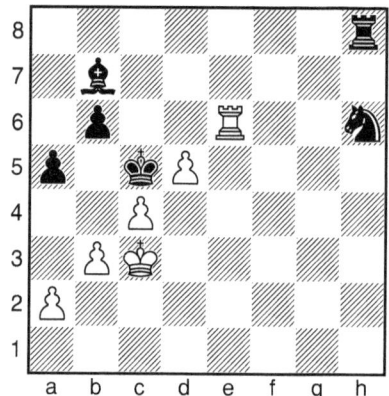

White immediately wins with the precise pawn move **1.a3!**, threatening a forced mate: **2.b4+ axb4+ 3.axb4#**. It's not hard to prove that black has no way to prevent 2.b4 with the subsequent seizing of this square and checkmate. We should point out that black does have a way to avoid white's planned mate in another two moves: by playing 1...a4, he falls to an even quicker checkmate – 2.b4#.

The position above clearly shows the lack of obvious difference between the threats of a mate in one move and a forced mate. If we remove the rook pawns from the board, black will still lose even if he is to move, because he still has no defense from the original mate threat. The only difference is that now white threatens to checkmate him on b4 in one move, rather than two.

17

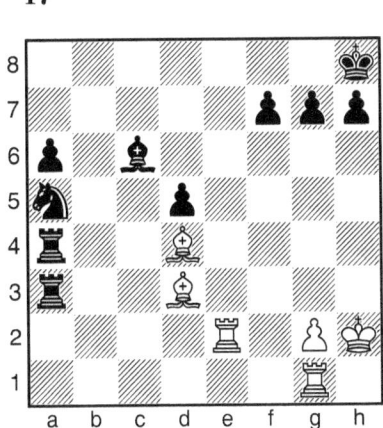

Both white bishops are en prise, but this doesn't make any difference here. After **1.♖ge1!**, he threatens a forced mate: **2.♖e8+ ♗xe8 3.♖xe8#**. It's easy to see that black has no defense against the white rook's mating incursion to the eighth rank. The only factor black can control is the number of moves he gets checkmated in: after 1...♗e8, 1...♗a8 or 1...♗b7 white mates in one, but after any other move, he mates in two.

In this example, as in the previous one, white uses the tactic of seizing the square; it didn't change the essence of the mate threat, but added one more move to the mating combination.

18

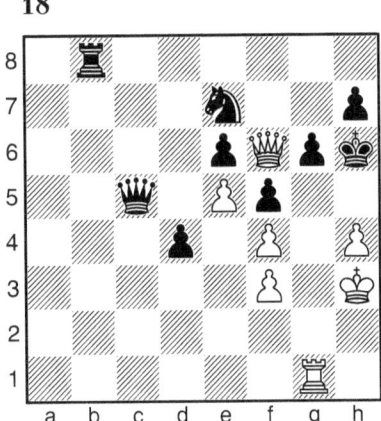

In this exercise, white is down a knight and pawn, but his pieces surrounded the black king, giving him clear conditions for the finishing mating blow. Indeed, after **1.♖g5!**, white creates the threat of a forced mate **2.♖h5+! ♔xh5 3.♕g5#**, which will be carried out on the next move, regardless of black's reply.

We should point out that the threat of a forced mate, like the threat of a mate in one, cannot be considered a mating combination in itself, because it doesn't always lead to the planned mating finale or even a good position. A mate threat just means that you are ready to deliver checkmate if it's your move, and it can lead to any result, depending on your opponent's defensive resources.

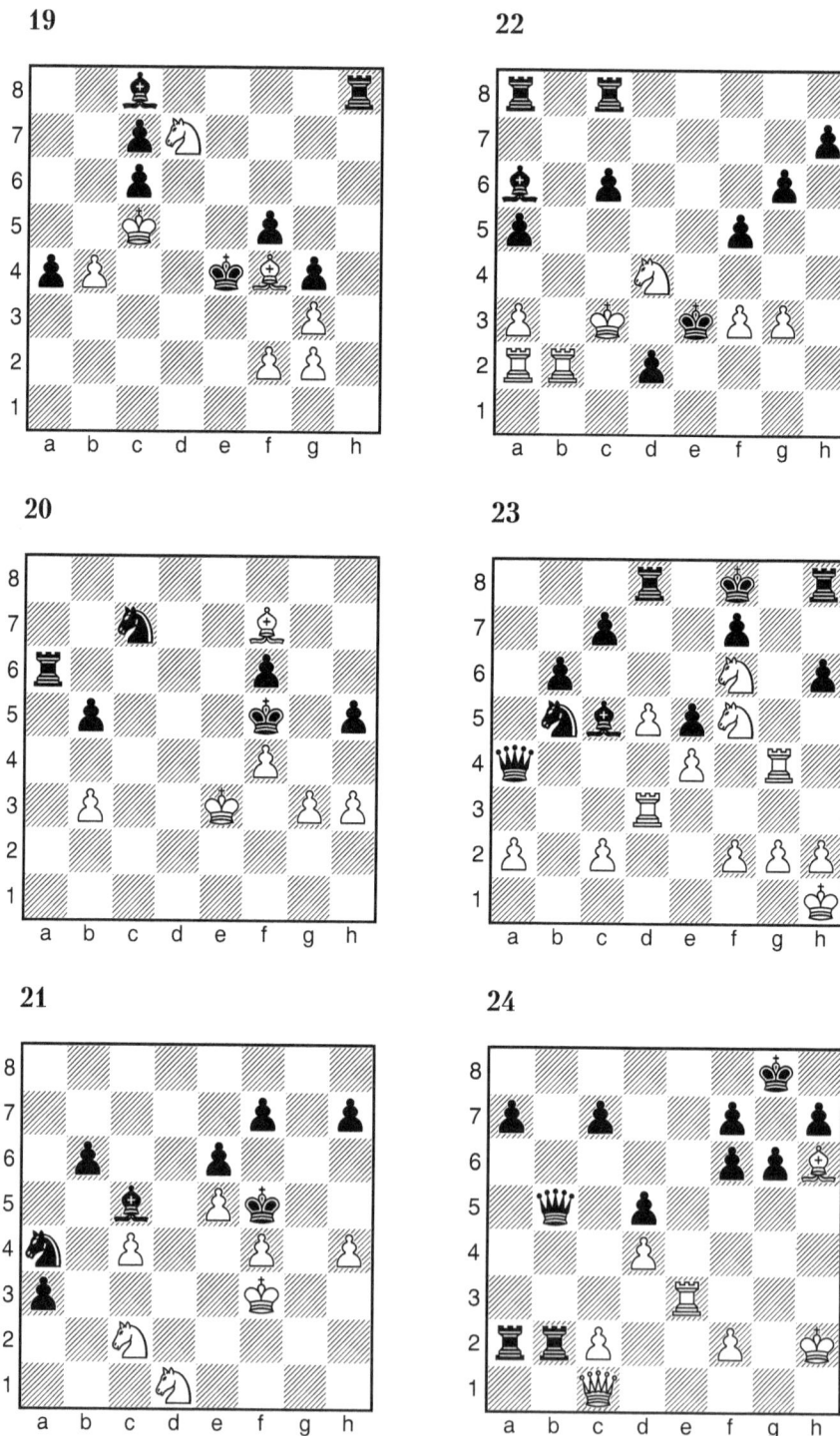

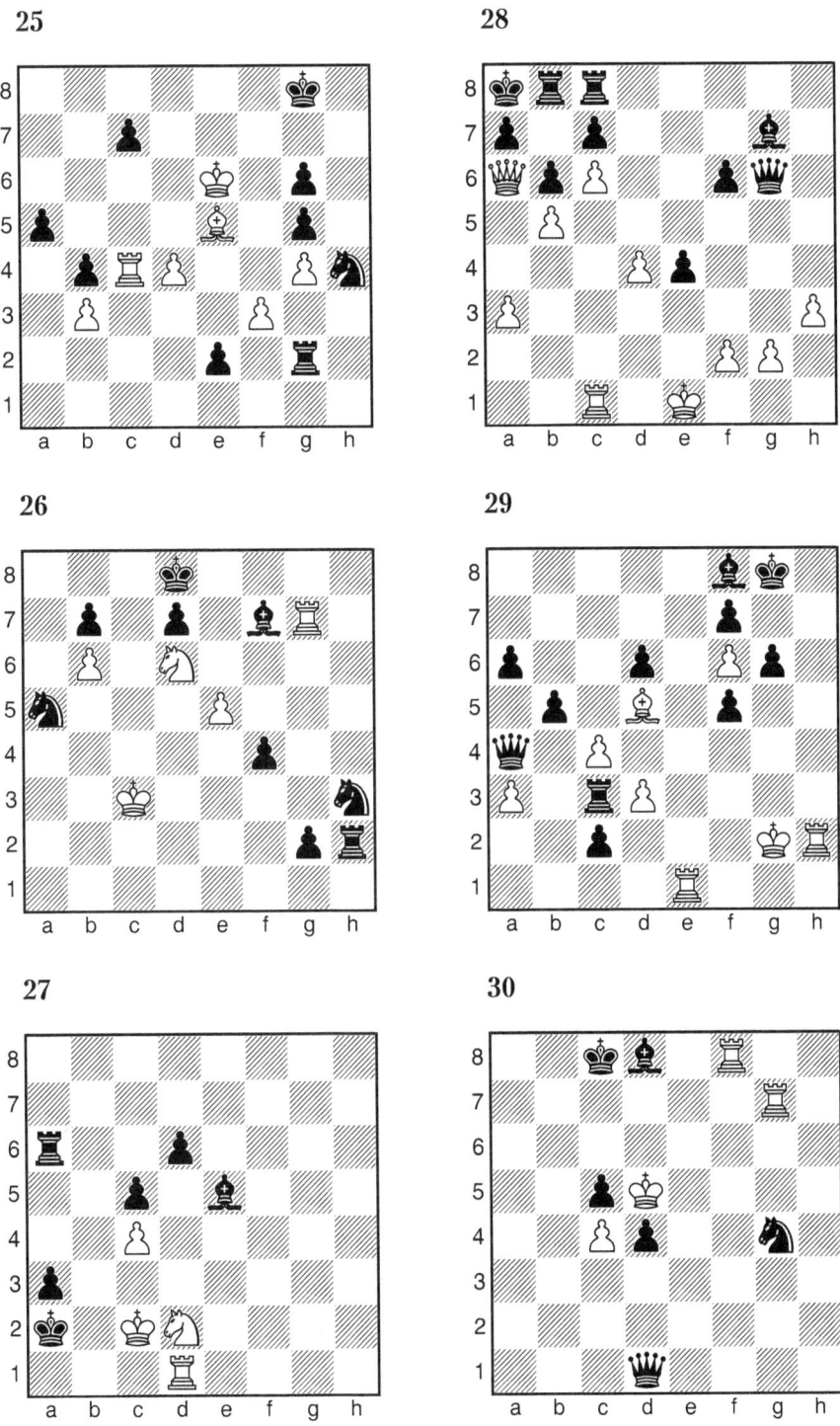

25

26

27

28

29

30

Chapter 3

DEFENDING AGAINST MATE THREATS

In chess, defense is finding countermeasures against the opponent's threats. To defend successfully, you should first identify what kind of threat your opponent has created, and then stop him from executing the threat with your next move. Defending from mate threats means finding successful countermeasures against your opponent's threat to checkmate you. Henceforth, the term "mate threat" means both the threat of a mate in one move and a forced mate in several moves, because both threats are the same for the defending side.

There are 9 defensive techniques in total, which can be divided into 3 groups: attack on your opponent's king ("counter-strike"), "countermeasures against your opponent's pieces", and "resources of your pieces". During the game, you should calculate your defensive resources in precisely this order!

A counter-strike against the mate threat is any attack on the opponent's king, including such tactics as forced mate, perpetual check (continuous attacks on the king) and stalemate ideas (forcing the opponent to stalemate you).

The second group of defensive tactics contains various countermeasures against the opponent's pieces: elimination, deflection, interference and pinning. Direct capture of the opponent's pieces can also be considered a specific case of elimination in the context of mate threats. The definitions of all these tactics should be well-known to the readers of *1500 Forced Mates*.

The third and final group, resources of your pieces, includes two more defensive tactics: escape and support, which mean escaping the danger zone with your king and supporting the potential mating squares with your pieces, respectively.

As part of a combination, defensive tactics can be used similarly to attacking ones: both separately and in conjunction. Tactics can be combined both sequentially, unfolding in a series of moves, or simultaneously, when a single move contains more than one tactical idea.

In each of the examples in this chapter, black has already created mate threats, but it's white to move, and he has just one way to defend, using one of the main defensive tactics.

31

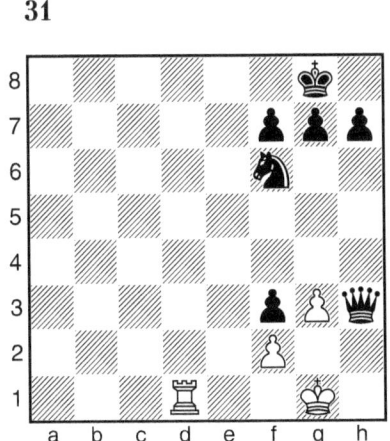

In the first position, black threatens 1...♕g2#. White defends with a forced mate of his own: **1.♖d8+! ♘e8 2.♖xe8#**.

32

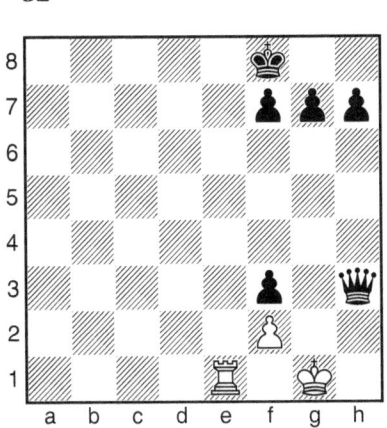

Black has created a mating net and threatens 1...♕g2#. However, unlike in the previous example, white uses a different counter-strike tactic: a stalemate idea. After the sudden **1.♖e8+! ♔xe8**, there's a stalemate on the board. Draw.

33

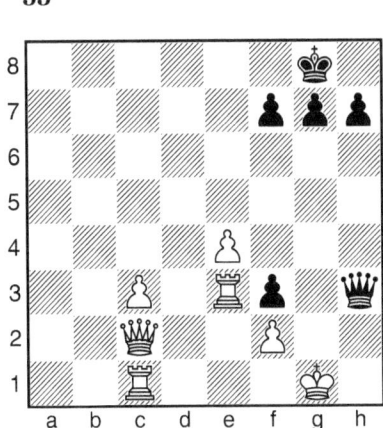

White has no checks, but he can use the elimination tactic: after **1.♖xf3!**, there's no mate threat anymore, and white still has extra material.

34

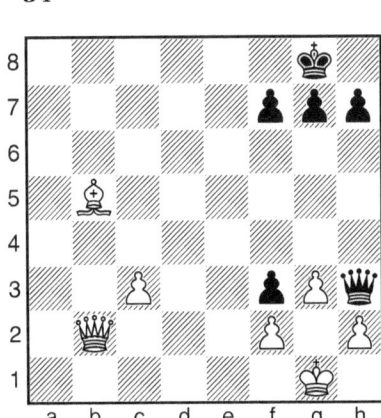

To defend, white needs to use "support": to gain control over the g2 mating square. He plays the accurate **1.♗f1!**, and black's position becomes hopeless.

35

38

36

39

37

40

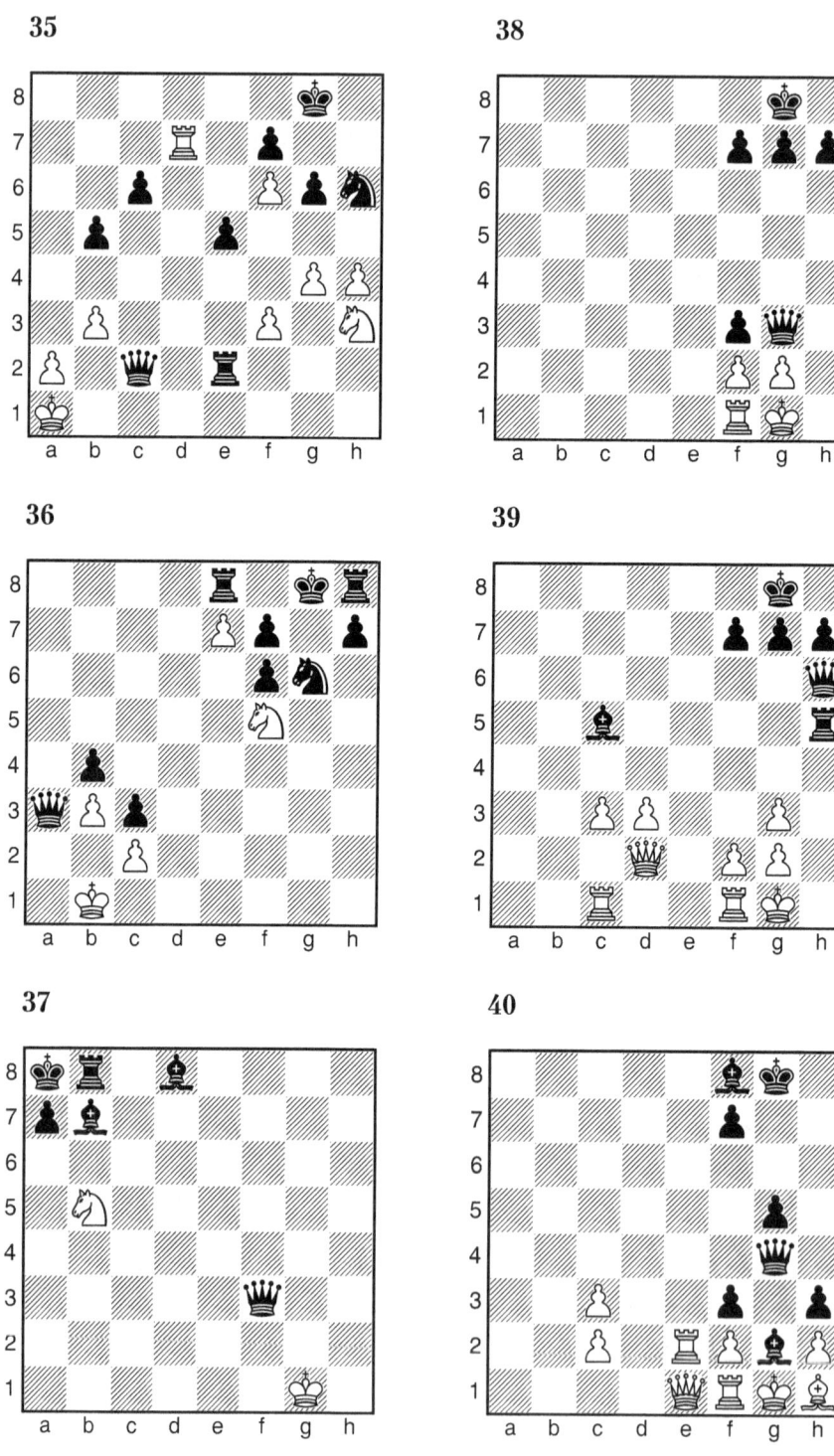

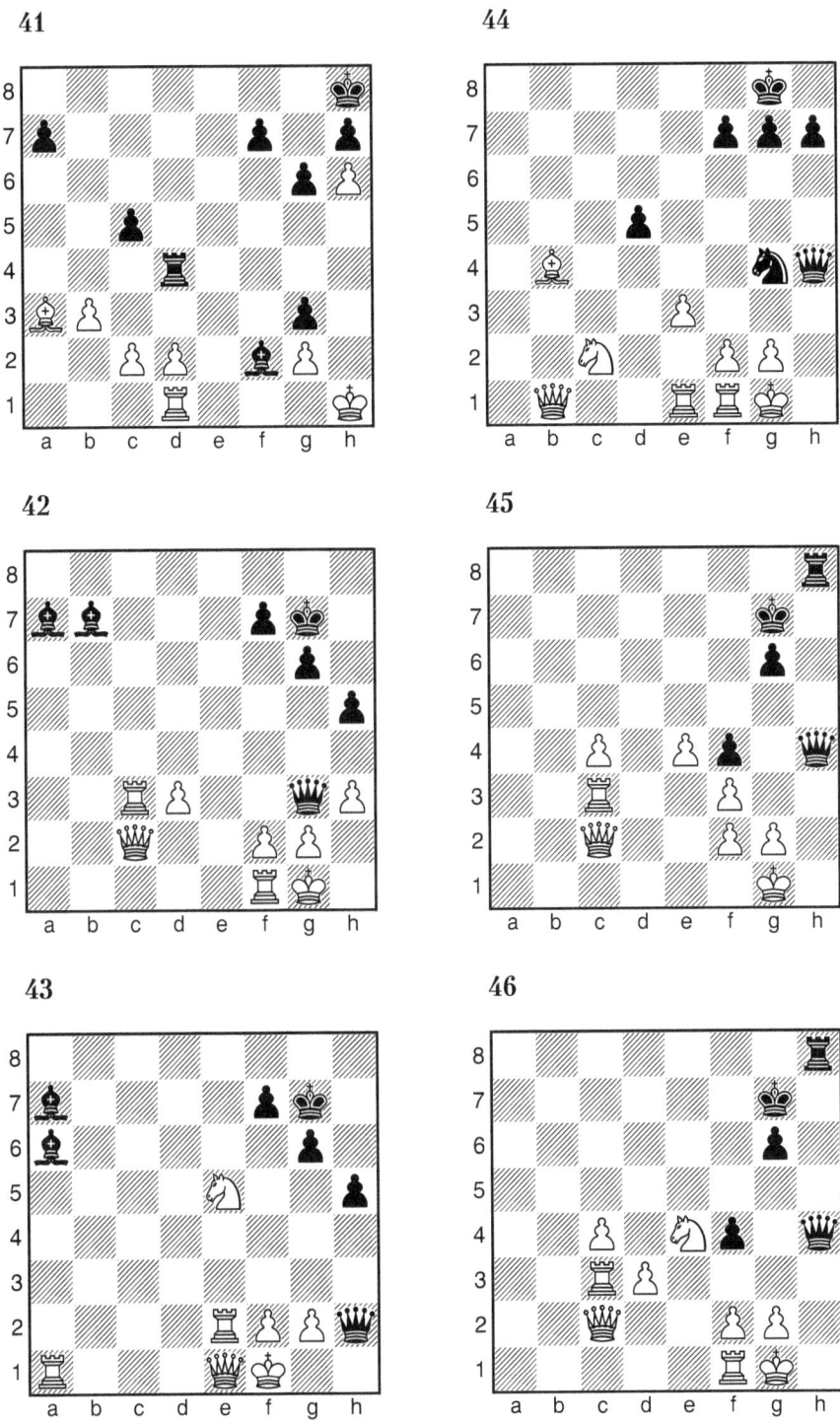

41

42

43

44

45

46

Chapter 4

SATISFACTORY DEFENSE

Satisfactory defense is a defensive tactic that ensures that the defending player's position is not hopeless even if his opponent plays perfectly. By contrast, if a move leads to a hopeless position, it usually isn't called a "defense" at all.

In the context of the possible creation of mate threats, the ability to determine whether a satisfactory defense exists plays a decisive role. A mate threat can be a tactical blow only if your opponent has no satisfactory defense. Otherwise, creating a mate threat can be essentially meaningless.

In each of the examples in this chapter, black has already created mate threats, but it's white to move, and he has several possible ways to prevent the impending mate. To solve the exercises correctly, it's recommended to find all possible moves that prevent immediate checkmate and then determine which of these moves constitute a "satisfactory defense". You should also try to find the best defense: in every exercise, one of the defending moves will always be much stronger than all the others.

47

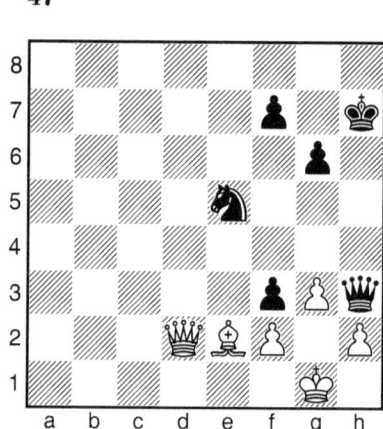

Black has created a mating net and threatens 1...♕g2#. White has to search for a defense, and the first thing he needs to do is check for counter-strikes, which only gives him a suicidal candidate move: 1.♕h6+. Then, checking for countermeasures against the opponent's pieces, white sees elimination – another suicidal move 1.♗xf3. Finally, checking for resources of his own pieces, white sees the support tactic – 1.♗f1. Technically, all three moves constitute defense from checkmate. However, the only satisfactory defense is **1.♗f1!** with a roughly equal position, and the other continuations obviously lose.

48

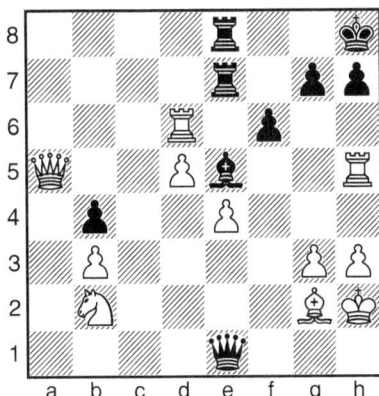

Black threatens mate in one: 1...♗xg3#. To find the best defense, let's look through all defensive resources available for white in the correct order.

You should always start your calculation with the search for counter-strikes, because white's forced play can turn out to be more dangerous than black's threat. However, the only available check in this position, 1.♖xh7+?, obviously loses.

The next defensive resource is attacking the pieces that threaten mate. As we start looking for ways to eliminate, deflect, pin or interfere with the black queen or bishop, we spot 1.♖xe5!?: this move eliminates the mate threat altogether and leads to a promising position for white.

The last stage of the search for defensive ideas is looking through the resources of your own pieces: supporting the potential mating squares or trying to escape the mating net with the king. The only way to

defend the g3 square is to put your rook en prise with 1.♖g5?, which is easily refuted with 1...fxg5. The king can escape the danger zone through the h3 or g2 squares, which gives us a number of possible but bad candidate moves: 1.h4?; 1.♗f1?; 1.♗f3? and 1.♗h1?. White, however, shouldn't spend too much time on calculating all these moves due to the same reply 1...♕xg3+ with a quick mate.

Therefore, **1.♖xe5!** is the only satisfactory defense from checkmate in this position; all other continuations lose quickly. Further line calculation allows us to evaluate this position as clearly in white's favor.

You should pay special attention to the order of defense resource calculation: counter-strike first, countermeasures against the opponent's pieces second, and resources of your own pieces last. After checking all the possibilities, you only have to choose the best among them, which is easy to do in this case.

49

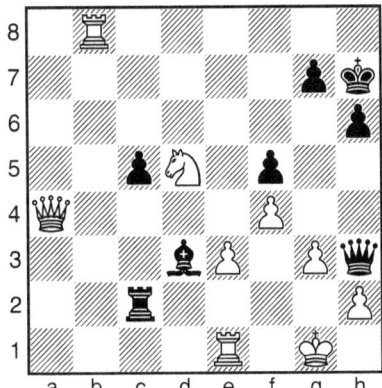

Black has created several mate threats, including 1...♛xh2#. To find the best defense to this move, let's compile a small list of candidate moves. First of all, we should look at counter-strikes; there are two in this position: 1.♖h8+ and 1.♞f6+. Then we see two more candidate moves as we search for countermeasures against enemy pieces – elimination 1.♛xc2 and interference 1.♖e2. Let's look at all four continuations in the "correct" order.

After the counter-strike 1.♖h8+!? ♚xh8 2.♛e8+ ♚h7, white can continue the attack with 3.♞f6+!, and after 3...gxf6 4.♛f7+ ♚h8 5.♛f8+ the game ends in a perpetual check. We should point out that white shouldn't stop immediately after calculating this line. He already has a guaranteed draw, but what if he has a winning move as well?

Finding the winning move shouldn't be difficult; after **1.♞f6+!**, black gets checkmated in all lines: **1...gxf6 2.♖b7+** and **3.♛e8#** after any reply, or **1...♚g6 2.♛e8+ ♚xf6 3.♖b6#**. A forced mate is always the best defense, therefore, there's no sense to calculate further lines in an actual game: white should just make the winning move.

Still, for the big picture, let's check the two remaining continuations. 1.♛xc2!? ♗xc2 leads to a complicated position that is roughly equal after the precise 2.♖b7!, while 1.♖e2? loses to 1...♖c1+! 2.♚f2 ♖f1#.

All in all, white has a choice between three satisfactory defensive resources – 1.♖h8+, 1.♞f6+ and 1.♛xc2. The best of these lines is the one that immediately leads to a win – **1.♞f6+!**.

Pay attention to the difference between the best and satisfactory defense. Best defense is the strongest move in a position that can still lead to any result, including defeat. Satisfactory defense is an opportunity for the defending side to avoid a loss. The player who creates a mate threat should be sure that his opponent has no way to avoid a hopeless position. Only in this case does a mate threat turn into a tactical combination!

50

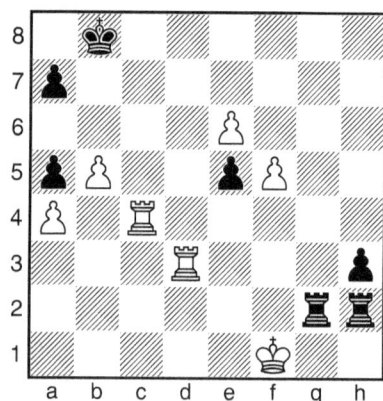

Black threatens 1...♖h1#. Calculating the defensive possibilities in the correct order, we find three candidate moves: 1.♖d8+; 1.♖c8+ and 1.♖xh3.

Counter-strike is considered the most important defensive resource, so we should start our calculations with 1.♖d8+!? After the forced

1...♔b7, white's attack continues: 2.♖d7+ ♔b8 (white quickly mates after 2...♔a8? 3.♖c8# or 2...♔b6? 3.♖c6#) 3.♖d8+ ♔b7 4.♖d7+ ♔b8 5.♖d8+, and the games ends in a perpetual check. The position after 1.♖d8+ is hence drawn.

The rook sacrifice 1.♖c8+? is also a counter-strike, attracting the black king to c8. However, after 1...♔xc8 black gains a decisive material advantage and white is simply lost.

Elimination of one of the threatening pieces with **1.♖xh3!** liquidates the mate threat, since 1...♖h1+?! is now met with 2.♔xg2 or 2.♖xh1 with an easy win for white. The trade 1...♖xh3 2.♔xg2 is no good for black either, because in the resulting rook endgame white has an extra pawn and a pair of very dangerous passed pawns, which tilts the evaluation in his favor. The only attempt for black is to create an attack on the king, but the threat of forced mate 1...♖a2!? (or 1...♖b2, or 1...♖d2) is again easily refuted by elimination 2.♖xh2!, and the perpetual check idea **1...♖f2+** doesn't work either due to **2.♔e1 ♖e2+ 3.♔d1 ♖d2+ 4.♔c1.** Thus, the position after 1.♖xh3! is evaluated as "white is better".

Comparing the evaluation of all three lines, we come to the conclusion that white has two satisfactory defenses from the checkmate threat: 1.♖xh3! and 1.♖d8+!?. **1.♖xh3!** is the best defense, because only this move gives white an advantage.

After choosing the strongest defensive move, you need to go back to your preferred line and search for your opponent's possible replies that you may not have accounted for.

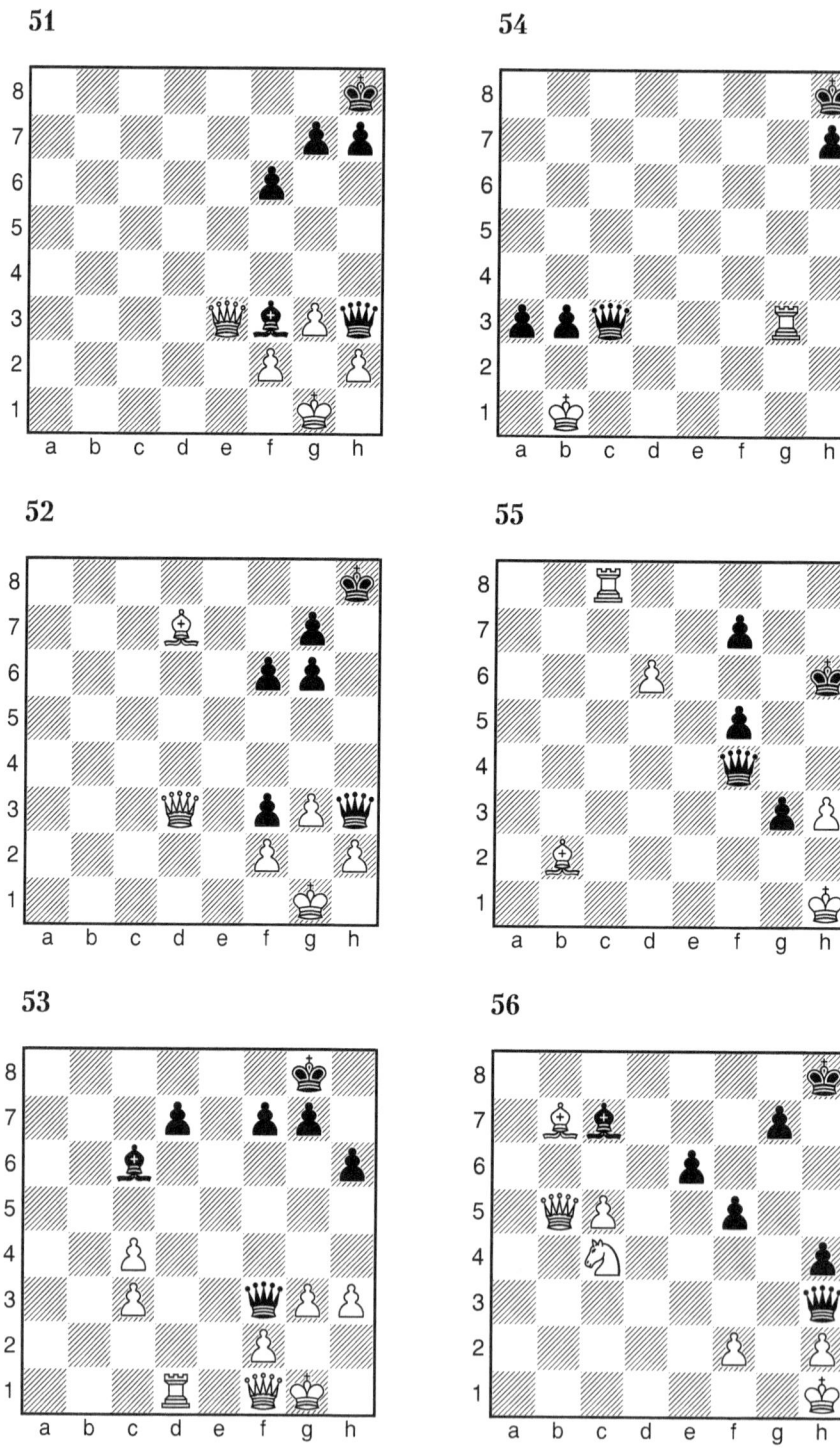

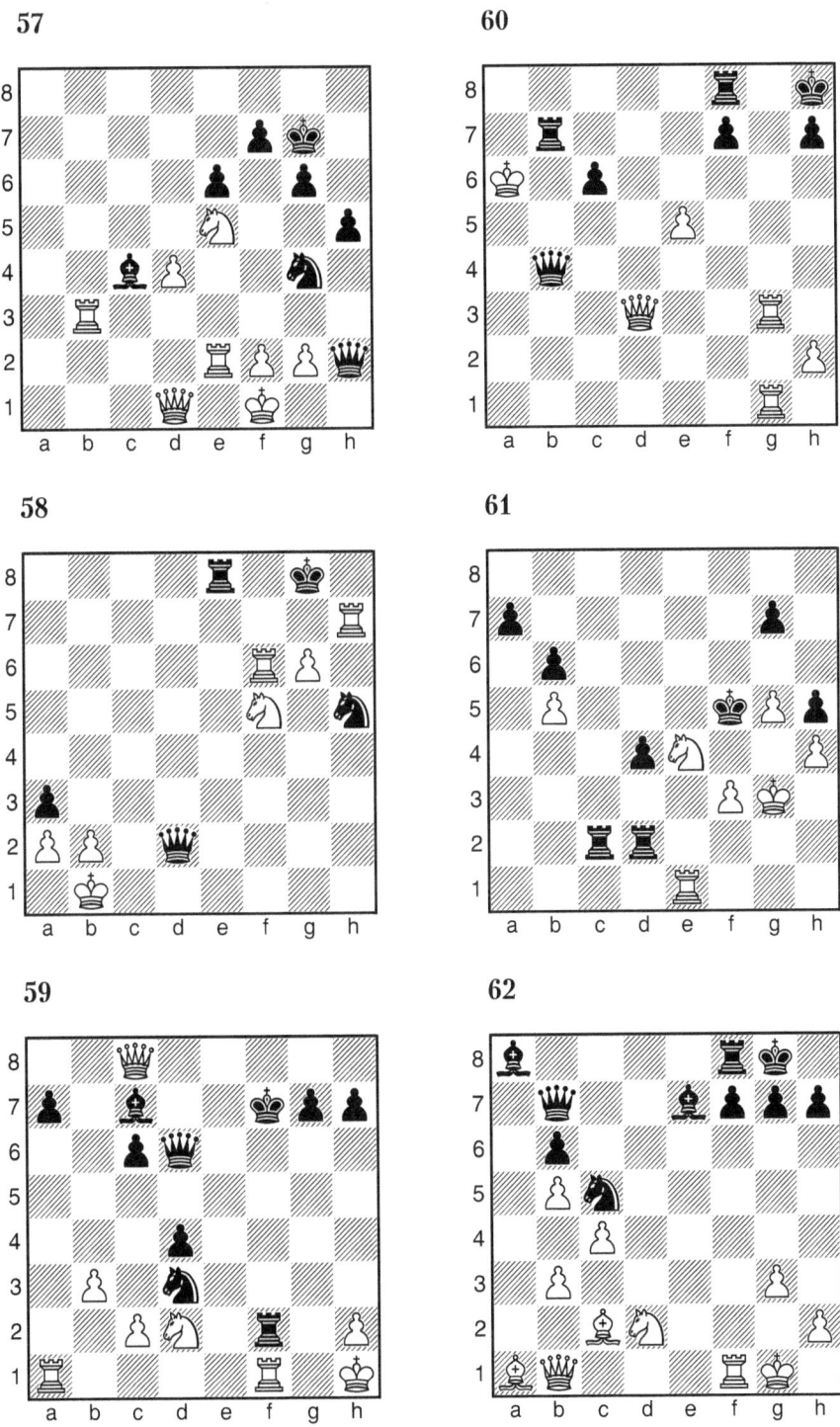

Part 2

Defense Against a Mate Threat.
Counter-Strike

The second part of this book focuses on defensive tactics involving a counter-attack against the opposing king. Such defensive actions are called in this book "counter-strikes". A counter-strike in chess is a broad concept implying a sudden transition from defense to attack. The purpose of a counter-strike is to deprive the attacking side of the time it needs to execute its threat by forcing it to defend. In case of a mate threat, the only feasible counter-strike is an attack on the opponent's king; otherwise, the mate threat will simply be acted upon, and the counter-attack will end before it even begins. In other words, if the opponent threatens to checkmate you, the only way to land a counter-strike is to give a check or execute a defensive tactic that consists solely of checks: forced mate, perpetual check or stalemate ideas. Each of these tactics is thoroughly examined in chapters 5, 6 and 7. Chapter 8 examines defensive combinations involving counter-strikes.

The process of calculating defensive lines should always start from possible counter-strikes, because a forced mate against the enemy king is the best defense to any kind of threat, checkmate included, if available. Still, you need to keep in mind that a counter-strike is not necessarily the best available defense. In practice, a check doesn't always provide defense from mate threats, and at times it can prove to be a poor and harmful decision, depriving the defending side of other good resources. Perpetual check and stalemate ideas can also be weaker than other continuations because they only guarantee you a draw.

We should point out that counter-strikes are often utilized as a part of defensive combinations and can be used to reposition your pieces without losing the right to move. Sometimes even a very small adjustment to the position of the pieces on the board can help you execute other kinds of defensive tactics. In many positions from the subsequent parts of this book white starts his defensive combination with several checks to the black king, and then goes for a different tactic, such as elimination, deflection, interference, pinning, escape or support.

Chapter 5

FORCED MATE

Forced mate is not just the best defensive tactic available – it's also an important outcome of an attacking combination; the author recommends his book *1500 Forced Mates* for further study of the subject.

In every exercise shown in this chapter, white can defend against black's mate threats by delivering a forced checkmate to the black king.

63

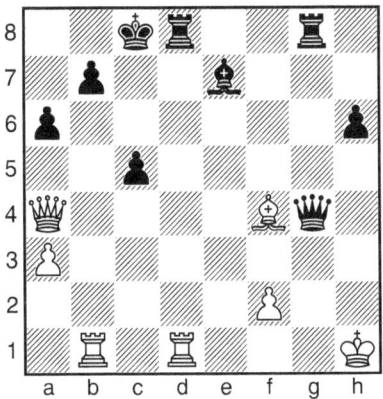

Black threatens 1...♕g2#, but white is one tempo faster: **1.♕c6+! bxc6 2.♖b8#**. There's no sense in trying to find any other defense for white.

64

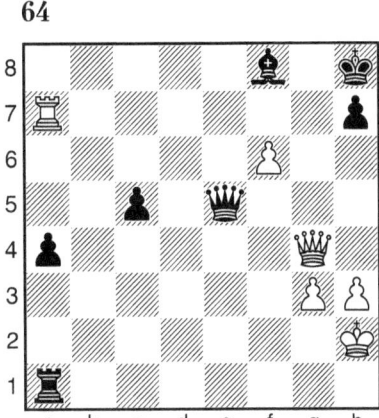

Black has two mate threats at once: a mate in two, 1...♕b2+! 2.♕e2 ♕xe2#, and 1...♖a2+!?, with a mate in three. Still, it's not necessary to study the quantity and quality of black's threats carefully: it's white to move, and he can reply with the best defense there is! White defends from the mate threat with **1.♕g7+!**, with simple lines: **1...♗xg7 2.♖a8+ ♕e8 3.♖xe8+ ♗f8 4.♖xf8#**. Other moves still can't save the game: 2...♗f8 3.♖xf8# or 2...♕b8 3.♖xb8+ ♗f8 4.♖xf8#.

We should point out again that after calculating a forced mate to the black king, white can stop his calculation right then and there: he won't find a stronger continuation anyway!

65

68

66

69

67

70

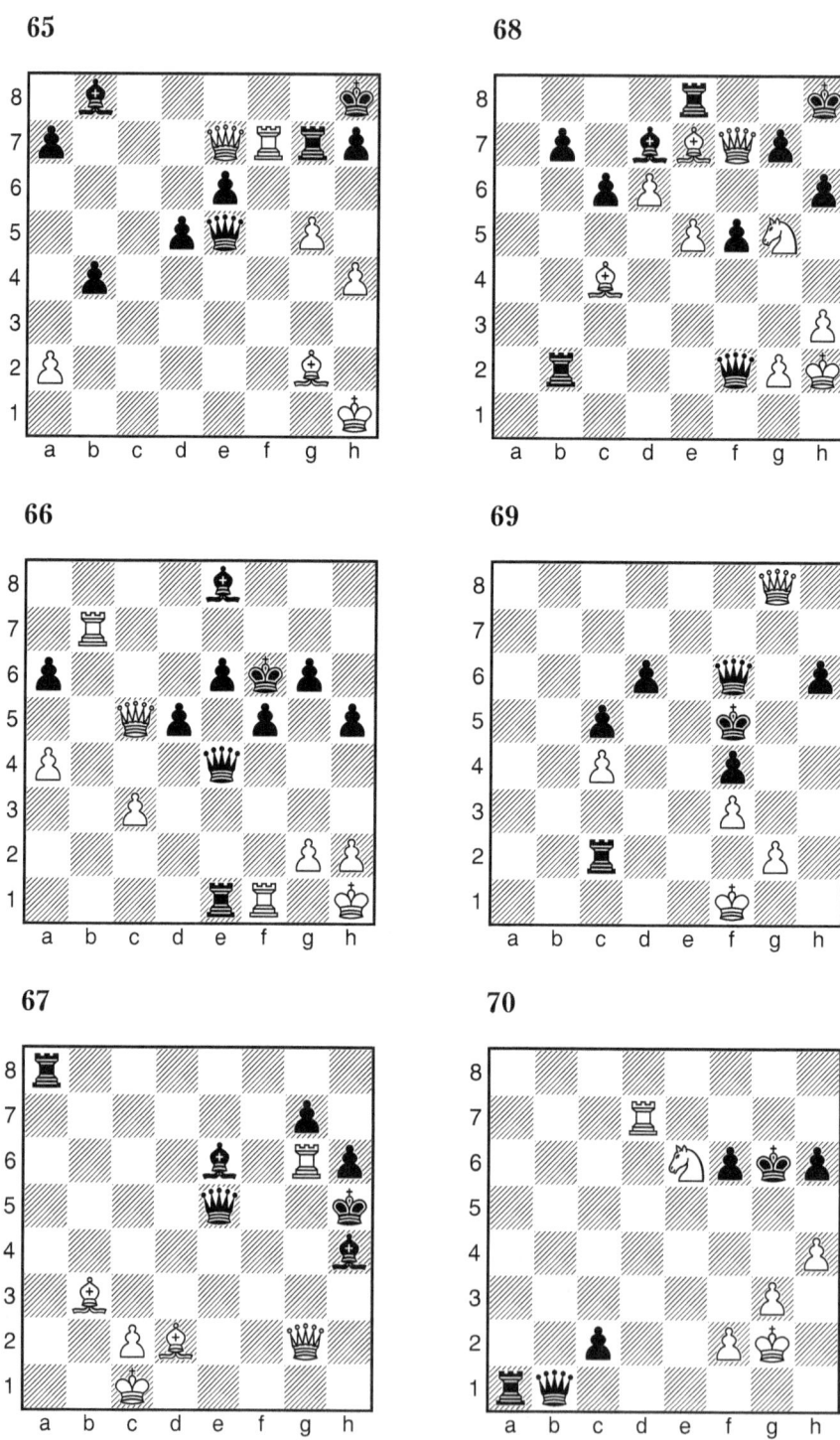

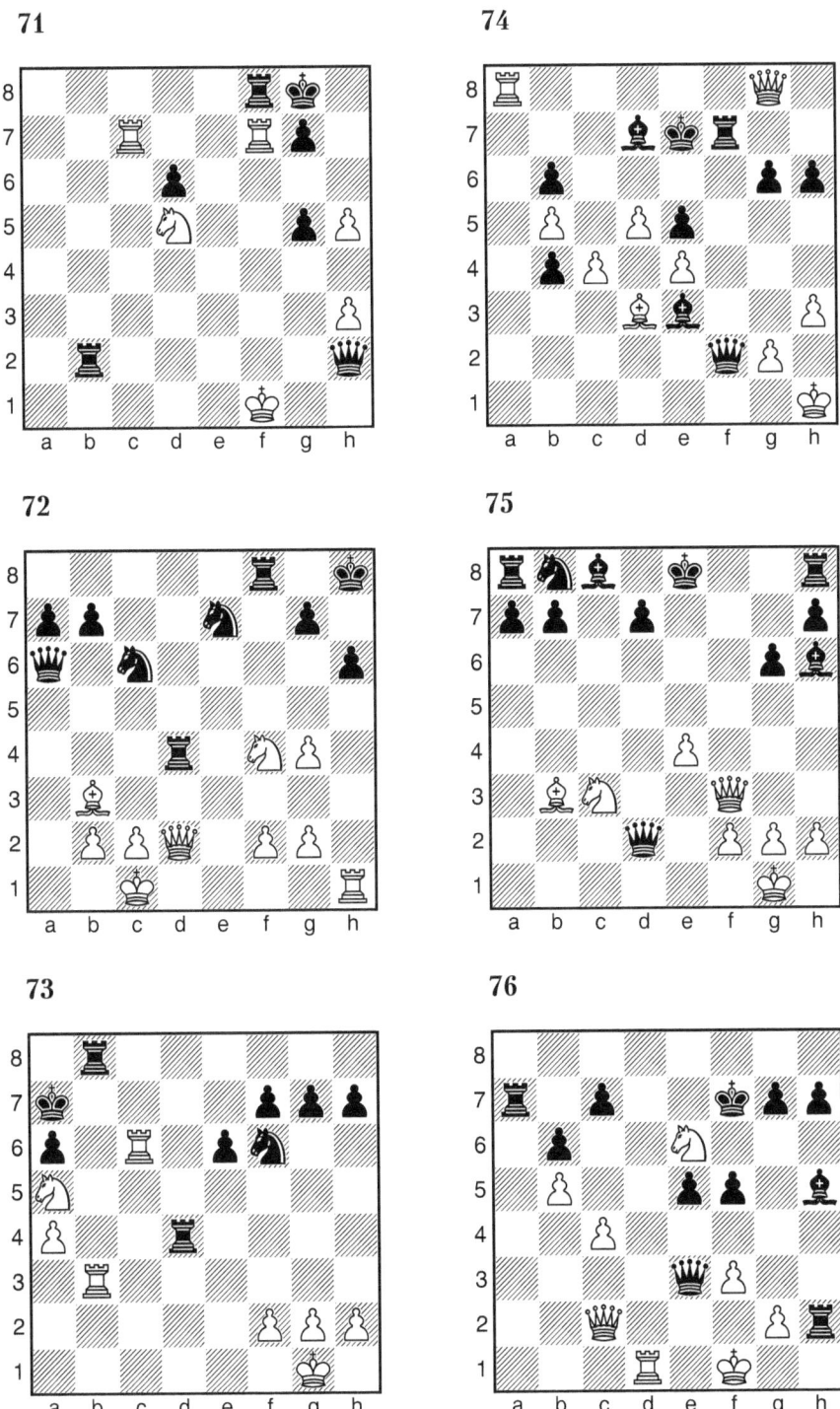

71

72

73

74

75

76

Chapter 6

PERPETUAL CHECK

Another active defensive tactic is perpetual check: a constant attack by one of your pieces on the opposing king that leads to threefold repetition and a draw. Unlike forced mate, perpetual check is not always the best possible defense. However, in many cases this tactic, which allows you to draw the game, is indeed the strongest continuation available.

In every exercise given in this chapter, white can defend against the mate threat with perpetual check.

77

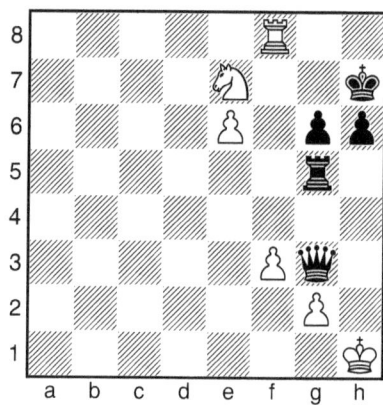

Black threatens 1...♕xg2# and 1...♕e1#. White has quite a few defensive resources, but after, say, 1.g3?!, his position remains completely hopeless. A counter-strike, however, saves white: **1.♕f7+!**

♔h8 **2.♕f8+!** ♔h7 **3.♕f7+!** with repetition. In this case, perpetual check is the only satisfactory defense against checkmate; all other moves quickly lose.

78

This example is similar to the previous one: white is again down on material, and black threatens 1...♕xg2#. To find the best defense, you need to first search for a counter-strike: a forced mate or a perpetual check. Simple calculation shows that after **1.♖f7+!** ♔h8, white doesn't have enough pieces for a checkmate, but just enough to harass the king endlessly! **2.♖f8+ ♔g7 3.♖f7+ ♔h8 4.♖f8+ ♔h7 5.♖f7+** etc.

Before considering the drawing line you found as the best possible solution, you need to check other possible defensive resources for white (countermeasures against opposing pieces, resources of your own pieces) on every move of this line. In the example above, such resources are nonexistent, so we can quickly conclude that perpetual check (and the draw) is indeed the best available choice.

79

82

80

83

81

84

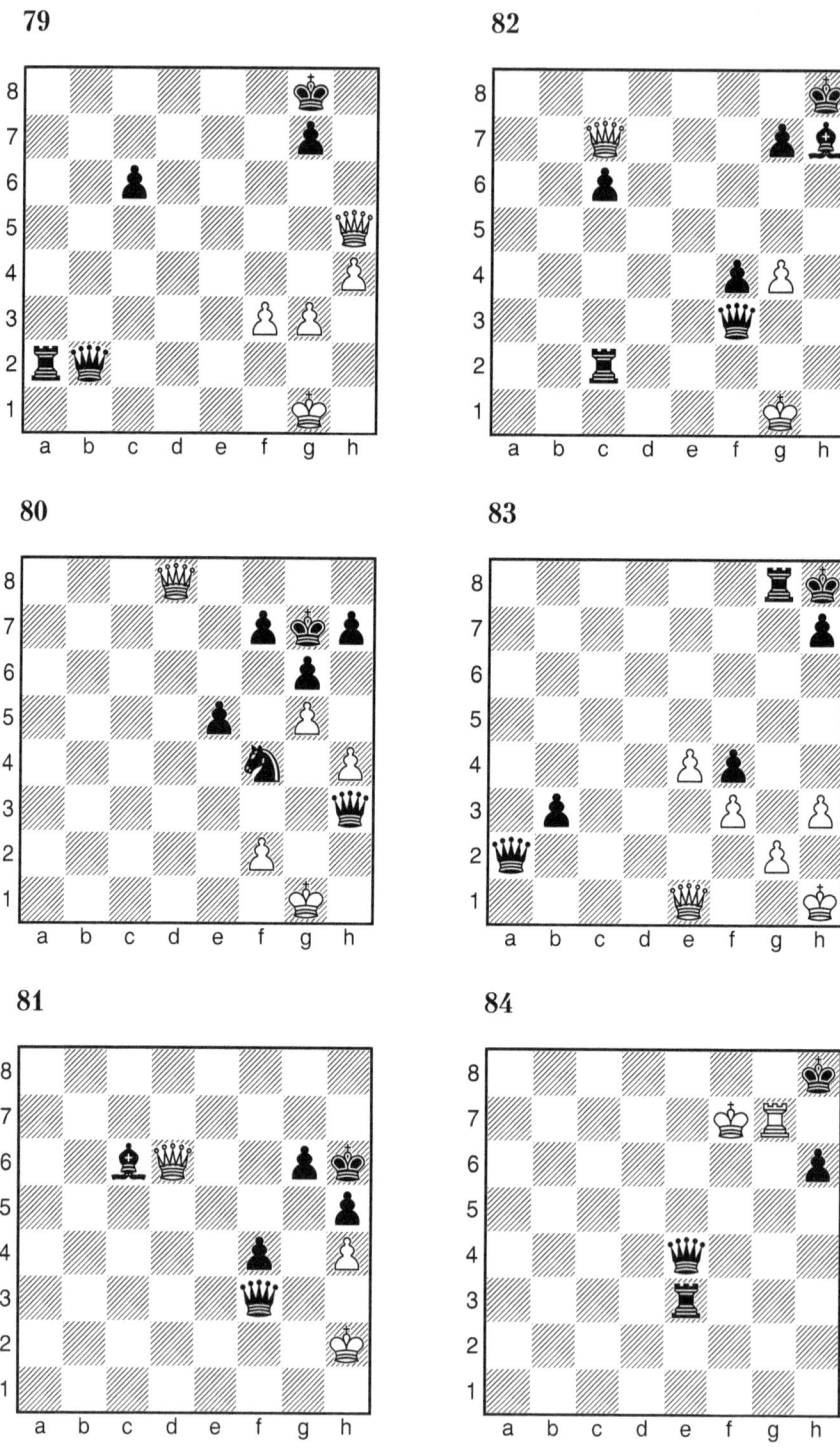

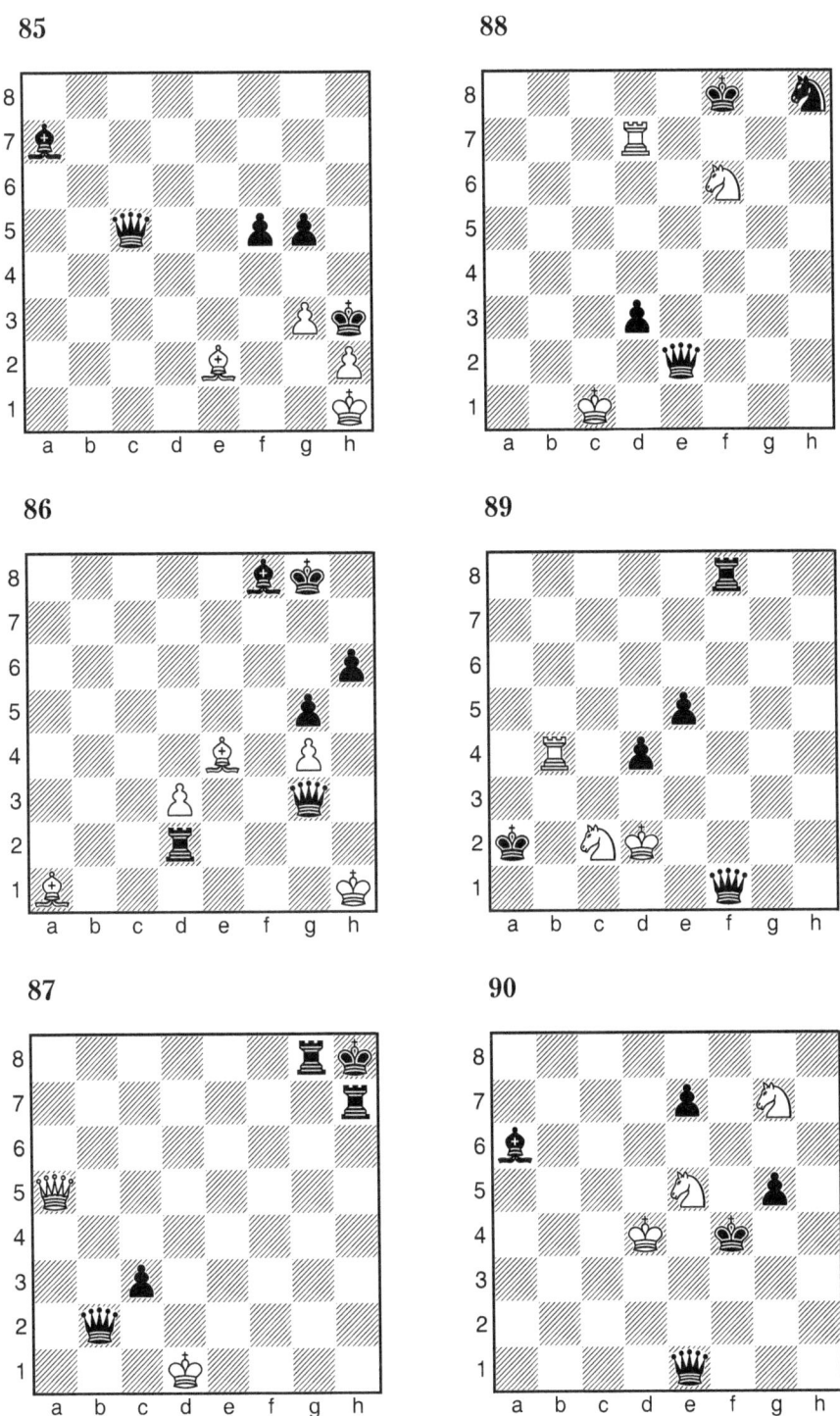

85

86

87

88

89

90

Chapter 7

STALEMATE IDEAS

Stalemate ideas are a rare, but spectacular defensive tactic that forces your opponent to stalemate you. Like perpetual check, stalemate only leads to a draw, therefore stalemate ideas cannot always be considered the best defense. Still, in many cases, a draw is indeed the best result of a defensive combination.

Stalemate ideas are most effectively used in positions where the defending side's king has no legal moves. To achieve stalemate in such positions, the defending side only needs to give up all his pieces that are still able to move. With very rare exceptions, you can only do this with checks, which allows us to classify stalemate ideas as counterstrikes: all the moves of the defensive combination will attack the king.

In every exercise included in this chapter, white can defend from his opponent's mate threats with stalemate ideas.

91

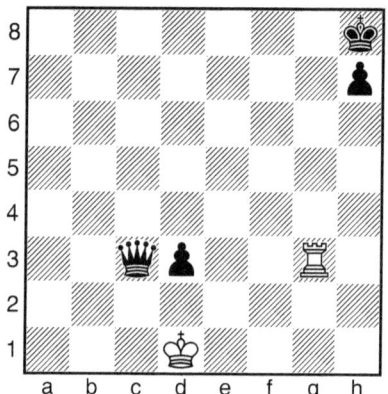

Black threatens to mate in two, but the white king cannot move, and so, after **1.♖g8+! ♔xg8**, there's stalemate on the board.

92

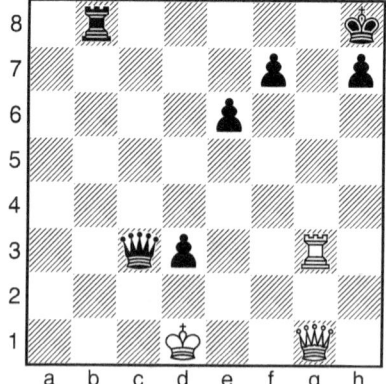

To achieve stalemate, white needs to give up both his strongest pieces – queen and rook. The best defense from checkmate is **1.♖g8+! ♖xg8 2.♕xg8+! ♔xg8**, stalemate. By the way, white cannot play 2.♕g7+? because of 2...♕xg7, and the "stalemate cage" around the white king comes apart.

If the defending side's king still has legal moves, then, to successfully execute stalemate tactics, you both need to give up your "extra" pieces and create a stalemate construction – i.e. you have to attract one or more of your opponent's pieces to squares where they block off the king's last moves. Again, the only way to do that, with rare exceptions, is to give checks to the opposing king.

93

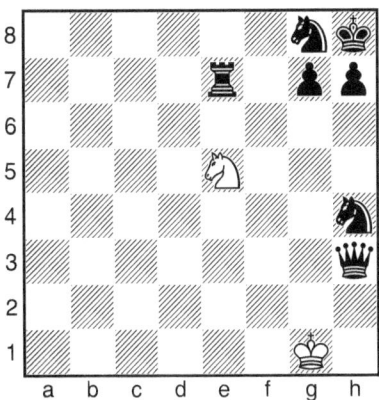

Black threatens mate with 1...♕g2# and also has a huge material advantage. After 1.♘g6+? hxg6 there's no stalemate. To execute the stalemate tactics, white needs to force black pieces to take control of the f2 square. He can do this with **1.♘f7+!**, and after the forced **1...♖xf7** there's stalemate on the board.

94

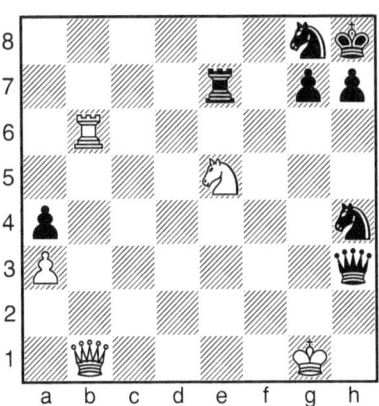

The position on the diagram is quite similar to the previous one. Black's material advantage is not as huge this time, but his extra knight and two pawns would be more than enough to win. In addition to material gains, black threatens 1...♕g2#. To achieve stalemate, white needs to deprive his own king of the f2 square and give up all his pieces that can still move – queen, rook and knight. To that end, he first plays **1.♘f7+! ♖xf7**, and then gives up all the "extraneous" pieces: **2.♕xh7+! ♔xh7 3.♖h6+!**, and any black reply leads to stalemate.

Please note that in all the exercises in this chapter, black cannot refuse the sacrifice of white pieces, which are put en prise just in time.

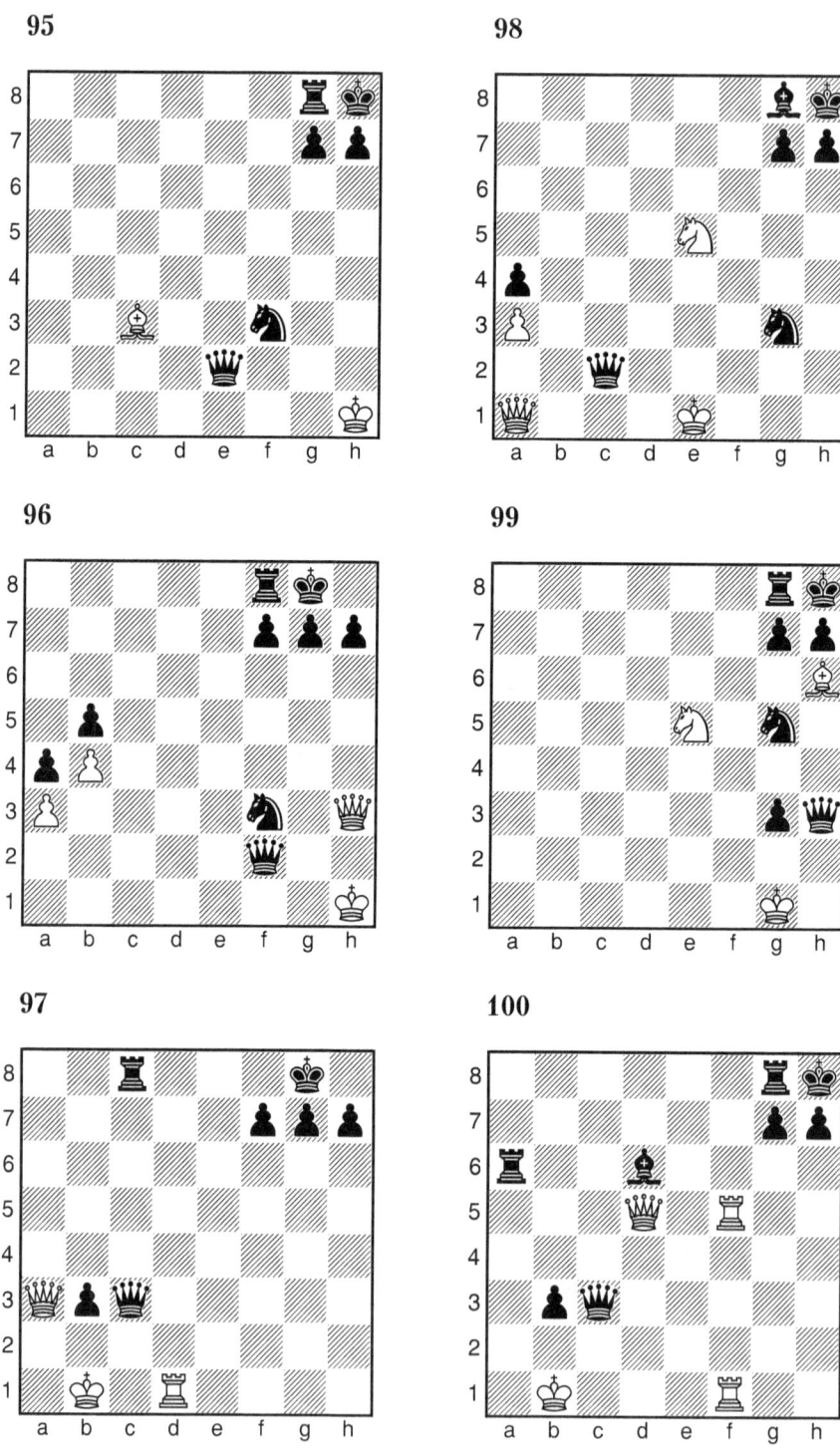

95

96

97

98

99

100

101

104

102

105

103

106

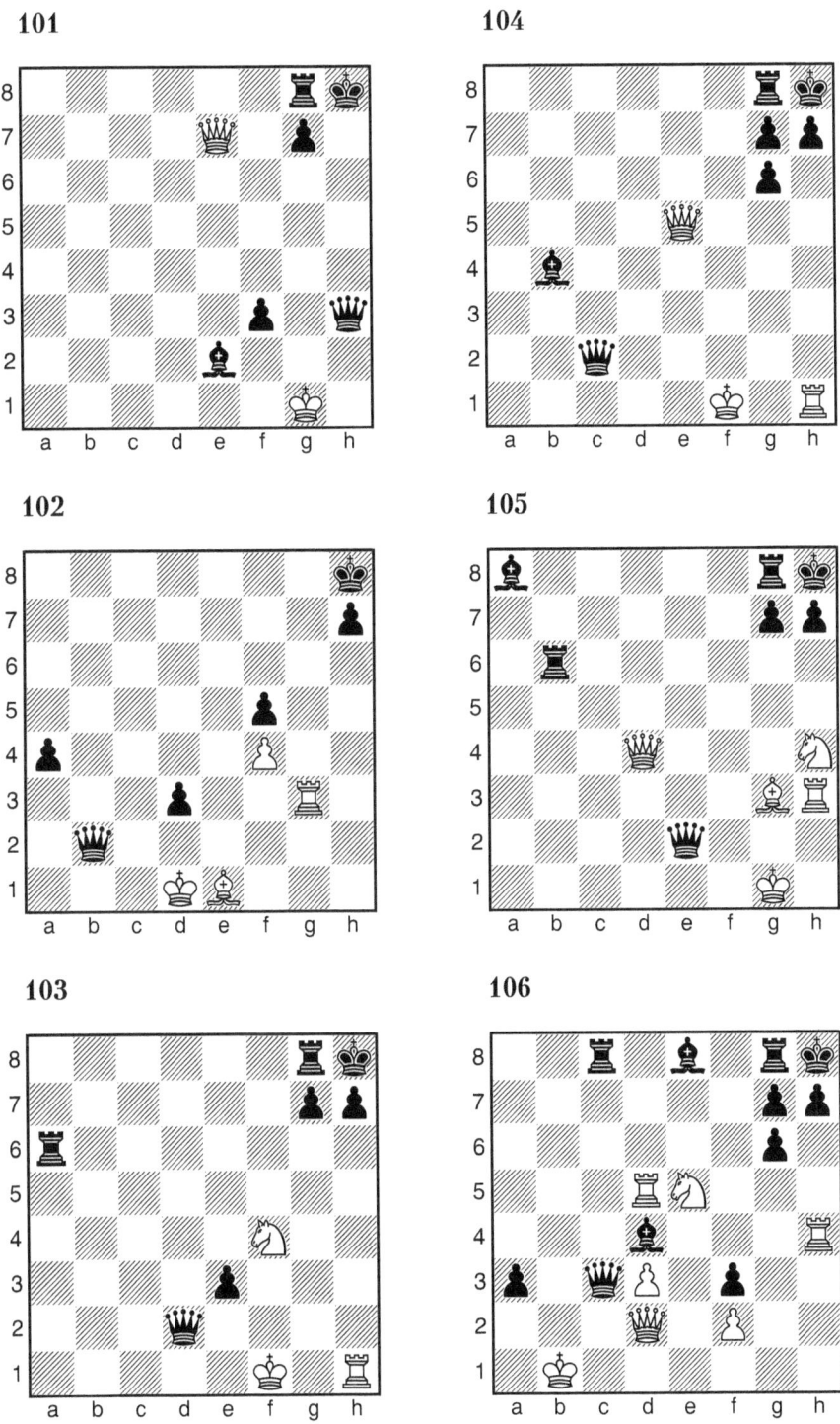

Chapter 8

COMBINATIONS

To solve the exercises in this chapter, you need to find the best defense against mate threats; to achieve that goal, white will have to use all the defensive tactics that we learned in the previous chapters, namely the three counter-strikes: forced mate, perpetual check and stalemate ideas. In other words, white needs to defend against mate solely by attacking the black king.

107

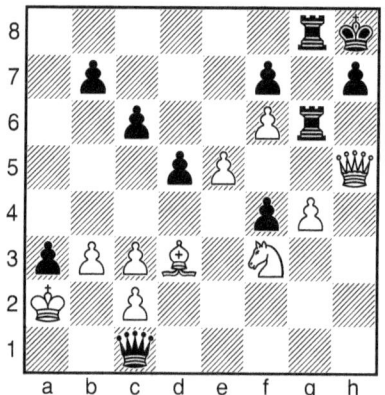

Black threatens 1...♕b2#, but it's white to move, and he manages to save the game with precise play! First he lands a counter-strike, **1.♕xh7+! ♔xh7**, and then gives perpetual check – **2.♘g5+ ♔h8 3.♘xf7+ ♔h7 4.♘g5+ ♔h8 5.♘f7+**, etc. It's easy to prove that this small defensive combination of

counter-strike and perpetual check is the best defense.

108

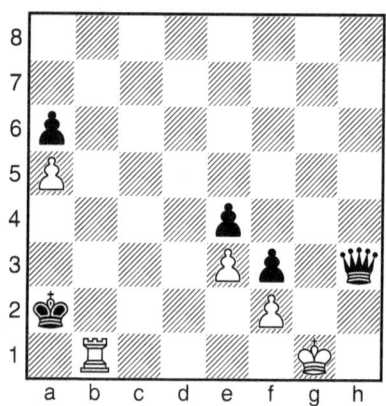

Black threatens 1...♕g2#, and white is also down on material. However, the white king and all pawns have no legal moves, which is a good reason to search for a stalemate idea. To get a stalemate, white needs to give up his rook! He can't do so immediately, because after **1.♖b2+!**, black won't accept the sacrifice: **1...♔a3**. However, that will be met with **2.♖b3+! ♔a4 3.♖b4+! ♔xa5 4.♖b5+! ♔a4 5.♖b4+! ♔a3 6.♖b3+!**, and the desperado rook will harass the black king until the game ends in a draw.

The line above is the only way to draw. After the careless 1.♖a1+?, black will play 1...♔b3!, and the king will subsequently get to d8, with the idea that the queen will capture the desperado rook. To defend against checkmate in this position, white used stalemate ideas and perpetual check.

109

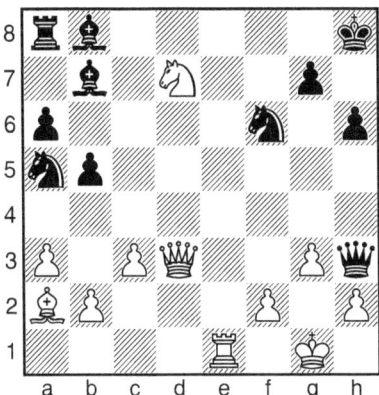

To defend from the threat 1... ♕g2# in the best way, white first attacks the black king with the counter-strike **1.♖e8+!**. Now, 1... ♘g8?? is a blunder: black gets checkmated with 2.♖xg8#. Thus, the strongest reply is **1...♘xe8**, which is met with another counter-strike – **2.♕h7+! ♔xh7**, and now white finishes off his combination with perpetual check – **3.♘f8+ ♔h8 4.♘g6+ ♔h7 5.♘f8+** with a draw.

If we list all the defensive tactics employed by white in this exercise, then we get a combination of counter-strike and perpetual check in one line and a forced mate in the other. It's worth noting that in the context of defensive counter-strikes, forced mate even theoretically cannot be used in conjunction with

other defensive tactics. However, it very often complements the solution, as happened in the position above.

110

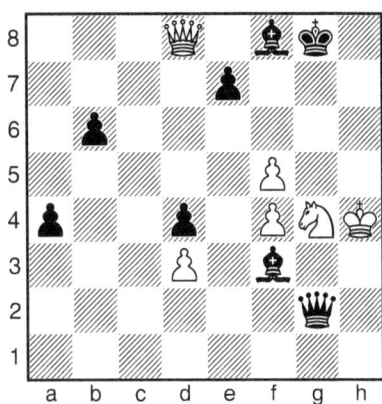

In the next position, white is again forced to use multiple counter-strikes to escape mate! After **1.♘f6+!**, the main line of the solution is **1...♔f7 2.♕e8+! ♔g7 3.♕xe7+! ♗xe7**, stalemate. Black has a lot of opportunities to get checkmated along the way: 3...♔h6? 4.♕h7#; 3... ♔h8? 4.♕h7#; 2...♔xf6? 3.♕xf8#; 1...♔h8? 2.♕xf8+ ♕g8 3.♕xg8#. For the complete solution, we also need to consider black's other possible replies. First, we have 1... ♔g7, which transposes to the main line after 2.♕xe7+!. Secondly, there's the capture 1...exf6, which leads to a position where white only has to give up his queen – 2.♕xf8+! ♔h7, and then either give perpetual check with the desperado queen, 3.♕h6+ ♔f8 4.♕f8+ ♔h7 5.♕h6+, or immediately end the game with 3.♕h8+! ♔xh8, stalemate.

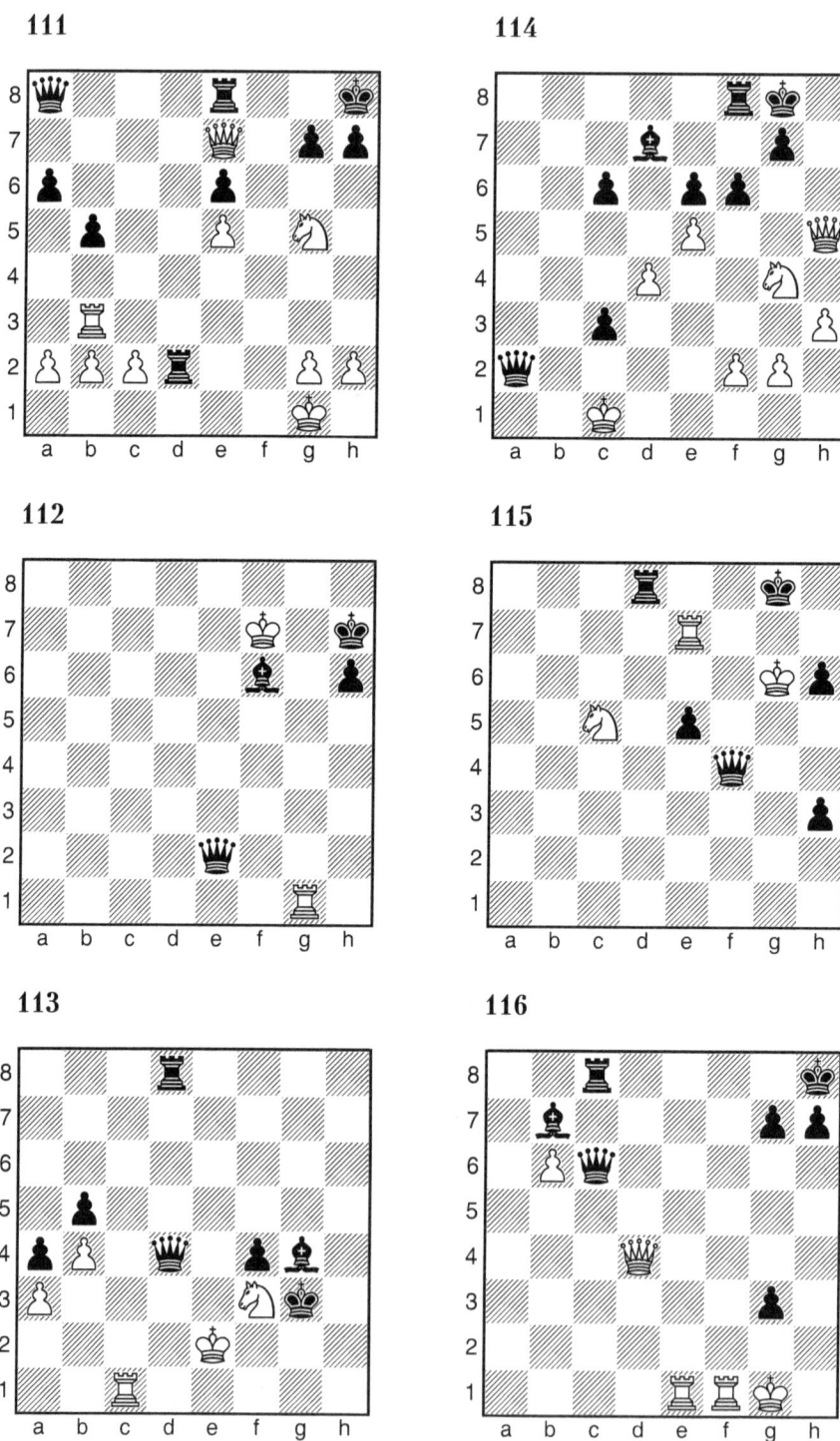

111

112

113

114

115

116

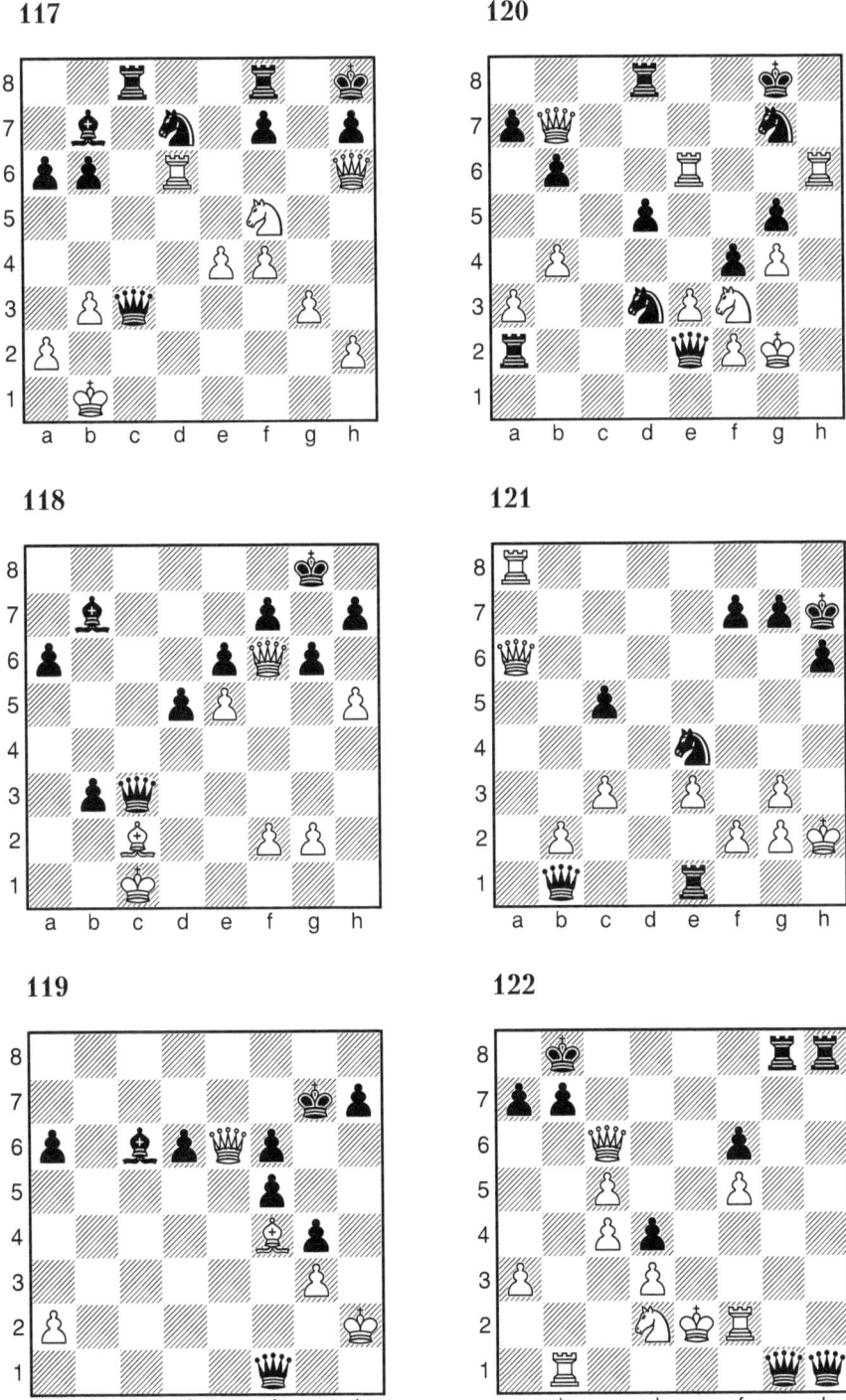

117

118

119

120

121

122

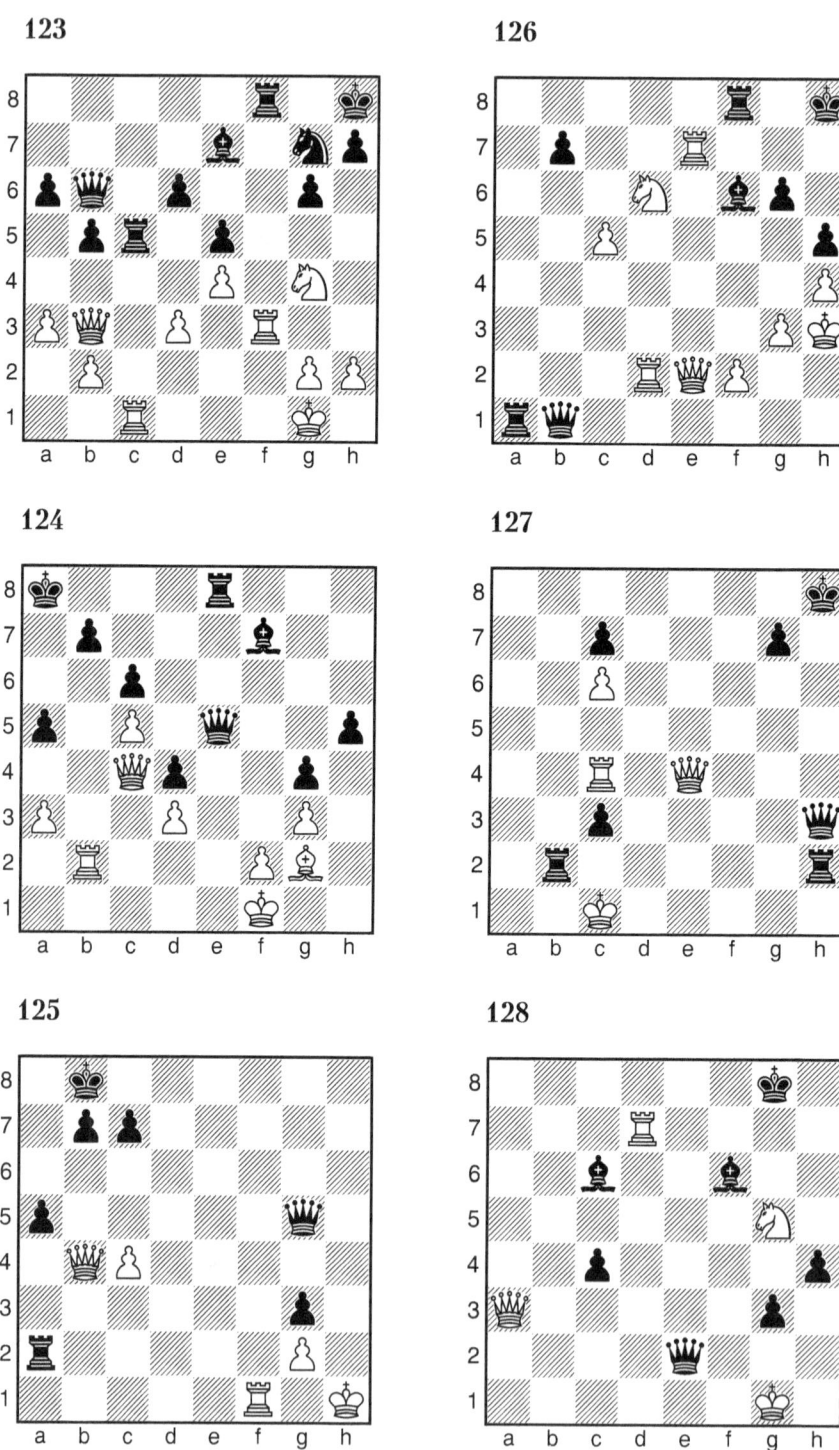

123

124

125

126

127

128

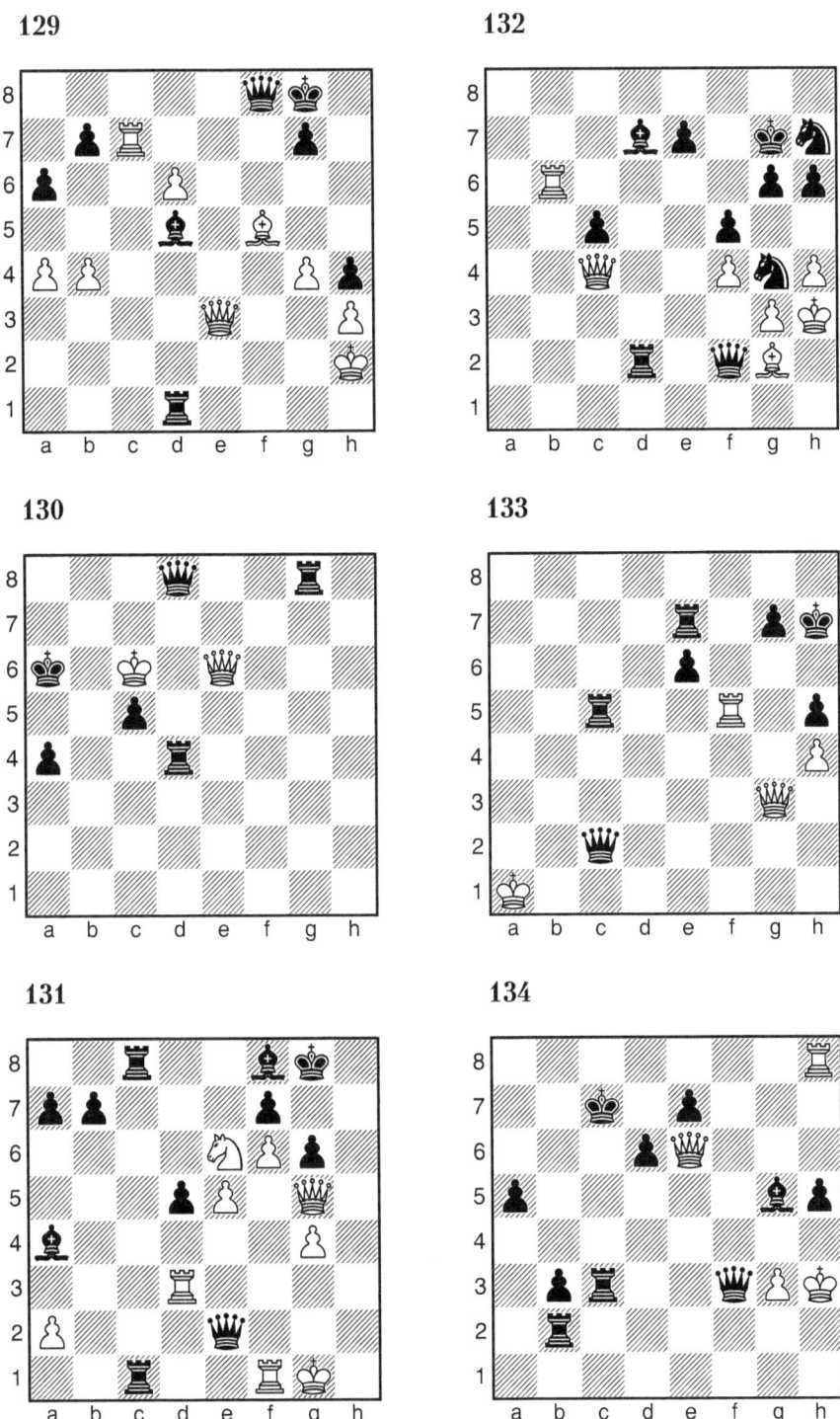

129

130

131

132

133

134

Part 3

Defense Against a Mate Threat. Countermeasures Against Your Opponent's Pieces

The third part of this book focuses on the defensive tactics used directly against the opponent's pieces that created mate threats. To stop a piece from delivering checkmate, only four tactics can be used: elimination, deflection, pinning and interference.

All the aforementioned tactics, as well as counter-strikes, belong to the category of active defense. The meaning of all these terms should be already known to readers of the book *1500 Forced Mates*. The defensive context only necessitates small theoretical changes: for instance, capturing the opponent's pieces in defense is not studied separately; unlike in forced mating, it's considered a particular case of elimination tactics. We should also note that even the defensive tactics of deflection, pinning or interference always entail a combination with another defensive tactic, most often elimination.

Active defense is much more promising than passive, therefore, checking for possible countermeasures against the opponent's pieces comes second in calculating defensive lines, right after the search for counter-strikes. An attack on the king can still turn out to be much more important than attacks on all other pieces.

Chapter 9

ELIMINATION

The simplest way to deal with the opposing pieces that created a mate threat is their direct elimination through capture, trade or sacrifice.

In every exercise shown in this chapter, white has a good opportunity to defend against the opponent's mate threats by using the elimination tactic.

135

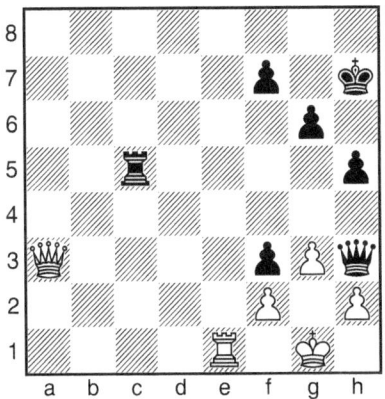

Here is a very simple example. Two black pieces have created the mate threat 1...♕g2#. After making sure that there are no counter-strikes, white has to search for possible countermeasures against the opponent's pieces that created the threat. The solution is to eliminate the threat with **1.♕xf3** – white captures the pawn and prevents

checkmate. Capturing the rook would be a blunder.

In the context of defending from mate threats, there is almost no distinction between capturing the piece "for free" and two other ways to eliminate it – trade and sacrifice. This is the main difference between defensive elimination and the similar tactic studied in the book *1500 Forced Mates.*

136

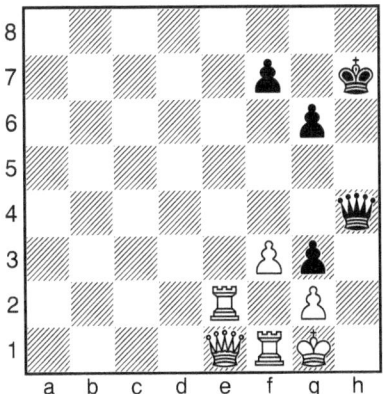

To prevent the mate threat 1...♕h2#, white has to sacrifice his queen. By eliminating one of the black pieces with **1.♕xg3!**, white can defend from checkmate on the next move. As we continue evaluating the position after **1...♕xg3**, we can say that it's roughly equal, which makes white's first move a satisfactory defense to checkmate. To be fair, if we don't count 1.♖ff2? with the subsequent 1...♛h2+ 2.♔f1 ♛h1#, then white has literally no other defenses against mate in one move.

137

140

138

141

139

142

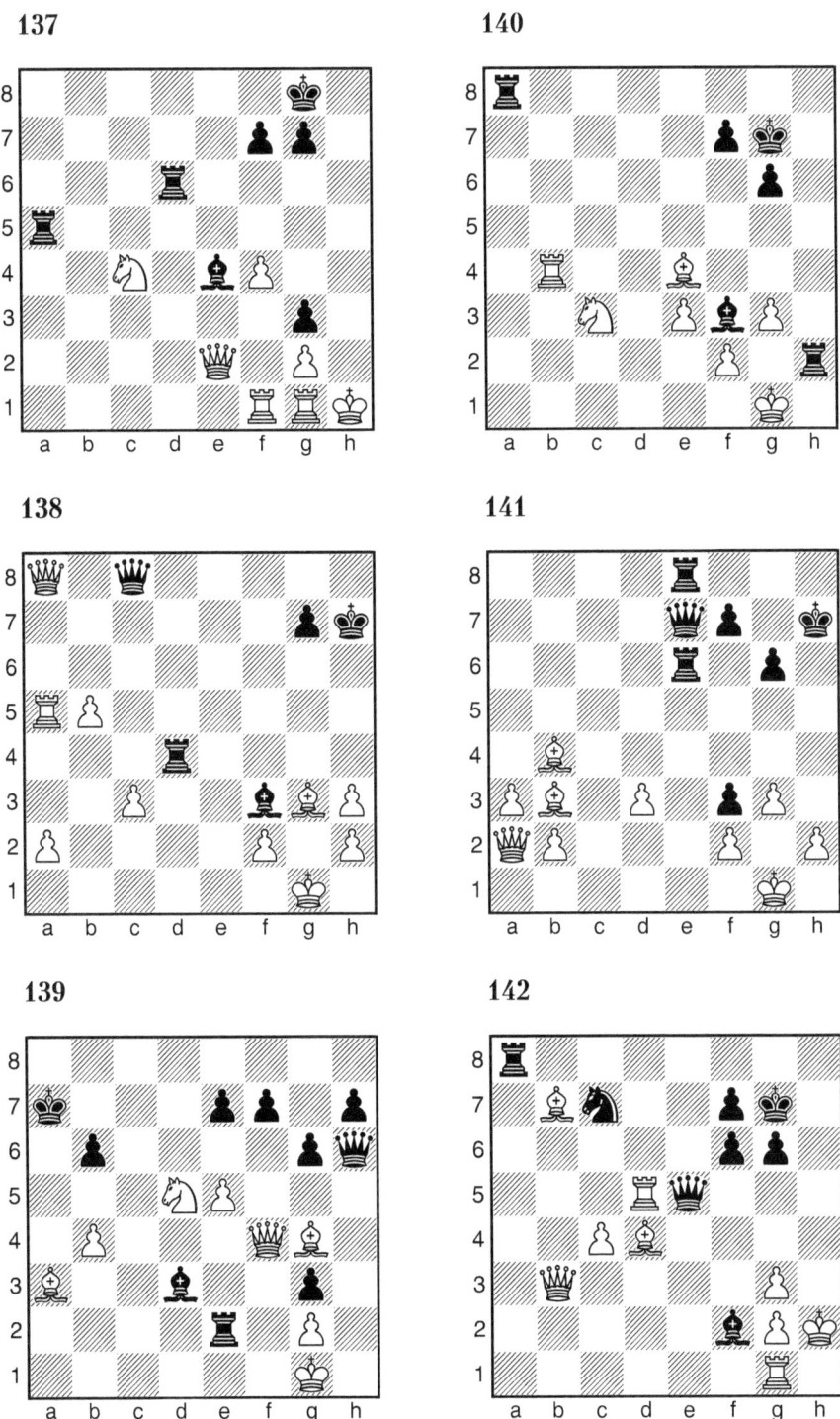

143

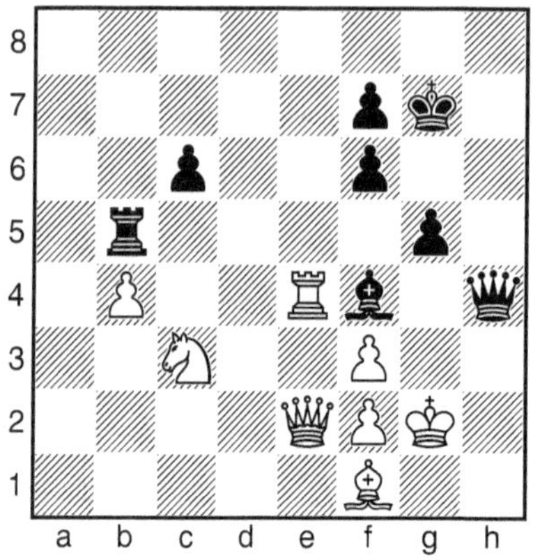

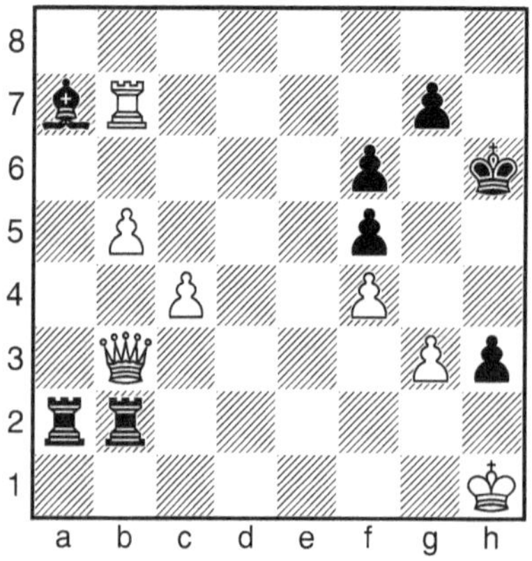

146

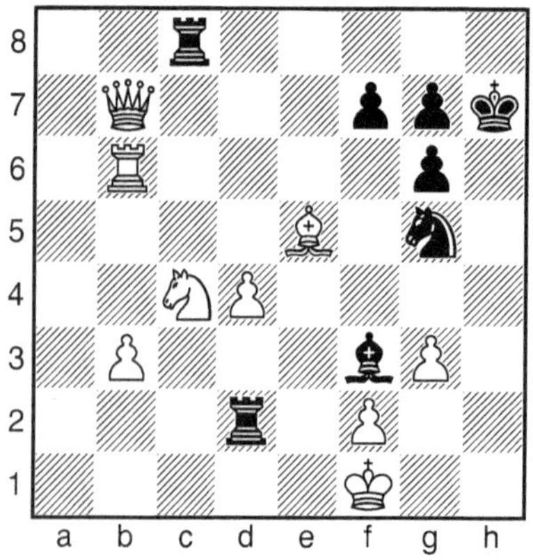

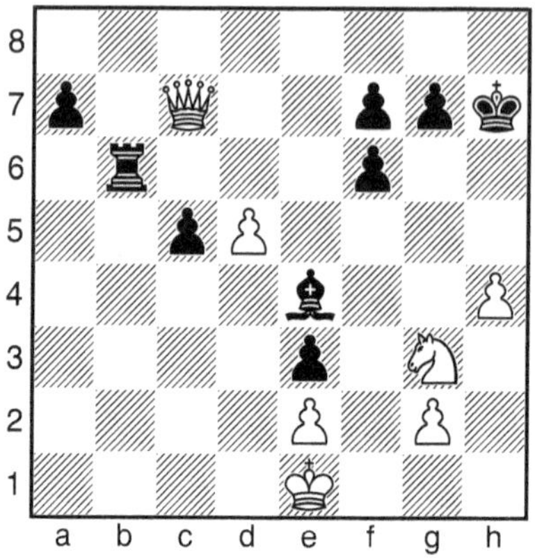

144

147

145

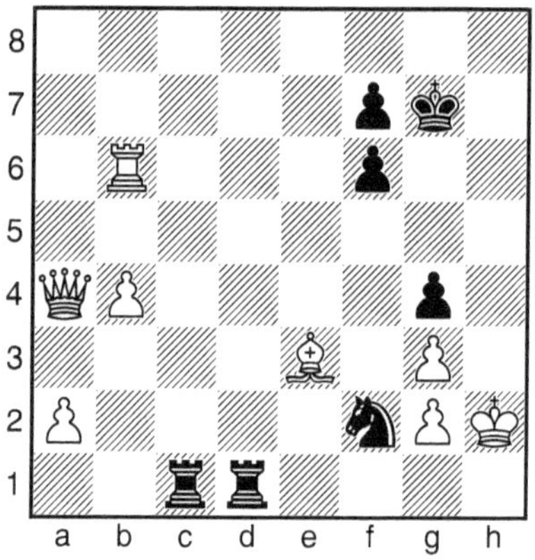

148

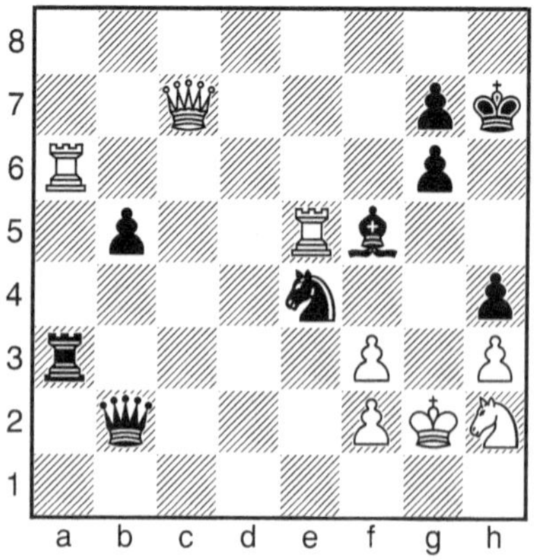

Chapter 10

COMBINATIONS

In this chapter, we study mixtures of elimination and all tactics that we have studied in the previous chapters. In every exercise presented in this chapter, white has an opportunity to defend against the opponent's mate threats by using elimination in various conjunctions with counter-strikes.

Defensive tactics, as well as attacking ones, can be used both in series or simultaneously. In the latter case, one move should execute more than one defensive idea; for instance, the elimination of a piece with check. Alternatively, defensive tactics can be executed one at a time on each move, separately from each other.

149

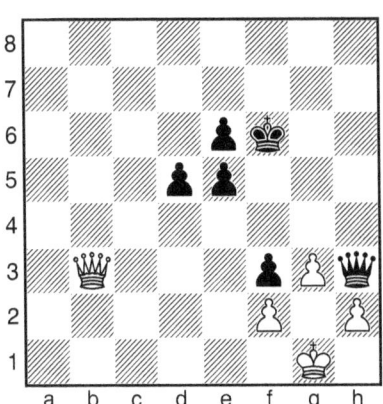

The only way for white to counter the threat 1...♛g2# is **1.♛xf3+!** – simultaneously eliminating a piece and executing a counter-strike.

150

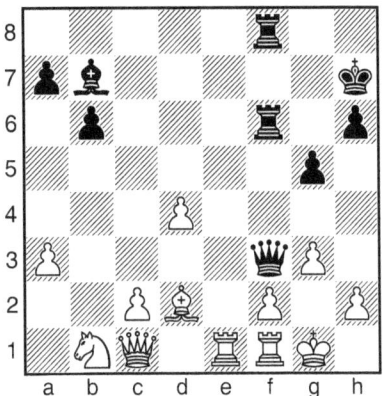

Black has created two mate-in-one threats: 1...♛h1# and 1...♛g2#. White has several defensive attempts, but most of them do not provide satisfactory defense. For the best defense, white first needs to use a counter-strike and then eliminate a piece. There follows **1.♖e7+!**, and the rook captures the black bishop on the next move, eliminating all mate threats to the white king. Black can play, for instance, **1...♖8f7 2.♖xb7!** with a big advantage for white.

We should note that the black king wasn't even the main target of the counter-strike in this exercise! With his first move, white changed his rook's position with check to obtain new defensive opportunities – to execute an elimination tactic.

151

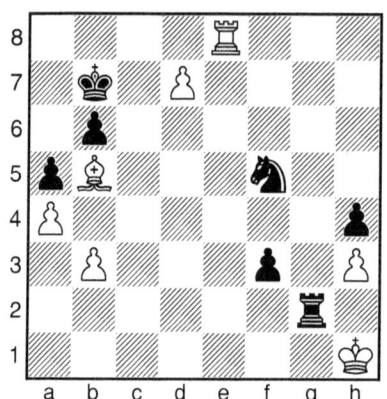

Black threatens 1...♘g3#. The first defensive ideas to consider are various counter-strikes: 1.♗a6+, 1.♗c6+, 1.d8=♘+ and 1.♖b8+. None of these moves can win the game for white if black plays correctly. However, after the strongest **1.♖b8+! ♔xb8?**, white can eliminate the black knight with checks: **2.d8=♕+ ♔b7 3.♕d7+ ♔b8 4.♕xf5**, achieving a decisive advantage. The strongest move here is 1...♔a7!, and after 2.♖a8+! ♔b7! 3.♖b8+!, the game ends with a perpetual check. Thus, in one line, white gives a perpetual check, and in the other, he uses several counter-strikes followed by elimination. Note that white had virtually no other defenses. For instance, the attempt to support the g3 square with 1.♖g8? led to a hopeless position after 1... ♖xg8.

152

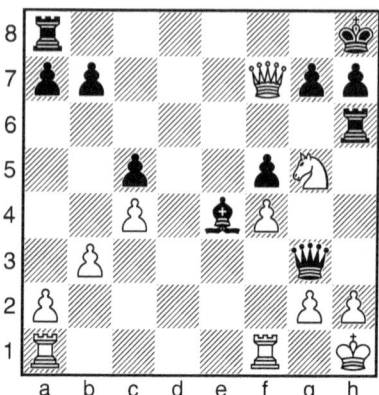

To solve this exercise, white will have to use defensive tactics both simultaneously and in series. Black has created a lot of mate threats, including 1...♕xg2# and 1...♕xh2#. The best way to defend is a nice combination: **1.♕e8+!** (counter-strike) **1...♖xe8 2.♘f7+!** (counter-strike) **2...♔g8 3.♘xh6+!** (counter-strike plus elimination) **3...gxh6 4.hxg3!** (elimination). White manages to capture two of the three most dangerous black pieces, liquidate the mate threats and get an endgame with good winning chances.

Defense is considered one of the most difficult chess skills. In the example above, only two defensive tactics were used. However, the solution cannot be called simple: it required a precise and quite long calculation.

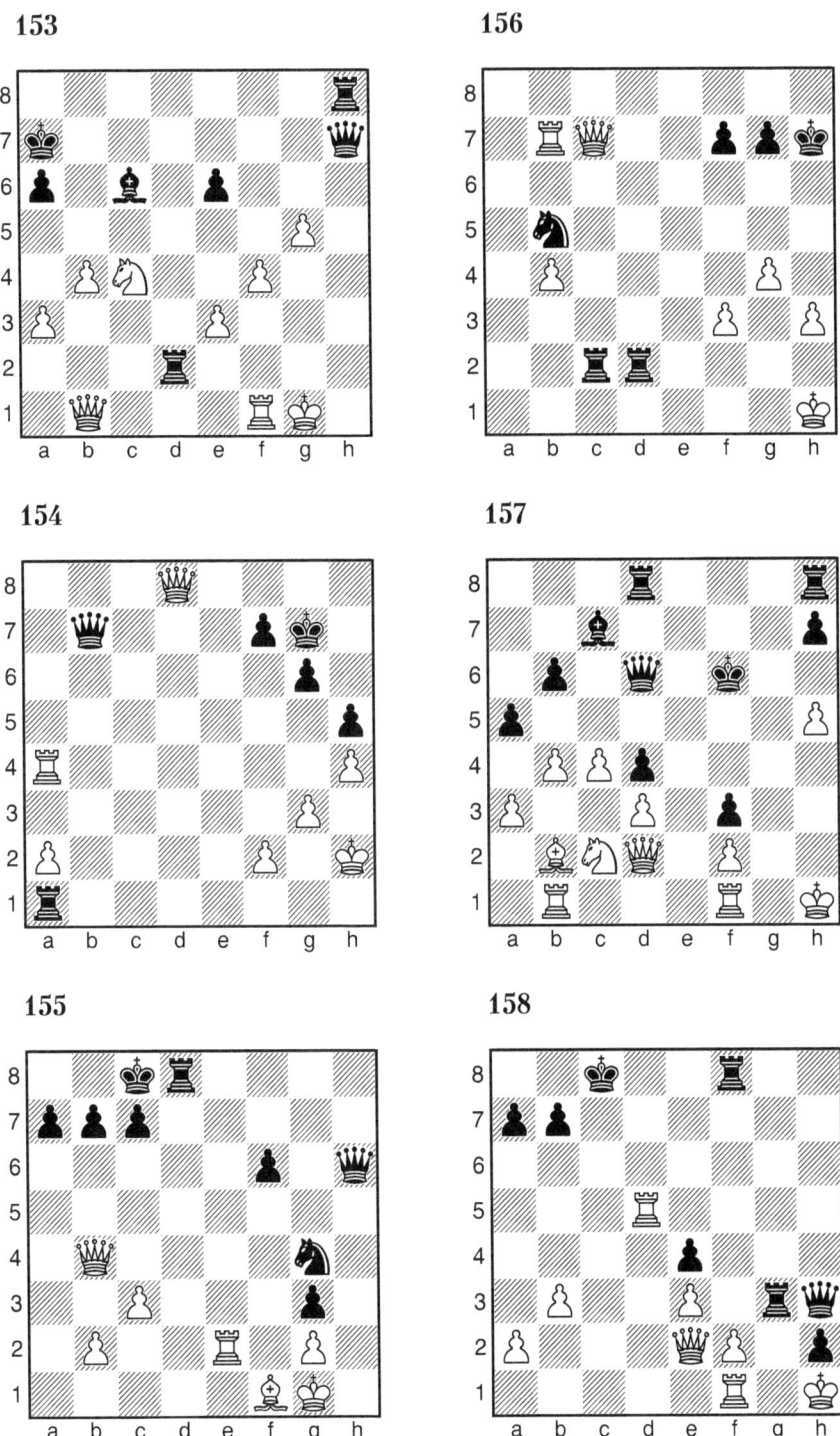

153

154

155

156

157

158

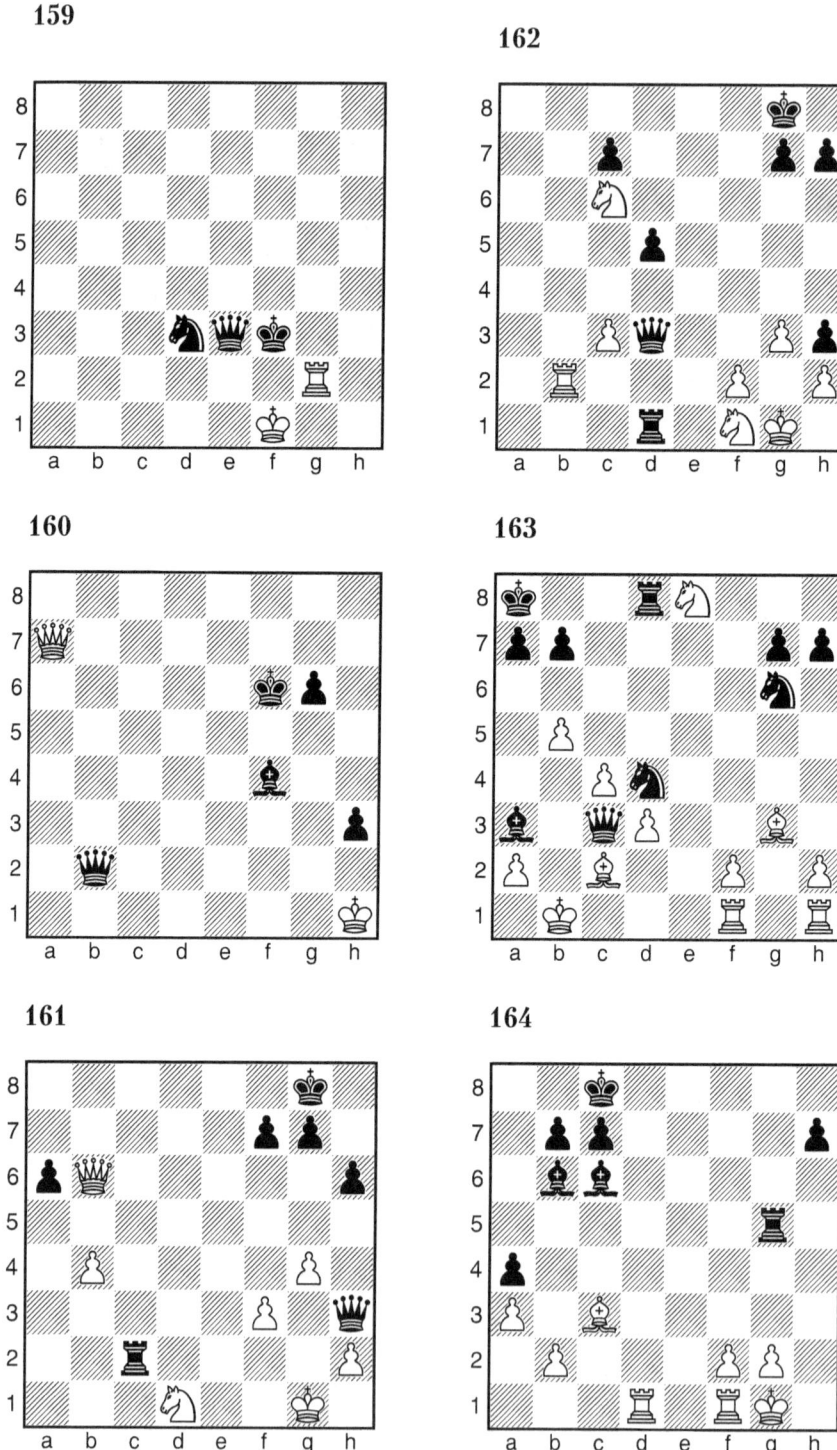

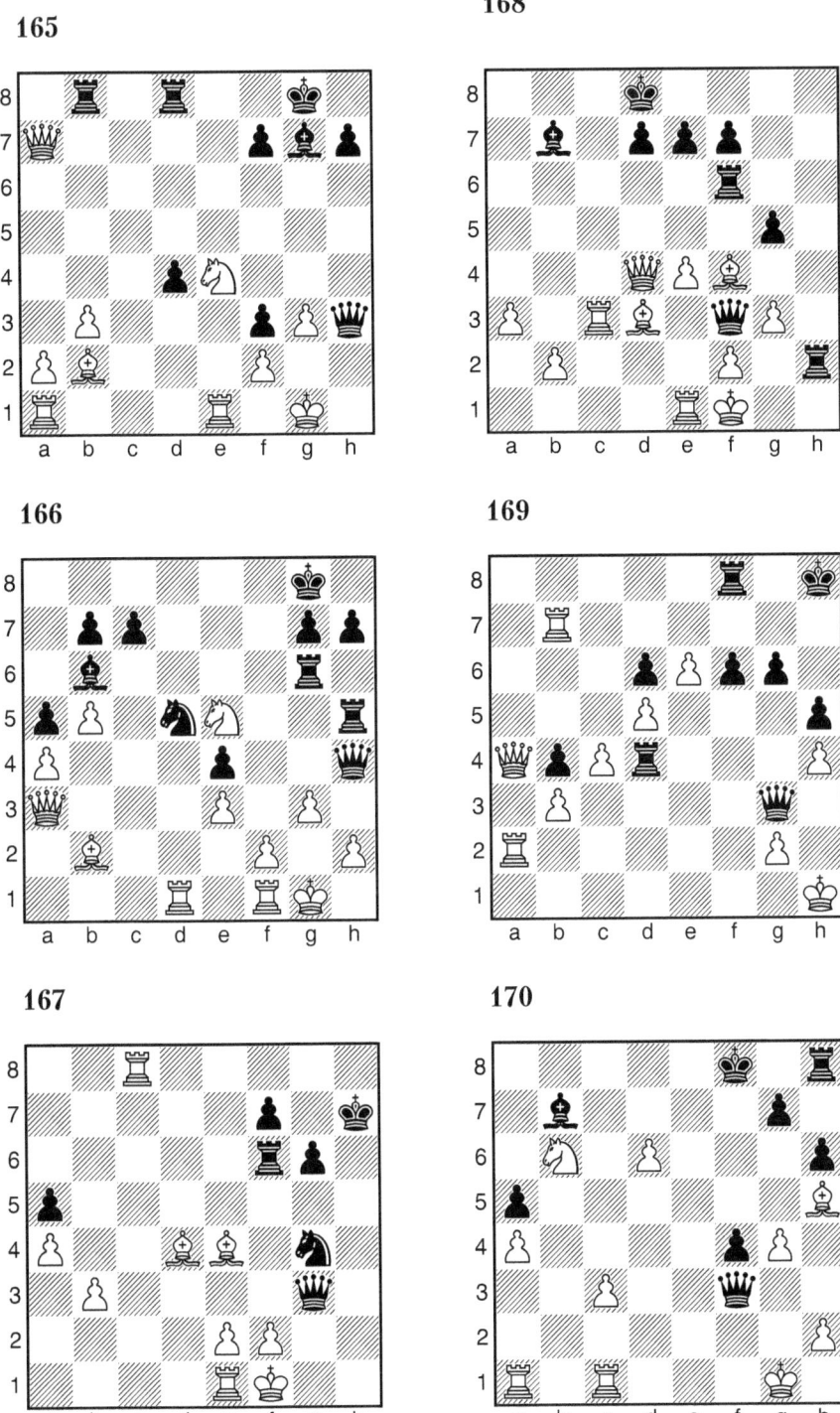

165

166

167

168

169

170

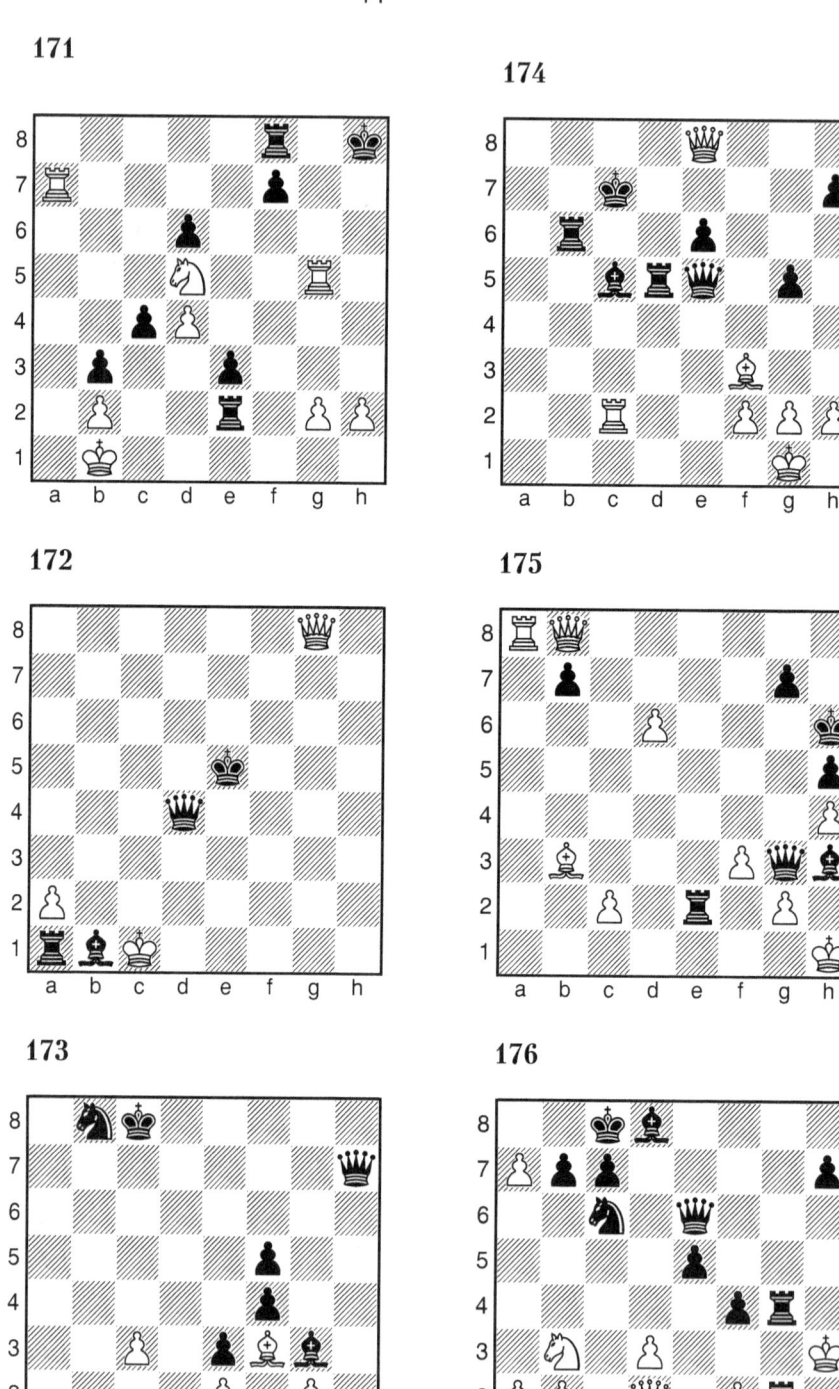

171

172

173

174

175

176

Chapter 11

DEFLECTION

Another defensive tactic that can be used against the opposing pieces is deflection. The essence of this tactic is to force the piece to move to another square, where it cannot take part in a mating combination.

In the context of defense against mate threats, "pure" deflection (not combined with counter-strikes) can only occur if the opponent threatens to checkmate you with a discovered check: in such positions, you can try to deflect the opponent's piece by attacking it. What's more, attacking a piece gives you an opportunity to eliminate it later.

177

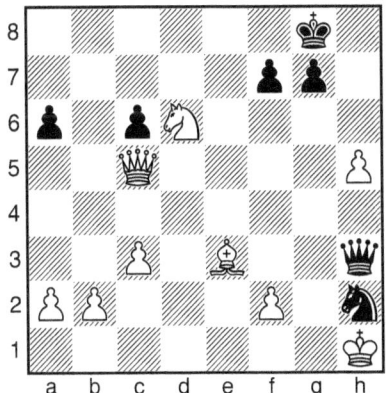

To defend from the mate 1...♘f3#, white needs to deflect the black queen. The only way to do that is

1.♕f5!, and now 1...♘f3+? 2.♕xh3 is plain bad, but even after the strongest reply **1...♘g4+!? 2.♔g1**, white's position is not worse at all.

178

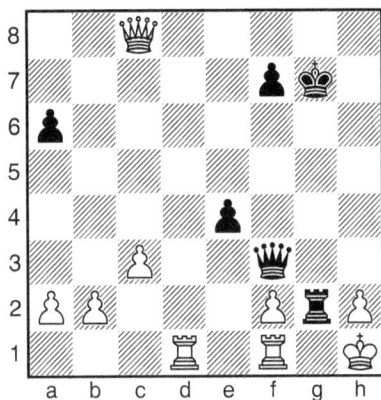

Black has four ways to deliver checkmate in one, for instance, 1...♖g3#. White can delay the checkmate for a few moves by giving up several of his pieces with checks: 1.♕g8+ ♔xg8 2.♖d8+ ♔g7 3.♖g8+ ♔xg8, even though it won't allow him to save the game. To neutralize the mate threat, white needs to deflect the black queen. This can be done in several ways. 1.♖d3? is poor, because after 1...exd3, the black queen remains in place, as well as all the mate threats. 1.♕h3? ♖g3+! 2.♕g2 ♕xg2# is no good either. The

best solution is the queen sacrifice
1.♕f5!, which prevents the direct
mate threat: 1...♖g3+? 2.♕xf3,
elimination, and after **1...♕xf5**
2.♔xg2, it's now black who needs to
think about how to salvage a draw.

179

180

181

182

183

184

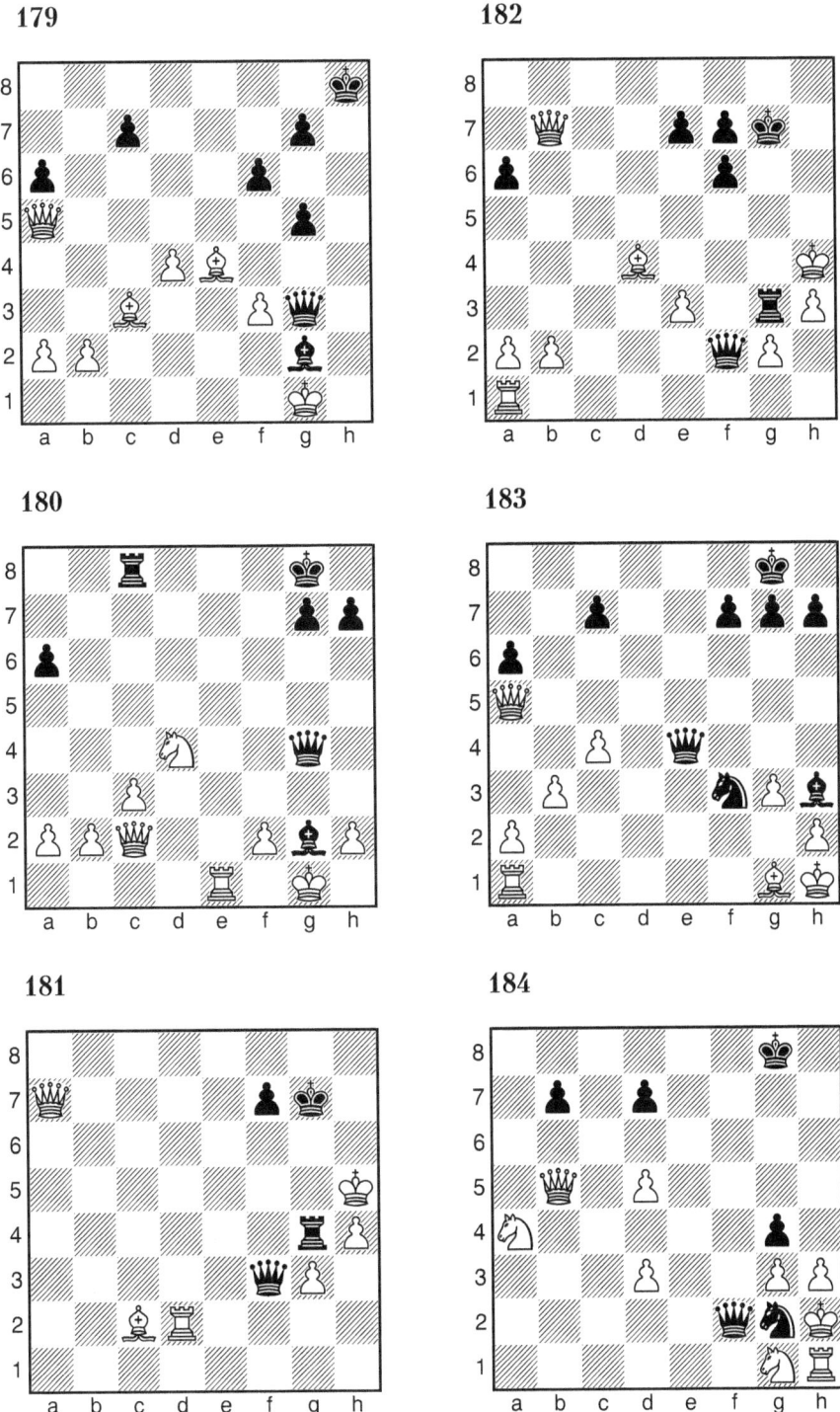

185

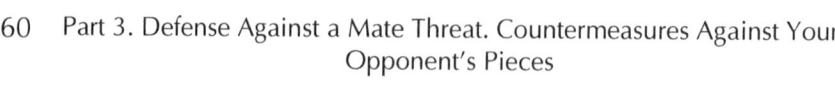

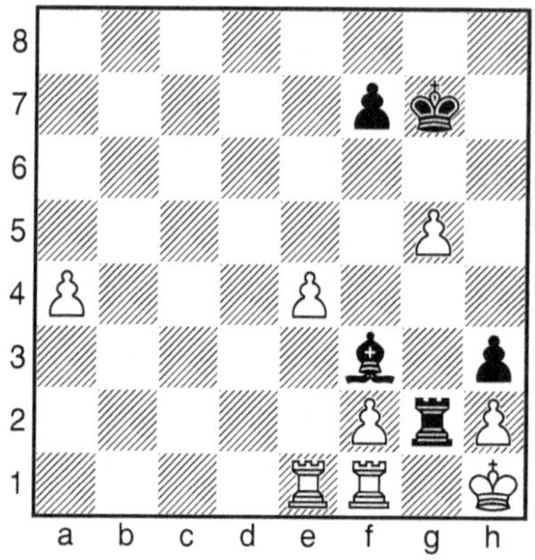

188

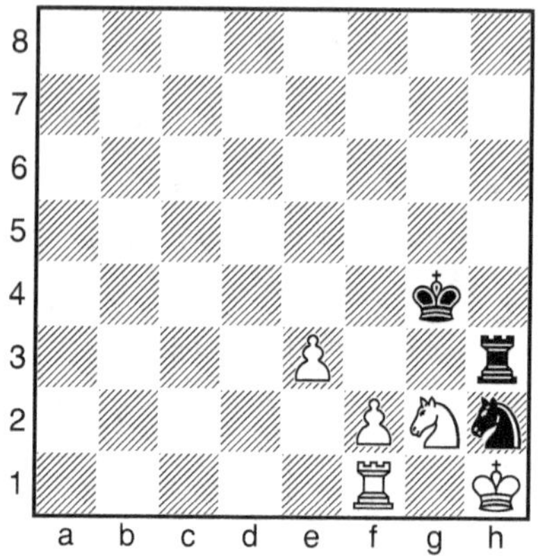

186

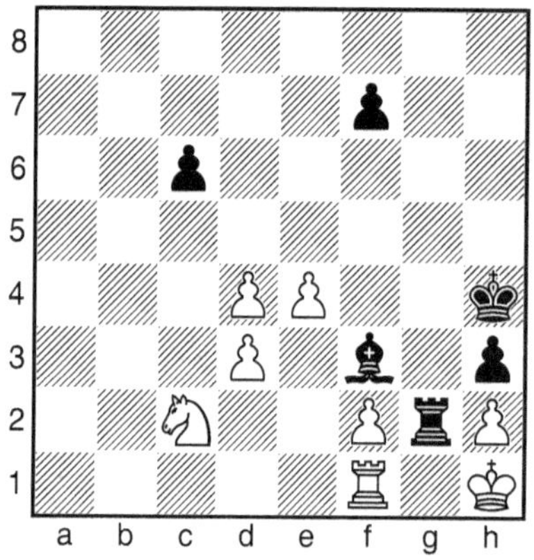

189

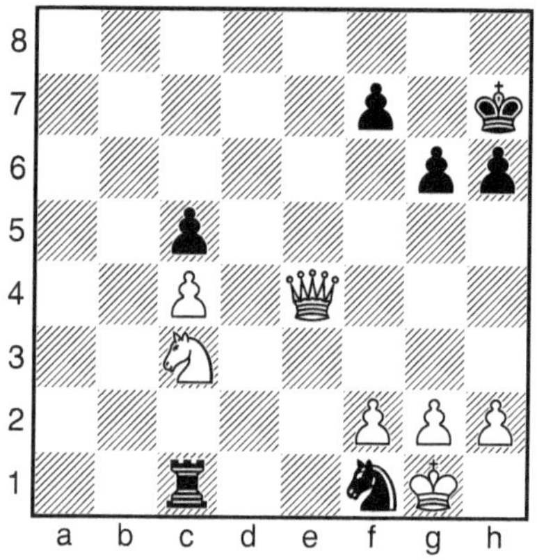

187

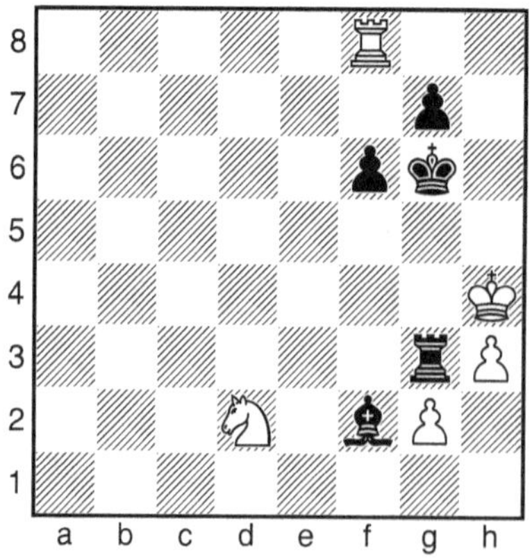

190

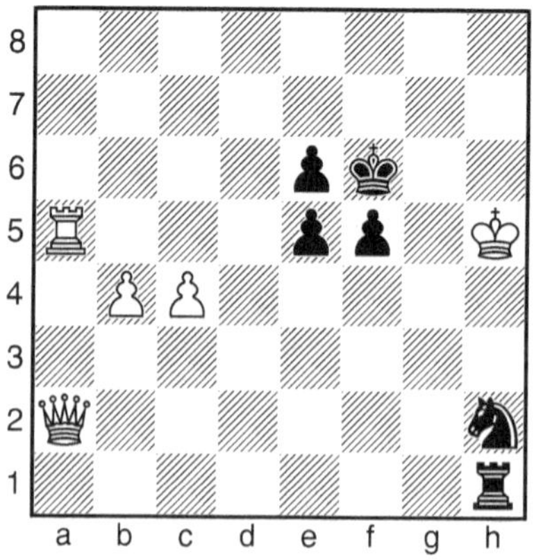

Chapter 12

COMBINATIONS

In this chapter, we study the conjunction of deflection and all the tactics we studied in the previous chapters. We should point out that in the context of defending from mate threats, deflection is often used in conjunction with counter-strikes. Defending your own king is a legitimate reason to drop whatever else you're doing!

In every exercise presented in this chapter, white has an opportunity to defend against the opponent's mate threats by using deflection in various conjunctions with counter-strikes and elimination.

191

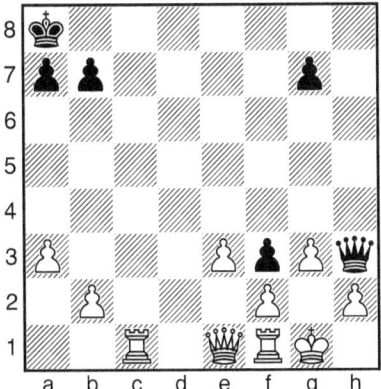

The mate threat 1...♛g2# can only be stopped by deflection and counter-strike used in conjunction. After

1.♜c8+!, the black queen is forced to divert its attention to the white rook **1...♛xc8**, which automatically eliminates black's mate threat. After that, it's easy for white to win.

192

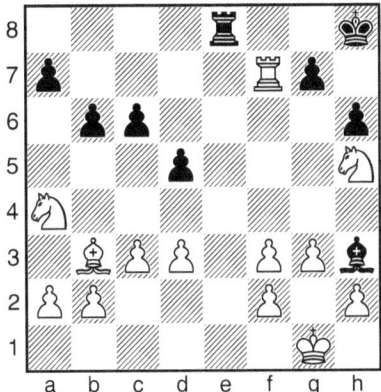

Black threatens 1...♜e1#. To defend, white may attempt to use interference 1.♜e7?, but this is easily refuted by simply capturing the undefended piece, 1...♜xe7. **1.♜f8+!** is much stronger; now, after 1...♚h7 2.♜xe8, white defends from the checkmate with counter-strike and elimination, while after **1...♜xf8**, it turns out that white used deflection and counter-strike in conjunction. Still, the exercise is not over yet: the black rook can return to e8 on the next move, renewing the mate threat.

To convert his material advantage, white needs to play **2.♘f4!**, either deflecting or eliminating another black piece, the bishop. Counter-strike, elimination and deflection tactics were used in this exercise.

193

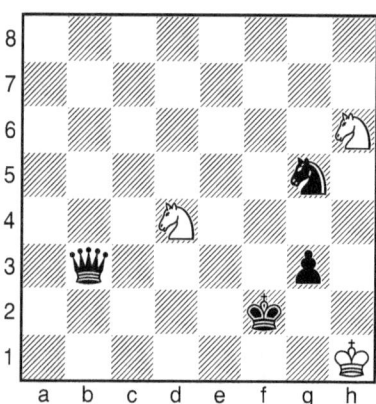

Black has created several mate threats: 1...♛b1#, 1...♛d1#, 1...♛b7+, which can be easily eliminated by capturing the queen. However, it turns out that 1.♘xb3? is met by another, slightly less obvious mate threat – 1...g2+! 2.♔h2 g1=♛#. To save the game, white needs to deliver a series of counter-strikes: **1.♘g4+! ♔f1 2.♘h2+!**, and now, after 2...♔f2 3.♘g4+!, the game ends in a perpetual check, while after both 2...♔e1 and **2...gxh2**, it turns out that white has managed to deflect one of two black pieces (either the queen or the pawn), and after eliminating the queen, **3.♘xb3!**, all mate threats disappear, and the game soon ends in a draw. To defend from checkmate, white had to use counter-strikes in conjunction with elimination and deflection.

194

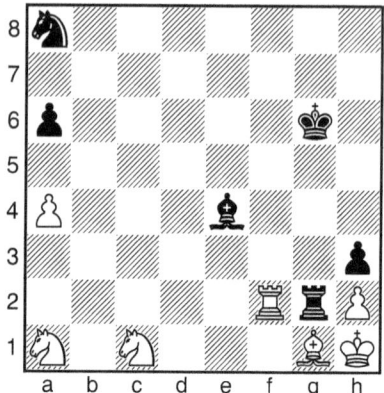

Black threatens to checkmate with a discovered bishop check by moving his rook. To save the game, white needs to use deflection. After **1.♖f4!**, the black bishop is under attack and cannot take part in the mating combination; for instance, 1...♖g4+ 2.♖xe4 ♖xe4 3.a5!? gives black nothing: white is at least no worse. To retain the mate threat, black needs to retreat with his bishop along the long diagonal, and white will use deflection again and again: **1...♗b7 2.♖b4! ♗c6 3.♖c4! ♗d5 4.♖d4! ♗f3**, and now it's simplest to play **5.♖f4**, repeating the position. White should be very precise: for instance, after 4.♖c5?, the black bishop finds a safe space, 4...♗b7!, and white is losing.

We should point out that white defends from checkmate only by attacking the bishop on every move. This tactic is called "perpetual attack" and can be used in other contexts as well, not only to defend from checkmate.

195

198

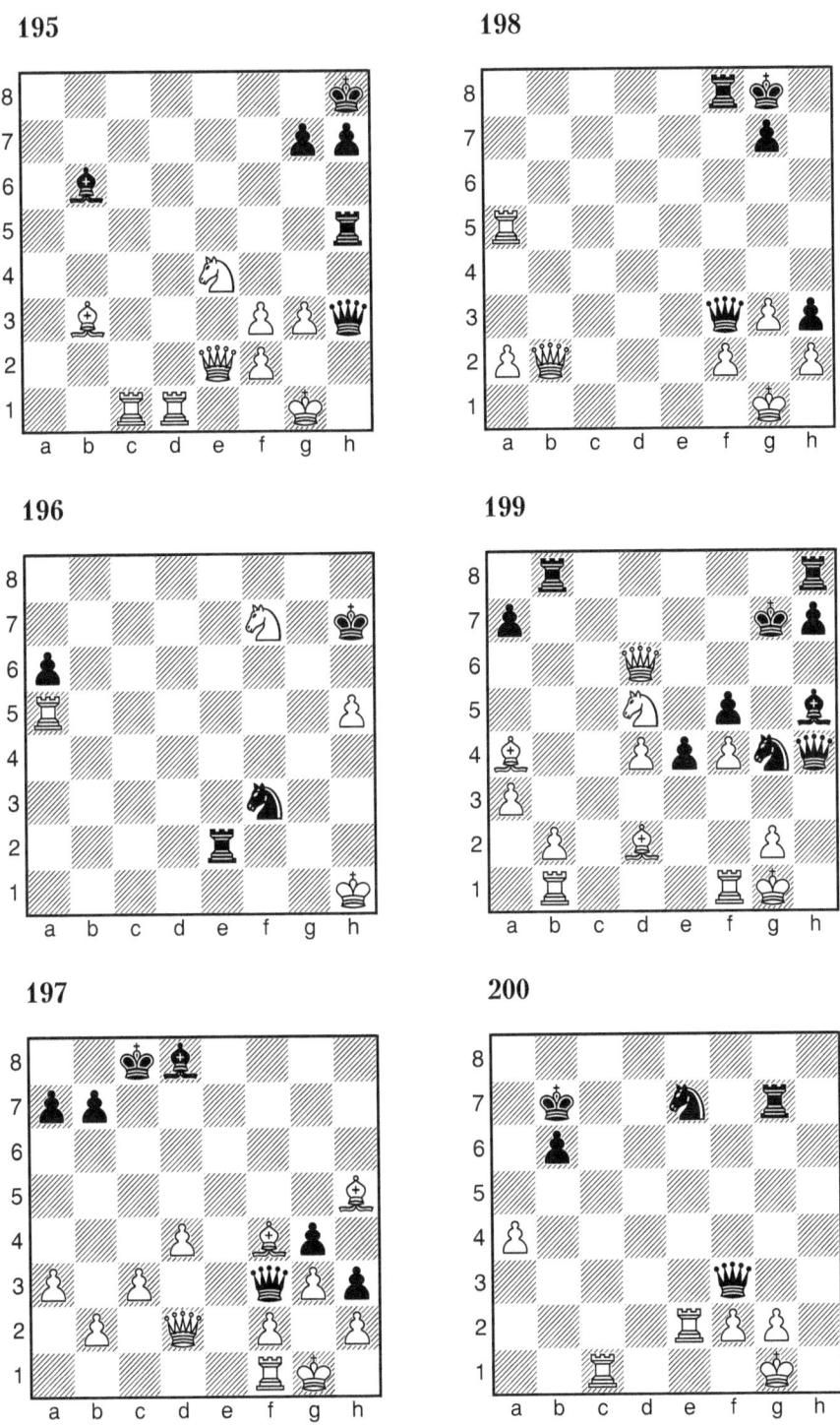

196

199

197

200

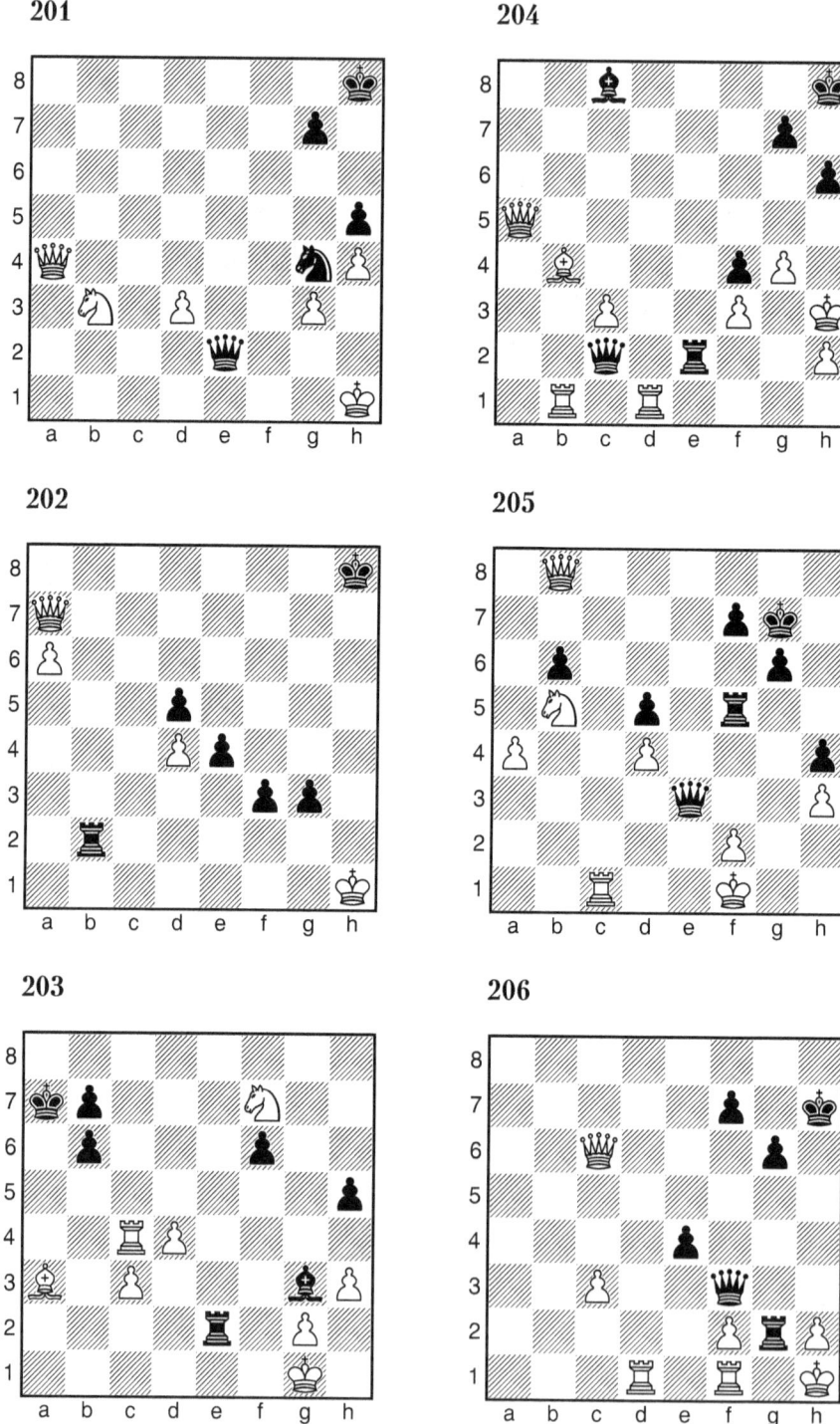

201

202

203

204

205

206

207

210

208

211

209

212

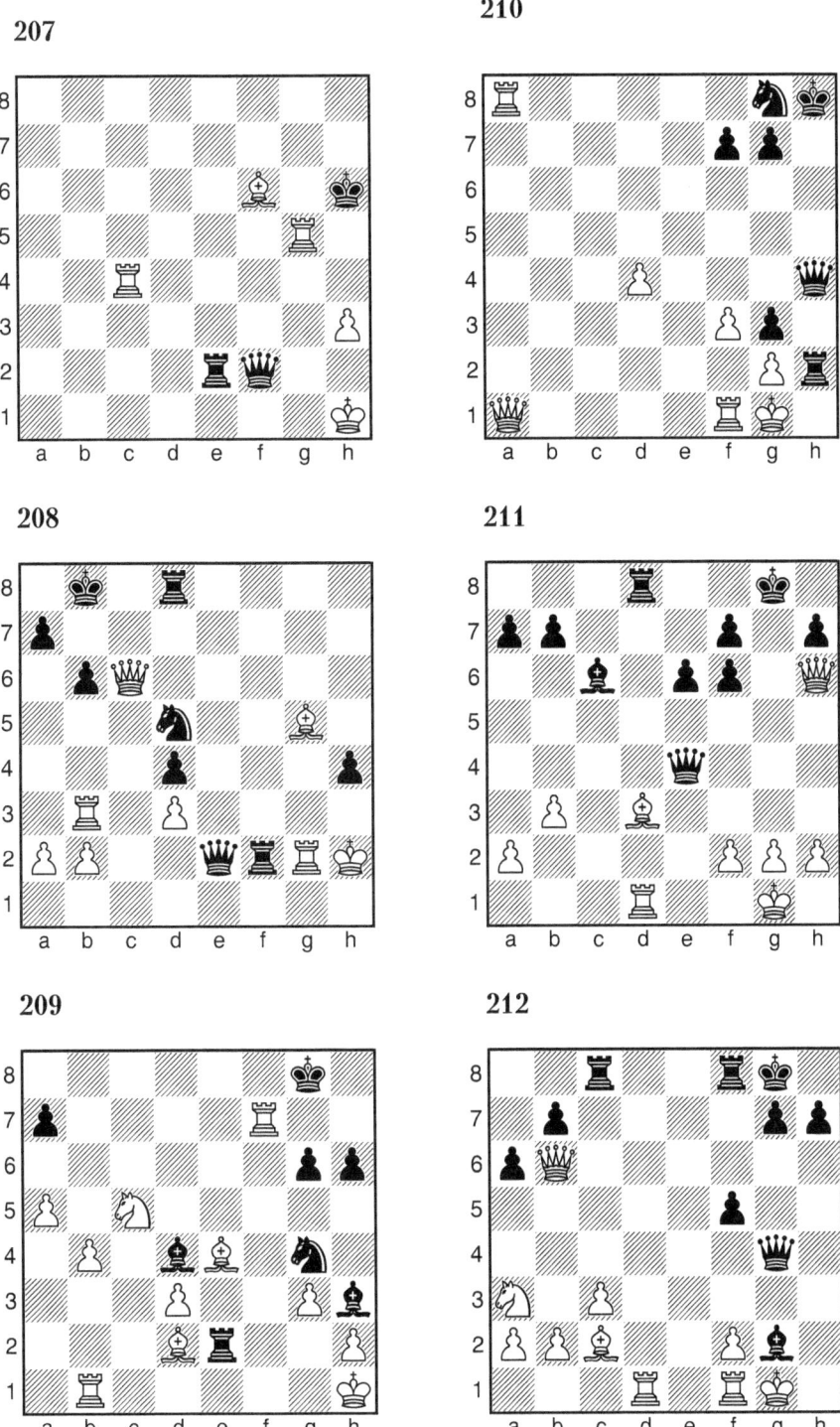

213

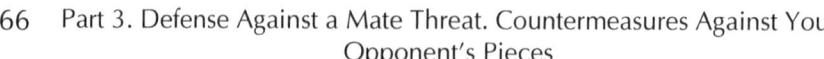

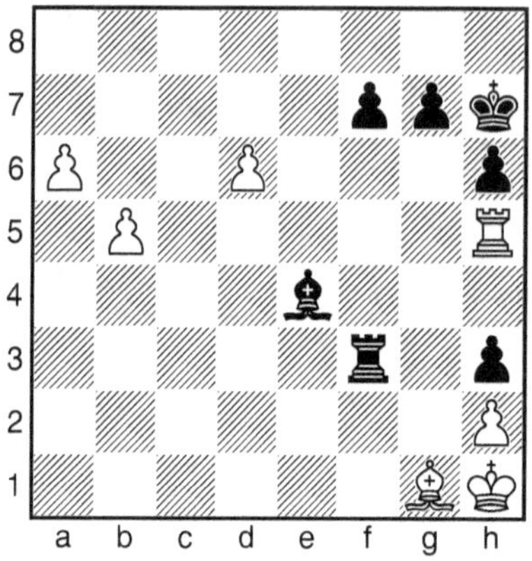

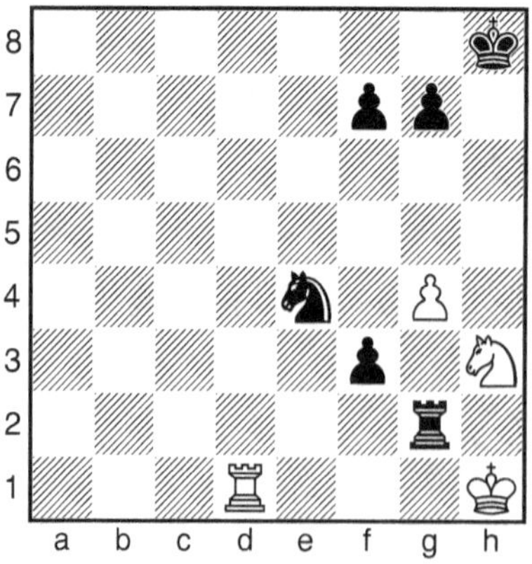

216

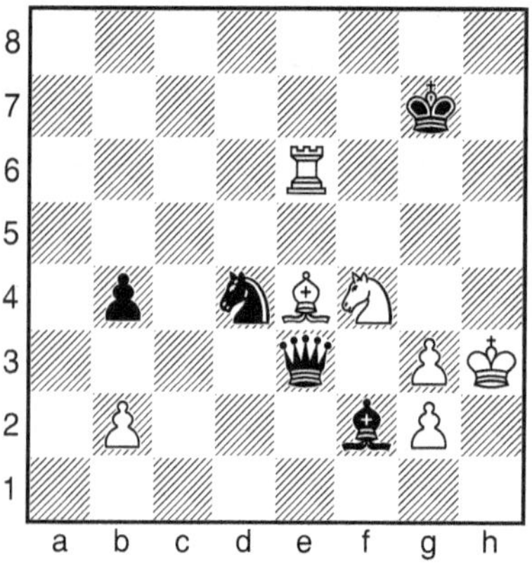

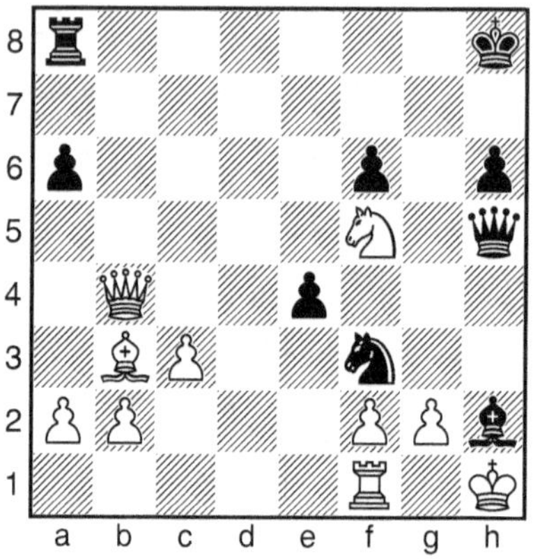

214

217

215

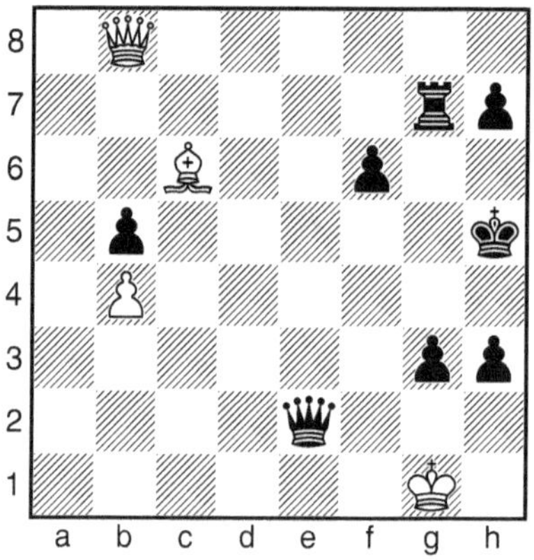

218

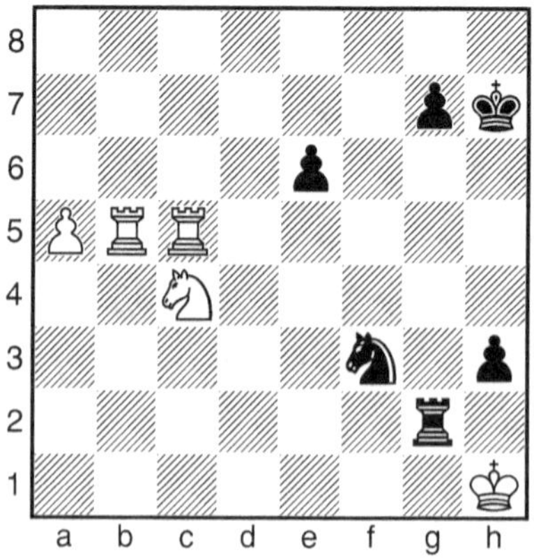

Chapter 13

PINNING

Another defensive countermeasure against pieces that create a mate threat is pinning. Pinning the opposing piece completely neutralizes it, stopping it from moving and taking part in any kind of mating combinations.

In the context of defense against mate threats, this tactic can only be used when the mating piece is pinned to its own king. We should also note that defending from checkmate with a pin often leads to subsequent elimination of the pinned piece.

219

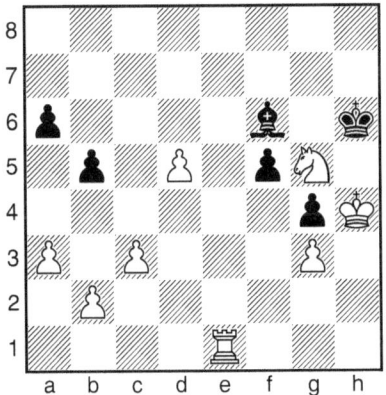

Black threatens 1...♗xg5#. The only defense is pinning the black bishop: **1.♖e6!**, and the white king is now completely safe.

220

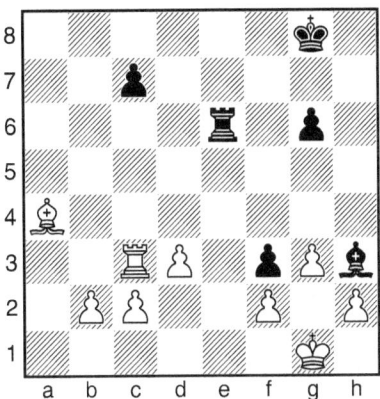

Black threatens 1...♖e1#. After **1.♗b3!**, the black rook cannot move, which means that the immediate mate threat is resolved. We should point out that after **1...♔g7** the pinned piece will be eliminated: **2.♗xe6!**, and white will convert his material advantage. This example clearly shows that in the context of the imminent checkmate, the pin, as well as deflection, is almost always used in conjunction with the subsequent elimination of the piece.

There's another theoretical subtlety here. If there was a black queen instead of a rook on e6, the move 1.♗b3! would still remain the only defense; however, since black can now play 1...♕xb3, it would have been considered a combination of pinning and deflection tactics.

221

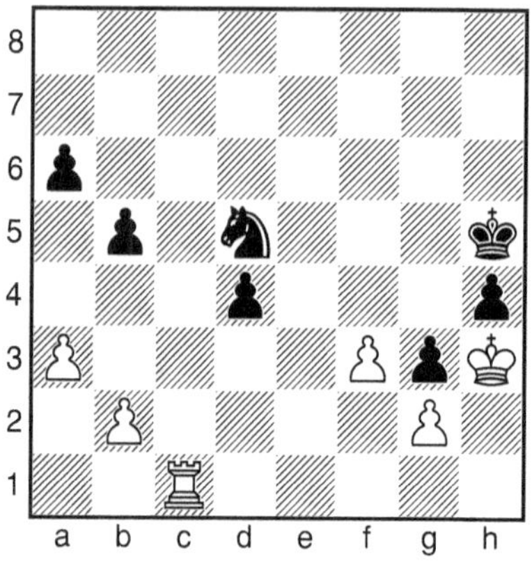

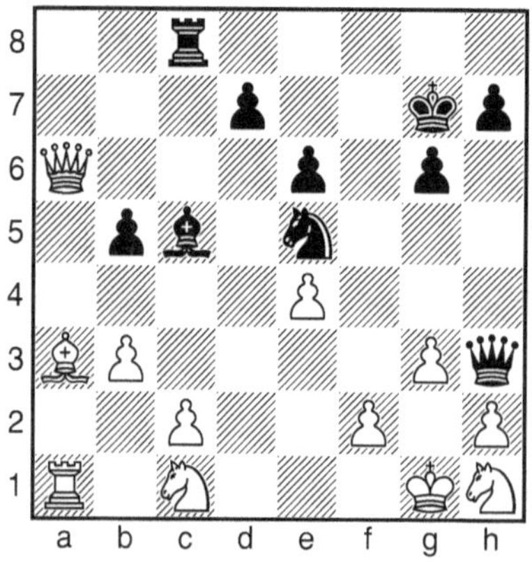

224

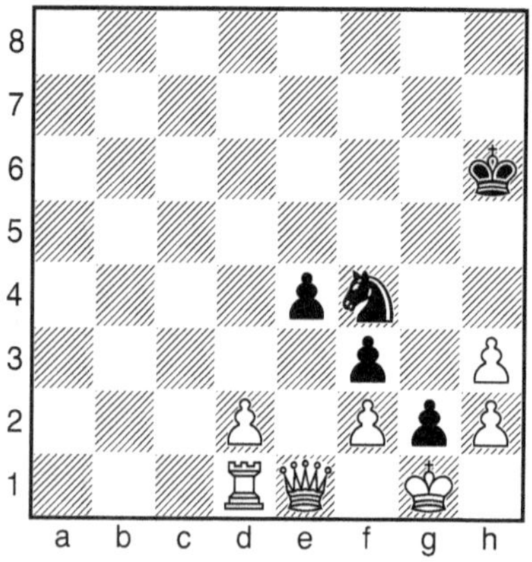

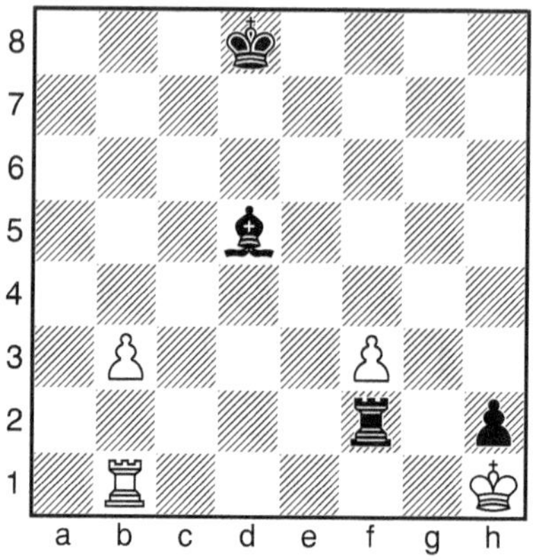

222

225

223

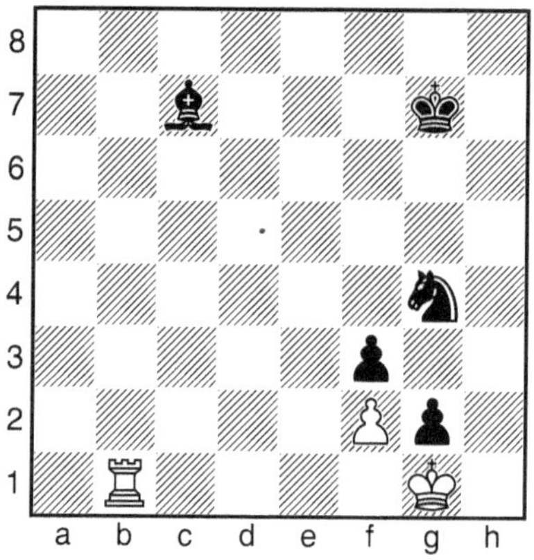

226

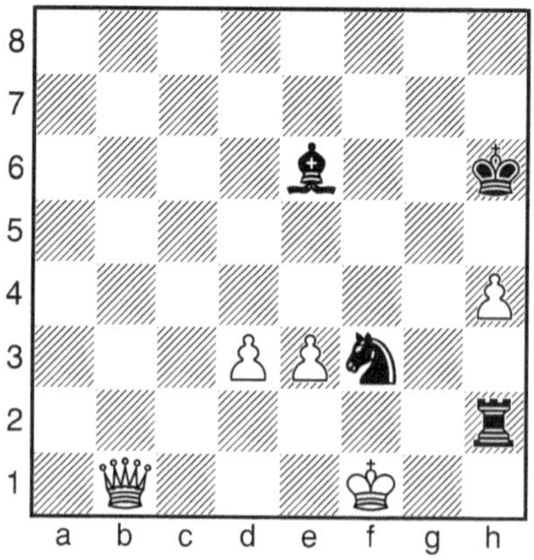

227

230

228

231

229

232

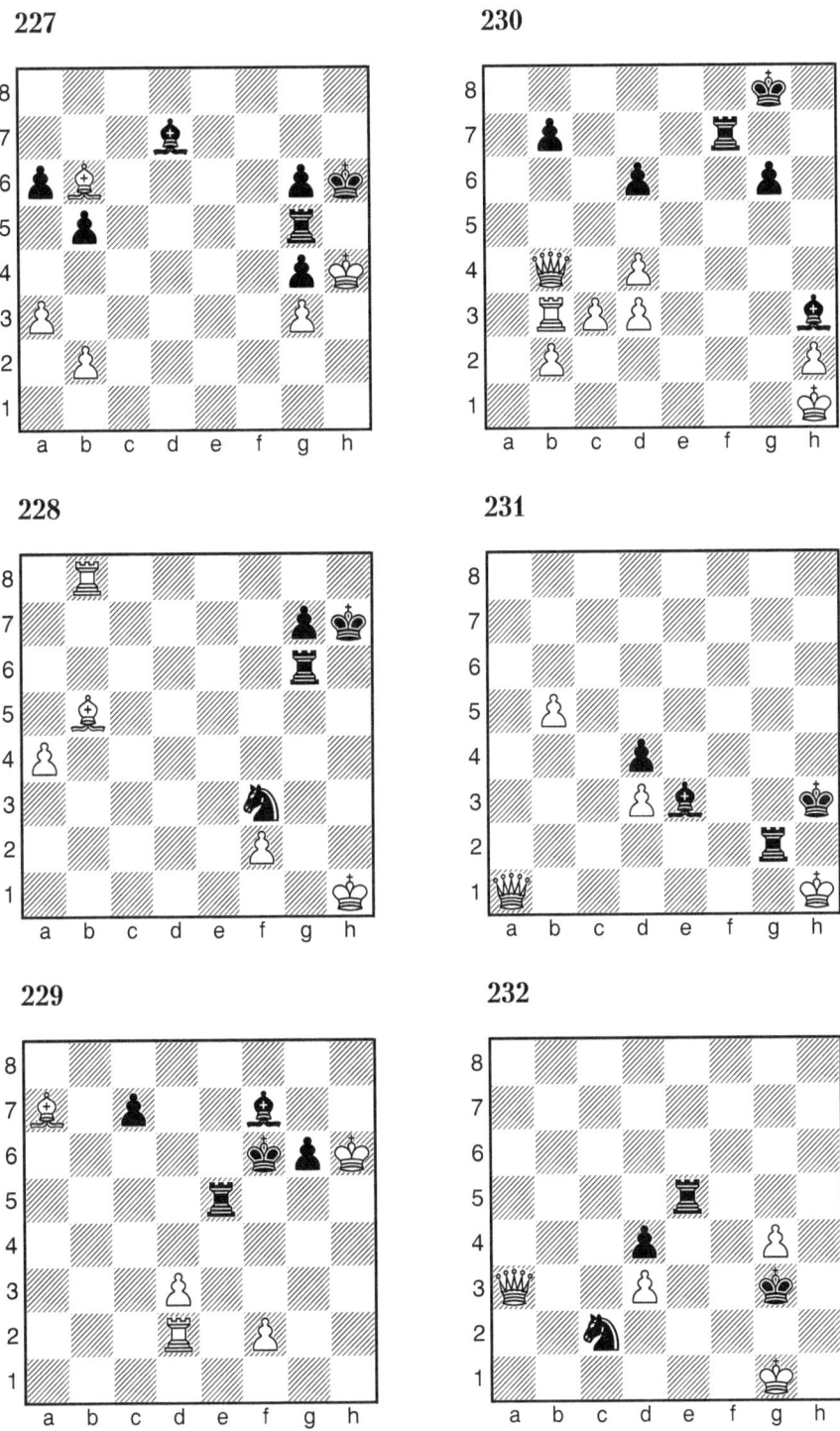

Chapter 14

COMBINATIONS

In this chapter, we study the conjunction of pinning and all the tactics we studied in the previous chapters.

In every exercise presented in this chapter, white has an opportunity to defend against the opponent's mate threats by using pins in various conjunctions with counter-strikes, elimination and deflection.

233

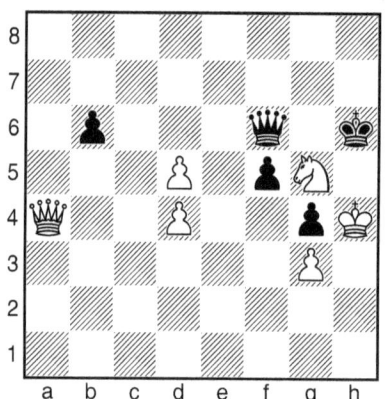

White can defend from checkmate 1...♕g5# with the precise **1.♕c6!**, and now the black queen is both pinned and attacked, which makes this defensive move a conjunction of pinning and deflection tactics. After the inevitable queen trade, white gets an extra piece and a totally won position.

234

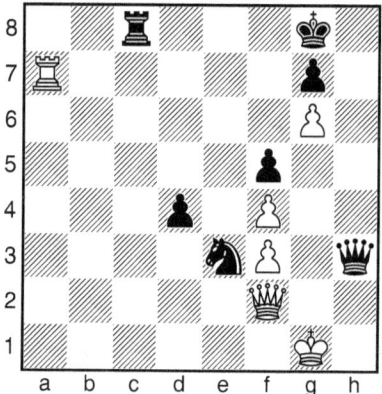

Black is a piece up and has created a forced checkmate threat: 1...♖c1+ 2.♕f1 ♖xf1#. The only satisfactory defense for white is first to use a pin and deflection in conjunction, **1.♖a8!** and after **1... ♖xa8**, use the "stalemating idea": **2.♕a2+! ♖xa2**, stalemate. Black can neither move his king, 2...♔f8 or 2...♔h8, nor interpose with his knight, 2...♘c4 or 2...♘d5, because of a mate in one. If black tries to search for an alternative on the first move, he will be hard-pressed to find a defense against 2.♖xc8#. Thus, to defend from checkmate, white used pinning and deflection in conjunction, stalemating ideas, forced mate and elimination. We should note that using a great number of different defensive tactics often does not make the solution any longer, even though it does make it a bit more complicated.

235

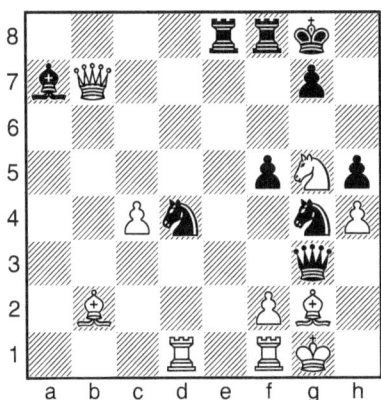

A lot of black pieces have gathered around the white king, creating several mate threats, including 1...♕h2# and 1...♘e2+ 2.♔h1 ♕h2#. Since the king is mated by the black queen in both lines, an attempt to eliminate it seems logical: 1.fxg3?, but it's easily refuted by 1...♘e2+ 2.♔h1 ♘xg3#. The strongest defense is the sudden counter-strike **1.♕xg7+!**. After the forced **1...♔xg7**, the black d4 knight is pinned and cannot take part in the mating combination anymore, which allows white to eliminate the queen with impunity: **2.fxg3!**. As a result of this defensive combination consisting of counter-strike, elimination and pin, white repels all mate threats and gets a big advantage.

236

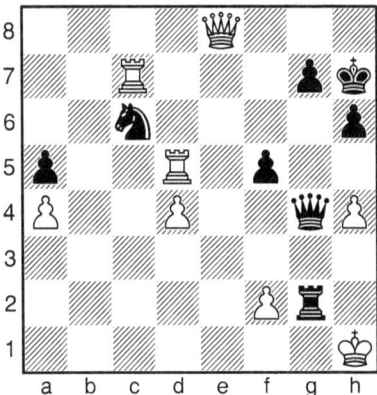

The white king is in big trouble once again. Black threatens both 1...♕h3# and 1...♖g1+ 2.♔h2 ♕g2#. However, this does not really change the evaluation of the position because white is to move! A powerful counter-strike **1.♖xg7+!** follows, after which black is either mated by force, 1...♔xg7 2.♖d7+ ♔f6 3.♕f7#, or plays **1...♕xg7** and, after **2.♖d7!**, all mate threats are gone, and he loses his queen due to the pin. There might follow **2...♖g1+ 3.♔h2 ♖g2+ 4.♔h3**, and black is out of checks. In the main line of the solution, white defended from mate threats by using a combination of counter-strike, pin and deflection, while in the sideline, he mated by force.

237

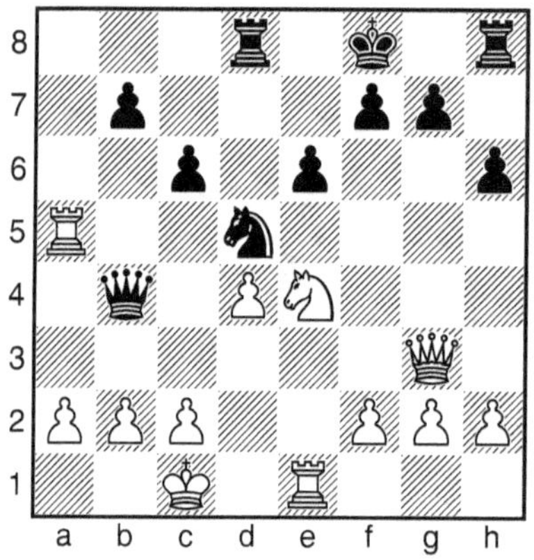

240

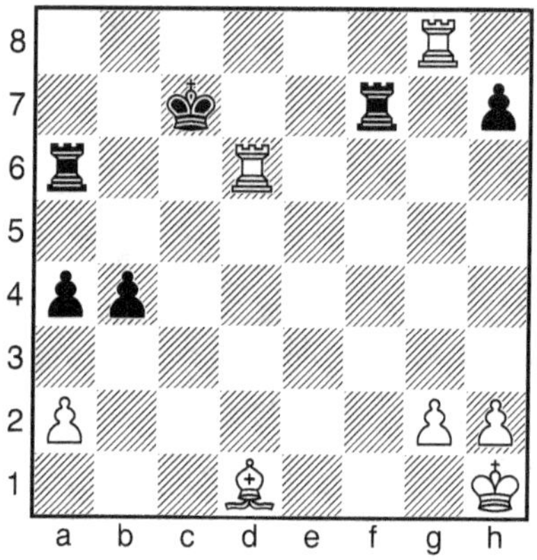

238

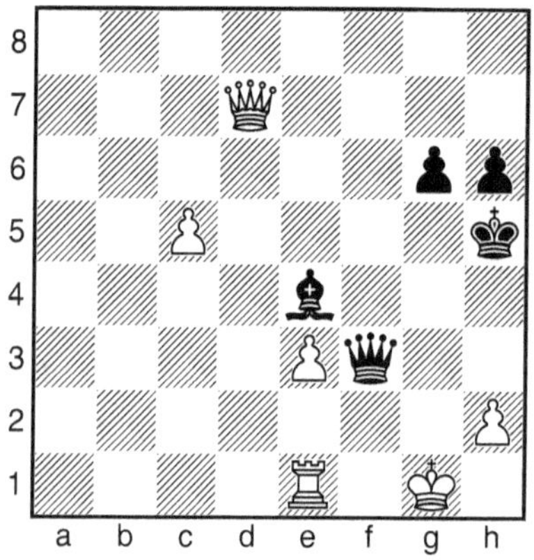

241

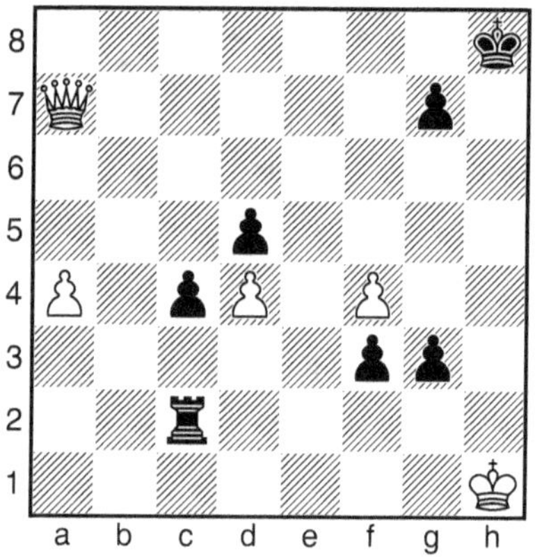

239

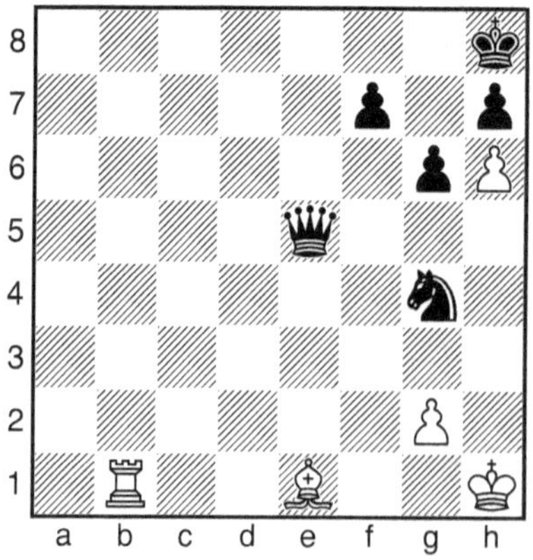

242

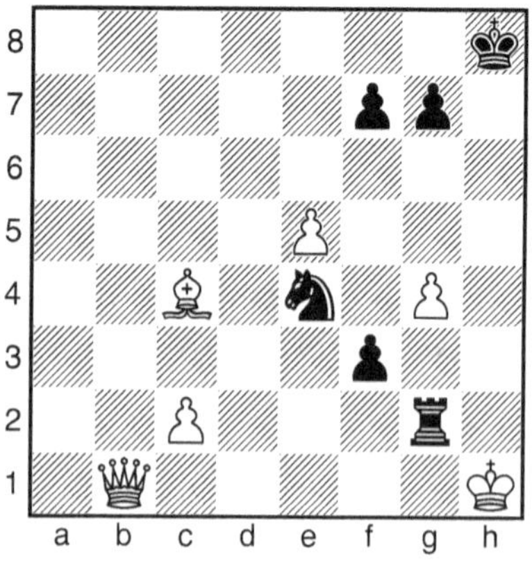

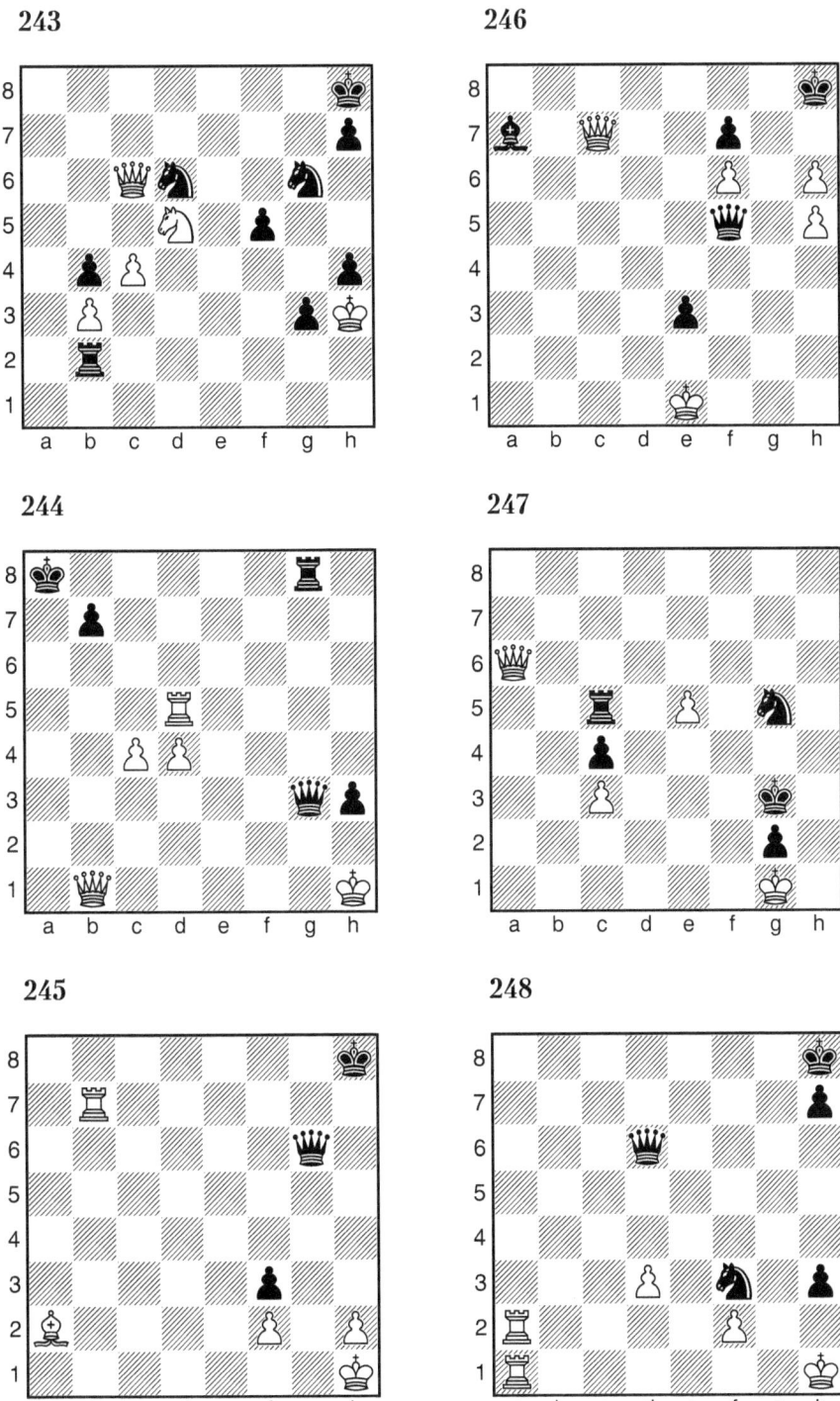

243

244

245

246

247

248

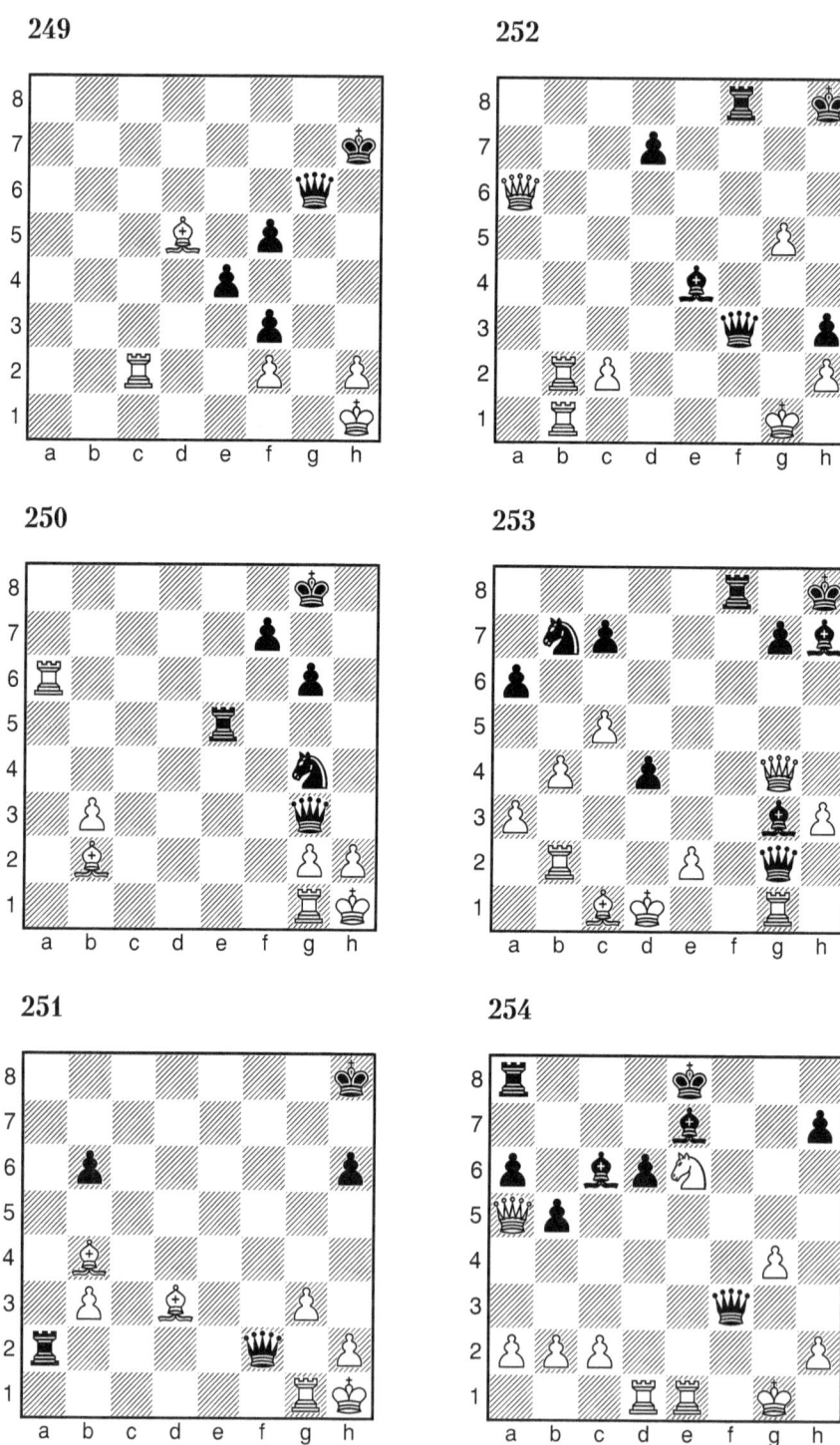

249

250

251

252

253

254

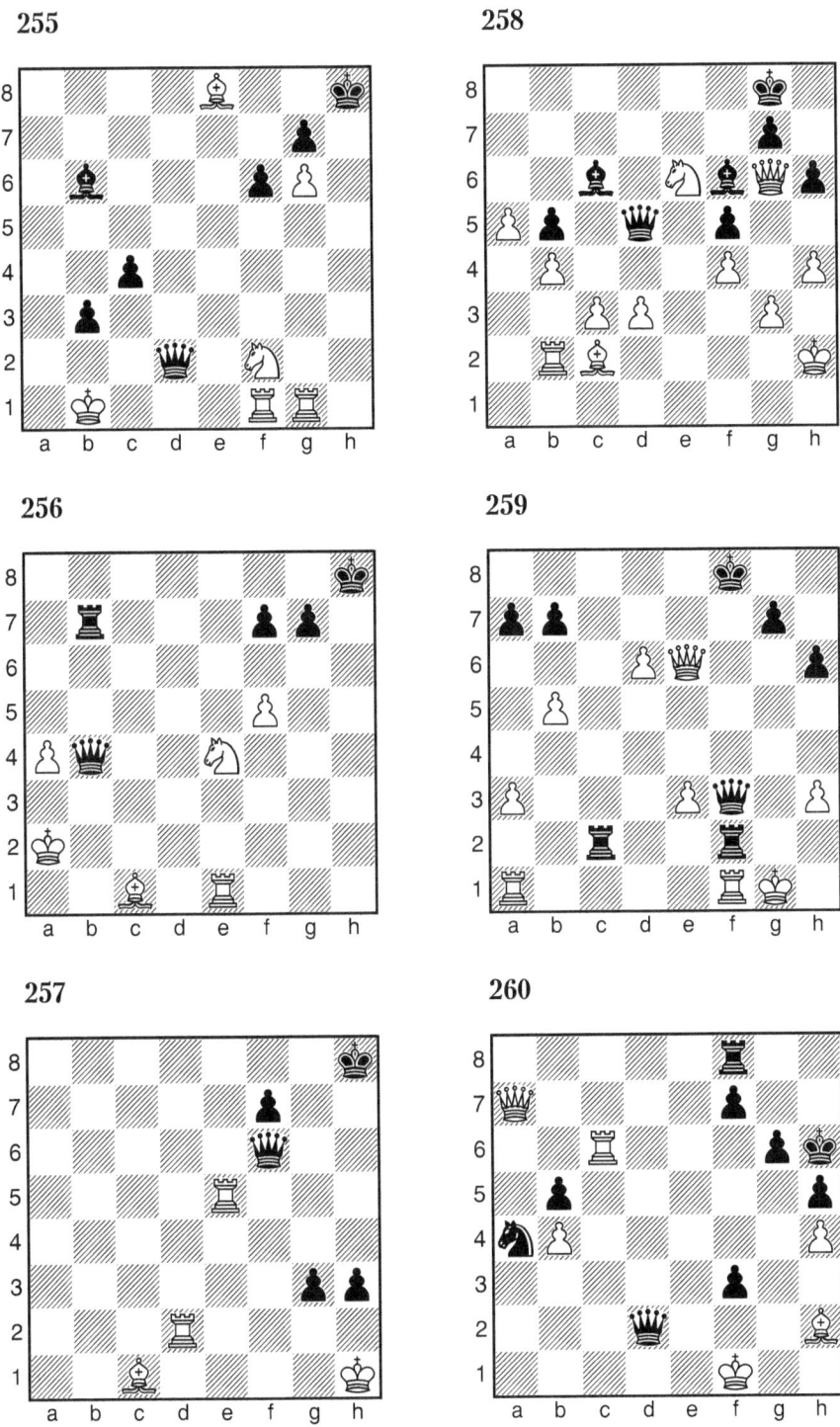

255

256

257

258

259

260

INTERFERENCE

Another defensive tactic used as a countermeasure against the opposing pieces that threaten to checkmate you is called interference. Interference is positioning one of your pieces on the line of action of the opposing long-range pieces to disrupt their attacking activity.

In the context of defending from mate threats, interference cannot be used separately from other defensive tactics. This happens because the interfering piece can always be captured by the attacking side.

261

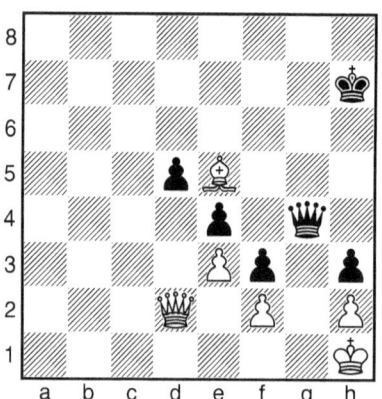

Black is threatening 1...♕g2#. The only defense is interference, **1.♗g3!**, cutting off the black queen's access to the g2 square. After **1...♕xg3**, the queen will be immediately eliminated, **2.hxg3** or **2.fxg3**, with an easy win.

262

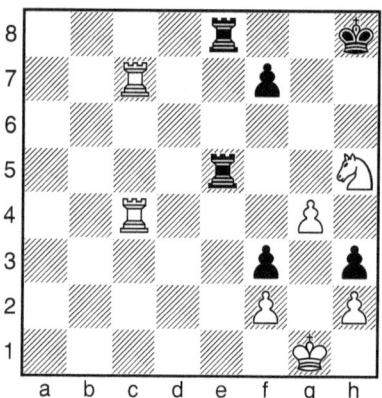

White needs to defend against the mate threat 1...♖e1#. He doesn't have many good defensive resources. For instance, he cannot play 1.♖c1? or 1.♖e7? because of 1...♖e1+ 2.♖xe1 ♖xe1#. Only interference can save white from checkmate, but an attempt to cut off the black rook from the e1 square, 1.♖e4?, turns out to be just a small and senseless delay, because after 1...♖xe4, black's mate threat remains the same. In actuality, unlike the previous example, white doesn't need to stop the piece that makes the threatening move. Instead, he needs to close off the first rank to stop the black rook from delivering checkmate! There follows **1.♘g3! ♖e1+ 2.♘f1**, and white retains an extra piece and a good position. After **2...♖xf1+?**, the rook is simply captured by the king **3.♔xf1**, winning.

263

266

264

267

265

268

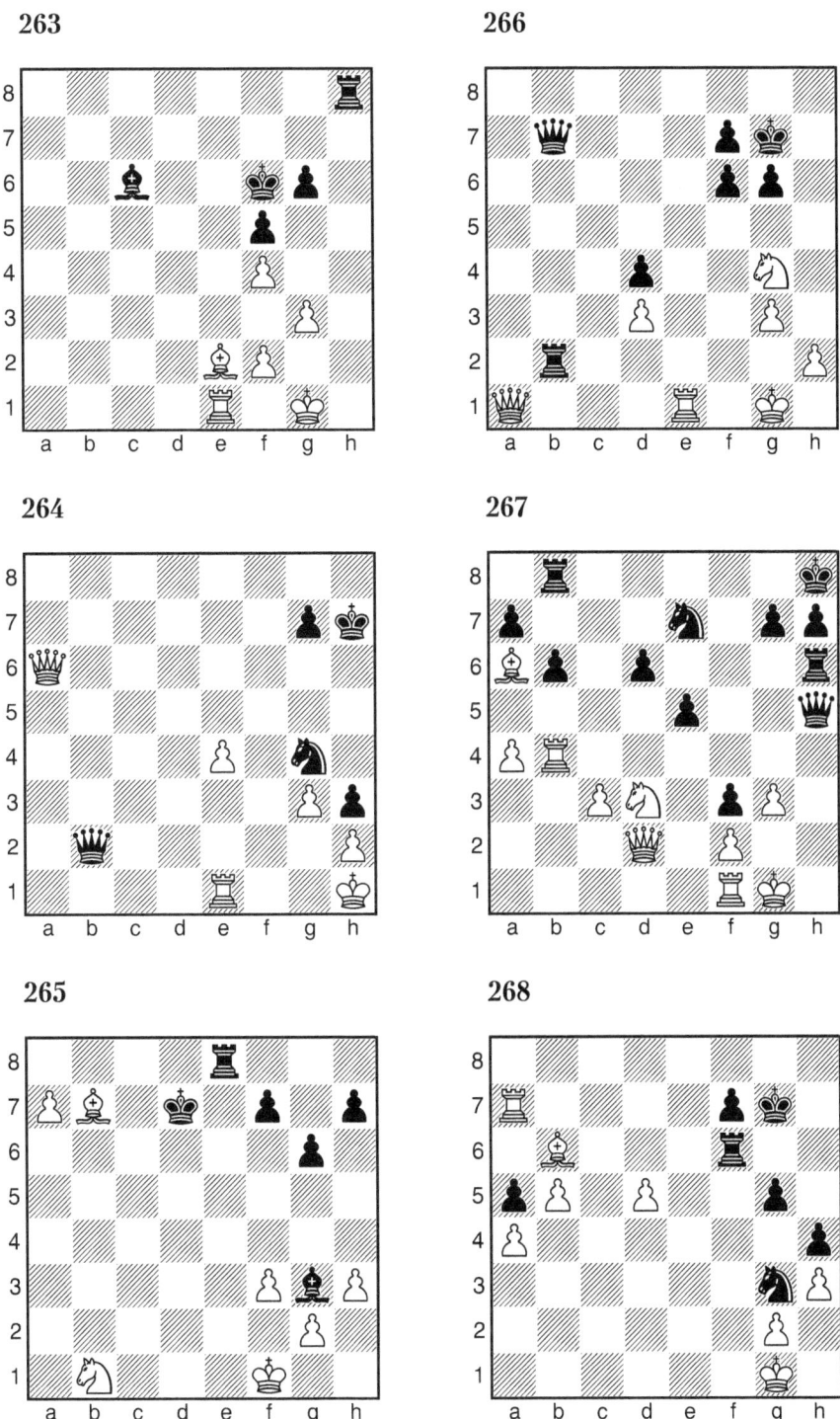

269

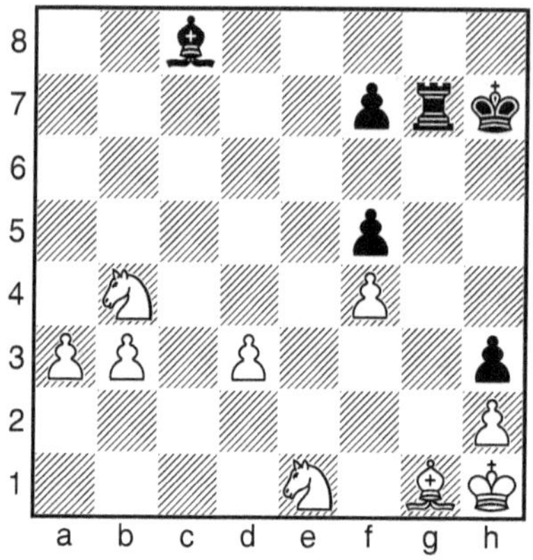

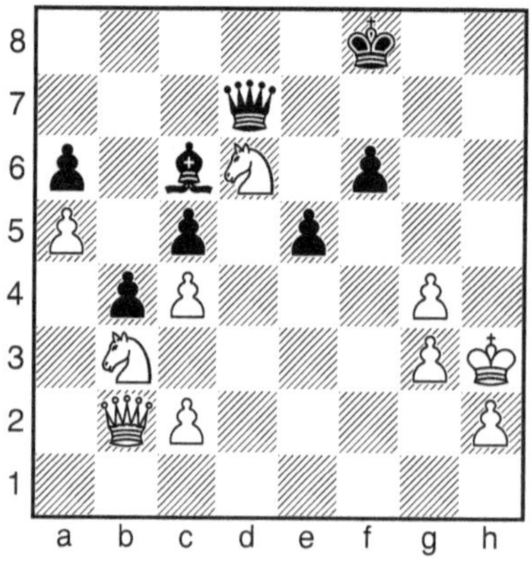

272

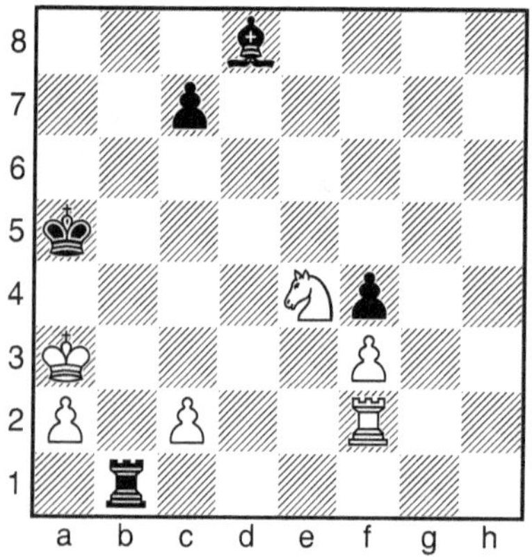

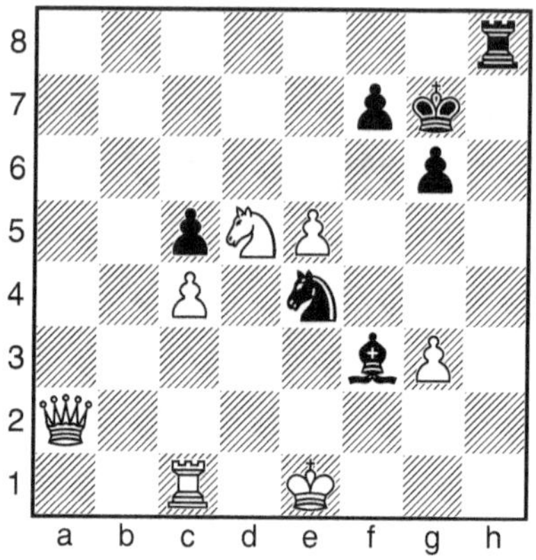

270

273

271

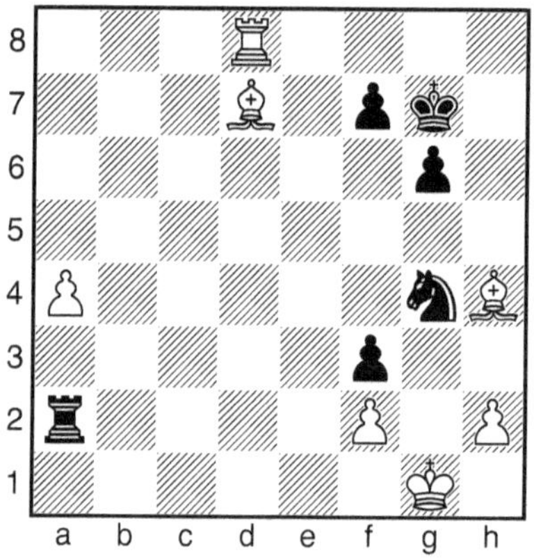

274

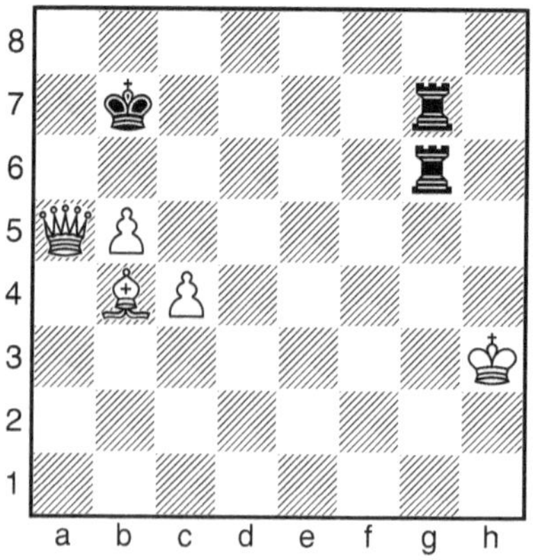

275

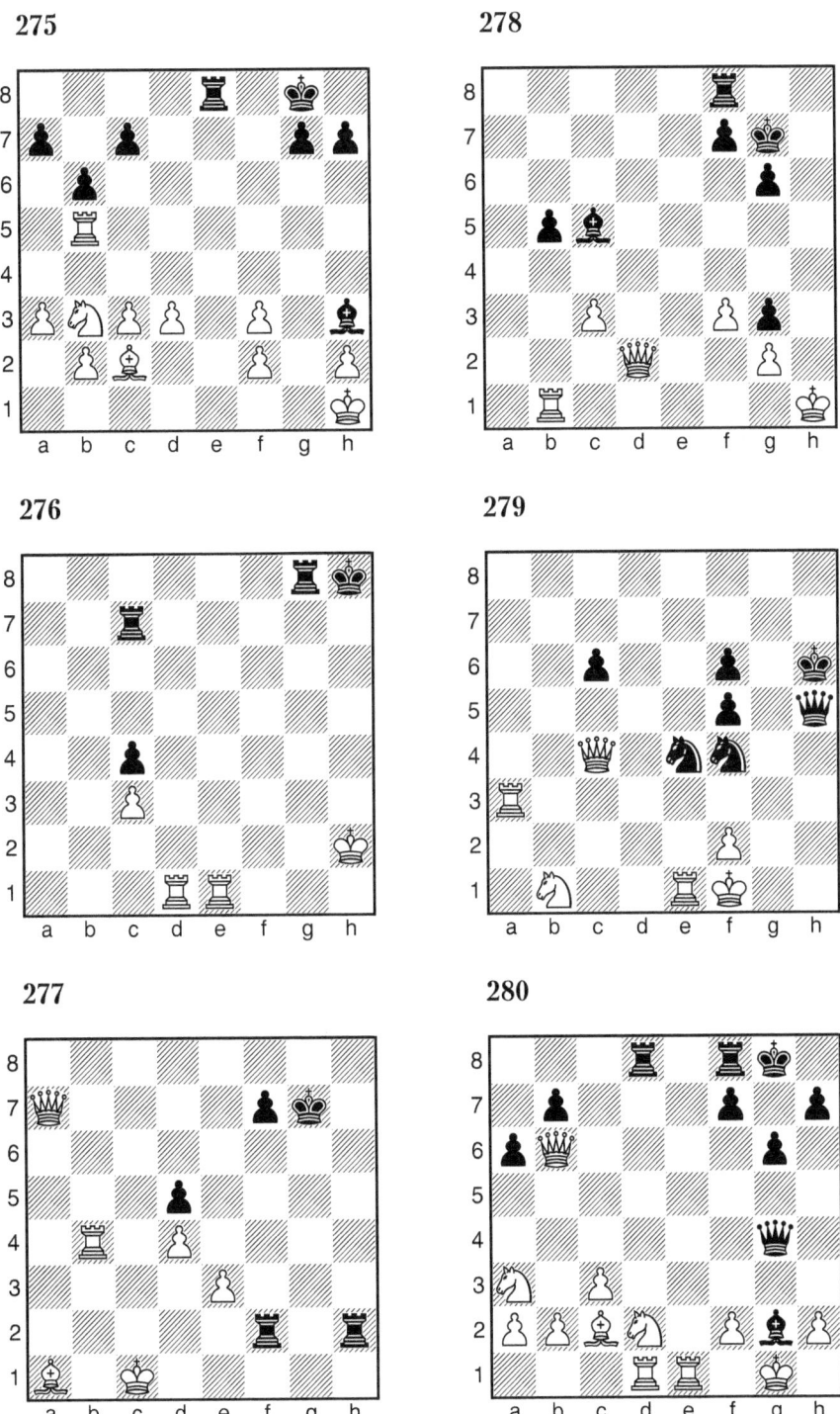

276

277

278

279

280

Chapter 16

COMBINATIONS

In this chapter, we study the conjunction of interference and all the tactics we studied in the previous chapters.

In every exercise presented in this chapter, white has an opportunity to defend against the opponent's mate threats by using interference in various conjunctions with counter-strikes, elimination, deflection and pinning.

281

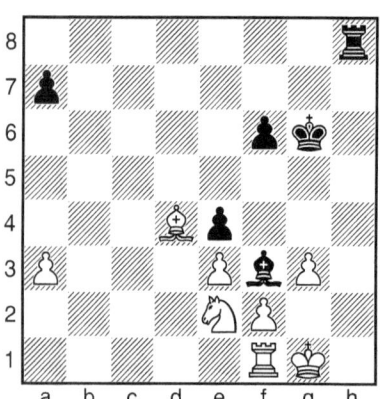

Black threatens 1...♖h1#. The only defensive resource available for white is the counter-strike **1.♘f4+!**, and after any king move, he can prevent the mate threat with interference – **1...♔f7 2.♘g2!** with an easy win. After closing off the black bishop's diagonal, white is ready to eliminate it with **2...♗xg2**

3.♔xg2. If white tries to close off the rook's file instead with 2.♘h3?, then, after 2...♖xh3, white will only have delayed the inevitable checkmate for a couple of moves.

282

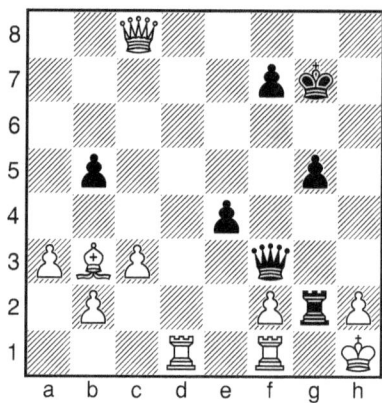

Black threatens to checkmate white with a discovered rook check – either by retreating along the g-file or playing 1...♖xf2#. We have already seen exercises with similar mating constructions in chapter 11, so we know that a discovered checkmate threat can be averted with deflection. White, for instance, can play 1.♕f5!?, and black has nothing better than 1...♕xf5 2.♔xg2 ♕g4+ 3.♔h1 ♕f3+ with perpetual check. Another way to deflect the queen is even stronger: **1.♖d3!**, and now **1...exd3** is met with another deflection – **2.♗d1!**. Now, after 2...♛f4, white eliminates the rook 3.♔xg2 and wins, so the queen has to retreat along the long diagonal. After **2...♛d5**, white has a choice between the perpetual attack 3.♗b3 ♛f3 4.♗d1 ♛d5 and interference **3.f3!** with an advantage for white. There can follow **3...♖xb2 4.♛g4!**, and white should eventually win. 2...♛e4 is also met with interference 3.f3!, leading to white's victory.

283

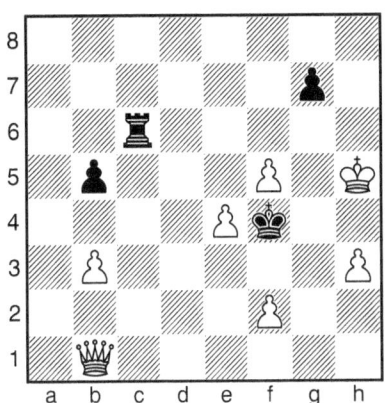

White is hoping to convert his extra material, but first he has to defend from the threat 1...♖h6#. Here, the combination of deflection and counter-strike 1.♛c1+? ♖xc1 just loses: black will now convert his extra rook. White is saved by interference **1.f6!**, and now, after 1...gxf6, the mate threat disappears as though it never existed, while after **1...♖xf6**, white is able to deliver the counter-strike **2.♛c1+!** with an easy win. In this exercise, white used interference in series with counter-strike.

We should note that white forced the black rook to move to a different square on the sixth rank with the interference, obtaining new defensive resources as a result. Such actions against an opposing piece is sometimes called "displacement".

284

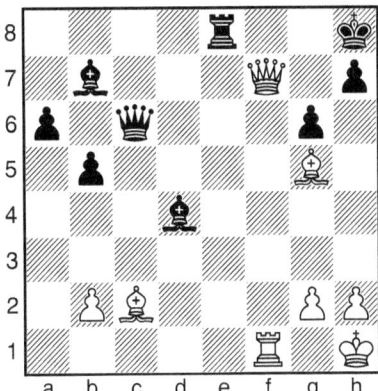

To find the best defense against 1...♛xg2#, white needs to check a lot of candidate moves. After the counter-strike 1.♗f6+? ♗xf6 2.♛xf6+ ♛xf6 3.♖xf6 he gets quickly checkmated: 3...♖e1+ 4.♖f1 ♖xf1#. Another attempt, 2.♗e4! ♛e6! 3.♛xe6 ♖xe6 4.♗xb7 ♗xb2 is not too good: black gets a decisive advantage. Interference 1.♖f3? ♖e1+ 2.♖f1 ♛xg2# or support 1.♖g1 ♛xg2+! 2.♖xg2 ♖e1# is just plain bad. 1.♛f3?! ♛xf3 2.gxf3 is more stubborn, but black still has a sizable advantage.

The only saving move is **1.♗e4!**, hoping for checkmate after 1...♖xe4?? 2.♛f8# or giving a perpetual check: **1...♛xe4 2.♗f6+! ♗xf6 3.♛xf6+ ♔g8 4.♛f7+ ♔h8 5.♛f6+**

etc. The purpose of 1.♗e4! is to displace the black queen, forcing it to move to another square on the long diagonal. Now that the black queen doesn't control the f6 square anymore, white can give perpetual check.

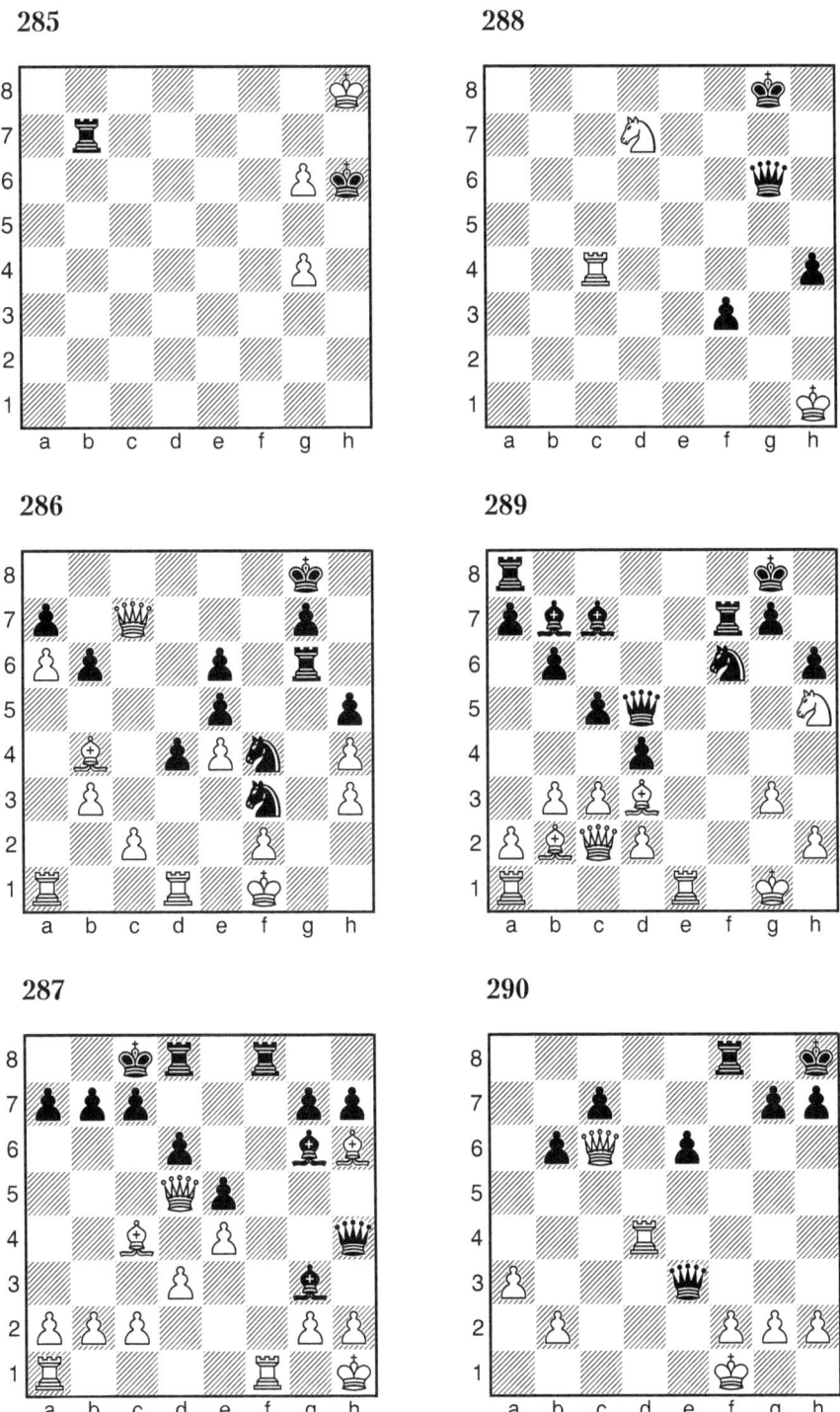

285

286

287

288

289

290

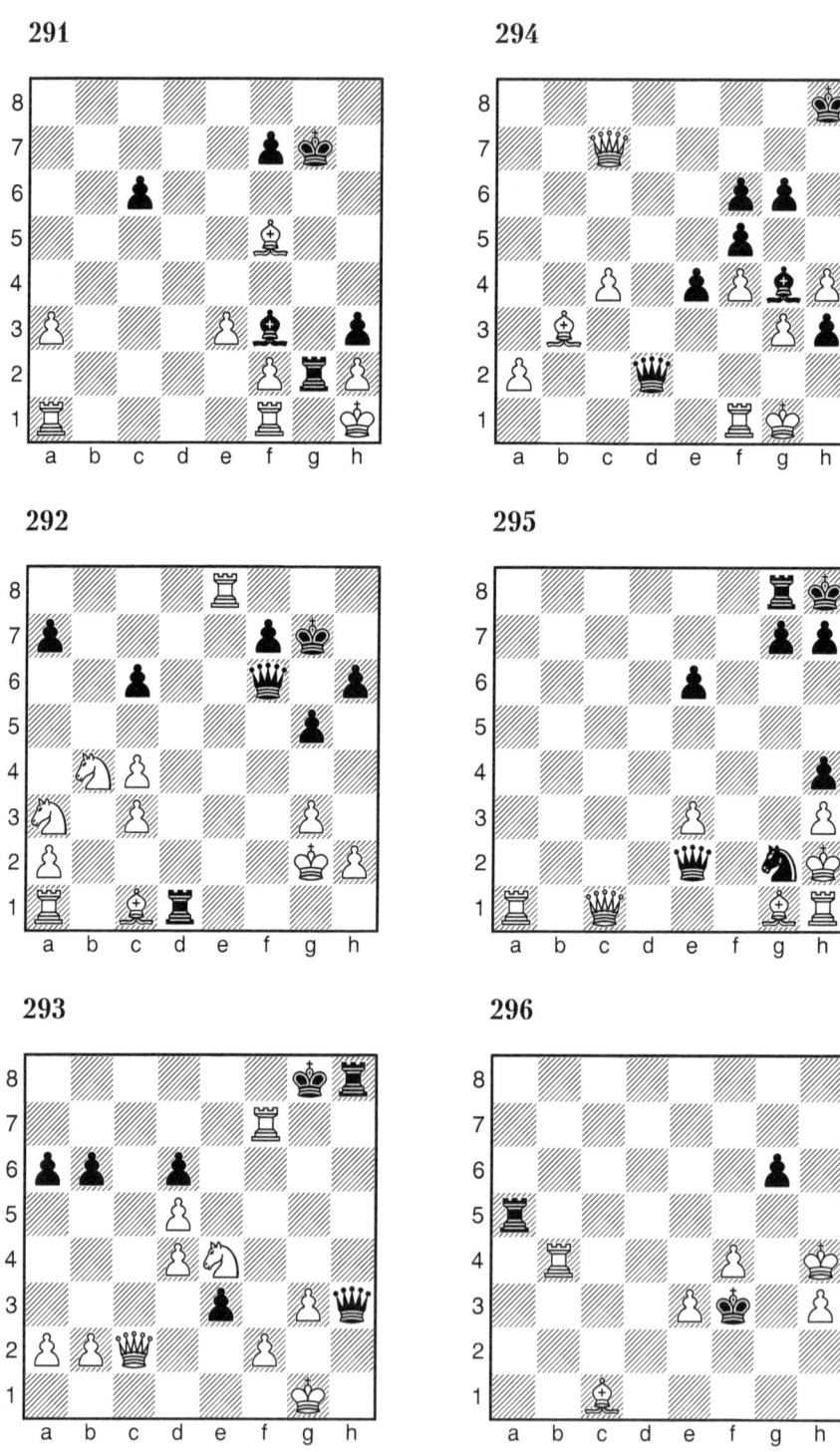

291

292

293

294

295

296

297

300

298

301

299

302

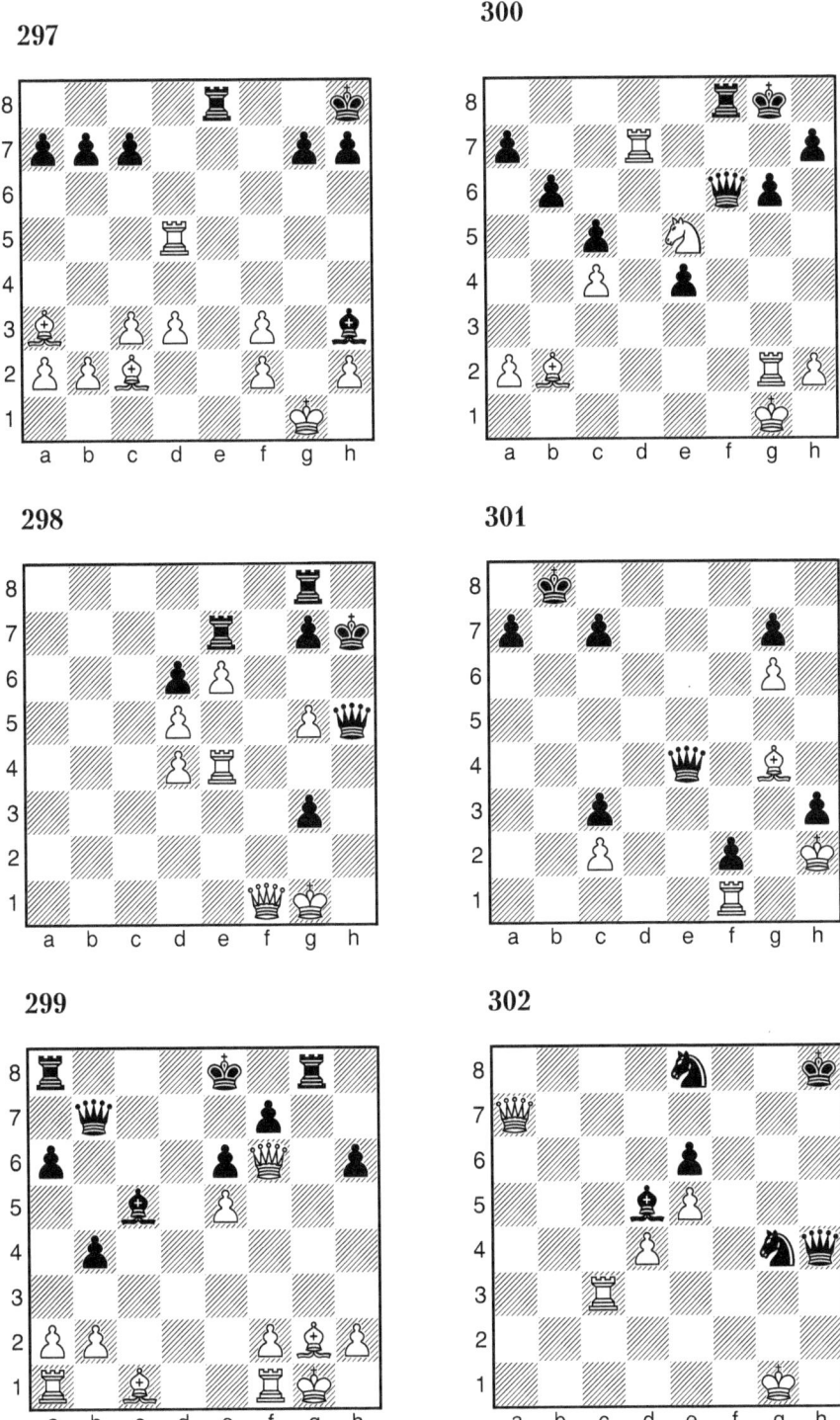

303

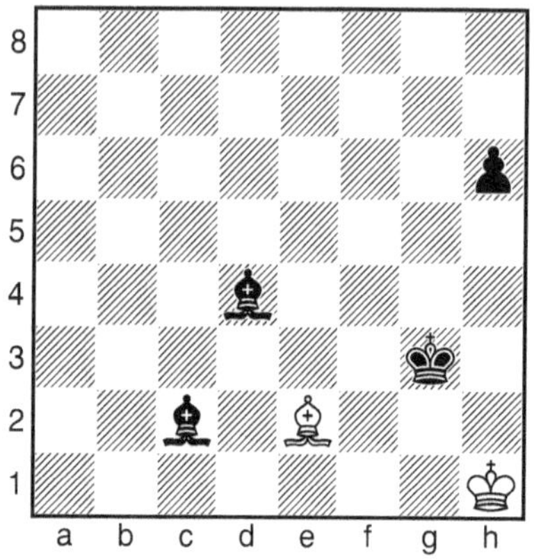

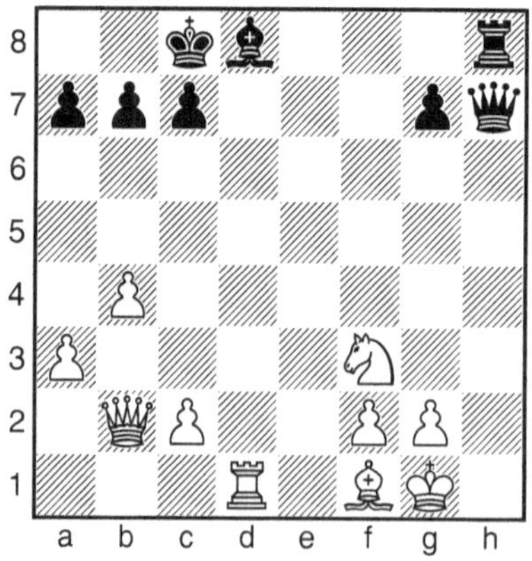

306

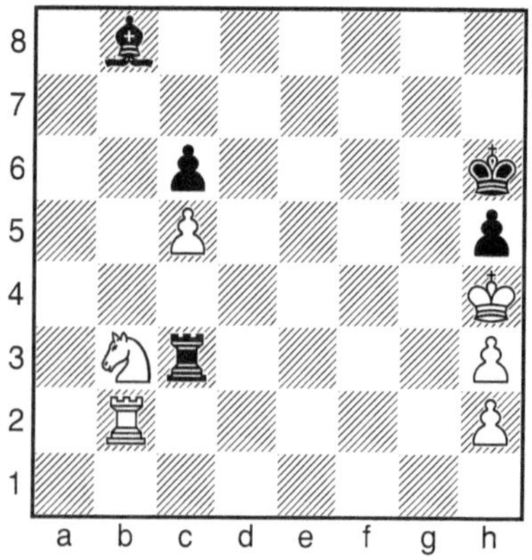

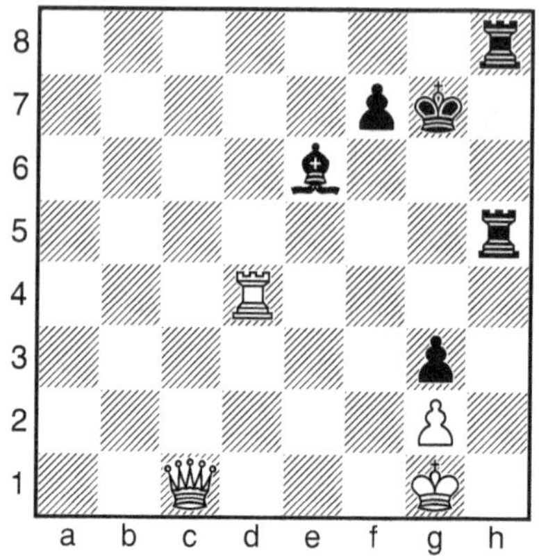

304

307

305

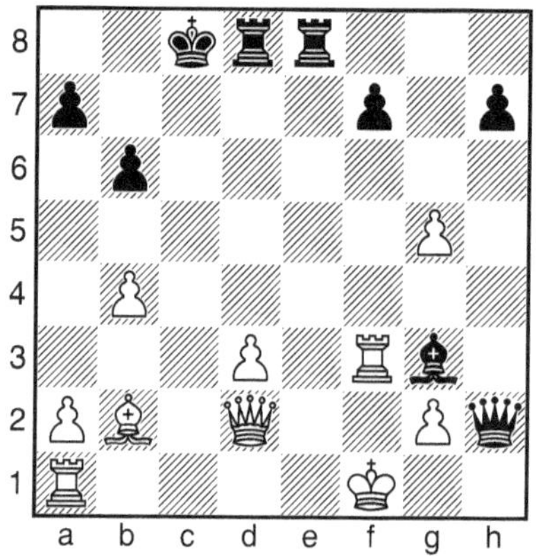

308

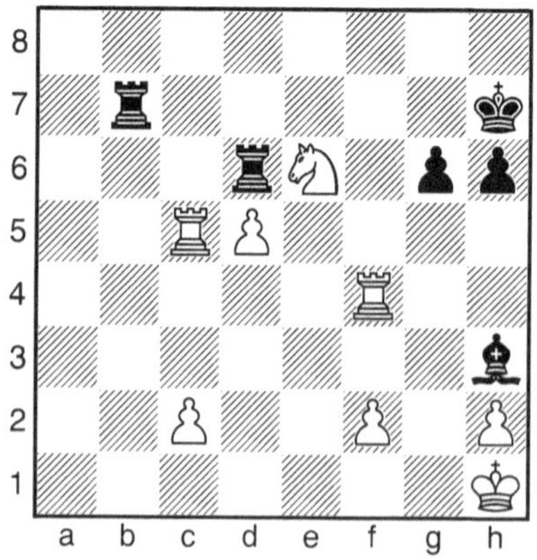

Part 4

Defense Against a Mate Threat. Resources of Your Own Pieces

The fourth part of this book focuses on defensive resources of your own pieces. It studies the final two defensive tactics, called support and escape. Support is having your piece take control over one or more squares that your opponent is threatening to use to deliver a mating combination. Escape is the immediate king move away from the danger zone or preparation of escape squares for the subsequent move away.

Both these tactics are classified as passive defense, so they are only checked at the very end when calculating possible defensive lines. On the other hand, sometimes you don't have to play actively to liquidate your opponent's mate threat with maximum efficiency! One accurate defensive king move can be much stronger than a whole defensive combination with several counter-strikes and sacrifices.

Chapter 17

SUPPORT

When defending against checkmate, resources of your own pieces can be used in two ways. The first defensive tactic is support: controlling one or more squares that your opponent intends to use to checkmate you.

Support is one of the most popular defensive tactics used in case of mate threats or threats against pieces. In every exercise presented in this chapter, white has an opportunity to defend against the opponent's mate threats using the support tactic.

309

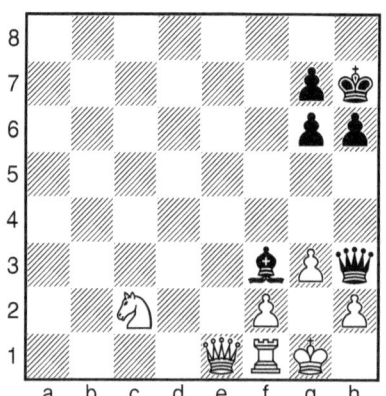

Black is threatening 1...♕g2#. The only defense is to support the g2 square, which black intends to use to checkmate you, with your knight – **1.♘e3!**. The white knight attacks the g2 square, rendering all of black's

threats harmless, and now white can easily convert his extra rook.

Sometimes you have to use some imagination to take control over a certain square.

310

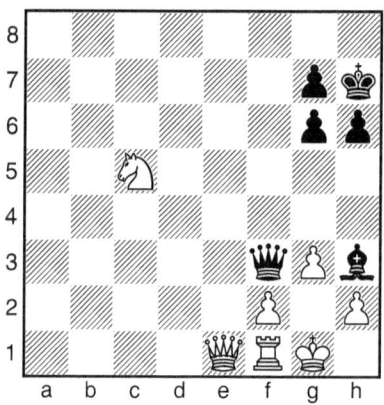

This example is analogous to the previous one, with one difference: no white piece can attack the g2 square directly on this move. The only defense against 1...♕g2# is to support that square with X-ray! After **1.♕e4!**, the white queen supports the key g2 square and defends from checkmate: **1...♕g2+?! 2.♕xg2**, winning.

In the book *1500 Forced Mates*, the opposition of two long-range pieces is a prerequisite for using the X-ray tactic. Take note that X-ray can be used both in attack and in defense, to support a square.

It's also important to remember that you can support several squares at once with one move!

311

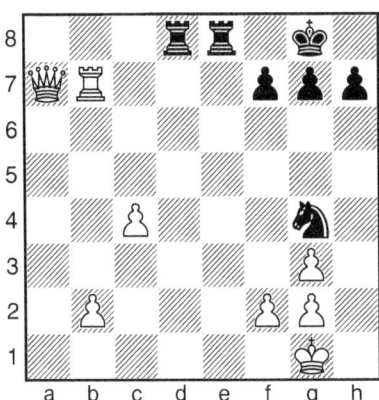

Black wants to checkmate white with either 1...♖d1# or 1...♖e1#. How can white defend? There are no counter-strikes – white doesn't have a single check. Interference is possible, but you can't stop two rooks at once: 1.♖d7 ♖e1#; 1.♖e7 ♖d1+ 2.♖e1 ♖exe1#; 1.♕e3 ♖d1+ 2.♕e1 ♖exe1#. Also, 1.♖b8 ♖e1# doesn't work either – you can pin only one rook, not two.

The best defense from checkmate is support **1.♕a1!**, taking control of both key squares, e1 and d1. In subsequent play, it's easy to see that white has a decisive advantage. We should also point out that supporting only one square, for instance, 1.♕a4, still doesn't stop black from delivering a checkmate, 1...♖e1#.

In case of a forced mate threat, the key problem in using support tactics is choosing which square to support. To avert the opponent's mate threat, it's sometimes enough to control just one square.

312

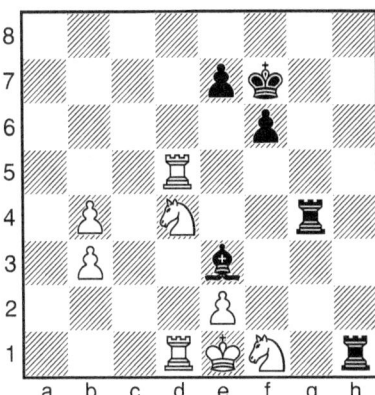

Black has created a threat of a mate in two: 1...♖xf1+ 2.♔xf1 ♖g1#. To defend, white can support either square from the line above. If he supports the f1 square with 1.♖f5, he prevents checkmate, but black can capture the knight, 1...♗xd4, achieving a roughly equal position. Nevertheless, white has a much better defense – he can take control of the g1 square with **1.♘f3!**, and now there's no mate: **1...♖xf1+ 2.♔xf1 ♖g1+ 3.♘xg1**. Of course, black doesn't have to give up his rooks like that, but white's position is still very good: he has repelled all mate threats and retained his extra material.

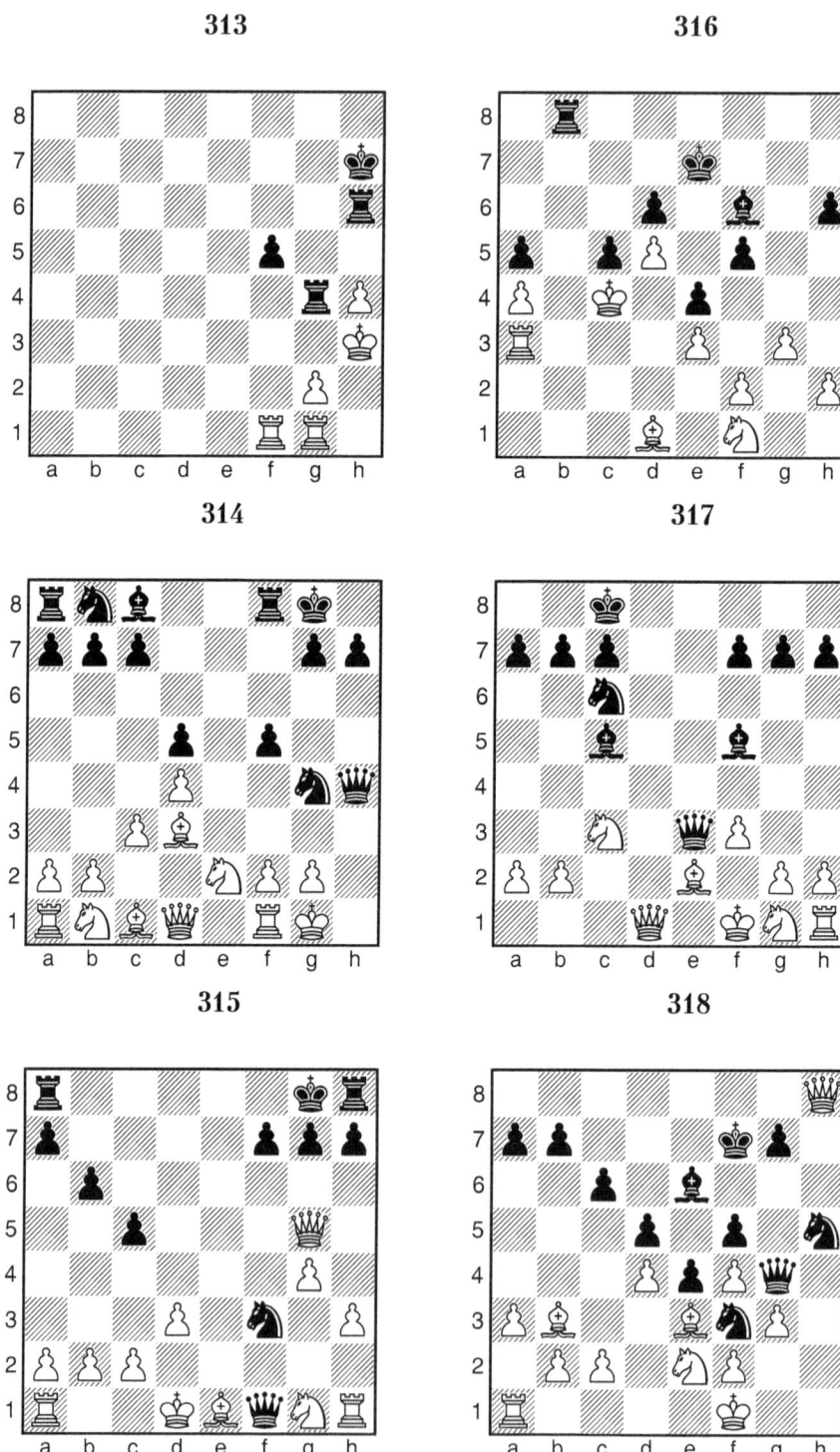

319

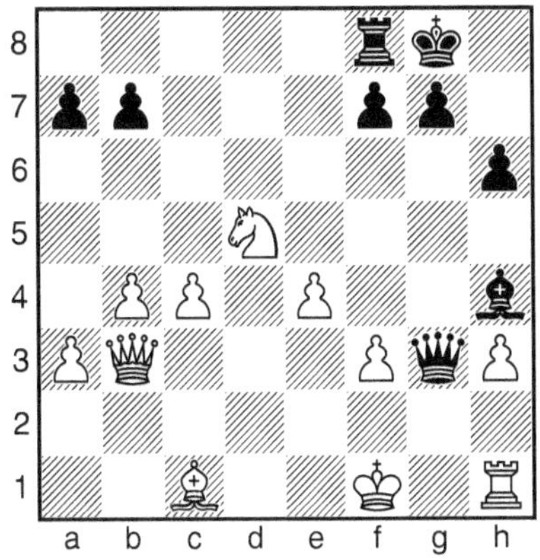

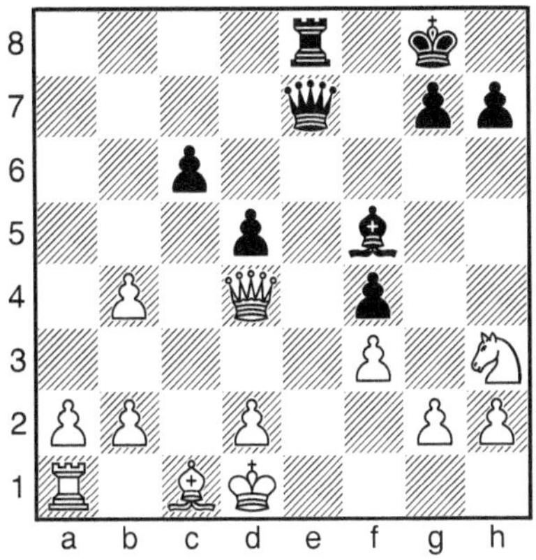

322

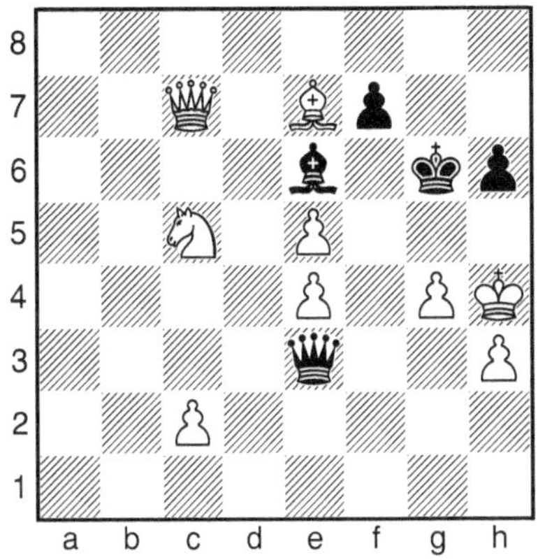

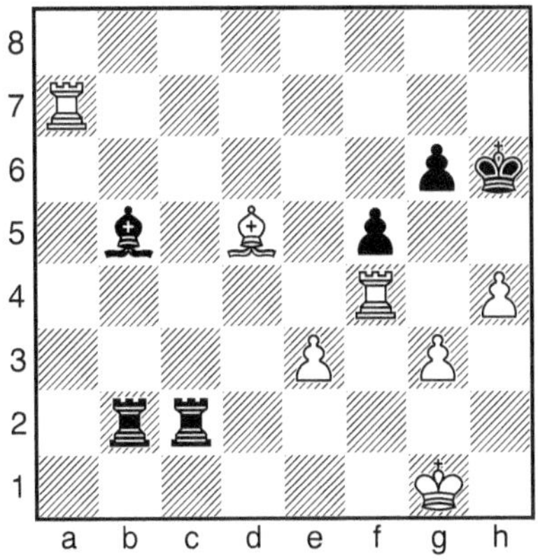

320

323

321

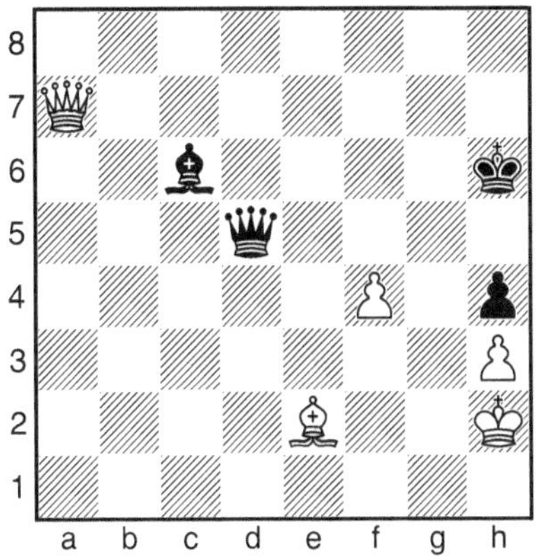

324

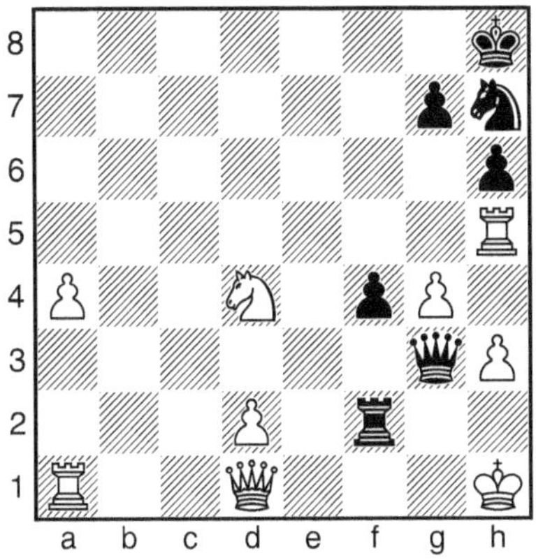

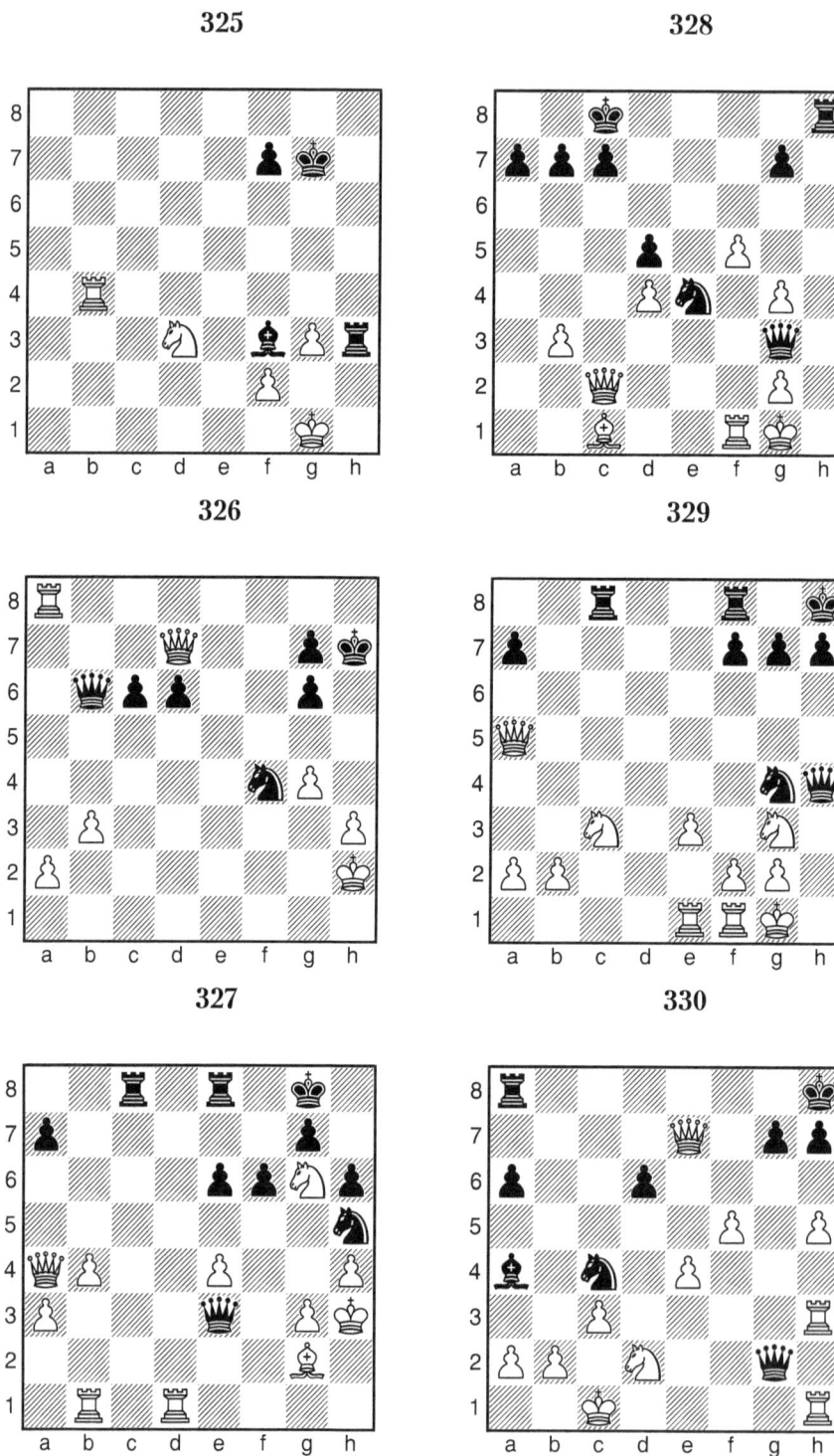

325

328

326

329

327

330

331

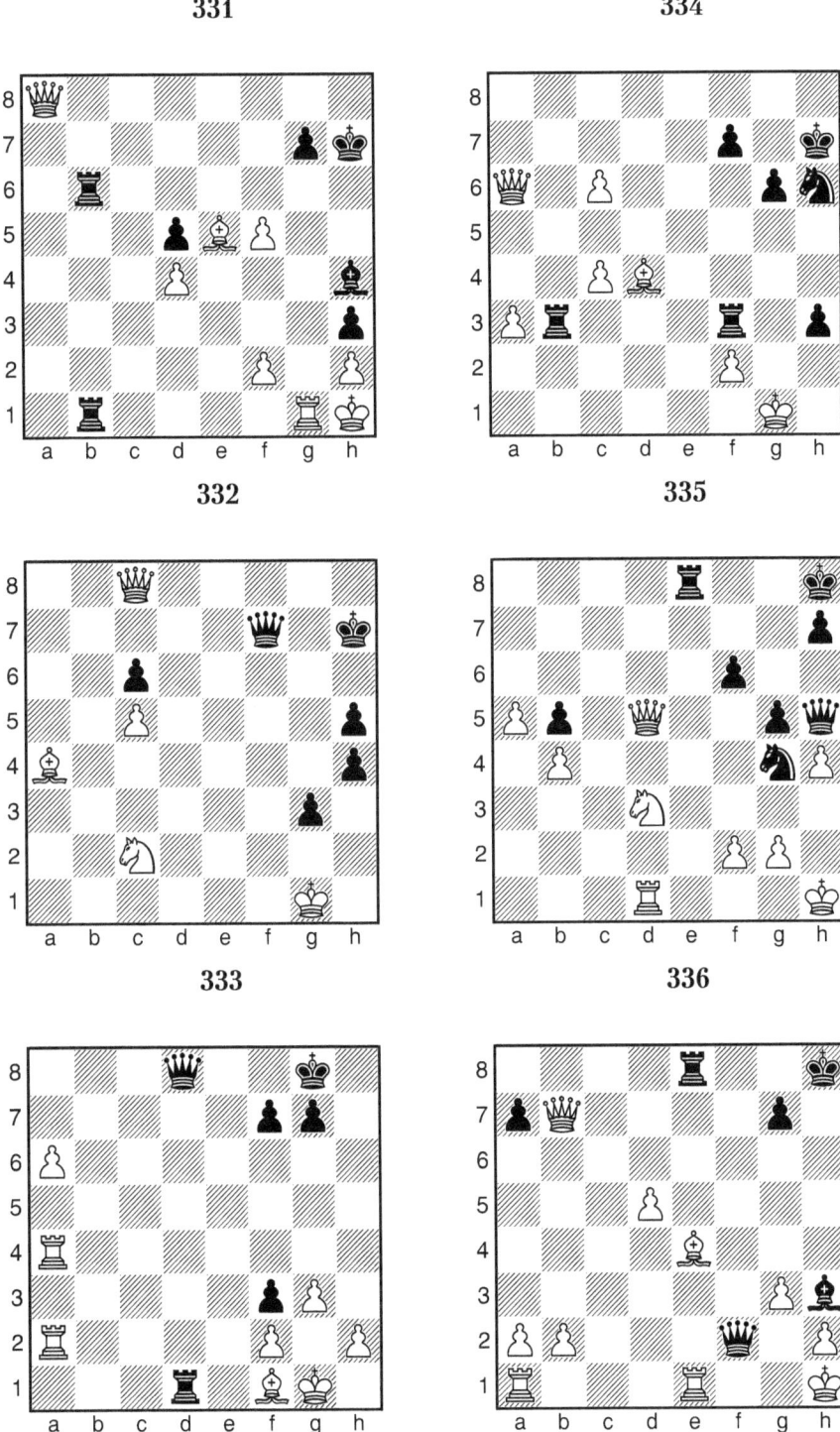

334

332

335

333

336

COMBINATIONS

In this chapter, we study the conjunction of support and all the tactics we studied in the previous chapters.

In every exercise presented in this chapter, white has an opportunity to defend against the opponent's mate threats by using support in various conjunctions with counter-strikes, interference, pins, deflection and elimination.

337

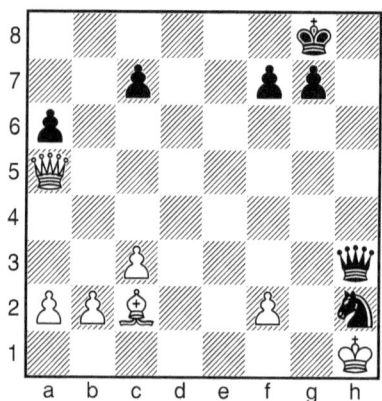

Black has created two mate threats: 1...♘f3# and 1...♘g4+ 2.♔g1 ♕h2+ 3.♔f1 ♕xf2#. White can play **1.♕f5!**, deflecting the black queen (and capturing it in the line 1...♘f3+ 2.♕xh3) and supporting the f2 square after **1...♘g4+ 2.♔g1 ♕h2+ 3.♔f1**. Black can continue the attack with 2...g6!?, but in reply,

white can win a pawn 3.♕c8+ ♔g7 4.♕xc7 and still support one of the squares that black wanted to use for his mating combination.

338

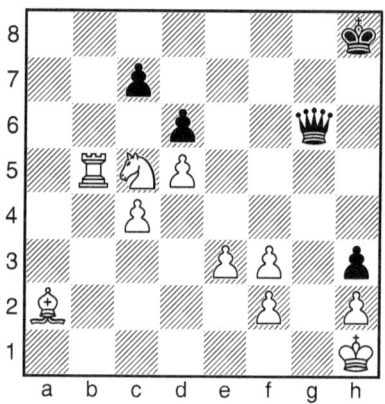

Black threatens 1...♕g2#. White starts with the counter-strike **1.♖b8+!**, and, in case of 1... ♔h7, defends with the pin **2.♗b1!**, winning the queen. In the line **1... ♔g7**, white saves the game with **2.♘e6+!**, and there's still the danger of 2...♔h7 3.♗b1; after 2...♔h6, white almost delivers a checkmate himself – 3.♖h8+!, deflecting and then capturing the black queen – 3... ♕h7 4.♖xh7+ with a win; finally, if the black king retreats to the f-file, **2...♔f6** or **2...♔f7**, there follows **3.♘f4!**, supporting the g2 square with the knight. Further analysis shows that white is much better in this position.

White's defensive combination included the following tactics: counter-strike, pin, deflection and support.

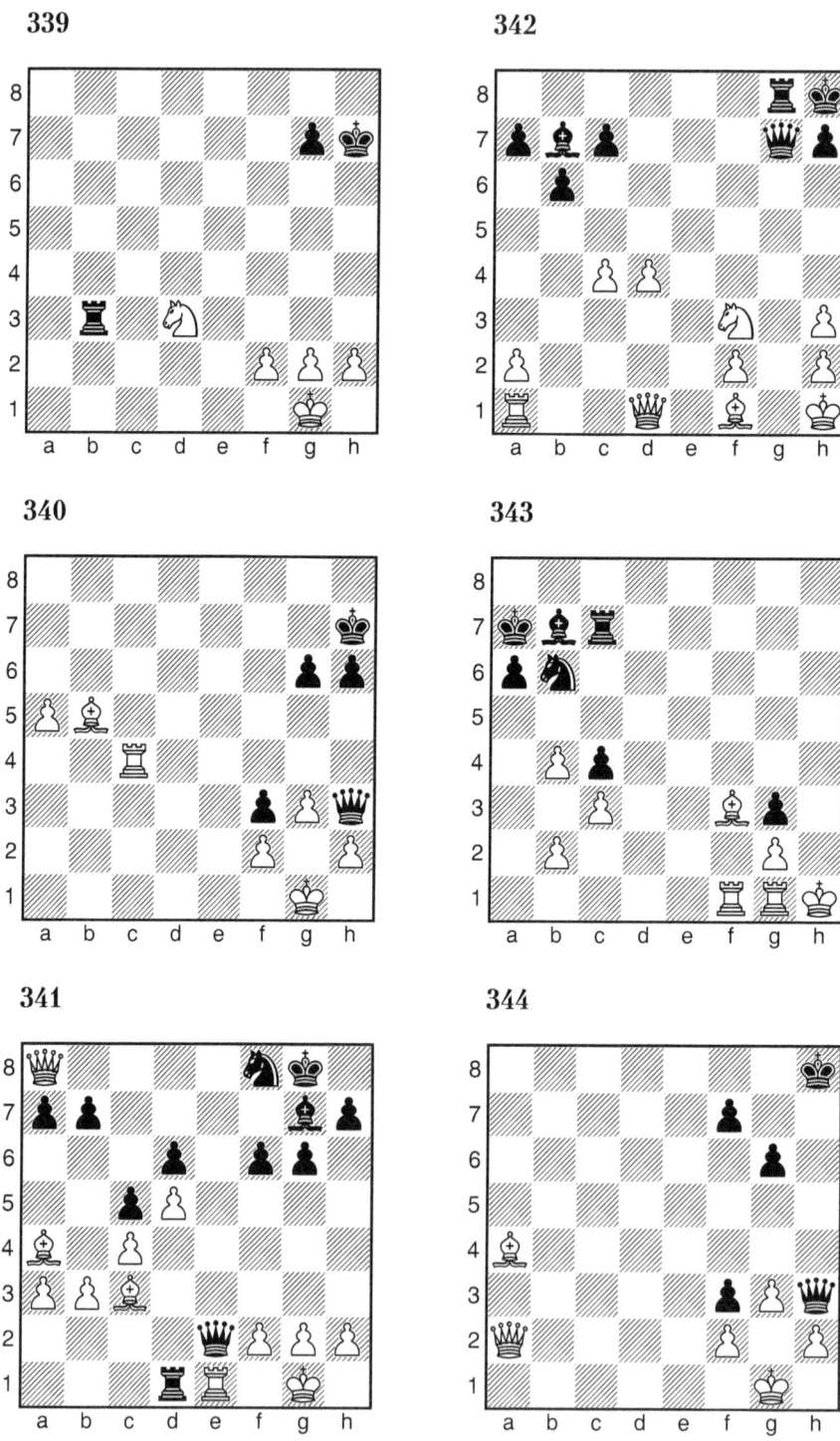

339

340

341

342

343

344

345

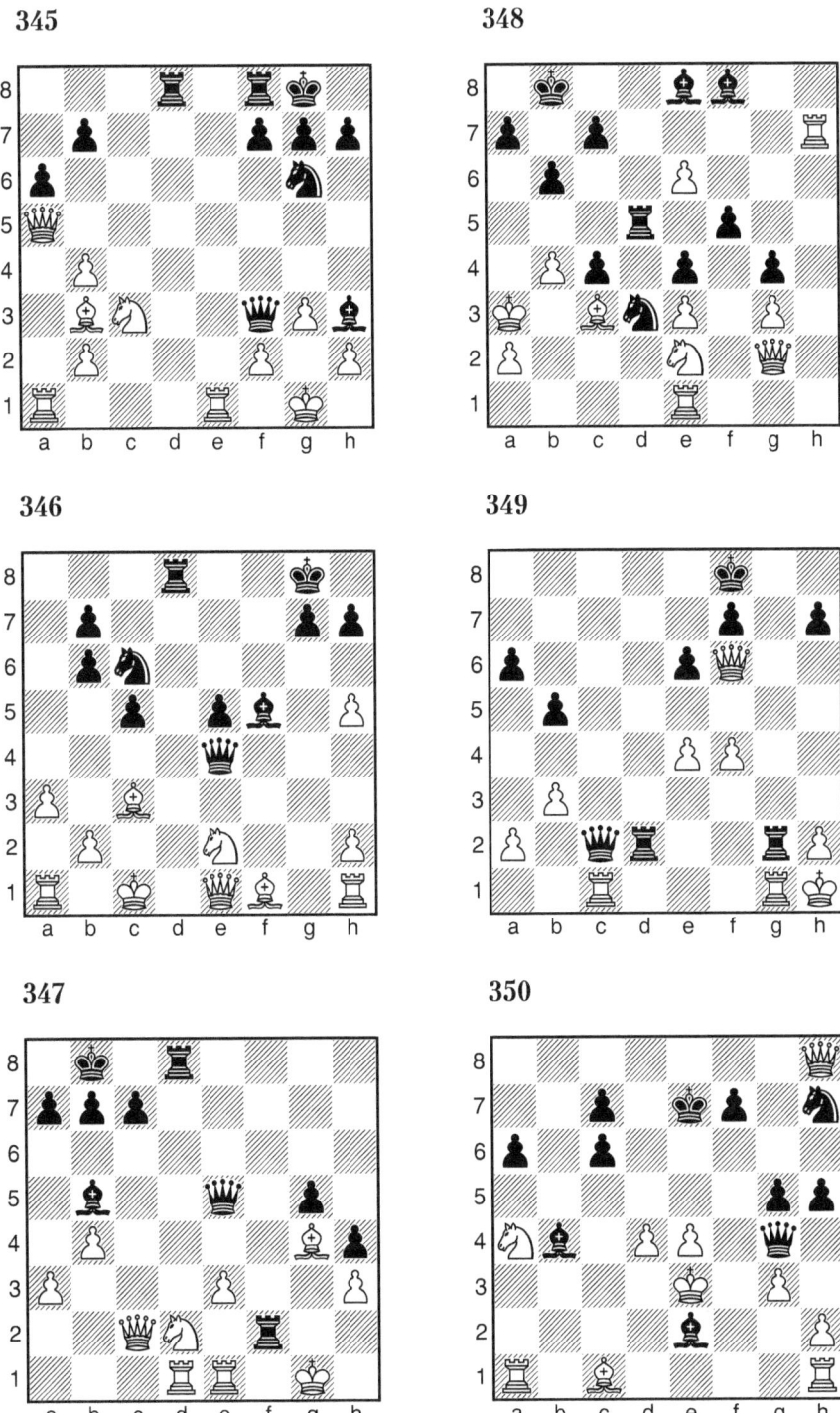

348

346

349

347

350

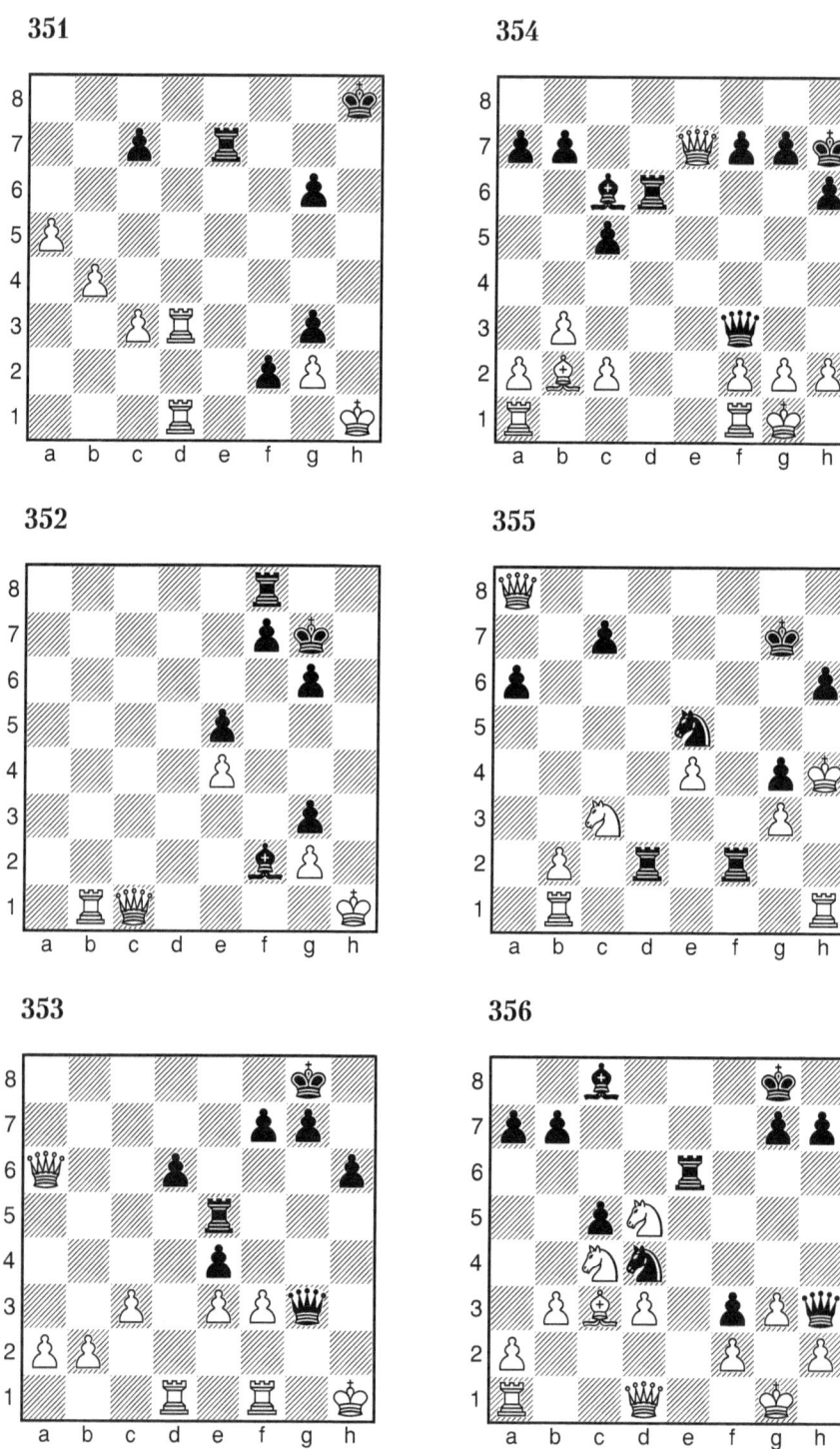

351

352

353

354

355

356

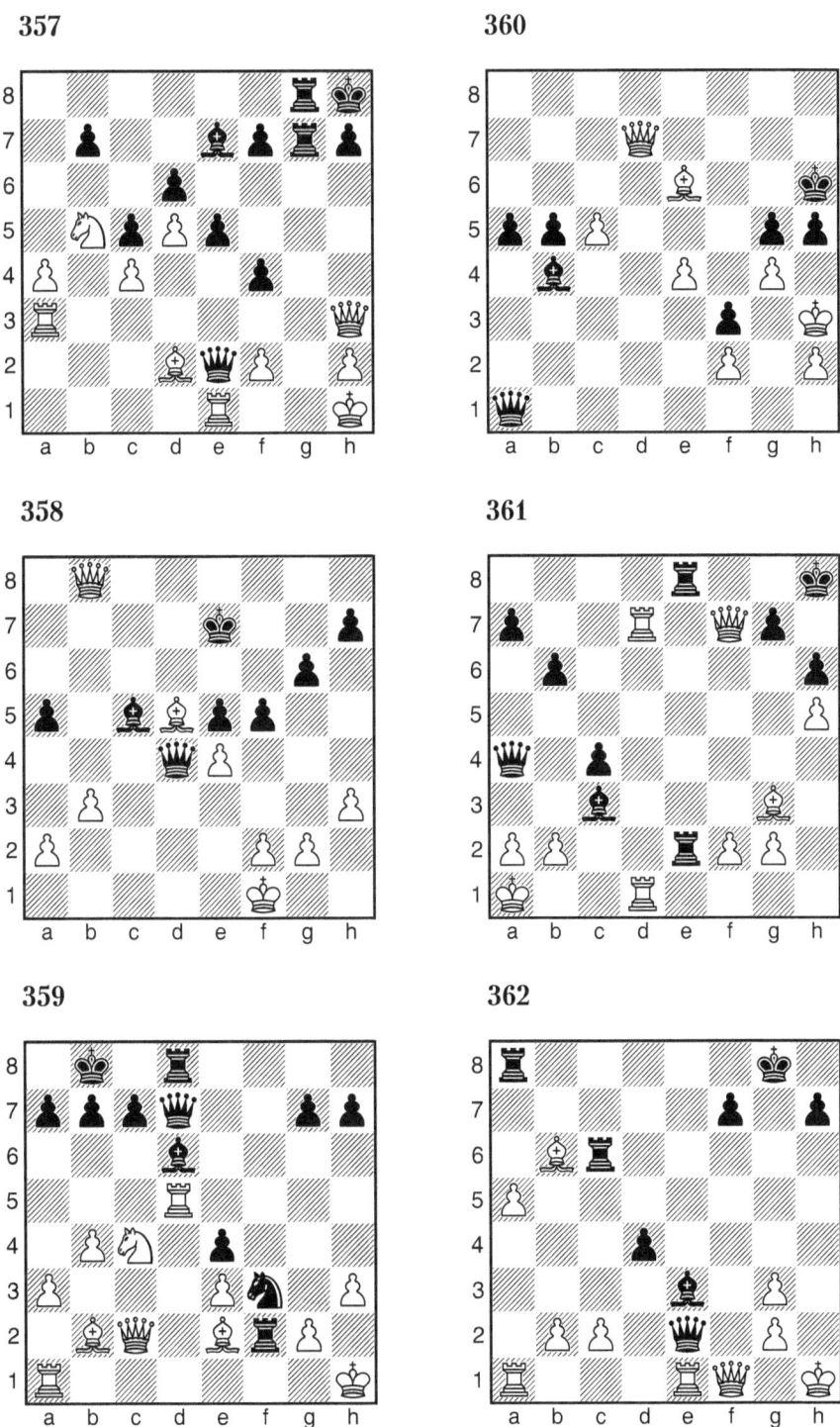

357

358

359

360

361

362

363

366

364

367

365

368

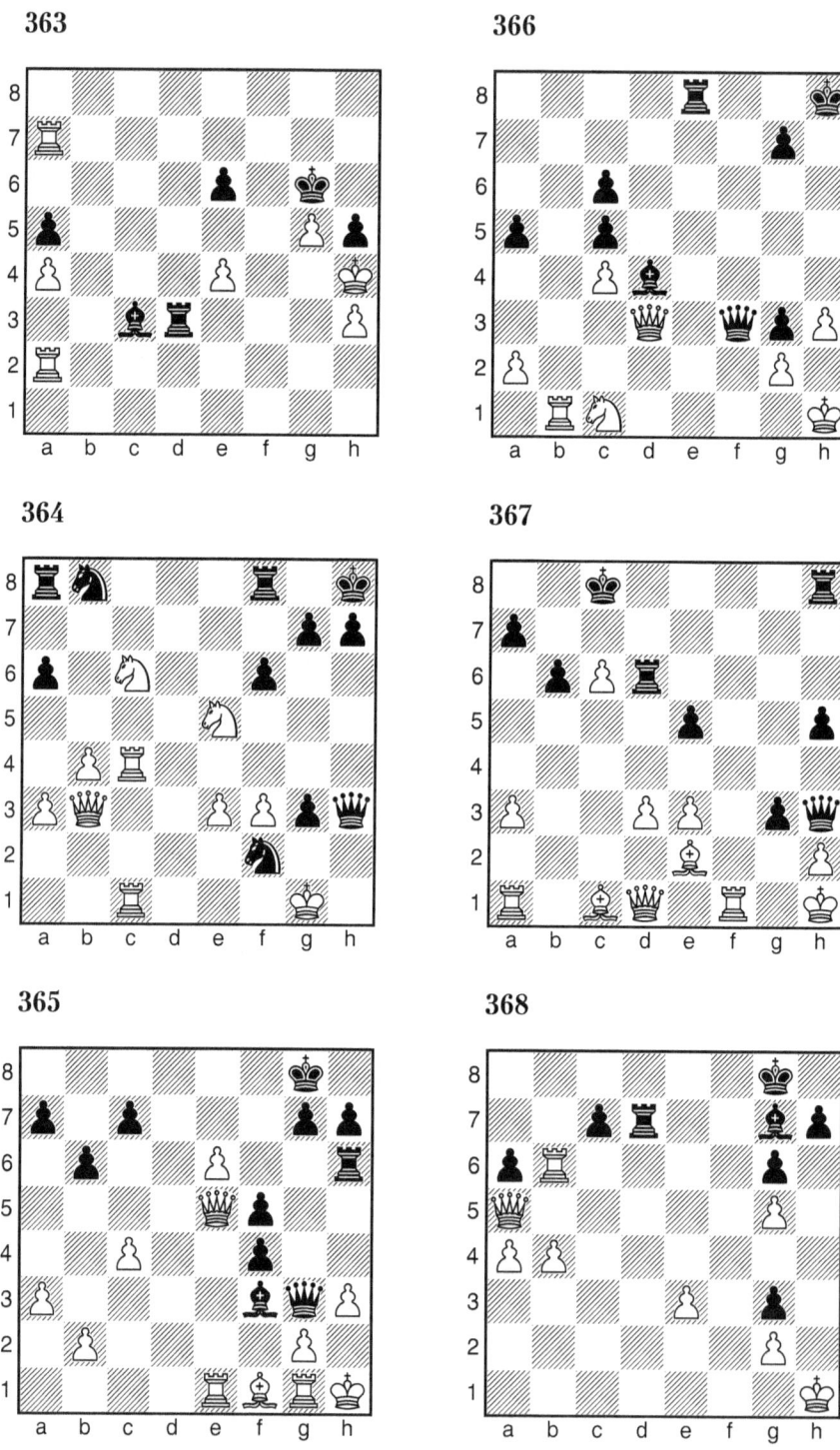

Chapter 19

ESCAPE

Another defensive tactic utilizing the resources of your own pieces is escape: immediately moving the king away from the danger zone or preparing an escape path for it.

In every exercise presented in this chapter, white has an opportunity to defend against the opponent's mate threats by using the escape tactic.

369

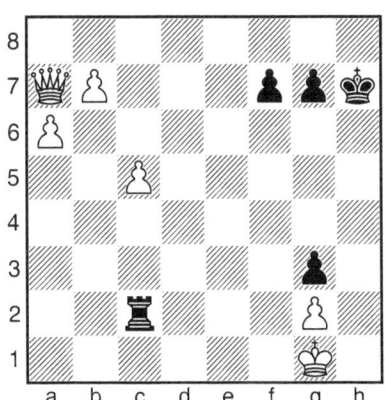

White has an overwhelming material advantage, but black threatens checkmate in one, 1...♖c1#. The only way to save the game is to escape: **1.♔f1!** – the white king leaves the mating net. **1...♖c1+ 2.♔e2** or 1...♖f2+ 2.♔e1. In both lines, white's position is completely won.

370

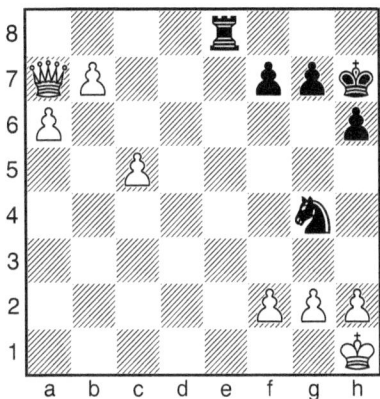

This example is similar to the previous one, because black again threatens a back-rank mate: 1...♖e1#. The immediate attempt to escape doesn't work – 1.♔g1 ♖e1#. To defend from checkmate, white has to prepare a safe escape route for his king. White plays **1.g3!**, and after **1...♖e1+**, the king flees to the prepared escape square, **2.♔g2**, with a decisive advantage for white.

371

374

372

375

373

376

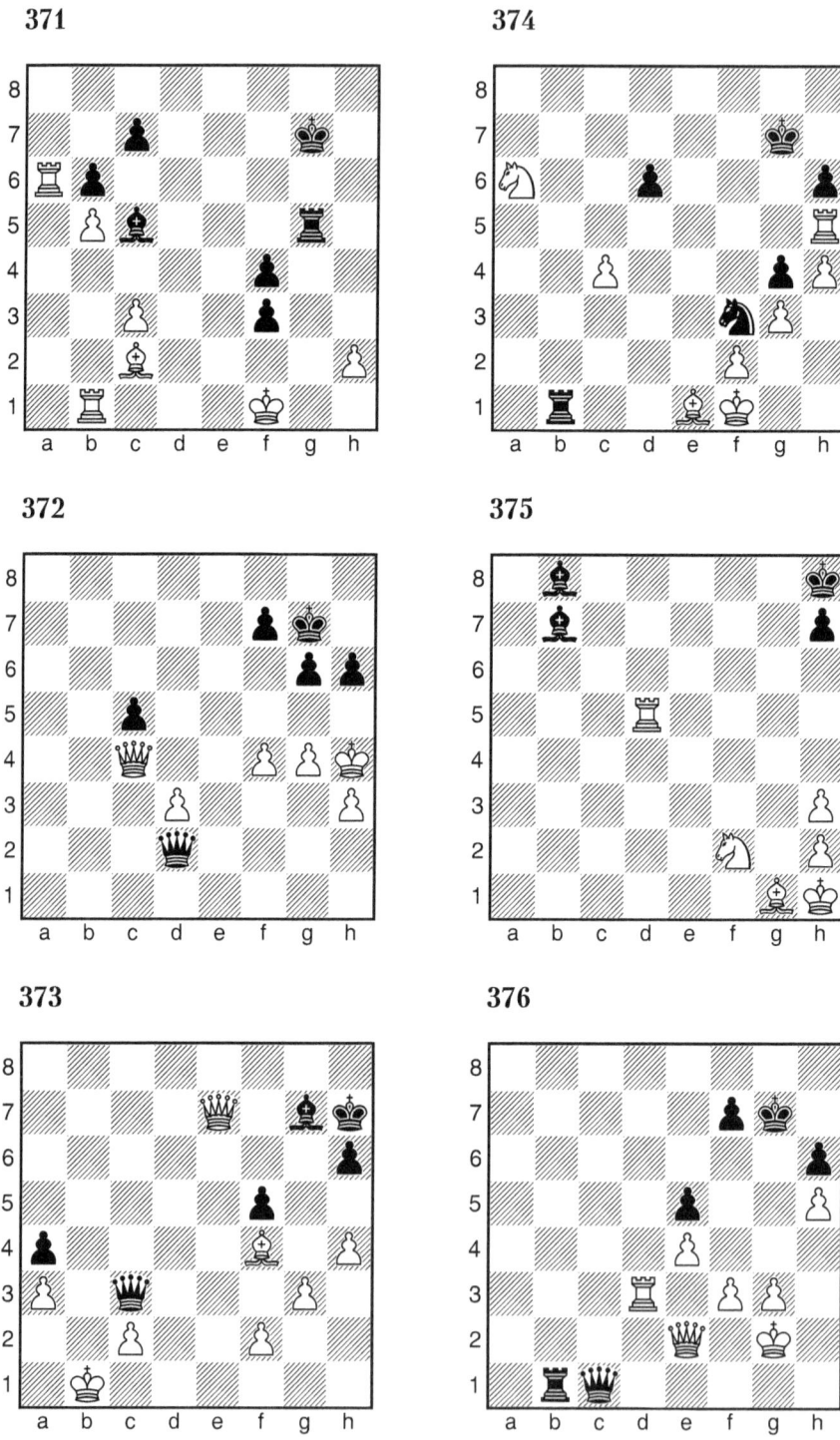

377

380

378

381

379

382

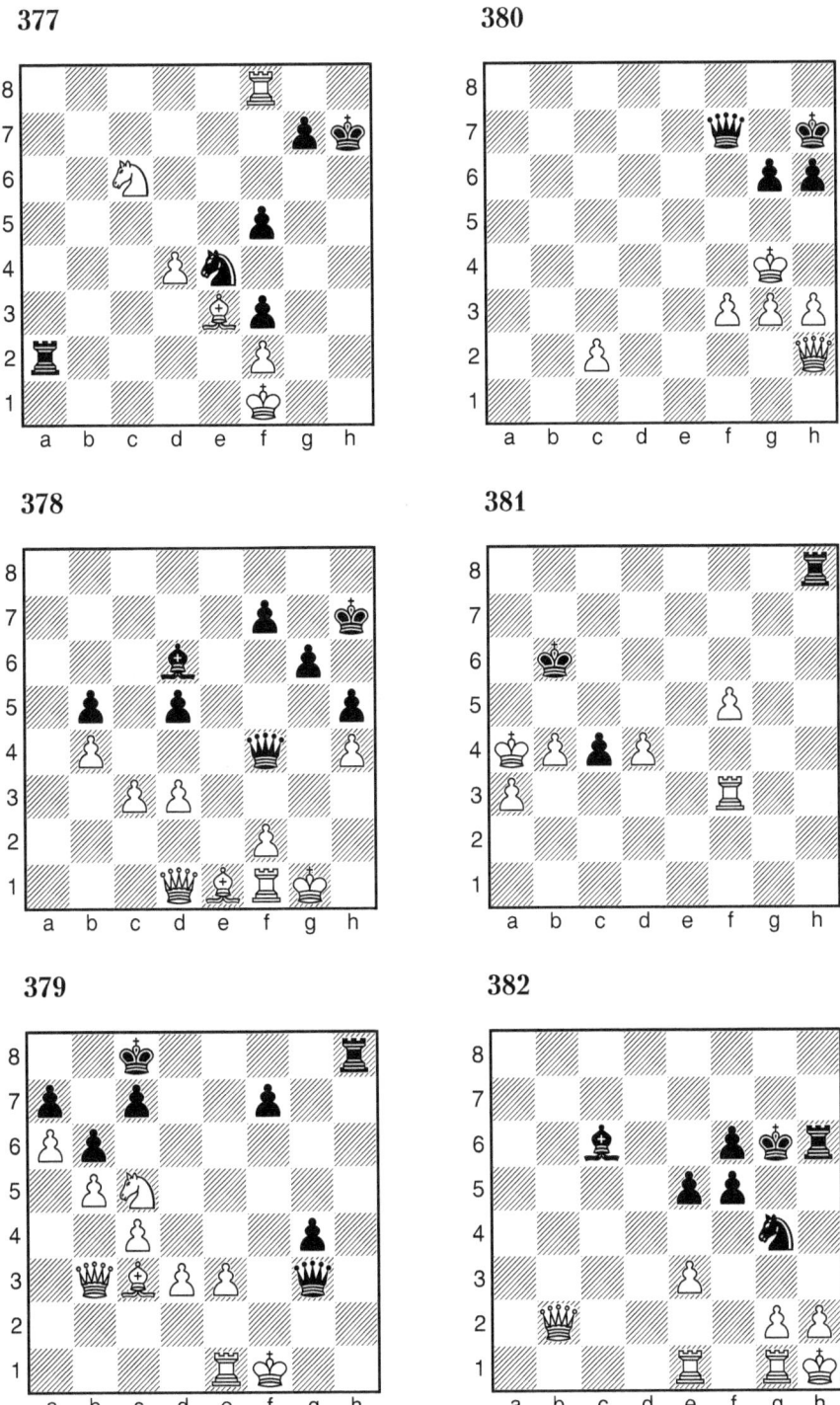

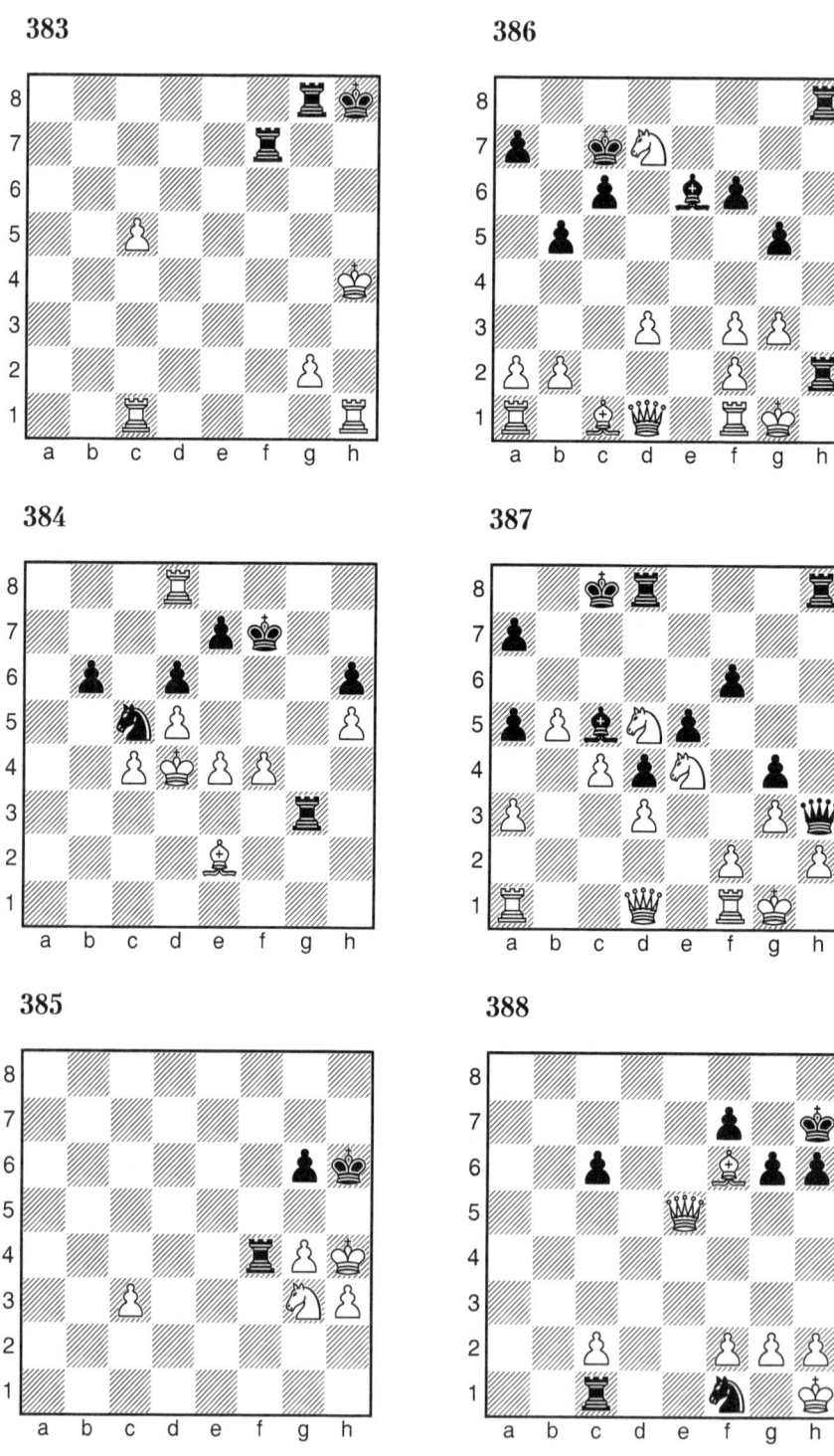

383

384

385

386

387

388

Chapter 20

COMBINATIONS

In this chapter, we study the conjunction of escape and all the tactics we studied in the previous chapters.

In every exercise presented in this chapter, white has an opportunity to defend against the opponent's mate threats by using escape in various conjunctions with counter-strikes, interference, pins, deflection, elimination and support.

389

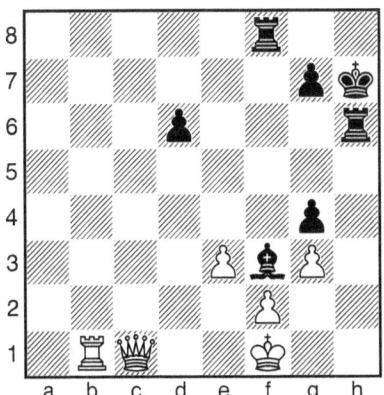

Black threatens 1...♖h1#. The logical attempt to escape the danger zone, 1.♔e1?, is met with 1...♖h1+ 2.♔d2 ♖xc1 – the extra piece gives black a decisive advantage. The best defense here is to combine escape with counter-strike! After **1.♕c2+!** and any king move by black, escape will save white from defeat. For instance, **1...♔h8 2.♔e1 ♖h1+ 3.♔d2** with a roughly equal position.

390

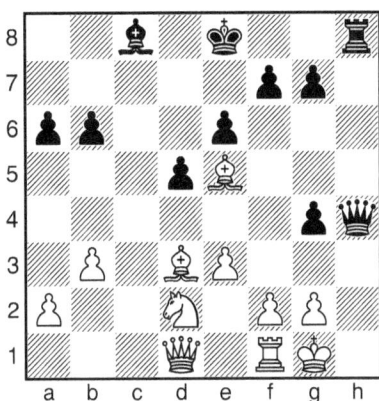

Black threatens 1...♕h1#. The only active defenses available to white are a dubious counter-strike 1.♗b5+? axb5 and an even more dubious interference 1.♗h2?? ♕xh2#. There's no way to support the h1 square – no white piece can take control over it on the next move. So, the only remaining attempt is to try and escape with the king, **1.f3!**. It turns out that after 1...♕h1+ 2.♔f2, black's attack fizzles out. He has a stronger reply **1...g3!?**, forcing white to resort to elimination, **2.♗xg3! ♕xg3**. Black has no more concrete mate threats; meanwhile, white has several moves that allow him to achieve a decisive advantage. For instance, he can play **3.♕e1!? ♕h2+ 4.♔f2 ♕h4+ 5.♔e2** – the white king escapes to safety. We should also note that another attempt to escape, 1.f4?, loses to 1...g3!, and the white king cannot escape the mating net.

391

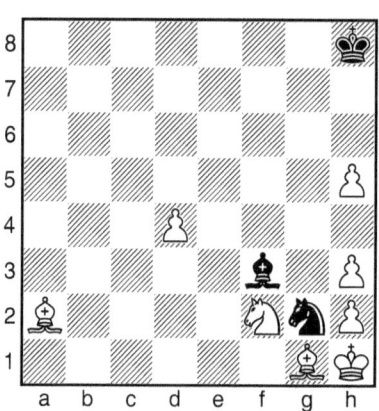

The next example may seem a bit strange at first. However, it's actually pretty straightforward: black threatens to deliver a discovered checkmate with his knight, 1... ♘e1#, 1...♘e3#, 1...♘f4# or 1... ♘h4#. To defend from such a mate, you first need to use deflection, **1.♗d5!**, forcing black to make an "extra" move with his bishop, **1... ♗xd5**. Then white closes off the long diagonal, **2.♘e4!**, delaying the execution for one more move. After **2...♗xe4**, the white king is finally able to escape the mating net: **3.♗f2!**, with the idea of meeting any knight move with **4.♔g1**. The resulting position is drawn.

392

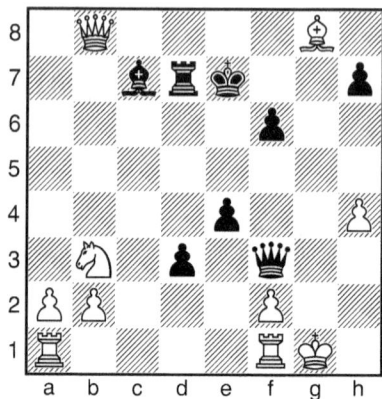

Black threatens to mate in three: 1...♕g4+ 2.♔h1 ♕h3+ 3.♔g1 ♕h2#; in addition, the white queen is under attack. To defend, white uses a counter-strike: **1.♕b4+!**, and after **1...♔e8**, delivers a beautiful tactical blow **2.♕xe4+!!**, deflecting the black queen with a check and essentially forcing black to reply **2...♕xe4**. It's not clear at first why white gave up his queen, since now he's forced to fend off two mate threats at once: in addition to the same idea 3...♕g4+, black now can also play 3...♖g7#. However, there follows **3.♖fe1!**, pinning the queen and freeing up the escape square for the king in the line **3...♖g7+ 4.♔f1**. White wins in a similar way after 1... ♗d6 2.♕xe4+ ♕xe4 3.♖fe1 or 1... ♖d6 2.♕xe4+ ♕xe4 3.♖fe1. And, of course, black just loses immediately after 1...♔d8? 2.♕f8#.

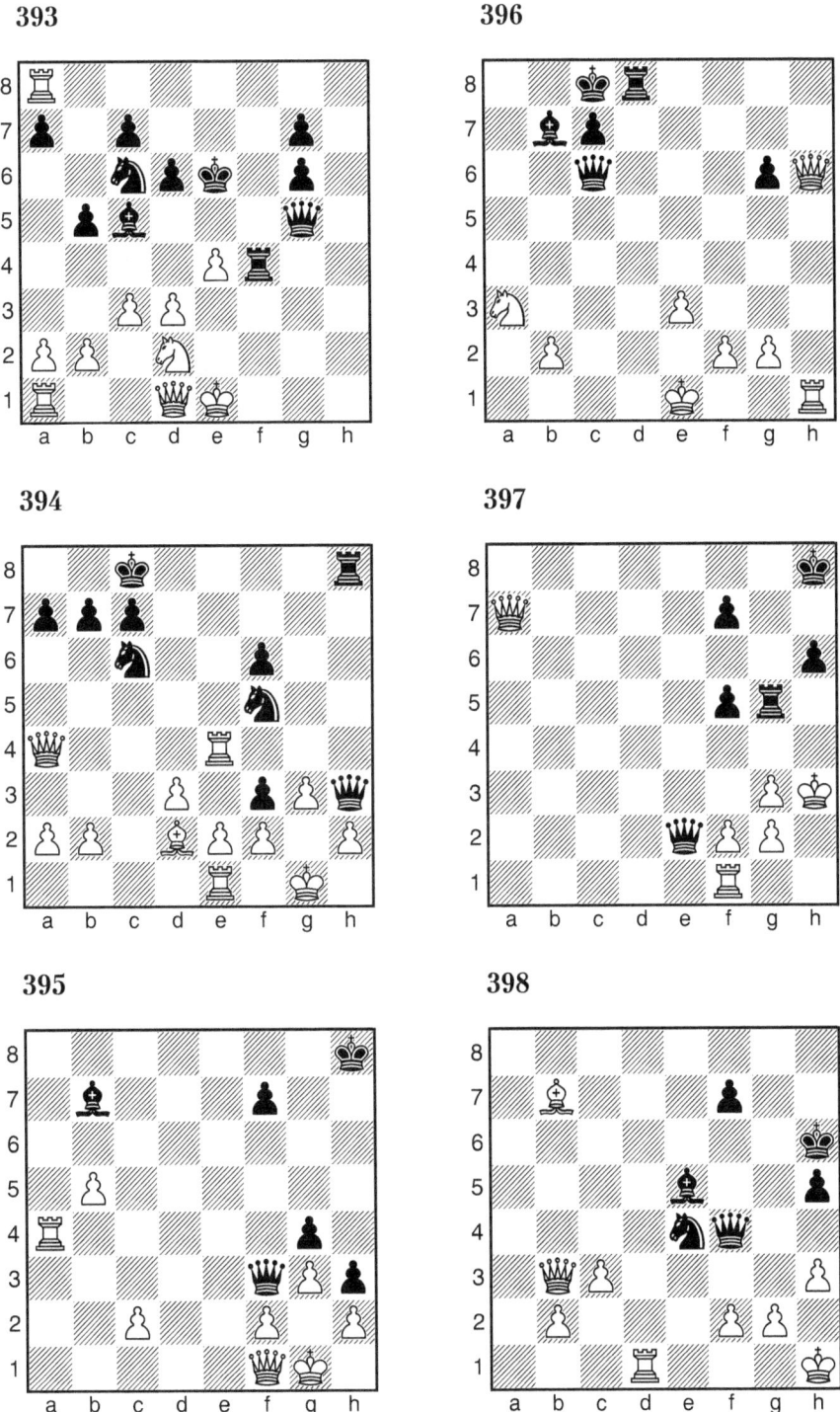

393

394

395

396

397

398

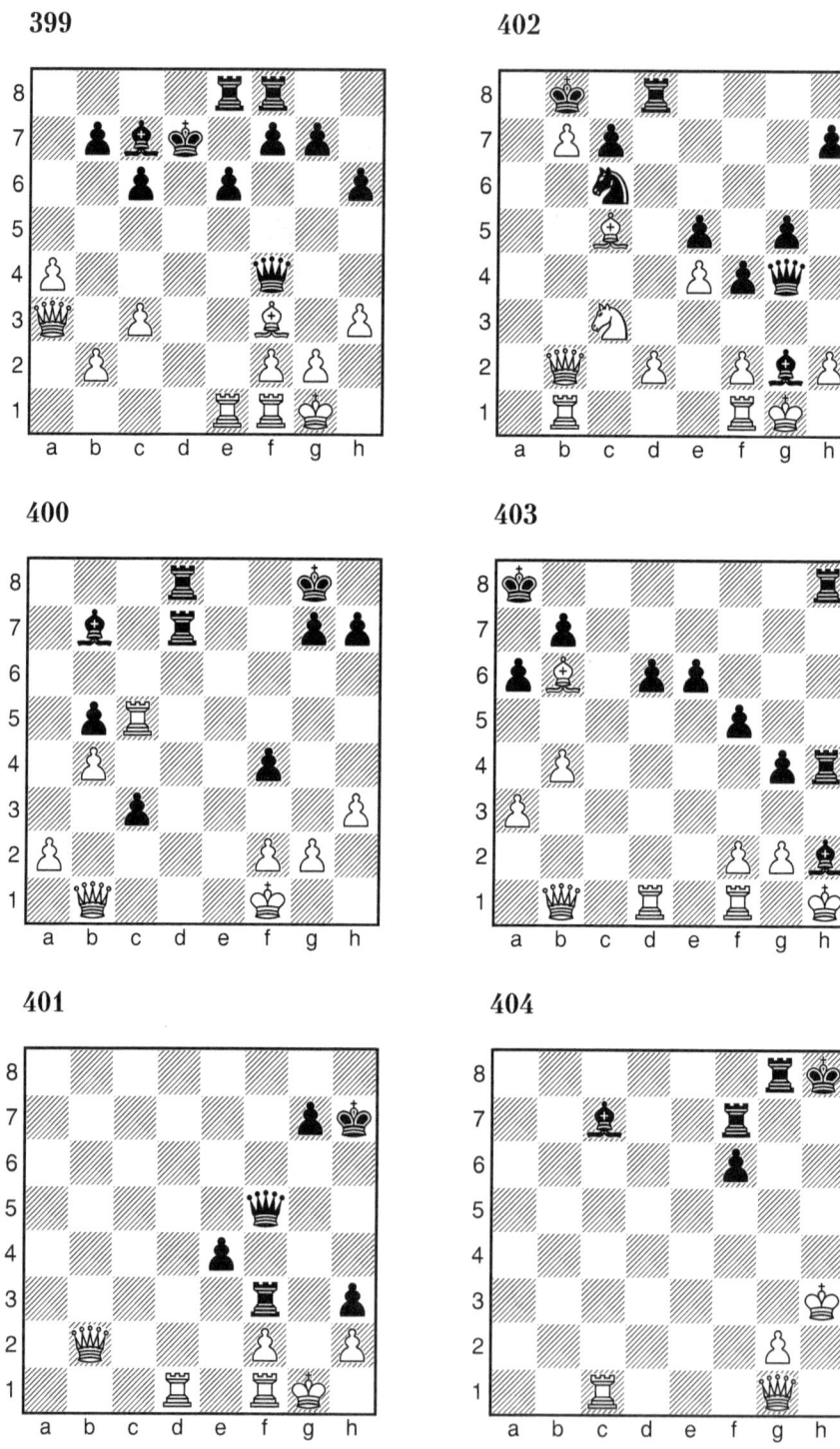

405

408

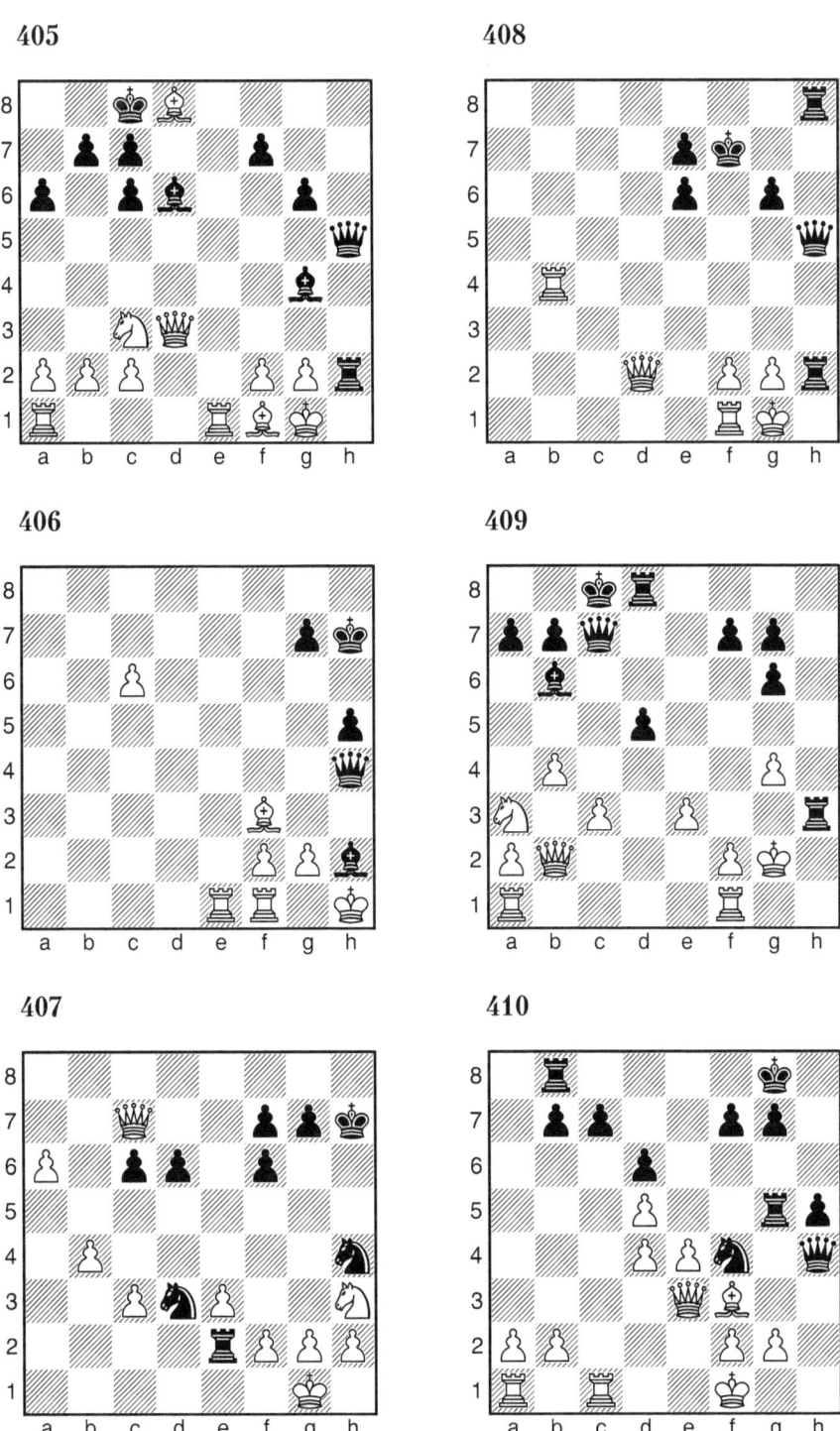

406

409

407

410

411

414

412

415

413

416

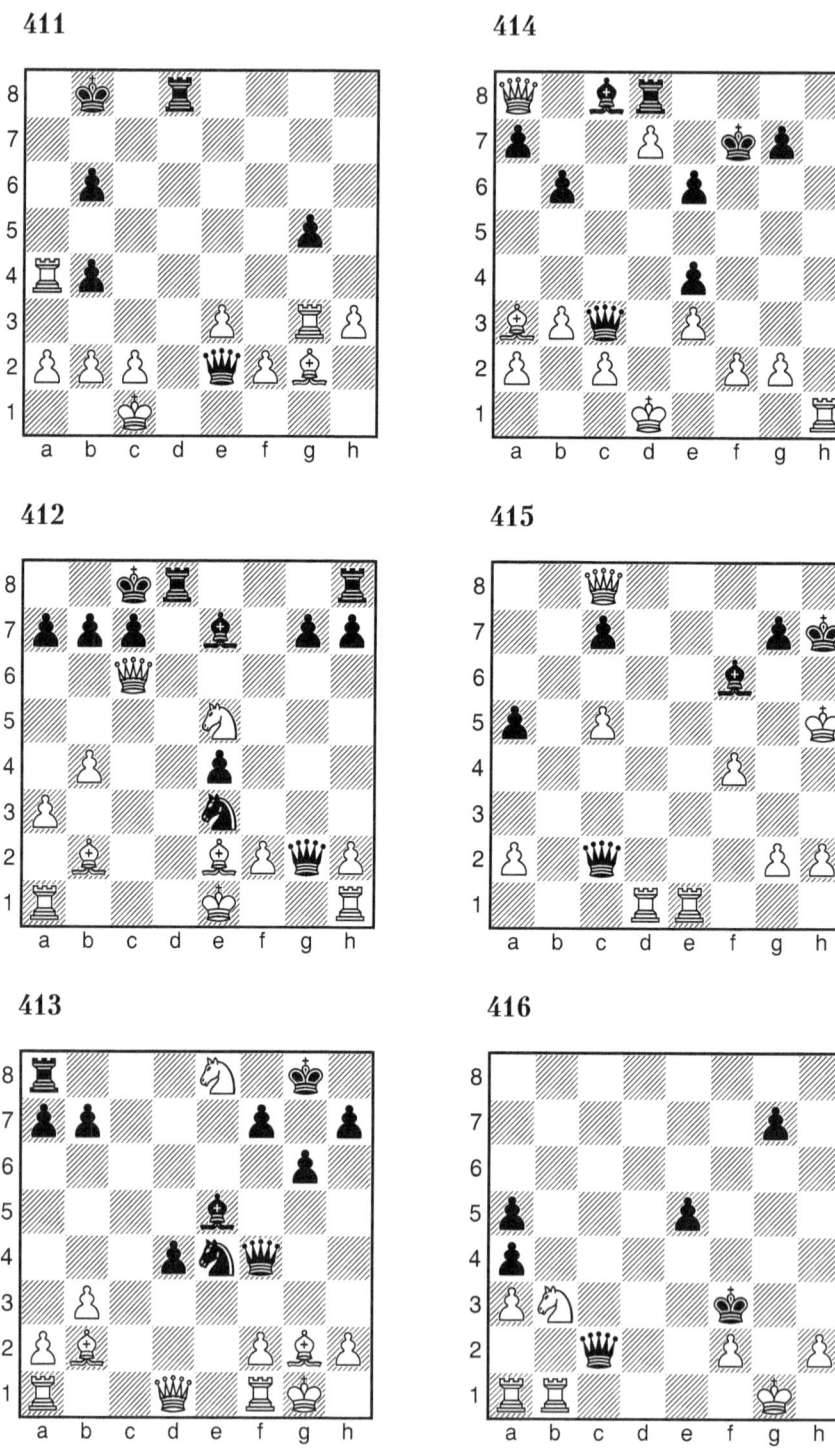

Part 5

Mate Threats and Combinations

The fifth part of this book focuses on attacks – mate threats and combinations. A mating combination in chess is a tactical blow that includes a forced mate or a winning mate threat. In this case, "winning mate threat" means two things: the opponent has no defense at all against the threat, which we call an "unstoppable mate", or he has no satisfactory defense against the threat! Unlike a forced mate, which the reader may know well from the *1500 Forced Mates* book, a winning mate threat does not always end with a checkmate – it may instead lead to material gain. A mating combination also often includes checks against the opponent's king, which usually work as a linking element between forced mate and various mate threats.

In this part, we are going to thoroughly study the most difficult element of mating combination – unstoppable mate, which will first be used on its own, and then in conjunction with checks to the king and forced mate. We define unstoppable mate separately from "forced mate" because in forced mate, all of the attacking player's moves are checks, unlike in unstoppable mate. In practice, no major distinction is made between unstoppable mate and mate threats without satisfactory defense, which are the two types of winning mate threat, but the former is usually much easier to calculate, so we shall consider them separately. In the concluding chapter of this part, you need to use several mate threats at once as part of a single mating combination.

Please note that while calculating any mate threats or combinations, you should take the strongest defensive resources of your opponent into account.

Chapter 21

UNSTOPPABLE MATE

An unstoppable mate in chess is the threat of a mate in one or more moves that your opponent cannot defend against. To check whether your mate threat is indeed unstoppable, you have to carefully consider all defensive resources of your opponent.

417

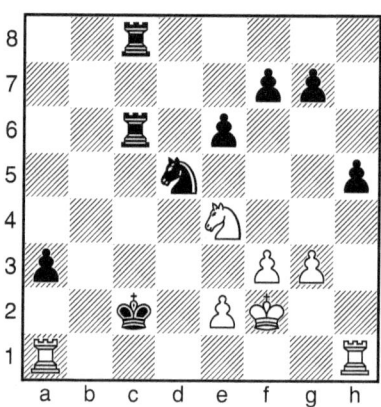

The black king has no moves, so it's enough to check it to win. After **1.g4!**, the white pawn cannot be stopped from delivering checkmate on the next move, **2.g5#**. To ensure that there is no defense, you have to check for all known defensive tactics: counter-strikes; elimination, deflection, pinning or interference against the mating pieces; support and escape. You have to calculate your opponent's defensive resources

before making the winning move over the board!

418

The black king has wandered deep into the opponent's camp, but it's not stuck in a mating net yet. In search for the strongest move, white should first check if a forced mate is available. For instance, after 1.♖hc1+? ♚b3 2.♖ab1+ ♚a4 it's clear that the black king is in grave danger, but there's still no win for white in sight. In this case, creating a mate threat is much stronger than giving checks! After **1.♖ab1!**, black has no defense against **2.♖hc1#**. It's easy to check black's defensive resources: he has no checks (counter-strikes), can't reach any of the white pieces on his next move, has nothing to support the c1 square with, and his king has no escape squares.

419

422

420

423

421

424

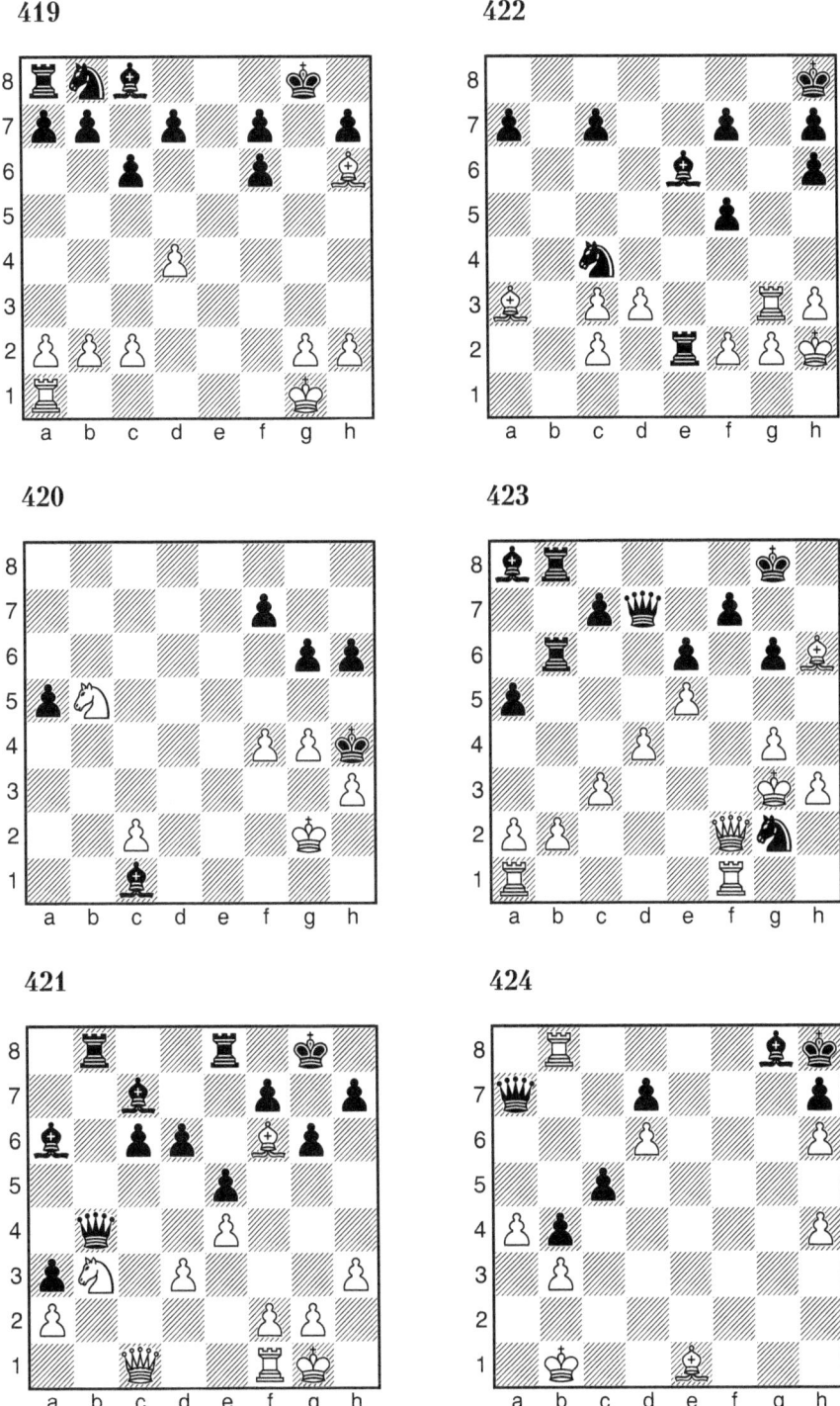

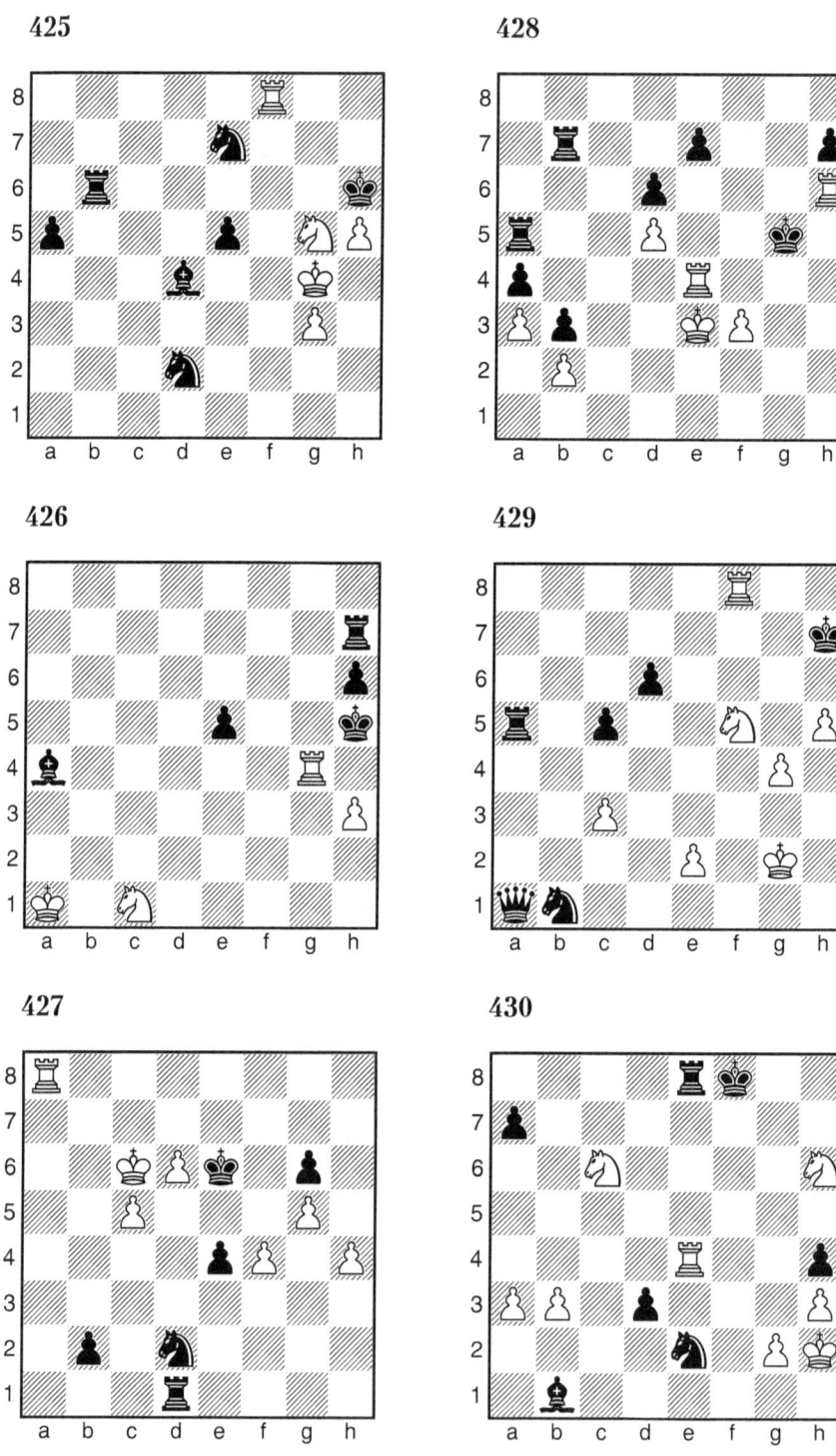

425

426

427

428

429

430

431

432

433

434

435

436

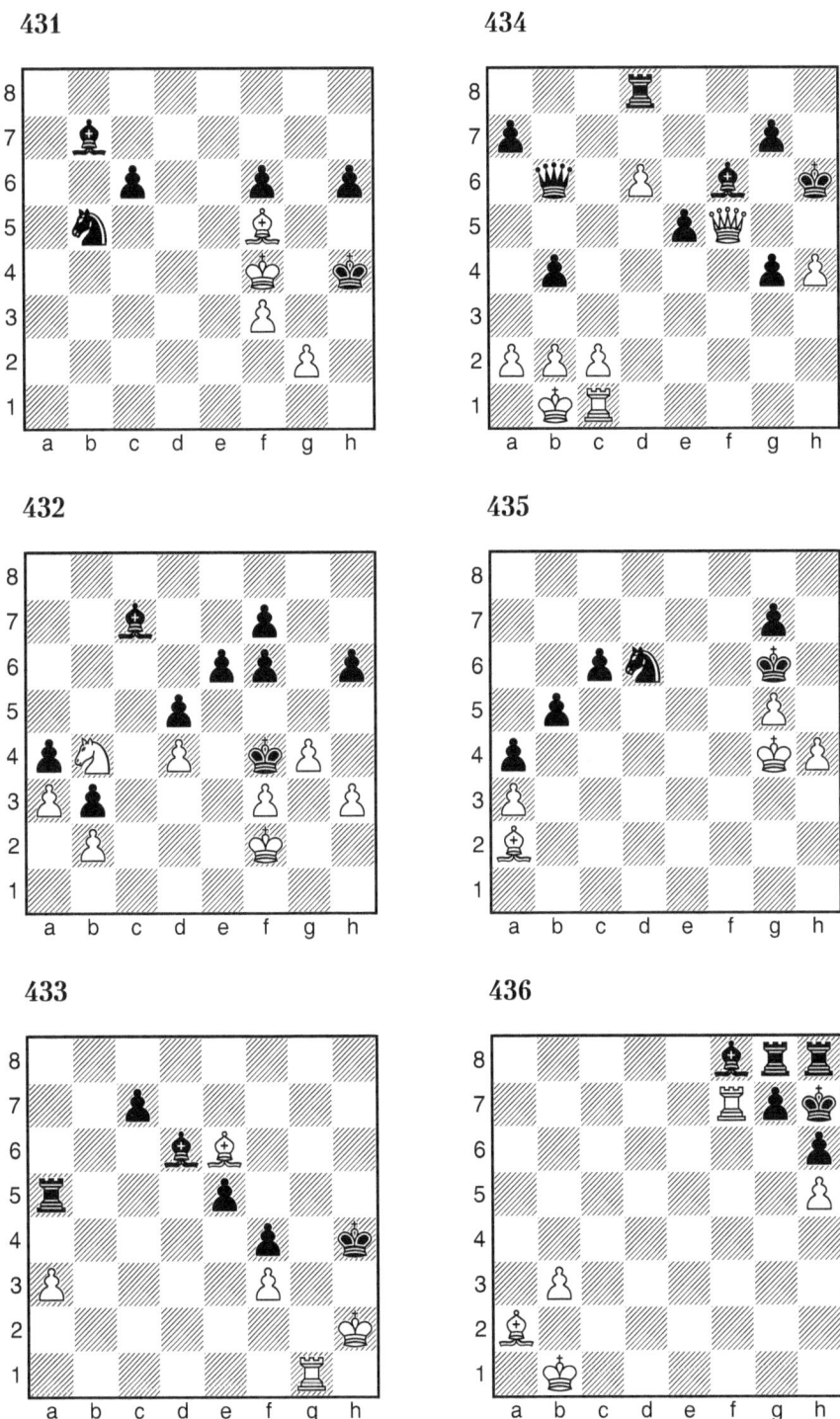

437

440

438

441

439

442

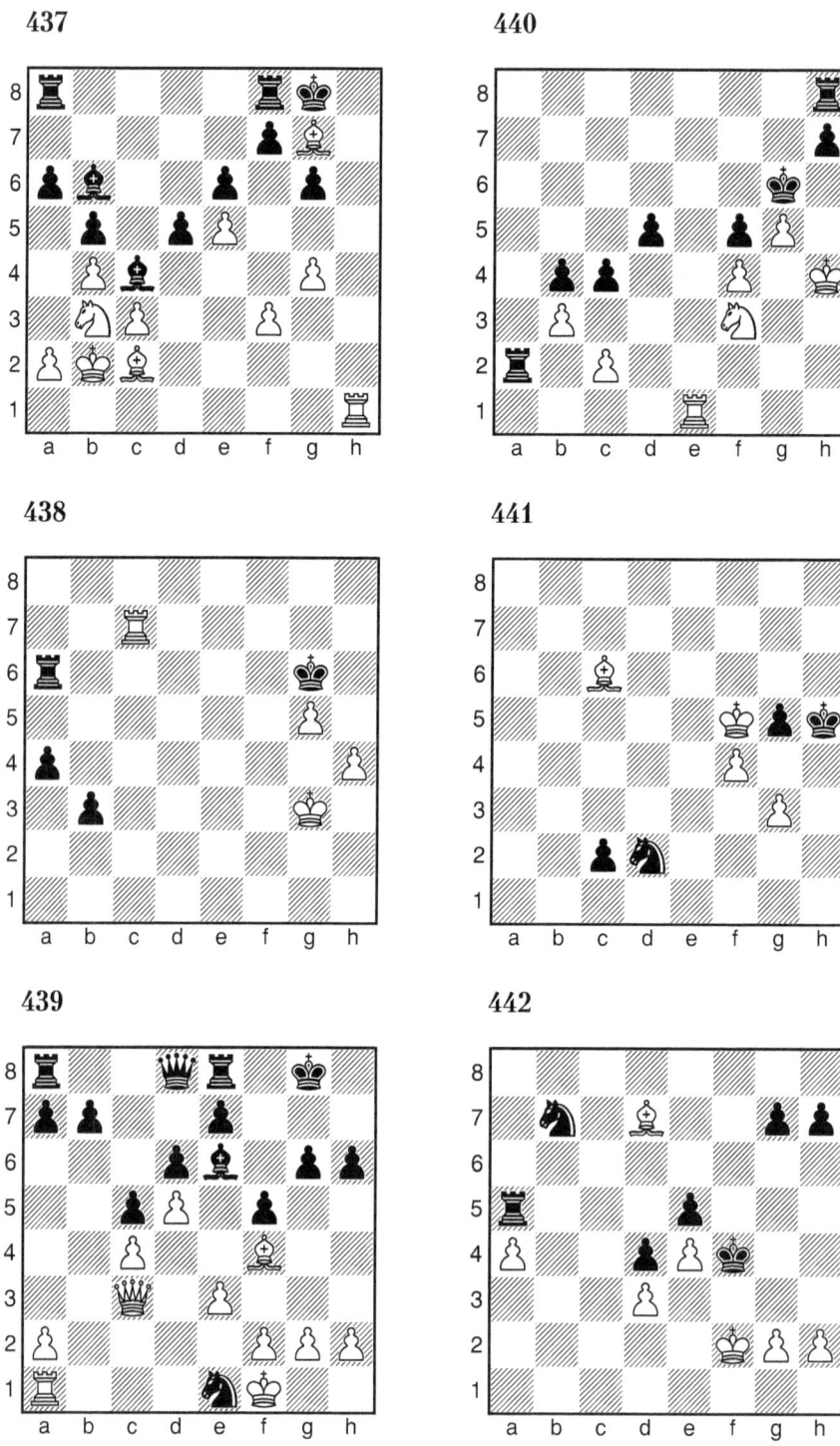

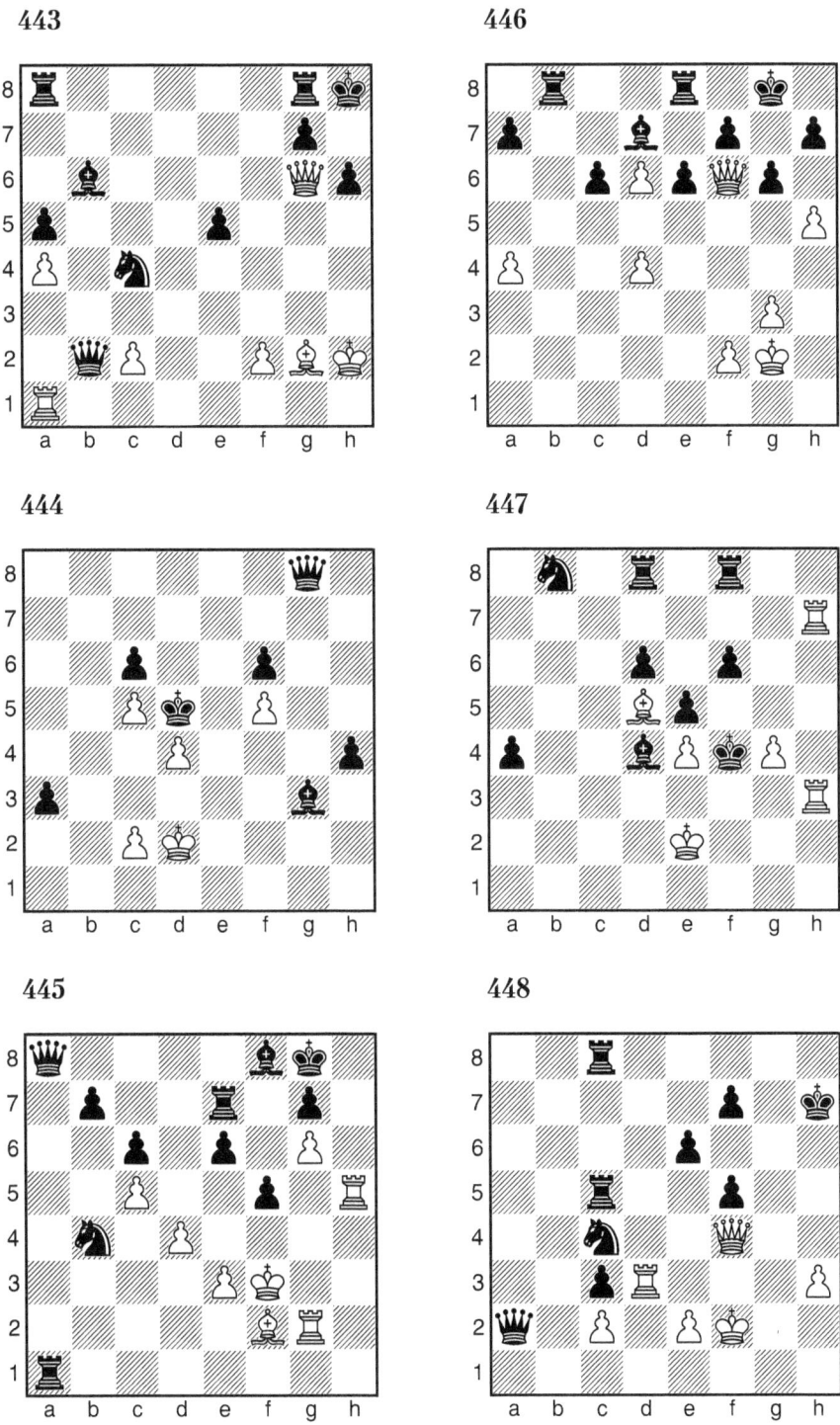

443

444

445

446

447

448

449

452

450

453

451

454

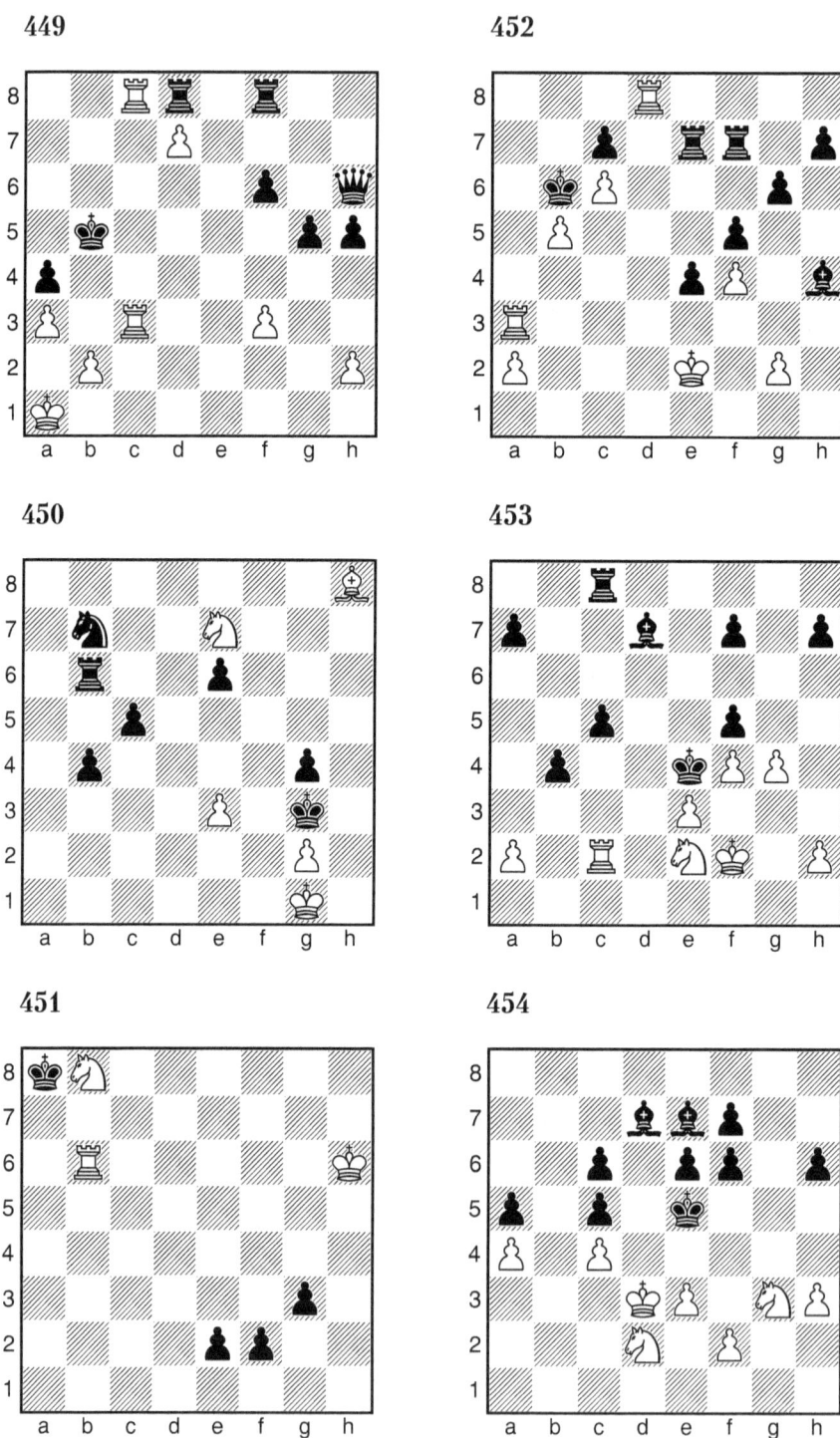

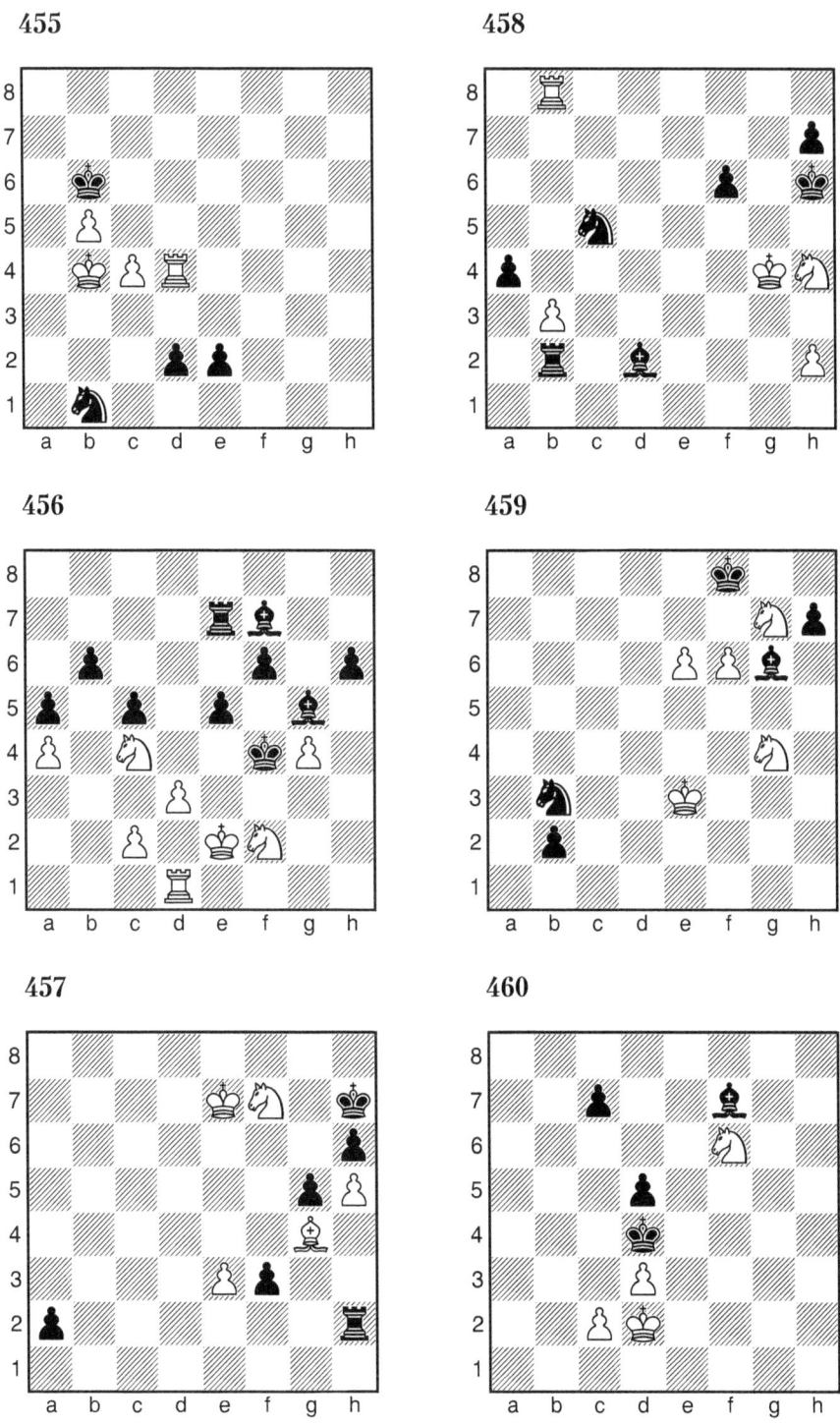

455

456

457

458

459

460

461

464

462

465

463

466

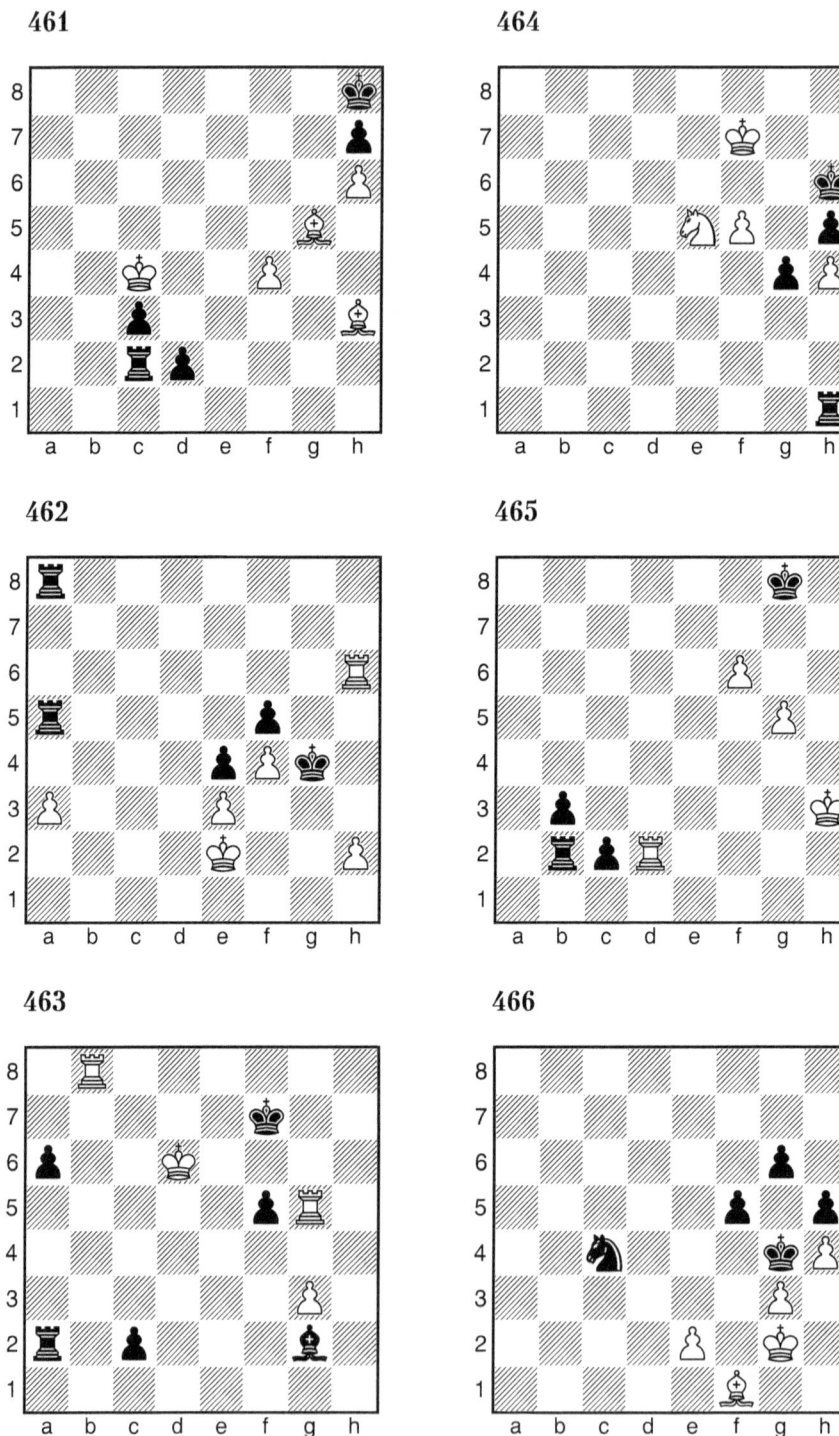

467

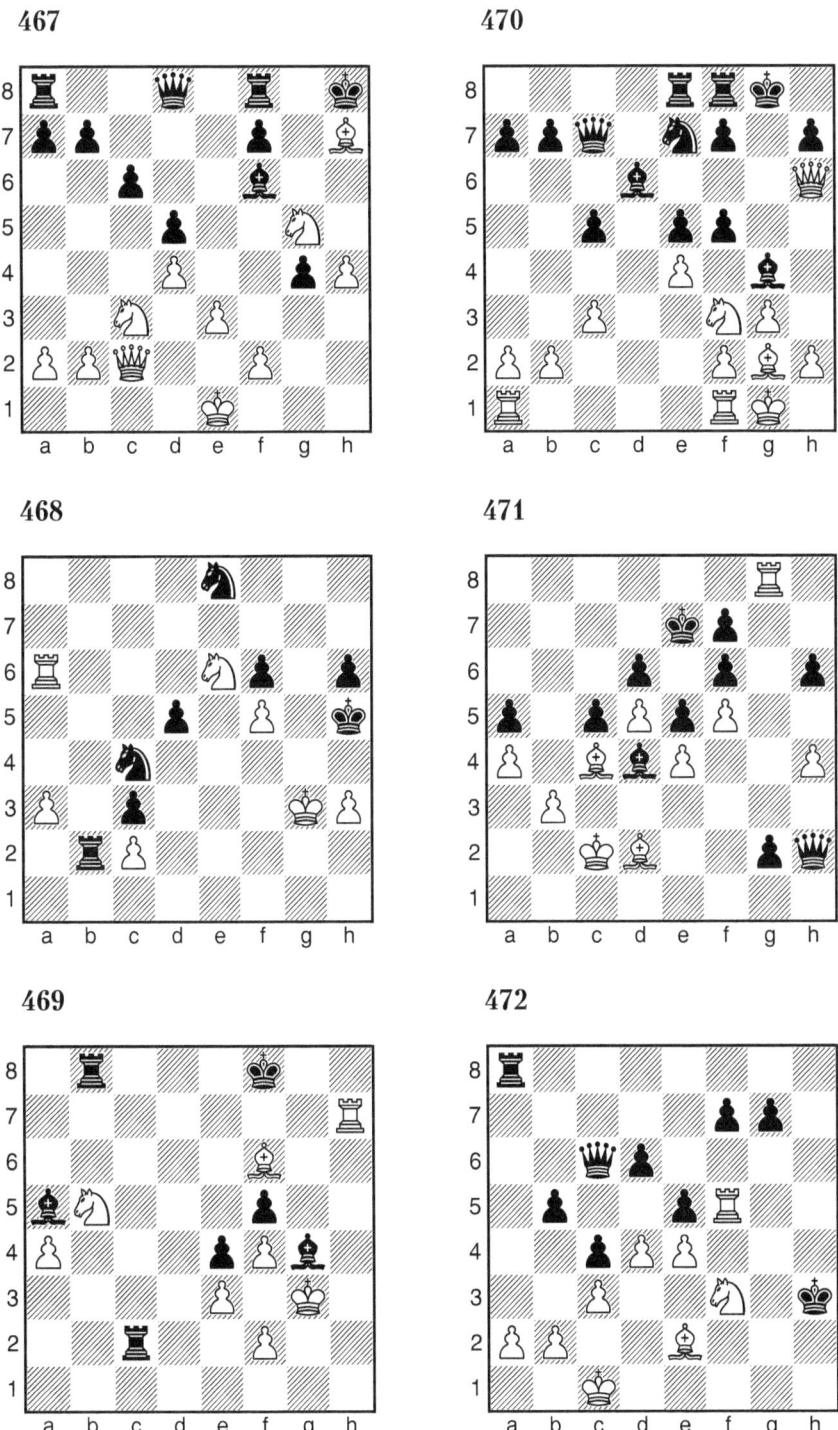

470

468

471

469

472

Chapter 22

COMBINATIONS

In this chapter, unstoppable mate is used in conjunction with forced mate and checks to the black king.

473

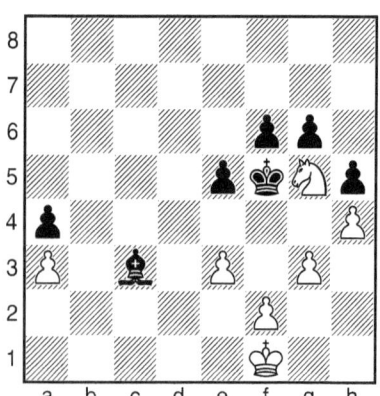

To weave a mating net, white needs to play **1.e4+ ♔g4 2.♔g2!** with unstoppable mate **3.f3#**. We should point out that 1.♔g2? also creates a mate threat – 2.e4+ ♔g4 3.f3#, but it can be easily repelled by the opponent, for instance, with 1...fxg5.

The difference between the two lines above is obvious: in the first case, white wins the game with a small mating combination, but in the second, he loses, hoping against hope that his opponent won't see the threat of a forced mate.

The following mating construction is encountered frequently in actual games.

474

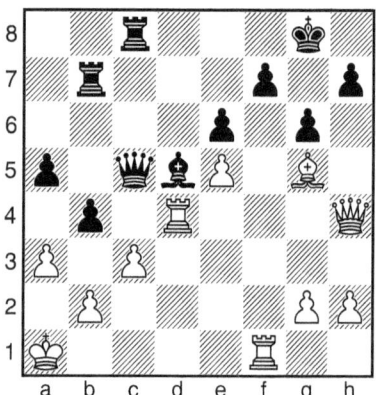

The opponents attack on different flanks, hoping to finish their attacks more quickly than the other player. White again has a choice between two mate threats. After 1.♗f6? with the threat of mate in three, 2.♕xh7+ ♔xh7 3.♖h4+ ♔g8 4.♖h8#, black has a great defense 1...h5!, and black is now better with correct play. The right move order is **1.♕xh7+! ♔xh7 2.♖h4+! ♔g8 3.♗f6!** with unstoppable mate **4.♖h8#**. In this line, it's necessary to calculate all possible black king retreats: 2...♔g7 3.♗f6+ ♔f8 4.♖h8# or 3...♔g8 4.♖h8#, and 1...♔f8 2.♕h8#. In all the lines above, black is mated by force.

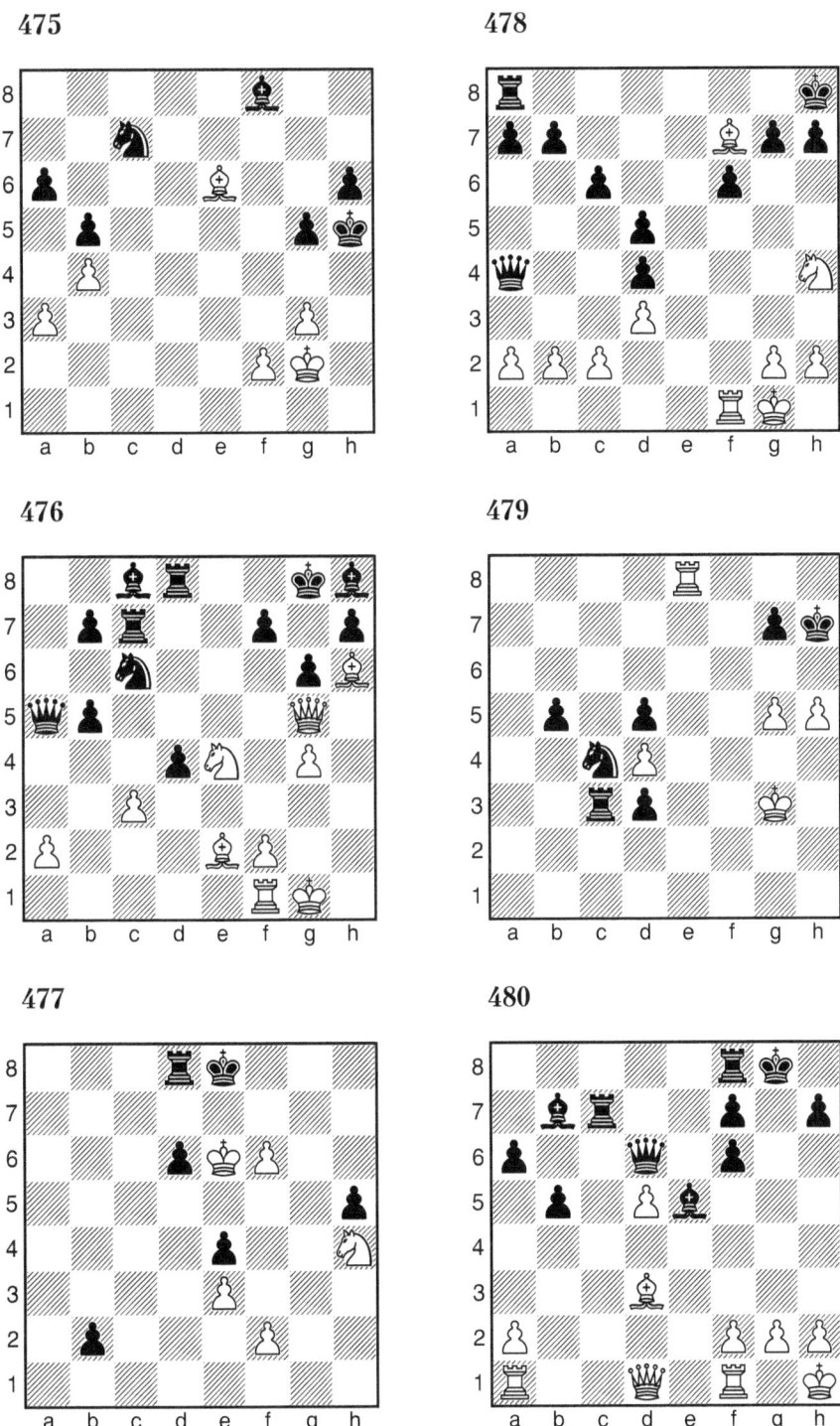

475

476

477

478

479

480

481

484

482

485

483

486

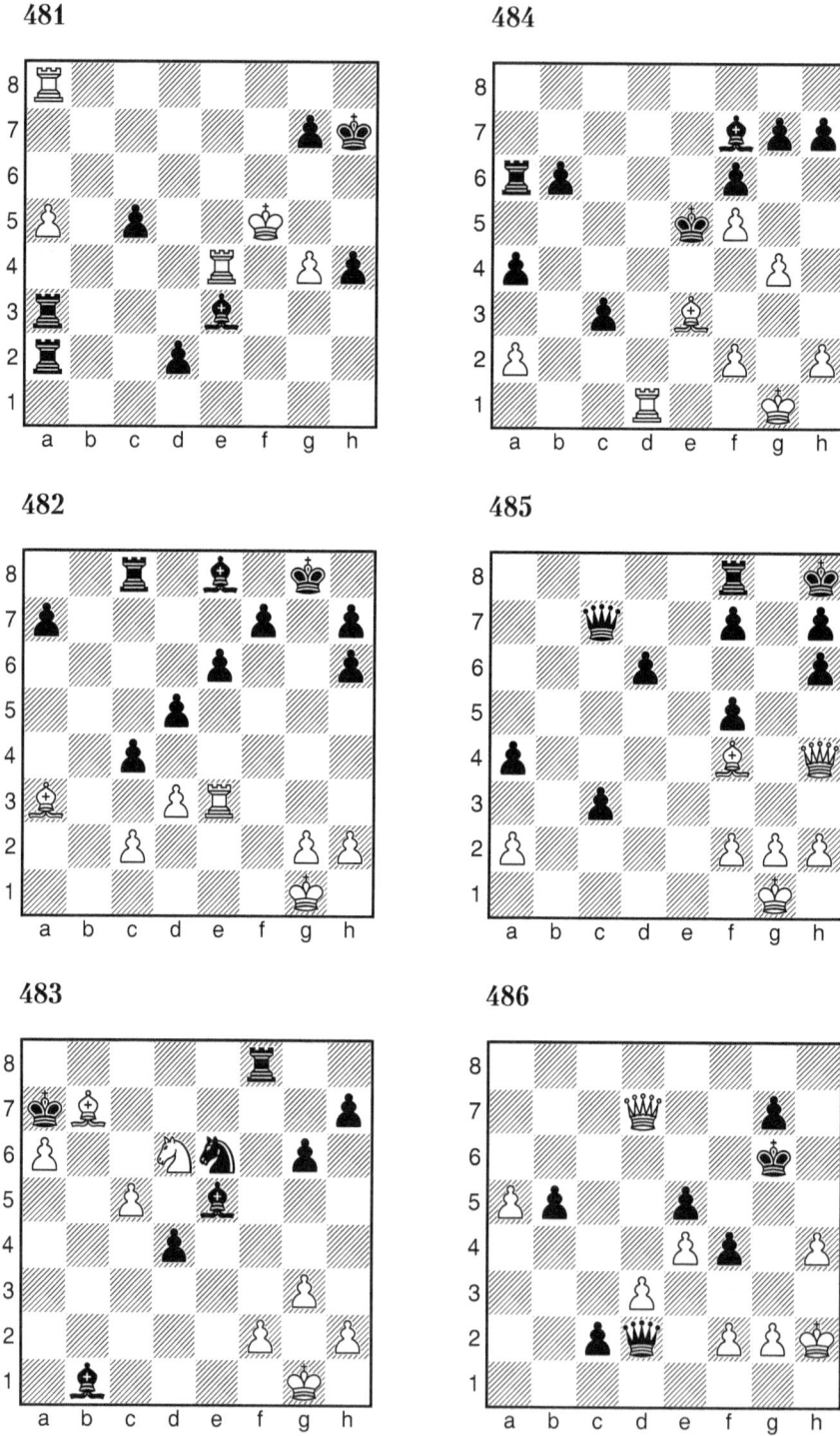

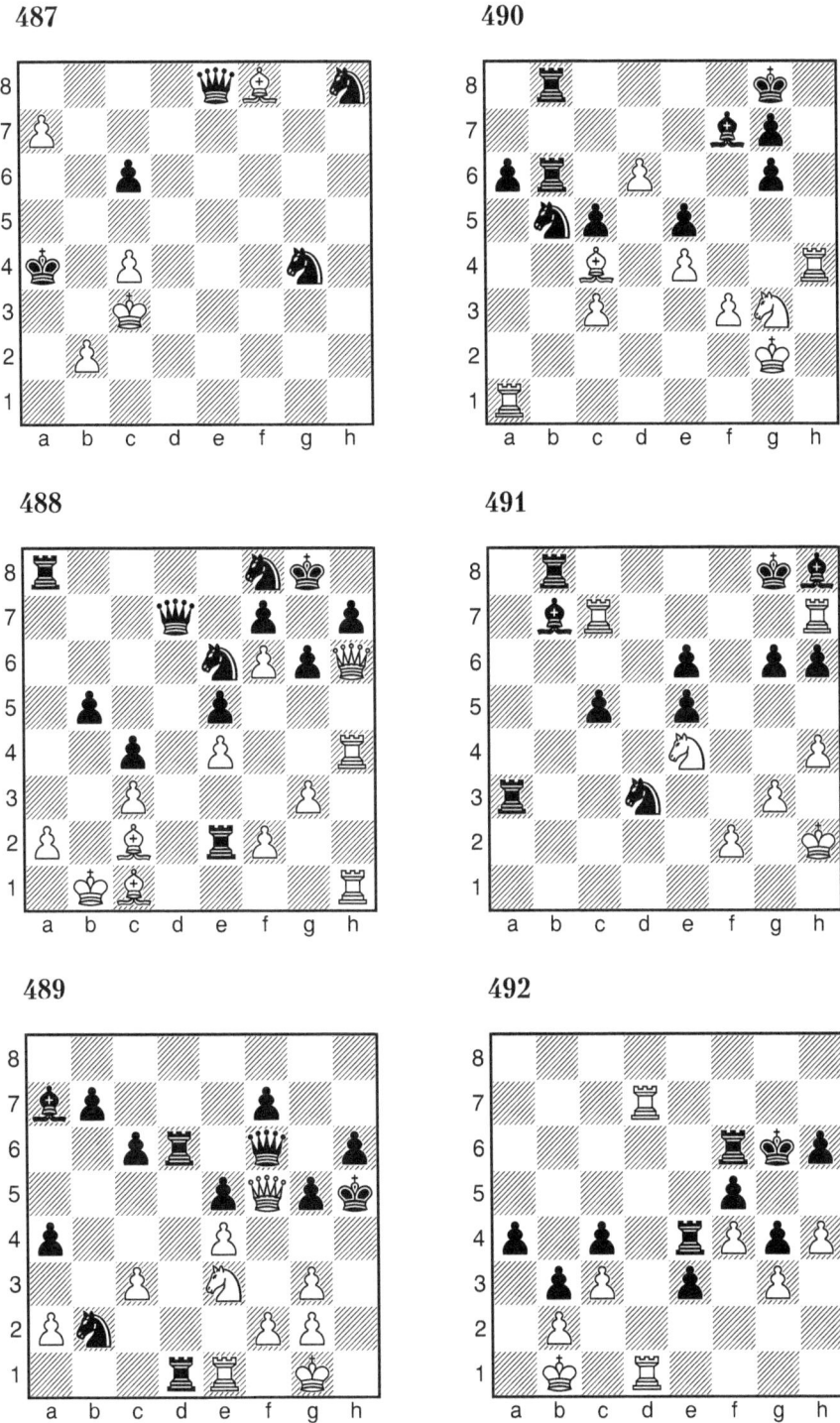

487

488

489

490

491

492

493

496

494

497

495

498

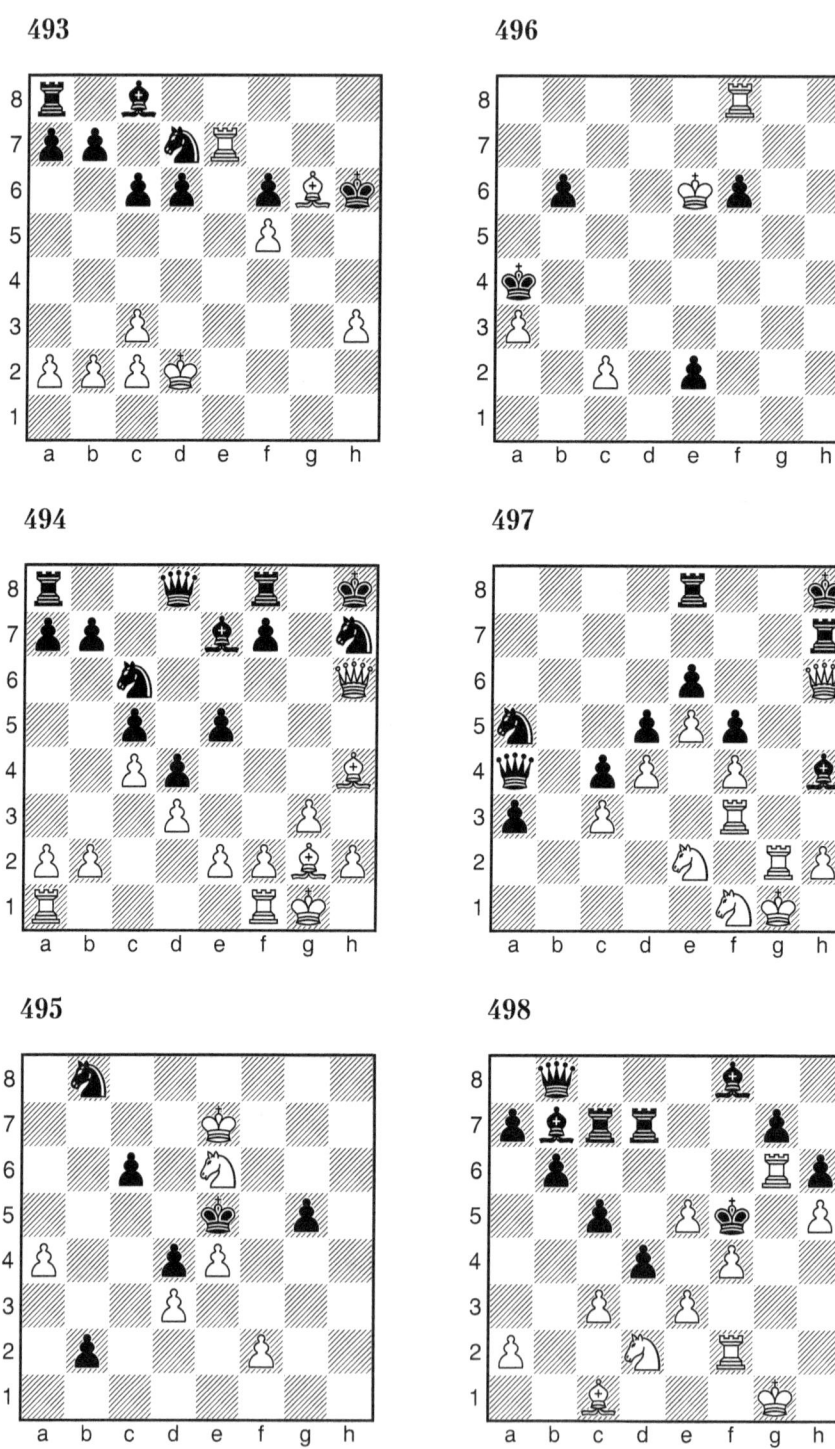

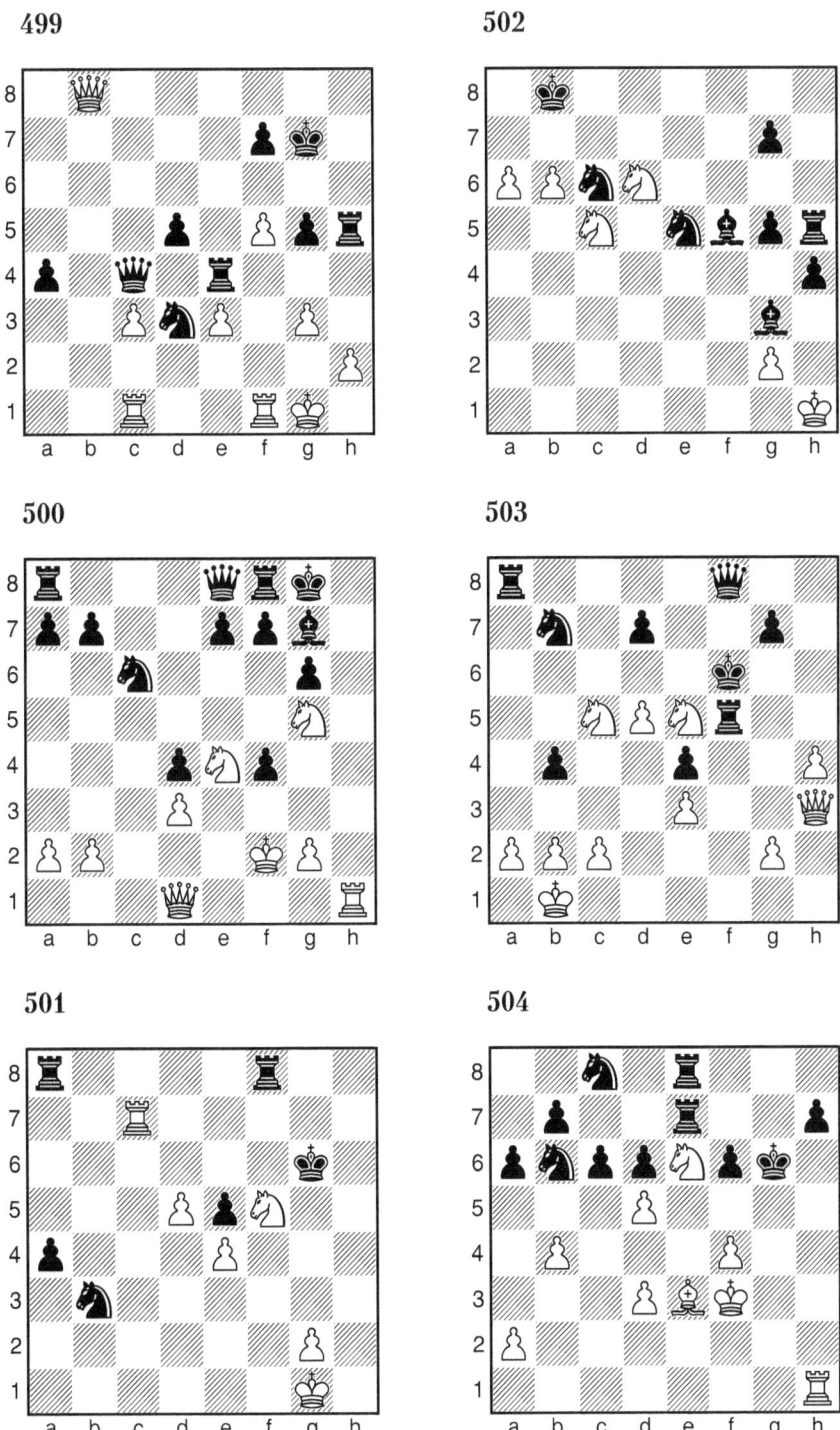

499

500

501

502

503

504

505

508

506

509

507

510

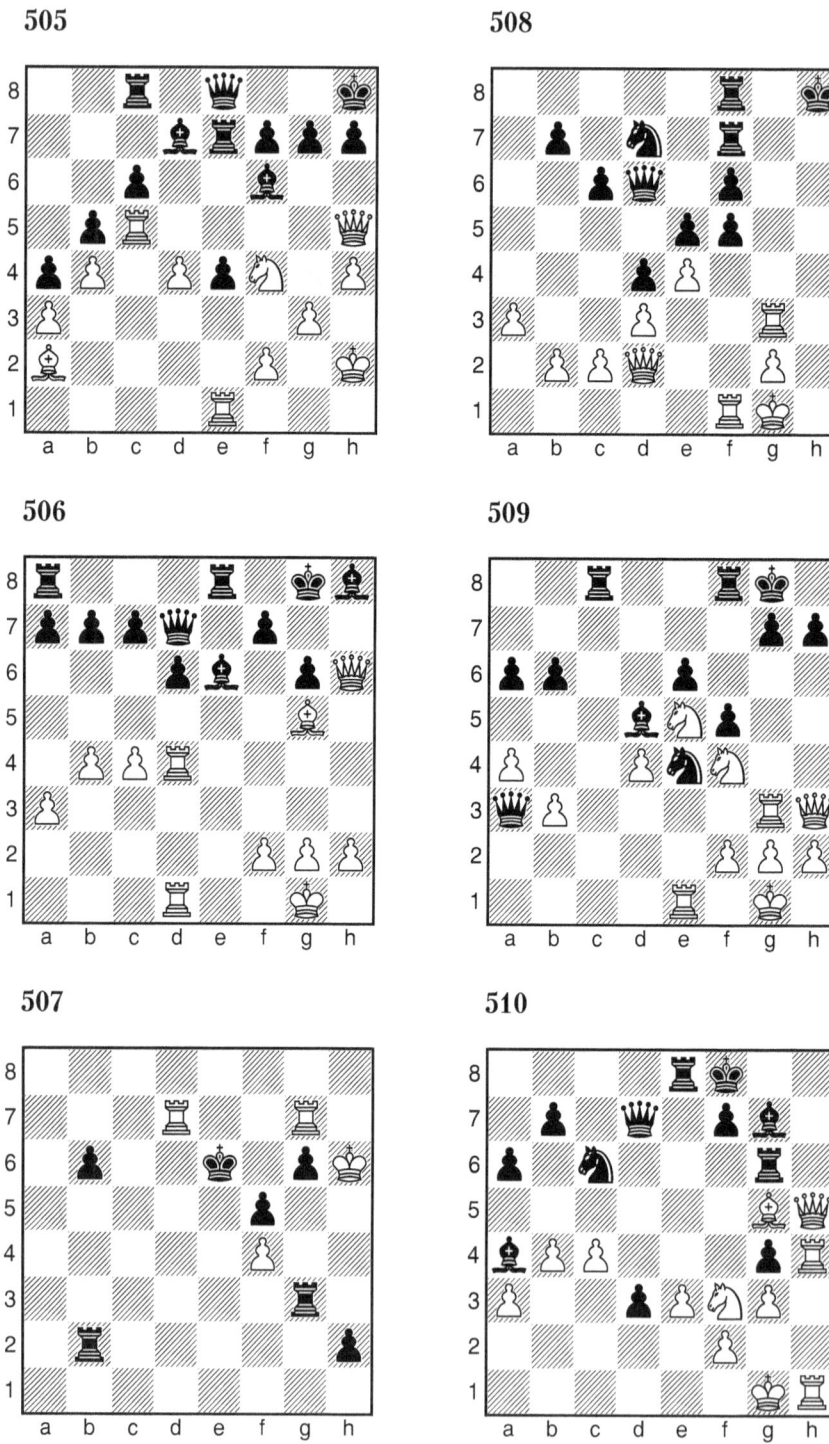

Chapter 23

MATE THREATS
WITHOUT SATISFACTORY DEFENSE

A mate threat without satisfactory defense is a threat of checkmate in one or more moves that leads to a hopeless position for the opponent, regardless of his defense.

511

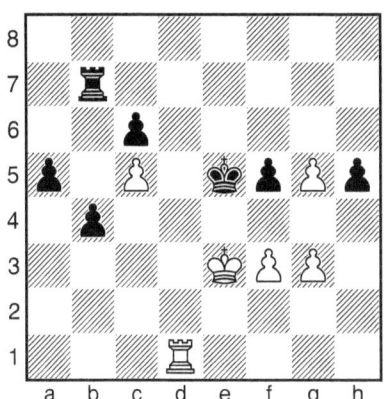

After **1.罝d6!**, white creates a dangerous mate threat: 2.f4#. The only way to stop this threat is to play **1...f4+**, which still leads to mate after **2.gxf4+ 含f5 3.罝f6#**. Thus, white's first move technically cannot be called an unstoppable mate threat, because black does have a defense against the immediate threat, but it's undeniable that after 1.罝d6!, black gets checkmated in all possible lines.

Often, the weaker side has no real defense from the mate threat, but he still has several checks that don't affect the position in any meaningful way, although they do delay checkmate for a few moves.

512

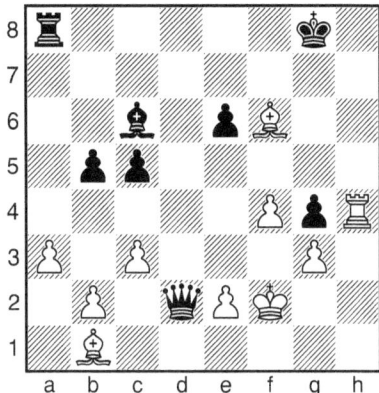

In this position, white should play **1.臬g6**, creating the mate threat 2.罝h8#. Black does not have to get checkmated on the second move; first, he can give some futile checks: 1...豐e1+ 2.含xe1; 1...豐e3+ 2.含xe3; 1...豐d4+ 2.cxd4; 1...豐xe2+ 2.含xe2 臬f3+ 3.含f2; **1...豐xf4+ 2.gxf4 g3+ 3.含xg3**. None of the above lines stop the final rook checkmate, but they do delay it for a couple of moves.

In many positions, the weaker side can defend from the immediate mate threat, but is forced to incur material losses – to give up one or more of his pieces.

513

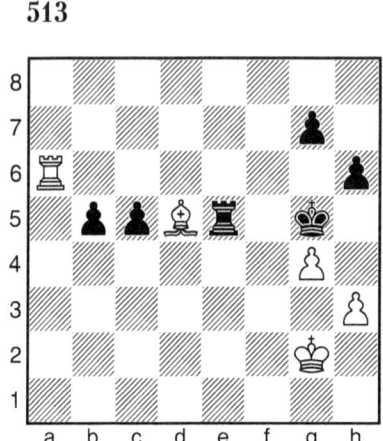

514

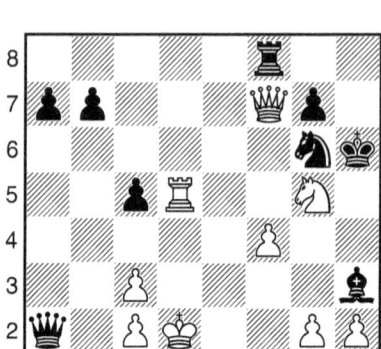

After **1.♔g3!**, white threatens 2.h4#. To avoid mate on the next move, black can close off the sixth rank with 1...♖e6? but then, after 2.♖xe6, he may as well resign due to the unstoppable mate threat 3.h4#. **1...♖e3+** is stronger, forcing white to defend. Counter-strikes have ruined many beautiful mating constructions, but this time, white has the precise reply **2.♗f3! ♖xf3+** – the rook sacrifices itself to destroy the mating net around the king. After **3.♔xf3**, the mate threats are eliminated, but the price of defense was too steep for black: white will have no problem converting his huge material advantage.

White wins with a beautiful mating combination: **1.♕g8!**, threatening 2.♕h7#. Black has more than a few defensive resources, but none of them are enough to save the game. The series of counter-strikes 1...♕xc2+ 2.♔xc2 ♗f5+ 3.♖xf5 is pointless: black pieces fall off the board, but all white's mate threats remain. After 1...♕xd5+!? 2.♕xd5, white has a decisive material advantage; however, in comparison with all of black's other defensive resources, this one should be considered the strongest. After **1...♖xg8**, white delivers a checkmate: **2.♘f7+ ♔h7 3.♖h5#**. Finally, if black tries to escape the mating net with 1...♔h5, white can play, for instance, 2.♕h7+ ♔g4 3.♕xh3+ ♔xf4 4.♕g3#.

515

518

516

519

517

520

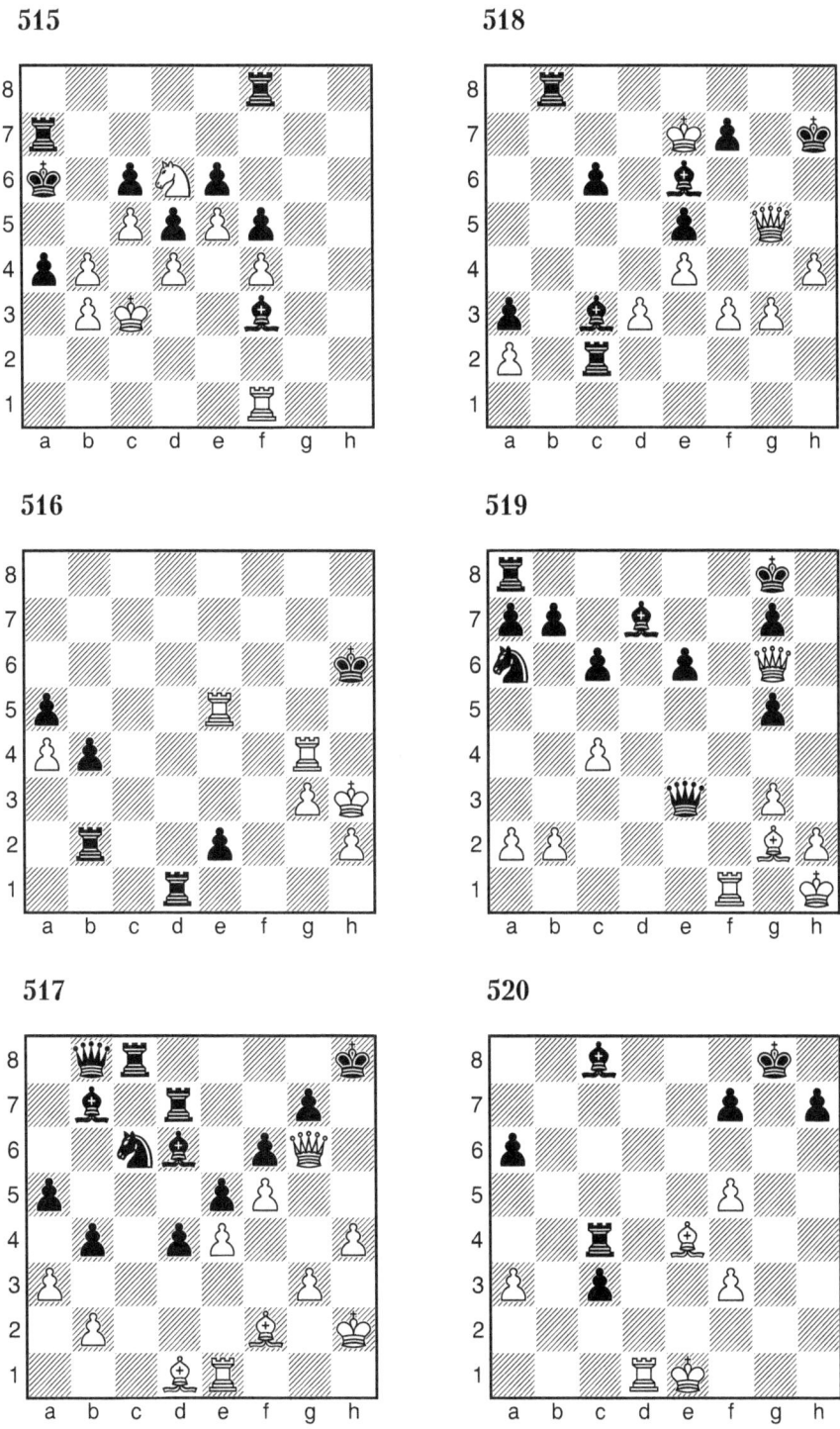

521

524

522

525

523

526

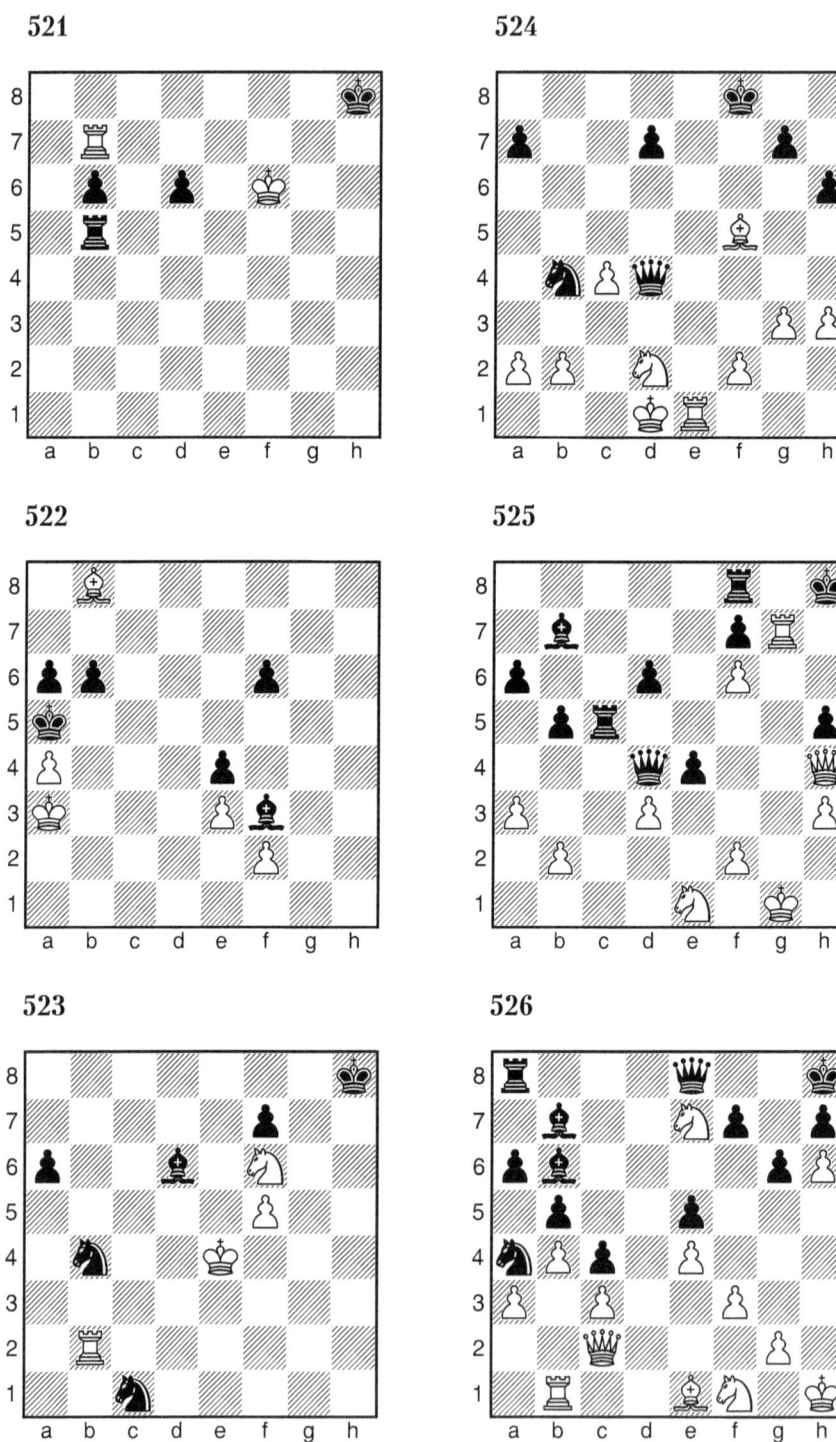

527

530

528

531

529

532

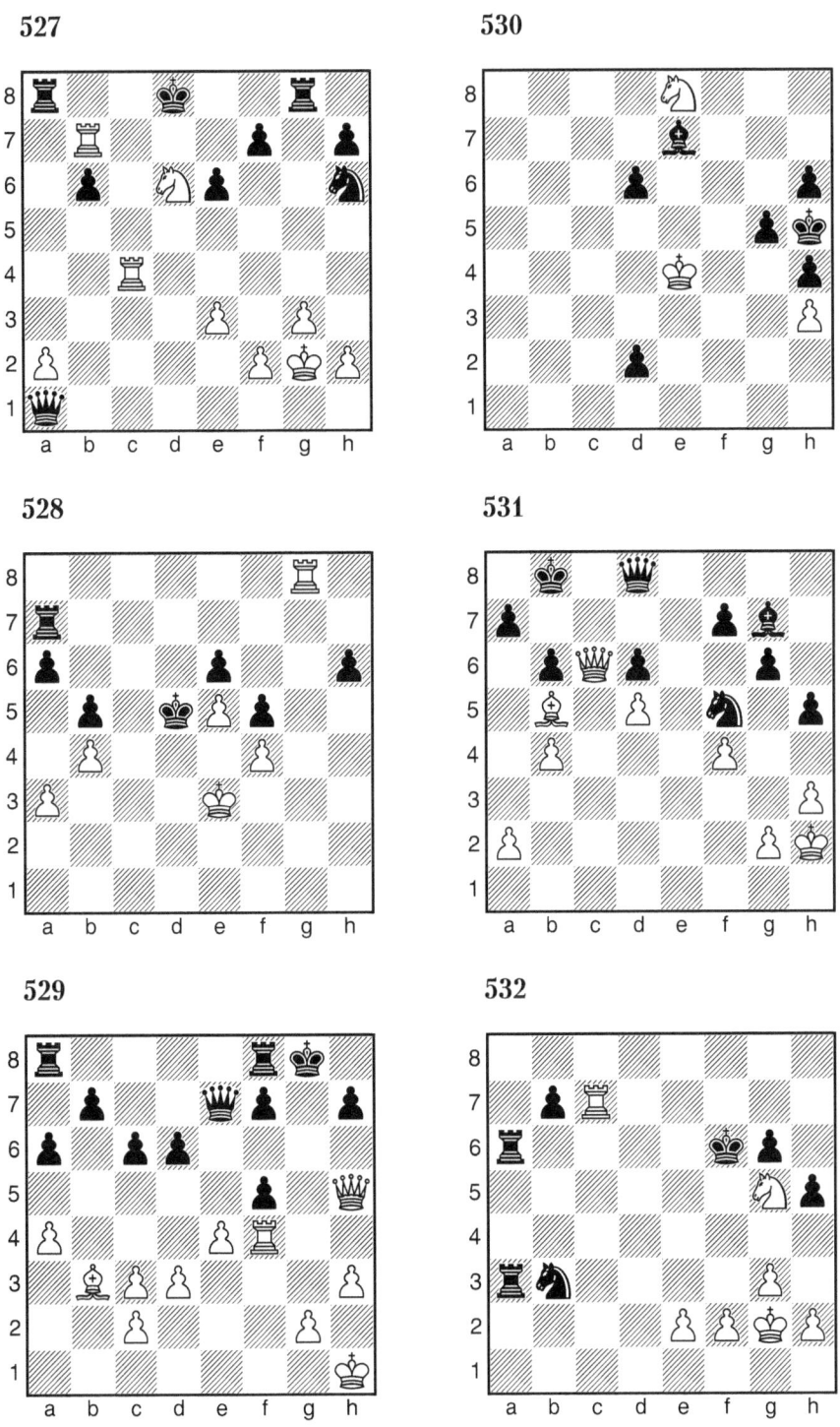

533

536

534

537

535

538

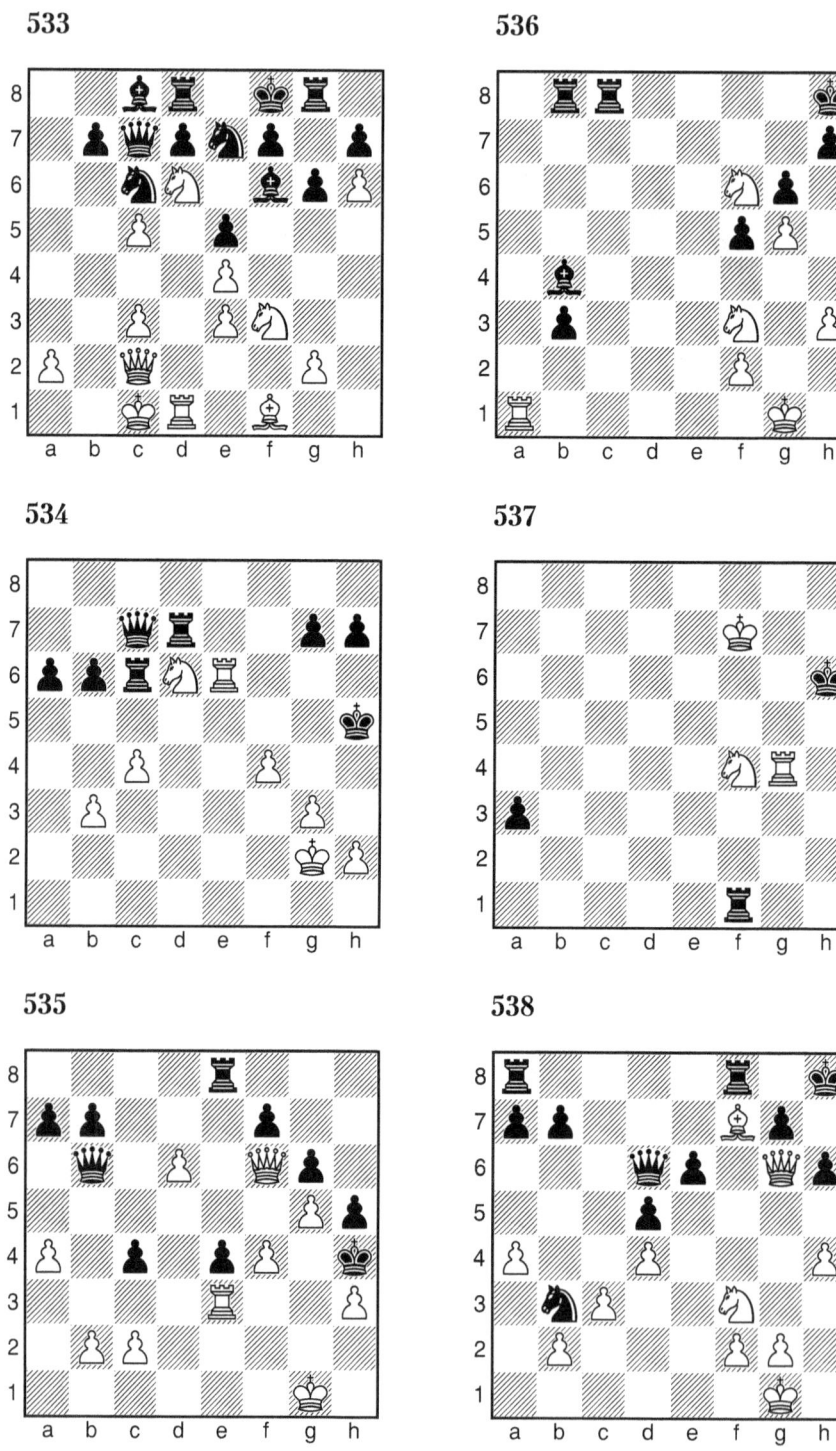

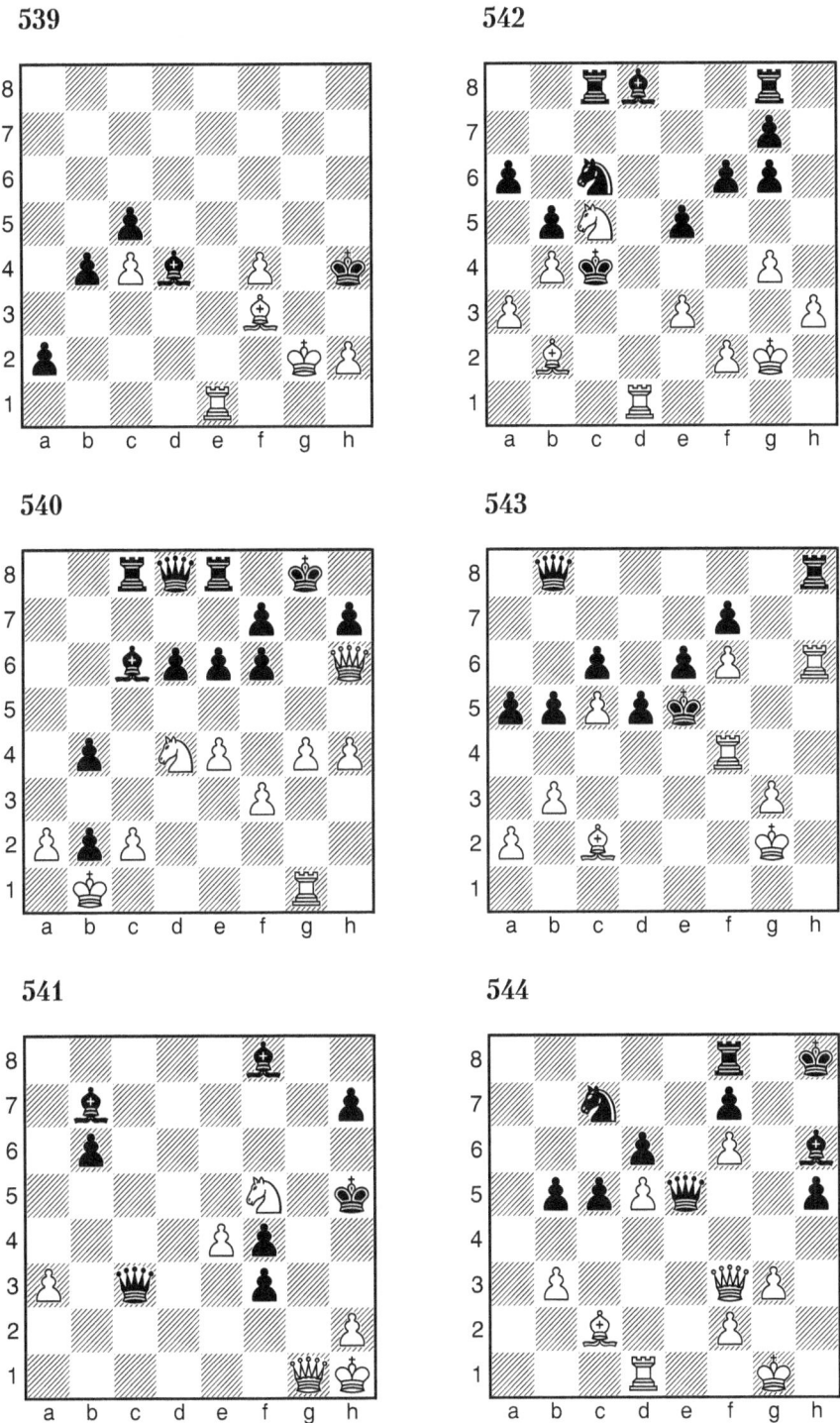

539

540

541

542

543

544

545

548

546

549

547

550

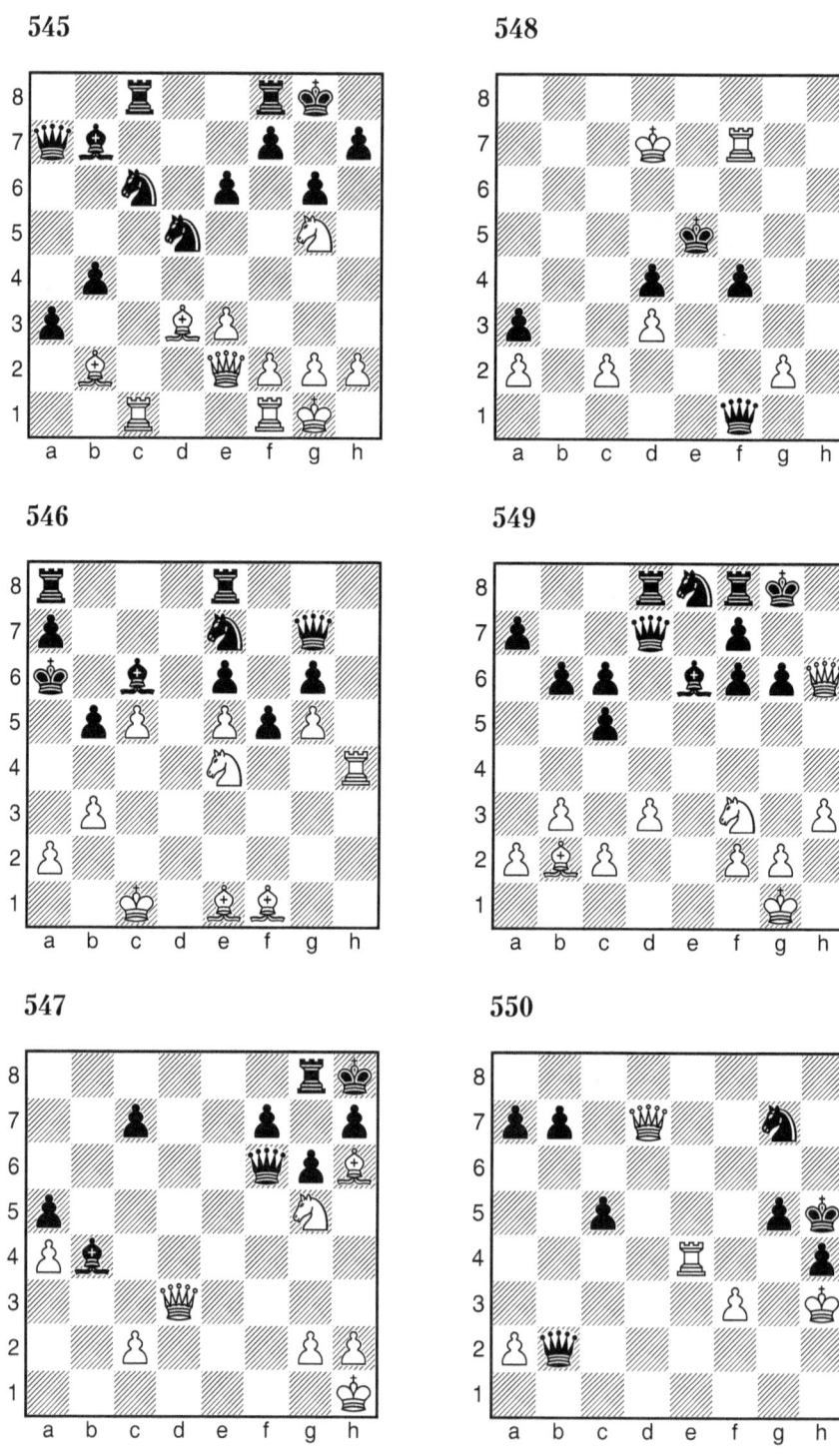

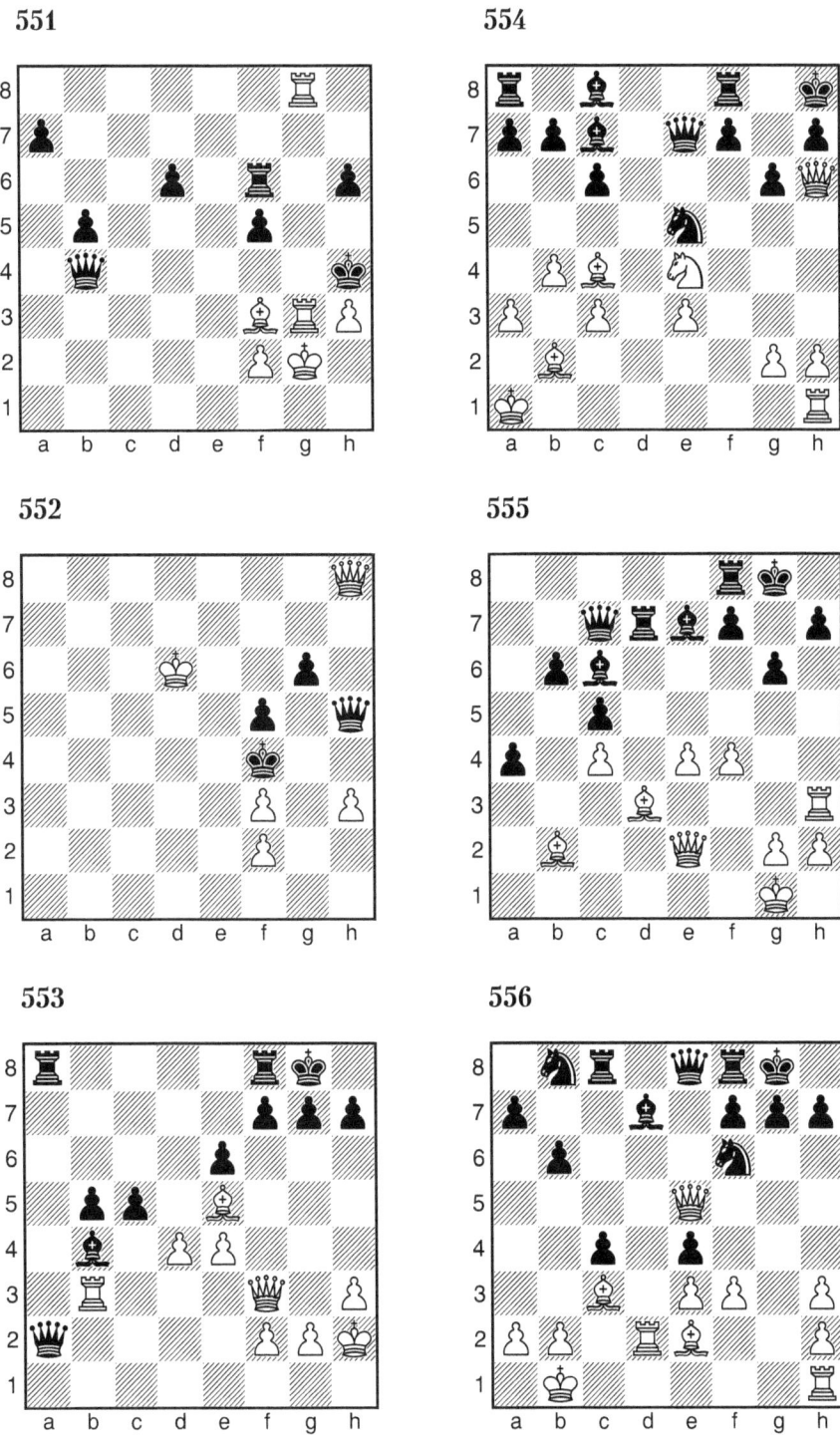

551

552

553

554

555

556

557

560

558

561

559

562

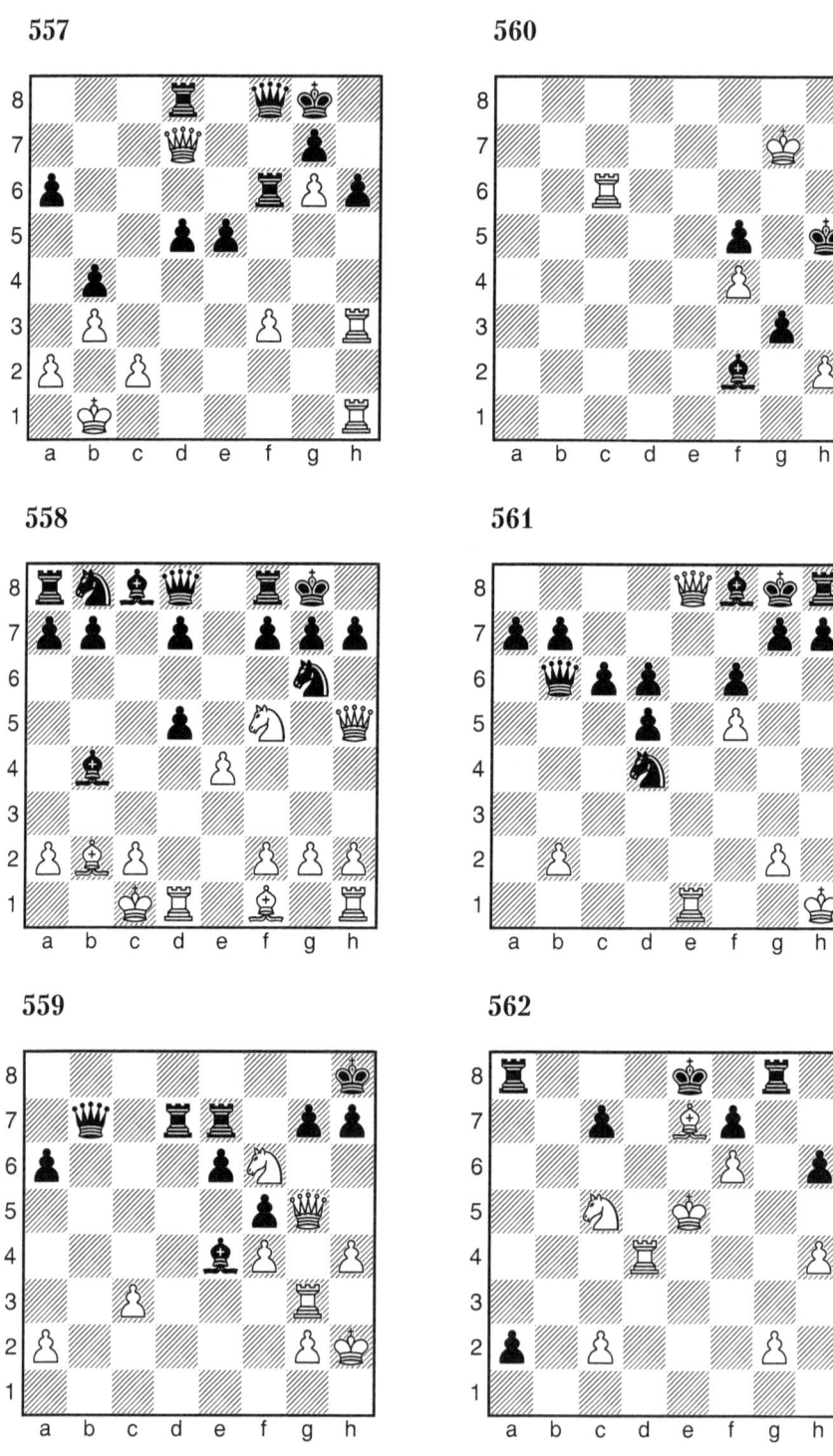

563

566

564

567

565

568

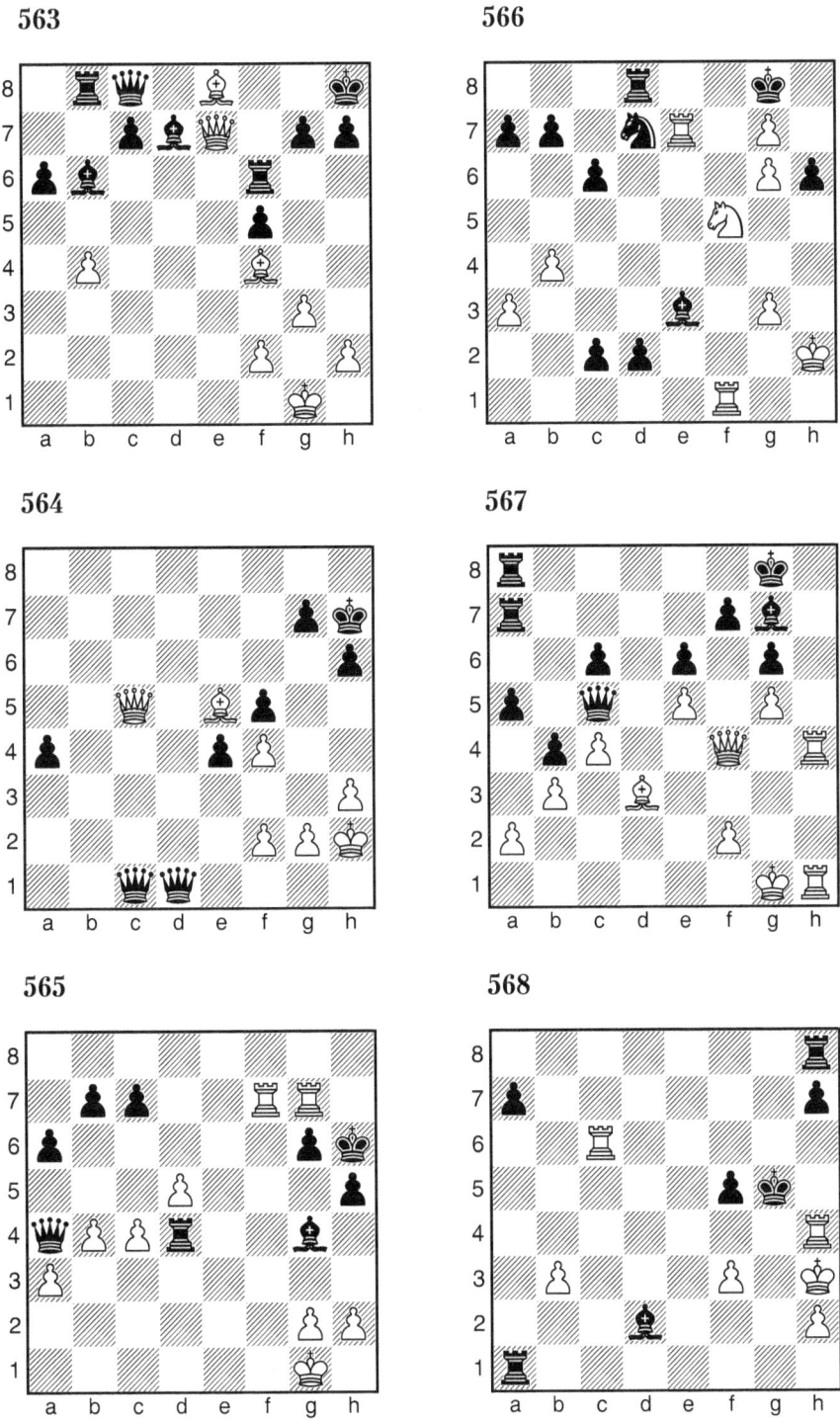

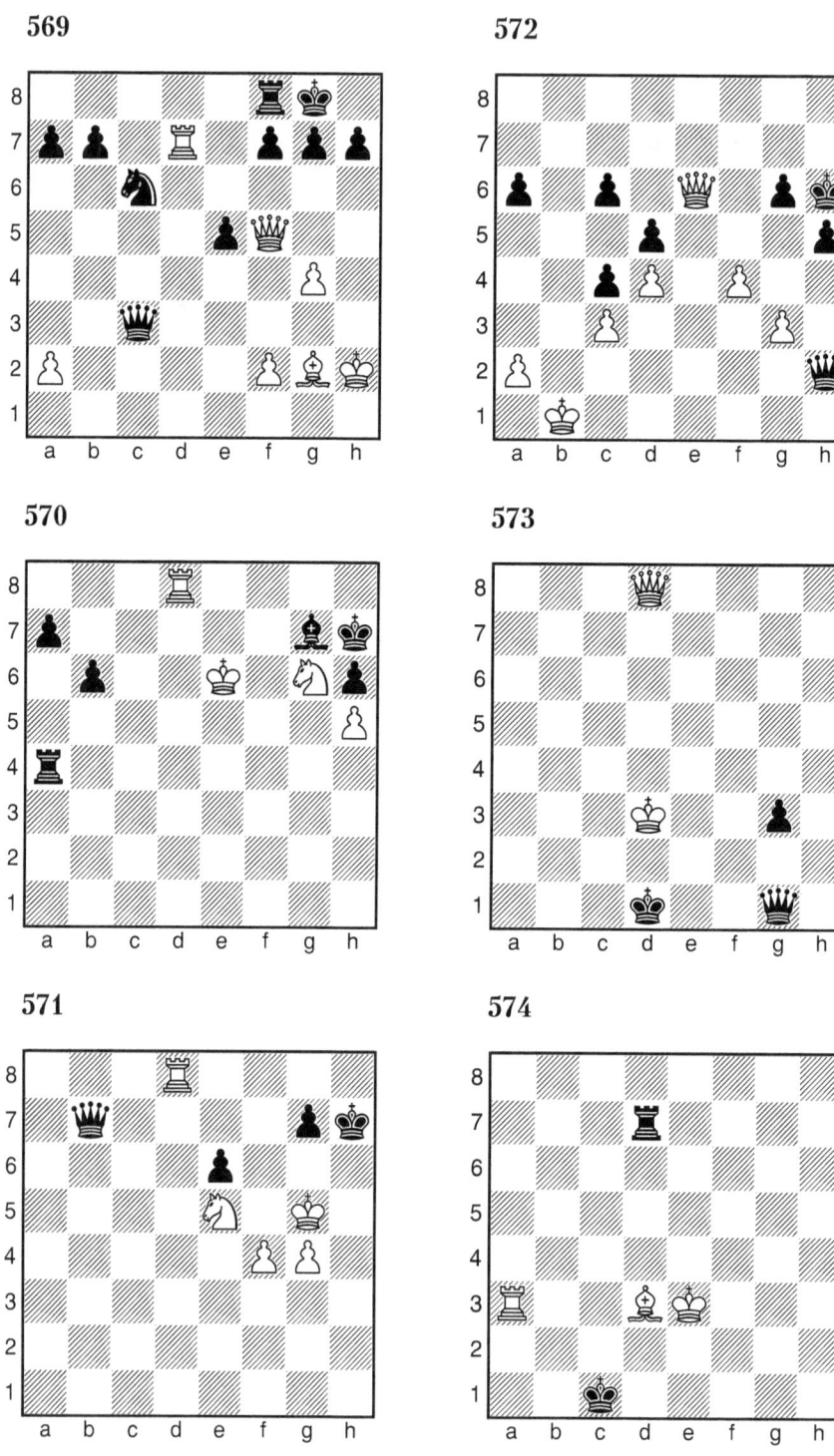

569

570

571

572

573

574

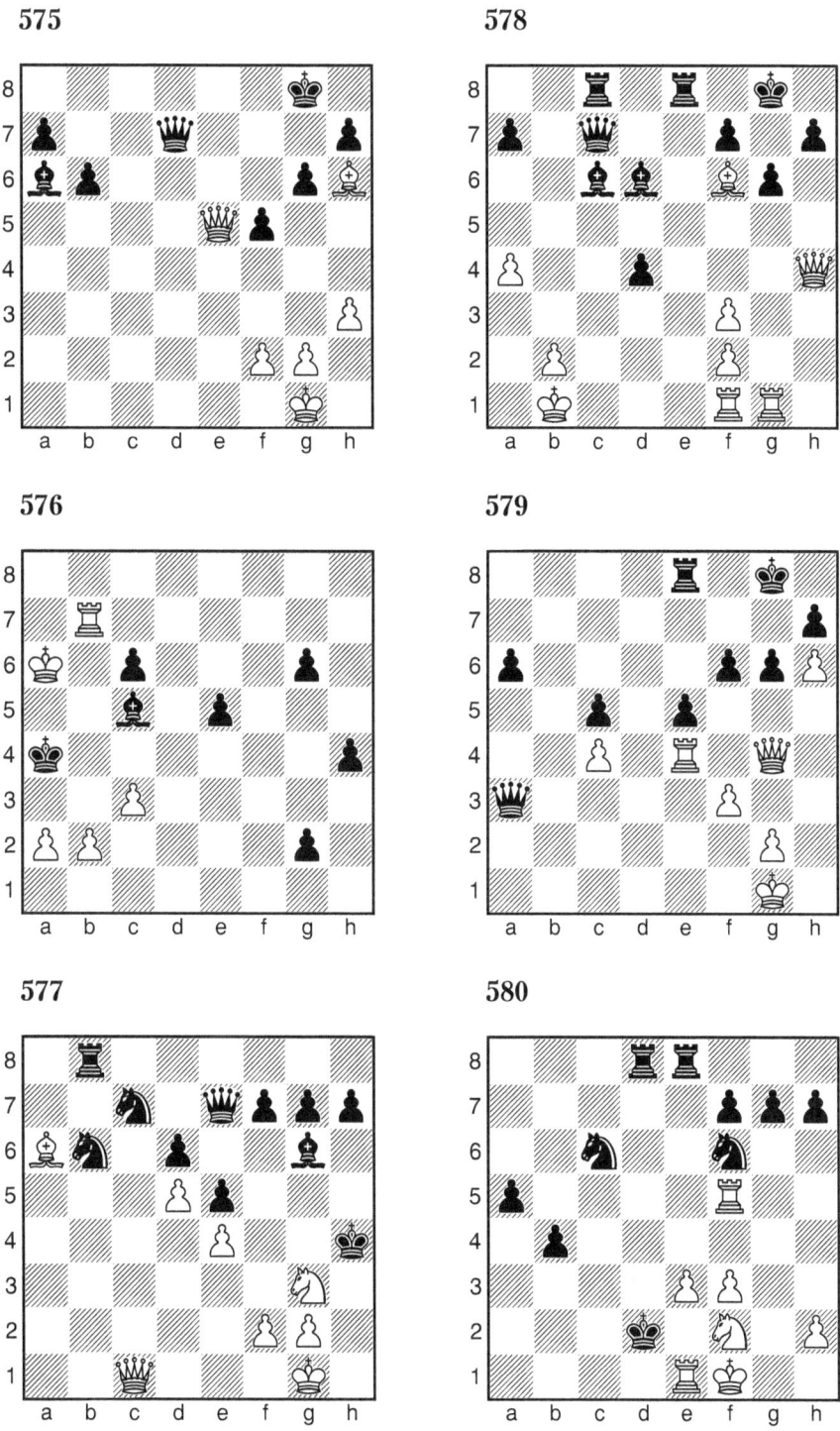

575

576

577

578

579

580

COMBINATIONS

In this chapter, the mate threat without satisfactory defense is used in conjunction with checks to the black king and forced checkmate.

581

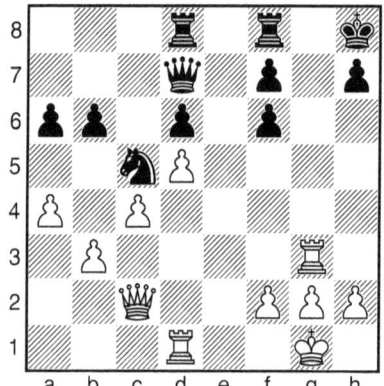

After **1.♕xh7+! ♔xh7 2.♖d4**, white creates a mate threat: 3.♖h4#. To defend from the imminent checkmate, black can only sacrifice a few of his pieces: 2...♘e4 3.♖xe4; 2...♕g4 3.♖dxg4; 2...♕h3 3.gxh3 or play **2...♕f5** and delay the checkmate by one move: **3.♖h4+ ♕h5 4.♖xh5#**. We should also point out that going for the immediate checkmate with 1.♖h3? doesn't work due to 1...f5! with an advantage for black.

582

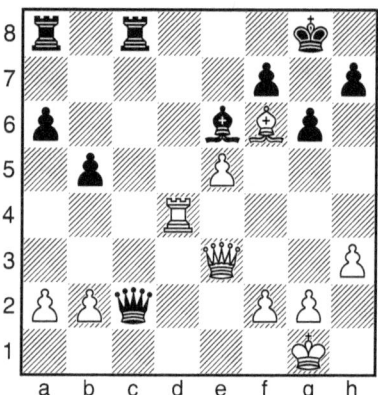

The weakness of the dark squares around the king makes white's mate threat quite obvious: 1.♕h6 with the idea 2.♕g7# looks logical. However, this move will be a serious mistake because black can meet 1.♕h6 with 1...♕c1+!, trading the white queen (2.♕xc1 ♖xc1+) and destroying the mating net. It's much stronger to first deflect the black rook – **1.♖d8+! ♖xd8**, and only then play **2.♕h6**. It turns out that the checks 2...♕d1+ 3.♔h2 or 2...♖d1+ 3.♔h2 ♖h1+ 4.♔xh1 are completely useless, and after the strongest reply **2...♕c1+! 3.♕xc1**, the mating combination allows white to win the queen for his rook. White now has a decisive advantage.

Note that mating combinations can be used for winning material, not only to deliver checkmate itself.

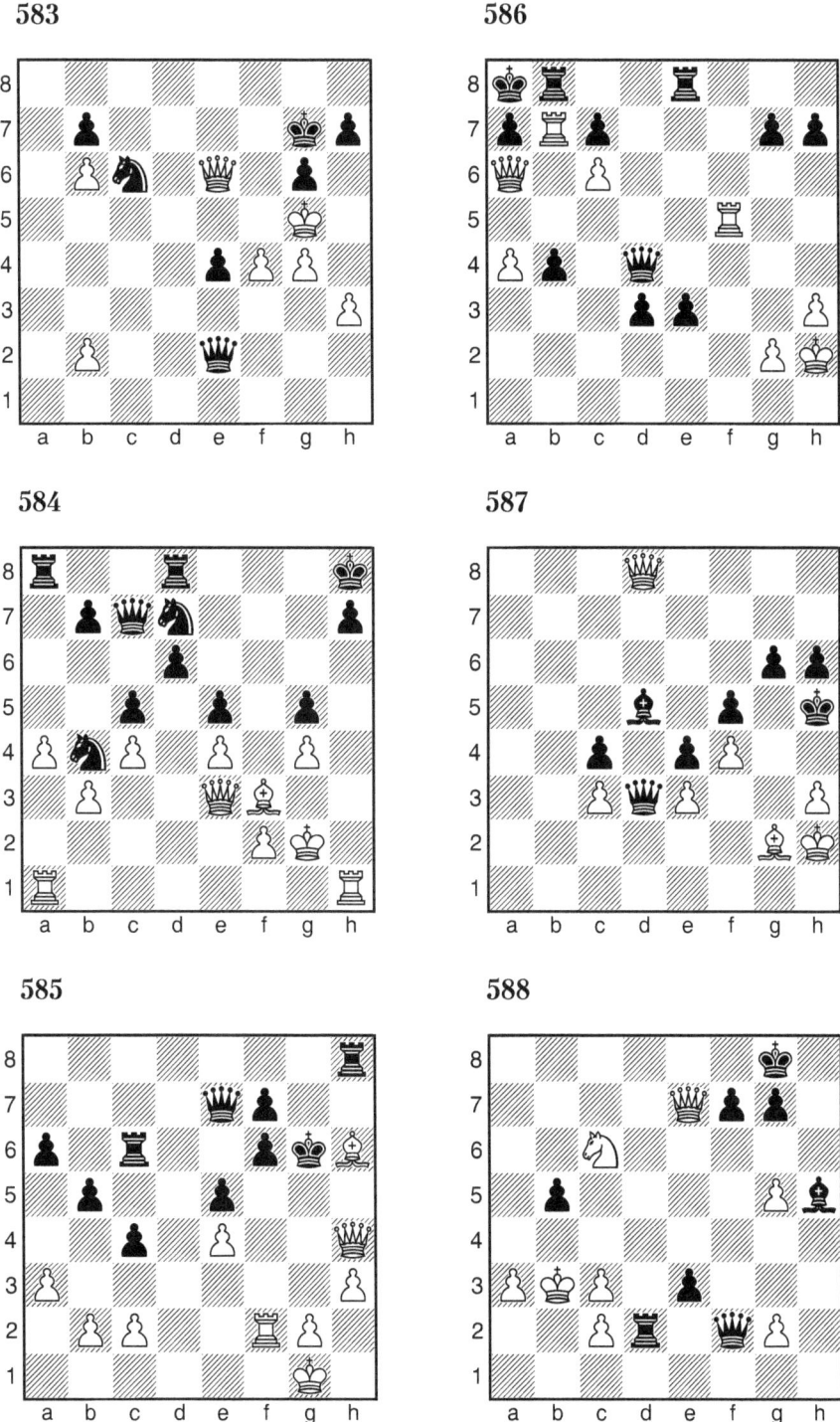

583

584

585

586

587

588

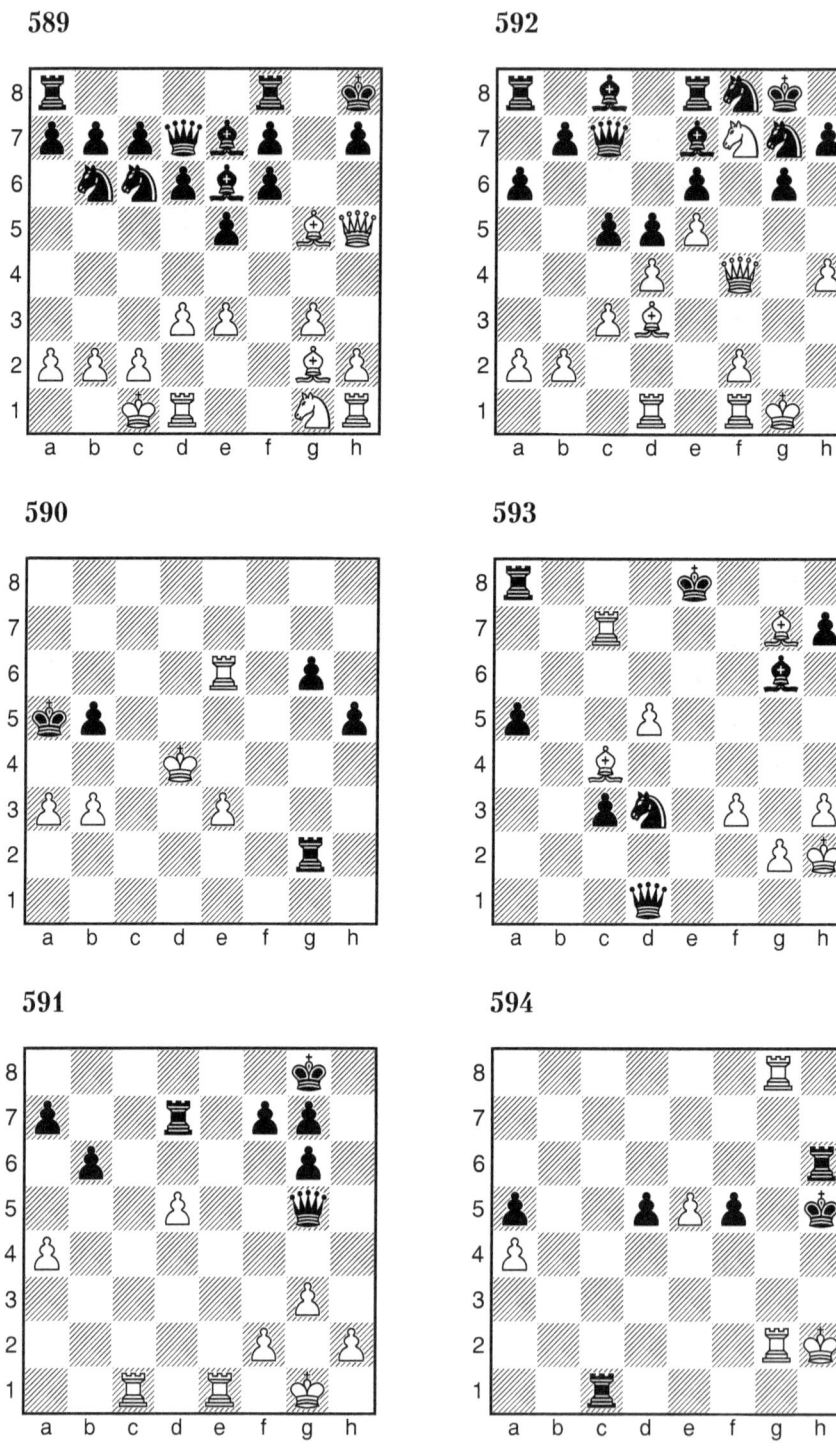

589

590

591

592

593

594

595

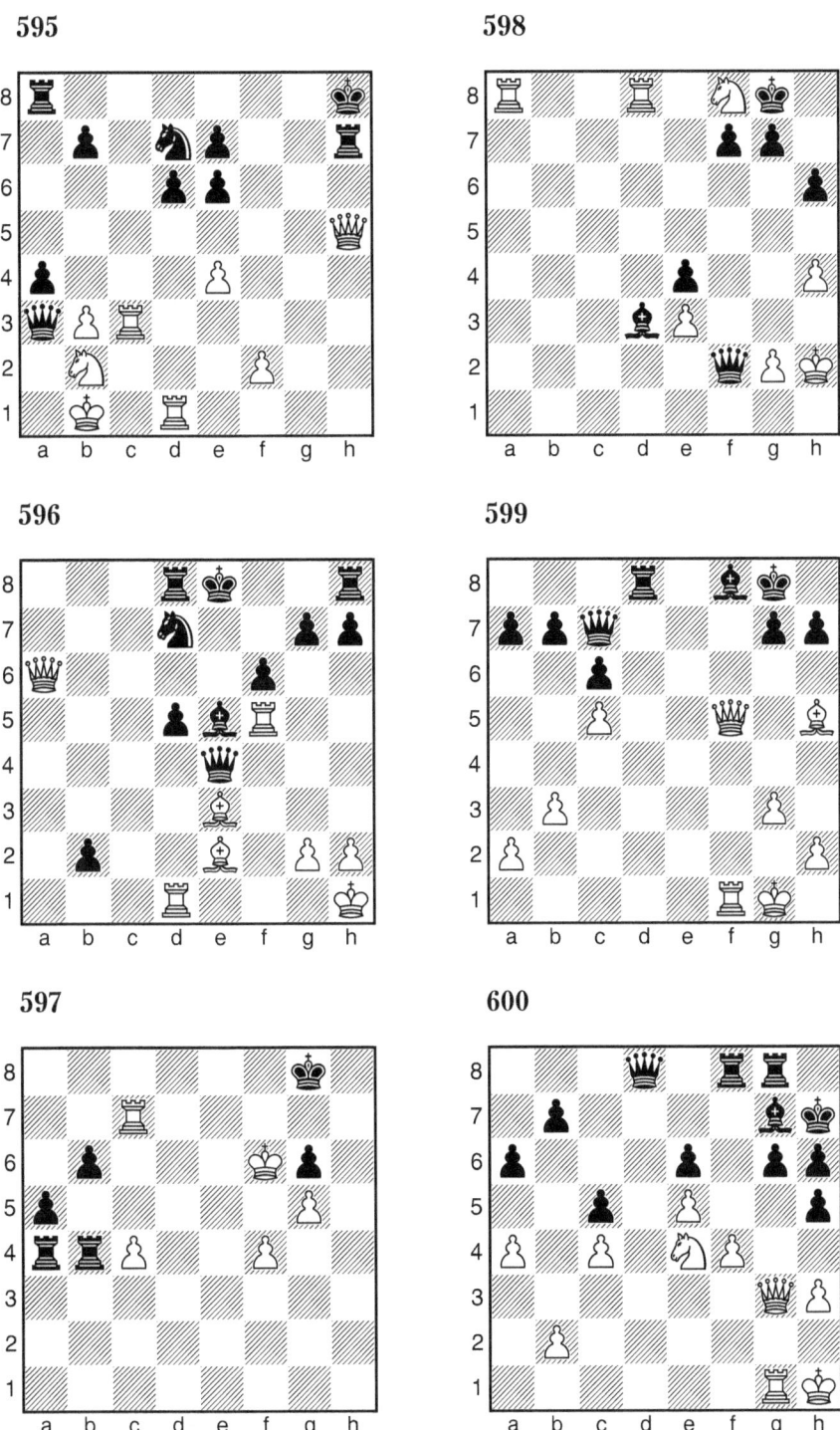

598

596

599

597

600

601

604

602

605

603

606

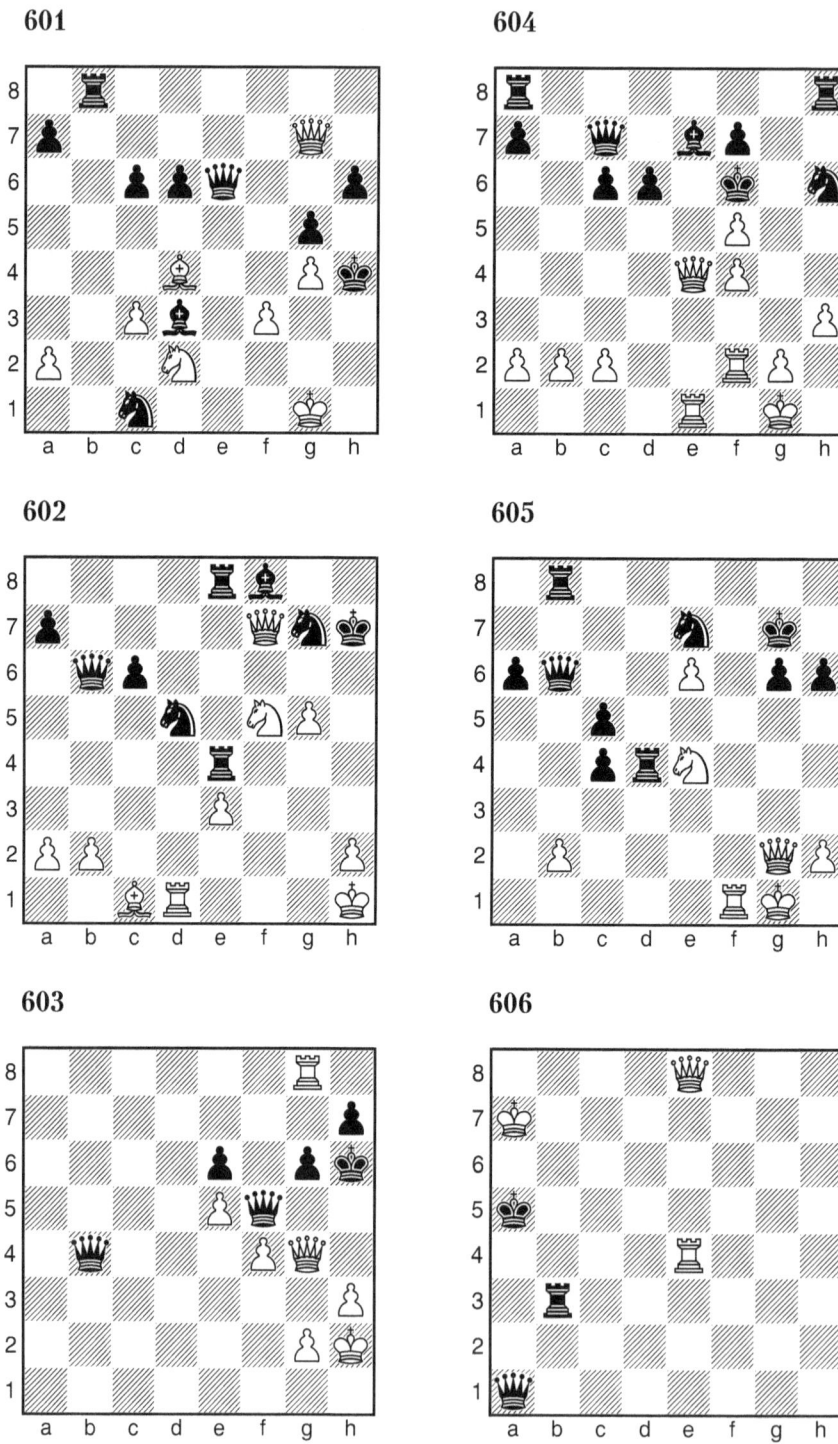

607

610

608

611

609

612

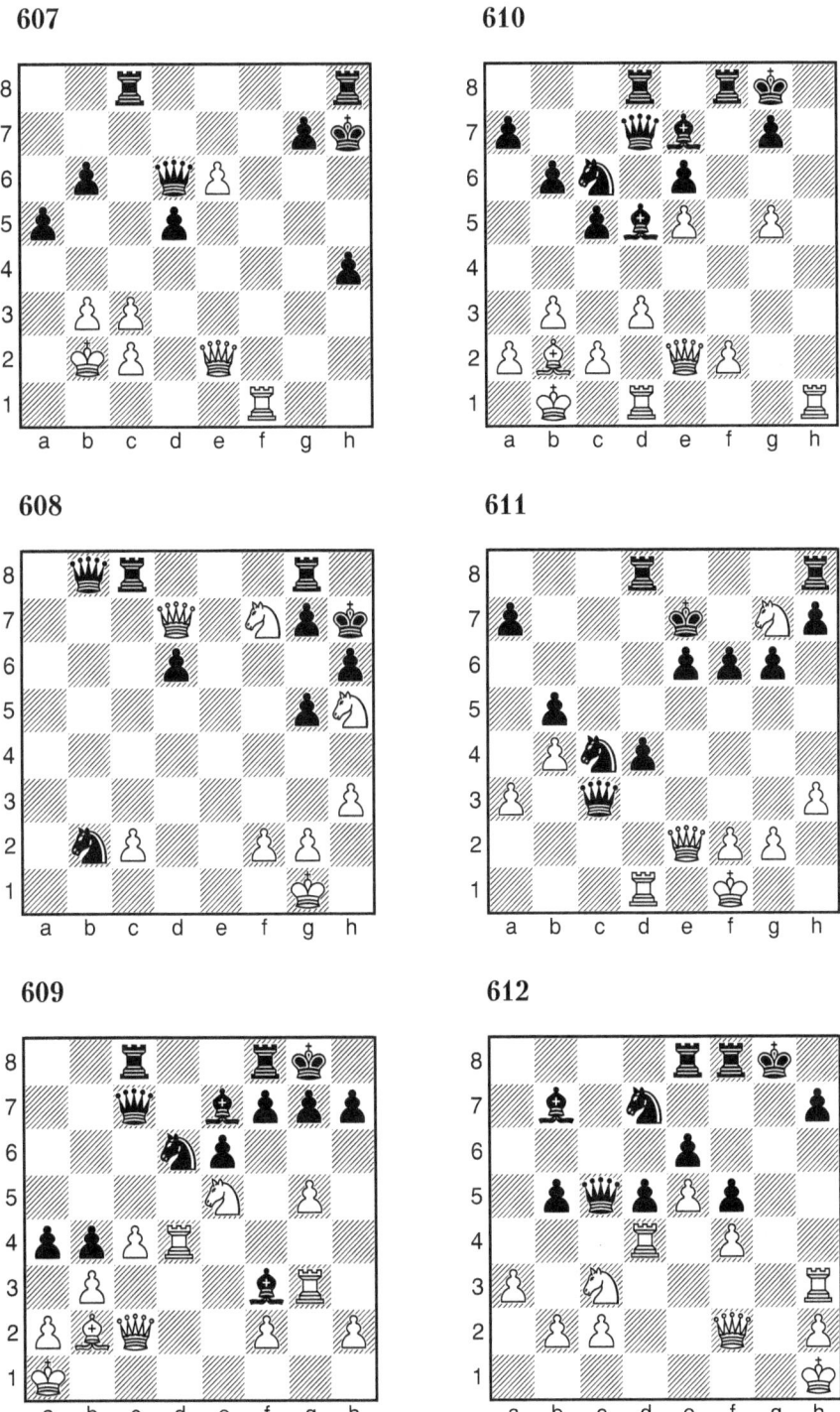

613

616

614

617

615

618

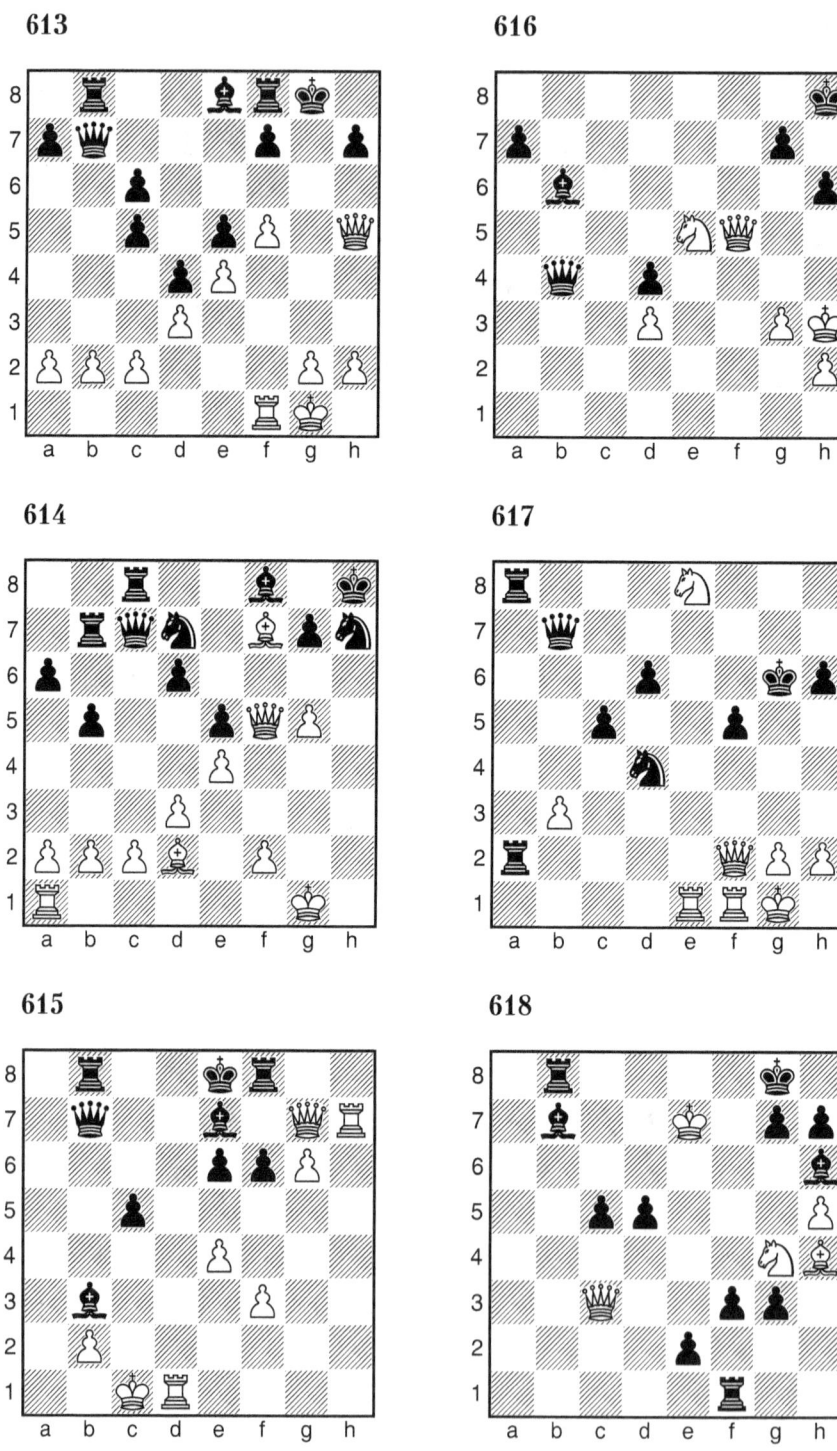

619

620

621

622

623

624

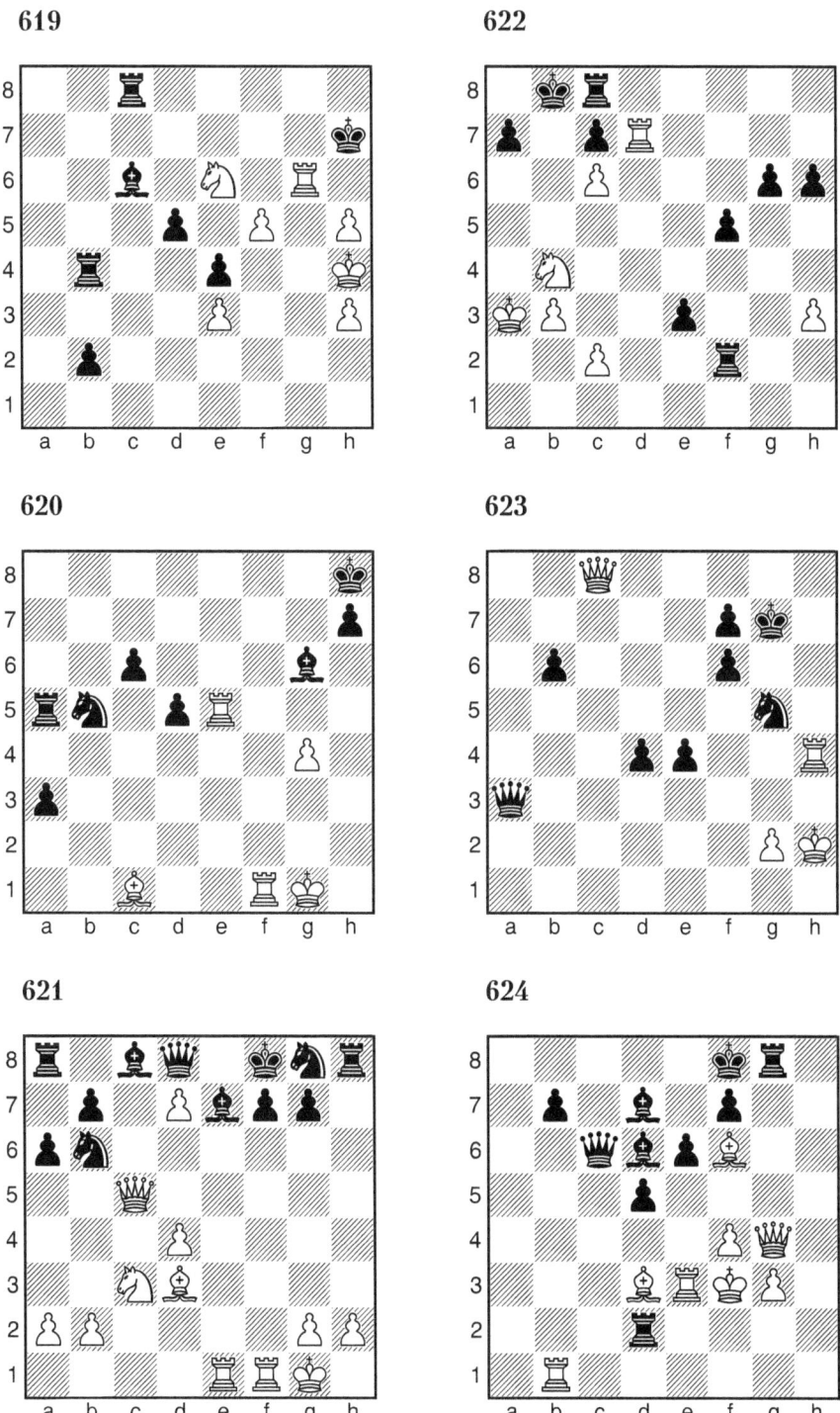

Chapter 25

MATING COMBINATIONS

In this chapter, we study mating tactics that combine several different mate threats with forced mate and checks to the black king. Mating threats in one combination can be used in series, one after the other, or simultaneously.

625

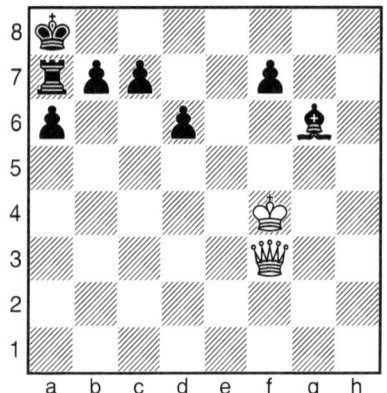

After **1.♕h3!**, white creates two mate threats at once: 2.♕c8# and 2.♕h8#. Black can defend from one of these threats or the other: for instance, 1...b5 prepares an escape square for the king after 2.♕h8+, but is easily refuted by 2.♕c8#. After 1...♔b8 or **1...f5** the white queen cannot give checkmate from c8, but quickly mates after **2.♕h8+! ♗e8 3.♕xe8#**. Such a situation – the creation of two threats at once – is usually called a "double attack", and

this term is applied to attacks on pieces as well.

626

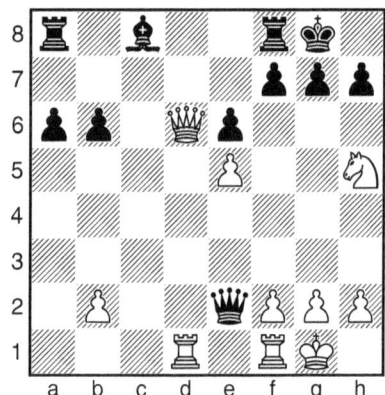

In this example, two mate threats are also made at once. After **1.♘f6+! gxf6 2.exf6!**, white threatens two forced mates: 3.♕xf8+ ♔xf8 4.♖d8# and 3.♕g3+ ♔h8 4.♕g7#. Black has a number of defenses against each of these threats, but he can't stop both at once: he will be checkmated in a few moves. There can follow, for instance: 2...♕g4 3.♕xf8+ ♔f8 4. ♖d8#; 2...♖e8 3.♕g3+ ♔f8 4.♕g7#; 2...♗b7 3.♕g3+ ♔h8 4.♕g7# etc. In addition to the lines above, black has some nonsensical queen sacrifices and the move 1...♔h8, which immediately loses to 2.♕xf8#.

In mating combinations, mate threats can occur in series as well as simultaneously.

627

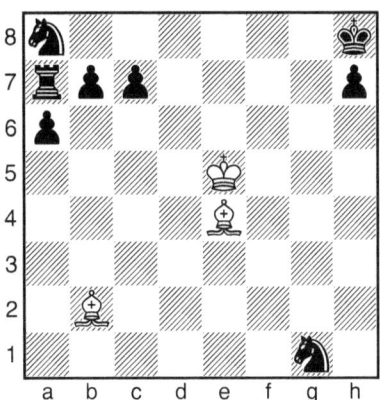

White plays **1.♔e1!**, creating the mate threat 2.♖g3#. It's easy to see that black has only two moves that prevent immediate checkmate. The pin 1...♖h1 saves black from checkmate, but leads to a completely hopeless position after the simple 2.♖xh1. Support **1...♖h3** also defends from checkmate; however, white can play **2.d5!**, creating another mate threat – **3.♘d4#**, which is completely unstoppable. Therefore, to solve this exercise, you need to create two mate threats in succession, not forgetting to calculate all possible defenses for black.

The number of mate threats in a combination is essentially unlimited. In the next example, white used three mate threats in succession.

628

After **1.♔f6!**, white threatens 2.♔f7#, so black is forced to reply **1...♔g8!** Now white gives a check and creates another mate threat: **2.♗d5+ ♔f8 3.♗f7!** with the idea of 4.♗a3+ c5 5.♗xc5#. Black has two ways to defend from this threat: 3...c5 and **3...b6**, but both of these defenses are refuted with **4.♗c1!** with the unstoppable mate threat **5.♗h6#**. After 2...♔h8, white plays 3.♔f7#. We should point out that despite the seeming simplicity of this line, the correct calculation of the combination becomes progressively more complex with each new mate threat.

629

632

630

633

631

634

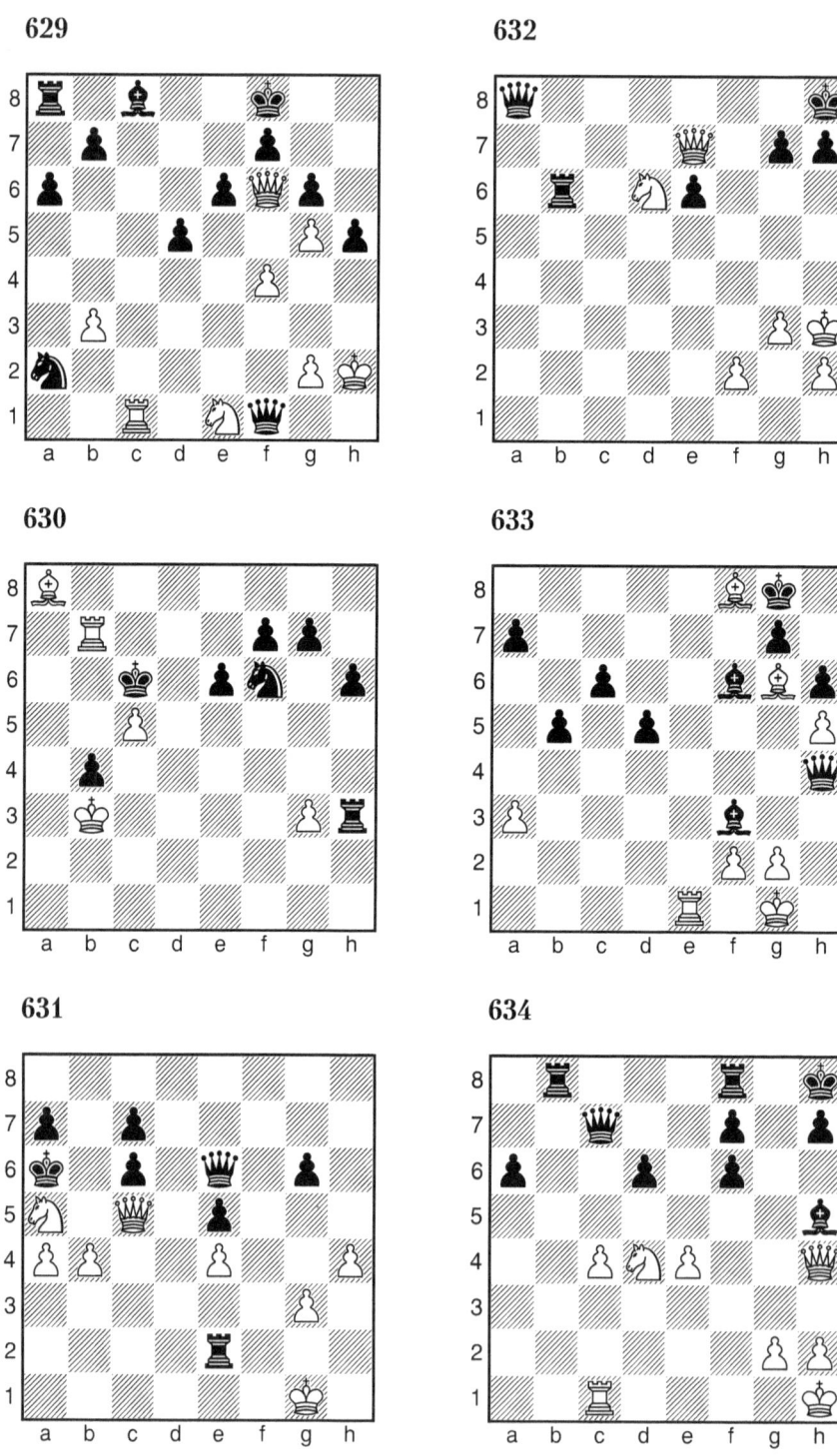

635

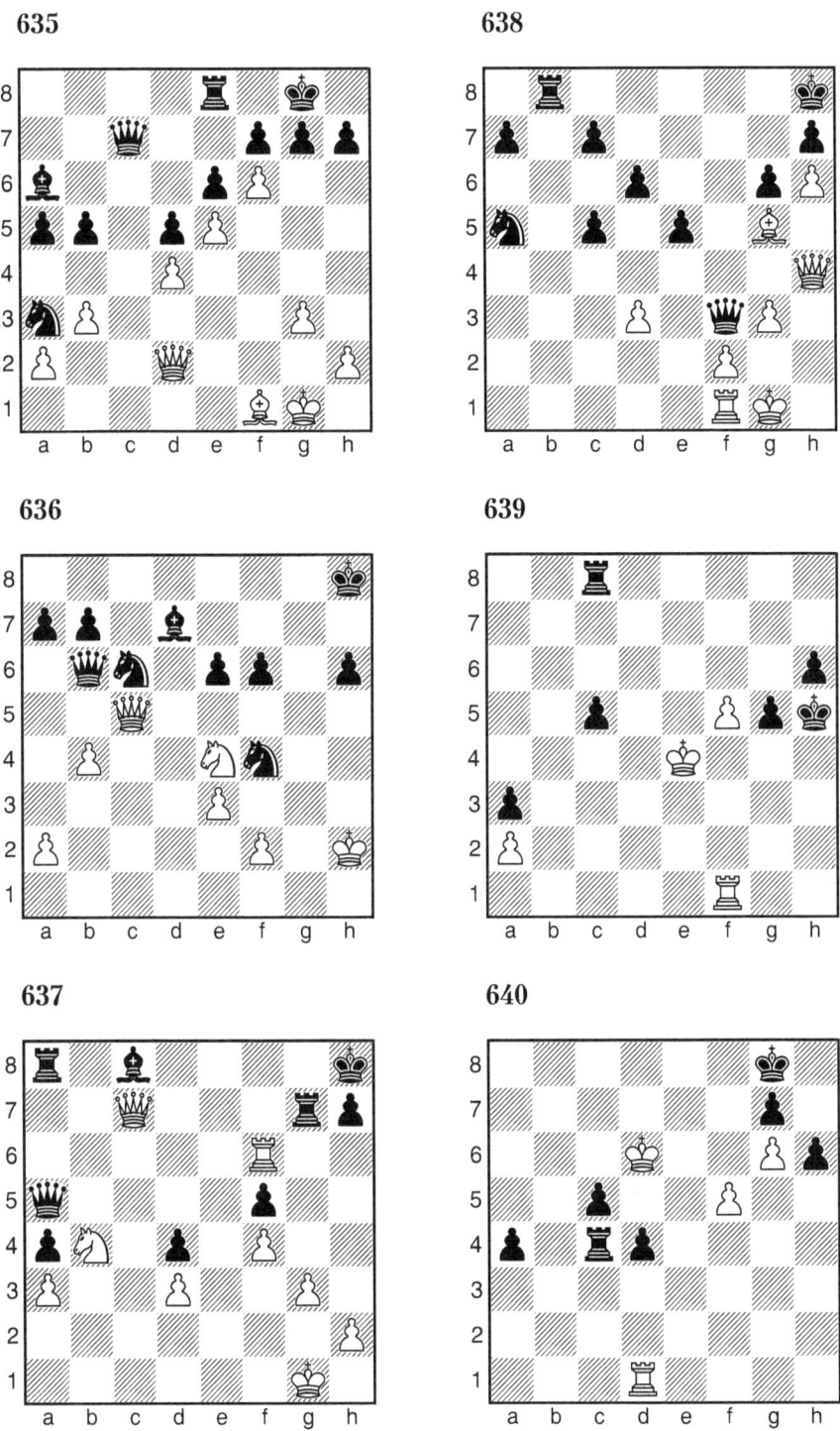

638

636

639

637

640

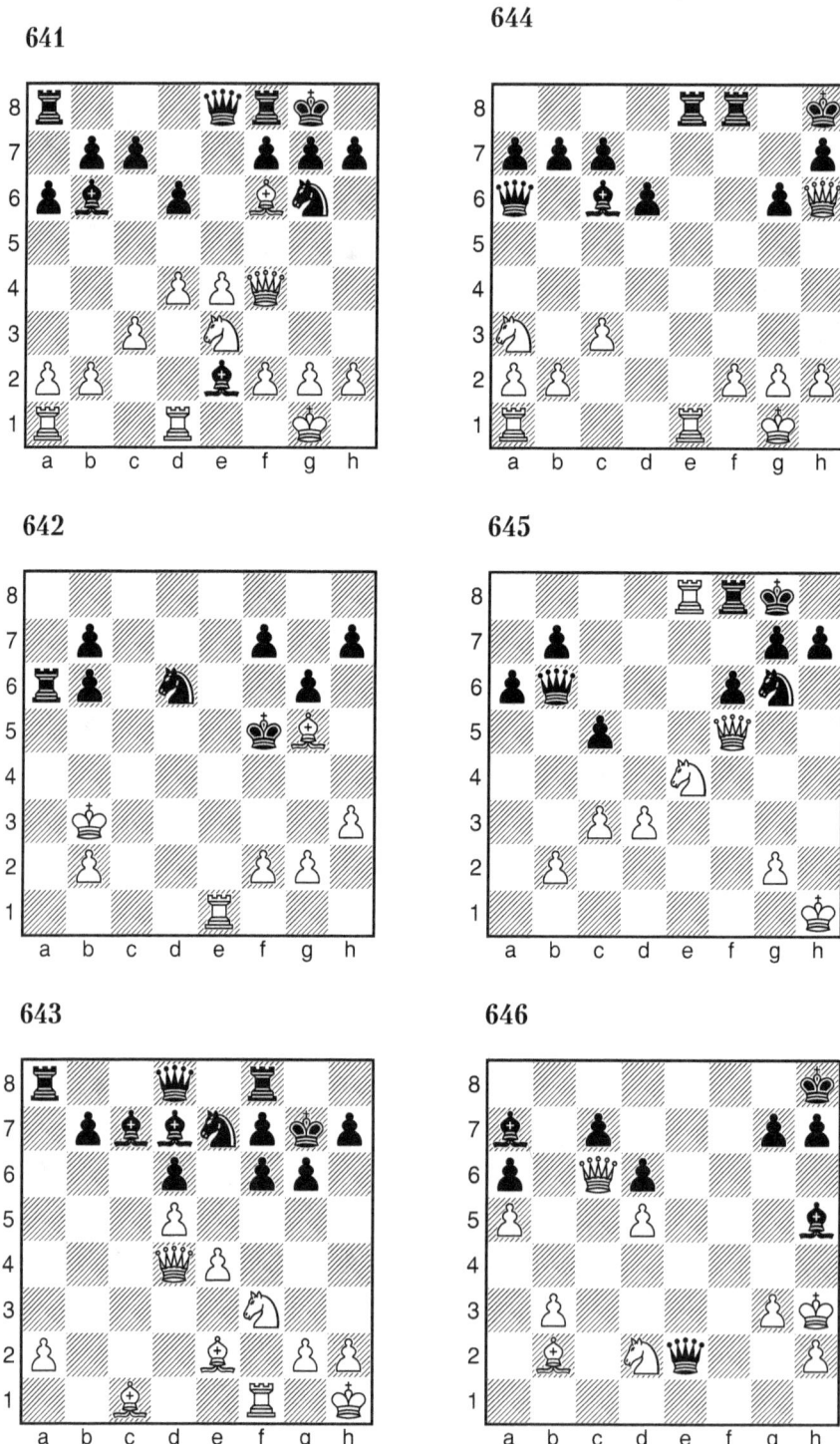

641

644

642

645

643

646

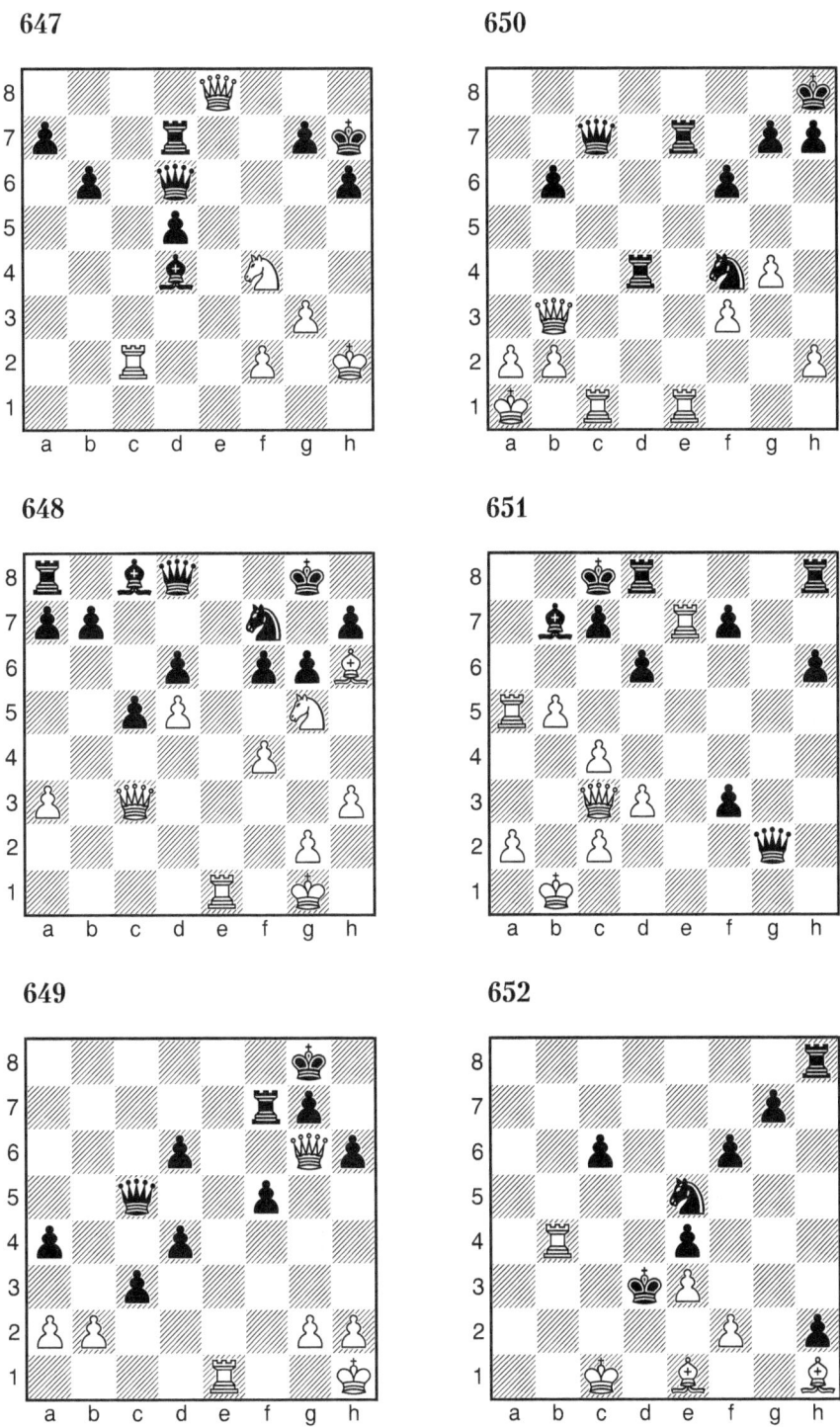

647

648

649

650

651

652

653

656

654

657

655

658

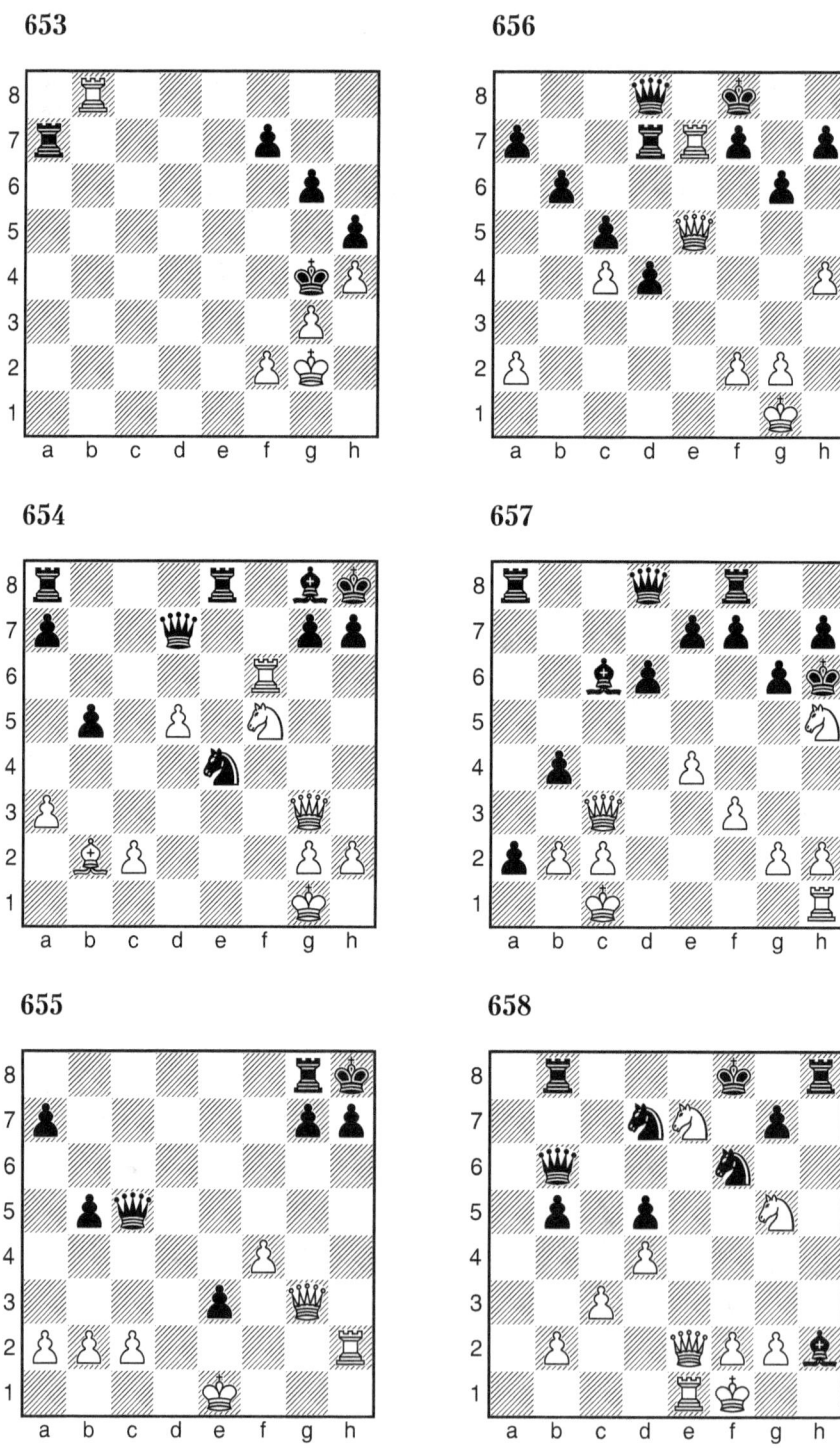

659

662

660

663

661

664

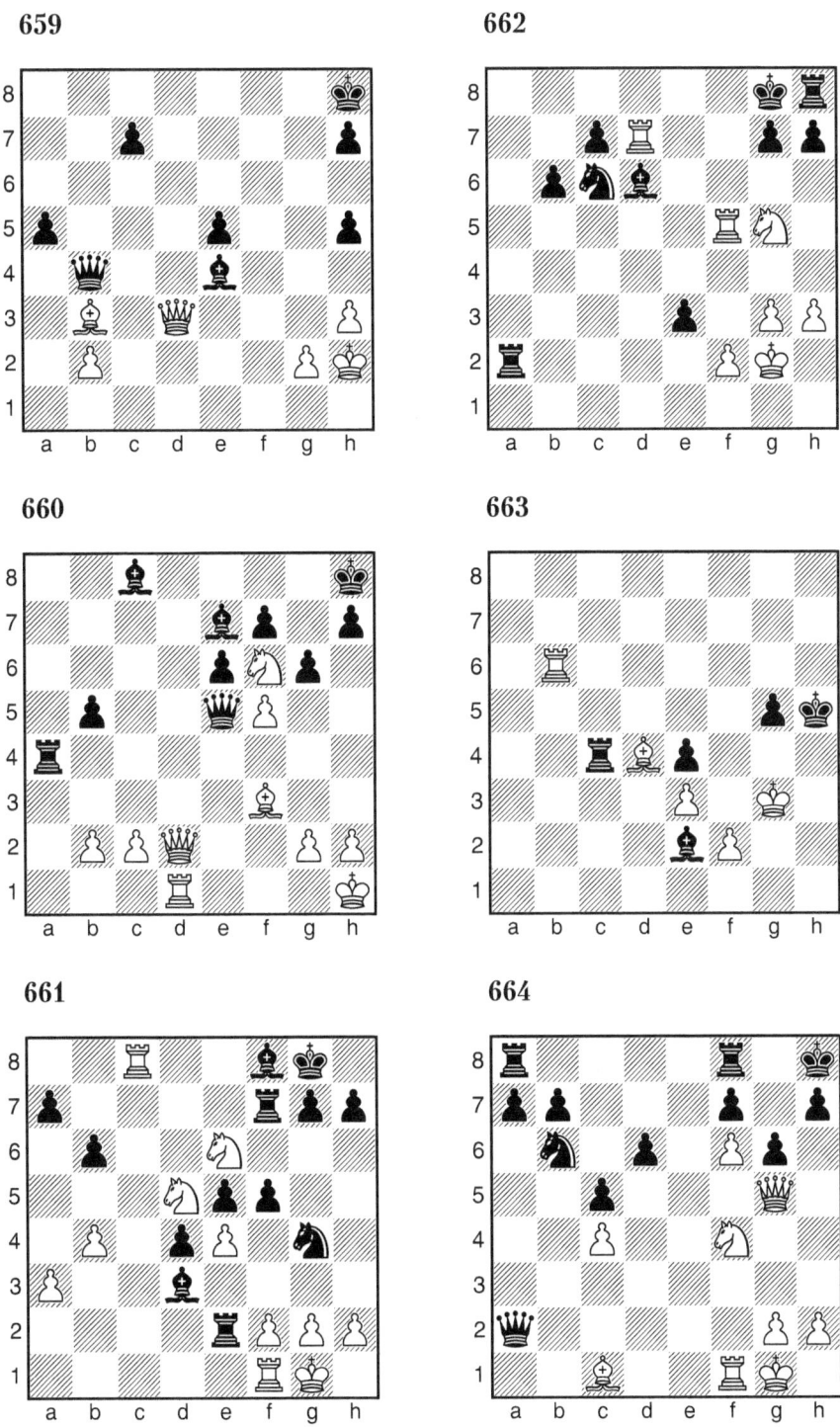

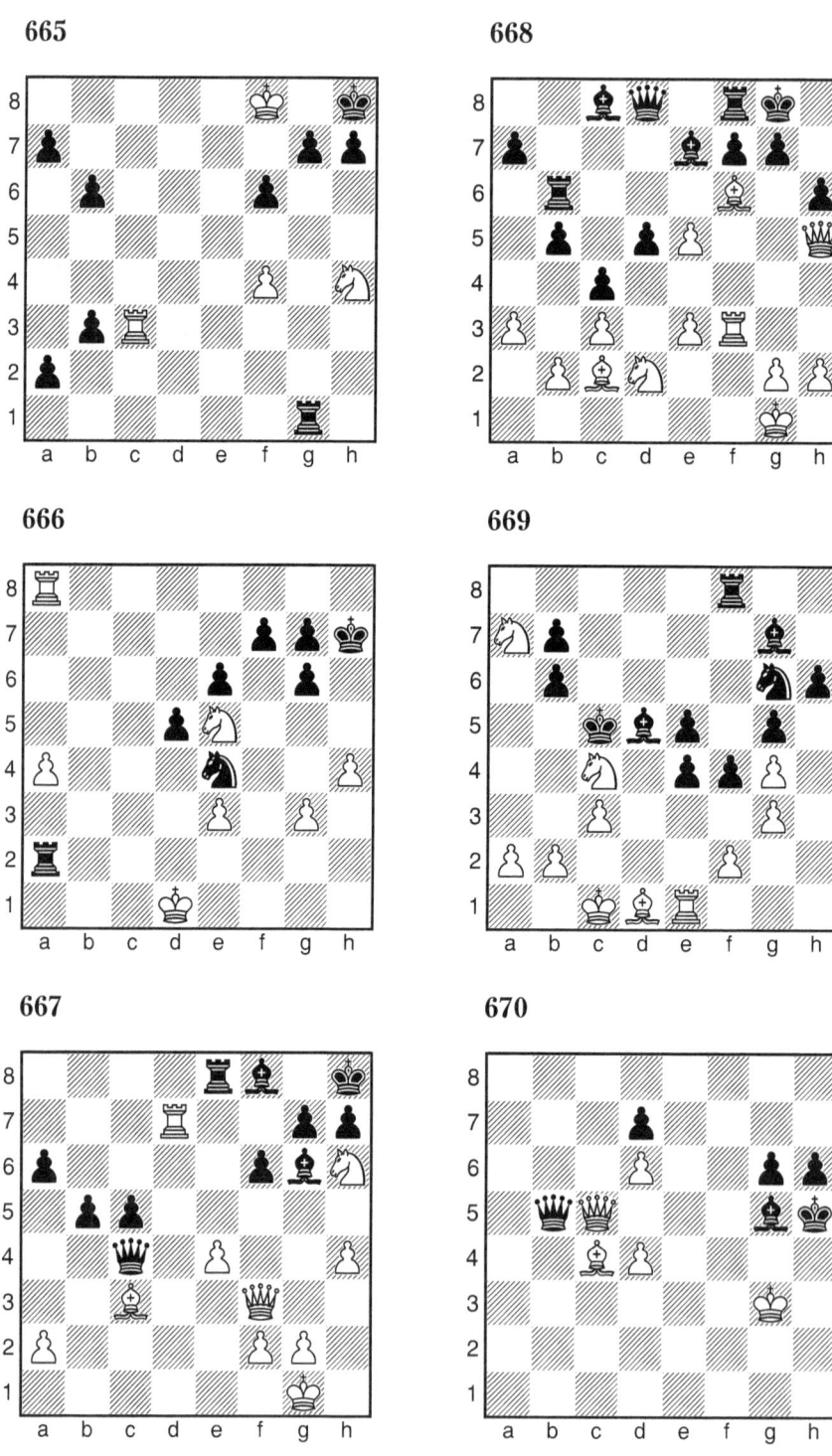

671

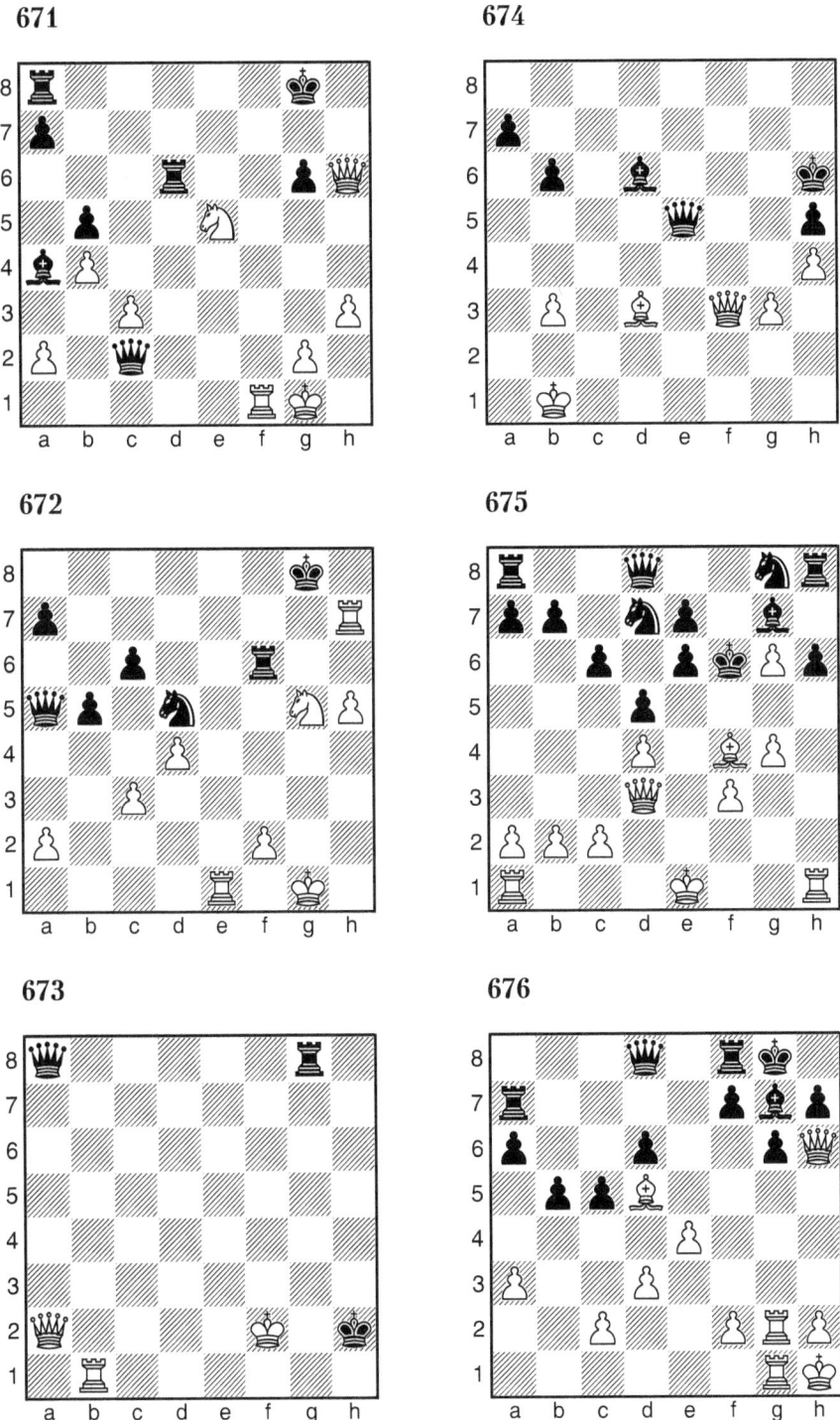

674

672

675

673

676

677

680

678

681

679

682

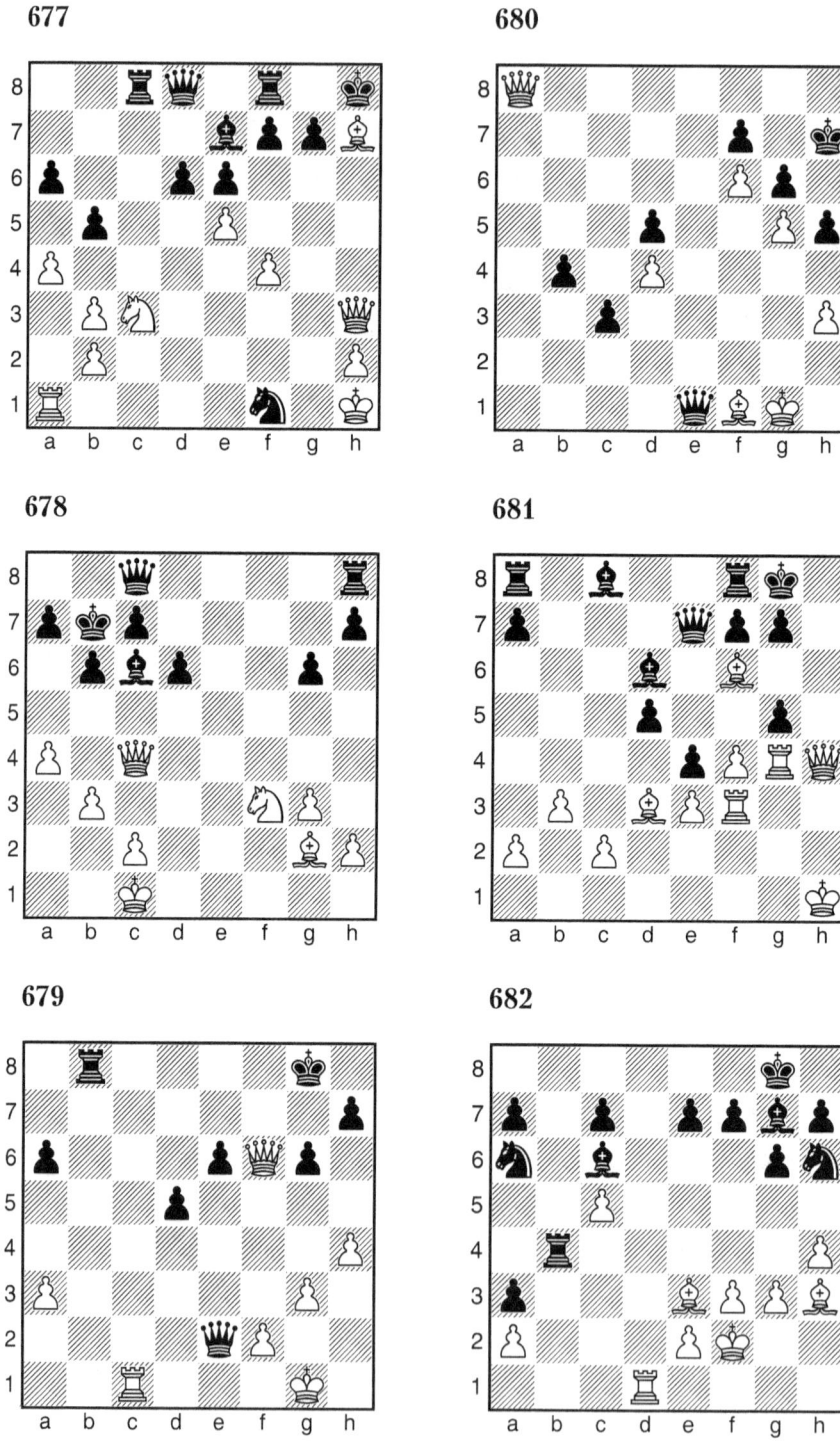

683

686

684

687

685

688

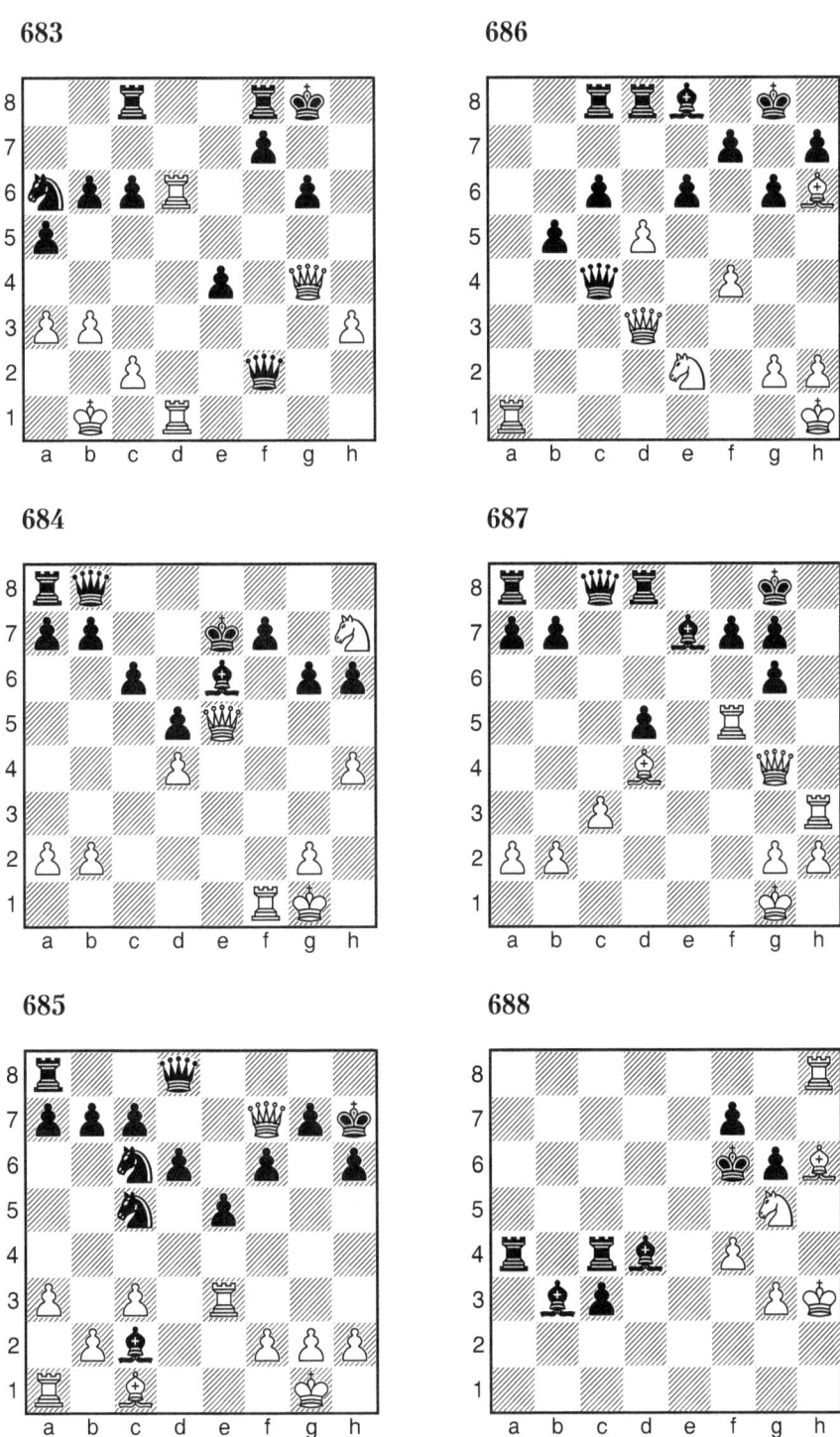

689

692

690

693

691

694

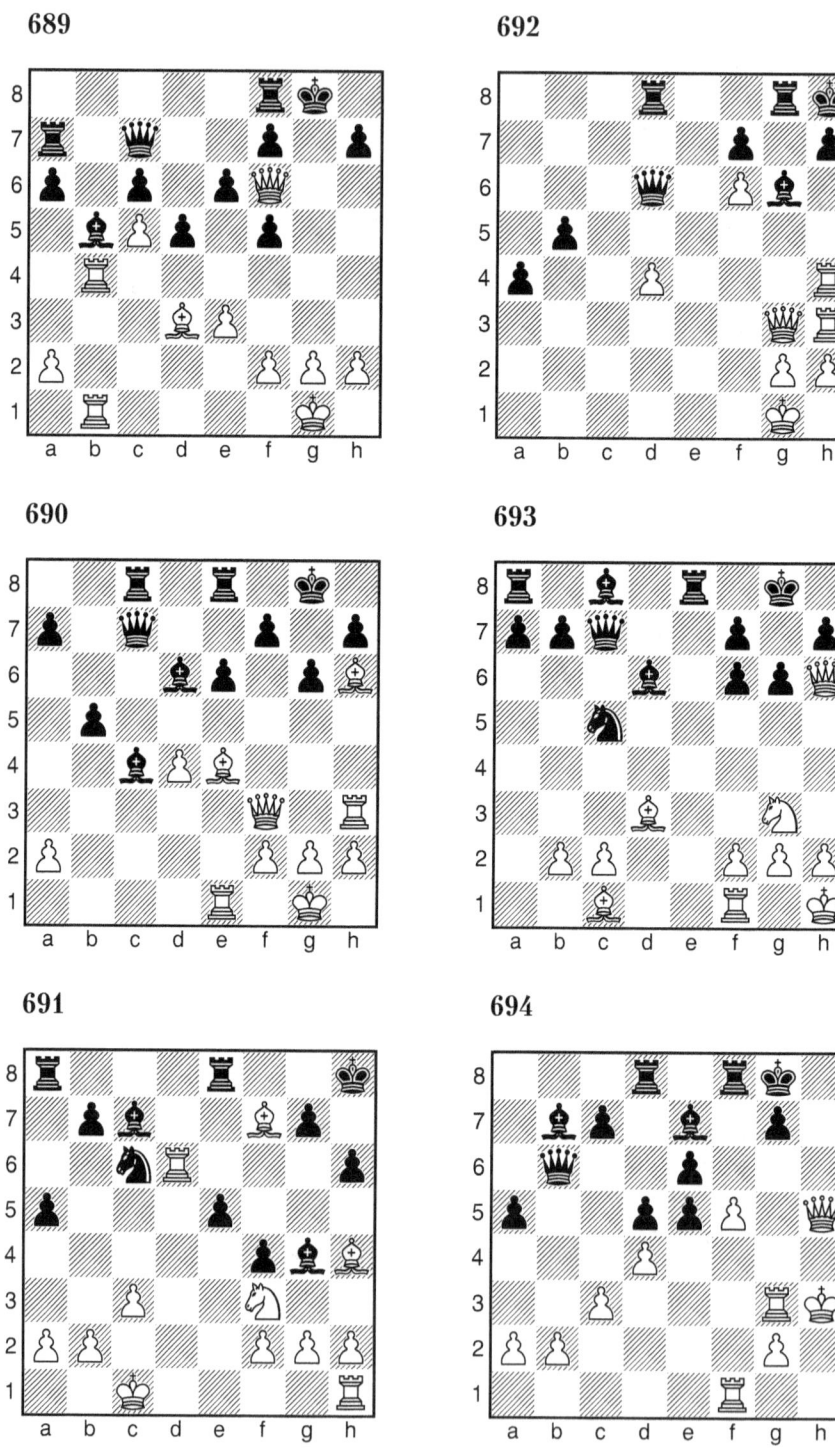

695

698

696

699

697

700

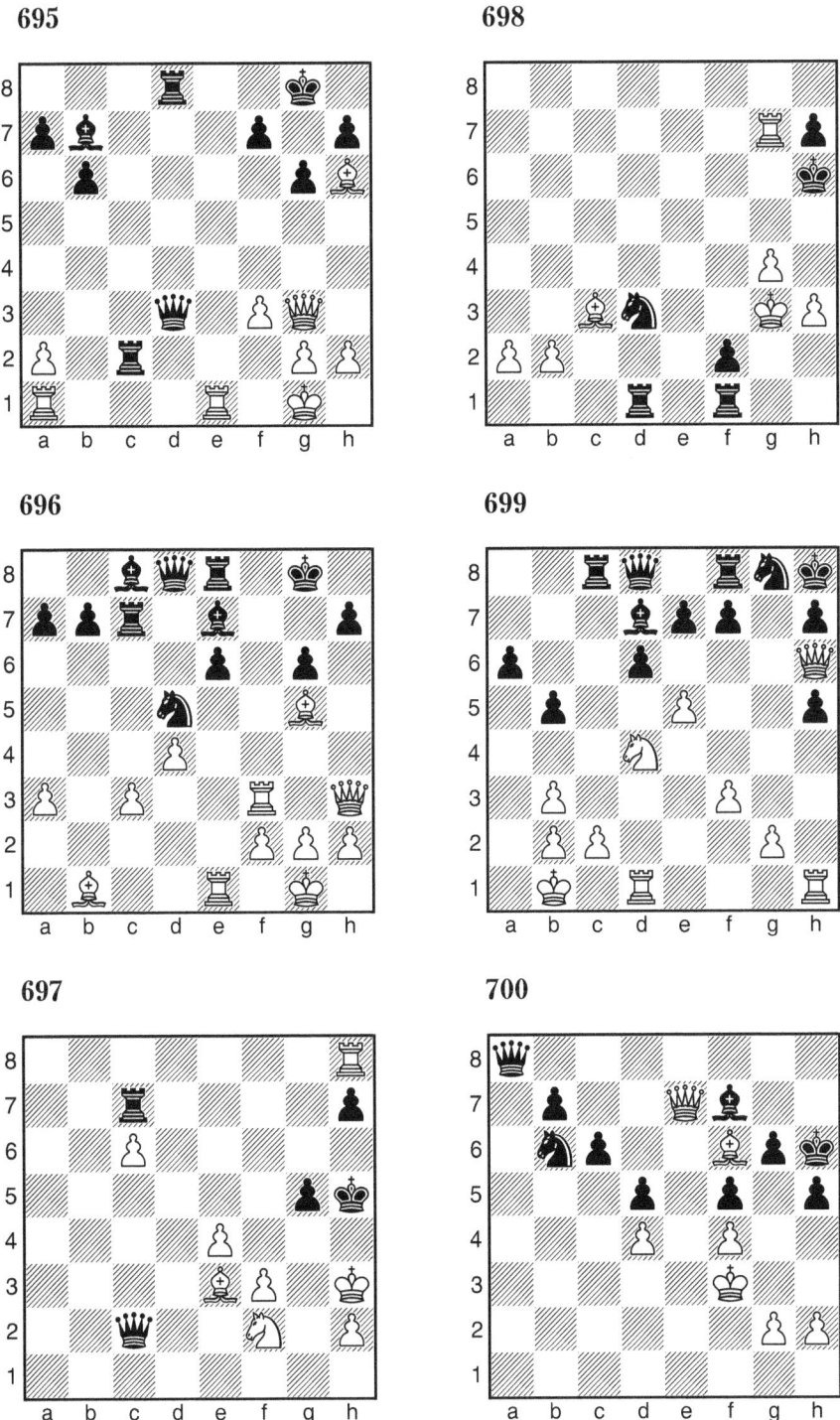

Part 6

Apply Your Knowledge!

The main purpose of the previous part of this book was thorough study of all existing tactics involving mate threats and defense against them. In parts 2 – 5, we have carefully studied all attacking and defensive resources of both sides that can theoretically play a role in mating or defending combinations.

The sixth part is a set of mixed tests that checks the your skills in executing mating combinations and finding the best defense against them. It also highlights your weaknesses – such as defensive technique that constantly escapes your attention or erroneous calculation of simple, but long lines. It contains 300 exercises split into three chapters: "Find the best defense", "Find the mating combination" and "Find the best continuation". When you tackle the exercises in part 6, you will not be told which tactic you are supposed to use. So you need to practice both precise calculation and confident use of all tactics and techniques you have studied in this book up to now.

The last chapter largely consists of difficult exercises; to find the correct solutions, even the strongest players will have to think hard!

Chapter 26

TEST YOURSELF! FIND THE MATING COMBINATION

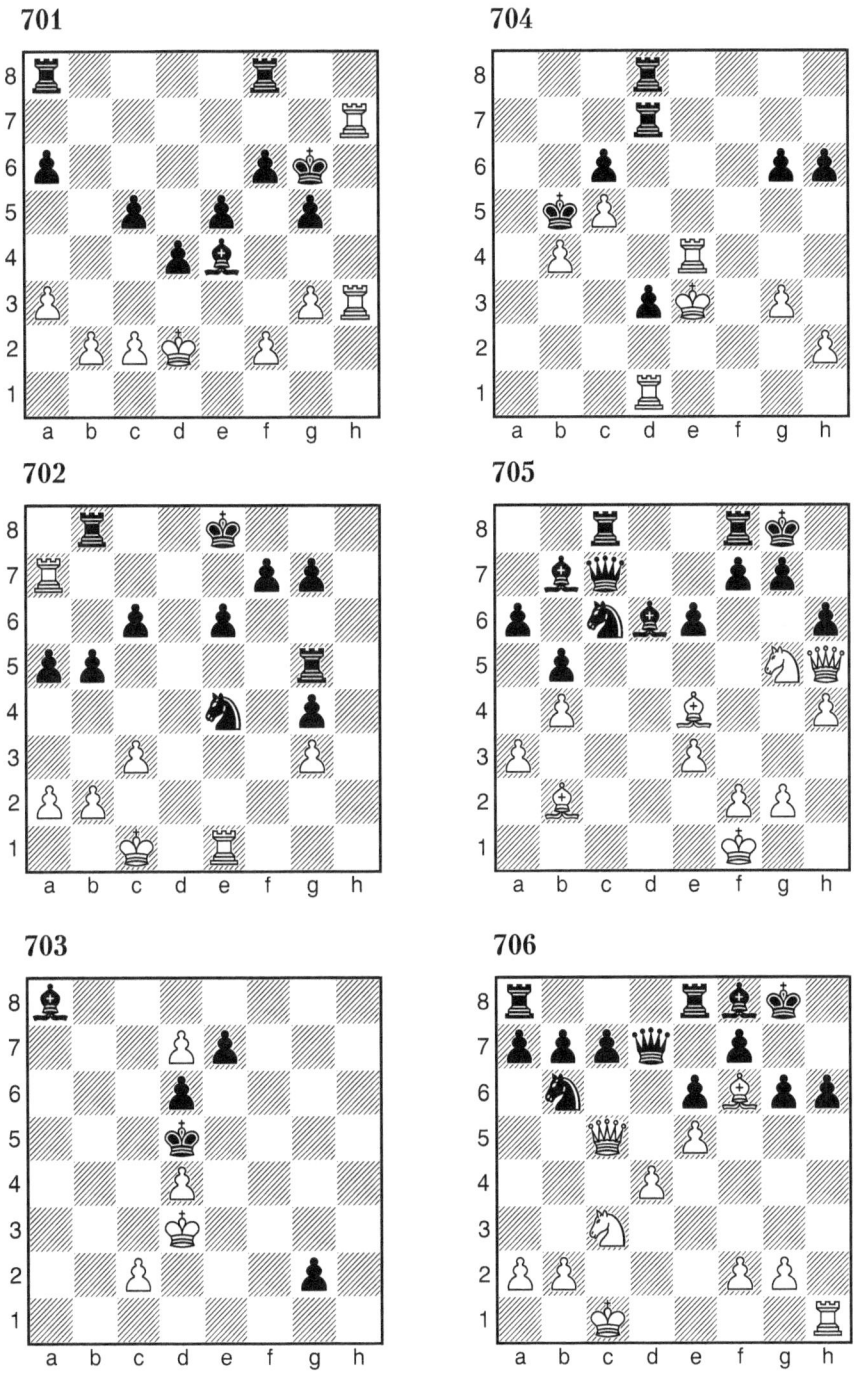

701

702

703

704

705

706

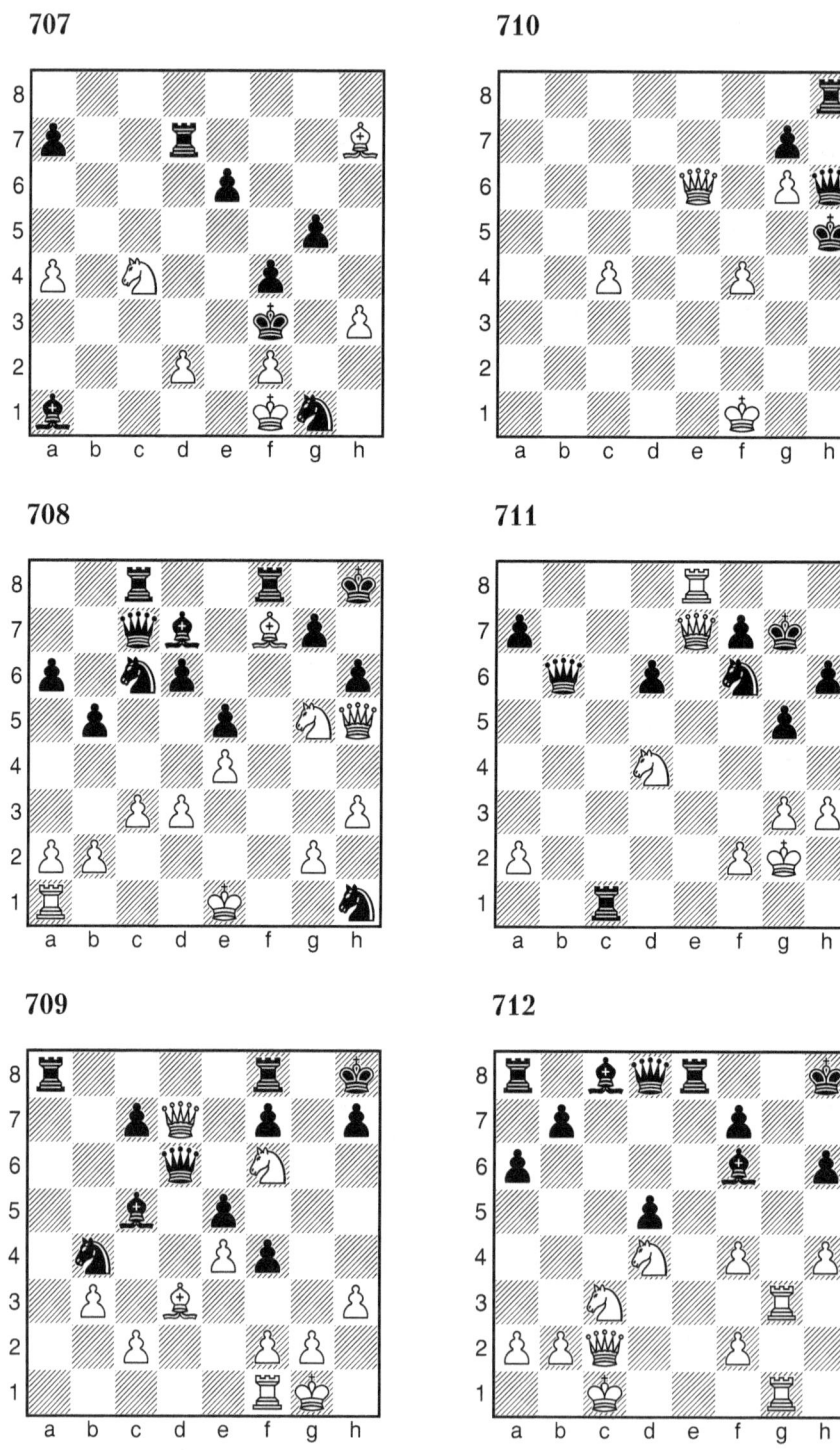

707

708

709

710

711

712

713

716

714

717

715

718

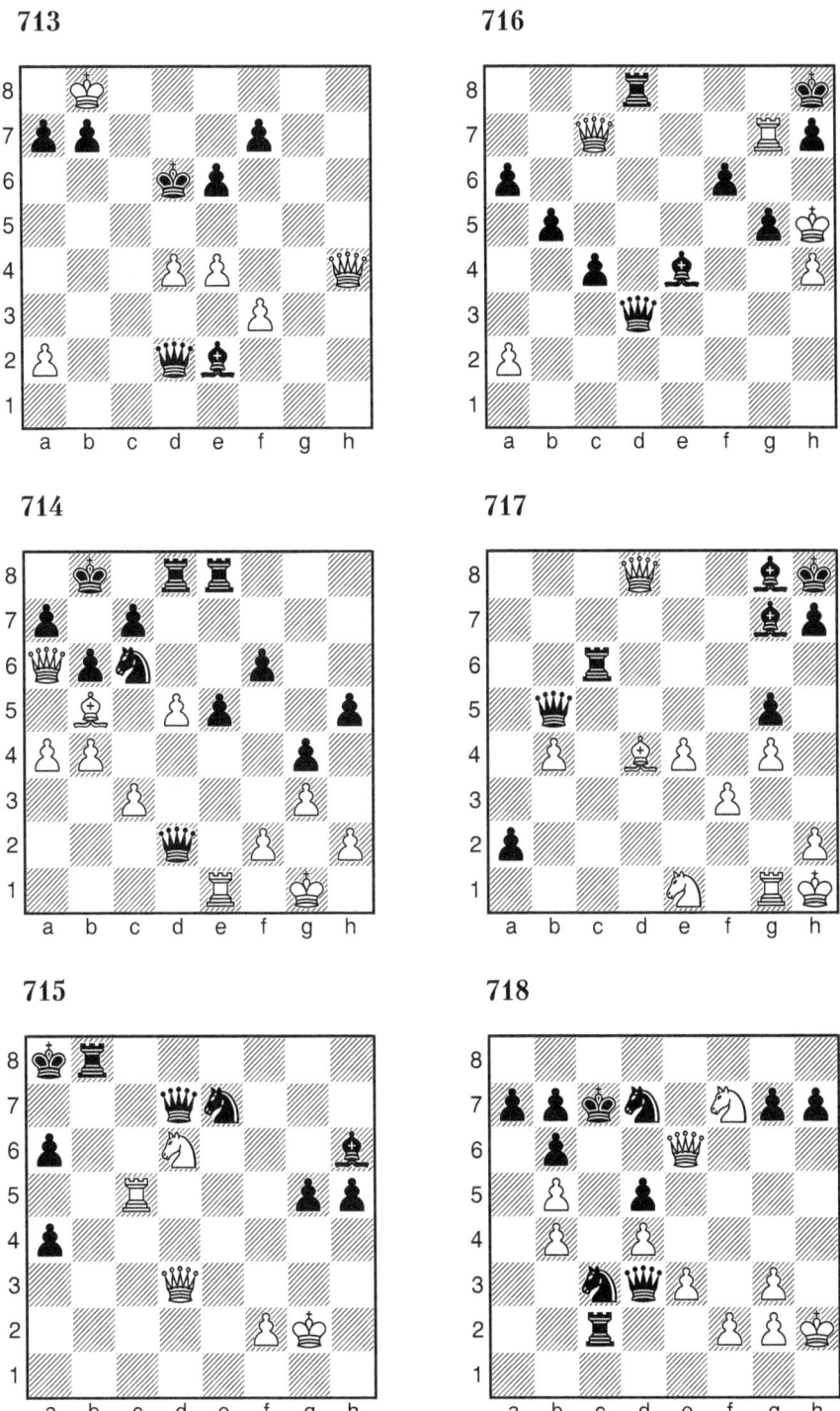

719

720

721

722

723

724

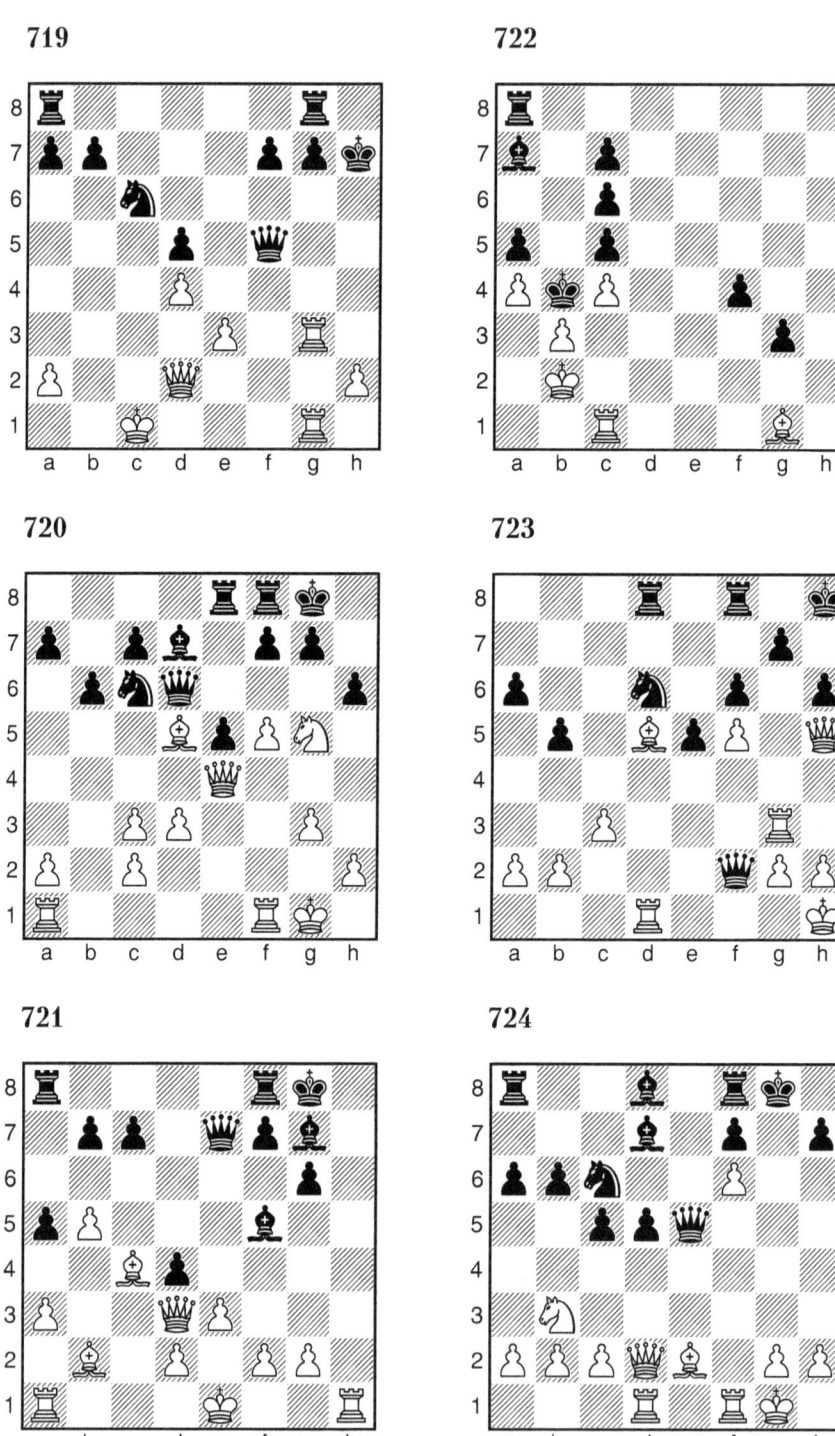

725

728

726

729

727

730

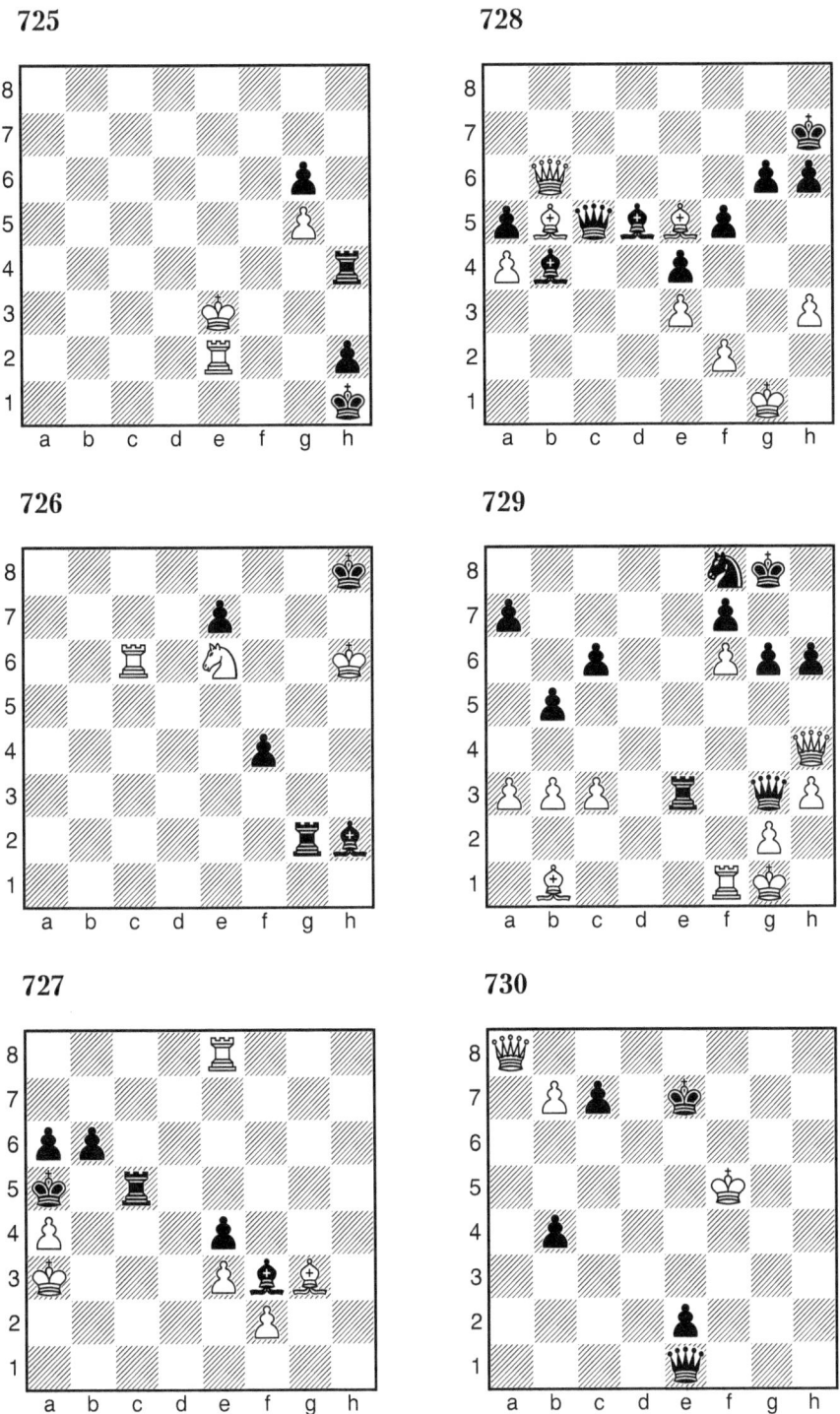

731

734

732

735

733

736

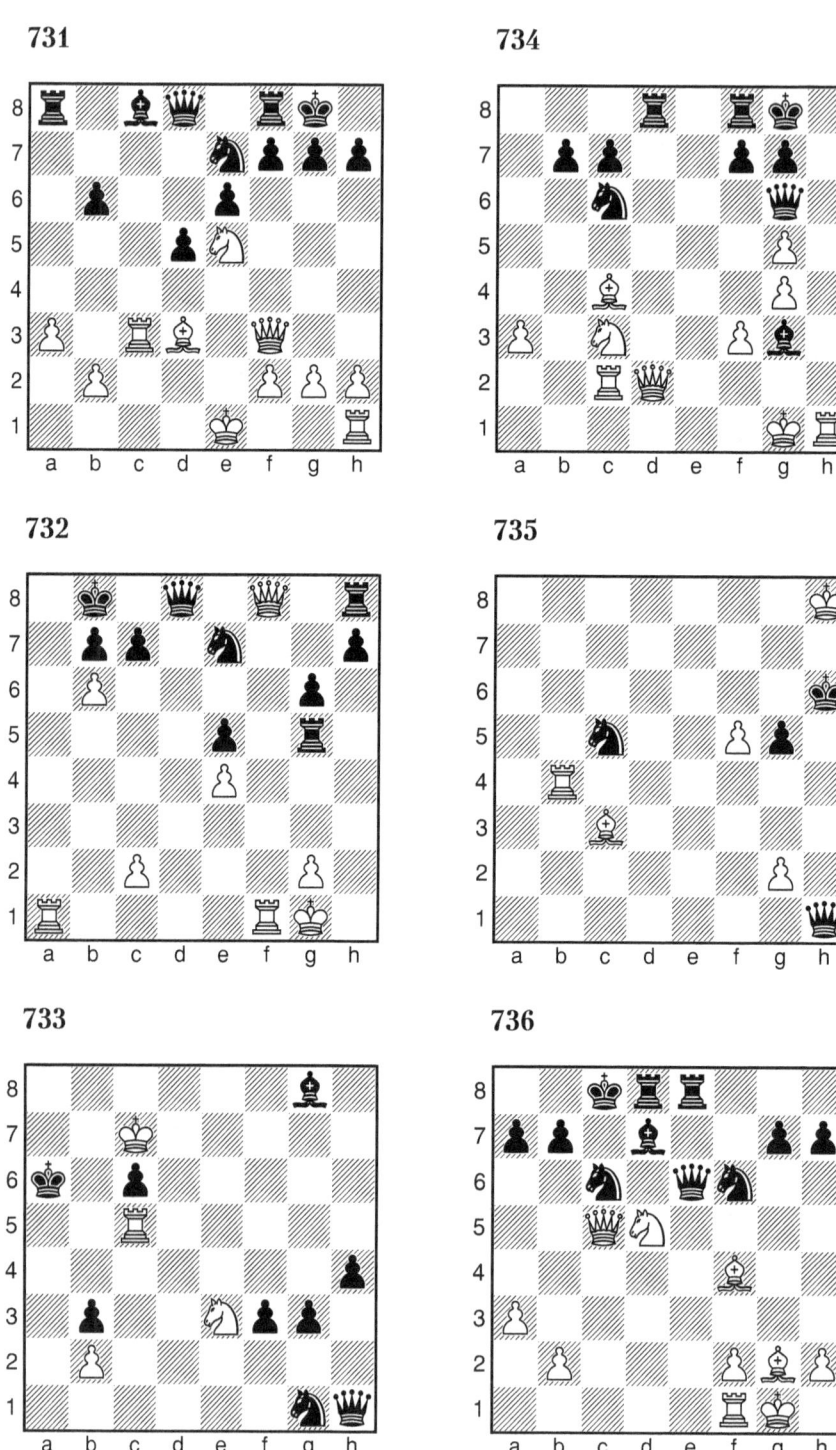

737

740

738

741

739

742

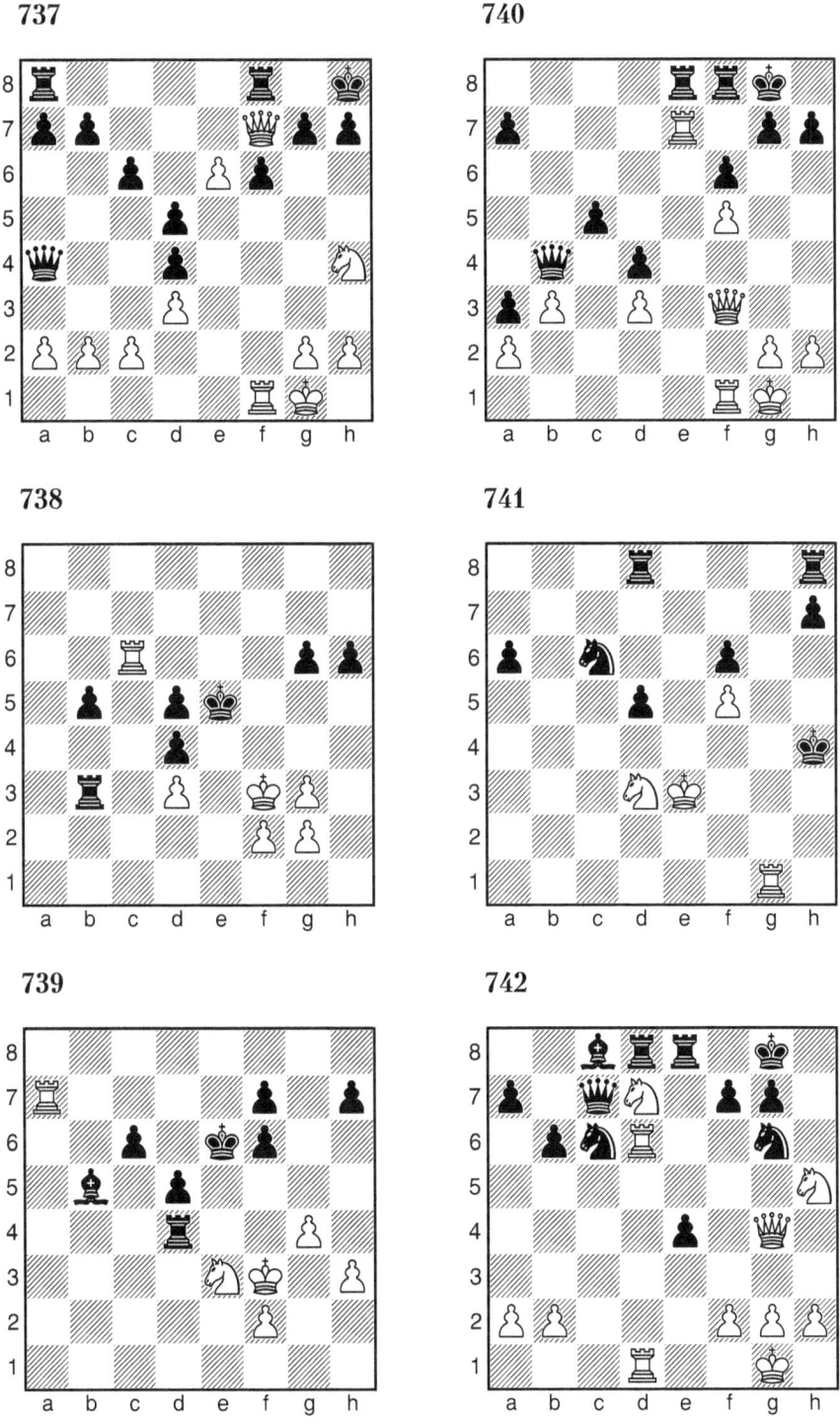

743

744

745

746

747

748

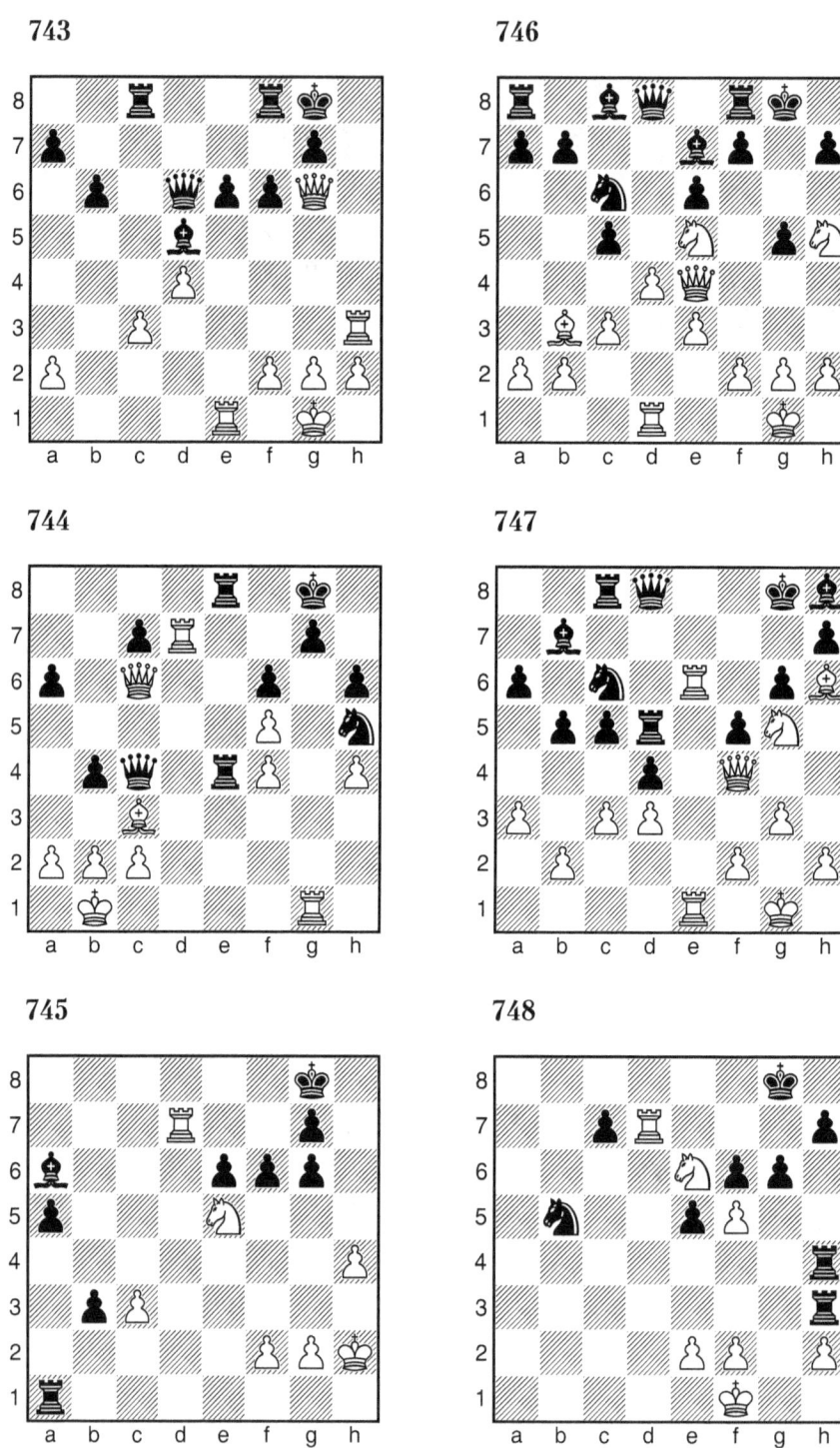

749

752

750

753

751

754

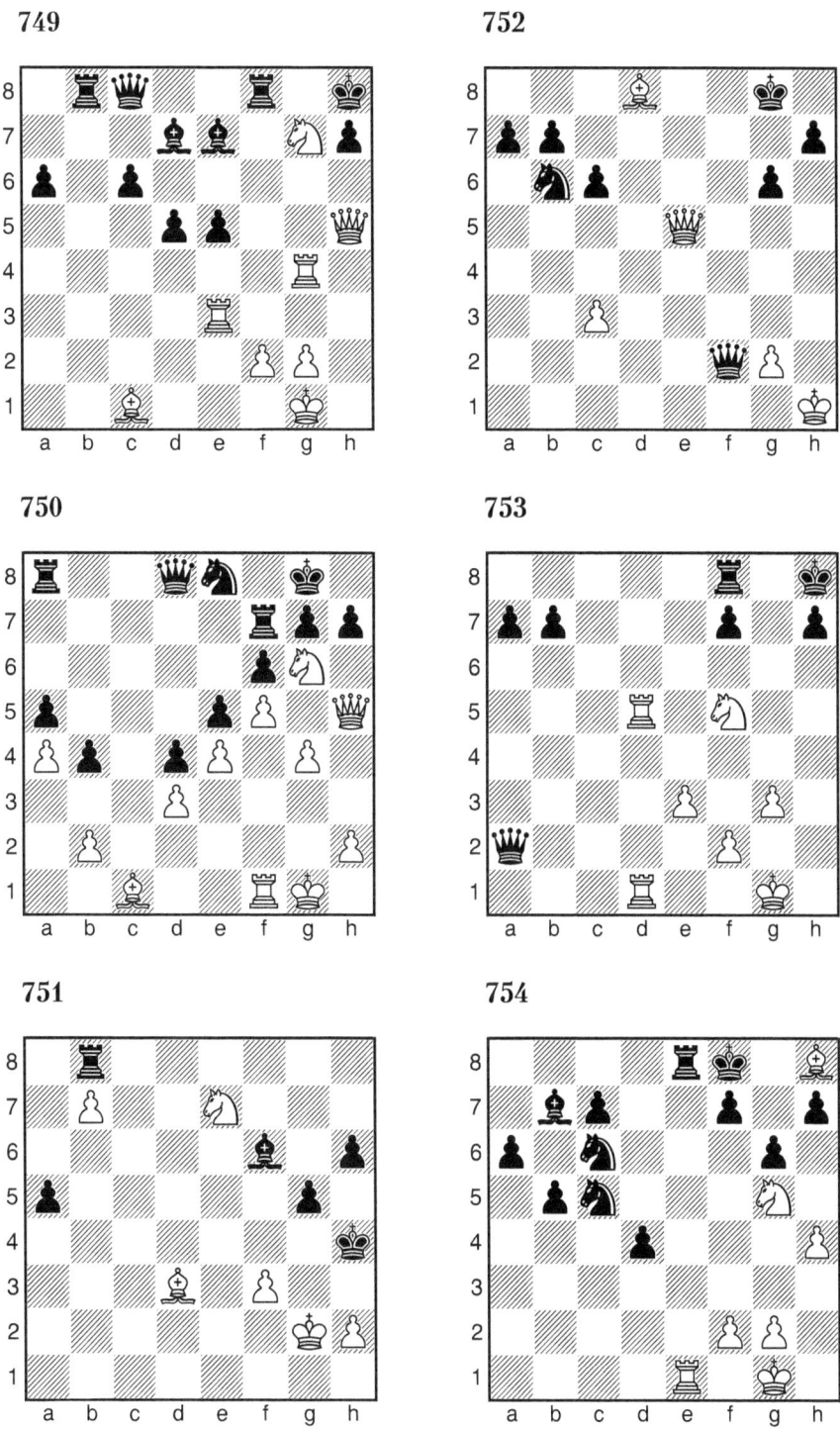

755

758

756

759

757

760

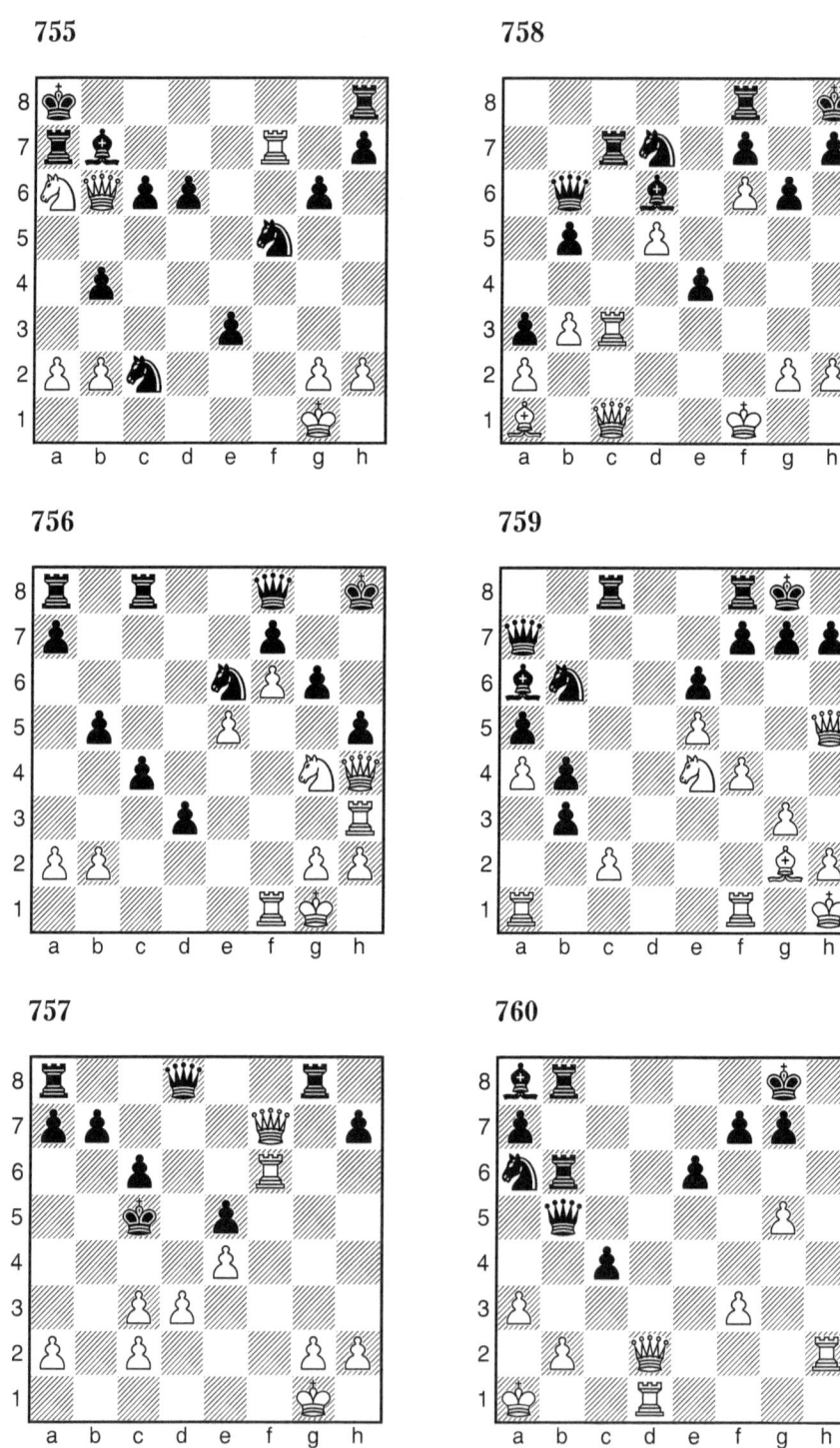

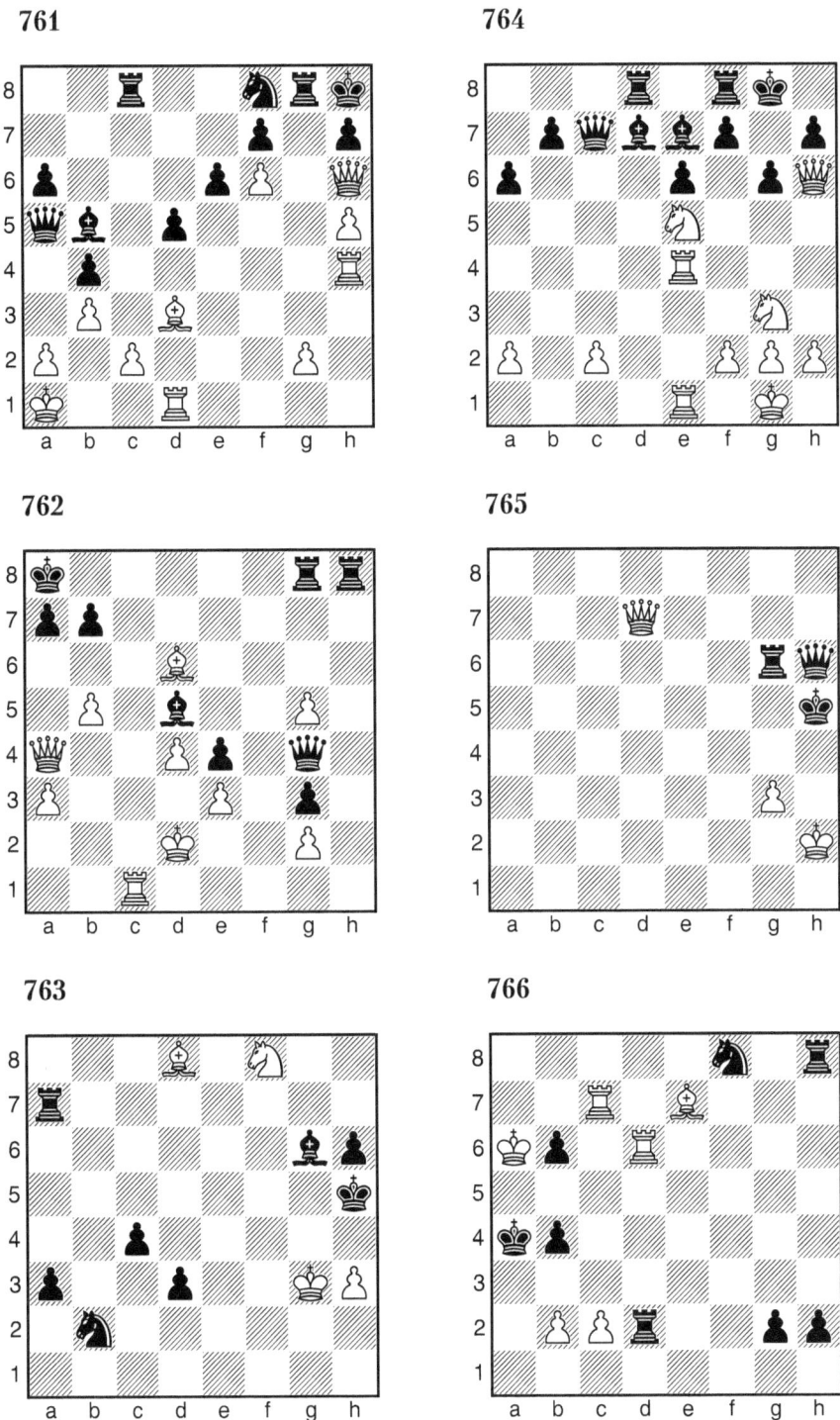

761

762

763

764

765

766

767

770

768

771

769

772

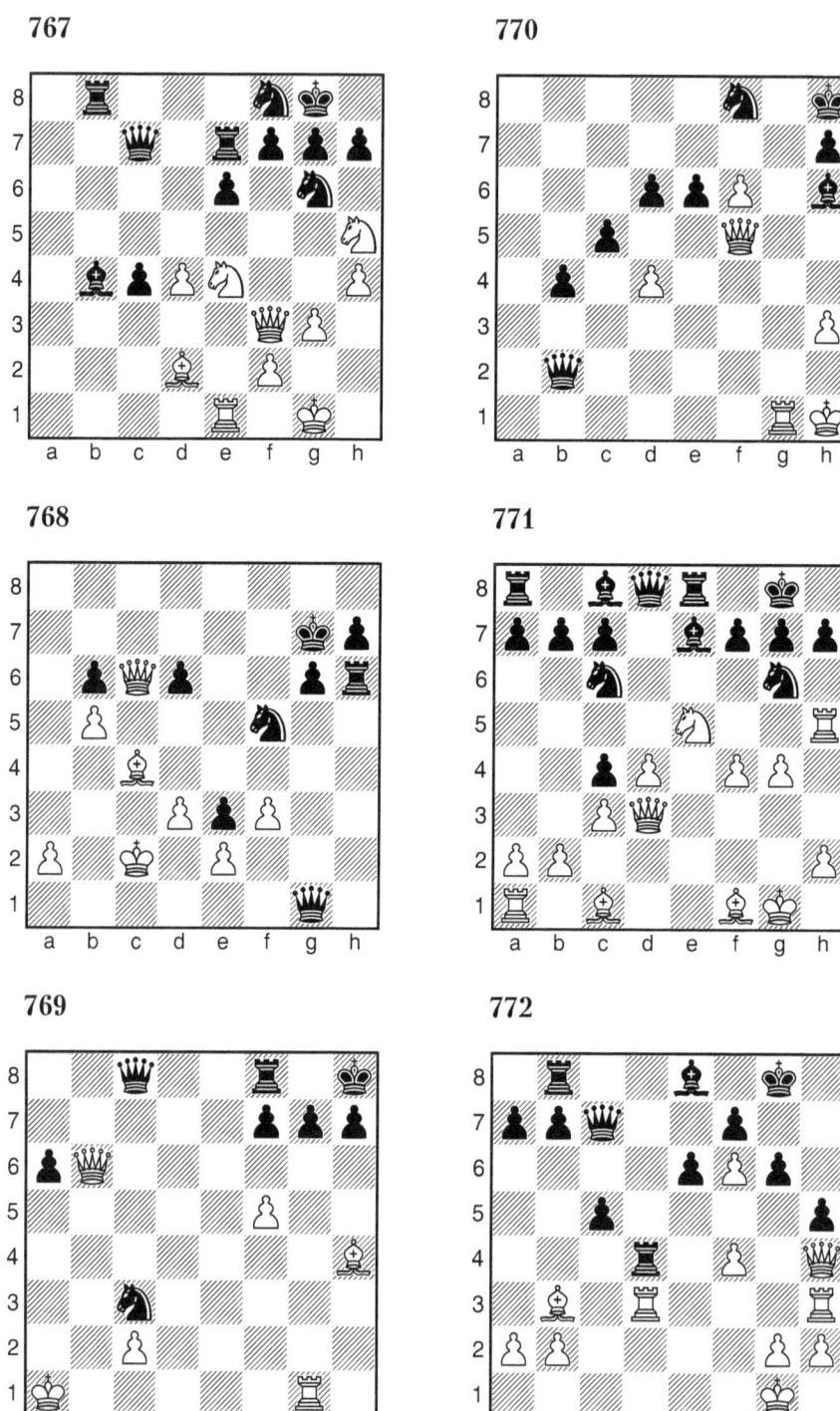

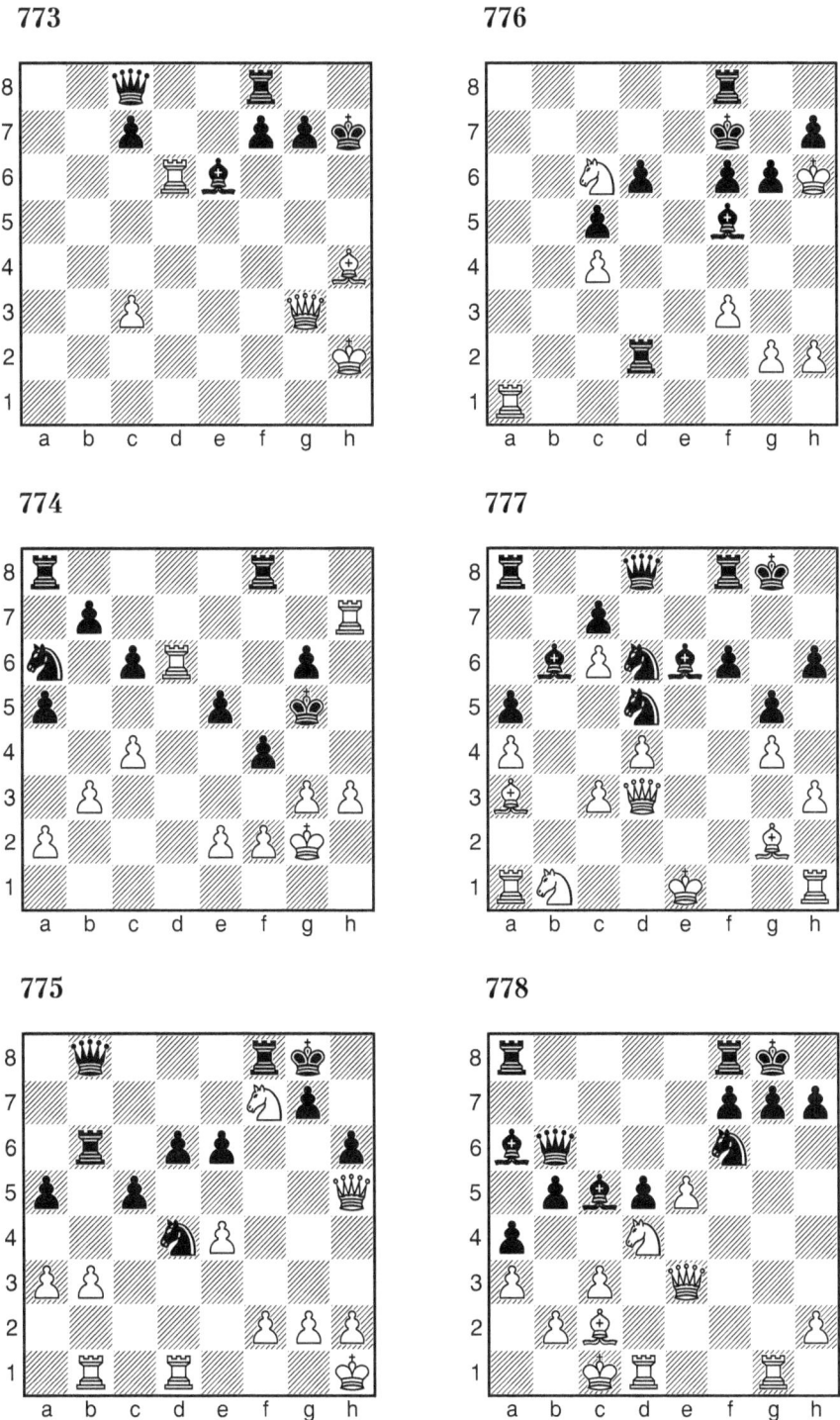

773

774

775

776

777

778

779

782

780

783

781

784

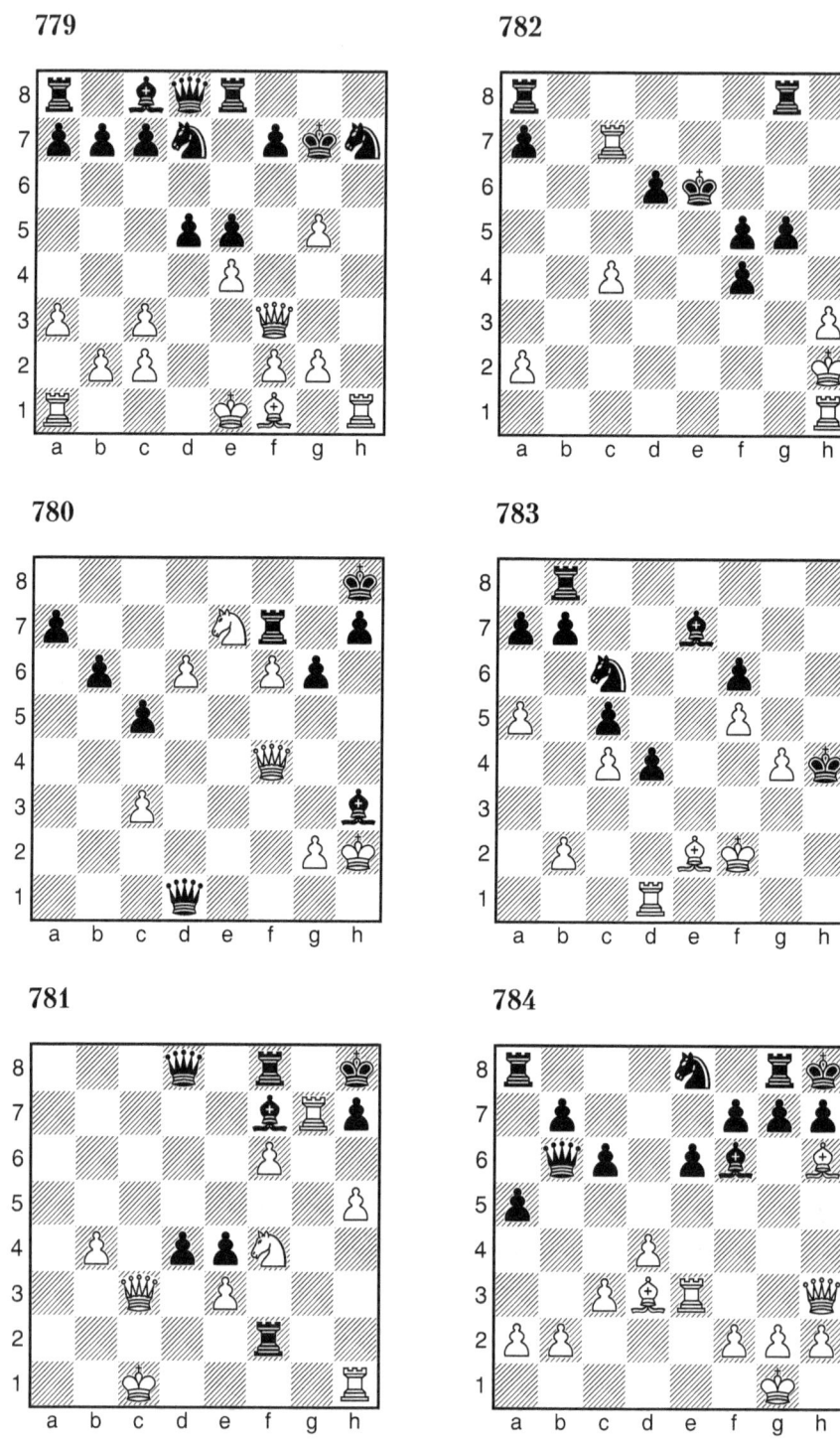

785

788

786

789

787

790

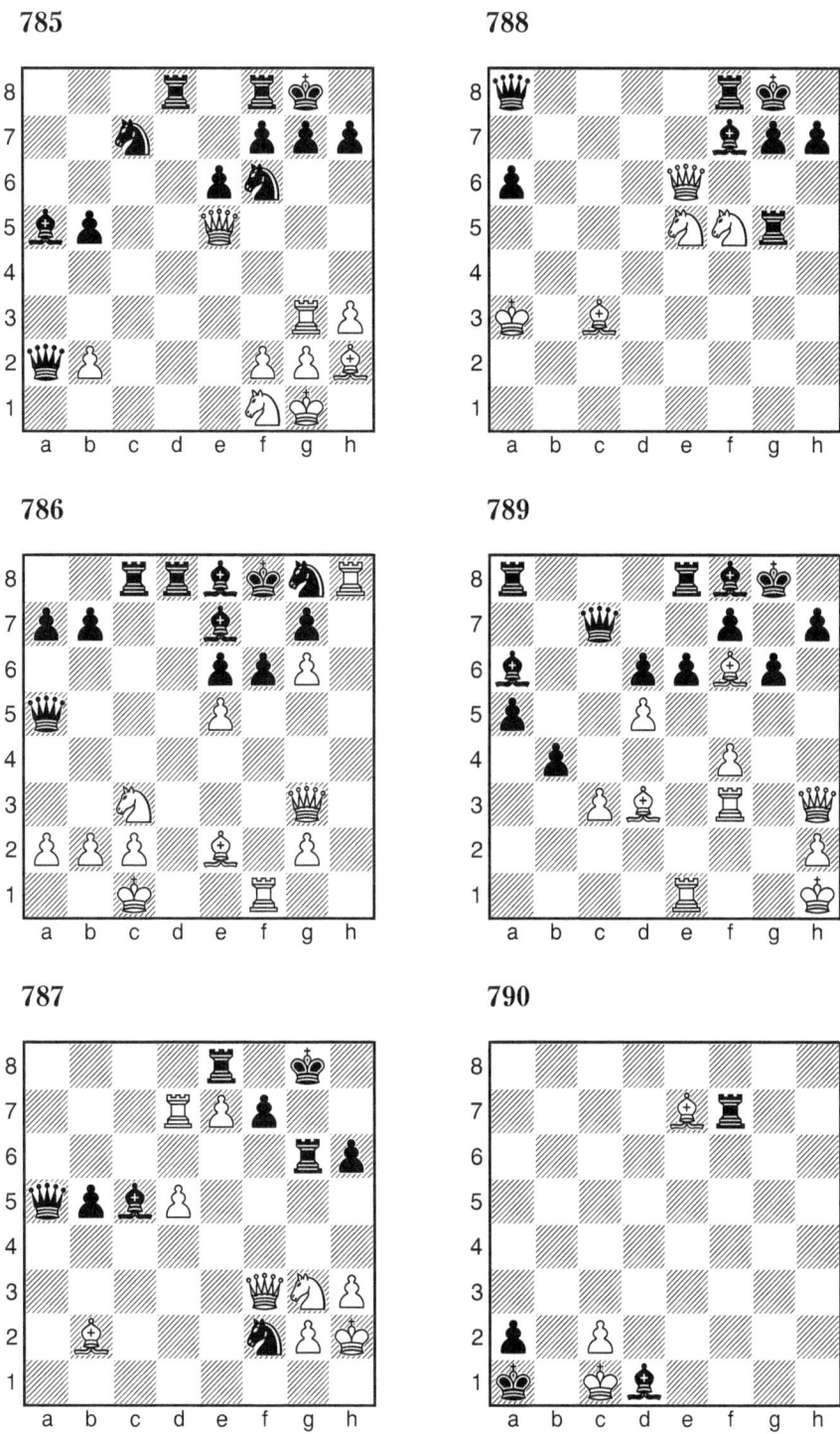

Chapter 27

TEST YOURSELF! FIND THE BEST DEFENSE AGAINST THE MATE THREAT

791

794

792

795

793

796

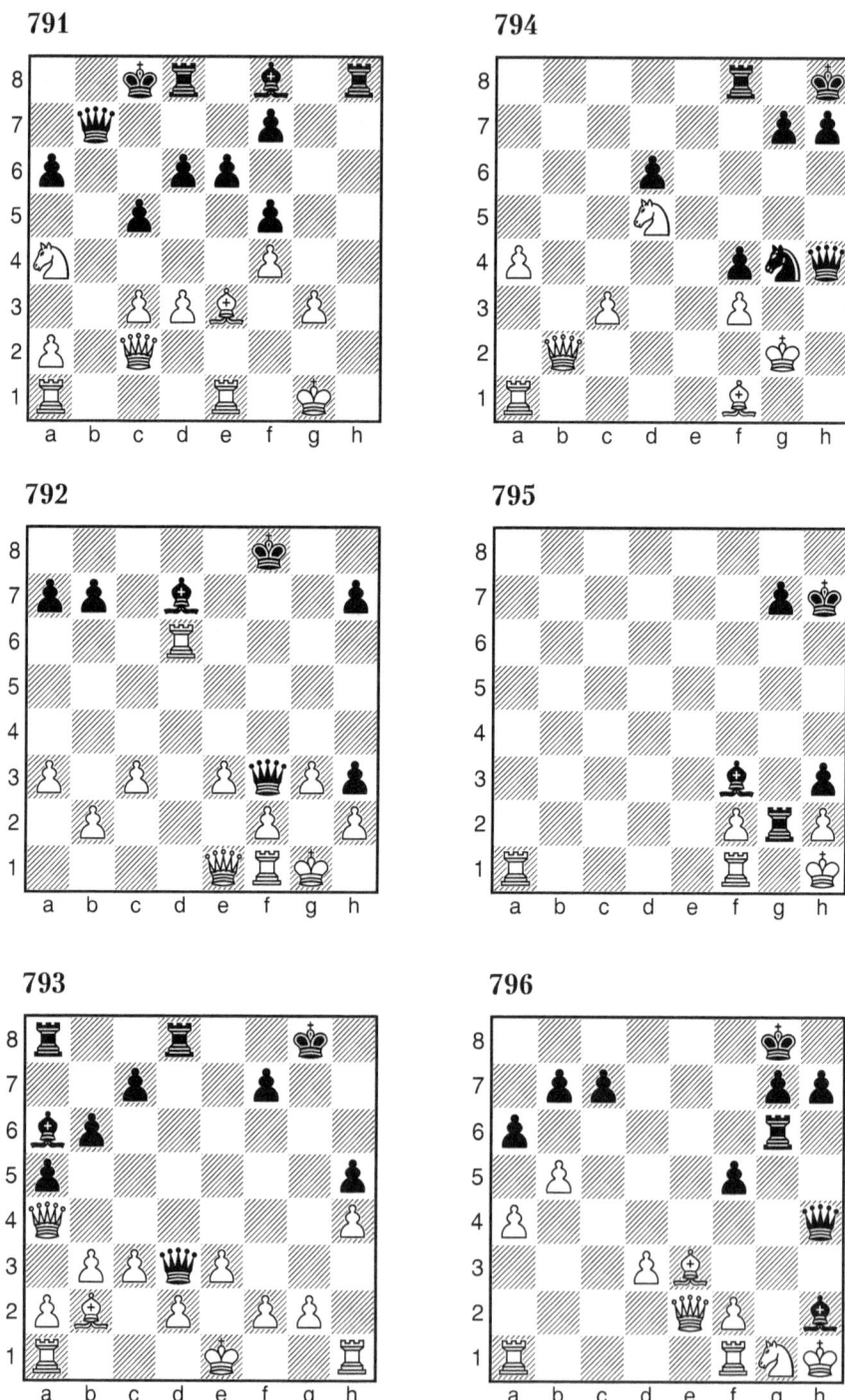

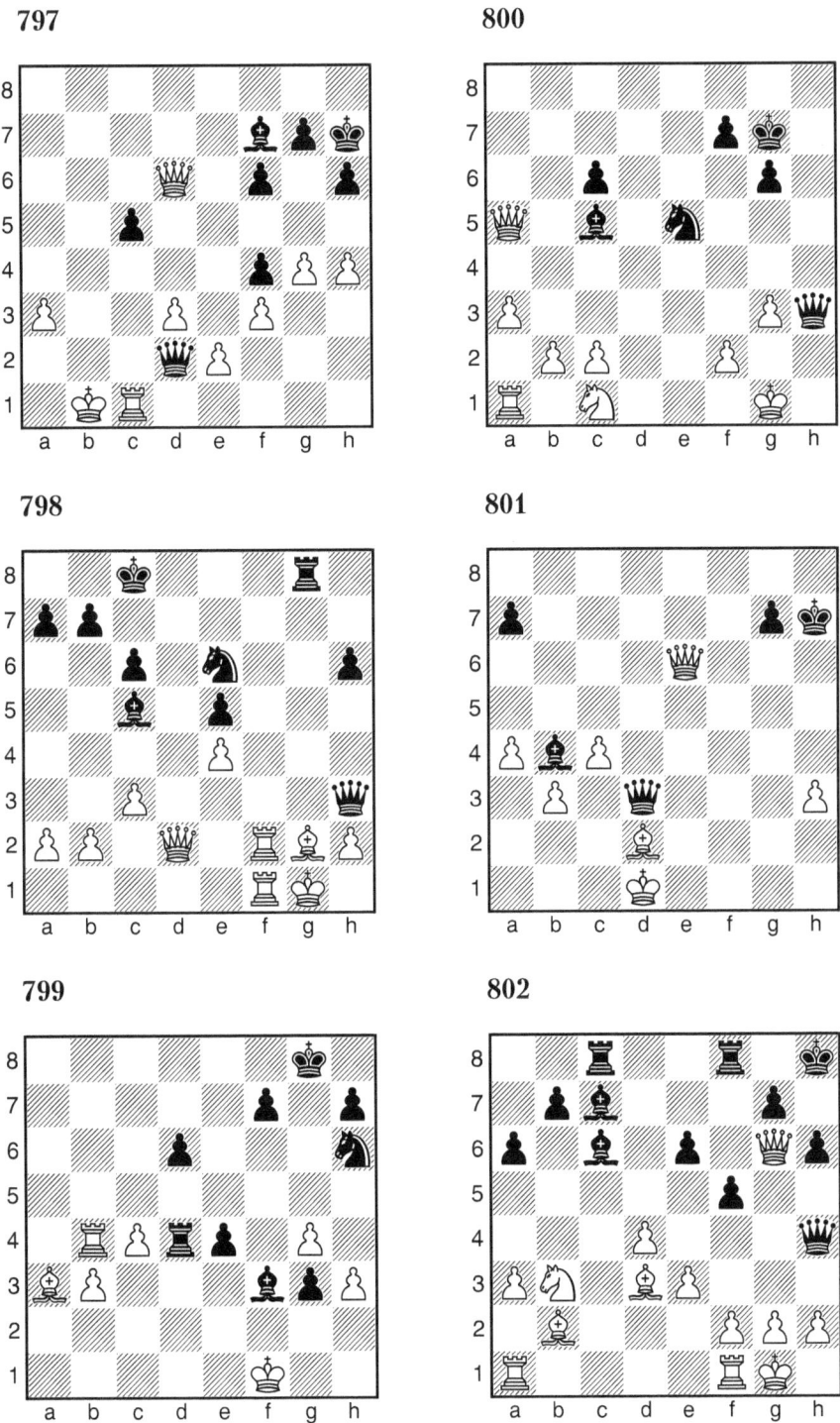

797

798

799

800

801

802

803

806

804

807

805

808

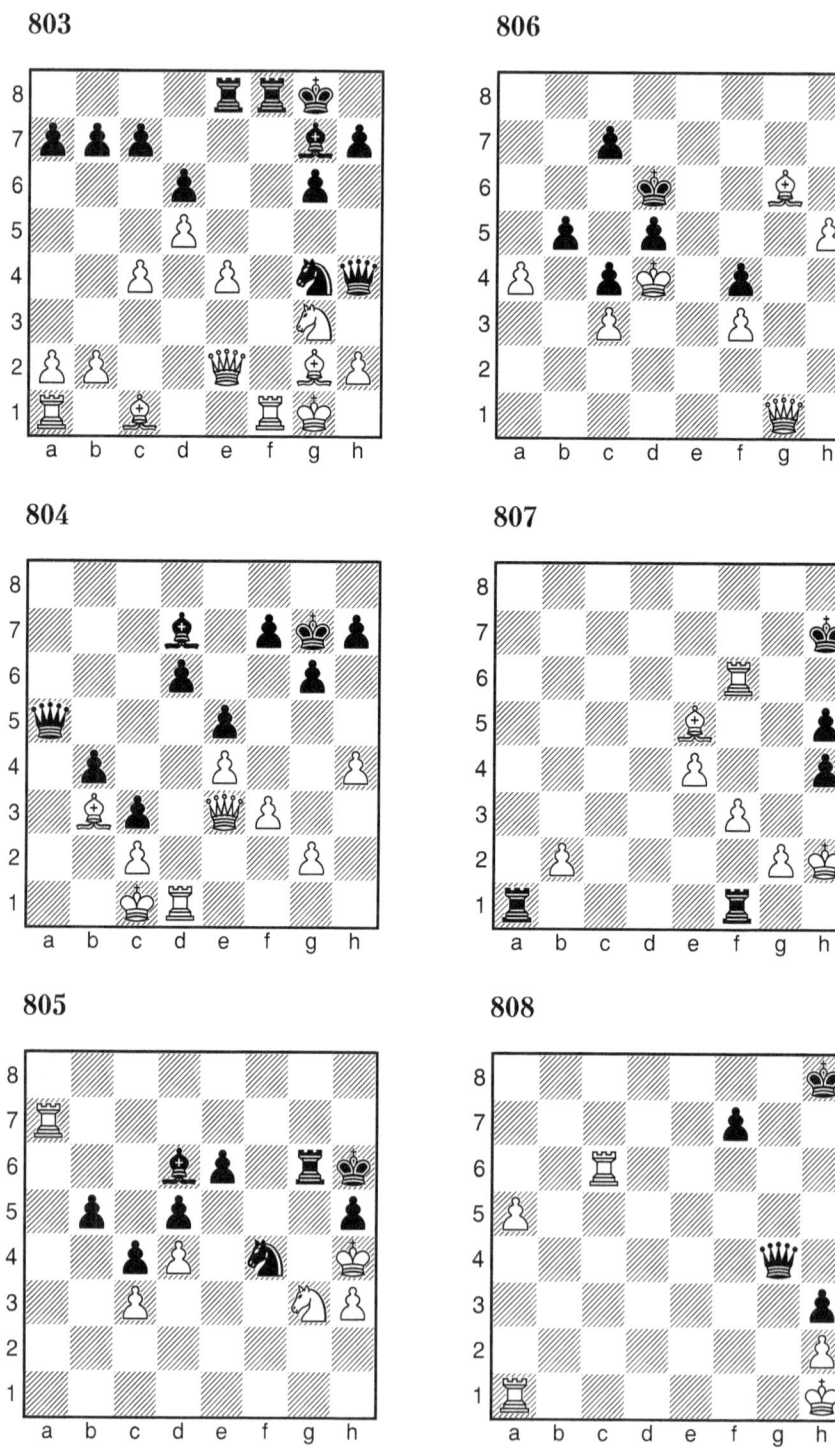

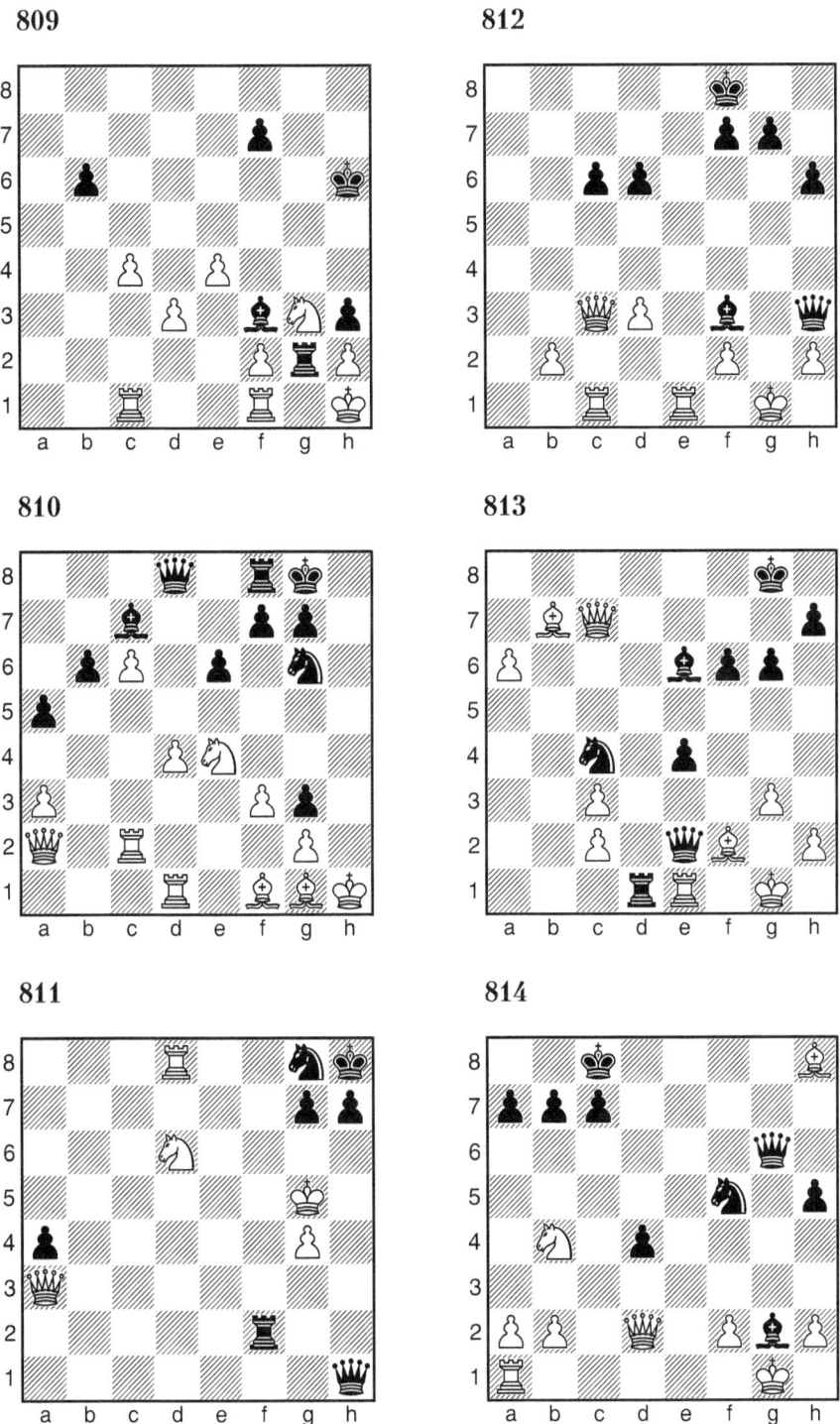

815

818

816

819

817

820

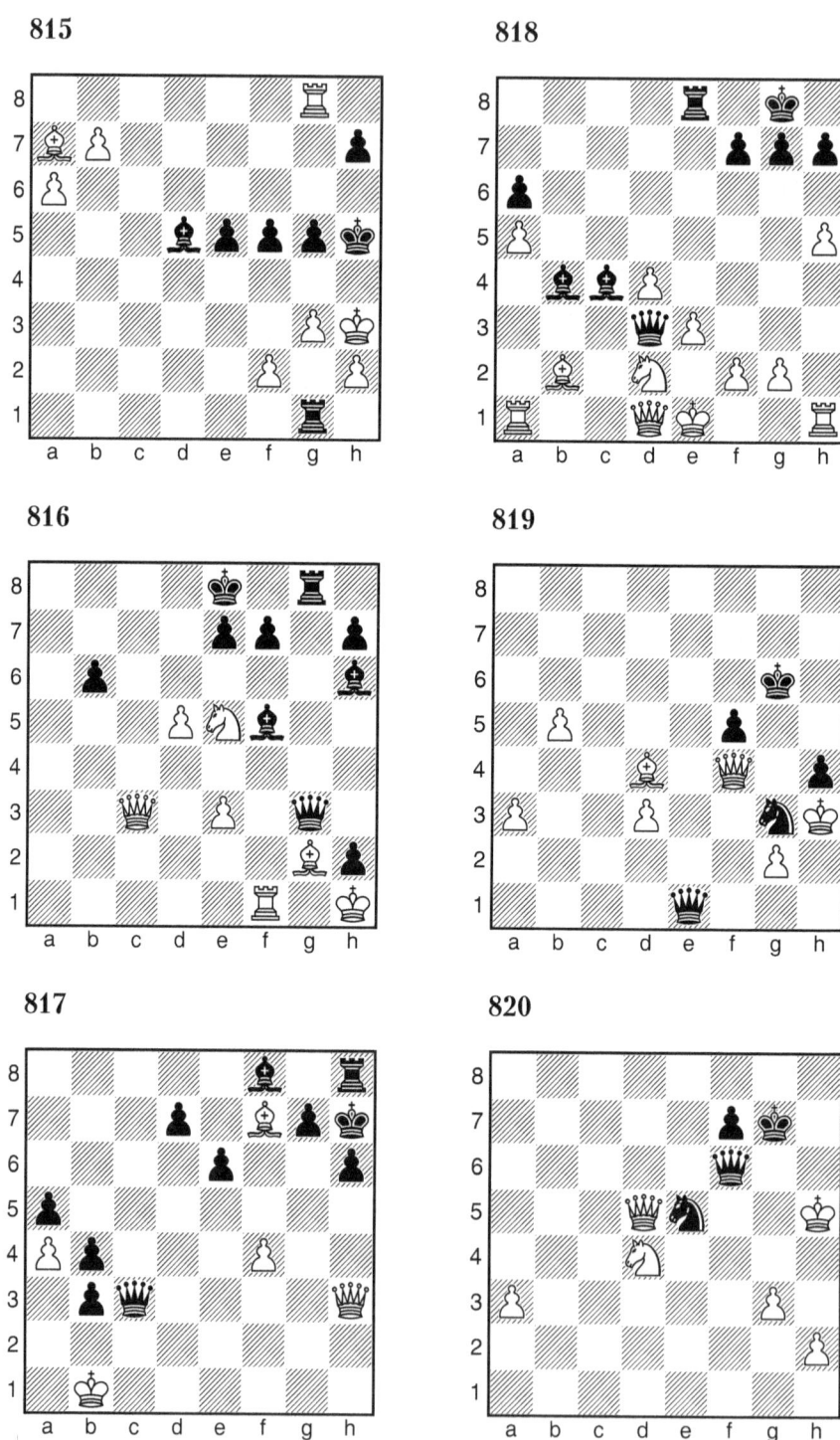

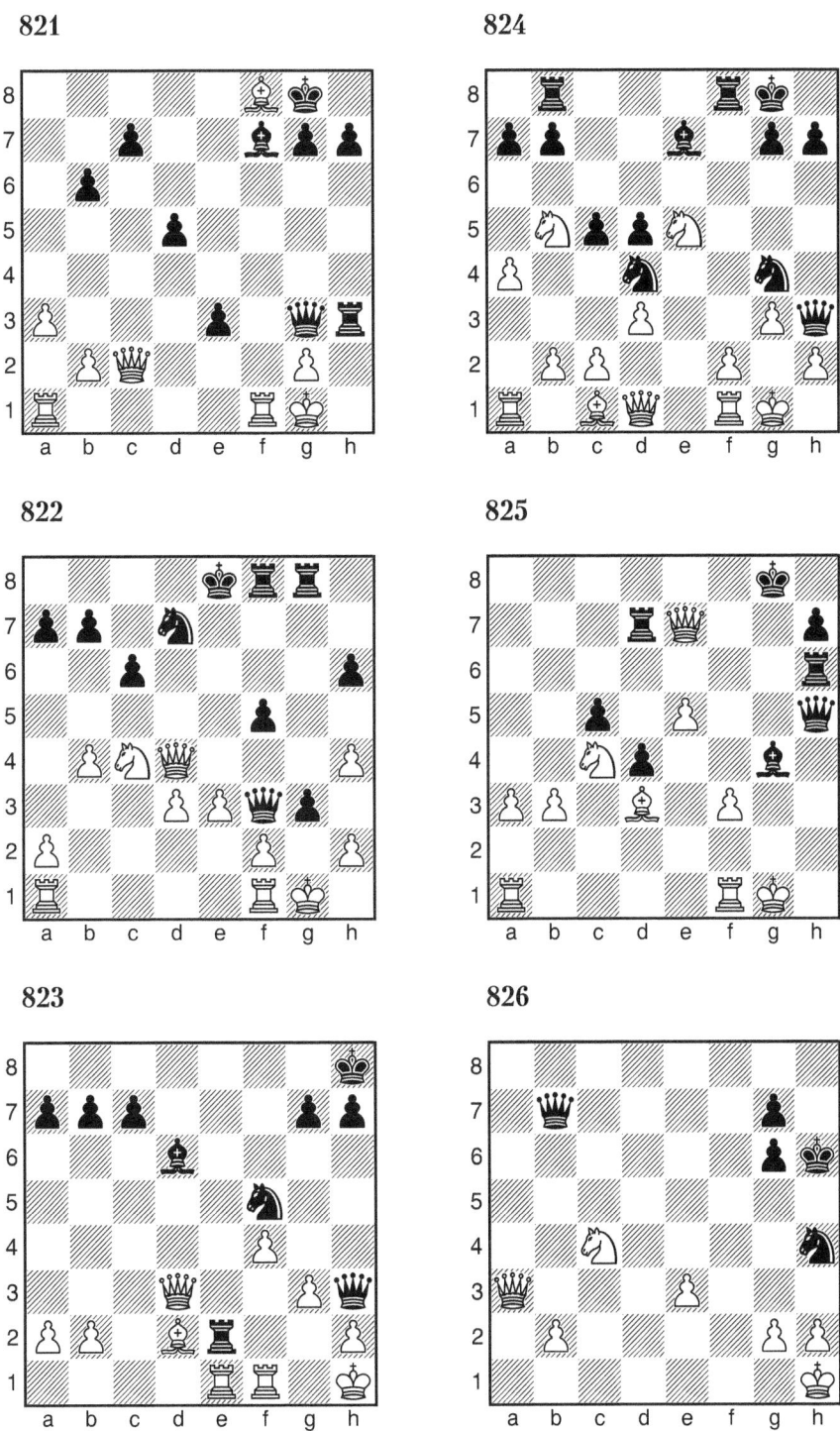

821

822

823

824

825

826

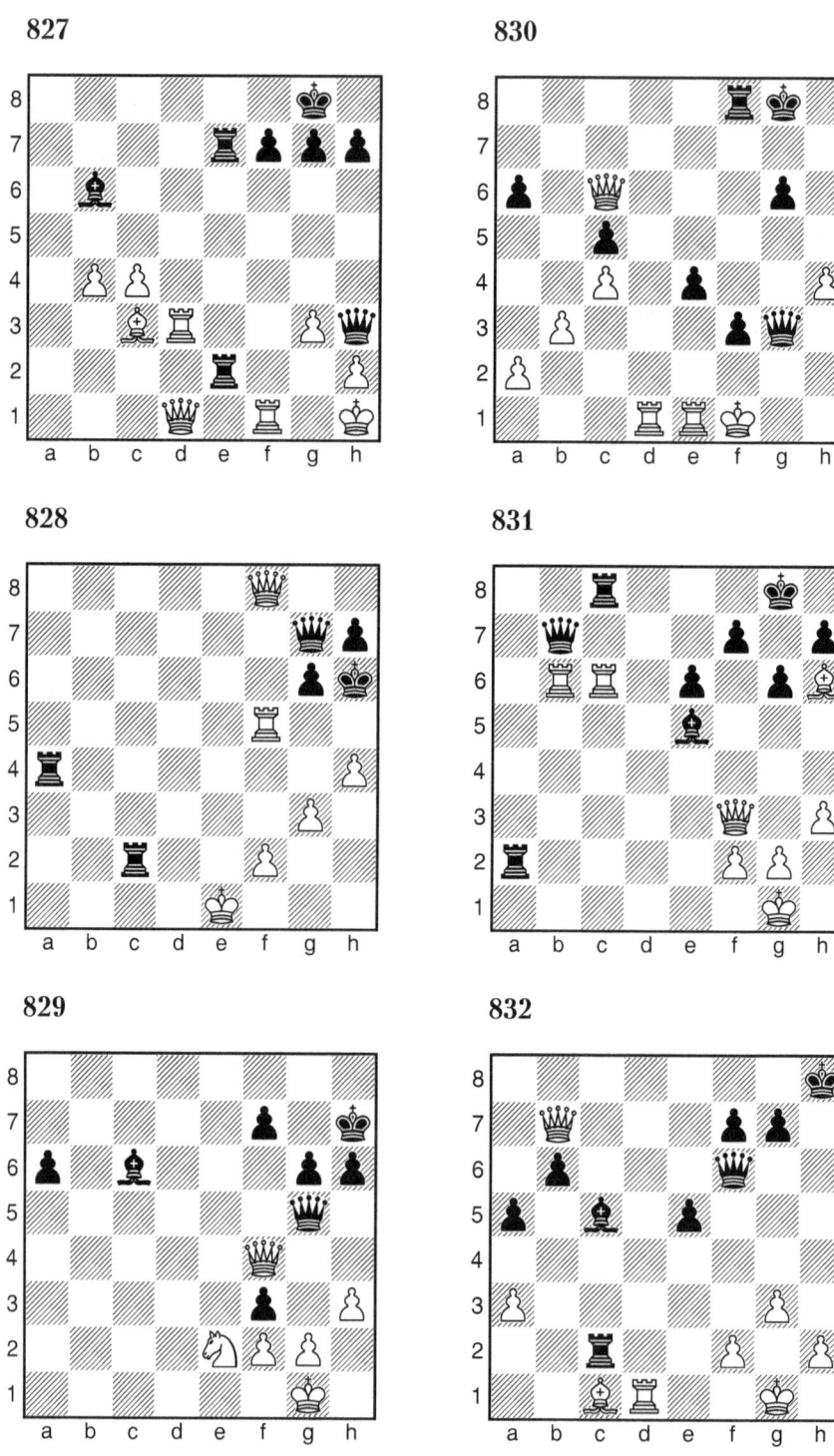

827

828

829

830

831

832

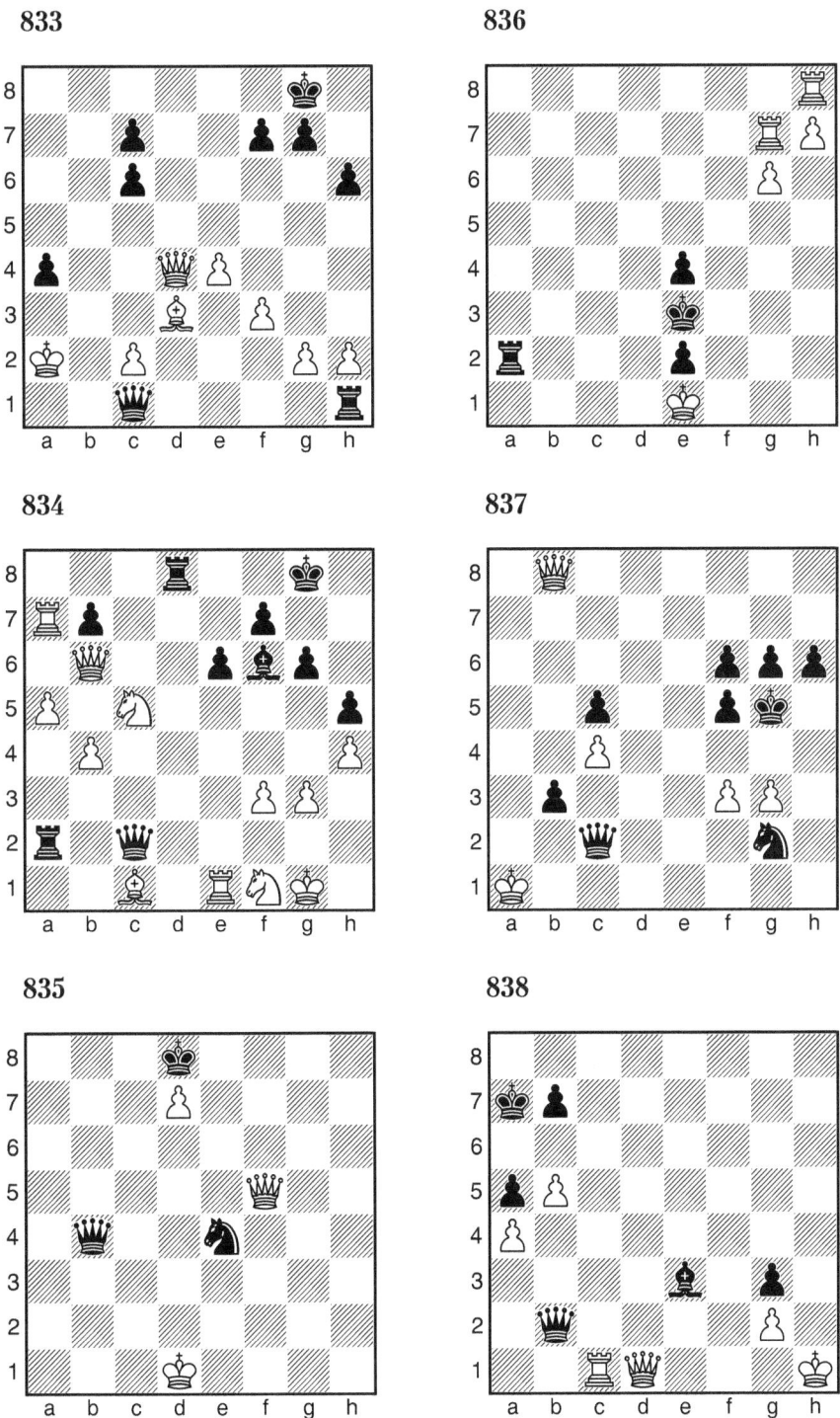

833

834

835

836

837

838

839

842

840

843

841

844

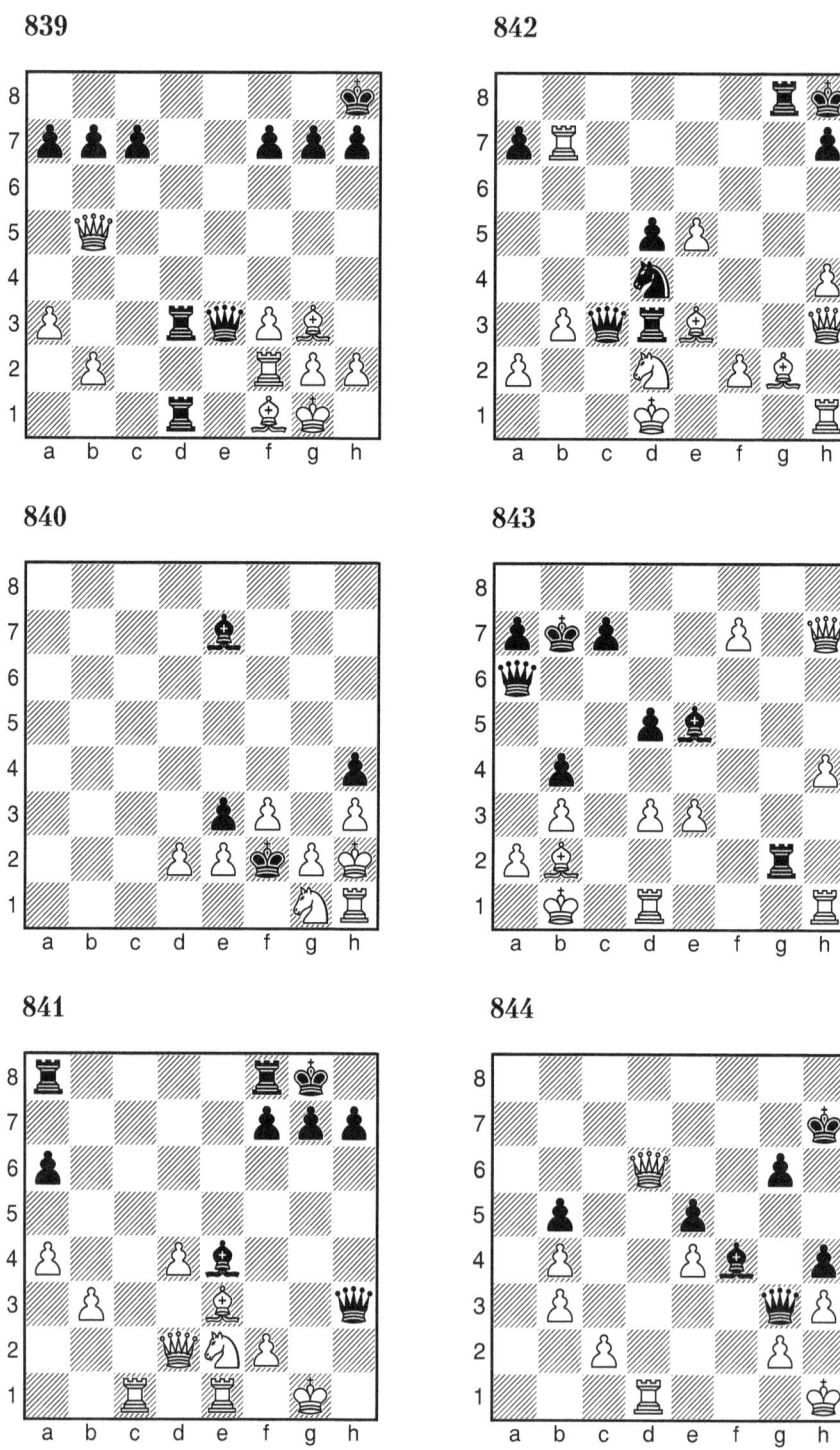

845

848

846

849

847

850

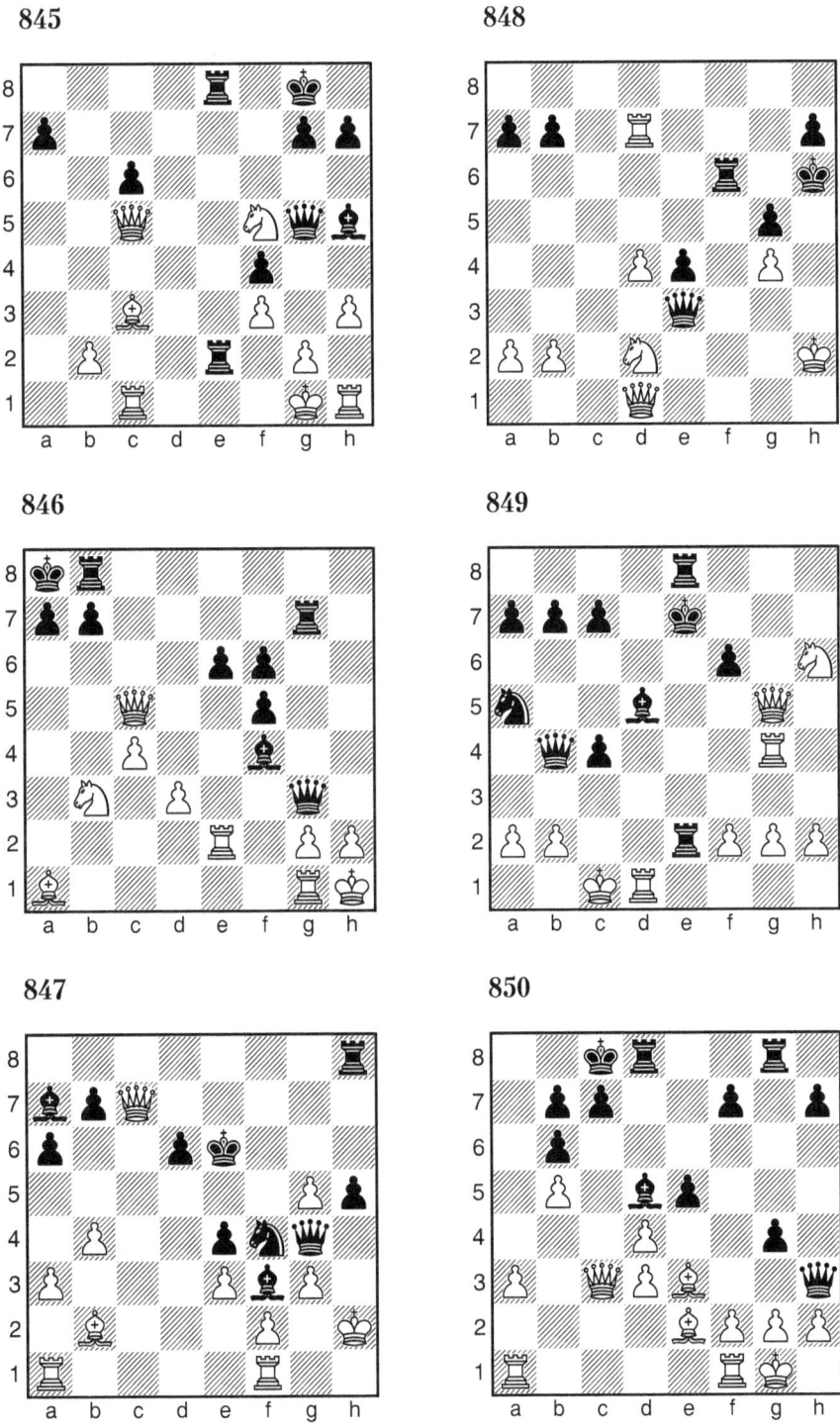

851

854

852

855

853

856

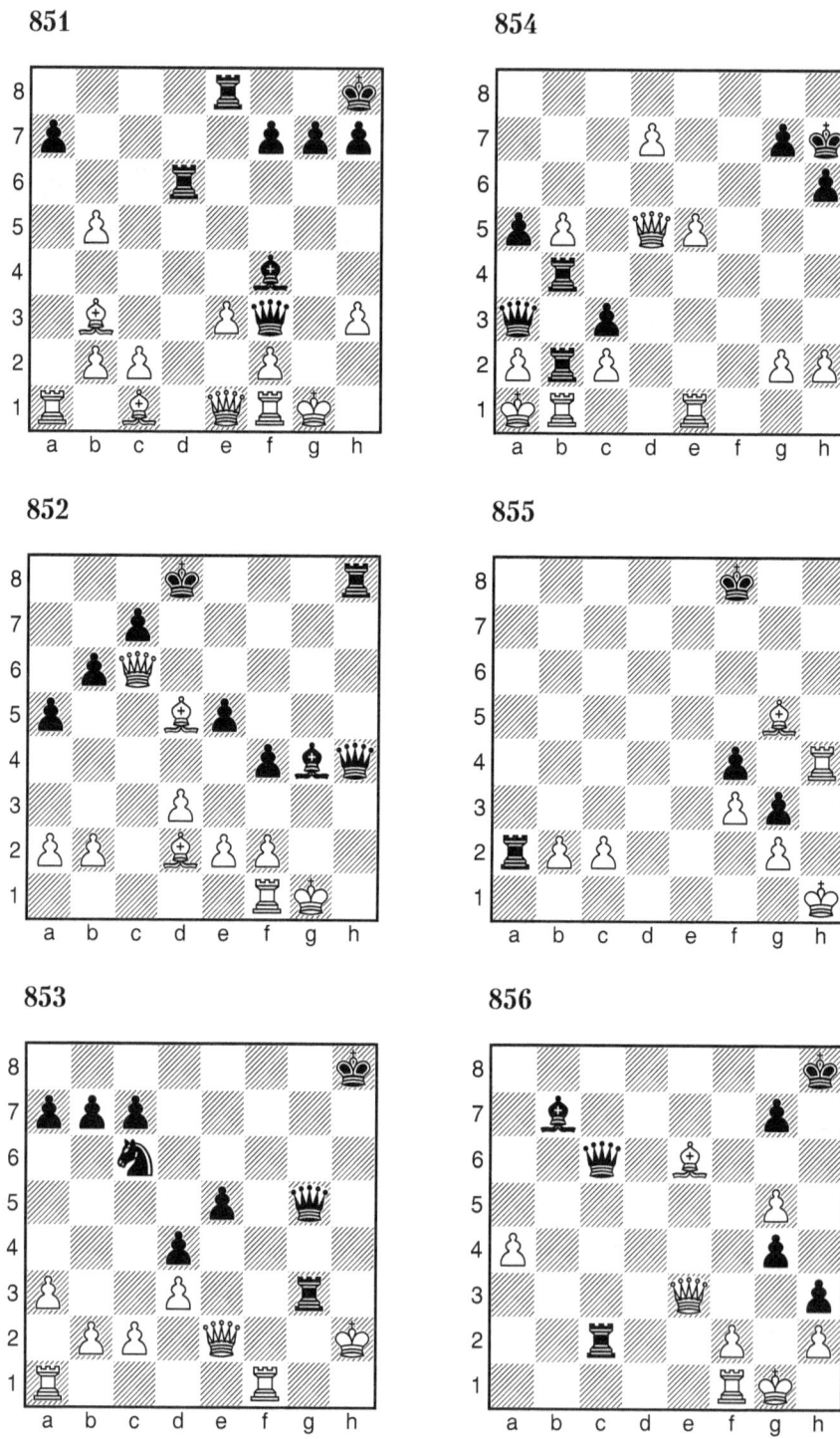

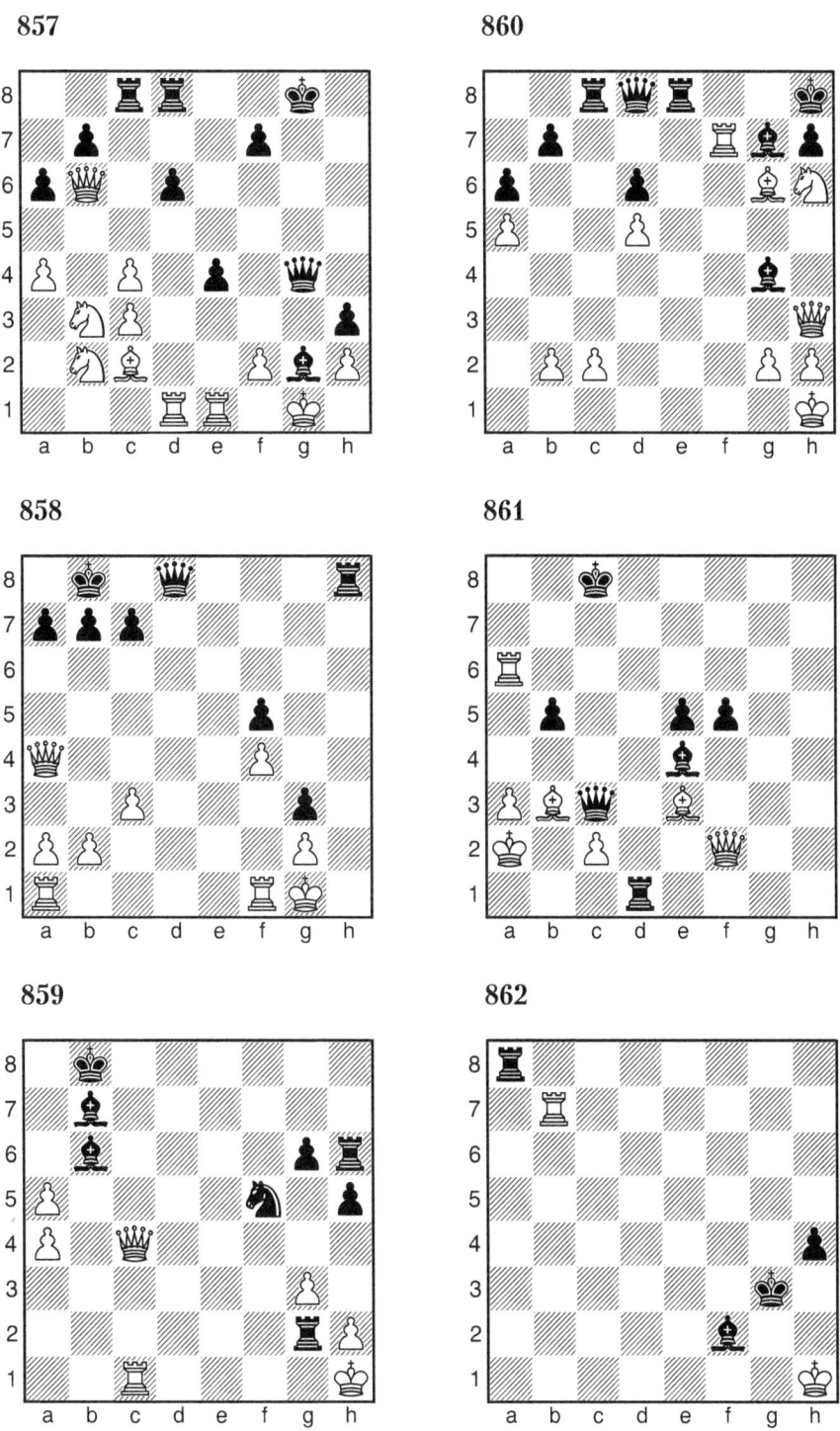

857

860

858

861

859

862

863

866

864

867

865

868

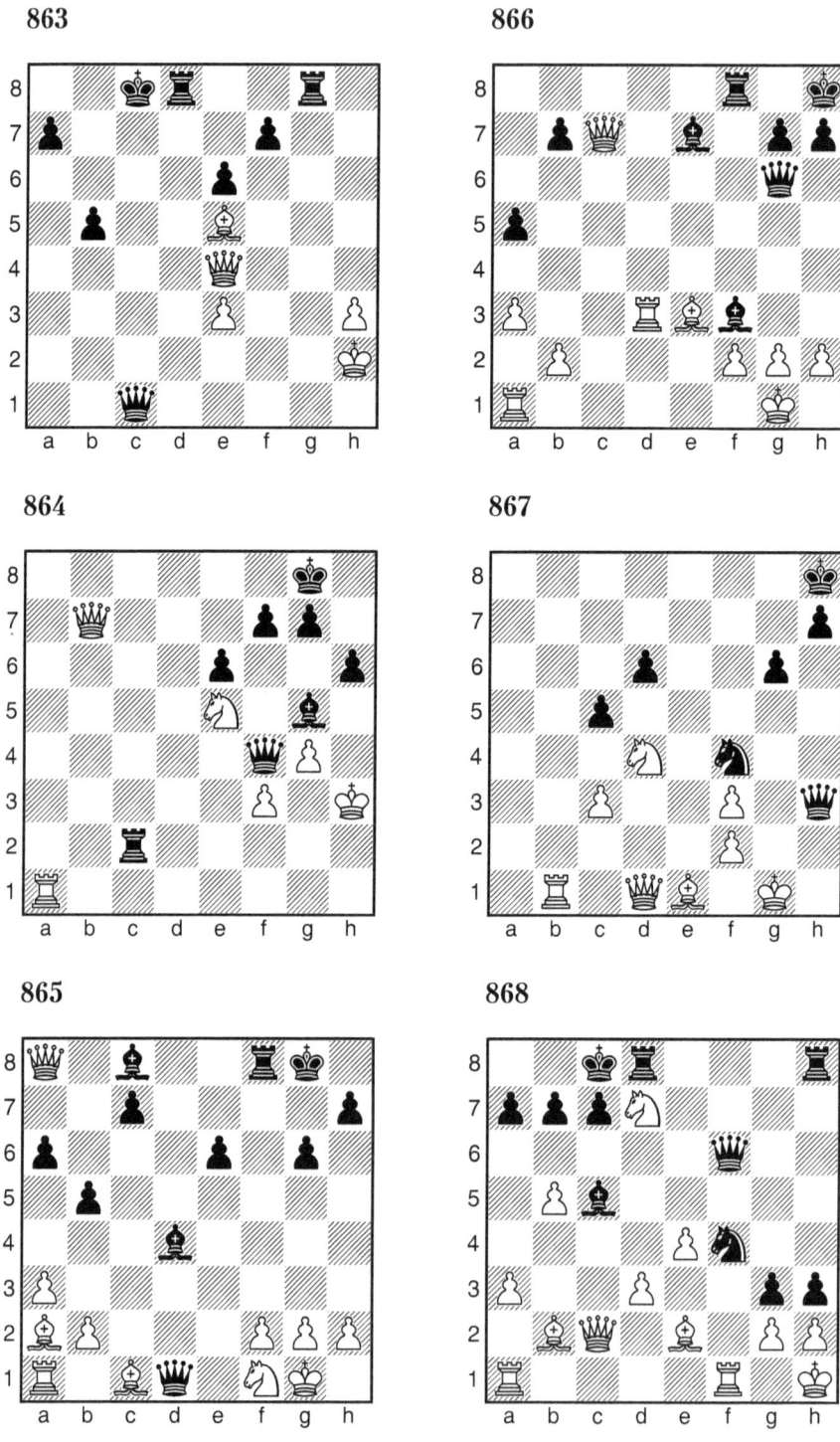

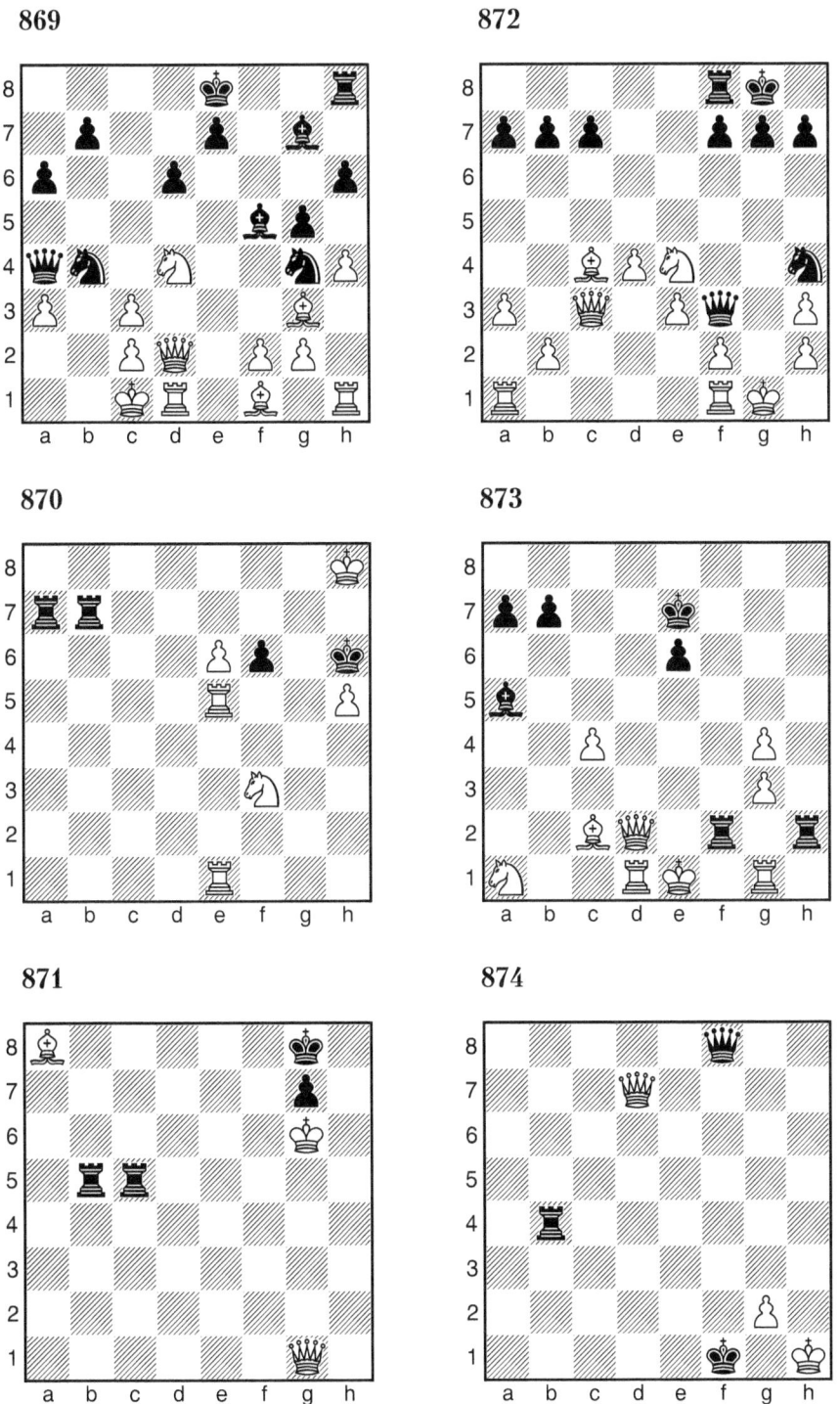

869

870

871

872

873

874

875

878

876

879

877

880

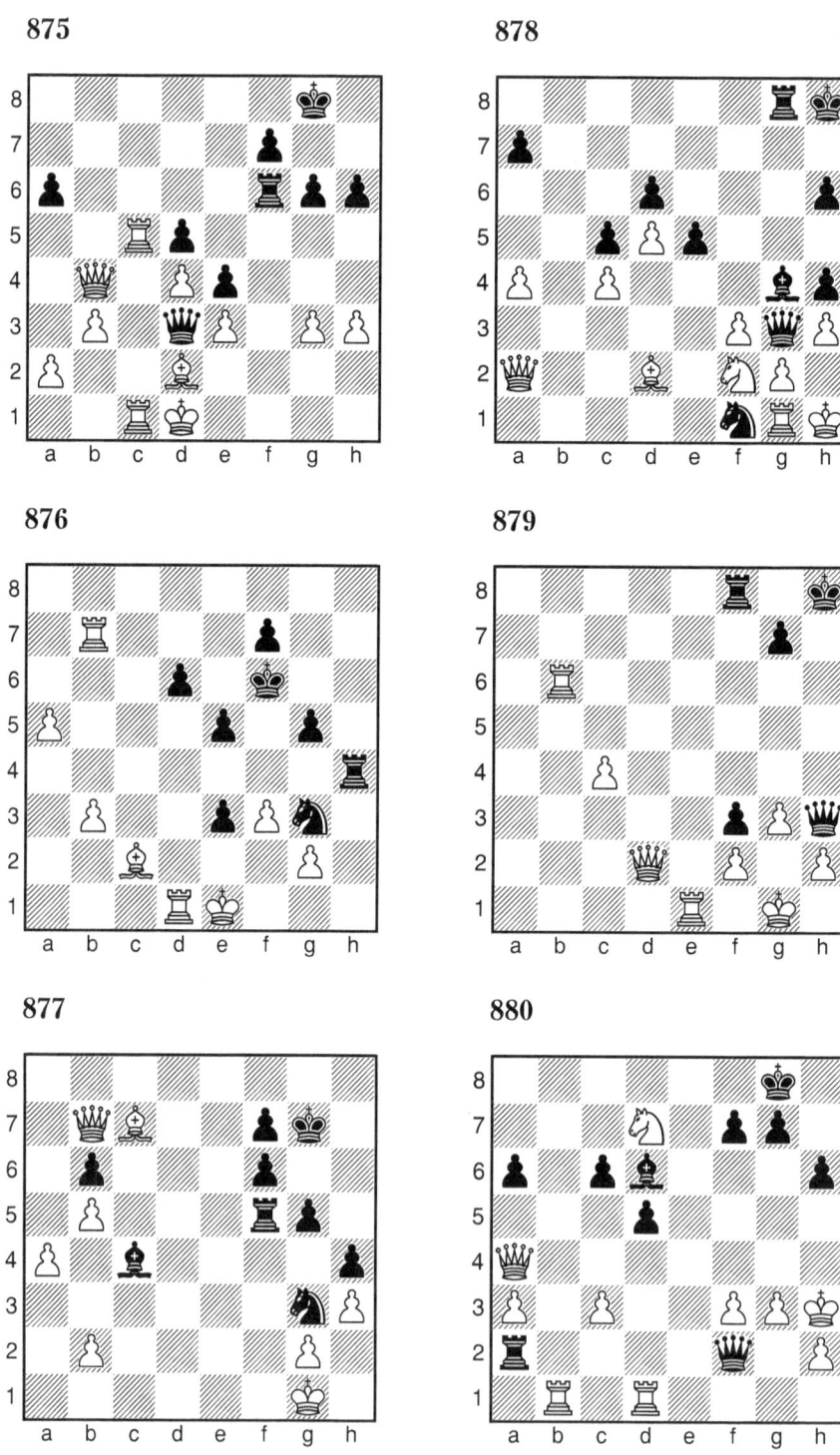

TEST YOURSELF! FIND THE BEST CONTINUATION

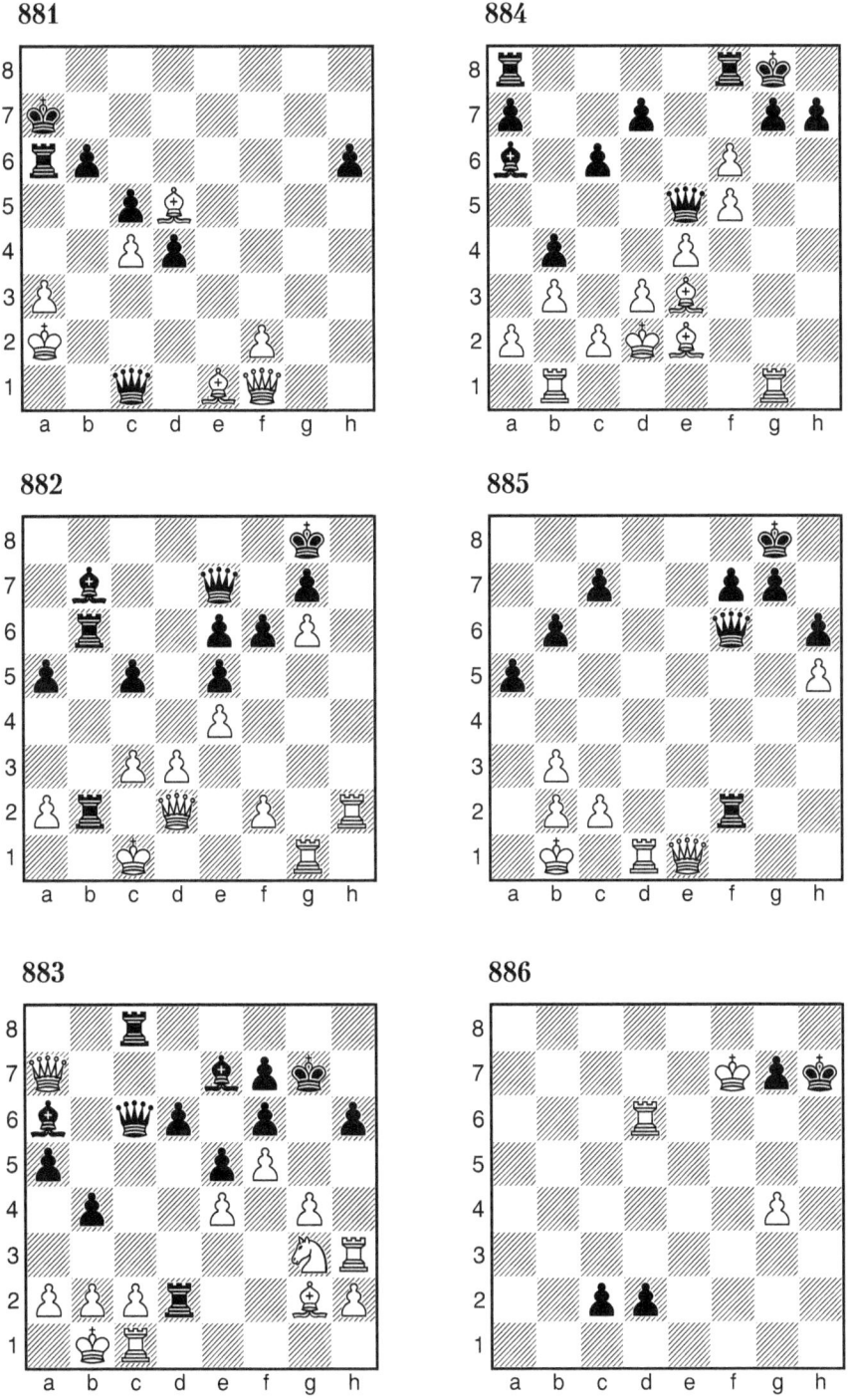

881

884

882

885

883

886

887

890

888

891

889

892

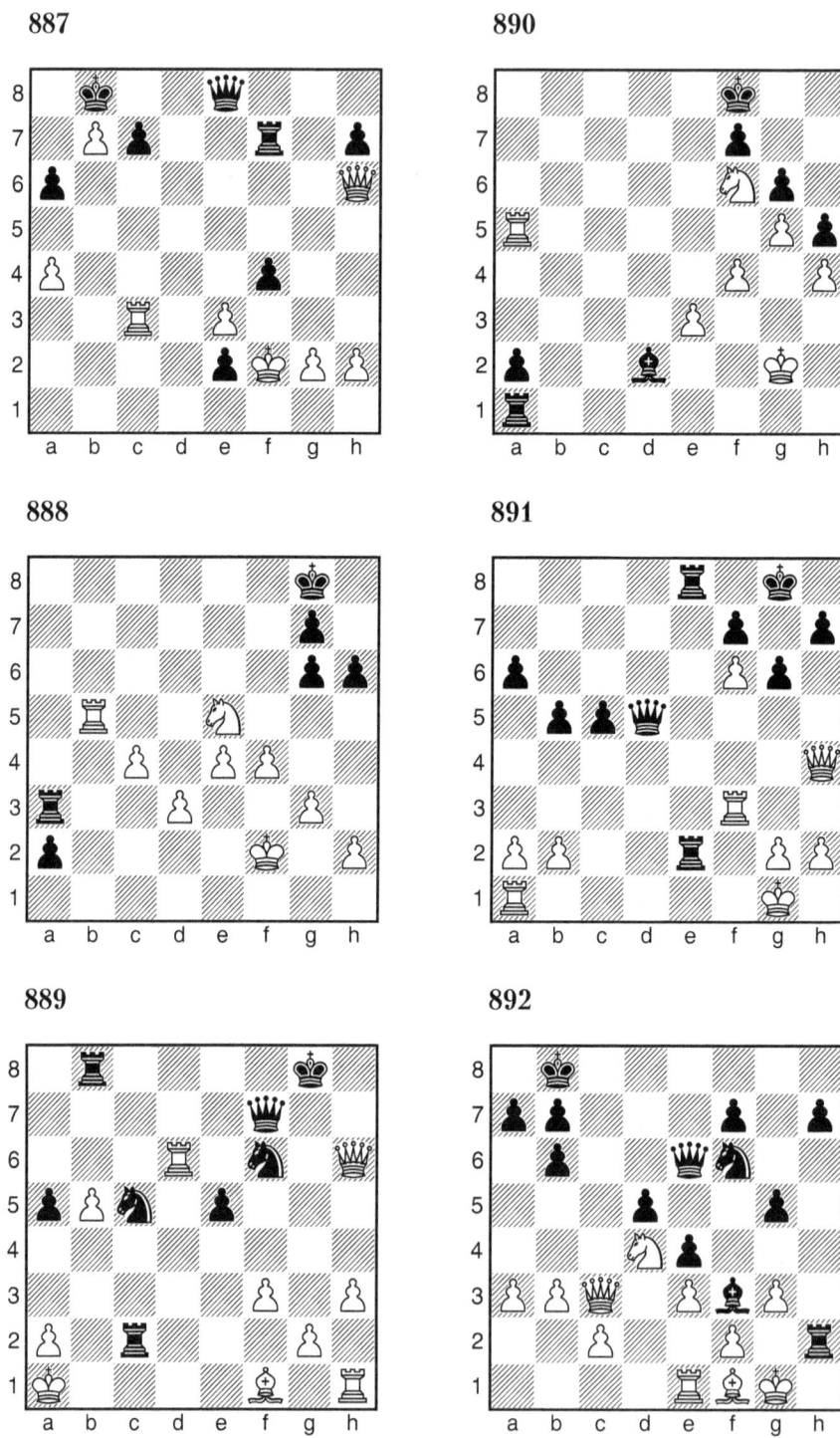

893

896

894

897

895

898

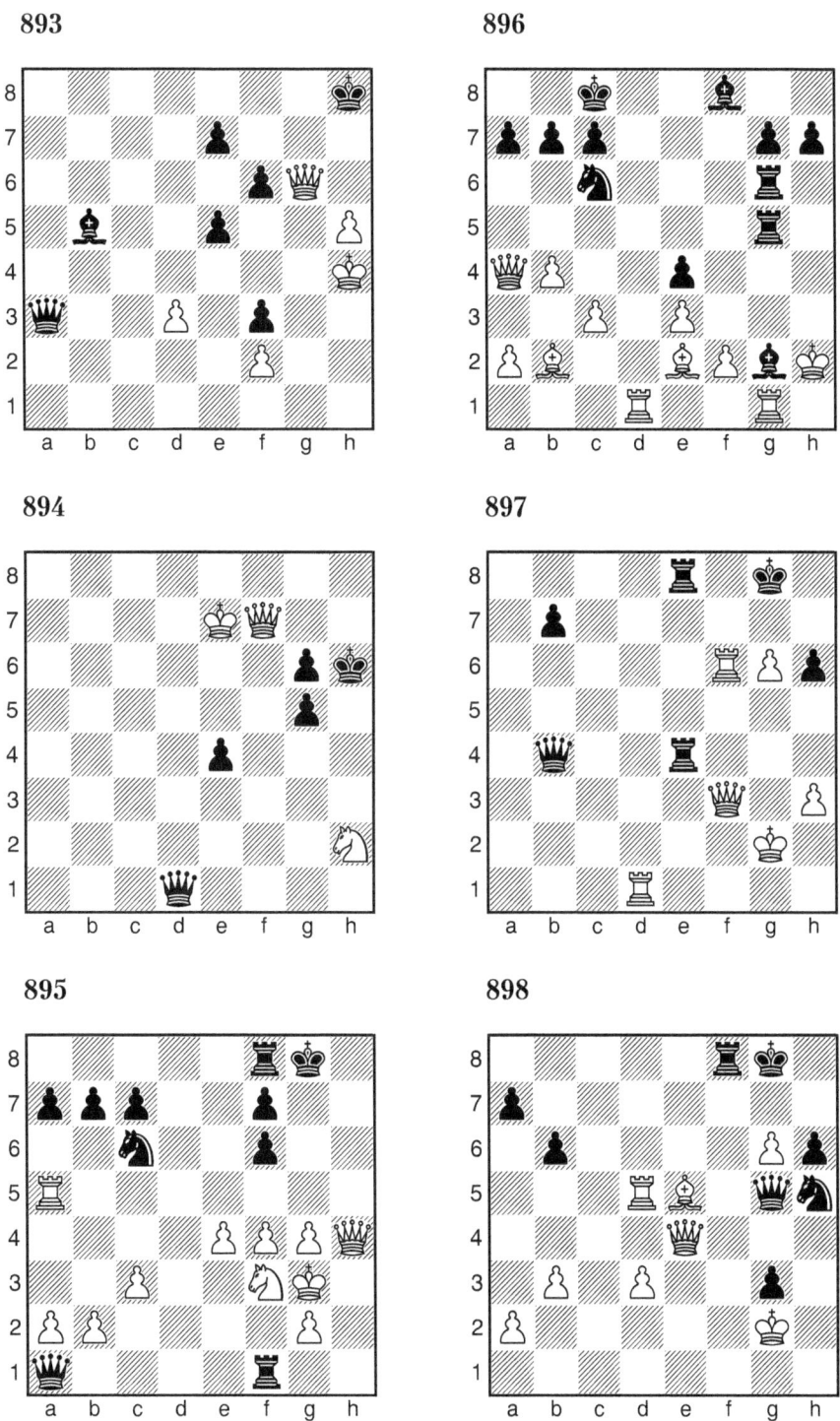

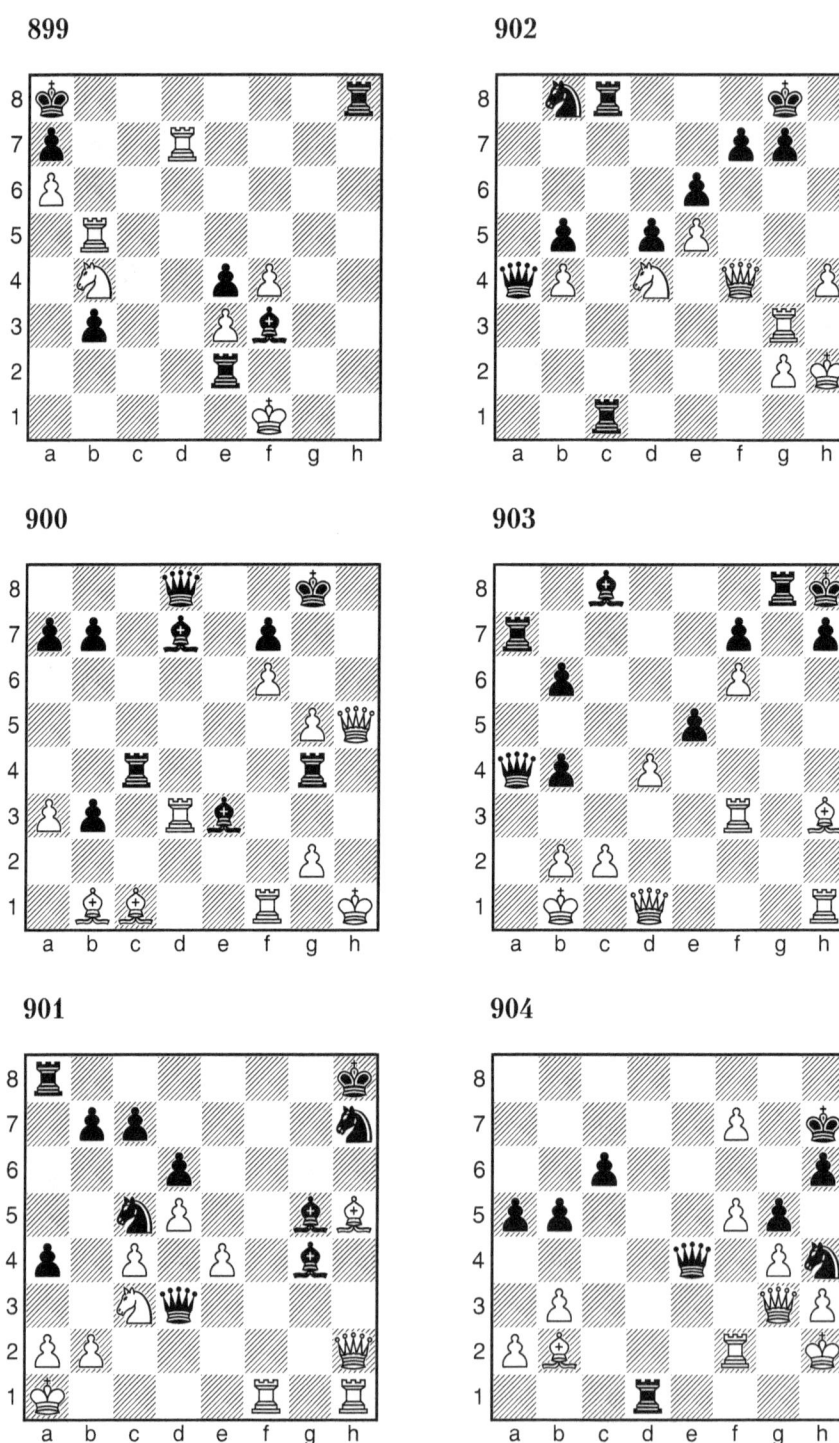

899

900

901

902

903

904

905

908

906

909

907

910

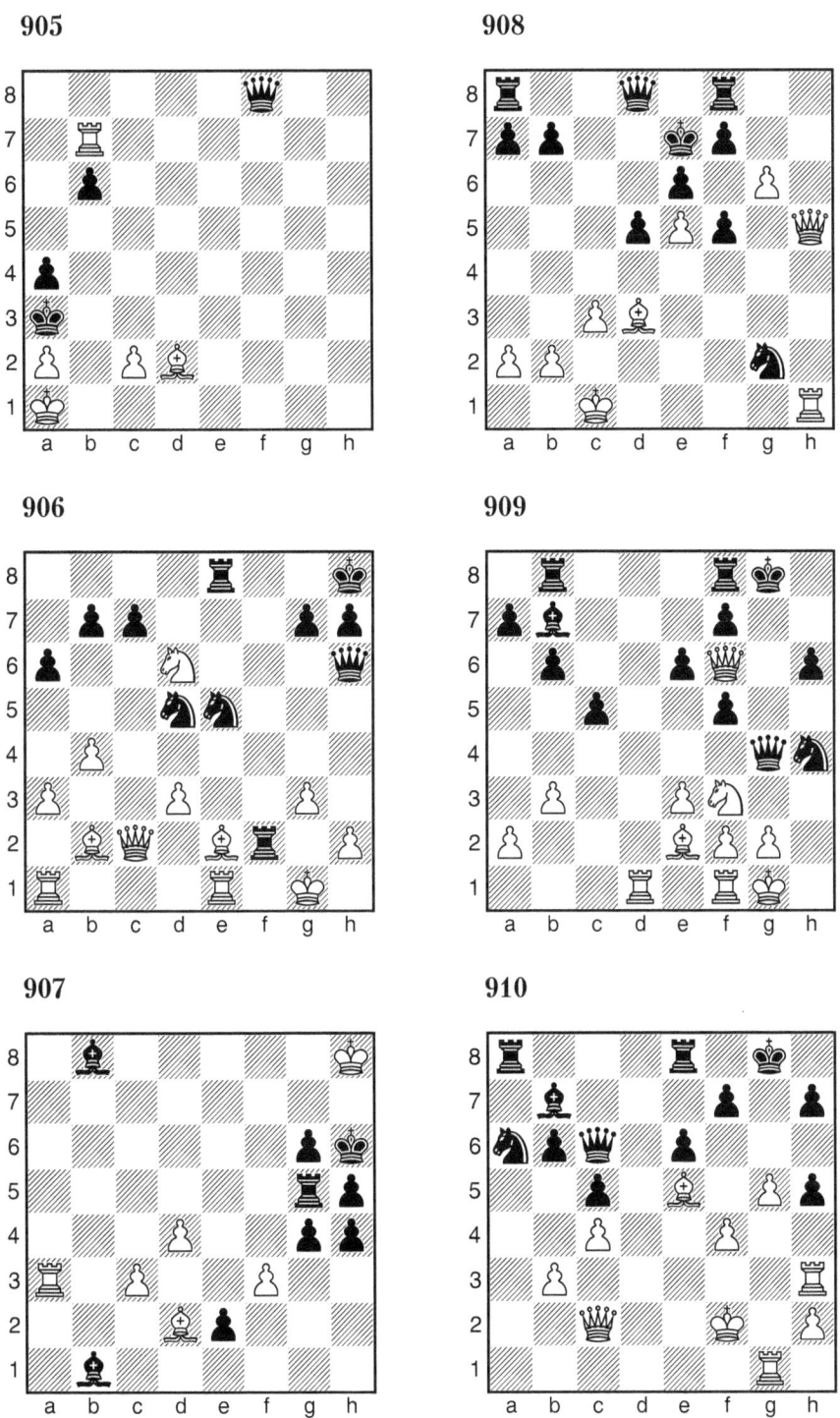

911

914

912

915

913

916

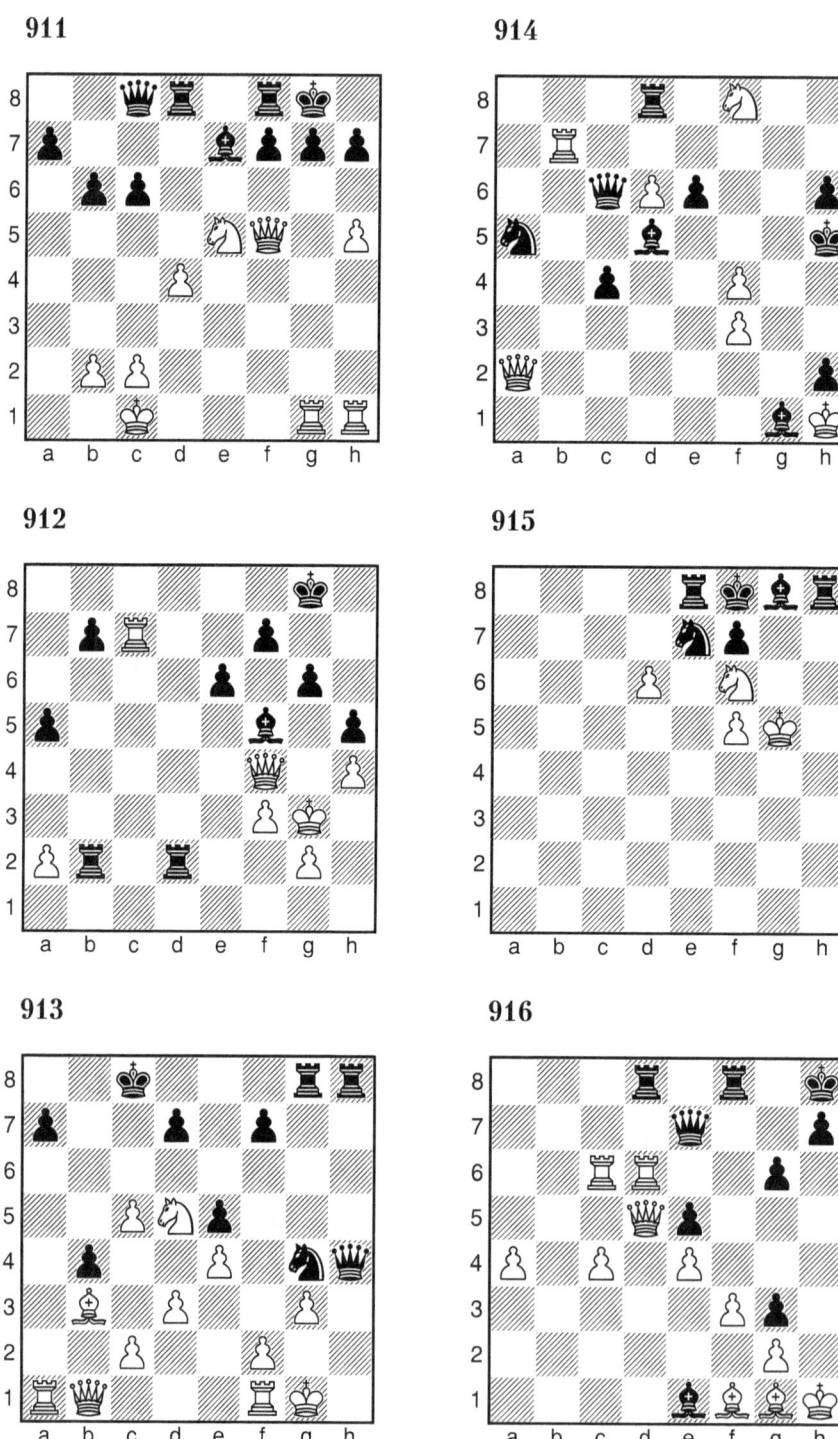

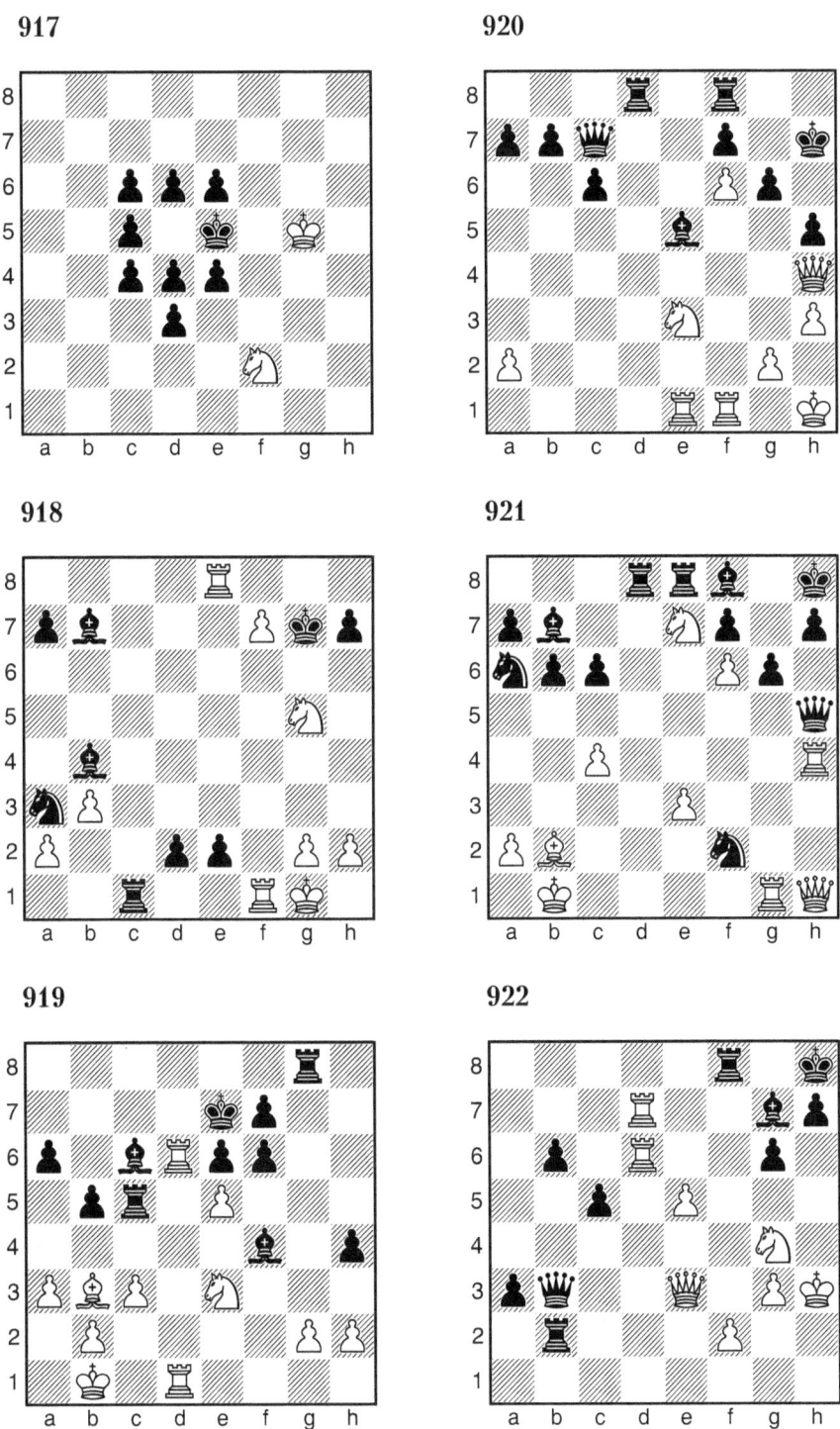

917

918

919

920

921

922

923

926

924

927

925

928

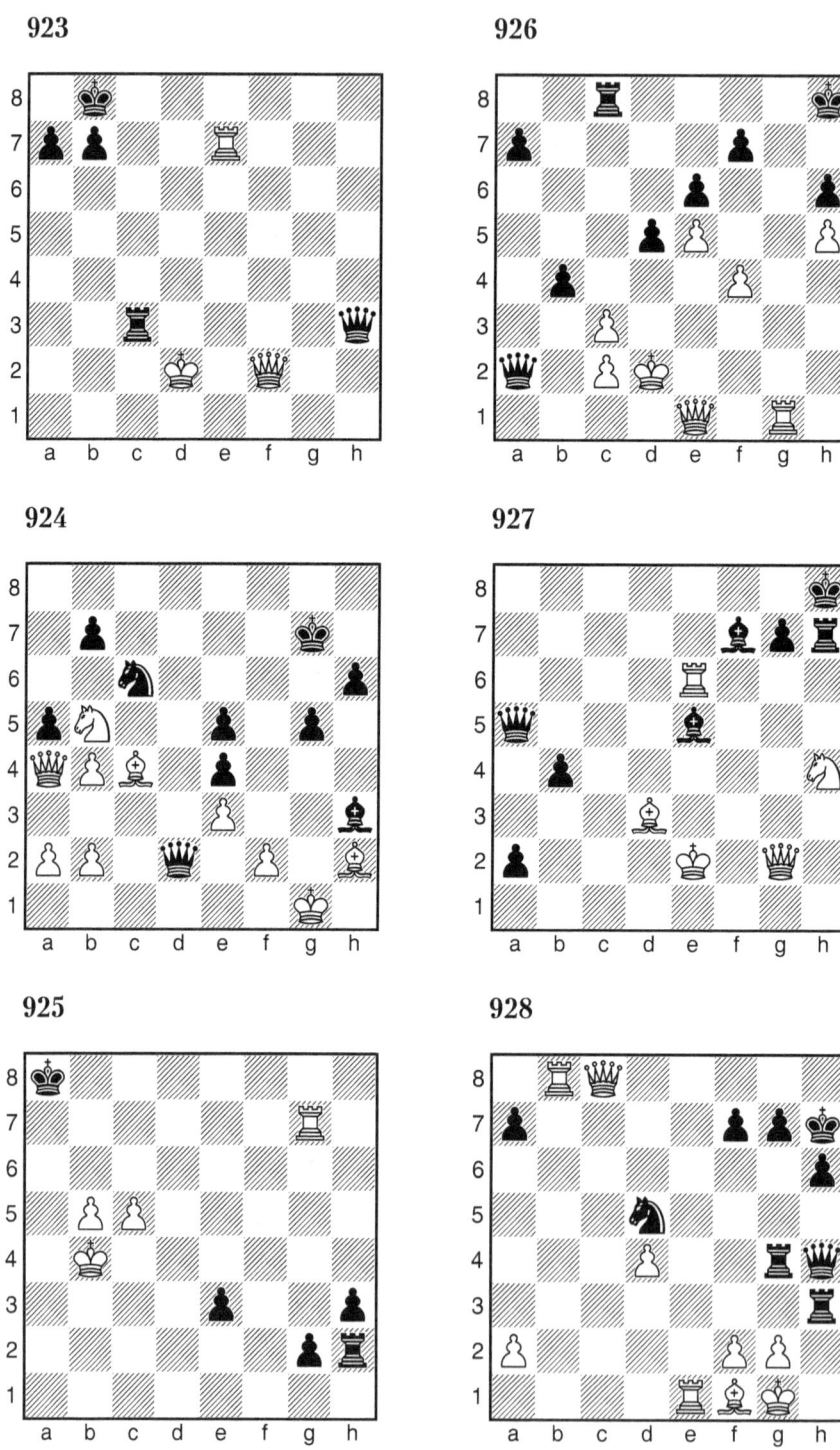

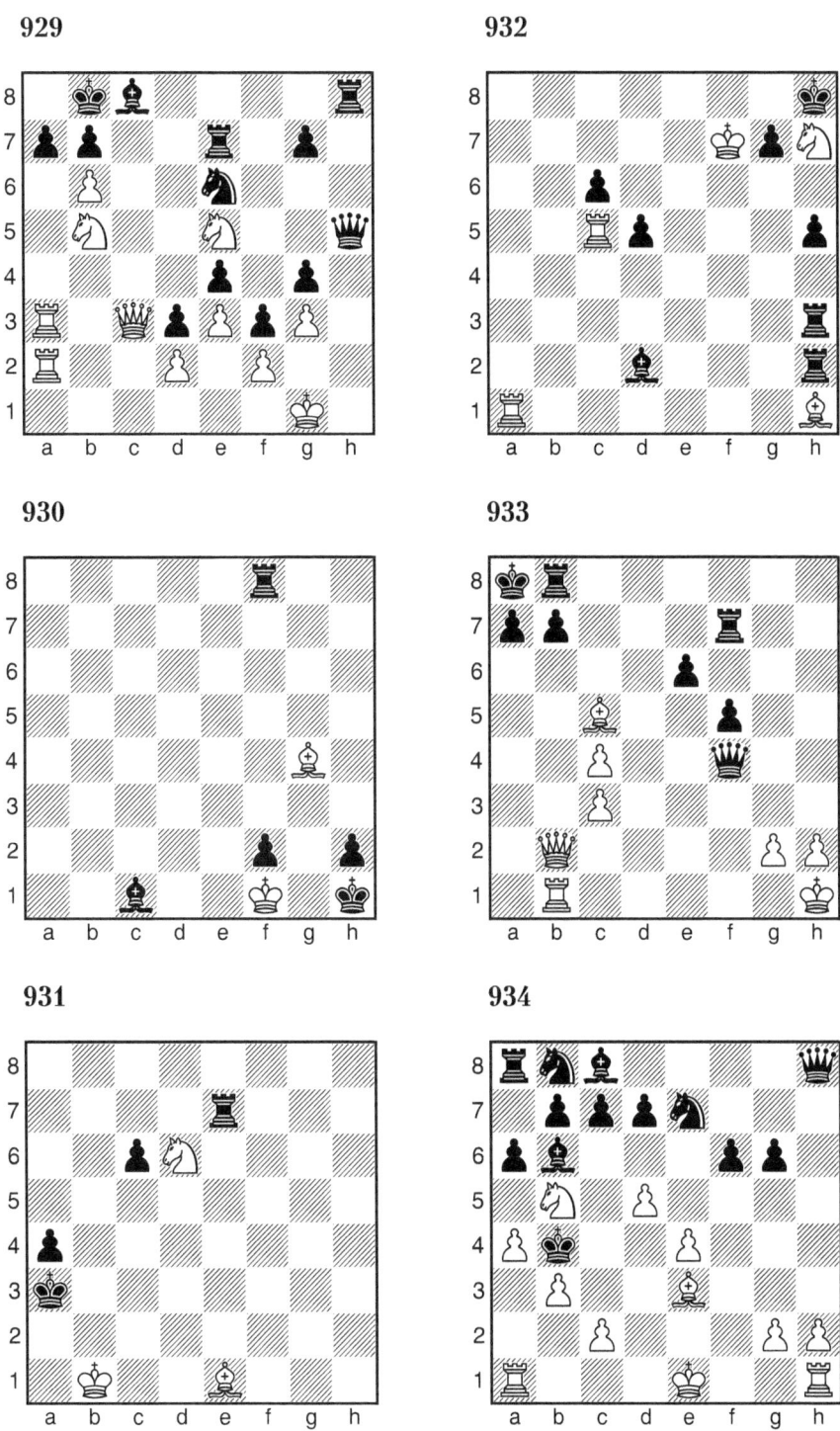

929

930

931

932

933

934

935

938

936

939

937

940

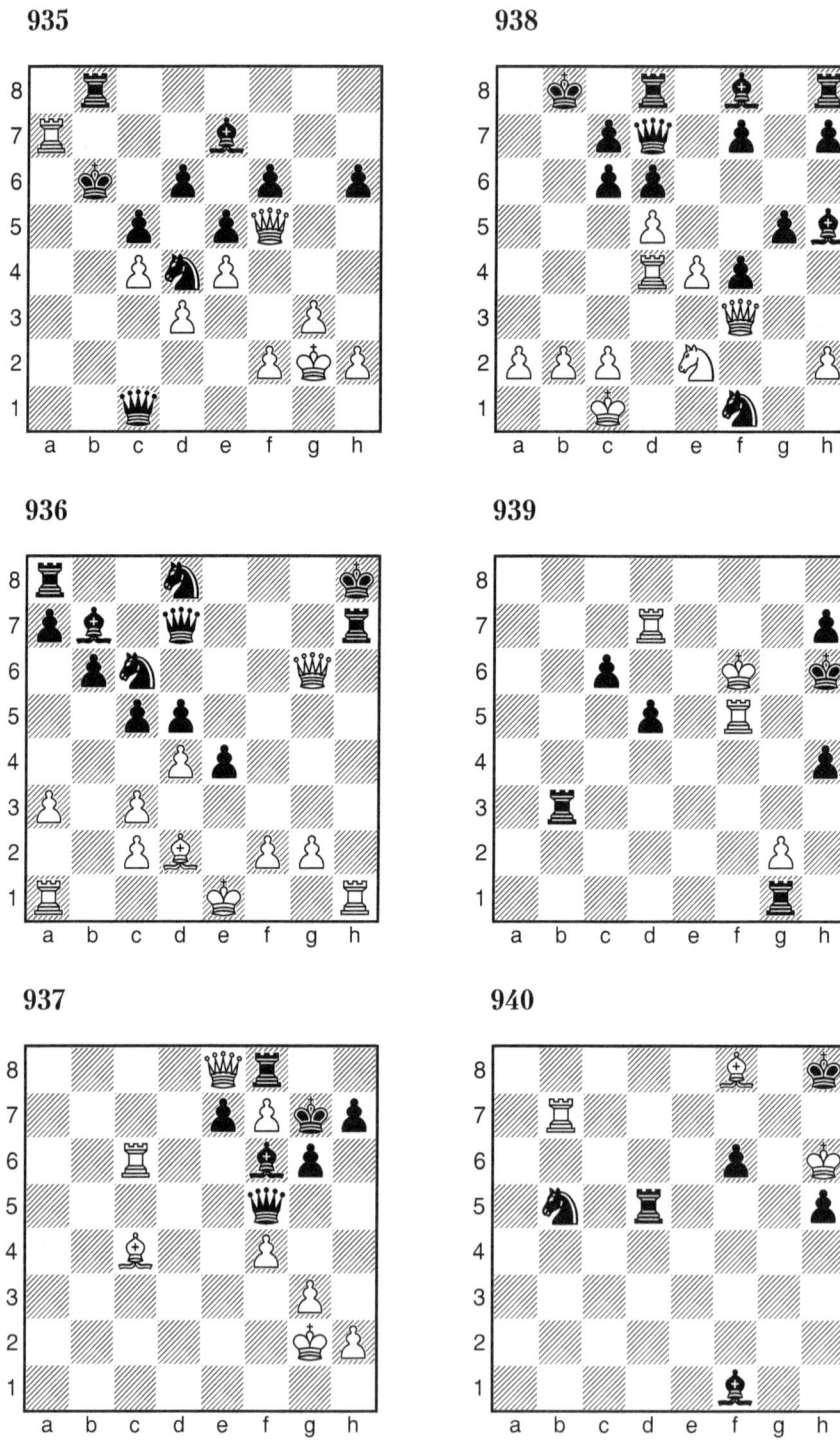

941

944

942

945

943

946

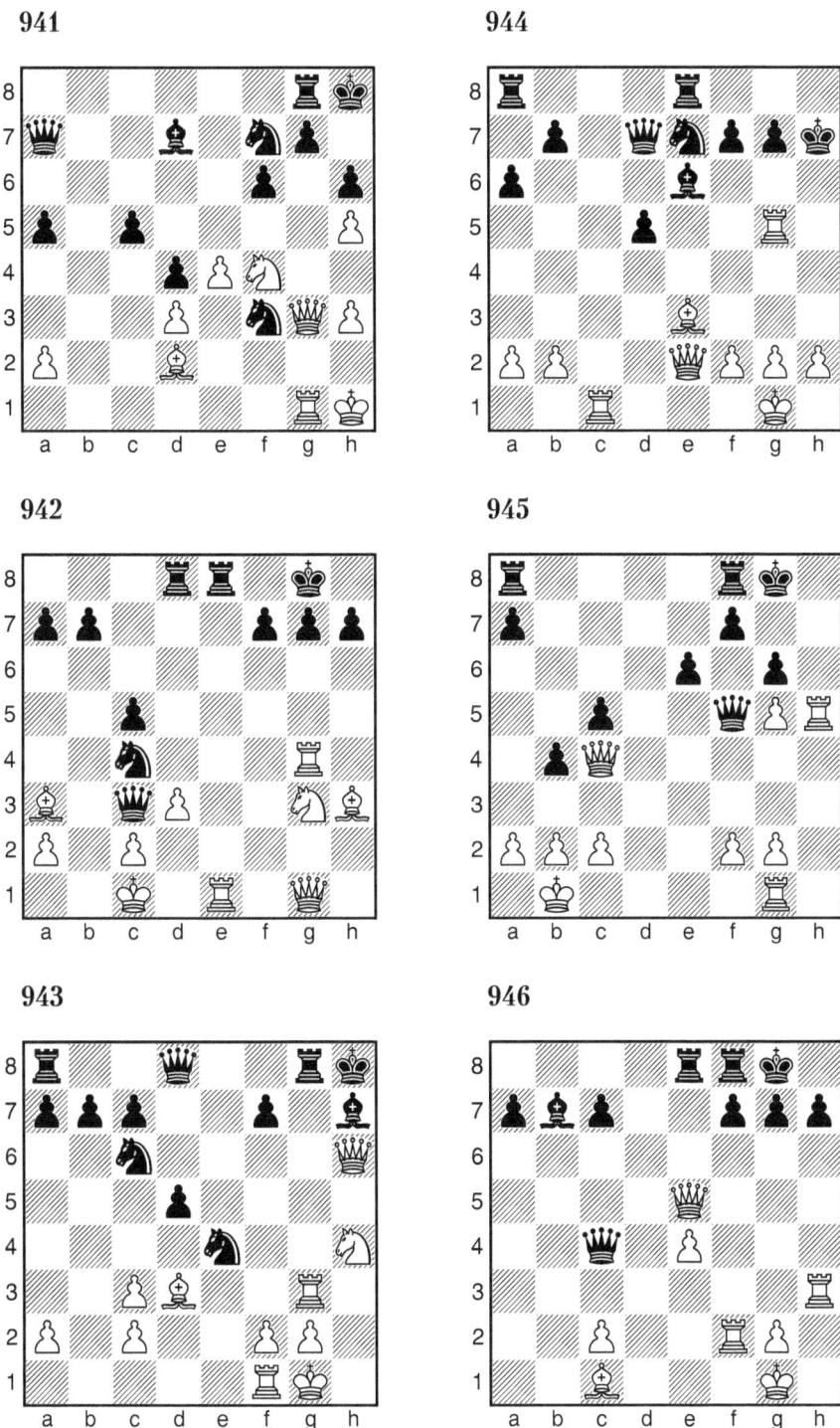

947

950

948

951

949

952

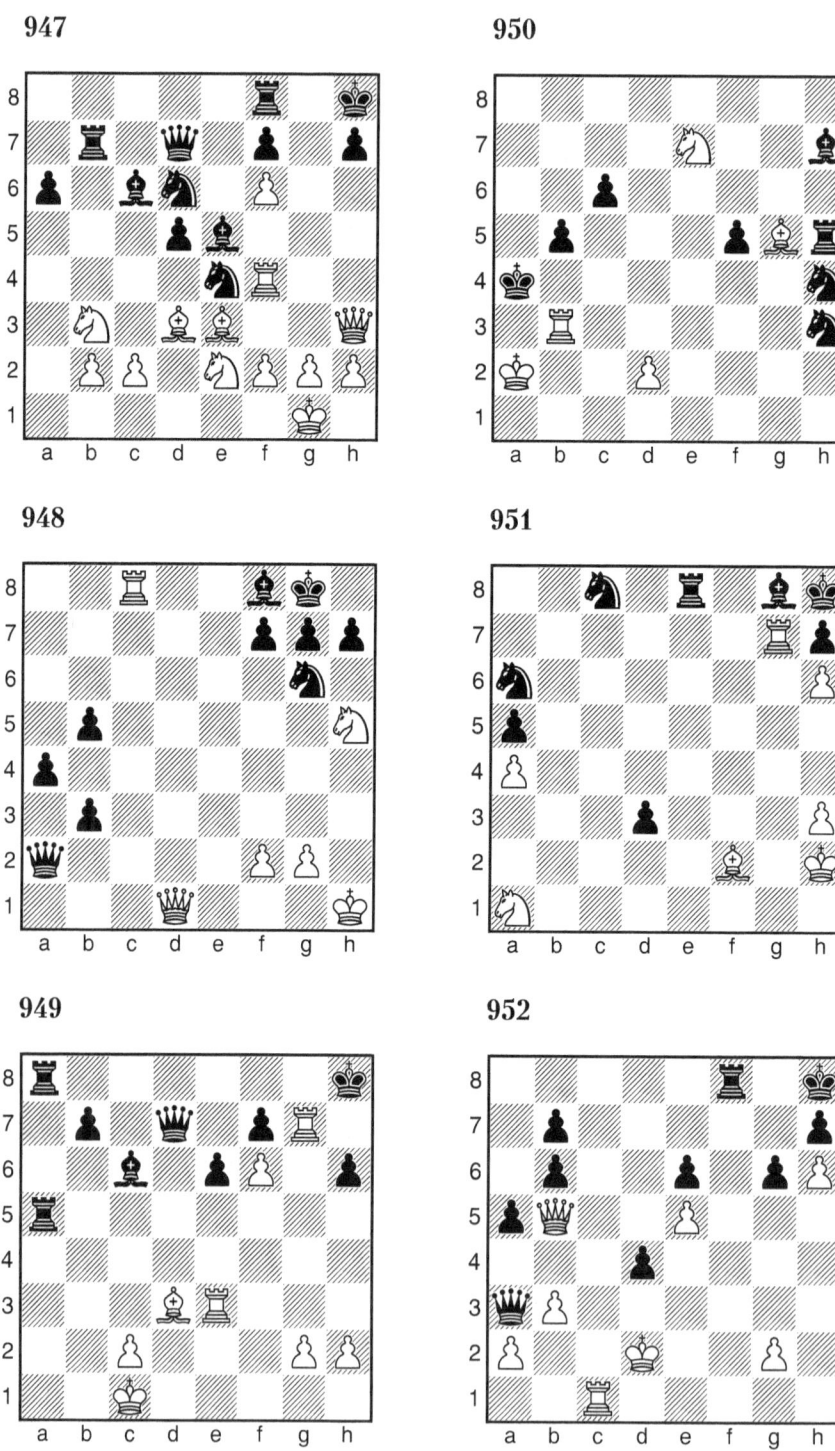

953

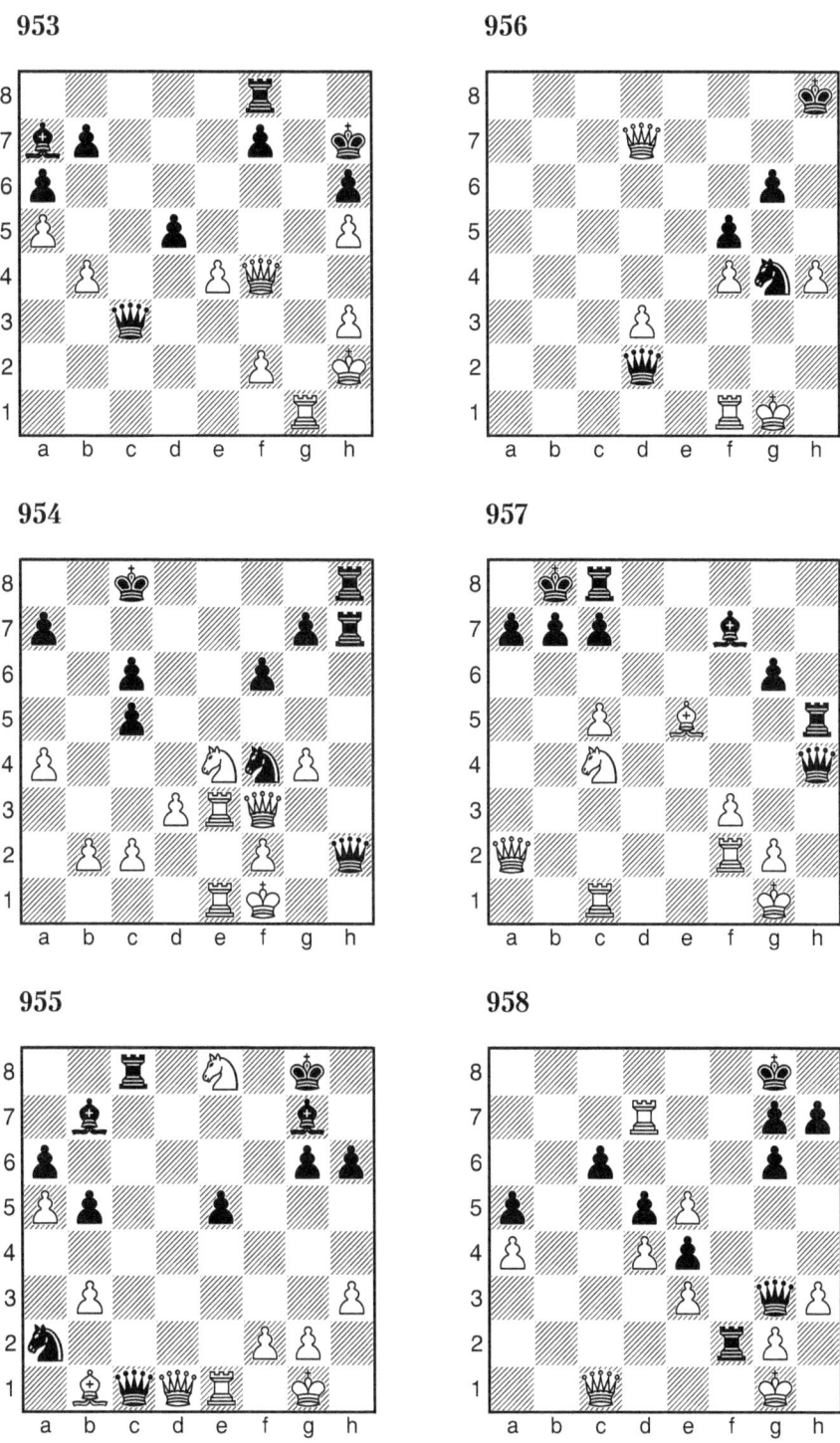

954

955

956

957

958

959

962

960

963

961

964

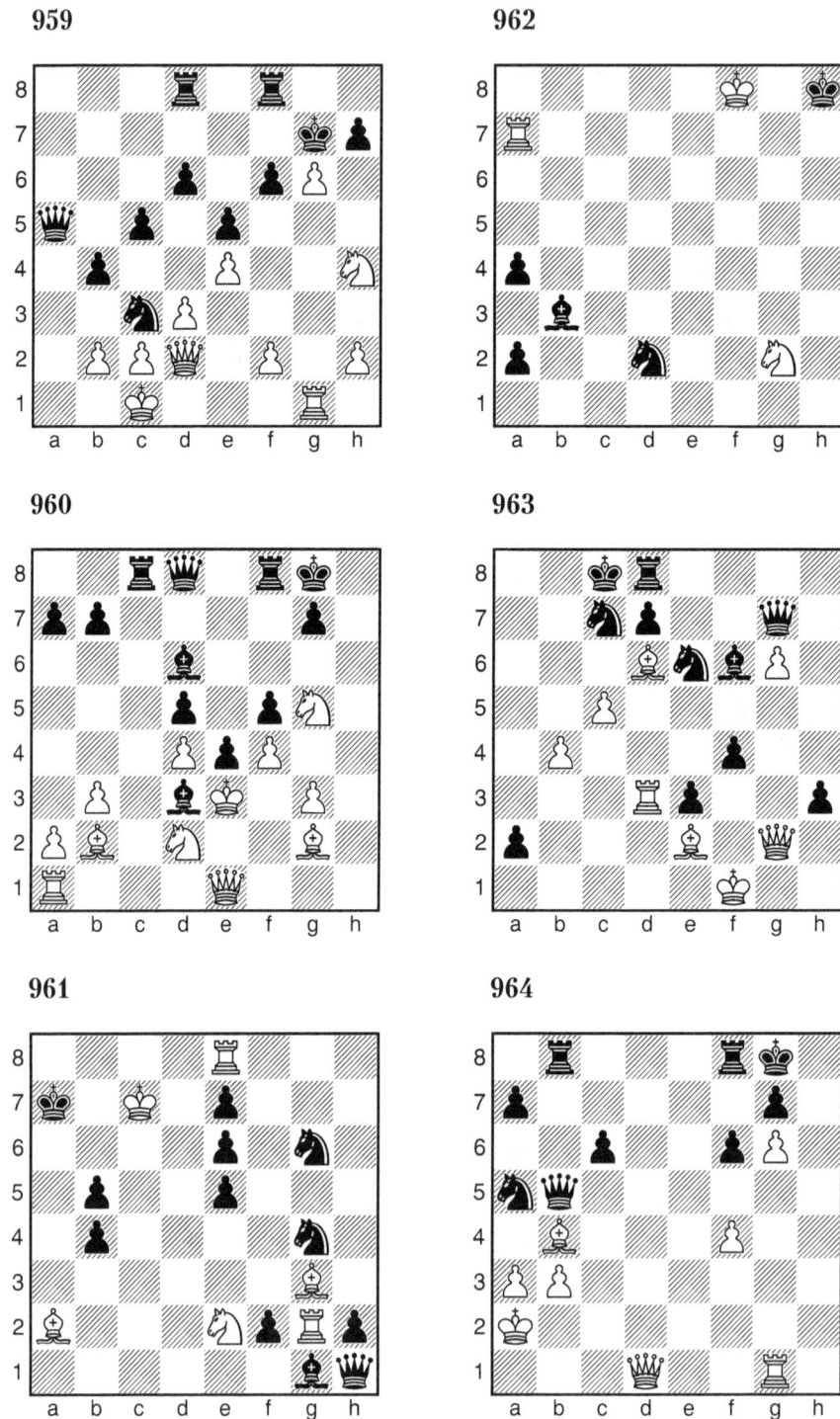

965

968

966

969

967

970

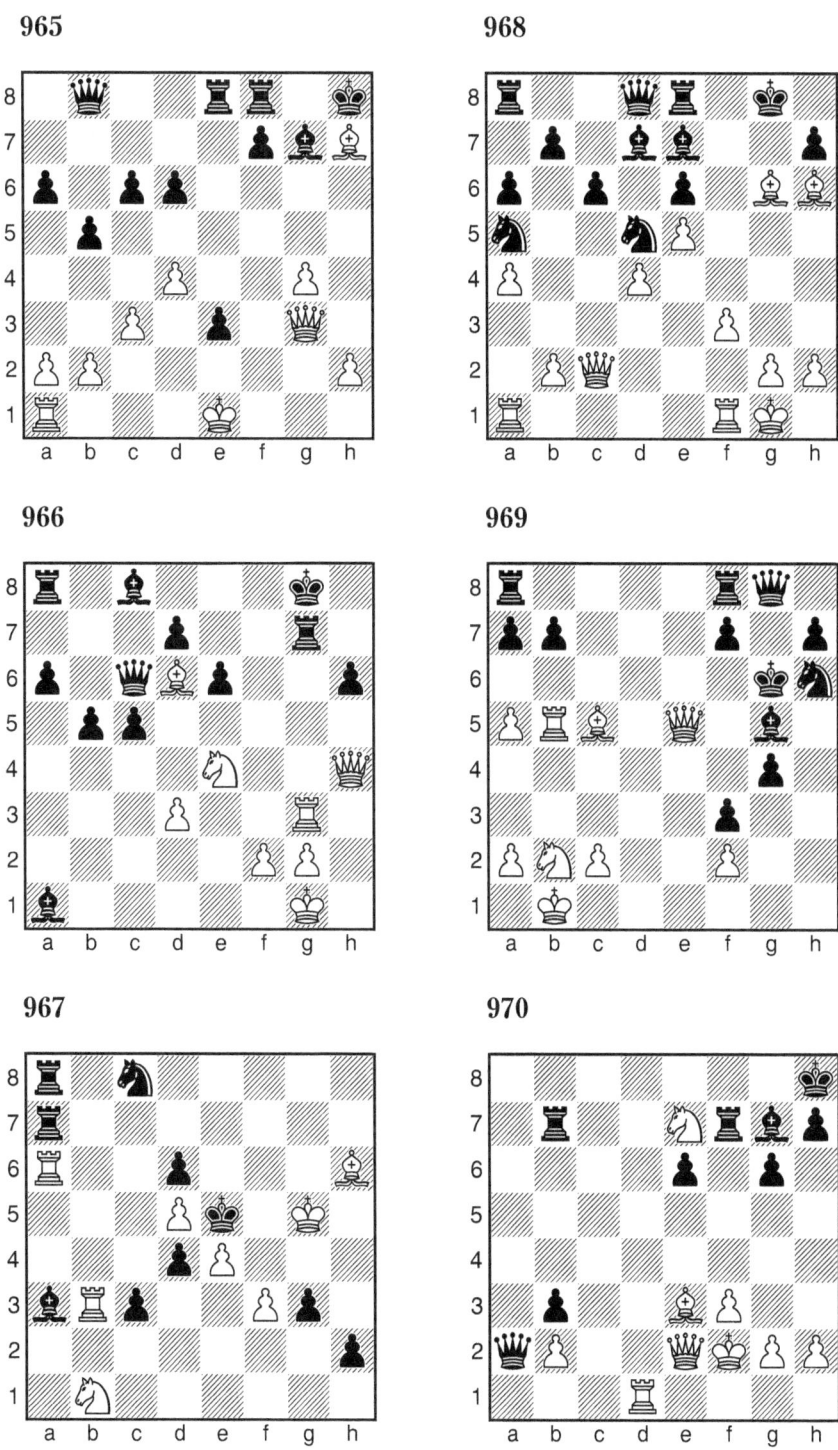

971

974

972

975

973

976

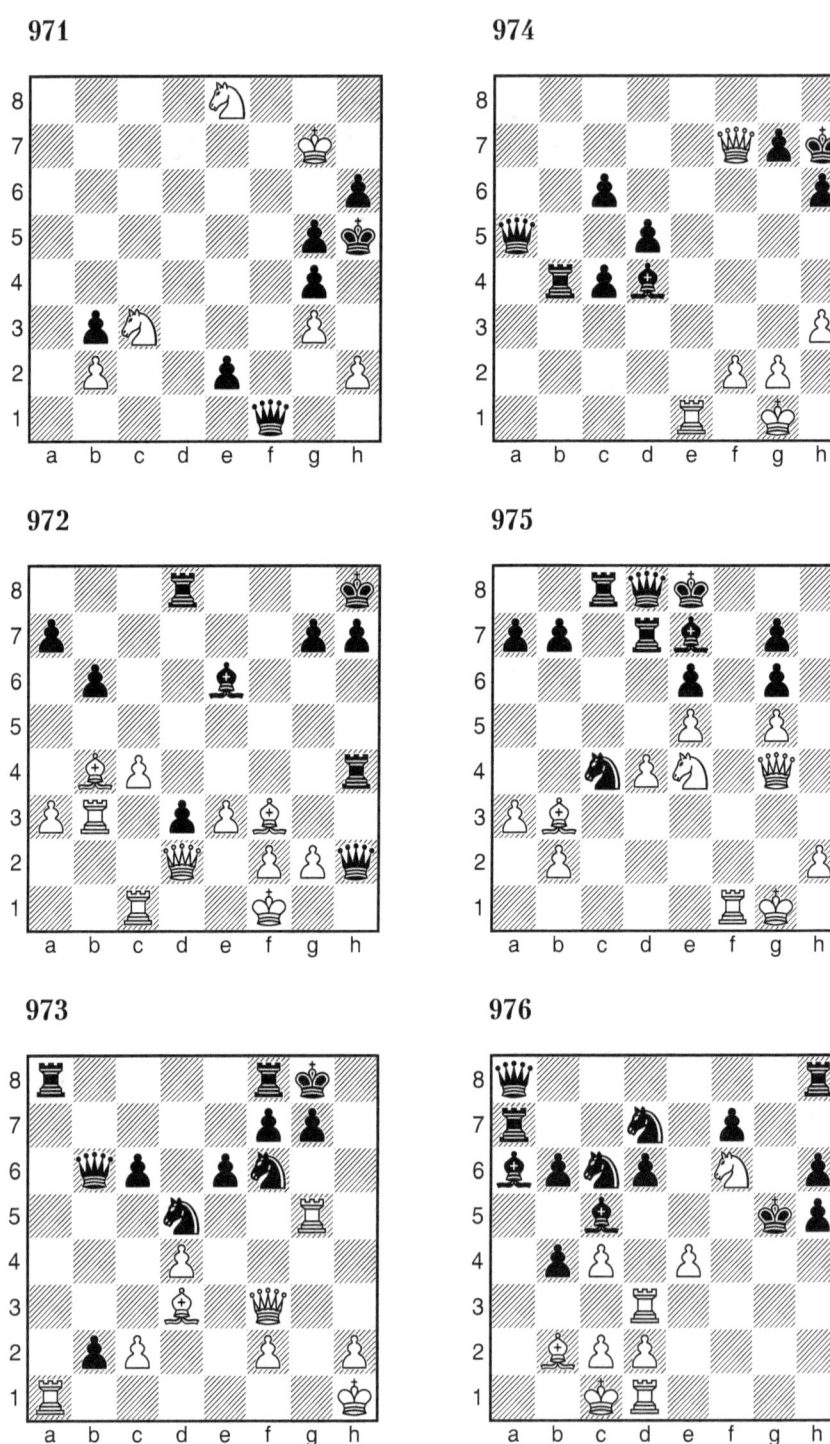

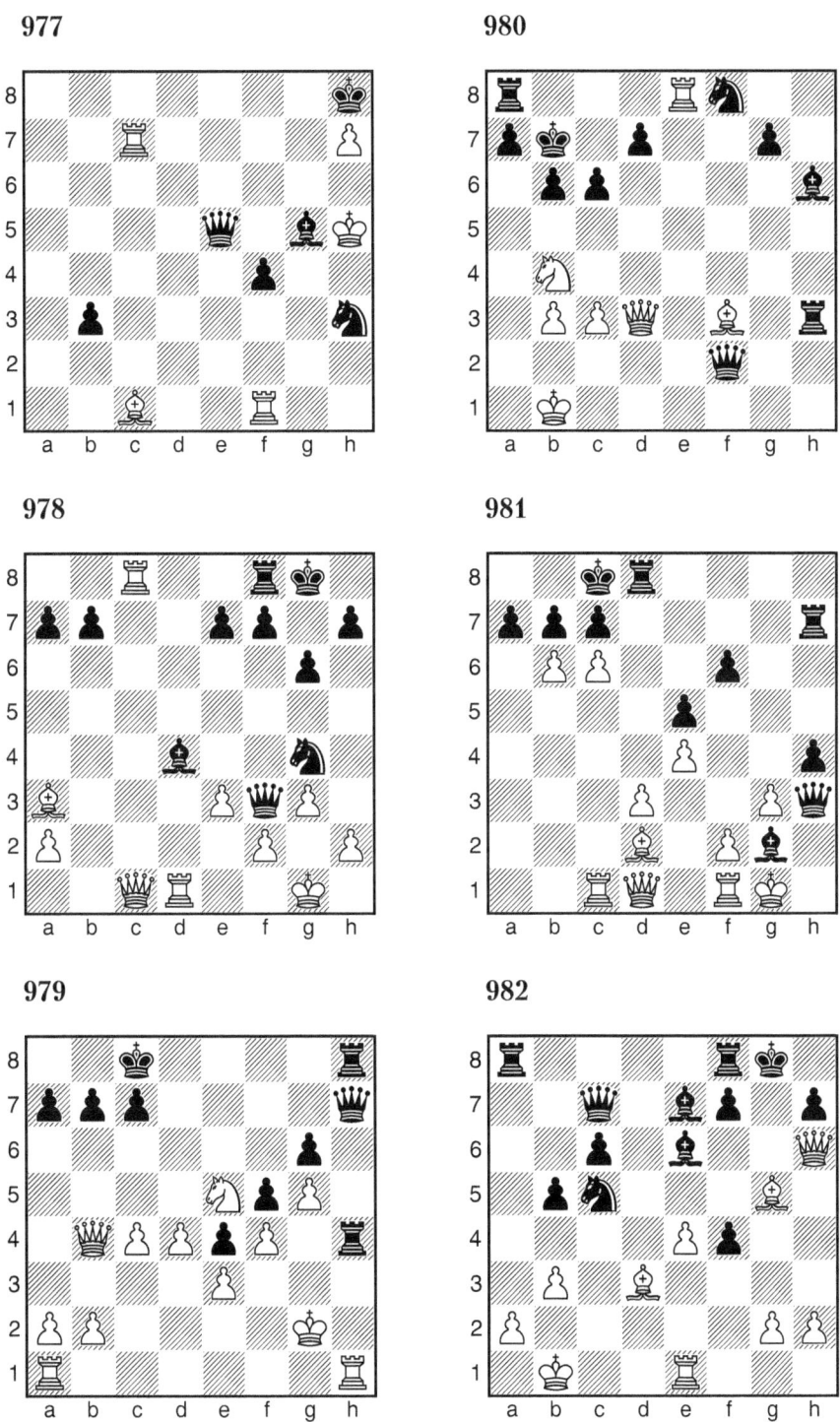

977

978

979

980

981

982

983

986

984

987

985

988

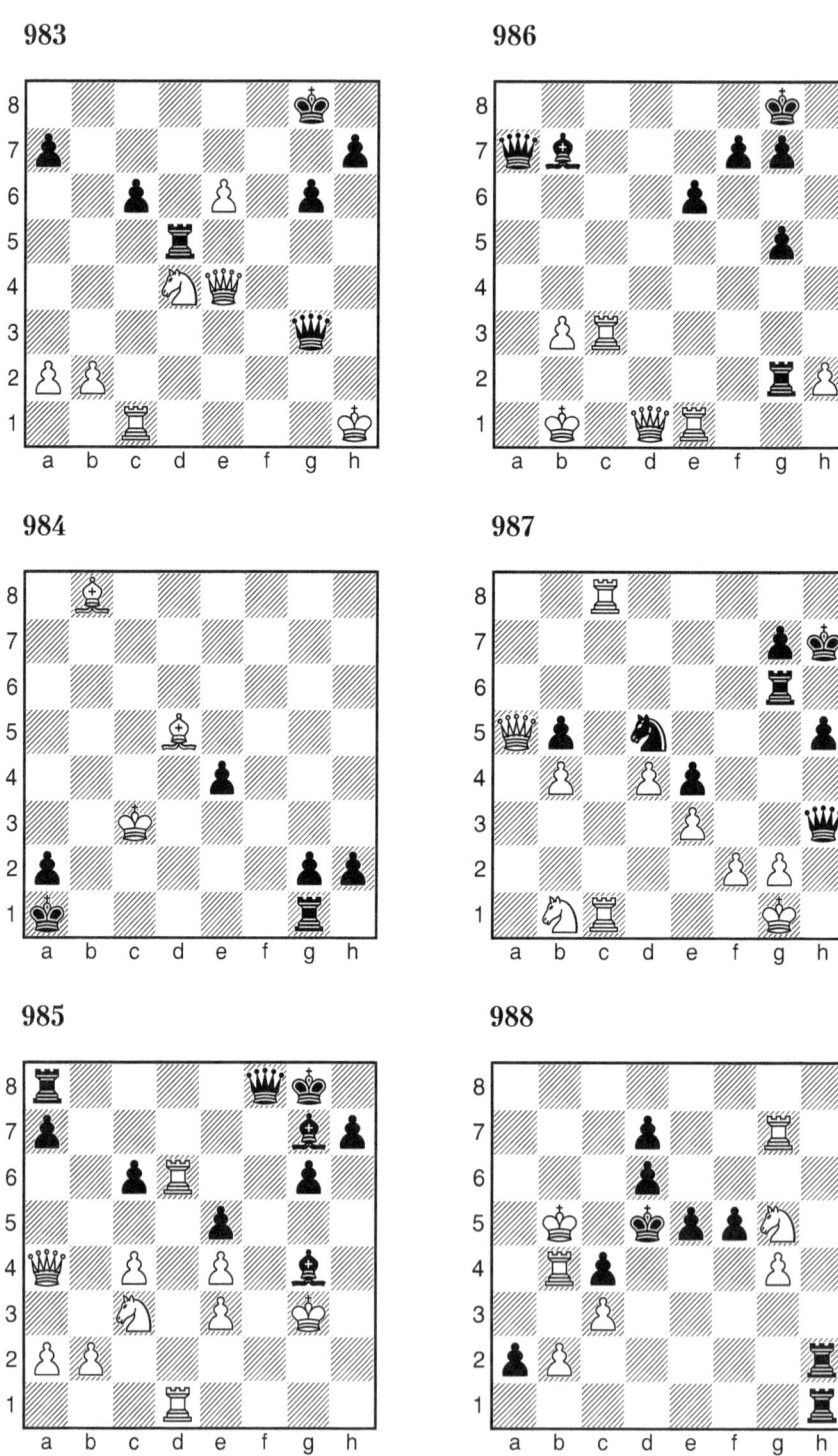

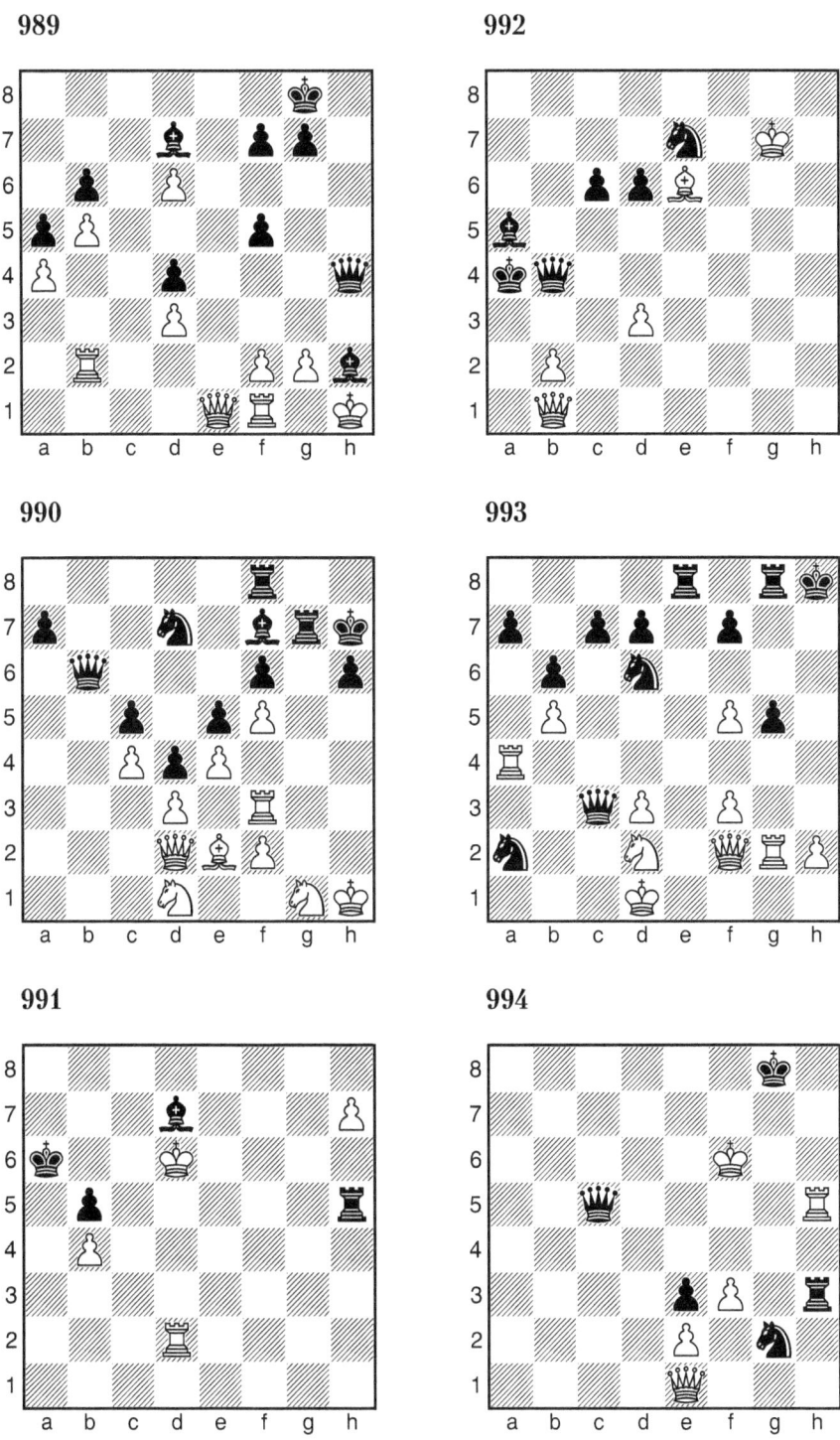

989

990

991

992

993

994

995

998

996

999

997

1000

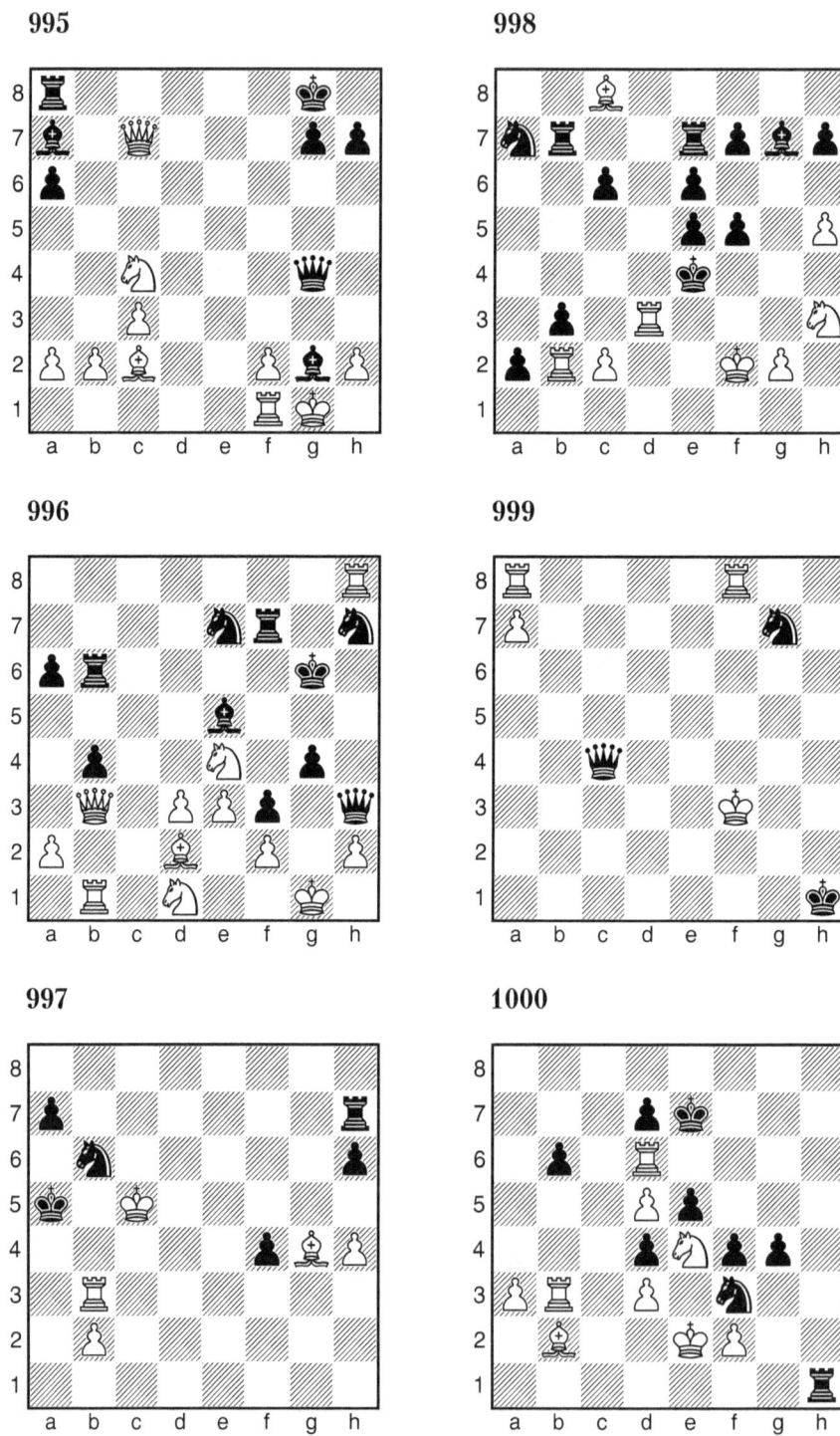

SOLUTIONS TO EXERCISES

Chapter 1

1 In total 2 threats. 1.♕d6! (1.♕e7? ♖xe7) 1...♖h8 2.♖a8#

2 In total 3 threats. 1.♗c1! (1.♗xf8? ♖xf8 2.♖g7+ ♔h8 3.♖7g6 ♗f7 4.♖xh6+ ♖h7 5.♖hg6; 1.♖g8? ♖xg8) 1...♗f7 2.♖xh6#

3 In total 2 threats. 1.♖xg4! (1.♖d7? ♖e4) 1...♖ed8 2.♖g8#

4 In total 2 threats. 1.♔g5! (1.♔f5? ♗xe4+) 1...♗xe4 2.♖f8#

5 In total 2 threats. 1.f5 (1.♔f5? g6+) 1...♖cxh2 2.♖c7#

6 In total 2 threats. 1.♘e8 (1.♘f5? ♗xf5) 1...♕xb4 2.♖xg7#

7 In total 2 threats. 1.♔f8 (1.♔f7? ♗c4+) 1...♗c4 2.♕xg7#

8 In total 2 threats. 1.♕h5 (1.♕h4? ♗xh4) 1...♖f6 2.♕h7#

9 In total 2 threats. 1.♘f6 (1.♖g7? ♔xg7) 1...♕e7 2.♖xh7#

10 In total 2 threats. 1.♖a7 (1.♗d7? ♗xd7+) 1...♗d5 2.♖a8#

11 In total 2 threats. 1.♖bf7 (1.e5? dxe5) 1...♕a6 2.♖3f6#

12 In total 3 threats. 1.♕b3 (1.♕e8? ♗xe8; 1.♕e6? ♗xe6) 1...♖g1 2.♕e3#

13 In total 3 threats. 1.♘g5 (1.♘f6? gxf6; 1.♘c5? bxc5) 1...♖e8 2.♘h7#

14 In total 5 threats. 1.♕d6 (1.♕g3? g6; 1.♕g4? g6; 1.♕g5? fxg5; 1.♕h6? gxh6) 1...♘f3 2.♕f8#

15 In total 7 threats. 1.♔f7 (1.♔f5? ♖f1+; 1.♖e4? ♖xh6+; 1.♖d4? ♖xh6+; 1.♖c4? ♖xh6+; 1.♖b4? ♖xh6+; 1.♖a4? ♖xh6+) 1...♖xh6 2.♖g8#

Chapter 2

16 1.a3 ♘f5 (1...a4 2.b4#) 2.b4+ axb4+ 3.axb4#

17 1.♖ge1 ♖xd4 (1...♖xd3 2.♖e8+ ♗xe8 3.♖xe8#; 1...♗b7 2.♖e8#) 2.♖e8+ ♗xe8 3.♖xe8#

18 1.♖g5 ♕c1 2.♖h5+ ♔xh5 3.♕xg5#

19 1.♘e5 ♖h2 2.f3+ gxf3 3.gxf3#

20 1.♔f3 ♖a3 (1...h4 2.g4#) 2.g4+ hxg4+ 3.hxg4#

21 1.h5 ♘b2 (1...♗e7 2.♘de3#) 2.♘ce3+ (2.♘de3+ ♗xe3 3.♘xe3#) 2...♗xe3 3.♘xe3#

22 1.♖xd2 c5 (1...♗b7 2.♖e2#) 2.♖e2+ ♗xe2 3.♖xe2#

23 1.♖dg3 ♕xc2 (1...h7 2.♖g8#) 2.♖g8+ ♖xg8 3.♖xg8#

24 1.♕e1 ♖xc2 (1...♗c4 2.♖e8#) 2.♖e8+ ♕xe8 3.♕xe8#

25 1.♖xc7 e1=♕ (1...♗f8 2.♖c8#) 2.♖c8+ ♔h7 3.♖h8#

26 1.♖xf7 g1=♕ 2.♖f8+ ♔e7 3.♖e8#

27 1.♘b3 ♖b6 (1...♗f4 2.♖a1#) 2.♖a1+ (2.♘c1+ ♔a1 3.♘b3+ ♔a2) 2...♗xa1 3.♘c1#

28 1.♖c4 ♕xg2 (1...♖b7 2.♕xb7#) 2.♕xa7+ ♔xa7 3.♖a4#

29 1.♖e8 c1=♕ 2.♖xf8+ ♔xf8 3.♖h8#

30 (Based on the game Castaldi –
Szabo, 1947) 1.♔d6 ♕a4 (1...
♔b8 2.♖xd8#) 2.♖c7+ ♔b8
3.♖xd8#

Chapter 3

31 1.♖d8+ ♞e8 2.♖xe8#
32 1.♖e8+ ♔xe8=
33 1.♖xf3+−
34 1.♗f1+−
35 1.♖d8+ ♔h7 2.♘g5#
36 1.♘h6+ ♔g7 2.♘f5+ ♔g8
3.♘h6+=
37 1.♘c7+ ♗xc7=
38 1.fxg3+−
39 1.♕xh6+−
40 1.♖e4+−
41 1.♗b2+−
42 1.♖c6+−
43 1.♘f3 ♕h1+ 2.♘g1+−
44 1.♗d6+−
45 1.♔f1+−
46 1.f3+−

Chapter 4

47 1.♗f1= (1.♕h6+? ♔xh6−+;
1.♗xf3? ♘xf3+ 2.♔h1 ♕xh2#)
48 1.♖xe5+− (1.♖xh7+? ♔xh7−+;
1.♖g5? fxg5−+; 1.♗f3? ♕xg3+
2.♔h1 ♕h2#; 1.♗f1? ♕xg3+
2.♔h1 ♕h2#; 1.♗h1? ♕xg3#;
1.h4? ♗xg3+ 2.♔h3 ♗xd6−+)
49 (Based on the game Xiong –
Vidit, 2021) 1.♘f6+ (1.♖h8+?!
♔xh8 2.♕e8+ ♔h7 3.♘f6+
gxf6 4.♕f7+ ♔h8 5.♕f8+=;
1.♕xc2?! ♗xc2 2.♖b7 ♗e4
3.♘f6+=; 1.♖e2? ♖c1+ 2.♔f2
♖f1#) 1...gxf6 (1...♔g6 2.♕e8+
♔xf6 3.♖b6#) 2.♖b7+ ♔g6 (2...

♔g8 3.♕e8#; 2...♔h8 3.♕e8#)
3.♕e8#

50 1.♖xh3 (1.♖d8+?! ♔b7 2.♖d7+
♔b8 (2...♔b6 3.♖c6#; 2...♔a8
3.♖c8#) 3.♖d8+ ♔b7 4.♖d7+=;
1.♖c8+? ♔xc8−+) 1...♖f2+
(1...♖a2 2.♖xh2+−; 1...♖xh3
2.♔xg2+−) 2.♔e1 ♖e2+ 3.♔d1
♖d2+ 4.♔c1+−
51 1.♕e8# (1.♕xf3?!=)
52 1.♗xh3+− (1.♕xf3?! ♕xd7=;
1.♕f1?! ♕xd7=)
53 1.♔h2+− (1.♖d5?! ♗xd5 2.cxd5
♕xd5=)
54 1.♖xc3+− (1.♖g8+?! ♔xg8=)
55 1.♗c1+− (1.♖h8+?! ♔g6
2.♖g8+ ♔h5 3.♖h8+ ♔g5
4.♖g8+=)
56 1.♘d6!+− (1.♕e8+?! ♔h7
2.♕h5+ ♔g8 3.♕e8+=; 1.♘e5?!
♗xe5 2.♕e8+ ♔h7 3.♕h5+=;
1.♔g1? ♗xh2+ 2.♔h1 ♗g3+
3.♔g1 ♕h2+ 4.♔f1 ♕xf2#)
57 1.♔h3+− (1.♔e1?!= ♕g1+
2.♔d2 ♕xd1+ 3.♔xd1 ♗xb3+=;
1.♘f3? ♕h1+ 2.♘g1 ♘h2+
3.♔e1 ♕xg1+ 4.♔d2 ♕xd1+
5.♔xd1 ♗xb3+−+)
58 1.♖f8+ (1.♘h6+?! ♕xh6
2.♖xh6 ♘xf6 3.bxa3=; 1.♖g7+?
♘xg7−+; 1.♖h8+? ♔xh8−+;
1.♘e7+? ♖xe7−+) 1...♔xf8 (1...
♖xf8 2.♘e7#) 2.♖h8#
59 1.♘f3+− (1.♖xf2+?! ♘xf2+=;
1.♕h3?! ♕d5+ 2.♔g1 ♕g5+
3.♔h1 ♕d5+ 4.♔g1=) 1...
♖xh2+? 2.♘xh2+
60 1.♕xh7+ (1.♖g8+?! ♖xg8
2.♖xg8+ ♔xg8 3.♕d8+ ♕f8 (3...
♔g7 4.♕g5+ ♔f8 5.♕d8+ ♔g7

6.♕g5+=) 4.♕g5+ ♔h8 (4...♕g7 5.♕d8+ ♕f8 6.♕g5+=) 5.♕f6+ ♕g7 (5...♔g8 6.♕g5+=) 6.♕d8+ ♕g8 7.♕f6+ ♕g7= 8.♕d8+) 1... ♔xh7 2.♖h3+ ♕h4 3.♖xh4#

61 1.♘d6+ (1.♘xd2?! ♖xd2=) 1...♔g6 2.♖e6+ ♔h7 3.g6+ ♔g8 (3...♔h8 4.♖e8#; 3...♔h6 4.♘f7#) 4.♖e8#

62 1.♗xh7+ (1.♖f3? g6−+; 1.♘f3?!=; 1.♘e4? ♘xe4−+; 1.♗e4? ♘xe4−+; 1.♔f2? ♖e8−+) 1...♔h8 2.♗xg7+! (2.♘f3?! ♘xb3 3.♗c3 ♗c5+ 4.♔g2 ♘d4 5.♗xd4 ♗xd4∓) 2...♔xg7 3.♖xf7+! ♖xf7 (3... ♔h8 4.♕a1+ ♗f6 5.♕xf6#; 3... ♔h6 4.♕g6#; 3...♔xf7 4.♕g6#) 4.♕g6+ ♔f8 5.♕g8#

Chapter 5

63 1.♕c6+ bxc6 2.♖b8#

64 1.♕g7+ ♗xg7 2.♖a8+ ♕e8 (2... ♗f8 3.♖xf8#; 2...♕b8 3.♖xb8+ ♗f8 4.♖xf8#) 3.♖xe8+ ♗f8 4.♖xf8#

65 1.♕f8+ ♖g8 2.♖xh7+ ♔xh7 3.♕h6#

66 1.♕e7+ (1.♕f8+?! ♔g5=; 1.♖g1?!=) 1...♔e5 2.♕g7+ (2.♕c7+ ♔f6 3.♕e7+ ♔e5) 2... ♔d6 3.♕c7#

67 1.♕g4+ ♗xg4 2.♖xh6+ gxh6 3.♗f7#

68 1.♕xg7+ ♔xg7 2.♗f6+ ♔f8 (2... ♔g6 3.♗f7#) 3.♘h7#

69 1.g4+ fxg3 (1...♔e5 2.♕d5#) 2.♕g4+ ♔e5 3.♕e4#

70 1.♘f4+ ♔f5 2.♖d5+ ♔e4 3.f3+ ♔e3 4.♖d3#

71 1.♘f6+ gxf6 (1...♔h8 2.♖xf8#) 2.♖g7+ ♔h8 3.♖h7+ ♔g8 4.♖cg7#

72 1.♘g6+ ♔h7 (1...♘xg6 2.♖xh6+ gxh6 3.♕xh6#) 2.♘xf8+ (2.♖xh6+?! gxh6 3.♘xf8+ ♔g7 4.♘e6+=) 2...♔h8 3.♖xh6+ gxh6 4.♕xh6#

73 1.♖c7+ ♔a8 (1...♖b7 2.♖bxb7+ ♔a8 3.♖c8#) 2.♖a7+ ♔xa7 3.♘c6+ ♔a8 4.♖xb8#

74 (Based on the game Bergamasco – Mazi, 2016) 1.♕d8+ ♔d6 2.c5+ ♔xc5 (2...bxc5 3.♖a6#; 2...♗xc5 3.♕b8+ ♔e7 4.♕xe5+ ♗e6 5.♕xe6#) 3.♕c7+ ♗c6 (3... ♔d4 4.♕c4#) 4.♕xc6+ ♔d4 5.♕c4#

75 1.♕f7+ ♔d8 2.♕f6+ ♔e8 (2... ♔c7 3.♘b5+) 3.♗f7+ ♔f8 4.♗xg6+ ♔g8 5.♕f7#

76 1.♕xf5+ ♔e7 (1...♔e8 2.♕f8#; 1...♔g8 2.♕f8#) 2.♖d7+ ♔xd7 (2...♔e8 3.♘xg7#) 3.♘c5+ ♔e7 (3...♔e8 4.♕e6+ ♔f8 5.♘d7#; 3...♔d6 4.♕f8#; 3...♔d8 4.♕d7#) 4.♕e6+ ♔f8 (4...♔d8 5.♕d7#) 5.♘d7#

Chapter 6

77 1.♕f7+ ♔h8 2.♕f8+ ♔h7 3.♕f7+=

78 1.♖f7+ ♔h8 2.♖f8+ ♔g7 3.♖f7+ ♔h8 4.♖f8+ ♔h7 5.♖f7+=

79 1.♕e8+ ♔h7 2.♕h5+ ♔g8 3.♕e8+=

80 1.♕f6+ ♔f8 2.♕d8+ ♔g7=

81 1.♕f8+ ♔h7 2.♕f7+ ♔h8 3.♕f8+ ♔h7 4.♕f7+=

82 1.♕d8+ ♗g8 2.♕h4+ ♗h7

3.Qd8+=

83 1.Qc3+ Rg7 2.Qc8+ Rg8 3.Qc3+=

84 1.Rg8+ Kh7 2.Rg7+ Kh8 3.Rg8+=

85 1.Bf1+ Kg4 2.Be2+ Kh3 3.Bf1+=

86 1.Bd5+ Kh7 2.Be4+ Kg8 3.Bd5+=

87 1.Qe5+ Rgg7 (1...Rhg7 2.Qh5+ Rh7 3.Qe5+=) 2.Qe8+ Rg8 3.Qe5+=

88 1.Nh7+ Kg8 (1...Ke8 2.Nf6+ Kf8 3.Nh7+=) 2.Nf6+ Kf8 3.Nh7+=

89 1.Ra4+ Kb1 (1...Kb2 2.Rb4+ Ka2 3.Ra4+=; 1...Kb3 2.Rb4+ Ka2 3.Ra4+=) 2.Rb4+ Ka2 3.Ra4+=

90 (Based on a position by Kamari, 1955) 1.Nh5+ Kf5 2.Ng7+ Kf6 (2...Kf4 3.Nh5+=) 3.Ne8+ (or 3.Nh5+ Ke6 (3...Kf5 4.Ng7+=) 4.Ng7+=) 3...Ke6 (3...Kf5 4.Ng7+=) 4.Ng7+ Kd6 (4...Kf6 5.Ne8+=) 5.Ne8+ Ke6 6.Ng7+=

Chapter 7

91 1.Rg8+ Kxg8=

92 1.Rg8+ Rxg8 2.Qxg8+ Kxg8=

93 1.Nf7+ Rxf7=

94 1.Nf7+ Rxf7 2.Qxh7+ Kxh7 3.Rh6+ Nxh6= (3...gxh6=; 3...Kxh6=)

95 1.Bxg7+ Rxg7= (1...Kxg7=)

96 1.Qxh7+ Kxh7=

97 1.Rd8+ (1.Qf8+? Kxf8 2.Rd8+ Ke7-+) 1...Rxd8 2.Qf8+ Kxf8= (2...Rxf8=)

98 1.Nf7+ (1.Ng6+? Qxg6-+) 1... Bxf7 2.Qxg7+ Kxg7=

99 1.Nf7+ (1.Ng6+? hxg6 2.Bxg7+ Kh7-+; 1.Bxg7+? Kxg7-+) 1...Nxf7 2.Bxg7+ Kxg7= (2... Rxg7=)

100 1.Qxg8+ Kxg8 2.Rf8+ Bxf8 3.Rxf8+ Kxf8=

101 1.Qh4+ Qxh4=

102 (Based on the game Fichtl – Blatny, 1956) 1.Bc3+ (1.Rg8+? Kxg8-+) 1...Qxc3 2.Rg8+ Kxg8=

103 1.Ng6+ (1.Rxh7+? Kxh7-+) 1...Rxg6 2.Rxh7+ Kxh7=

104 1.Rxh7+ Kxh7 2.Qh2+ Qxh2=

105 1.Ng6+ Rxg6 2.Rxh7+ Kxh7 3.Qxg7+ Kxg7= (3...R8xg7=; 3...R6xg7=)

106 1.Nf7+ Bxf7 2.Rxh7+ Kxh7 3.Rh5+ gxh5 4.Qh6+ gxh6= (4... Kxh6=)

Chapter 8

107 (Based on the game Stojanovsky – Guzel, 1958) 1.Qxh7+ Kxh7 2.Ng5+ Kh8 (2...Kh6 3.Nxf7+ Kh7 4.Ng5+ Kh6 (4...Kh8 5.Nf7+=) 5.Nf7+=) 3.Nxf7+ Kh7 4.Ng5+ Kh8 (4...Kh6 5.Nf7+=) 5.Nf7+=

108 1.Rb2+ (1.Ra1+? Kb3-+) 1...Ka3 (1...Ka1 2.Rb1+ Ka2 (2...Kxb1=) 3.Rb2+=; 1...Kxb2=) 2.Rb3+ (2.Ra2+? Kb4-+) 2...Ka4 (2...Ka2 3.Rb2+=; 2...Kxb3=) 3.Rb4+ (3.Ra3+? Kb4-+) 3...Kxa5 (3...Ka3 4.Rb3+=; 3...Kxb4=) 4.Rb5+

♔a4 (4...axb5=; 4...♔xb5=)
5.♖b4+ ♔a3 (5...♔a5 6.♖b5+=;
5...♔xb4=) 6.♖b3+ ♔a2 (6...
♔a4 7.♖b4+=; 6...♔xb3=)
7.♖b2+ ♔a1 (7...♔a3 8.♖b3+=;
7...♔xb2) 8.♖b1+ ♔a2 (8...
♔xb1=) 9.♖b2+=

109 (Based on the game Neimann
– NN, 1956) 1.♖e8+ ♘xe8 (1...
♘g8? 2.♖xg8#) 2.♕h7+ ♔xh7
3.♘f8+ ♔h8 4.♘g6+ ♔h7
5.♘f8+=

110 (Based on the game McNab –
Groszpeter, 1992) 1.♘f6+ ♔f7
(1...♔g7 2.♕xe7+ ♗xe7=; 1...
exf6 2.♕xf8+ ♔h7 (2...♔xf8=)
3.♕h8+ ♔xh8=; 1...♔h8?
2.♕xf8+ ♕g8 3.♕xg8#) 2.♕e8+
♔g7 (2...♔xf6? 3.♕xf8#)
3.♕xe7+ ♗xe7= (3...♔h8?
4.♕h7#; 3...♔h6? 4.♕h7#)

111 1.♘f7+ ♔g8 2.♘h6+ ♔h8 (2...
gxh6? 3.♖g3+ ♔h8 4.♕g7#)
3.♘f7+=

112 1.♖g7+ ♔h8 (1...♗xg7=)
2.♖g8+ ♔h7 3.♖g7+=

113 1.♖g1+ ♔h3 (1...♕xg1=)
2.♖h1+ ♔g3 (2...♔g2 3.♖g1+
♔h3 (3...♕xg1=) 4.♖h1+=)
3.♖g1+ ♔h3 (3...♕xg1=)
4.♖h1+=

114 1.♘h6+ gxh6 (1...♔h7? 2.♘f5+
♔g8 3.♘e7#; 1...♔h8? 2.♘f5+
♔g8 3.♘e7#) 2.♕g6+ ♔h8
3.♕xh6+ ♔g8 4.♕g6+ ♔h8
5.♕h6+=

115 1.♖g7+ ♔f8 (1...♔h8 2.♖h7+
♔g8 3.♖g7+=) 2.♘e6+ ♔e8
3.♘c7+ ♔f8 4.♘e6+=

116 1.♕d8+ ♖xd8 (1...♕e8

2.♖xe8#) 2.♖e8+ ♖xe8 (2...
♕xe8 3.♗f8+ ♕xf8=) 3.♗f8+
♖xf8=

117 (Based on the game Perez-
Garcia – Zechevich, 1986)
1.♕xh7+ ♔xh7 2.♖h6+ ♔g8
3.♘e7+ ♔g7 4.♘f5+ ♔g8
5.♘e7+=

118 1.♕d8+ ♔g7 2.h6+ (2.♕f6+?
♔h6–+) 2...♔xh6 3.♕h4+ ♔g7
4.♕f6+ ♔g8 (4...♔h6 5.♕h4+=;
4...♔f8 5.♕d8+ ♔g7 6.♕f6+=)
5.♕d8+ ♔g7 6.♕f6+=

119 (Based on the game Gonzales –
Martinez, 1991) 1.♗h6+ ♔xh6
(1...♔g6 2.♕g8+ ♔xh6 (2...♔h5
3.♕f7+ ♔xh6 4.♕xf6+ ♔h5
5.♕f7+=) 3.♕f8+ ♔g6 (3...♔g5
4.♕g7+=; 3...♔h5 4.♕f7+=)
4.♕g8+ ♔h6 5.♕f8+=; 1...♔h8?
2.♕xf6+ ♔g8 3.♕g7#) 2.♕xf6+
♔h5 3.♕f7+ ♔h6 (3...♔g5
4.♕g7+ ♔h5 5.♕f7+=) 4.♕f6+=

120 1.♕xg7+ ♔xg7 2.♖hg6+
(2.♖eg6+? ♔f7 3.♖f6+ ♔e7
4.♖e6+ ♔d7 5.♖d6+ ♔c7
6.♖c6+ ♔b7–+) 2...♔h8 (2...
♔h7? 3.♘xg5+ ♔h8 4.♖h6+
♔g8 (4...♔g7 5.♖eg6+ ♔f8
6.♖h8++–) 5.♖eg6+ ♔f8
6.♖h8+ ♔e7 7.♖h7+ ♔f8 (7...
♔e8 8.♖g8#) 8.♘e6+ ♔e8
9.♖g8#; 2...♔f7 3.♘xg5+
(3.♖gf6+=) 3...♔f8 4.♘h7+
♔f7 5.♘g5+=; 2...♔f8
3.♖gf6+) 3.♖h6+ ♔g8 (3...♔g7
4.♖hg6+=) 4.♖hg6+ ♔h7 (4...
♔h8 5.♖h6+=) 5.♖h6+ ♔g7
6.♖hg6+=

121 1.♖h8+ ♔xh8 2.♕c8+ ♔h7

3.♕f5+ g6 (3...♚g8 4.♕c8+ ♚h7
5.♕f5+=; 3...♚h8 4.♕c8+ ♚h7
5.♕f5+=) 4.♕xf7+ ♚h8 5.♕f8+
(5.♕e8+ ♚g7 6.♕e7+=) 5...♚h7
6.♕f7+= (6.♕e7+=)

122 (Based on the game Kasparian
– Chekhover, 1936) 1.♖xb7+
♚a8 2.♖xa7+ ♚xa7 (2...
♚b8? 3.♕c7#) 3.♕b6+ ♚a8
4.♕a6+ ♚b8 5.♕d6+ (5.♕b6+?
♕b7–+) 5...♚c8 (5...♚a8
6.♕a6+=; 5...♚a7 6.♕b6+ ♚a8
7.♕a6+=) 6.♕e6+ (6.♕a6+?
♕b7–+) 6...♚c7 (6...♚b8
7.♕d6+=; 6...♚b7 7.♕b6+; 6...
♚d8 7.♕d6+ ♚e8 (7...♚c8
8.♕e6+=) 8.♕e6+ ♚f8 9.♕xf6+
♚e8 10.♕e6+ ♚d8 11.♕d6+=)
7.♕d6+ ♚b7 (7...♚c8 8.♕e6+=)
8.♕b6+ ♚c8 (8...♚a8 9.♕a6+=)
9.♕e6+=

123 (Based on the game Kratkowski
– Lapschis, 1982) 1.♖xf8+ ♗xf8
2.♕g8+ ♗xg8 3.♘h6+ ♚h8
4.♘f7+ ♚g8 5.♘h6+=

124 (Based on a position by V.
Berezin) 1.♕a6+ bxa6 (1...♚b8?
2.♕xb7#) 2.♗xc6+ ♚a7 3.♖b7+
♚a8 4.♖b6+ (4.♖b5+ ♚a7
5.♖b7+=; 4.♖b4+ ♚a7 5.♖b7+=;
4.♖b3+ ♚a7 5.♖b7+=; 4.♖b2+
♚a7 5.♖b7+=; 4.♖b1+ ♚a7
5.♖b7+=; 4.♖xf7+? ♚b8–+) 4...
♚a7 5.♖b7+=

125 (Based on a position by Lolli)
1.♖f8+ ♚a7 (1...♕d8? 2.♖xd8+
♚a7 3.♕c5+ b6 (3...♚a6
4.♖a8#) 4.♕xc7+ ♚a6 5.♖a8#)
2.♕c5+ (2.♖a8+? ♚xa8 3.♕f8+
♚a7 4.♕c5+ ♚a6–+) 2...

♕xc5 (2...♚a6? 3.♖a8#; 2...b6?
3.♕xc7+ ♚a6 4.♖a8#) 3.♖a8+
♚b6 (3...♚xa8=) 4.♖a6+ ♚xa6=
(4...bxa6=)

126 1.♘f7+ ♚g8 (1...♚g7? 2.♘g5+
♗xe7 (2...♚h6 3.♖h7#; 2...
♚h8 3.♖h7+ ♚g8 4.♕e6+ ♖f7
5.♕xf7#; 2...♚g8 3.♕e6+ ♚h8
4.♖h7#) 3.♕xe7+ ♖f7 (3...
♚h6 4.♕h7#; 3...♚h8 4.♕h7#)
4.♕xf7+ ♚h8 (4...♚h6 5.♕h7#)
5.♕h7#; 1...♚h7? 2.♘g5+ ♚g8
(2...♚h6 3.♖h7#; 2...♚h8 3.♖h7+
♚g8 4.♕e6+ ♖f7 5.♕xf7#)
3.♕e6+ ♖f7 (3...♚h8 4.♖h7#)
4.♕xf7+ ♚h8 5.♕h7#; 1...
♖xf7? 2.♖d8+ ♚g7 (2...♚h7
3.♖xf7+ ♗g7 4.♖xg7+ ♚xg7
5.♕e7+ ♚h6 6.♖h8#) 3.♖xf7+
♚xf7 4.♕e8+ ♚g7 5.♕f8+ ♚h7
6.♖d7+ ♗g7 (6...♗e7 7.♖xe7#)
7.♕xg7#) 2.♘h6+ ♚h8 3.♘f7+=

127 1.♕e8+ ♚h7 2.♖h4+ (2.♕e4+?
♚h6 3.♕f4+ ♚g6–+) 2...♕xh4
3.♕h5+ ♚g8 (3...♕xh5=)
4.♕e8+ ♚h7 5.♕h5+=

128 1.♕f8+ ♗xf8 2.♘h7+ ♚g8 (2...
♚e8 3.♘xf6+ ♚f8 4.♘h7+=)
3.♘xf6+ ♚f8 (3...♚h8 4.♖h7#)
4.♘h7+ ♚g8 (4...♚e8 5.♘f6+=)
5.♘f6+=

129 1.♖xg7+ ♕xg7 (1...♚xg7?
2.♕g5+ ♚h8 (2...♚f7 3.♕g6#)
3.♕h5+ ♚g7 (3...♚h6 4.♕xh6+
♚g8 5.♗h7+ ♚h8 6.♗g6+
♚g8 7.♕h7+ ♚f8 8.♕h8+
♗g8 9.♕h6#; 3...♚g8 4.♕h7#)
4.♕g6+ ♚h8 5.♕h7#) 2.♕e8+
♕f8 3.♕g6+ ♕g7 (3...♚h8?
4.♕h7#) 4.♕e8+=

130 (Moravec J, 1952) 1.Qc4+ Ka7 (1...Rxc4=; 1...Ka5? 2.Qb5#) 2.Qxc5+ Ka8 (2...Ka6? 3.Qb5+ Ka7 4.Qb7#; 2...Qb6+? 3.Qxb6+ Ka8 4.Qb7#; 2...Rb8? 3.Qb5+ Qb6+ (3...Ka8 4.Qb7#; 3...Ka7 4.Qb7#; 3...Kc8 4.Qb7#) 4.Qxb6+ Ka8 (4...Kc8 5.Qc7#) 5.Qb7#) 3.Qa5+ Qxa5= (3...Rb8? 4.Qb5+ Ka8 5.Qb7#)

131 (Based on the game Osmanagic – Gligoric, 1963) 1.Qxg6+ fxg6 (1...Bg7? 2.Qxg7#; 1...Kh8? 2.Rh3+ Bh6 3.Rxh6#) 2.f7+ Kh7 (2...Kh8? 3.Rh3+ Bh6 4.Rxh6#) 3.Rh3+ Bh6 4.Ng5+ Kg7 (4...Kh8? 5.Rxh6+ Kg7 6.Rh7+ Kf8 7.Ne6+ Ke7 8.f8=Q+ Kxe6 9.Rxe7#) 5.Ne6+ Kh7 (5...Kh8? 6.Rxh6#) 6.Ng5+ Kg7 7.Ne6+=

132 (Based on the game Byrne R – Evans, 1962) 1.Rxg6+ Kxg6 (1...Kh8? 2.Qg8#; 1...Kf8? 2.Qg8#) 2.Qg8+ Kf6 (2...Kh5? 3.Qf7#) 3.Qh8+ Ke6 (3...Kg6 4.Qg8+=; 3...Kf7 4.Qxh7+ Ke6 (4...Kf8 5.Qh8+ Kf7 6.Qh7+=; 4...Kf6 5.Qh8+ Ke6 6.Qg8+=; 4...Ke8? 5.Qg8#) 5.Qg8+ Kd6 6.Qb8+ Ke6 7.Qg8+=) 4.Qg8+ Kd6 (4...Kf6 5.Qh8+=) 5.Qb8+ Ke6 6.Qg8+=

133 1.Qg6+ (1.Rxh5+? Kg8-+) 1...Kxg6 (1...Kg8 2.Rf8+ Kxf8 3.Qf7+ (3.Qe8+=; 3.Qf6+=; 3.Qxg7+=) 3...Kxf7= (3...Rxf7=) ; 1...Kh8 2.Rf8#) 2.Rf6+ Kh7 (2...gxf6=; 2...Kxf6=) 3.Rh6+ Kg8 (3...gxh6=; 3...Kxh6=) 4.Rh8+ Kf7 (4...Kxh8=) 5.Rf8+ Kg6 (5...Kxf8=) 6.Rf6+=

134 (Based on the game Frolyanov – Nepomniachtchi, 2010) 1.Rc8+ (1.Qc8+? Kb6-+) 1...Kb6 (1...Kb7?! 2.Qd7+!? (2.Rb8+=; 2.Rc7+=; 2.Qxe7+=) 2...Rc7 (2...Kb6 3.Qxd6+; 2...Ka6 3.Qxd6+) 3.Rb8+!? (3.Qxc7+=; 3.Qb5+=; 3.Rxc7? Kb6-+) 3...Kxb8 (3...Ka7? 4.Qxc7+ Ka6 5.Rb6#; 3...Ka6? 4.Qb5+ Ka7 5.Qb6#) 4.Qxc7+ (4.Qd8+=; 4.Qe8+=; 4.Qc8+=) 4...Ka8 (4...Kxc7=) 5.Qa7+ Kxa7=) 2.Qxd6+! (2.Rc6+? Qxc6-+; 2.Rb8+? Qb7! 3.Rxb7+ Kxb7-+) 2...exd6 (2...Rc6 3.Rb8+ Ka6 4.Ra8+ Kb5 5.Rxa5+=; 2...Kb5 3.Rb8+ Kc4 4.Rb4+ axb4 5.Qd5+ Kxd5= (5...Kxd5=) ; 2...Kb7? 3.Rb8+ Ka7 4.Qb6#; 2...Ka7 3.Ra8+ Kxa8 (3...Qxa8 4.Qb6+ Kxb6=) 4.Qb8+ Kxb8=; 2...Rc6 3.Rb8+ Ka6 4.Ra8+ Kb5 5.Rxa5+=) 3.Rc6+ Kb5 (3...Ka7 4.Rc7+ Ka8 (4...Qb7 5.Rxb7+=) 5.Rc8+ Kb7 6.Rc7+ Kb6 7.Rc6+=; 3...Qxc6=; 3...Rxc6=; 3...Qxc6=; 3...Kb7 4.Rc7+ Kb8 5.Rc8+ Ka7 6.Rc7+=) 4.Rc5+ Kb4 (4...Kb6 5.Rc6+=; 4...Ka6 5.Rc6+=; 4...dxc5=; 4...Rxc5=; 4...Ka4 5.Rc4+ Ka3 (5...Rxc4=; 5...Kb5 6.Rc5+=) 6.Ra4+ Kxa4=) 5.Rc4+ Ka3 (5...Kb5 6.Rc5+=;

5...♖xc4=; 5...♔xc4=) 6.♖a4+ ♔xa4=

Chapter 9

135 1.♕xf3+−

136 1.♕xg3 ♕xg3=

137 1.♘xd6 (1.♕xe4? ♖h5#; 1.♘xa5? ♖h6+ 2.♕h5 ♖xh5#) 1...♖h5+ 2.♕xh5+−

138 1.♕xf3+− (1.cxd4 ♕c1#; 1.♕xc8 ♖d1#)

139 1.♕xg3 (1.♕xh6 ♖e1#; 1.♗xe2 ♕h2+ 2.♔f1 ♕h1#) 1...♖a2 2.♕xd3+−

140 1.♗xf3+− (1.♔xh2 ♖h8+ 2.♔g1 ♖h1#; 1.♗xa8 ♖h1#)

141 1.♗xe6 (1.♗xe7? ♖e1#; 1.h4? ♖e1+ 2.♔h2 ♕e2−+) 1...♕xe6 2.♕xe6 ♖xe6 3.a4!?+−

142 1.♗xa8 (1.♗xe5? ♖h8#; 1.♖xe5? ♖h8+ 2.♖h5 ♖xh5#) 1...♘xd5 2.♗xe5+−

143 1.♖xf4 (1.♘xb5? ♕h2#) 1...gxf4 2.♘xb5+−

144 1.♕xf3 (1.♕xc8 ♖d1#; 1.♘xd2 ♖c1#) 1...♘xf3 2.♘xd2+−

145 1.♕xb2 (1.♖xa7 ♖h2+ 2.♔g1 ♖ag2+ 3.♔f1 ♖h1#; 1.♕xa2 ♖xa2) 1...♖xb2 2.♖xa7+−

146 1.♕xb6 (1.♘xe4 ♖b1#) 1...axb6 2.♘xe4+−

147 1.♕xd1 (1.♗xc1 ♖h1#) 1...♖xd1 2.♗xf2+−

148 1.♖xe4 (1.fxe4 ♗xh3+ 2.♔h1 ♕b1+; 1.♖xa3 ♕xf2+ 2.♔h1 ♘g3#) 1...♗xe4 (1...♖xa6 2.♖xh4++−) 2.♖xa3 ♕xa3 3.fxe4+−

Chapter 10

149 1.♕xf3+=

150 1.♖e7+ ♖8f7 (1...♔g8 2.♖xb7+−; 1...♔h8 2.♖xb7+−; 1...♔g6 2.♖xb7+−; 1...♖6f7 2.♖xb7+−) 2.♖xb7+−

151 (Based on the game Gruenfeld – Saemisch, 1925) 1.♖b8+ (1.d8=♘+? ♔c7 2.♘e6+ ♔d6−+) 1...♔a7 (1...♔xb8? 2.d8=♕+ ♔b7 (2...♔a7 3.♕c7+ ♔a8 4.♗c6#) 3.♕d7+ ♔b8 4.♕xf5+−; 1...♔c7? 2.d8=♕#) 2.♖a8+ ♔b7 3.♖b8+=

152 1.♕e8+ ♖xe8 2.♘f7+ ♔g8 3.♘xh6+ gxh6 (3...♔h8 4.hxg3+−; 3...♔f8 4.hxg3+−) 4.hxg3+−

153 1.♕xh7+ ♖xh7 2.♘xd2+−

154 1.♕d4+ ♔h7 (1...♔h6? 2.♕h8#; 1...f6 2.♕xa1+−; 1...♔g8 2.♕xa1+−; 1...♔f8 2.♕xa1+−) 2.♕xa1+−

155 1.♕xg4+ ♔b8 (1...f5 2.♕xg3+−; 1...♔d7 2.♖e8#) 2.♕xg3+− (2.♕h3? ♕f4−+)

156 1.♕xc2+ ♖xc2 2.♖xb5+−

157 1.♕h6+ (1.♗xd4+? ♔f7) 1...♔f7 (1...♔e7 2.♕xd6++−; 1...♔f5 2.♕xd6+−; 1...♔e5 2.♕xd6++−) 2.♕xd6+−

158 1.♖c1+ ♔b8 2.fxg3+−

159 1.♖g3+ ♔f4 (1...♔xg3=) 2.♖xe3 ♔xe3=

160 1.♕b6+ ♕xb6= (1...♔f7? 2.♕xb2+−)

161 (Based on the game Girmay – Namaganda, 2015) 1.♕d8+ ♔h7 2.♕d3+ g6 (2...♔h8 3.♕xc2+−; 2...♔g8 3.♕xc2+−; 2...f5 3.♕xc2+−) 3.♕xc2+−

162 1.♖b8+ ♔f7 2.♘e5+ ♔e7

(2...♔f6 3.♘xd3+−; 2...♔e6
3.♘xd3+−) 3.♘xd3+−

163 1.♘c7+ ♔b8 2.♘d5+ ♔c8 (2...
♕a8 3.♘xc3+−) 3.♘xc3+−

164 (Based on the game Lanc
– Novikov, 1985) 1.♖d8+!
(1.♔h2?!=; 1.g4?!=; 1.♔h1?
♗xg2+∓) 1...♖xd8 2.♗f6+ ♔c8
(2...♔d7 3.♗xg5+−; 2...♔e8
3.♗xg5+−) 3.♗xg5+−

165 (Based on the game
Chvedtchikov – Estrin,
1977) 1.♕xf7+ ♔xf7 (1...
♔h8 2.♕xf3+−) 2.♘g5+ ♔g8
(2...♔f8 3.♘xh3+−; 2...♔f6
3.♘xh3+−; 2...♔g6 3.♘xh3+−)
3.♘xh3+−

166 (Based on the game Georghiu
– Polugaevsky, 1973) 1.♕f8+
♔xf8 2.♘xg6+ hxg6 (2...♔g8
3.♘xh4+−; 2...♔f7 3.♘xh4+−;
2...♔e8 3.♘xh4+−) 3.gxh4+−

167 (Based on the game Markowski
– Lalic, 1995) 1.♖h8+ ♔xh8 (1...
♔g7 2.♗xf6+ ♘xf6 (2...♔xf6
3.fxg3+−) 3.fxg3+−) 2.♗xf6+
♘xf6 (2...♔g8 3.fxg3+−; 2...♔h7
3.fxg3+−) 3.fxg3+−

168 (Based on the game Leko –
Piket, 1997) 1.♕xd7+ ♔xd7
2.♗b5+ ♔c6 (2...♔e6 3.♖xf3+−;
2...♔d8 3.♖xf3+−; 2...♖c6
3.♖xf3+−) 3.♗xc6+ (3.♖xf3?
♗xb5+−+) 3...♖xc6 4.♖xf3+−

169 1.♖h7+ ♔g8 (1...♔xh7?
2.♕a7+ ♖f7 (2...♔h8
3.♕xd4+−; 2...♔g8 3.♕xd4+−;
2...♔h6 3.♕xd4+−) 3.♕xf7+
(3.♕xd4+−) 3...♔h6 (3...♔h8
4.♖a8#) 4.♕f8+ ♔h7 5.♖a7#)

2.♖g7+ ♔h8 (2...♔xg7? 3.♕a7+
♖f7 (3...♔g8 4.♕xd4+−; 3...♔h8
4.♕xd4+−; 3...♔h6 4.♕xd4+−)
4.♕xf7+ (4.♕xd4+−) 4...♔h6
(4...♔h8 5.♖a8#) 5.♕f8+ ♔h7
6.♖a7#) 3.♖h7+=

170 1.♘d7+ ♔g8 2.♗f7+ ♔h7 (2...
♔xf7? 3.♘e5+ ♔g8 (3...♔f6
4.♘xf3+−; 3...♔e6 4.♘xf3+−;
3...♔e8 4.♘xf3+−; 3...♔f8
4.♘xf3+−) 4.♘xf3+−) 3.♗g6+
♔g8 (3...♔xg6? 4.♘e5+ ♔f6
(4...♔g5 5.♘xf3++−; 4...♔h7
5.♘xf3+−) 5.♘xf3+−) 4.♗f7+=

171 1.♖h5+ ♔g7 (1...♔g8 2.♖g5+
♔h7 (2...♔h8 3.♖h5+=) 3.♖h5+
♔g6? (3...♔g8 4.♖g5+=; 3...
♔g7 4.♖g5+=) 4.♘f4+ ♔g7
5.♘xe2+−) 2.♖g5+ ♔h6
(2...♔h8 3.♖h5+=; 2...♔h7
3.♖h5+=) 3.♖h5+ ♔g7 (3...
♔xh5? 4.♘f4+ ♔h4 (4...♔g4
5.♘xe2+−; 4...♔g5 5.♘xe2+−;
4...♔h6 5.♘xe2+−) 5.♘xe2+−;
3...♔g6? 4.♘f4+ ♔f6 (4...♔g7
5.♘xe2+−) 5.♘xe2+−) 4.♖g5+
♔h6 (4...♔h7 5.♖h5+=; 4...♔h8
5.♖h5+=) 5.♖h5+=

172 (Maximovskikh, 1978)
1.♕g7+ ♔d5 (1...♔e4 2.♕g4+
♔e3 (2...♔d3 3.♕d1+=;
2...♔e5 3.♕g7+=; 2...♔d5
3.♕d7+=) 3.♕g1+ ♔d3 (3...
♔f4? 4.♕xd4++−; 3...♔e2?
4.♕xd4+−; 3...♔f3? 4.♕xd4+−;
3...♔e4 4.♕g4+=) 4.♕d1+ ♔c4
(4...♔e4 5.♕g4+=; 4...♔c3?
5.♕b3#; 4...♔e3 5.♕g1+=)
5.♕a4+ ♔c5 (5...♔c3? 6.♕b3#;
5...♔d3 6.♕d1+=; 5...♔d5

6.♕d7+=) 6.♕a7+ ♚d5 (6...♚c4
7.♕a4+=; 6...♚b5? 7.♕xd4+−;
6...♚b4? 7.♕xd4++−; 6...
♚c6? 7.♕xd4+−; 6...♚d6?
7.♕xd4++−) 7.♕d7+ ♚e5
(7...♚c5 8.♕a7+=; 7...♚c4
8.♕a4+=; 7...♚e4 8.♕g4+=)
8.♕g7+=; 1...♚f5? 2.♕xd4+−;
1...♚f4? 2.♕xd4++−; 1...
♚e6? 2.♕xd4+−; 1...♚d6?
2.♕xd4+) 2.♕d7+ ♚c5 (2...♚e5
3.♕g7+=; 2...♚e4 3.♕g4+=;
2...♚c4 3.♕a4+=) 3.♕a7+
♚c4 (3...♚d5 4.♕d7+=; 3...
♚d6? 4.♕xd4++−; 3...♚c6?
4.♕xd4+−; 3...♚b5? 4.♕xd4+−;
3...♚b4? 4.♕xd4++−) 4.♕a4+
♚d3 (4...♚c3? 5.♕b3#; 4...♚c5
5.♕a7+=; 4...♚d5 5.♕d7+=)
5.♕d1+ ♚e3 (5...♚c3? 6.♕b3#;
5...♚c4 6.♕a4+=; 5...♚e4
6.♕g4+=) 6.♕g1+ ♚e4 (6...♚d3
7.♕d1+=; 6...♚e2? 7.♕xd4+−;
6...♚f3? 7.♕xd4+−; 6...♚f4?
7.♕xd4++−) 7.♕g4+ ♚e5
(7...♚e3 8.♕g1+=; 7...♚d3
8.♕d1+=; 7...♚d5 8.♕d7+=)
8.♕g7+=

173 1.♖xb8+ ♚xb8 (1...♚d7?
2.♖b7+ ♚d6 3.♖xh7+−; 1...
♚c7? 2.♖b7+ ♚d6 3.♖xh7+−)
2.♖a8+ ♚c7 3.♖a7+ ♚d6
(3...♚b6 4.♖xh7+−; 3...♚b8
4.♖xh7+−; 3...♚c8 4.♖xh7+−;
3...♚d8 4.♖xh7+−) 4.♖xh7+−
174 (Based on the game Richter –
Grob, 1935) 1.♖xc5+ (1.♕e7+?
♚b8 2.♕e8+ ♚a7 3.♖a2+
♖a6−+; 1.g3? ♖b2−+) 1...
♖xc5 (1...♚d6? 2.♕f8+ ♚d7

3.♕c8+ ♚e7 (3...♚d6 4.♕c7#)
4.♖c7++−) 2.♕e7+ ♚c8 (2...
♚b8? 3.♕d8+ ♚a7 (3...♖c8
4.♕xb6#) 4.♕a8#) 3.♕e8+
(3.♕f8+ ♚d7 4.♕f7+=) 3...♚c7
4.♕e7+=
175 1.♕h8+ ♚g6 2.♕xg7+
(2.♗f7+? ♚f6 3.♕d8+ ♚xf7−+)
2...♚xg7 (2...♚f5 3.♖f8#)
3.♖g8+ ♚f6 (3...♚h7 4.♖xg3+−;
3...♚h6 4.♖xg3+−) 4.♖xg3+−
176 1.a8=♕+ (1.a8=♖+? ♘b8−+)
1...♘b8 (1...♚d7 2.♘c5+
♚e7 (2...♚d6 3.♘xe6+−; 2...
♚e8 3.♘xe6+−) 3.♘xe6+−)
2.♕xb7+ ♚xb7 (2...♚d7 3.♘c5+
♚d6 (3...♚e7 4.♘xe6+−; 3...
♚e8 4.♘xe6+−) 4.♘xe6+−)
3.♘c5+ ♚c8 (3...♚a8
4.♘xe6+−; 3...♚c6 4.♘xe6+−;
3...♚a7 4.♘xe6+−; 3...♚b6
4.♘xe6+−) 4.♘xe6+−

Chapter 11

177 1.♕f5! ♘g4+! 2.♚g1±
178 1.♕f5 ♕xf5 (1...♖xh2+ 2.♚xh2
♕xf5=; 1...♖g1+ 2.♚xg1 ♕xf5=)
2.♚xg2=
179 1.♗e1+−
180 1.♕f5+−
181 1.♖f2+−
182 1.♖f1 ♕xf1 2.♚xg3+−
183 1.♕d5+−
184 1.♕b2+−
185 1.♖e3 ♖g3+ 2.♖xf3 ♖xf3
3.♖a1!?+−
186 1.♘e1 ♖g3+! 2.♘xf3+ ♖xf3=
187 1.♘e4=
188 1.♘f4=
189 1.♕b1 (1.♘e2? ♖e1−+;

1.♘a2?! ♘d2+ 2.♘xc1 ♘xe4=)
1...♖xb1 2.♘xb1+−
190 1.♕g2+−

Chapter 12
191 1.♖c8++−
192 1.♖f8+ ♖xf8 (1...♔h7
2.♖xe8+−) 2.♘f4+−
193 (Based on a position by
Nadareshvili) 1.♘g4+ (1.♘xb3?
g2+ 2.♔h2 g1=♕#) 1...♔f1 (1...
♔e1 2.♘xb3=) 2.♘h2+ gxh2
(2...♔f2 3.♘g4+=; 2...♔e1
3.♘xb3=) 3.♘xb3=
194 1.♖f4 ♗b7 (1...♗c6 2.♖c4=; 1...
♗d5 2.♖d4=) 2.♖b4 ♗c6 (2...
♗f3 3.♖f4=; 2...♗d5 3.♖d4=)
3.♖c4 ♗d5 (3...♗b7 4.♖b4=; 3...
♗f3 4.♖f4=) 4.♖d4 ♗f3 (4...♗c6
5.♖c4=; 4...♗b7 5.♖b4=) 5.♖f4=
195 1.♖c8++−
196 1.♘g5+=
197 1.♗xg4++−
198 1.♕b3++−
199 1.♕e7++−
200 1.♖xe7+ ♖xe7 (1...♔a6
2.♖xg7+−; 1...♔b8 2.♖xg7+−;
1...♔a8 2.♖c8#) 2.gxf3+−
201 1.♕a8+ ♔h7 (1...♕e8?
2.♕xe8++−) 2.♕e4+ ♕xe4+
3.dxe4 ♘f2+ 4.♔g2 ♘xe4=
202 1.♕a8+ ♔h7 (1...♔g7
2.♕b7++−; 1...♔b8 2.♕xb8++−)
2.♕b7++−
203 1.♖a4+ ♔b8 2.♗d6++−
204 1.♕d8+ (1.♖h1?! ♗xg4+
2.♔xg4 ♕g6+ 3.♔xf4 ♕f6+=)
1...♔h7 (1...♖e8 2.♕xe8++−)
2.♕d3++−
205 (Based on the game Lputian –

Mikhalchishin, 1984) 1.♕e5+
♖xe5 (1...♕xe5 2.dxe5+−; 1...
♔h7 2.♕xe3+−) 2.fxe3+−
206 1.♖d3 (1.♕f6? ♖xh2+ 2.♔xh2
♕xf6−+) 1...♖xd3 (1...exd3?
2.♕xf3+−) 2.♔g2 ♕f3+ 3.♔g1
♕g4+ 4.♔h1 ♕f3+=
207 1.♖h4+ ♕xh4 2.♗g6+ ♔xg6
(2...♔h5 3.♗xh4=; 2...♔h7
3.♗xh4=) 3.♗xh4=
208 (Based on the game Efimenko
– Berndt, 2004) 1.♗f4+
(1.♖xb6+? axb6 2.♗f4+
♔a7−+) 1...♘xf4 (1...♖xf4?
2.♖xe2+−; 1...♕e5? 2.♗xe5++−;
1...♖d6? 2.♗xd6++−; 1...♘c7?
2.♕xc7+ ♔a8 3.♕c6#) 2.♖xb6+
axb6 3.♕xb6+ ♔c8 (3...♔a8
4.♕a6+ ♔b8 5.♕b6+=) 4.♕c6+
♔b8 5.♕b6+=
209 (Based on a position by V.
Berezin) 1.♖f8+ ♔h7 (1...♔xf8?
2.♘e6+ ♔g8 3.♘xd4+−; 1...
♔g7? 2.♘e6+ ♔h7 3.♘xd4+−)
2.♖f7+ ♔h8 (2...♗g7? 3.♗c3+−;
2...♔g8 3.♖f8+=) 3.♖f8+
♔h7 (3...♔g7? 4.♘e6+ ♔h7
5.♘xd4+−) 4.♖f7+=
210 1.♖xg8+ ♔h7 (1...♔xg8
2.♕a8+ ♔h7 (2...♔d8?
3.♕xd8++−) 3.♕e4+=) 2.♖h8+
♔xh8 (2...♔g6? 3.♖xh4+−)
3.♕a8+ ♔h7 (3...♔d8?
4.♕xd8++−) 4.♕e4++−
211 (Based on a position by V.
Berezin) 1.♕xh7+! (1.f3?! ♕d4+
2.♔h1 f5∓) 1...♔f8 (1...♕xh7
2.♗xh7+ ♔xh7 3.♖xd8+−)
2.♕h8+ (2.♕xe4?! ♗xe4
3.♗c2=) 2...♔e7 3.♕xd8+ ♔xd8

4.♗xe4++−

212 (Based on the game Chigorin – Gunsberg, 1890) 1.♕e6+ ♔h8 (1...♖f7 2.♕xc8+ ♖f8 3.♕c4++−) 2.♗xf5! ♕g5 (2...♖xf5 3.♕xc8+ ♖f8 4.♕xf8#; 2...♕xf5 3.♕xf5 ♖xf5 4.♔xg2+−) 3.f4! ♕g3 (3...♖xf5 4.♕xf5 ♖xf5 5.♔xg2+−) 4.♕e1!+−

213 1.♖e5 ♗a8 (1...♗d3? 2.d7+−) 2.♖e8! (2.b6? ♖b3+ 3.b7 ♖xb7−+) 2...♗d5 3.♖e5 ♗a8 4.♖e8=

214 1.♖e7+ ♔h6 (1...♔f6 2.♘d5++−; 1...♔f8 2.♘g6+ ♔g8 3.♗d5+ ♘e6 (3...♕e6+ 4.♗xe6++−) 4.♗xe6+ ♕xe6+ 5.♖xe6+−; 1...♔h8 2.♘g6+ ♔g8 3.♗d5+ ♘e6 (3...♕e6+ 4.♗xe6++−) 4.♗xe6+ ♕xe6+ 5.♖xe6+−; 1...♔g8 2.♗h7+ ♔h8 (2...♔f8 3.♘g6#) 3.♘g6#) 2.♖h7+ ♔g5 3.♖h5+ ♔f6 4.♘d5+ ♔e6 (4...♔f7 5.♘xe3+−; 4...♔g7 5.♘xe3+−) 5.♘xe3+−

215 1.♖d8+ ♔h7 2.♘g5+ ♘xg5 (2...♔g6 3.♘xe4=; 2...♔h6 3.♘xe4=) 3.♖h8+ ♔g6 (3...♔xh8=) 4.♖h6+ ♔xh6= (4...gxh6=)

216 1.♘g7 (1.♗f7? ♕xf5−+) 1...♔xg7 (1...♕h4 2.♘f5 ♕g4 (2...♕h5 3.♘g7=) 3.♘e3 ♕h5 (3...♕h4 4.♘f5=) 4.♗f7 ♕h4 5.♘f5 ♕g4 6.♘e3 ♕h4 7.♘f5=; 1...♕g6? 2.♗f7! (2.♕b7!?+−) 2...♕xg7 (2...♕xf7 3.♕xe4+−) 3.♕xe4+−) 2.♕e7+ ♔h8 (2...♔g6? 3.♗f7++−; 2...♕f7?

3.♕xf7++−) 3.♕xf6+ ♔h7 4.♕e7+ (4.♗f7? ♕g5∓) 4...♔h8 (4...♔g6? 5.♗f7++−; 4...♕f7? 5.♕xf7++−) 5.♕f6+=

217 1.♗f3+ ♕xf3 (1...♔h6? 2.♗xe2+−; 1...♔g5? 2.♗xe2+−; 1...♔g6? 2.♗xe2+−; 1...♖g4? 2.♗xe2 h2+ 3.♔g2!+−; 1...♔h4? 2.♕f4+ ♖g4 3.♕xg4#) 2.♕e5+ f5 (2...♔g4 3.♕g5+=; 2...♔h6 3.♕g5+=; 2...♔h4 3.♕g5+=; 2...♕f5? 3.♕xf5++−; 2...♔g6 3.♕g5+ ♔f7 4.♕xg7+=; 2...♖g5 3.♕xg5+=; 2...fxe5=) 3.♕e8+! (3.♕xf5+? ♕xf5−+) 3...♖g6 (3...♔h4 4.♕e7+=; 3...♔g5 4.♕e7+=; 3...♔g4 4.♕g6+=; 3...♔h6 4.♕g6+=; 3...♖f7 4.♕xf7+=) 4.♕xg6+ ♔h4 (4...♔xg6=; 4...hxg6=) 5.♕g5+ ♔xg5=

218 1.♖h5+ ♔g6 (1...♔g8 2.♖b8+ ♔f7 3.♘e5++−) 2.♘e5+ ♔xh5 (2...♖xe5 3.♖bxe5+−; 2...♔f6 3.♘xf3+−) 3.♘xf3++− ♔g4 4.♖g5+!? ♔xf3 5.♖xg2 hxg2+ 6.♔g1+−

Chapter 13

219 1.♖e6+−
220 1.♗b3+−
221 1.♖c5+−
222 1.♕e3+−
223 1.♗b2+−
224 1.♖d1=
225 1.♖b7=
226 1.♕b6+−
227 1.♗e3=
228 1.♗d3+−
229 1.♗d4+−

230 1.♕c4+−
231 1.♕f1+−
232 1.♕d6+− (1.♕c1? ♖e1+
2.♕xe1+ ♘xe1 3.g5 ♘f3+−+)
1...♔f4 2.♕f6+!?

Chapter 14
233 1.♕c6+−
234 1.♖a8 ♖xa8 (1...♕g4+? 2.fxg4±;
1...♖f8? 2.♕a2+ ♘d5 (2...♘c4
3.♕xc4+ ♔h8 4.♖xf8#; 2...
♔h8 3.♖xf8#) 3.♕xd5+ ♔h8
4.♖xf8#; 1...♕h5? 2.♖xc8#)
2.♕a2+ ♖xa2= (2...♘c4?
3.♕xa8#; 2...♘d5? 3.♕xa8#;
2...♔h8? 3.♕xa8#; 2...♔f8?
3.♕f7#)
235 (Based on the game Kramnik –
Short, 1995) 1.♕xg7+ (1.fxg3?
♘e2+ 2.♔h1 ♘xg3#) 1...♔xg7
2.fxg3+−
236 1.♖xg7+ ♔xg7 (1...♔xg7
2.♖d7+ ♘e7 (2...♔f6 3.♕f7#)
3.♖xe7+ ♔f6 4.♕f7#) 2.♖d7+−
237 1.♕a3+−
238 1.♕d1+−
239 1.♗c3+− ♕xc3 2.♖b8+ ♔c8
3.♖xc8#
240 1.♖g7 ♖xd6 (1...♖xg7
2.♖xa6+−) 2.♖xf7++−
241 1.♕b8+ ♔h7 2.♕b1+−
242 1.♕b8+ ♔h7 2.♗d3+−
243 1.♕a8+ ♔g7 (1...♘f8 2.♕xf8#;
1...♘c8 2.♕a1+−; 1...♘e8
2.♕a1+−) 2.♕a1+−
244 1.♕a2+ ♔b8 (1...♕a3?
2.♕xa3++−) 2.♕h2=
245 1.♖b8+ ♔g7 (1...♔h7
2.♗b1+−) 2.♖g8+ ♔h6 (2...♔f6
3.♖xg6++−; 2...♔h7 3.♖xg6+−)

3.♖xg6++−
246 1.♕d8+ ♔h7 2.♕d3 ♕xd3=
(2...♔xh6? 3.♕xf5+−)
247 1.♕g6 ♖xe5 (1...♔g4 2.♔xg2=;
1...♔h4 2.♔xg2=; 1...♔f4
2.♔xg2=) 2.♕xg5+ ♖xg5=
(2...♔f3 3.♕xe5+−; 2...♔h3
3.♕xe5+−)
248 1.♖a8+ ♔g7 (1...♕b8
2.♖xb8++−; 1...♔d8
2.♖xd8++−; 1...♕f8 2.♖xf8++−)
2.♖1a7+ (2.♖8a7+ ♔h8
3.♖a8+ ♔g7) 2...♔f6 (2...♔g6
3.♖a6+−; 2...♔h6 3.♖a6+−;
2...♕c7 3.♖xc7++−; 2...
♕d7 3.♖xd7++−; 2...♕e7
3.♖xe7++−) 3.♖a6+−
249 1.♖c7+ ♔h8 (1...♔h6?
2.♖c6+−; 1...♕g7? 2.♖xg7++−;
1...♕f7? 2.♖xf7++−) 2.♖c8+
♔h7 (2...♔g7? 3.♖g8+; 2...
♕e8? 3.♖xe8++−; 2...♕g8?
3.♖xg8++−) 3.♖c7+=
250 1.♖a8+ ♔h7 (1...♕e8 2.♖xe8+
♔h7 3.♖h8#; 1...♔g7 2.hxg3+−)
2.♖h8+ ♔xh8 (2...♔g7 3.hxg3)
3.hxg3+−
251 1.♗c3+ ♔g8 (1...♕d4?
2.♗xd4++−; 1...♕f6?
2.♗xf6++−) 2.♗c4+ ♔h7
(2...♔f8? 3.♖f1+−; 2...♕f7?
3.♗xf7++−) 3.♗d3+ ♔g8 (3...
♕f5? 4.♗xf5++−) 4.♗c4+=
252 1.♕h6+ ♔g8 (1...♔h7 2.♕xf8+
♕xf8 (2...♗g8 3.♕xf3+−)
3.♖b8+−) 2.♕xf8+ ♔xf8
(2...♕xf8 3.♖b8+−; 2...♔h7
3.♕xf3+−) 3.♖f1+−
253 (Based on the game Nogueiras
– Arencibia, 1996) 1.♕xg7+

(1.♖xg2? ♖f1+ 2.♔d2 ♗e1+
3.♔d1 ♗c3#) 1...♔xg7
2.♖xg2+−

254 1.♘g7+ (1.♘c7+? ♔d7−+;
1.♖d2? ♕h1+ 2.♔f2 ♗h4+
3.♔e3 ♕e4#) 1...♔d7 (1...♔f8
2.♖f1+−; 1...♔f7 2.♖f1+−)
2.♖xe7+ ♔xe7 (2...♔c8
3.♕c7#) 3.♕c7+ ♔f8 (3...♗d7
4.♕xd6++−; 3...♔f6 4.♖f1+−)
4.♖f1+− (4.♘e6+ ♔e8 5.♘g7+
♔f8)

255 1.♖h1+ ♔g8 (1...♕h6
2.♖xh6++−) 2.♗f7+ ♔f8
3.♖h8+ ♔e7 4.♖e8+ ♔d7
(4...♔d6 5.♖d1+−) 5.♖d1+−
(5.♖d8+?! ♔xd8 6.♖d1=)

256 1.♖h1+ ♔g8 2.♘f6+ gxf6 (2...
♔f8? 3.♖h8+ (3.♗a3+−) 3...
♔e7 4.♘d5+ ♔d7 (4...♔d6
5.♘xb4+−) 5.♘xb4+−) 3.♖g1+
♔f8 (3...♔h7 4.♖h1+ ♔g7
(4...♔g8 5.♖g1+=) 5.♖g1+
♔f8 (5...♔h8 6.♖h1+=; 5...
♔h7 6.♖h1+=) 6.♗a3 ♔e8!=;
3...♕g4? 4.♖xg4++−) 4.♗a3
♔e8!= (4...♕xa3+? 5.♖xa3+−;
4...♕e7? 5.♖e1+−)

257 1.♖h5+ ♔g8 (1...♔g7?
2.♗b2+−; 1...♕h6? 2.♖xh6++−)
2.♖h8+! (2.♖g5+? ♕xg5−+;
2.♖d8+? ♕xd8−+; 2.♔g1?
♕b6+−+) 2...♕xh8 (2...♔xh8?
3.♗b2+−; 2...♔g7? 3.♗b2+−)
3.♖d8+ ♔h7 (3...♔g7? 4.♗b2+
f6 5.♗xf6+ ♔xf6 6.♖xh8+−)
4.♖xh8+ ♔xh8 5.♗f4=

258 1.♕h7+ (1.♕e8+? ♗xe8
2.♗b3 ♕d6!−+) 1...♔xh7 (1...
♔f7? 2.♘d8+ (2.♘g5++−)

2...♔xd8 (2...♔e8 3.♘xc6+−;
2...♔e7 3.♘xc6++−; 2...♔f8
3.♘xc6+−; 2...♖xd8 3.♗b3++−)
3.♗b3+−) 2.♘f8+ ♔h8 (2...
♔g8? 3.♗b3+−) 3.♘g6+ ♔h7
(3...♔g8? 4.♗b3+−) 4.♘f8+=

259 (Based on the game McCardle
– Hold, 1993) 1.♕c8+!
(1.♕e7+? ♔g8 2.♕e6+ ♔h7−+)
1...♔f7 (1...♖xc8 2.♖xf2=)
2.♕c4+ (2.♕c7+? ♔g8−+) 2...
♔f8 (2...♔f6? 3.♕h4+ ♔g6
4.♖xf2 ♖xf2 5.♕xf2+−; 2...♔g6?
3.♕xc2+ ♖xc2 4.♖xf3+−; 2...
♔e8? 3.♕g8+ ♔d7 4.♕xg7+
♔xd6 5.♖ad1++−; 2...♖xc4
3.♖xf2=) 3.♕c8+! ♖xc8 (3...♔f7
4.♕c4+ ♔f8 5.♕c8+=) 4.♖xf2
♕xf2+ 5.♔xf2 ♖c2+!=

260 1.♗f4+ ♕xf4 (1...♔h7?
2.♗xd2+−; 1...♔g7? 2.♗xd2+−)
2.♕e3 ♕xe3 (2...♔g7?
3.♕xf4+−) 3.♖xg6+ ♔h7 (3...
fxg6=; 3...♔xg6=) 4.♖g7+
(4.♖h6+? ♕xh6−+) 4...♔h8
(4...♔xg7=; 4...♔h6 5.♖g6+=)
5.♖g8+ (5.♖h7+ ♔g8 6.♖g7+=)
5...♔h7 (5...♖xg8=; 5...♔xg8=)
6.♖g7+=

Chapter 15

261 1.♗g3+−
262 1.♘g3 ♖e1+ 2.♘f1+−
263 1.f3= (1.♗f3? ♗xf3−+; 1.♗h5?
♖xh5−+)
264 1.♕e2+− (1.♖e2? ♕c1+ 2.♖e1
♕xe1+ 3.♕f1 ♕xf1#)
265 1.♗e4+−
266 1.♘f2+− (1.♖e2? ♖xe2−+;
1.♕xb2? ♕xb2−+)

267 1.♖h4+− (1.♕xh6? ♕xh6−+)

268 1.♗f2+− (1.♔h2? ♖xb6−+;
1.♗d4? ♘e2+ 2.♔h2 ♘xd4−+)

269 1.d4 (1.♘c6? ♗b7−+; 1.♘d5?
♗b7−+; 1.♘f3? ♗b7−+) 1...
♗b7+ 2.d5+−

270 1.c4 (1.♘c5? ♗e7−+; 1.♘d6?
♗e7−+) 1...♗e7+ 2.c5=

271 1.♘f5 ♕h7+ 2.♘h4+−

272 1.♘e3 (1.♕f2?! ♘xf2 2.♔xf2=;
1.♕e2? ♗xe2 2.♔xe2 ♘xg3+∓)
1...♖h1+ 2.♘f1+−

273 1.♗b5 ♖a1+ 2.♗f1+−

274 1.♗e1 (1.♕d8?! ♖h7+ 2.♕h4=;
1.♕a6+?! ♖xa6 2.bxa6+=) 1...
♖g1 (1...♖h6+ 2.♗h4+−; 1...
♖h7+ 2.♗h4+−) 2.♕a6++−

275 1.♖g5 (1.♖e5? ♖xe5−+) 1...
♖e1+ 2.♖g1+−

276 1.♖e3 (1.♖d7? ♖xd7−+;
1.♖d3? cxd3−+) 1...♖h7+
2.♖h3=

277 1.♕a4 (1.♗c3? ♖h1+ 2.♗e1
♖xe1#) 1...♖h1+ (1...♖f1+
2.♕d1 ♖xd1+ 3.♔xd1 ♖h1+=)
2.♕d1 ♖xd1+ 3.♔xd1 ♖f1+=

278 1.♕d7 (1.♕d4+? ♗xd4−+;
1.♕h6+? ♔xh6−+) 1...♖h8+
2.♕h3+−

279 1.♕g8 ♕h1+ (1...♘g5
2.♕h8++−) 2.♕g1+−

280 1.♕c7 (1.♘f1? ♗f3+ 2.♔g3
♕h3−+; 1.♘e4? ♗xe4+ 2.♔f1
♗g2+ 3.♔g1 ♗f3+ 4.♔f1 ♕g2#;
1.♖e3? ♗f3+ 2.♔f1 ♖xd2!−+)
1...♗f3+ 2.♕g3+−

Chapter 16

281 1.♘f4+ ♔f7 (1...♔g7 2.♘g2+−;
1...♔g5 2.♘g2+−; 1...♔f5

2.♘g2+−) 2.♘g2+−

282 1.♖d3 (1.♕f5?! ♕xf5 2.♔xg2
♕g4+ 3.♔h1 ♕f3+ 4.♔g1
♕g4+=) 1...exd3 2.♗d1 ♕d5
(2...♕e4 3.f3+−) 3.f3+−
(3.♗b3?! ♕e4 4.♕h3 ♖xf2+
5.♔g1 g4 6.♕g3 ♖xf1+ 7.♔xf1
♕e2+ 8.♔g1 d2=)

283 1.f6 ♖xf6 2.♕c1++−

284 1.♗e4! (1.♖f3? ♖e1+ 2.♖f1
♕g2#; 1.♕f3? ♕xf3−+; 1.♗f6+
♗xf6 2.♗e4 (2.♔xf6+ ♕xf6
3.♖xf6 ♖e1+ 4.♖f1 ♖xf1#) 2...
♕e6! 3.♕xe6 ♖xe6 4.♗xb7
♗xb2−+) 1...♕xe4 (1...♖xe4?
2.♕f8#; 1...♕e6? 2.♕xe6 ♖xe6
3.♗xb7+−) 2.♗f6+ ♗xf6
3.♕xf6+ ♔g8 4.♕f7+ ♔h8
5.♕f6+=

285 1.g7 (1.g5+? ♔xg6−+) 1...♖xg7
(1...♖b8+ 2.g8=♕ (2.g8=♖=;
2.g8=♗=; 2.g8=♘+? ♔g6 3.g5
♖b7−+) 2...♖xg8+ 3.♔xg8
♔g5=) 2.g5+ ♔xg5 (2...♖xg5=;
2...♔g6=; 2...♔h5 3.♔xg7
♔xg5=) 3.♔xg7=

286 1.♕d8+ ♔h7 2.♕g5+−

287 1.♕e6+ ♔b8 (1...♖d7
2.♖xf8++−) 2.♕h3= (2.h3?
gxh6−+)

288 1.♖g4 (1.♖c8+? ♔g7−+) 1...
♕xg4 (1...♔h7? 2.♘f8++−;
1...♔f7? 2.♘e5++−; 1...♔g7
2.♖xg6+=) 2.♘f6+ ♔f7 (2...♔g7
3.♘xg4=; 2...♔h8 3.♘xg4=; 2...
♔f8 3.♘xg4=) 3.♘xg4=

289 1.♘xf6+ ♖xf6 (1...gxf6
2.♗e4+−) 2.♗c4+− (2.♗e4?!
♕g5 3.♗xb7 ♗xg3=)

290 1.♕f3 ♕xf3 (1...♖xf3? 2.♖d8+

♖f8 3.♖xf8#; 1...♕c1+ 2.♖d1=)
2.gxf3=

291 1.♗e4 (1.♖g1? ♖g5+ 2.♖g2
♗xg2+ 3.♔g1 ♖xf5–+) 1...♗xe4
2.f3+–

292 1.♗f4 ♖xa1 (1...gxf4 2.♖xd1+–;
1...♕xf4 2.gxf4+–) 2.♗e5+–

293 1.♖h7 (1.♖g7+?! ♔xg7
2.♕c7+=) 1...♖xh7 (1...
exf2+ 2.♕xf2 ♖xh7 3.♘f6+
♔g7 4.♘xh7+–; 1...♔xh7
2.♘g5++–; 1...♕xh7 2.♘f6+
♔g7 3.♘xh7+–) 2.♘f6+ ♔g7
3.♘xh7 (3.♕xh7+? ♕xh7
4.♘xh7 e2–+) 3...exf2+ (3...
♕xh7 4.♕xh7+ ♔xh7 5.fxe3+–)
4.♕xf2+–

294 1.♕b8+ (1.♕c8+? ♔h7
2.♕c7+ ♔h6–+; 1.♖f2?
♕e1+–+) 1...♔g7 (1...♕d8?
2.♕xd8++–; 1...♔h7 2.♕a7+
♔h6 (2...♔h8 3.♕f2+–; 2...♔g8
3.♕f2+–) 3.♕f2+–) 2.♕a7+
♔h6 (2...♔f8 3.♕f2+–; 2...♔g8
3.♕f2+–; 2...♔h8 3.♕f2+–)
3.♕f2+– (3.♖f2? ♕e1+ 4.♔h2
e3–+)

295 1.♕f1 (1.♔d1?! ♕b2 2.♔d4
♕b8+ 3.♔xg2 ♕g3+ 4.♔f1
♖f8+ 5.♔e2 ♕g2+ 6.♔d3
♕xh1=) 1...♕b2 (1...♕d2
2.♕f2+–; 1...♕c2 2.♕f2+–)
2.♕f2 (2.♗f2? ♘xe3–+; 2.♕c1?
♕e5+ 3.♔xg2 ♕g3+ 4.♔f1
♖f8+ 5.♔e2 ♕g2+–+) 2...♕xa1
3.♔xg2+–

296 1.f5 ♖xf5 2.♖f4+ ♖xf4+
3.exf4+–

297 1.♗e7 ♖xe7 (1...h6 2.♖d8+–)
2.♖d8+ ♖e8 3.♖xe8#

298 1.♖h4 ♕xh4 2.h3 ♕xh3 (2...
♕h6 3.gxh6=; 2...♔g6 3.♕xh4=;
2...♖a8 3.♕xh4+=; 2...♖a7
3.♕xh4+=) 3.g6+ ♔xg6= (3...
♔h8=; 3...♔h6=)

299 1.♗g5 ♖xg5 (1...♕c7
2.♕xh6+–; 1...hxg5 2.♗b7+–)
2.♕xg5 hxg5 3.♗b7+–

300 (Based on the game Olafsson
– Kristiansen, 1985) 1.♘f3
(1.h3?! ♕f1+=; 1.h4?! ♕f1+=;
1.♖d1?! ♕f4∓; 1.♔h1? ♕e6∓;
1.♖g7+? ♕xg7 2.♘g4 ♖f1+!
3.♔xf1 ♕f7+ 4.♔g1 ♕xc4∓)
1...♕xf3 (1...exf3 2.♗xf6+–; 1...
♕xb2 2.♖xb2+–) 2.♖g7+ ♔h8
3.♖7xg6+ (3.♖f7++–) 3...♕f6
(3...♕c3 4.♗xc3+ ♖f6 5.♗xf6#;
3...♖f6 4.♖g8#) 4.♗xf6+ ♖xf6
5.♖g8#

301 1.♖b1+ ♔a8 (1...♕b4?
2.♖xb4+ ♔a8 3.♗f3+ c6
4.♗xc6#; 1...♕b7? 2.♖xb7+
♔xb7 3.♗xh3+–) 2.♗f3 ♕xf3
(2...f1=♘+ 3.♖xf1+–) 3.♖b8+
♔xb8=

302 1.♖h3 ♕xh3 (1...♕h6?
2.♖xh6+ ♘xh6 3.♕b8+–)
2.♕g7+ ♔xg7= (2...♘xg7=)

303 1.♗d3 ♗b3 (1...♗d1 2.♗e2
♗c2 3.♗d3=; 1...♗a4 2.♗b5 ♗c2
3.♗d3=) 2.♗c4 (2.♗e4?–+) 2...
♗a4 (2...♗c2 3.♗d3=; 2...♗d1
3.♗e2=) 3.♗b5 ♗d1 (3...♗b3
4.♗c4=; 3...♗c2 4.♗d3=) 4.♗e2
♗c2 (4...♗b3 5.♗c4=; 4...♗a4
5.♗b5=) 5.♗d3=

304 1.♘d4 ♖c4 (1...♗e5 2.♘f5+
♔g6 3.♘e7+=; 1...♗f4 2.♘f5+
♔g6 3.♘e7+=; 1...♗c7 2.♘f5+

♔g6 3.♘e7+=) 2.♖xb8 (2.♖b4?
♗g3+! (2...♖xb4=) 3.♔xg3
(3.hxg3 ♖xb4−+) 3...♖xb4
4.♘xc6 ♖c4−+; 2.♖d2? ♗e5−+)
2...♖xd4+ 3.♔g3=

305 1.♖xd8+ ♔xd8 (1...♖xd8
2.♕e5+−) 2.♕d4+ (2.♘h4?
♕xh4−+) 2...♕c8 (2...♕e7
3.♕e5+ ♔d8 4.♘h2+−; 2...♔e8
3.♕e5+ ♔d8 4.♘h2+−) 3.♕g4+
♔b8 (3...♔d8 4.♕h3+−; 3...♕f5
4.♕xf5++−) 4.♕h3+−

306 1.♖h4 ♖xh4 2.♕g5+ ♔f8
(2...♔h7 3.♕xh4+=) 3.♕d8+
(3.♕c5+? ♔e8−+; 3.♔f1?
♖g4−+) 3...♔g7 4.♕g5+=

307 1.♗d4 (1.♖xg3? ♕xg3−+)
1...♖xd4 (1...♕h1+ 2.♗g1=)
2.♕c3+ ♔b8 (2...♖c4 3.♕xc4+
♔b8 4.♕d4=; 2...♔b7 3.♕xd4=;
2...♔d8?! 3.♕xd4+±; 2...♗c7?
3.♕xd4+−; 2...♔d7? 3.♖xf7+
♔e6 4.♖f6++−) 3.♕xd4= ♕h1+
4.♕g1

308 1.♖b5 (1.♖c7+? ♖xc7 2.♘xc7
♖b6-+) ♖xb5 (1...♖a7 2.♖a5
(2.♖b1=) 2...♖b7 3.♖b5=
(3.♖a1=) ; 1...♖db6 2.♖xb6
♖xb6 3.♖f7+ ♔h8 (3...♔g8?
4.♖g7+ ♔h8 5.♖xg6 ♖b1+
6.♖g1+−) 4.♖f8+ ♔h7 5.♖f7+=;
1...♖bb6 2.♖xb6 ♖xb6 3.♖f7+
♔h8 (3...♔g8? 4.♖g7+ ♔h8
5.♖xg6 ♖b1+ 6.♖g1+−) 4.♖f8+
♔h7 5.♖f7+=; 1...♖e7 2.♖f3±)
2.♖f7+ ♔g8 (2...♔h8 3.♖f8+
♔h7 4.♖f7+=) 3.♖f8+ ♔h7
4.♖f7+=

Chapter 17

309 1.♘e3+−
310 1.♕e4+−
311 1.♕a1+−
312 1.♘f3+− (1.♖f5?! ♗xd4=)
313 1.g3+−
314 1.♗f4+− (1.♖e1? ♕xf2+
2.♔h1 f4−+)
315 1.♕e3+− (1.♕e7?! ♘g1
2.♕e3 ♕f3+=; 1.♘xf3? ♕xf3+
2.♔d2 ♕xh1−+)
316 1.♖b3+−
317 1.♕e1+− (1.♘h3?! ♗xh3
2.♘e4 ♗e6=)
318 1.♘g1+− (1.♔g2?! ♘h4+=;
1.♘c3? ♕h3+ 2.♔e2 ♘xg3+
3.fxg3 ♕xh8−+)
319 1.♕e3+− (1.♕c2?! ♕e1+
2.♔g2 ♕g3+=; 1.♕b2?! ♕e1+
2.♔g2 ♕g3+=; 1.♕a2?! ♕e1+
2.♔g2 ♕g3+=; 1.♘e7+?
♗xe7−+; 1.♔e2? ♕g2−+)
320 1.♘d3+−
321 1.♕f2+−
322 1.♖a1= (1.♖f1? ♗xf1−+;
1.♖f2? ♖xf2)
323 1.♕g1=
324 1.♕g1+−
325 1.♖h4+−
326 1.♕a7+− (1.♔h1? ♕f2−+;
1.♖h8+? ♔xh8 2.♕e8+ ♔h7−+)
327 1.♖b3 (1.♔h2? ♕xg3+ 2.♔g1
♕xg6−+; 1.♕b3? ♖c3−+;
1.♖d3? ♕xd3−+) 1...♖c3
2.♕xe8++−
328 1.♗f4+− (1.♖d1? ♕h2+ 2.♔f1
♕h1−+; 1.♖f3? ♕h2+ 2.♔f1
♕h1−+)
329 1.♕h5+−
330 1.♖3h2+− (1.♕xd6? ♘xd6−+;
1.♖1h2? ♕g1+ 2.♘f1 ♕xf1#;

1.♖d3? ♕xh1+ 2.♘f1 ♕xf1+
3.♖d1 ♕xd1#; 1.♖d1? ♗xd1−+)

331 1.♕a2 (1.♕a1? ♖xa1 2.♖xa1
♗xf2−+; 1.♕b8? ♖xb8 2.♗xb8
♖xb8−+) 1...♖6b2 (1...♖xg1+
2.♔xg1+−) 2.♕xb1 ♖xb1
3.♖xb1+−

332 1.♔h3 (1.♔h1? ♕f1#−+) 1...
♕f2+ 2.♔h1= ♕f3+!? 3.♔g1
♕f2+

333 1.♖a1+− (1.h4? ♖xf1+−+
2.♔h2 (2.♔xf1 ♕d1#) 2...
♖h1+!? 3.♔xh1 ♕d1+ 4.♔h2
♕f1−+; 1.h3? ♖xf1+ 2.♔h2
(2.♔xf1 ♕d1#) 2...♕d1−+)

334 1.♕c8 (1.♔h2? ♘g4+ 2.♔h1
(2.♔g1 ♖b1#) 2...♖b1#; 1.♕b5?
♖xb5−+; 1.♕b7? ♖xb7 2.cxb7
♖b3−+) 1...♖b1+ 2.♔h2+−

335 (Based on the game Shvedova –
Contreras, 2021) 1.♕d6 (1.♔g1?
♘e3−+; 1.♕f3?! ♕xh4+ 2.♕h3
(2.♔g1? ♕h2+ 3.♔f1 ♕h1#)
2...♘xf2+ 3.♘xf2 ♕xf2=; 1.g3?
♘e3−+; 1.♘f4? ♕xh4+ (1...
♘xf2+−+) 2.♘h3 ♘xf2+−+) 1...
♕xh4 2.♔g1+−

336 1.♕b4 (1.d6? ♗g2+ 2.♗xg2
♖xe1+ 3.♗xe1 (3.♗f1 ♕xf1#)
3...♕xe1+ 4.♗f1 ♕xf1#) 1...
♖xe4 (1...♗g2+ 2.♗xg2+−)
2.♕xe4+−

Chapter 18

337 1.♕f5 (1.♗f5? ♘g4+ 2.♔g1
♕h2+ 3.♔f1 ♕xf2#) 1...
♘g4+ (1...♕xf5?! 2.♗xf5+−)
2.♔g1 g6! (2...♕h2+ 3.♔f1
♕h3+ 4.♔e2 g6 5.♕c8+ ♔g7
6.♕xc7+−) 3.♕c8+ ♔g7

4.♕xc7±

338 1.♖b8+ ♔g7 (1...♕e8
2.♖xe8++−; 1...♔g8 2.♖xg8++−;
1...♔h7 2.♗b1+−) 2.♘e6+ ♔f7
(2...♔f6 3.♘f4 ♕c2 4.♘xh3+−;
2...♕xe6 3.dxe6+−; 2...♔h7
3.♗b1+−; 2...♔h6 3.♖h8+ ♕h7
4.♖xh7++−) 3.♘f4 (3.♖f8+ ♔e7
4.♘f4 ♕c2) 3...♕c2 4.♘xh3+−

339 1.♘e1 ♖b1 2.♔f1=

340 1.♖c7+ ♔h8 (1...♔g8 2.♗f1+−;
1...♕d7 2.♖xd7++−) 2.♗f1+−

341 1.♕e8 (1.g3? ♖xe1+−+;
1.♖xd1? ♕xd1+ 2.♗e1 ♕xe1#)
1...♕xe8 (1...♖xe1+ 2.♗xe1=;
1...♕xe1+? 2.♗xe1+−) 2.♗xe8
♖d3!? (2...♖xe1+ 3.♗xe1±)
3.♖e3=

342 1.d5+−

343 1.♗h5 (1.♗e4? ♗xe4−+) 1...
♖h7 2.♖f5+−

344 1.♕a1+ (1.♕b2+? ♔h7−+) 1...
♔h7 (1...♔g8 2.♕f1+−; 1...f6
2.♕f1+−) 2.♕f1+−

345 1.♗d5 (1.♕d5? ♖xd5−+) 1...
♕g4± (1...♖xd5? 2.♕xd5+−)

346 (Based on the game Arnason –
Agdestein, 1987) 1.♘d4 (1.♕d2?
♖xd2−+; 1.♕d1? ♖xd1+−+) 1...
cxd4 (1...♖xd4 2.♕xe4+−; 1...
♕f4+ 2.♕d2+−; 1...exd4 2.♕xe4
(2.♗c4+ ♔h8 3.♕xe4 ♗xe4
4.♖e1+−) 2...♗xe4 3.♗c4+ ♔h8
4.♖e1+−; 1...♘xd4 2.♕xe4 ♗xe4
3.♗c4+ ♔h8 4.♖e1+−) 2.♕xe4
(2.♗c4+ ♔h8 3.♕xe4 ♗xe4
4.♖e1+−) 2...♗xe4 3.♗c4+ ♔h8
4.♖e1+−

347 (Based on the game Adams –
Ftacnik, 1993) 1.♘f1 (1.♔xf2?

♕g3#; 1.♘f3? ♕g3+ 2.♔h1
♕g2#) 1...♖xf1+ (1...♖df8
2.♕xf2+−; 1...♖xc2 2.♖xd8#)
2.♖xf1 ♕xe3+ (2...♕g3+
3.♕g2+−) 3.♕f2+−

348 1.e7 ♗xe7 2.♖xe7+−

349 (Based on the game Oud – Le
Blancq, 1989) 1.♕h6+ (1.♖xg2?
♕xc1+ 2.♖g1 ♕c2−+; 1.♖xc2?
♖xh2#) 1...♔e8 (1...♔e7
2.♖xc2+−; 1...♔g8 2.♖xc2+−;
1...♖g7 2.♖xc2+−) 2.♖xc2+−

350 1.♕e5+ ♔d8 (1...♔f8 2.♕f5+−;
1...♔d7 2.♕f5++−; 1...♕e6
2.♕xe6++−) 2.♕f5+−

351 1.♖d8+ ♔g7 (1...♖e8
2.♖xe8++−; 1...♔h7 2.♖8d7+−)
2.♖8d7 ♖xd7 (2...f1=♕+ 3.♖xf1
♖xd7 4.a6+−; 2...♔f6 3.♖xe7+−)
3.♖xd7+ ♔f6 4.♖d1+−

352 1.♖b8 (1.♕h6+? ♔xh6 2.♖b8
♗c5!−+) 1...♖xb8 (1...♖h8+?
2.♖xh8+−) 2.♕h6+ ♔g8 (2...
♔xh6=) 3.♕h8+ (3.♕g7+
♔xg7=; 3.♕h7+=; 3.♕xg6+=)
3...♔xh8=

353 1.♕c8+ (1.♕a8+? ♔h7
2.♕xe4+ (2.♖d5? exf3−+) 2...
♖xe4 3.fxe4 ♕h4+∓; 1.♖d5?
exf3−+) 1...♔h7 (1...♖e8
2.♕xe8++−) 2.♕g4+−

354 (Based on the game Ahues –
NN, 1954) 1.♕g5 (1.gxf3? ♖g6+
2.♔h1 (2.♕g5 ♖xg5+ 3.♔h1
♗xf3#) 2...♗xf3#) 1...♖g6 (1...
hxg5 2.gxf3+−) 2.♕xg6+ ♔xg6
(2...fxg6 3.gxf3+−; 2...♔g8
3.♕xg7#; 2...♔h8 3.♕xg7#)
3.gxf3+−

355 (Based on the game Gomes –

Speelman, 1996) 1.♖h3 (1.♘e2?!
♖dxe2 2.♖h3 gxh3=) 1...♖h2
(1...gxh3 2.♕e8+−) 2.♖h1 ♖xh1
3.♖xh1+−

356 1.♘f4 (1.♘ce3? ♘e2+ (1...
♖h6−+) 2.♔h1 (2.♕xe2
fxe2−+) 2...♕xh2+ 3.♔xh2
♖h6#; 1.♕f1? ♘e2+ 2.♔h1
(2.♕xe2 ♕g2#) 2...♕xh2+
3.♔xh2 ♖h6+; 1.♘de3? ♘e2+
(1...♖h6−+) 2.♔h1 (2.♕xe2
fxe2−+) 2...♕xh2+ 3.♔xh2
♖h6#) 1...♘e2+ 2.♕xe2
(2.♘xe2? ♕g2#) 2...fxe2 (2...
♖xe2 3.♘xh3+−) 3.♘xh3+−

357 (Based on the game Gagarin –
Pozin, 1998) 1.♕xh7+ (1.♖xe2?
♖g1#; 1.♖aa1? ♕xd2−+;
1.♕f1? ♕xd2−+) 1...♔xh7 (1...
♖xh7 2.♖xe2 ♖hg7 3.♖h3++−)
2.♖h3+ ♔g6 (2...♕h5 3.♖xh5+
♔g6 4.♖h3+−; 2...♗h4 3.♖xh4+
♕h5 (3...♔g6 4.♖xe2+−)
4.♖xh5+ ♔g6 5.♖h3+−) 3.♖xe2
♔f5 (3...♔f6 4.♖e1+−) 4.♖e1+−

358 (Based on the game Schlaeger
– Hautcoeur, 2008) 1.♕b7+
(1.♕c7+? ♔f6 2.♕c6+ ♔g5−+;
1.♔g1? ♕xf2+ 2.♔h2 ♕f4+
3.♔h1 ♕f1+ 4.♔h2 ♗g1+
5.♔h1 ♗f2+ 6.♔h2 ♕g1#;
1.♔e2? ♕b2+!?−+; 1.♔e1?
♗b4+!?−+) 1...♔f6 (1...♔f8?
2.♕f7#; 1...♔d6 2.♕c6+ ♔e7
3.♕b7+=; 1...♔e8 2.♕c8+ ♔e7
3.♕b7+=; 1...♔d8 2.♕b8+ ♔d7
(2...♔e7 3.♕b7+=) 3.♕b7+
♔d6 (3...♔d8 4.♕b8+=; 3...
♔e8 4.♕c8+=) 4.♕c6+ ♔e7
5.♕b7+=) 2.♕a6+ (2.♕c6+?

♔g5–+; 2.♔e2? ♛xf2+–+)
2...♔g7 (2...♗b6 3.♔e2=; 2...
♔e7 3.♔e2=; 2...♔g5 3.♔e2=)
3.♔e2= (3.♔b7+? ♔h6–+)

359 1.♗e5 (1.♖h5? ♛e8!? (1...
♛e6–+) 2.♖xh7 ♛g6 3.♖xg7
♛h6–+; 1.♘xd6? ♛xh3+ 2.gxh3
♖h2#) 1...♛xh3+ (1...♘xe5
2.♘xe5+–; 1...♗xe5 2.♖xd7+–)
2.gxh3 ♖h2+ 3.♗xh2+–

360 (Based on the game Ivkov
– Mecking, 1967) 1.♗c4
(1.♕f7? ♛f1+ 2.♔g3 ♛g2#;
1.♕d3? ♛h1–+; 1.gxh5?
♛g1–+; 1.♕xb5? ♛g1–+) 1...
bxc4 2.♕e6+ ♔h7 (2...♛f6?
3.♕xf6++–; 2...♔g7 3.♕e7+=)
3.♕f5+! (3.♕f7+? ♛g7–+) 3...
♔g8 (3...♔h6 4.♕e6+=; 3...♔h8
4.♕f8+ ♔h7 5.♕f5+=; 3...♔g7
4.♕d7+=) 4.♕c8+ (4.♕e6+=)
4...♔g7 (4...♛f7 5.♕d7+=; 4...
♔h7 5.♕f5+=) 5.♕d7+ ♔f6
6.♕d6+=

361 (Based on the game Miles
– Pritchett, 1982) 1.♗e5
(1.♕xe8+? ♖xe8–+; 1.♕g6?
♗xb2+ 2.♔b1 ♗c3–+; 1.♖b1?
♗xb2+!? (1...♛c2–+) 2.♖xb2
♖e1+ 3.♖b1 ♖xb1+ 4.♔xb1
♖e1+ (4...♛b4+–+) 5.♔b2
♛b4+ 6.♔c2 ♖e2+–+; 1.♖7d2?
♖xd2–+) 1...♗xe5 (1...♖8xe5
2.♕xg7#; 1...♖2xe5 2.♕xg7#;
1...♗xb2+ 2.♗xb2+–; 1...
♖xb2 2.♕xg7#) 2.♕xe8+ ♔h7
3.♕g6+ ♔h8 (3...♔g8 4.♖d8+
♛e8 5.♖xe8#) 4.♖d8+ ♛e8
5.♖xe8#

362 1.♕f4 (1.♕xe2? ♖h6+ 2.♔h5

♖xh5#; 1.♖xe2? ♖h6#; 1.♗d8?
♖xd8–+; 1.♕f5? ♖h6+–+) 1...
♕h5+ (1...♖h6+? 2.♕xh6 ♗xh6
3.♖xe2; 1...♛xc2 2.♖xe3=; 1...
♛xe1+ 2.♖xe1 ♗xf4 3.gxf4 ♖xc2
4.♗xd4=) 2.♕h4 ♖h6 (2...♛d5?!
3.c4±) 3.♖xe3!=

363 1.♖f2 (1.♖e2? ♗e5 2.♖g2
♖e3–+; 1.♖f7? ♔xf7–+) 1...
♗e5 (1...♗e1 2.♖af7=; 1...♖e3
2.♖e7!?=) 2.♖f6+ (2.♖g2?
♖e3–+) 2...♗xf6 3.gxf6=

364 1.♖h4! (1.♘f7+? ♖xf7 2.♖h4
♛xh4–+; 1.♘g6+? hxg6 2.♖h4+
♛xh4–+) 1...♛xh4 (1...fxe5
2.♖xh3 ♘xh3+ 3.♔g2 ♘xc6
4.♔xh3+–) 2.♕g8+ ♔xg8
(2...♖xg8 3.♘f7#) 3.♘e7+
♔h8 4.♘f7+ ♖xf7 5.♖c8+ ♖f8
6.♖xf8#

365 (Based on the game NN –
Ragaz, 1927) 1.♕xg7+ (1.gxf3?
♖xh3+ 2.♗xh3 ♛xh3#) 1...
♔xg7 (1...♛xg7 2.gxf3+–)
2.gxf3+–

366 1.♖b8 (1.♕xf3? ♖e1+ 2.♕f1
♖xf1#; 1.gxf3? ♖e1+ 2.♕f1
(2.♔g2 ♖g1#) 2...♖xf1+
3.♔g2 ♖g1#) 1...♛f8 (1...♛h5
2.♖xe8+ ♛xe8 3.♕xg3=; 1...
♛f7 2.♖xe8+ ♛xe8 3.♕xg3=; 1...
♖xb8? 2.♕xf3+–) 2.♖xe8 ♛xe8
3.♕xg3=

367 (Based on the game Malakhov
– Gabrielian, 2002) 1.♗g4+
(1.♖f2? gxf2–+) 1...hxg4 (1...
♕xg4 2.♕xg4++–) 2.♖a2+–
(2.♕e2?!=)

368 1.♖b8+ ♔f7 (1...♗f8 2.♖xf8+
♔xf8 3.♕c5++–; 1...♖d8

2.♖xd8++−) 2.♖d8 (2.♕xc7?
♖xc7+−; 2.♖f8+? ♗xf8−+) 2...
♖xd8 (2...♖d1+ 3.♖xd1+−)
3.♕xc7+ ♚e8 (3...♚e6
4.♕xd8+−) 4.♕xg3+−

Chapter 19

369 1.♔f1 ♖c1+ (1...♖f2+
2.♔e1+−) 2.♔e2+−

370 1.g3 (1.h3? ♖e1#) 1...♖e1+
2.♔g2+−

371 1.♔e1+−

372 1.♔g3= (1.g5? ♕f2+ 2.♔g4
h5#)

373 1.♔c1= (1.♗e5? ♕xe5−+)

374 1.♔e2 (1.♔g2 ♖xe1−+) 1...
♖xe1+ 2.♔d3=

375 1.♔g2 (1.♘e4? ♗xd5−+)
1...♗xd5+ 2.♔f1= (2.♘e4?
♗xe4+−+)

376 1.♔h3 (1.f4? ♖b2−+; 1.g4?
♖b2−+) 1...♕h1+ 2.♔g4=
(2.♕h2? ♕f1+ 3.♕g2 ♕xd3−+)

377 1.♔g1 ♖a1+ 2.♔h2+−

378 1.♔g2 ♕h2+ 2.♔f3 ♕f4+
3.♔e2 ♕g4+ 4.♔d2 ♗f4+
5.♔c2+−

379 1.♔e2 (1.♗xh8? ♕f3+ 2.♔g1
♕g3+ 3.♔h1 (3.♔f1 ♕f3+=)
3...♕h3+ 4.♔g1 ♕g3+=) 1...
♕f3+ (1...♖h2+ 2.♔d1 ♕f3+
3.♔c1+−) 2.♔d2 ♖h2+
3.♔c1+−

380 1.f4 ♕f5+ 2.♔f3 ♕d5+!=

381 1.b5 ♖a8+ 2.♔b4+−

382 1.♖gf1 (1.h3? ♖xh3#) 1...♘xh2
(1...♖xh2+ 2.♔g1+−) 2.♔g1+−

383 1.g4 ♖h7+ 2.♔g3+−

384 1.e5 (1.♗d1? ♖d3#) 1...♘b3+
2.♔e4=

385 1.♘e2 (1.♘h1? ♖f1−+ 2.♘g3
g5#; 1.♘e4? ♖xe4−+; 1.♘f5+?
gxf5−+; 1.♘h5? gxh5−+) 1...♖e4
(1...g5+ 2.♔g3=) 2.♘d4 (2.♘g1
♖e3 3.g5+=) 2...♖e3 3.g5+=

386 1.g4 (1.f4? ♖h1+ 2.♔g2 ♗d5+
3.f3 (3.♕f3 ♖8h2#) 3...♖8h2#;
1.♖e1? ♖h1+ 2.♔g2 ♖8h2#) 1...
♖h1+ 2.♔g2 ♖8h2+ (2...♖1h2+
3.♔g1 ♖h1+ 4.♔g2=) 3.♔g3
♖h3+ 4.♔g2 ♖3h2+ 5.♔g3=

387 1.♖e1 ♕xh2+ 2.♔f1 ♕h1+
3.♔e2 ♕f3+ 4.♔d2+−

388 1.h3 (1.h4? ♘e3+ 2.♔h2 ♘g4+
3.♔g3 ♘xe5−+; 1.♕a1? ♘g3#;
1.♕e1? ♖xe1−+; 1.♕g1? ♘e3#;
1.g3? ♘e3#) 1...♘g3+ (1...♘e3+
2.♔h2 ♘f1+=; 1...♘d2+ 2.♔h2
♘f1+=) 2.♔h2 ♘f1+ 3.♔h1=
(3.♔g1=)

Chapter 20

389 1.♕c2+ (1.♔e1? ♖h1+
2.♔d2 ♖xc1−+) 1...♔h8 (1...
g6 2.♔e1=; 1...♔g8 2.♔e1=)
2.♔e1=

390 1.f3 (1.f4? g3−+; 1.♗b5+?!
axb5 2.f3 g3 3.♗xg3 ♕xg3∓;
1.♗h7?! ♖xh7 2.f3 g3 3.♗xg3
♕xg3∓) 1...g3 (1...♕h1+
2.♔f2+−) 2.♗xg3 (2.♗b5+?!
axb5 3.♗xg3 ♕xg3∓) 2...♕xg3
(2...♕h1+ 3.♔f2+−) 3.♗e1
♕h2+ 4.♔f2 ♕h4+ 5.♔e2+−

391 1.♗d5 ♗xd5 2.♘e4 (2.h4?
♘f4+ 3.♘e4 ♗xe4#) 2...♗xe4
(2...♘f4 3.♗f2 ♗xe4+ 4.♔g1=)
3.♗f2 (3.♗e3? ♘xe3+−+) 3...
♘f4+ 4.♔g1=

392 (Based on the game Moura −

Rinaldi, 1983) 1.♕b4+ (1.♕xc7? ♖xc7−+; 1.♖fd1? ♗xb8−+) 1...♔e8 (1...♔d8 2.♕f8#; 1...♗d6 2.♕xe4+ ♕xe4 3.♖ae1+−; 1...♖d6 2.♕xe4+ ♕xe4 3.♖fe1+−) 2.♕xe4+ (2.♗f7+? ♔xf7−+) 2...♕xe4 (2...♗e5 3.♕xf3+−) 3.♖fe1 (3.♖ae1? ♖g7#) 3...♖g7+ 4.♔f1+−

393 (Based on the internet game soilsh – yasir01, 2014) 1.♕b3+ (1.♕e2? ♖f2−+; 1.♘f1? ♖xf1+ 2.♔xf1 (2.♔e2 ♕g2#) 2...♕g1+ 3.♔e2 ♕f2#) 1...♔e7 (1...♔f6 2.0-0-0+−; 1...♔d7 2.0-0-0+−; 1...d5 2.0-0-0+−; 1...♕d5 2.♕xd5++−; 1...♔e5 2.0-0-0+−) 2.0-0-0+−

394 1.exf3 (1.♖e8+? ♖xe8−+) 1...♕xh2+ (1...♘cd4 2.♖e8+ ♖xe8 3.♖xe8#) 2.♔f1 ♕h1+ 3.♔e2+−

395 1.♕a1+ ♔g8 (1...♔h7 2.♔f1+−; 1...♕c3 2.♕xc3++−; 1...f6 2.♔f1+−; 1...♕f6 2.♕xf6++−) 2.♔f1+−

396 1.♕h3+ (1.0-0? ♕xg2#) 1...♔b8 (1...♖d7 2.0-0+−; 1...♕d7 2.♕xd7++−; 1...♕e6 2.♕xe6++−) 2.0-0+−

397 1.♕a1+ (1.♔h2? ♕xf1−+; 1.♕xf7? ♖h5+ 2.♕xh5 ♕xh5#) 1...♔h7 (1...♔g8 2.♔h2=; 1...♖g7 2.♔h2=; 1...f6 2.♕xf6+ (2.♔h2=) 2...♔h7 (2...♔g8 3.♕d8+=) 3.♕f7+ ♔h8 4.♕f6+=) 2.♔h2 (2.g4? ♕xg4+ 3.♔h2 ♕xg2#) 2...♕h5+ (2...♕h5+ 3.♔g1=) 3.♔g1=

398 1.♕b6+ (1.♔g1? ♕xf2+ 2.♔h1 ♘g3+ 3.♔h2 ♘e2+ 4.♔h1

♕f4−+; 1.g3? ♕f3+ 2.♔h2 (2.♔g1 ♕xf2+ 3.♔h1 ♘xg3#) 2...♕xf2+ 3.♔h1 ♘xg3#) 1...♔g7 (1...♔h7 2.♗xe4++−; 1...♗d6 2.♕g1+−; 1...f6 2.♕g1+−; 1...♔g5 2.♕g1+−) 2.♕g1 ♕h2+ 3.♔f1 ♕h1+ 4.♔e2+−

399 1.♖d1+ (1.g3? ♕xf3−+; 1.♗xc6+? bxc6−+) 1...♔c8 (1...♗d6? 2.♖xd6+ ♕xd6 3.♖d1+−) 2.♖fe1 (2.g3? ♕xf3−+) 2...♕h2+ (2...♖d8!?=) 3.♔f1 ♕h1+ 4.♔e2 ♕h2=

400 1.♕b3+ (1.♔g1? ♖d1+−+; 1.♔e2? ♖d2+ 2.♔e1 f3!?−+; 1.♕e1? ♖d1−+; 1.♔e1? f3!?−+) 1...♔h8 2.♕g1! (2.♕xc3?! ♖d3 3.♕c2 (3.♕b2 ♖d2 4.♕c3 ♖2d3=) 3...♖d2 4.♕c3 ♖8d3 (4...♖2d3=) 5.♗c8+ ♗xc8 6.♕xc8+ ♖d8=; 2.♖e5?! ♖d1+ 3.♗e1 ♗xg2+ 4.♔xg2 ♖xe1∓) 2...♖d1+ 3.♔h2+−

401 1.♔h1 (1.♕b8? ♕g4+ 2.♕g3 ♖xg3+ 3.fxg3 ♕e2−+) 1...♕g4 2.♖g1+−

402 1.f3 (1.♖fc1? ♗h3+ 2.♔h1 ♕g2#) 1...♗xf3+ (1...♗h3+ 2.fxg4+−) 2.♔f2 ♕h4+ (2...♕g2+ 3.♔e1+−) 3.♔xf3 ♕xh2 4.♖f2! ♖d3+ 5.♔e2+−

403 1.g3 (1.♗d8?! ♗g3+ 2.♗xh4 ♖xh4+ 3.♔g1 ♗h2+ 4.♔h1 ♗g3+=) 1...♖xg3+ (1...♗g1+ 2.gxh4+−; 1...♖h3 2.♔g2+−; 1...♖4h5 2.♔g2+−; 1...♖4h6 2.♔g2+−; 1...♖4h7 2.♔g2+−) 2.♔g2 (2.♔g1? ♗f4−+) 2...♖h2+ (2...♗f4 3.♖h1+−; 2...♗e5 3.♖h1+−) 3.♔xg3 (3.♔g1?

♗f4–+) 3...♖8h3+ 4.♔f4+–

404 1.♖xc7 (1.g3? ♖h7+ 2.♔g2
♗xg3–+) 1...♖xc7 (1...♖h7+?
2.♖xh7++–) 2.g3 ♖h7+ 3.♔g2=

405 (Based on the internet game
Obama – xNEPHILIMx, 2008)
1.f4 (1.f3? ♗g3–+; 1.♗h4?
♕xh4–+) 1...♗c5+ (1...♗xf4
2.♗f6+–; 1...♖h1+ 2.♔f2+–)
2.♖e3 ♖h1+ 3.♔f2+–

406 1.♗e4+ (1.g3? ♗xg3+ 2.♔g1
(2.♔g2 ♕h2#) 2...♕h2#) 1...
g6 (1...♔h6 2.♗f5!? (2.g3=) 2...
♗c7+ 3.♗h3=; 1...♔h8? 2.♗f5±;
1...♔g8? 2.♗f5±) 2.g3 ♗xg3+
3.♔g2=

407 1.♘g5+ (1.♔h1? ♖e1+ 2.♘g1
♘xf2#) 1...fxg5 (1...♔g6
2.♘f3+–; 1...♔g8 2.♕c8#; 1...
♔h8 2.♕c8#) 2.h3 ♖e1+ (2...
♖xf2 3.♕xc6+–) 3.♔h2 ♘xf2
4.♕xc6+–

408 1.♖f4+! (1.f3? ♕c5+ 2.♕d4
(2.♖d4 e5–+) 2...♖h1+ 3.♔f2
♕c2+ 4.♔g3 (4.♔e3 ♖xf1–+)
4...♖8h3+! 5.gxh3 ♕h2+ 6.♔g4
♕xh3+ 7.♔f4 ♖xf1–+; 1.g3?
♖h1+ 2.♔g2 ♕h3+ 3.♔f3
♖xf1–+) 1...♕e8 (1...♔g7 2.f3
♖h1+ (2...♕c5+ 3.♕d4+=)
3.♔f2 ♕c5+ 4.♕d4+=; 1...♔g8
2.f3 (2.♕d8+ ♔g7 3.♕xe7+
♔h6 4.f3=) 2...♕c5+ (2...♖h1+
3.♔f2 ♕c5+ 4.♕d4=) 3.♕d4
♖h1+ 4.♔f2 ♕c2+ 5.♔e3=
♖xf1? 6.♕d8+ ♔g7 7.♕xe7+
♔h6 8.♖h4#) 2.f3 ♕c5+ (2...
♖h1+ 3.♔f2 ♕c5+ 4.♕d4=; 2...
♕e5 3.♖g4!=) 3.♕d4 ♖h1+
4.♔f2= ♕c2+ 5.♔e3 ♖xf1?

6.♕xh8+ ♔d7 7.♖d4++–

409 1.♔xh3 (1.♖h1? ♖xh1∓) 1...
♖h8+ 2.♔g2 ♖h2+ (2...♖h2+
3.♔f3+–) 3.♔f3 ♖h3+ 4.♔e2+–

410 1.g3 (1.♔g1?!=) 1...♕h3+
2.♔e1 (2.♔g1? ♖g4!–+) 2...
♘g2+ (2...♗xg3 3.fxg3 ♕xg3+
4.♔d2+–) 3.♗xg2 ♕xg2
4.♕xg5+–

411 1.♖a8+ (1.b3? ♕e1+ 2.♔b2
♕c3+ 3.♔c1 (3.♔b1 ♖d1#) 3...
♕a1#) 1...♔c7 2.♖xd8 (2.♖a7+?
♔d6 3.b3 ♕xf2–+) 2...♖xd8
(2...♕e1+? 3.♖d1+–; 2...♕xf2?
3.♖f3 ♕xg2 4.♖df8±) 3.b3 ♕e1+
(3...♕xf2 4.♖g4=) 4.♔b2 ♕xf2
5.♖g4=

412 (Based on the game Peltonen
– Lampela, 1963) 1.♗a6!
(1.♕e6+? ♔b8 2.♘d7+ ♖xd7
3.♕xd7 ♖d8–+; 1.♗f3? exf3–+;
1.♗f1? ♕xh1–+) 1...♕xh1+
(1...bxa6 2.♕a8#; 1...♘c2+
2.♔e2+–) 2.♔e2+–

413 (Based on the game Gelfand –
Timman, 2000) 1.♘f6+ (1.♖e1?
♕xf2+ 2.♔h1 ♕f4 3.♘f6+
♔h8!–+; 1.♕h5? gxh5–+;
1.♗xe4 ♕xh2#) 1...♘xf6
(1...♔h8 2.♘g4+–; 1...♗xf6
2.♕f3+–; 1...♖xf6 2.♗xe4+–)
2.♖e1 (2.f3? ♕xh2+ 3.♔f2
♗g3+ 4.♔e2 ♕xg2+ 5.♔d3
♕xb2–+) 2...♕xh2+ (2...♘g4
3.♕xg4!?+–) 3.♔f1+–

414 (Based on the game Ivanchuk
– Motwani, 1992) 1.♗b2
(1.♕xc8? ♕xc8–+; 1.♖c1?
♕a1+ 2.♔d2 ♖xd7+ 3.♔e2
♕xh1–+) 1...♕xb2 (1...♖xd7+

2.♔c1+−) 2.♕xc8 ♕b1+ (2...
♔e7 3.♖h8!?+−; 2...♖xc8
3.dxc8=♕+−) 3.♔d2 (3.♔e2
♕xh1 4.♕xd8+−) 3...♕xh1
4.♕xd8+−

415 (Based on the game Fischer –
Larsen, 1971) 1.♖d3! (1.♔g4?
♕xg2+−+; 1.f5? ♕xg2−+) 1...
♕xd3 (1...♕xg2 2.♖g3+−; 1...
g6+ 2.♔g4) 2.♔g4+−

416 1.♘d2+ (1.♖f1? ♕g6+ 2.♔h1
♕g2#; 1.♔h1? axb3−+) 1...
♕xd2 2.♔h1 (2.♖f1? ♕g5+
3.♔h1 ♕g2#) 2...♕xf2 (2...♕d5
3.♖d1=; 2...♕xf2? 3.♖f1+−; 2...
♕g5?! 3.♖g1±) 3.♖f1+! (3.♖d1?
♕e2−+) 3...♔e2 (3...♔e3?
4.♖ae1+ ♔d3 5.♖d1+−) 4.♖g1!=

Chapter 21

417 1.g4+−
418 1.♖ab1+−
419 1.♖e1+−
420 1.♘d4+−
421 1.♕h6+−
422 1.♗e7+−
423 1.♕f6+−
424 1.♗g3+−
425 1.♖f7+−
426 1.♘e2+−
427 1.♖f8+−
428 1.♖eh4+−
429 1.g5+−
430 1.♖g4+−
431 1.♗g4+−
432 1.h4+−
433 1.♗f7+−
434 1.h5+−
435 1.♗g8+−
436 1.♔a1+−

437 1.♗f6+−
438 1.♔g4+−
439 1.♗xh6+−
440 1.♖e7+−
441 1.fxg5+−
442 1.h4+−
443 1.♗e4+−
444 1.♔d3+−
445 1.♖gh2+−
446 1.h6+−
447 1.♖g7+−
448 1.♖g3+−
449 1.♖8c6+−
450 1.♘g6+−
451 1.♘c6+−
452 1.♖d5+−
453 (Based on the game Schaefer –
Siegert, 2015) 1.♖d2+−
454 1.♘de4+−
455 1.♖d7+−
456 1.♖g1+−
457 1.♔f8+−
458 1.♖g8+−
459 1.♘h6+−
460 1.♘d7+−
461 1.♗e6+−
462 1.♔f2+−
463 1.♖gg8+−
464 1.♔g8+−
465 1.g6+−
466 1.♔h2+−
467 1.♗g8+−
468 1.h4+−
469 1.♘d6+−
470 1.♘g5+−
471 1.♗b5+−
472 1.♖g5+−

Chapter 22
473 1.e4+ ♔g4 2.♔g2+−

474 1.♕xh7+ (1.♗f6? h5) 1...♔xh7 (1...♔f8 2.♕h8#) 2.♖h4+ ♔g8 (2...♔g7 3.♗f6+ ♔f8 (3...♔g8 4.♖h8#) 4.♖h8#) 3.♗f6+−

475 1.♗f7+ ♔g4 2.♗g6+−

476 1.♘f6+ ♗xf6 2.♕xf6+−

477 1.f7+ ♔f8 2.♗f6+−

478 1.♘g6+ hxg6 2.♖f3+−

479 1.g6+ ♔h6 2.♔h4+−

480 (Based on the internet game nyuweyber – Jeegeey, 2014) 1.♕g4+ ♔h8 2.♕f5+−

481 1.♖h8+ ♔xh8 2.♔g6+−

482 1.♖g3+ ♔h8 2.♗e7+−

483 1.♘b5+ ♔b8 2.c6+−

484 1.f4+ ♔e4 2.♔f2+−

485 1.♕f6+ ♔g8 2.♗xh6+−

486 1.♕f5+ ♔h6 2.h5+−

487 1.a8=♕+ (1.a8=♖+ ♕xa8 2.♗b4+−) 1...♕xa8 2.♗b4+−

488 1.♕xh7+ ♘xh7 2.♖xh7+−

489 1.g4+ ♔h4 2.♔h2+−

490 (Based on the game Georgiev K. – Socko B., 2007) 1.♖h8+ ♔xh8 2.♗xf7+−

491 1.♖xh8+ ♔xh8 2.♘f6+−

492 1.h5+ ♔xh5 2.♖g7+−

493 1.♖h7+ ♔g5 2.♔e3+−

494 1.♗f6+ ♗xf6 2.♗e4+−

495 (Based on a position by Wotawa) 1.f4+ gxf4 2.♘f8+−

496 (Based on a position by Wotawa) 1.♖a8+ ♔b5 2.♔d5+−

497 1.♕xh7+ ♔xh7 2.♖h3+−

498 1.e4+ ♗xe4 2.♘f1+−

499 1.f6+ ♔h7 (1...♔g6 2.♕g8+ ♔h6 3.♕g7#; 1...♔h6 2.♕h8+ ♔g6 3.♕g7#) 2.♕f8+−

500 1.♖h8+ ♗xh8 (1...♔xh8 2.♕h1+ ♗h6 (2...♔g8 3.♕h7#)

3.♕xh6+ ♔g8 4.♕h7#) 2.♕h1+−

501 1.♖g7+ ♔f6 (1...♔h5 2.g4#) 2.g4+−

502 1.a7+ ♔a8 (1...♘xa7 2.♘a6+ ♔a8 3.b7#) 2.♘a6+−

503 1.♕xf5+ ♔xf5 (1...♔e7 2.♕xd7+ ♔f6 3.♕e6#) 2.♘cxd7+−

504 (Based on the internet game Naymin – Blauesross, 2009) 1.♖g1+ ♔h5 (1...♔f5 2.♘d4#; 1...♔f7 2.♖g7#; 1...♔h6 2.f5+ ♔h5 3.♖h1#) 2.f5+−

505 (Based on the game Reshevsky – Ivanovic, 1976) 1.♕xh7+ ♔xh7 2.♖h5+ ♔g8 3.♘g6+−

506 1.♕xh8+ ♔xh8 2.♗f6+ ♔g8 (2...♔h7 3.♖h4+ ♔g8 4.♖h8#) 3.♖h4+−

507 1.♖ge7+ ♔f6 2.♖f7+ ♔e6 3.♔g7+−

508 1.♕h6+ ♖h7 2.♕xh7+ ♔xh7 3.♔f2+−

509 (Based on the game Naumkin – Zverev, 2021) 1.♕xh7+ ♔xh7 2.♖h3+ ♔g8 3.♘fg6+−

510 1.♕h8+ ♗xh8 2.♖xh8+ ♖g8 (2...♔g7 3.♖1h7#) 3.♖xg8+ ♔xg8 4.♗f6+−

Chapter 23

511 1.♖d6 f4+ (1...b3 2.f4#) 2.gxf4+ ♔f5 3.♖f6#

512 1.♗g6 ♕xf4+ (1...♕xe2+ 2.♔xe2 ♗f3+ 3.♔f2+−; 1...♕e1+ 2.♔xe1+−; 1...♕e3+ 2.♔xe3+−; 1...♕d4+ 2.cxd4+−) 2.gxf4 g3+ 3.♔xg3+−

513 (Based on the game Demchenko

– Halkias, 2017) 1.Kg3 Re3+ (1...Re6 2.Rxe6+−) 2.Bf3 Rxf3+ (2...Re6 3.Rxe6+−) 3.Kxf3+−

514 1.Qg8 Rxg8 (1...Qxd5+ 2.Qxd5+−; 1...Kh5 2.Qh7+ Kg4 3.Qxh3+ Kxf4 4.Qf3#; 1...Qxc2+ 2.Kxc2 Bf5+ 3.Rxf5+−) 2.Nf7+ Kh7 3.Rh5#

515 1.Ra1 Be2 (1...a3 2.Rxa3#) 2.Rxa4#

516 1.Kh4 e1=Q (1...Rd5 2.Rxd5+−) 2.Rh5#

517 1.Bb3 Ne7 (1...Rf7 2.Bxf7+−) 2.Qh5#

518 1.Kf6 Rg8 (1...Ba5 2.Qg7#) 2.Qh5#

519 (Based on the internet game jptica – ntbinh_ctu 2011) 1.Be4 Rf8 (1...Qxe4+ 2.Qxe4+−; 1...Qf4 2.gxf4+−) 2.Qh7#

520 1.f6 Be6 (1...Bd7 2.Rxd7+−; 1...Rd4 2.Rxd4+−) 2.Rd8#

521 1.Kg6 Re5 (1...Rg5+ 2.Kxg5+−; 1...Rb1 2.Rb8#) 2.Rb8+ Re8 3.Rxe8#

522 1.Bd6 Bd1 (1...b5 2.Bc7#) 2.Bb4#

523 1.Rg2 Be7 (1...Bg3 2.Rxg3+−) 2.Rg8#

524 1.Bg6 Qf6 (1...Qg4+ 2.hxg4+−; 1...Qxd2+ 2.Kxd2+−; 1...Qe3 2.Rxe3+−; 1...Qe5 2.Rxe5+−; 1...Qe4 2.Rxe4+−) 2.Re8#

525 1.Qf4 Rc1 (1...Qxf2+ 2.Kxf2+−; 1...Rg5+ 2.Qxg5+−; 1...Qxf6 2.Qxf6+−; 1...Qe3 2.Qxe3+−) 2.Qh6#

526 1.Bh4 Bd8 (1...Qxe7 2.Bxe7+−; 1...g5 2.Bxg5+−; 1...Qc6 2.Nxc6+−) 2.Bf6#

527 1.Rcc7 Nf5 (1...Qf1+ 2.Kxf1+−; 1...Rg1+ 2.Kxg1+−; 1...Qh1+ 2.Kxh1+−; 1...Rxg3+ 2.hxg3+−) 2.Rd7#

528 1.Rc8 Rg7 (1...Rc7 2.Rxc7+−) 2.Rc5#

529 1.Rh4 Qf6 (1...Qxh4 2.Qxh4+−; 1...Rfe8 2.Qxh7+ Kf8 3.Qh8#) 2.Qxh7#

530 1.Kf5 d1=Q (1...Bf8 2.Nf6#; 1...Bf6 2.Nxf6#) 2.Ng7#

531 1.Ba6 Qc7 (1...Nd4 2.Bb7#; 1...Qd7 2.Qxd7+−) 2.Qe8+ Qc8 3.Qxc8#

532 1.f4 Kf5 (1...R6a5 2.Rf7#) 2.e4+ Kg4 (2...Kf6 3.Rf7#) 3.h3#

533 1.Qb3 Na5 (1...Qxd6 2.cxd6+−; 1...Rg7 2.hxg7++−; 1...Nd5 2.Qxd5+−) 2.Qxf7#

534 1.Kh3 g6 (1...Rcxd6 2.g4#) 2.g4+ Kh6 3.Nf5#

535 (Based on the internet game Willpower13 – rplobos, 2014) 1.Qc3 Qxd6 (1...Qb4 2.Qxb4+−; 1...Qa5 2.Qxa5+−; 1...Qxe3+ 2.Qxe3+−) 2.Qe1#

536 1.Ra7 Rc1+ (1...Be7 2.Rxe7+−; 1...Rb7 2.Rxb7+−; 1...Rc7 2.Rxc7+−) 2.Kg2 Rbc8 3.Rxh7#

537 1.Kg8 a2 (1...Rg1 2.Rxg1 a2 3.Rg6#; 1...Rxf4 2.Rxf4+−) 2.Rg6#

538 1.Ng5 hxg5 (1...Qh2+ 2.Kxh2+−; 1...Qf4 2.Qh7#) 2.Qh5#

539 (Based on the game Ekinci – Hasanoglu, 2018) 1.Re7 a1=Q

(1...♗g7 2.♖xg7+−) 2.♖h7#

540 1.♘f5 exf5 (1...♔h8 2.♕g7#)
2.gxf5+ ♔h8 3.♕g7#

541 1.h3 f2 (1...♕e1 2.♕xe1+−;
1...♕c1 2.♕xc1+−; 1...♕g7
2.♘xg7++−; 1...♕a1 2.♕xa1+−)
2.♕g4#

542 1.e4 ♘xb4 (1...♘d4 2.♖c1+
♘c2 3.♖xc2#; 1...♗e7 2.♖c1#)
2.♖c1+ ♘c2 3.♖xc2#

543 1.♗h7 d4 (1...♖g8 2.♖h5+ ♖g5
3.♖xg5#; 1...♖xh7 2.♖xh7 ♕h8
3.♖xh8+−) 2.♖h5#

544 1.♕d3 ♕xf6 (1...♕e1+
2.♖xe1+−; 1...♕e4 2.♕xe4+−;
1...♕f5 2.♕xf5+−; 1...♕xg3+
2.fxg3+−) 2.♕h7#

545 1.♕h5 gxh5 (1...♘f6 2.♗xf6+−;
1...h6 2.♕xh6+−; 1...♖fd8
2.♕xh7+ ♔f8 3.♕xf7#)
2.♗xh7#

546 1.♘d6 ♗e4 (1...f4 2.♖xf4+−;
1...♕xe5 2.♖a4#) 2.♗xb5#

547 (Based on the game
Maksimenko – Petelin, 1993)

548 1.♕d4 ♕xd4 (1...♖g7
2.♕xf6+−; 1...♗e7 2.♘xf7#; 1...
♗c3 2.♘xf7#) 2.♘xf7#

549 (Based on a position by
Wotawa) 1.g4! ♕h3 (1...fxg3
2.♖xf1+−; 1...♕xd3 2.cxd3+−)
2.♖f5#

550 (Based on the game Ramirez
– Morozevich, 2002) 1.♖e6
♘xe6 (1...♕f2 2.♕f7#; 1...♕h2+
2.♔xh2+−; 1...♕g2+ 2.♔xg2+−;
1...♕f6 2.♖xf6+−; 1...g4+ 2.fxg4+
♔g5 3.♕d5++−) 2.♕h7#

551 1.♖3g5 hxg5 (1...♕f4 2.♖h5#;
1...♕g4+ 2.hxg4+−; 1...♖g6

2.♖8xg6+−) 2.♖h8+ ♖h6
3.♖xh6#

552 1.♕c3! ♕xf3 (1...♕xh3
2.♕e3#; 1...♔g5 2.f4+ ♔xf4 (2...
♔h4 3.♕g3#; 2...♔h6 3.♕h8#)
3.♕e3#) 2.♕c1+ ♔e4 (2...♕e3
3.♕xe3#) 3.♕c4#

553 1.♕f6 gxf6 (1...♕xb3 2.♕xg7#)
2.♖g3+ ♔h8 3.♗xf6#

554 1.♘f6 ♕xf6 (1...♗f5 2.♕xh7#)
2.♕xf8#

555 1.♕h5 ♗h4 (1...gxh5 2.♖g3+
♗g5 3.♖xg5#; 1...f6 2.♕xh7#;
1...♖fd8 2.♕xh7+ ♔f8 3.♕h8#)
2.♕xh7+ ♔xh7 3.♖xh4+ ♔g8
4.♖h8#

556 1.♕xf6 gxf6 (1...♕e5
2.♗xe5+−; 1...♕e6 2.♕xg7#)
2.♖g1+ ♗g4 3.♖xg4+ ♔h8
4.♗xf6#

557 1.♖xh6 gxh6 (1...♖xd7 2.♖h8#)
2.♕h7#

558 (Based on the game Lvov –
Radchenko, 1957) 1.♕h6 gxh6
(1...♗c3 2.♖xc3+−; 1...♕g5+
2.♕xg5+−; 1...f6 2.♕xg7#)
2.♘xh6#

559 1.♕h6 gxh6 (1...♕b8 2.♕xh7#)
2.♖g8#

560 (Based on the game Herbrig
– Sponheim, 2014) 1.h3 ♗d4+
(1...♔h4 2.♖h6#; 1...g2 2.♖h6#)
2.♔h7 ♗f6 (2...♔h4 3.♖h6#; 2...
g2 3.♖h6#) 3.♖xf6 g2 (3...♔h4
4.♖h6#) 4.♖h6#

561 1.♖e7 h5 (1...h6 2.♖xg7+
♔xg7 3.♕g6#; 1...♕b3 2.♕f7#)
2.♖xg7+ ♔xg7 3.♕g6#

562 1.♘a6 ♖xa6 (1...♖g5+
2.hxg5+−; 1...♖c8 2.♘xc7+

Rxc7 3.Rd8#; 1...a1=Q 2.Nxc7#) 2.Rd8#

563 (Based on the game Katalymov – Mnatsakanian, 1959) 1.Bh6 gxh6 (1...Bxf2+ 2.Kxf2+−; 1...Rxh6 2.Qf8#; 1...Qxe8 2.Qxg7#) 2.Qxf6+ Kg8 3.Qf7+ (3.Bf7++−) 3...Kh8 4.Qf8#

564 (Based on the game Belyakov – Geller, 2012) 1.Qe7 Qh1+ (1...Qg4 2.hxg4+−; 1...Qd7 2.Qxd7+−; 1...Qc7 2.Qxc7+−; 1...Qxf4 2.Bxf4+−; 1...Qg1+ 2.Kg3 Qxf2+ (2...Qg2+ 3.Kxg2+−) 3.Kxf2 Qd2+ 4.Kg1 Qe1+ (4...Qe3+ 5.Kh2+−) 5.Kh2+−) 2.Kg3 Qxf4+ (2...Qe3+ 3.fxe3+−; 2...Qa3+ 3.Qxa3+−; 2...Qc3+ 3.Bxc3+−; 2...Qxg2+ 3.Kxg2+−) 3.Bxf4+−

565 1.h4 Rd1+ (1...Qd1+ 2.Kh2+−; 1...Qe8 2.Rh7#) 2.Kh2 Rh1+ 3.Kxh1 Qd1+ 4.Kh2+−

566 1.Qf4 Bxf4 (1...d1=Q 2.Nxh6#; 1...Bg1+ 2.Kh3+−) 2.gxf4 d1=Q 3.Nxh6#

567 1.Qf6 Bxf6 (1...Rd7 2.Rh8+ Bxh8 3.Rxh8#; 1...Qxf2+ 2.Kxf2+−; 1...Kf8 2.Rh8+ Bxh8 3.Rxh8#) 2.gxf6 Qxe5 (2...Qxf2+ 3.Kxf2+−; 2...Kf8 3.Rh8#) 3.Rh8#

568 1.Rch6 Rb1 (1...Bf4 2.R4h5#; 1...Be1 2.f4#; 1...f4 2.R4h5#) 2.f4+ Bxf4 3.R4h5#

569 (Based on the game Saldano – Bianchi 1995) 1.Rxf7 Rxf7 (1...Rd8 2.Bf8+ Rxf8 3.Bd5++−; 1...Qc5 2.Rxf8+ Qxf8 3.Bd5++−;

1...Qh3+ 2.Kxh3+−; 1...g6 2.Rxf8++−) 2.Qc8+ Rf8 (2...Nd8 3.Qxd8+ Rf8 4.Bd5+ Kh8 5.Qxf8#) 3.Bd5+ Kh8 4.Qxf8#

570 1.Kf7 Ra1 (1...Rf8 2.Nxf8+ Kh8 3.Ng6+ Kh7 4.Rh8#; 1...Rf4+ 2.Qxf4) 2.Rh8+ Bxh8 3.Nf8#

571 1.Ng6 Qb5+ (1...Qd5+ 2.Rxd5+−; 1...Qe7+ 2.Nxe7+−) 2.f5 Qe2 (2...exf5 3.Rh8#; 2...Qxf5+ 3.gxf5+−; 2...Qb8 3.Rxb8++−) 3.Rh8#

572 1.Qg8 Qg1+ (1...Qxg3 2.Qh8#) 2.Kb2 Qf2+ (2...Qxg3 3.Qh8#) 3.Ka3 Qxg3 (3...Qxd4 4.cxd4+−; 3...Qb2+ 4.Kxb2+−; 3...Qxa2+ 4.Kxa2+−; 3...Qxf4 4.gxf4+−) 4.Qh8#

573 1.Qf6! Ke1 (1...Qd4+ 2.Qxd4+−; 1...Qe3+ 2.Kxe3+−; 1...g2 2.Qa1#) 2.Qe5+ (2.Qe6++−; 2.Qe7++−) 2...Kf2 (2...Kf1 3.Qe2#; 2...Kd1 3.Qa1#; 2...Qe3+ 3.Qxe3+) 3.Qe2#

574 (Based on the game Truskavetsky – Grebeniuk, 2006) 1.Rb3 Re7+ (1...Rb7 2.Rxb7+−; 1...Rxd3+ 2.Kxd3+−) 2.Be4 Rd1 (2...Rxe4+ 3.Kxe4+−; 2...Rb7 3.Rxb7+−) 3.Rb1#

575 (Based on the internet game gmflashy – fisherekb, 2014) 1.Qf6 Qf7 (1...Bb5 2.Qf8#; 1...Qd1+ 2.Kh2+−) 2.Qd8+ Qe8 (2...Qf8 3.Qxf8#) 3.Qxe8#

576 (Based on positions by Wotawa) 1.Rb3 g1=Q (1...Ba3

2.♖xa3#) 2.♖a3+ ♗xa3 3.b3#

577 (Based on positions by Nunn)
1.♗e2 ♕g5 (1...♘bxd5 2.♘f5+ ♗xf5 3.g3+ ♔h3 4.♕f1#)
2.♘f5+ ♗xf5 (2...♕xf5 3.g3+ ♔h3 4.♕f1#) 3.g3+ ♕xg3+ (3...♔h3 4.♕f1#) 4.fxg3+ ♔h3 (4...♔xg3 5.♕g5+ ♔h3 6.♗f1#) 5.♕f1+ ♔xg3 6.♕f2+ ♔h3 7.♕h2#

578 1.♕h6 ♗e4+ (1...♗f8 2.♕xh7+ ♔xh7 3.♖h1+ ♗h6 4.♖xh6+ ♔xh6 5.♖h1+ ♕h2 6.♖xh2#; 1...♖e1+ 2.♖xe1+−; 1...♗e5 2.♕g7#) 2.♔a1 ♗f8 (2...♕c1+ 3.♖xc1+−) 3.♕xh7+ ♔xh7 4.♖h1+ ♗h6 (4...♕h2 5.♖xh2++−; 4...♔g8 5.♖h8#) 5.♖xh6+ ♔xh6 (5...♔g8 6.♖h8#) 6.♖h1+ ♕h2 7.♖xh2#

579 (Based on the internet game robi2 – veljomedic, 2008) 1.♕d7 ♕c1+ (1...♖e7 2.♕xe7+−; 1...♕a1+ 2.♔h2+−; 1...♕e3+ 2.♖xe3+−) 2.♔f2 ♕b2+ (2...♕d2+ 3.♕xd2+−; 2...♕xh6 3.♕xe8++−; 2...♖e7 3.♕xe7+−; 2...♕c2+ 3.♔g3+−) 3.♔g3+−

580 1.♖c5 ♘d4 (1...♖xe3 2.♖d1#) 2.♖d1+ ♔xe3 3.♖d3+ ♔f4 4.♘h3#

Chapter 24

581 1.♕xh7+ ♔xh7 2.♖d4 ♕h3 (2...♕f5 3.♖h4+ ♕h5 4.♖xh5#; 2...♕g4 3.♖dxg4+−; 2...♖g8 3.♖h4#; 2...♘e4 3.♖xe4+−) 3.gxh3 (3.♖xh3+? ♔g6=) 3...♖g8 4.♖h4#

582 1.♖d8+ ♖xd8 2.♕h6 ♕c1+ (2...♖d1+ 3.♔h2 ♖h1+ 4.♔xh1 ♕d1+ 5.♔h2+−; 2...♕d1+ 3.♔h2+−) 3.♕xc1+−

583 1.♕f6+ ♔g8 2.♕h6 ♕f2 (2...♕xb2 3.♕xb2+−) 3.♕g7#

584 (Based on the internet game woodbking – hopeimnotapawn, 2013) 1.♖xh7+ ♔xh7 2.♕xg5 ♘f6 (2...♖g8 3.♖h1#) 3.♖h1+ ♘h5 4.♖xh5#

585 (Based on the internet game gabesten – asador, 2009) 1.♕g4+ ♔xh6 (1...♔h7 2.♕g7#) 2.♖f5 ♕c5+ (2...♔e6 3.♖h5#) 3.♔h1 ♕e3 4.♖h5#

586 (Based on the game Capablanca – Raubitschek, 1906) 1.♖xa7+ ♕xa7 2.♖a5 ♕xa6 (2...♖b7 3.♕xb7#; 2...♖b6 3.♕xa7#) 3.♖xa6#

587 1.♗f3+ exf3 2.♔g3 g5 (2...♕xe3 3.♕h4#) 3.♕e8+ ♗f7 4.♕xf7#

588 (Based on the game Hamdouchi – Leyva, 2006) 1.♕e8+ ♔h7 2.♘e7 ♖d8 (2...♖xc2 3.♕g8#) 3.♕xd8 ♗g6 (3...♕xc2+ 4.♔xc2+−) 4.♕g8#

589 1.♗xf6+ ♗xf6 2.♗e4 ♖g8 (2...♗f5 3.♗xf5+−; 2...h6 3.♕xh6+ ♔g8 4.♕h7#) 3.♕xh7#

590 (Based on the internet game Charlie61554 – vanthao311, 2012) 1.b4+ ♔a4 2.♔c3 ♔xa3 (2...♖c2+ 3.♔xc2+−) 3.♖a6#

591 1.♖e8+ ♔h7 2.♖cc8 ♖d8 (2...♕xd5 3.♖h8#) 3.♖exd8! (3.♖cxd8? ♕c1+ 4.♔g2 g5=) 3...♕d2 (3...♕xd8 4.♖xd8+−) 4.♖h8#

592 1.♘h6+ ♔h8 2.♕f7 ♘d7 (2...

♗d8 3.♕g8#) 3.♕g8+ ♖xg8
4.♘f7#

593 1.♗b5+ ♔d8 2.d6 ♘f4 (2...
♕h1+ 3.♔xh1+−; 2...♕e2
3.♗f6+ ♕e7 4.♗xe7#; 2...♕xf3
3.gxf3+−; 2...♕g1+ 3.♔xg1+−;
2...♕e1 3.♗f6+ ♕e7 4.♗xe7#)
3.♗f6#

594 (Based on the game Ciocaltea
– Rogulj, 1979) 1.♖8g5+ ♔h4
2.♖5g3 ♖hc6 (2...♖c3 3.♖xc3+−;
2...♖h1+ 3.♔xh1) 3.♖h3#

595 1.♕xh7+ ♔xh7 2.♖g3 ♖a5 (2...
♕xb2+ 3.♔xb2+−; 2...♕a1+
3.♔xa1+−; 2...♕a2+ 3.♔xa2+−;
2...♕xb3 3.♖h1#) 3.♖h1+ ♖h5
4.♖xh5#

596 1.♕e6+ ♔f8 2.♗h5 g6 (2...
♕xg2+ 3.♔xg2+−; 2...b1=♕
3.♕f7#) 3.♕h6#

597 1.♖c8+ ♔h7 2.f5 ♖xc4 (2...gxf5
3.g6+ ♔h6 4.♖h8#) 3.fxg6#

598 1.♘g6+ ♔h7 2.h5 (2.♘f8+
♔g8+−) 2...fxg6 (2...♕h4+
3.♘xh4+−; 2...♕xg2+
3.♔xg2+−; 2...♕f4+ 3.exf4+−)
3.♖h8#

599 (Based on the game Reti –
Bogoljubov, 1924) 1.♗f7+
♔h8 (1...♕xf7 2.♕xf7++−)
2.♗e8 ♗e7 (2...h6 3.♕xf8++−;
2...♖xc5+ 3.♕xc5+− ♖xe8
4.♖f8+ ♖xf8 5.♕xf8#; 2...♕e7
3.♕xf8+ ♕xf8 4.♖xf8#; 2...
♕xg3+ 3.hxg3+−) 3.♕f8+ ♗xf8
4.♖xf8#

600 1.♕xg6+ ♔h8 2.♘g5 hxg5
(2...♕d5+ 3.cxd5+−; 2...♕xg5
3.fxg5+−; 2...♕d3 3.♕xd3+−;
2...♕e8 3.♕h7#) 3.♕xh5+ ♗h6

4.♕xh6#

601 1.♕xh6+ ♕xh6 (1...♔g3
2.♕h2#) 2.♔h2 ♘e2 (2...♕e6
3.♗f2#) 3.♗f2+ ♘g3 4.♗xg3#

602 1.g6+ ♔h8 2.♘h6 ♗c5 (2...♗c7
3.♕g8#) 3.♕g8+ ♖xg8 4.♘f7#

603 (Based on the game Odinaeva –
Basnayake, 2012) 1.♕h4+ ♕h5
2.♕f6 ♕f5 (2...♕e2 3.♕g5#; 2...
♕xf4+ 3.♕xf4++−; 2...♕xh3+
3.♔xh3+−; 2...♕xe5 3.♕xe5+−)
3.♕g7+ ♔h5 4.♕xh7#

604 1.♕d4+ ♔xf5 2.♕g7 ♖ag8
(2...♗f6 3.g4+ ♘xg4 4.hxg4#;
2...♘g4 3.hxg4#) 3.g4+ ♘xg4
4.hxg4#

605 (Based on the game Muzychuk
A. – Schmidt, 2006) 1.♖f7+ ♔h8
(1...♔g8 2.♘f6+ ♔h8 3.♖h7#)
2.♘f6 ♖d1+ (2...♕xe6 3.♖h7#)
3.♕f1 ♖xf1+ (3...♕xe6 4.♖h7#)
4.♔xf1 ♕xe6 5.♖h7#

606 1.♕h5+ (1.♖g4? ♖b7+!=) 1...
♖b5 (1...♕e5 2.♕xe5+ ♖b5
3.♕a1#) 2.♕g6 ♕c3 (2...♕g7+
3.♕xg7+−; 2...♖b7+ 3.♔xb7+−)
3.♕a6#

607 1.♕h5+ ♔g8 2.♕f7+ ♔h7
3.♖f5 ♖hf8 (3...♕xe6 4.♕xe6+−;
3...♕f4 4.♖xf4+−; 3...♕a3+
4.♔xa3+−; 3...♕e5 4.♖xe5+−)
4.♖h5#

608 1.♕f5+ g6 2.♕f6 ♖c7 (2...♖gf8
3.♕g7#) 3.♕g7+ ♖xg7 4.♘f6#

609 1.♕xh7+ ♔xh7 2.♖h3+
(2.♖h4+ ♔g8 3.♖gh3+−) 2...
♔g8 3.♖dh4 ♗xg5 (3...♗h5
4.♖xh5+−; 3...g6 4.♖h8+ ♔g7
5.♖3h7#) 4.♖h8#

610 1.♖h8+ ♔xh8 (1...♔f7 2.♕h5+

g6 3.♕h7+ ♔e8 4.♕xg6#)
2.♕h5+ ♔g8 3.g6 ♖f5 (3...♗f3
4.♕h7#) 4.♕h7+ ♔f8 5.♕h8#

611 1.♕xe6+ ♔f8 2.♕xf6+ ♔g8
3.♘e6 ♘d2+ 4.♔g1 (4.♖xd2?
♕a1+ 5.♔e2 d3+−+) 4...♖d7
(4...♕c7 5.♖xc7; 4...♘f3+ 5.gxf3;
4...d3 5.♕xc3) 5.♕f8#

612 (Based on the game Geller –
Golod, 2007) 1.♕g2+ ♔h8 (1...
♔f7 2.♖xh7#) 2.♖xh7+ ♔xh7
3.♖d3 ♖g8 (3...♘f6 4.♖h3+ ♘h5
5.♖xh5#; 3...♕e3 4.♖xe3+−;
3...♕g1+ 4.♔xg1+−; 3...♕xc3
4.bxc3+−; 3...♖f6 4.exf6+−)
4.♖h3#

613 1.♕g5+ ♔h8 2.♕f6+ ♔g8
3.♖f3 ♕xb2 (3...h6 4.♖g3+ ♔h7
5.♕g7#; 3...h5 4.♖g3+ ♔h7
5.♕g7#) 4.♖g3#

614 1.♕xh7+ ♔xh7 2.g6+ ♔h8
3.♔g2 ♘f6 (3...♗e7 4.♖h1+
♗h4 5.♖xh4#; 3...♘b6 4.♖h1#)
4.♖h1+ ♘h7 (4...♘h5 5.♖xh5#)
5.♖xh7#

615 (Based on the game Chigaev –
Iljushonok, 2021) 1.♕f7+ ♖xf7
2.gxf7+ ♔f8 3.♖g1 ♗d8 (3...♗d6
4.♖g8+ ♔e7 5.f8=♕#; 3...♕a6
4.♖g8#) 4.♖g8+ ♔e7 5.f8=♕#

616 1.♘g6+ ♔g8 (1...♔h7
2.♘e7+ ♔h8 (2...g6 3.♕xg6+
♔h8 4.♕g8#) 3.♕f8+ ♔h7
4.♕g8#) 2.♘e6+ ♔h7 3.♘e7
h5 (3...♗d8 4.♕g8#; 3...♕xe7
4.♕xe7+−; 3...♕c4 4.dxc4+−; 3...
♕b3 4.♕xb3+−) 4.♕g6+ ♔h8
5.♕xh5#

617 (Based on the game Toth
– Aarland, 1974) 1.♕g3+

(1.♖e6+? ♔f7−+) 1...♔h7
2.♘f6+ ♔h8 3.♕g6 ♕g7 (3...
♖xg2+ 4.♕xg2+−; 3...♘f3+
4.♖xf3+−; 3...♖a7 4.♕xh6+
♕h7 5.♘xh7+−; 3...♖xg2+
4.♕xg2+−) 4.♖e8+ ♖xe8
5.♕xe8+ ♔g8 6.♕xg8#

618 1.♘xh6+ gxh6 (1...♔h8 2.♘f7+
♔g8 3.♕xg7+ ♔xg7 4.♗f6+
♔g8 5.♘h6#) 2.♕h8+! ♔xh8
3.♔f7 ♖g8 (3...♖f8+ 4.♔xf8+−;
3...d4 4.♗f6#) 4.♗f6+ ♖g7+
5.♗xg7#

619 1.♘g5+ ♔h8 2.♘f7+ ♔h7 3.f6
♖g8 (3...♗e8 4.♖g7#) 4.♖h6#

620 (Based on a position by Del
Rio) 1.♖f8+ ♔g7 2.♗h6+ ♔xh6
3.♖g8 ♖a4 (3...♗e4 4.♖h5#)
4.♖h5+ ♗xh5 5.g5#

621 1.♖xf7+ ♔xf7 2.♕f5+ ♘f6 (2...
♗f6 3.♕g6+ ♔f8 4.♖e8+ ♕xe8
5.dxe8=♕#) 3.♕e6+ ♔f8 4.♗g6
♕xd7 (4...♕e8 5.dxe8=♕+
♘xe8 6.♕f7#) 5.♕f7#

622 1.♘a6+ ♔a8 2.♘xc7+ ♔b8
(2...♖xc7 3.♖d8+ ♖c8 4.♖xc8#)
3.♘a6+ ♔a8 4.♖b7 ♖xc2 (4...
♖xc6 5.♖b8#) 5.♖b8+ ♖xb8
6.♘c7#

623 (Based on the game Khalil –
Mahrous, 2016) 1.♕h8+ ♔g6
2.♖h6+ ♔f5 3.♕xf6+ ♔g4
4.♕f2 ♕e3 (4...♘f3+ 5.gxf3++−;
4...♕d6+ 5.♖xd6+−; 4...♘e6
5.♕h4+ ♔f5 6.♕f6+ ♔g4
7.♖h4#) 5.♖h4#

624 1.♕xg8+ ♔xg8 2.♖h1 d4+ (2...
♖h2 3.♖xh2+−) 3.♗e4 ♖f2+!
(3...♕xe4+ 4.♖xe4+−; 3...♖h2
4.♖xh2+−) 4.♔g4! (4.♔xf2?

dxe3+ 5.♔e2 ♛c4+ 6.♔f3
♛xe4+ 7.♔xe4 ♝c6+−+) 4...e5+
(4...♖h2 5.♖xh2+−) 5.♔g5 ♝e7
(5...♖h2 6.♖xh2+−) 6.♖h8#

Chapter 25

625 1.♕h3 ♝f5 (1...b5 2.♕c8#; 1...
♔b8 2.♕h8#) 2.♕h8+ ♝c8
3.♕xc8#

626 1.♘f6+ gxf6 (1...♔h8 2.♕xf8#)
2.exf6 ♖e8 (2...♕g4 3.♕xf8+
♔xf8 4.♖d8#; 2...♕xf1+
3.♔xf1+−) 3.♕g3+ ♔f8 (3...
♔h8 4.♕g7#; 3...♕g4 4.♕xg4+)
4.♕g7#

627 (Based on the game Chevalier
– Lopez Jorge, 1990) 1.♔e1 ♖h3
(1...♖h1 2.♖xh1+−) 2.d5 ♘xd5
3.♘d4#

628 1.♔f6 ♔g8 2.♝d5+ ♔f8 3.♝f7
b6 (3...c5 4.♝c1 b5 5.♝h6#)
4.♝c1 c5 5.♝h6#

629 (Based on the internet game
sandyp626 – King_William,
2008) 1.♖c7 ♔g8 (1...♕xf4+
2.♕xf4+−; 1...♕h1+ 2.♔xh1+−;
1...♕g1+ 2.♔xg1+−; 1...♕xg2+
2.♘xg2+−; 1...♝d7 2.♖xd7+−)
2.♕xf7+ ♔h8 3.♕g7#

630 (Based on the game Fischer –
Petrosian, 1961) 1.♔c4 ♘d5 (1...
♖h4+ 2.gxh4+−) 2.♖a7#

631 (Based on the game Dueball
– Partos, 1974) 1.♘xc6 ♔b7
(1...♕h3 2.♕b5#; 1...♖e1+
2.♔f2+−) 2.♘d8+ ♔c8
3.♘xe6+−

632 (Based on the internet game
doublexclam – raskolnnikov,
2013) 1.♘e8 ♕b7 (1...♕f3

2.♕xg7#; 1...♕g2+ 2.♔xg2+−)
2.♕f8#

633 1.♖e8 ♕e4 (1...♕xf2+
2.♔xf2+−; 1...♕h1+ 2.♔xh1+−;
1...♕h2+ 2.♔xh2+−) 2.♝e7#

634 1.♕xf6+ ♔g8 2.♘f5 h6 (2...
♖fe8 3.♕g7#) 3.♕g7#

635 1.♕g5 g6 (1...♕c3 2.♕xg7#)
2.♕h6 ♕c3 3.♕g7#

636 1.♕f8+ ♔h7 2.♕f7+ ♔h8
3.♘xf6 ♕d8 (3...♘e5 4.♕h7#)
4.♕h7#

637 (Based on the game Davies –
Rendle, 2008) 1.♖f8+ ♖g8 2.♕f7
♝e6 (2...♖xf8 3.♕xf8#; 2...♕b6
3.♕xg8#) 3.♕f6#

638 1.♝f4 ♖f8 (1...♔g8 2.♕f6+−;
1...♕xf4 2.gxf4+−; 1...♕xf2+
2.♖xf2+−; 1...g5 2.♕xg5+−;
1...exf4 2.♕e7+−) 2.♕e7 ♖xf4
(2...♕xf2+ 3.♖xf2+−; 2...♖f7
3.♕e8+ ♖f8 4.♕xf8#; 2...♕xf4
3.♕g7#) 3.♕g7#

639 1.♔f3 g4+ (1...♖d8 2.♖h1#)
2.♔f4 ♖d8 3.♖h1#

640 1.♖e1 ♔f8 (1...d3 2.♖e8#)
2.♖d7 d3 3.♖e8#

641 (Based on the game Nechesany
– Vashichek, 1947) 1.♕h6
gxh6 (1...gxf6 2.♘f5+−; 1...♕e6
2.♕xg7#) 2.♘f5+−

642 1.f4 ♘e4 (1...h5 2.♖e5#; 1...f6
2.g4#; 1...♖a3+ 2.bxa3+−) 2.g4+
♔e6 3.♖xe4++−

643 1.♕xf6+ ♔g8 (1...♔xf6
2.♝b2#) 2.♝b2 ♘f5 3.♕h8#

644 1.♖e7 ♖xe7 (1...♔f7 2.♖xf7
♖e1+ 3.♖xe1+−; 1...♕f1+
2.♖xf1+−) 2.♕xf8#

645 (Based on the internet game

TekWz – jmhet42, 2009) 1.♕d5+ ♔h8 (1...♕e6 2.♕xe6++−) 2.♕f7 h6 (2...♖xe8 3.♕xe8+ ♘f8 4.♕xf8#; 2...♕d8 3.♖xd8+−; 2... ♕d6 3.♘xd6+−) 3.♕xg6+−

646 1.♕d7 ♗g4+ (1...♗g4+ 2.♕xg4 ♕xg4+ 3.♔xg4+−; 1...♕e8 2.♕xg7#; 1...♗d4 ♗xd4+−; 1... ♗f7 2.♕xf7+−) 2.♕xg4 ♗xg4+ 3.♔xg4+−

647 1.♖c8 g5 (1...♕xf4 2.gxf4+−; 1...♖d8 2.♖xd8+−; 1...♕f8 2.♕xf8+−) 2.♕g8#

648 1.♕xf6 ♕xf6 (1...♕f8 2.♗xf8+−; 1...♘xh6 2.♕xd8+) 2.♖e8#

649 1.♖e8+ ♖f8 2.♖e7 ♕e5 (2...♖f7 3.♕xf7+ ♔h8 4.♕xg7#; 2...cxb2 3.♕xg7#) 3.♖xe5 dxe5 4.bxc3+−

650 (Based on the game Teschner – Portisch, 1969) 1.♕f7 ♖xf7 (1... ♖de4 2.♕f8#; 1...h6 2.♕xe7+−) 2.♖e8+ ♖f8 3.♖xf8#

651 1.♖a8+ ♗xa8 2.♕a5 ♕g1+ (2...♗b7 3.♕xc7#; 2...♔b8 3.♕xc7#; 2...♖d7 3.♕xa8#) 3.♔b2 ♕b6 (3...♕d4+ 4.♔b3+−; 3...♖d7 4.♕xa8#; 3...♔b8 4.♕xc7#; 3...♗b7 4.♕xc7#; 3... ♕a7 4.♕xa7+−) 4.♕xa8+ ♕b8 5.♖xc7+ ♔xc7 6.♕c6#

652 1.♔d1 ♘f3 (1...f5 2.♖d4#; 1... c5 2.♗xe4#) 2.♗xf3 exf3 3.♖d4#

653 1.♖b5 ♖a2 (1...f6 2.f3#) 2.♖g5#

654 1.♖f7 ♕xf7 (1...♗xf7 2.♕xg7#; 1...♘xg3 2.♗xg7#) 2.♗xg7+ (2.♕xg7+ ♕xg7 3.♗xg7#) 2... ♕xg7 3.♕xg7#

655 1.♕g6 h6 (1...♕b4+ 2.c3+−; 1...♕h5 2.♖xh5+−; 1...♗d8

2.♕xh7#; 1...h5 2.♖xh5+ ♕xh5 3.♕xh5#) 2.♖xh6+ gxh6 3.♕xh6#

656 1.♕f6 ♕xe7 (1...♖xe7 2.♕h8#; 1...♕e8 2.♖xe8++−; 1...d3 2.♕xf7#) 2.♕h8#

657 (Based on the internet game Mani999 – piratephan, 2014) 1.♕g7+ ♔xh5 (1...♔g5 2.h4+ ♔xh5 3.♕xh7#) 2.h4 a1=♕+ (2...a1=♖+ 3.♔d2 ♖xh1 4.♕xh7#; 2...♖h8 3.g4#; 2...f5 3.♕xh7#) 3.♔d2 ♕xh1 (3...♖h8 4.g4#; 3...f5 4.♕xh7#; 3...♕c1+ 4.♔xc1+−; 3...♕d1+ 4.♔xd1+−; 3...♕e1+ 4.♔xe1+−) 4.♕xh7#

658 1.♘g6+ ♔g8 2.♕e7 ♖f8 (2... ♕d6 3.♕f7#; 2...♘e5 3.♕f8+ ♖xf8 4.♘e7#) 3.♕xf8+ ♘xf8 4.♘e7#

659 (Based on the internet game Nedjib – JPatSoCal, 2013) 1.♕g3 ♕f8 (1...♕d6 2.♕g8#; 1...♕xb3 2.♕xb3+−; 1...♗d5 2.♗xd5+−; 1...♕c4 2.♗xc4+−) 2.♕e5+ ♕g7 3.♕e8+ ♕g8 4.♕xg8#

660 1.♕h6 ♕xf6 (1...♗xf6 2.♕f8#; 1...♕e1+ 2.♖xe1+−; 1...♕xh2+ 2.♔xh2+−) 2.♖d8+ ♗xd8 3.♕f8#

661 (Based on the internet game Visconde – thomsonfam, 2013) 1.♘e7+ ♔h8 (1...♖xe7 2.♕xf8#) 2.♘xf8 g6 (2...♖xe7 3.♘g6#) 3.♘e6+ ♖f8 4.♕xf8#

662 1.♘e6 ♗e7 (1...♖xf2+ 2.♖xf2 exf2 3.♖xg7#) 2.♖xe7 ♘xe7 (2... ♖xf2+ 3.♖xf2+−) 3.♖f8#

663 (Based on the internet game

QTexx – Aikiigm, 2017) 1.♗g7
g4 (1...♖c6 2.♖xc6+−) 2.♔f4
♖c7 (2...♖c6 3.♖xc6+−) 3.♖h6#

664 1.♕h6 ♖g8 (1...♕c2 2.♕g7#)
2.♖f3 ♕c2 (2...♕xg2+
3.♔xg2+−; 2...♕f2+ 3.♔xf2+−;
2...♕b3 3.♖xb3+−; 2...♖g7
3.♕xg7#) 3.♕xh7+ ♔xh7
4.♖h3#

665 (Based on a position by
Wotawa) 1.♘g6+ ♖xg6 (1...hxg6
2.♖h3#) 2.♔f7 h5 (2...a1=♕
3.♖c8#; 2...h6 3.♔xg6 a1=♕
4.♖c8#) 3.♔xg6 a1=♕ (3...♔g8
4.♖c8#) 4.♖c8#

666 1.♘xf7 g5 (1...♘c3+ 2.♔e1
♖a1+ 3.♔d2! (3.♔f2? ♘e4+=)
3...♘e4+ 4.♔c2+−; 1...♘f2+
2.♔c1 ♘d3+ 3.♔b1 ♖b2+
4.♔a1+−) 2.h5 g6 (2...♘c3+
3.♔e1 ♖a1+ 4.♔d2 ♘e4+
5.♔c2+−; 2...♘f2+ 3.♔c1 ♘d3+
4.♔b1 ♖b2+ 5.♔a1+−) 3.h6
♘c3+ (3...♘f2+ 4.♔c1 ♘d3+
5.♔b1 ♖b2+ 6.♔a1+−) 4.♔e1
♖a1+ 5.♔d2 ♘e4+ 6.♔c2+−

667 (Based on the game Lahlum
– Madsen, 1995) 1.♕xf6 gxf6
(1...♕xc3 2.♕xc3+−; 1...♕d4
2.♗xd4+−; 1...♕g8 2.♕f4!?
♕e6 3.♕xf8+ ♖xf8 4.♗xg7#; 1...
♗f7 2.♗xf7+−) 2.♗xf6+ ♗g7
3.♗xg7#

668 1.♕xh6 gxh6 (1...♗xf6 2.♕h7#;
1...♖xf6 2.♕h7#) 2.♖g3+ ♗g4
3.♖xg4#

669 (Based on the game Klukin –
Ziaziulkina, 2014) 1.b4+ ♔xc4
2.♔d2 e3+ (2...fxg3 3.♗b3#)
3.fxe3 fxe3+ 4.♖xe3 ♖f2+

5.♖e2 ♖f3 (5...♖xe2+ 6.♗xe2#)
6.♗b3#

670 1.♕f5 ♕xf5 (1...gxf5 2.♗f7#;
1...♕b3+ 2.♗xb3 gxf5 3.♗f7#;
1...♕e5+ 2.dxe5 gxf5 3.♗f7#; 1...
♕b2 2.♕f3#) 2.♗e2+ ♕g4+ (2...
♕f3+ 3.♗xf3#) 3.♗xg4#

671 (Based on the internet game
Extant_MC1R – Mazama,
2014) 1.♖f7 ♖d1+ (1...♕xg2+
2.♔xg2+−; 1...♖c1+ 2.♕xc1+−;
1...♕d1+ 2.♔h2+−; 1...♕b1+
2.♔h2+−) 2.♔h2 ♖h1+ (2...
♕xg2+ 3.♔xg2+−) 3.♔xh1
♕d1+ 4.♔h2+−

672 1.♖e8+ ♖f8 2.h6 ♖xe8 (2...♕a3
3.♗g7+ ♔h8 4.♘f7#; 2...♕c7
3.♖h8+ ♔xh8 4.♖xf8#; 2...♘f6
3.♖g7+ ♔h8 4.♘f7#) 3.♗g7+
♔f8 (3...♔h8 4.♘f7#) 4.♘h7#

673 (Based on a position by Stubbs)
1.♖h1+ ♔xh1 (1...♕xh1
2.♕xg8+−) 2.♕b1+ ♔h2 (2...
♖g1 3.♕xg1#) 3.♕h7#

674 (Based on the game
Mikhailovsky – Yashmetov,
2018) 1.♕f7 ♕g7 (1...♕e1+
2.♔c2+−; 1...♕h8 2.♕g6#)
2.♕e6+ ♕g6 3.♕xg6#

675 (Based on the game Bujakin
– Livschin, 1966) 1.♖h5 ♗f8
(1...♕a5+ 2.c3+−) 2.♖f5+ exf5
(2...♔xg6 3.♖g5+ ♔f7 (3...♔f6
4.♕g6#) 4.♕g6#) 3.♕xf5+ ♔g7
4.♕f7#

676 (Based on the internet game
rgarrido – C_4, 2009) 1.♖xg6
hxg6 (1...♕f6 2.♖xg7++−)
2.♕xg6 (2.♖xg6? ♕f6∓) 2...♕h4
(2...♕f6 3.♕xf6+−) 3.♕xg7#

677 (Based on the game Ramaswamy – Mongontuul, 2007) 1.Qh5 g6 (1...Ng3+ 2.hxg3+–; 1...Bg5 2.fxg5 Qxg5 3.Qxg5+–; 1...f5 2.Bg6+ Kg8 3.Qh7#) 2.Bxg6+ Kg7 (2...Kg8 3.Qh7#) 3.Qh7#

678 1.Qxc6+ Kxc6 (1...Ka6 2.Bf1+ Ka5 3.Qb5#; 1...Kb8 2.Nd4 d5 3.Bxd5+–) 2.Ne5+ Kc5 3.Nd3+ Kd4 4.Kd2+–

679 (Based on the game Cordara – Rombaldoni, 2010) 1.Rc7 Rb1+ (1...Qe1+ 2.Kh2+–; 1...Qd1+ 2.Kh2+–) 2.Kh2 Rh1+ (2...Qxf2+ 3.Qxf2+–; 2...Qf1 3.Qg7#) 3.Kxh1 Qf1+ 4.Kh2+–

680 (Based on the game Ender – Oezdemir, 2017) 1.Qf8 Qe3+ (1...Qg3+ 2.Kh1 Qf3+ 3.Bg2 Qd1+ 4.Kh2+–) 2.Kh1 (2.Kh2? Qf4+=) 2...Qe4+ (2...Qf3+ 3.Bg2 Qd1+ 4.Kh2+–) 3.Bg2 Qe1+ (3...Qb1+ 4.Kh2+–) 4.Kh2+–

681 1.Rh3 gxh4 (1...Qxf6 2.Qh8#) 2.Rxg7+ Kh8 3.Rxh4#

682 1.Rd8+ Bf8 (1...Ke8 2.Rxe8++–) 2.Bxh6 Rb8 (2...Be8 3.Rxe8+–) 3.Bc8 Rxc8 (3...Be8 4.Rxe8+–) 4.Rxc8 Nxc5 5.Rxf8#

683 1.Rxg6+ fxg6 (1...Kh7 2.Qh5#; 1...Kh8 2.Qh5#) 2.Qxg6+ Kh8 3.Rd7 Qh4 (3...Qf7 4.Rxf7 Rxf7 5.Qxf7+–; 3...Rf7 4.Rxf7 Qxf7 5.Qxf7+–) 4.Qg7#

684 (Based on the game Najer – Sokolov, 2014) 1.Rxf7+ Kxf7

(1...Kd8 2.Qh8#; 1...Ke8 2.Qxe6+ Kd8 3.Qd7#) 2.Qf6+ Ke8 (2...Ng8 3.Qxg6+ Kh8 4.Nf6+–) 3.Qxe6+ Kd8 4.Nf6 (4.Nf8? Qc7=) 4...Qc8 (4...Qc7 5.Qe8#; 4...Kc7 5.Qe7+ Kb6 6.Nd7++–) 5.Qd6+ Qd7 6.Qxd7#

685 (Based on the internet game blaze777 – jonnyp, 2007) 1.Rh3 Kh8 (1...Qe8 2.Rxh6#) 2.Bxh6 Qg8 (2...gxh6 3.Rxh6+ Bh7 4.Qxh7#) 3.Bxg7#

686 (Based on the internet game Michodov – pumareal2000, 2014) 1.Qa3 b4 (1...c5 2.Qb2+–; 1...Bd7 2.Qb2+–; 1...Qb4 2.Qxb4+–; 1...Qc5 2.Qxc5+–; 1...Ra8 2.Qf8#) 2.Qb2 e5 (2...Qc3 3.Nxc3+–; 2...f6 3.Qxf6+–; 2...Qd4 3.Qxd4+–) 3.Qxe5 f6 4.Qxf6+–

687 1.Rfh5 f6 (1...Bh4 2.Rh8+ Kxh8 3.Qxh4+ Kg8 4.Qh8#; 1...f5 2.Qxg6+–) 2.Qxg6 Qxh3 (2...Bc5 3.Rh8#) 3.Rxh3+–

688 1.Re8 Bd1 (1...Bc5 2.Nh7+ Kf5 3.g4#) 2.g4 (2.Ne4+? Kf5 3.Nd6+ Kf6=) 2...Bxg4+ (2...Bc5 3.Nh7#) 3.Kxg4 Bc5 4.Nh7#

689 1.Rg4+ (1.Qg5+ Kh8 2.Qf6+ Kg8) 1...fxg4 2.Qg5+ Kh8 3.Qh6 (3.Qf6+ Kg8 4.Qg5+ Kh8) 3...Rg8 (3...Qxh2+ 4.Kxh2+–; 3...f5 4.Qxf8#) 4.Qxh7#

690 (Based on the game Goswami – Murugan, 1999) 1.Qf6 Bf8 (1...Be5 2.dxe5+–; 1...Qe7

2.♕g7#) 2.♗xf8 ♖xf8 (2...♔xf8
3.♖xh7+−) 3.♖xh7 ♔xh7 (3...
♕d8 4.♖h8#) 4.♗e3 ♔g8 (4...
♕xh2+ 5.♔xh2+−; 4...♕g3
5.♖xg3+−; 4...♕f4 5.♕xf4+−;
4...♕d8 5.♖h3+ ♔g8 6.♖h8#)
5.♖h3 ♕d8 6.♖h8#

691 1.♖xh6+ gxh6 2.♗f6+ ♔h7
3.♘g5+ hxg5 4.h4 ♗h3 (4...♗h5
5.hxg5+−; 4...gxh4 5.♖xh4+ ♗h5
6.♖xh5#; 4...♖f8 5.hxg5+ ♗h5
(5...♗h3 6.♖xh3#) 6.♖xh5#)
5.hxg5 (5.♖xh3? g4−+) 5...♗d8
6.♖xh3#

692 1.♕xg6 (1.♕g5? ♕xd4+
2.♖xd4 ♖xd4 3.♕xb5 ♖d1+
4.♔f2 ♖d2+=) 1...♕xd4+! (1...
♖xg6 2.♖xh7+ ♔g8 3.♖h8#; 1...
fxg6 2.♖xh7#) 2.♖xd4 fxg6 (2...
♖xg6 3.♖xd8++−) 3.♖xh7+!
♔xh7 4.♖h4#

693 (Based on the game Fuderer –
Donner, 1952) 1.♘h5 gxh5 (1...
♗f8 2.♘xf6+ ♔h8 3.♕xh7#; 1...
♘e6 2.♘xf6+ ♔h8 3.♕xh7#;
1...♗e5 2.♕g7#) 2.♗xh7+ ♔h8
3.♗g6+ ♔g8 4.♕h7+ ♔f8
5.♗h6+ ♔e7 6.♕xf7+ ♔d8
7.♕xe8#

694 1.♖xg7+ ♔xg7 2.♕g6+
♔h8 3.♖h1 (3.♕h6+ ♔g8
4.♕g6+ ♔h8) 3...exf5 (3...♗h4
4.♔xh4+−; 3...♖xf5 4.♔g3+
♖h5 5.♖xh5#) 4.♔g3+ ♗h4+
5.♖xh4#

695 (Based on the internet game
Southlandstag – CarlD82, 2014)
1.♕e5 ♖xg2+ (1...♕d4+ 2.♕xd4
♖xd4 3.♖e8#; 1...f6 2.♕e6+ ♔h8
3.♕xf6+ ♔g8 4.♕g7#) 2.♔h1

(2.♔xg2 ♕xf3+ 3.♔g1 ♕g2#)
2...♖xh2+ (2...♕d4 3.♕e8+ ♖xe8
4.♖xe8#; 2...f6 3.♕e6+ ♔h8
4.♕xf6+ ♔g8 5.♕g7#; 2...♖g1+
3.♔xg1+−) 3.♔xh2 ♕c2+ (3...
♕d2+ 4.♗xd2+−) 4.♔g3+−

696 (Based on the game Hort
– Scotland, 1981) 1.♖f7 h5
(1...♘f6 2.♗xf6+−; 1...♔xf7
2.♕xh7+ ♔f8 3.♗h6#) 2.♕d3
(2.♗xg6? ♗xg5 3.♕xh5 ♘f6−+)
2...♔xf7 (2...♘f4 3.♗xf4+−; 2...
♗xg5 3.♕xg6+ ♔h8 4.♕h7#)
3.♕xg6+ ♔f8 4.♗h6#

697 1.♖g8 h6 (1...♕c5 2.♗xc5+−;
1...♕xf2 2.♗xf2+−; 1...♕c3
2.♖xg5+ ♔h6 3.♘g4#) 2.♘h1
♕xc6 (2...g4+ 3.fxg4#; 2...
♕xh2+ 3.♔xh2+−; 2...♕g2+
3.♔xg2+−; 2...♖g7 3.♖xg7+−;
2...♕f2 3.♗xf2+−) 3.♘g3#

698 1.♔h4 ♖g1 (1...♘e5 2.♗xe5
♖d4 3.♗xd4+−; 1...♘f4 2.g5#)
2.g5+ (2.♖g5? ♘e5 3.♖xe5
(3.♗xe5? ♖d7−+) 3...♖d6=)
2...♖xg5 3.♖xg5 ♘e5 (3...f1=♕
4.♗g7#) 4.♗xe5 ♖d7 5.♖f5+−

699 (Based on the internet game
Matalino – frank713, 2008)
1.♕xh5 h6 (1...♗h3 2.♖xh3+−;
1...♗f5 2.♘xf5+−; 1...♘h6
2.♕xh6+−) 2.♕g5 ♔h7 (2...
♗h3 3.♖xh3+−; 2...e6 3.♖xh6+
♘xh6 4.♕xh6+ ♔g8 5.♖h1+−)
3.♖xh6+ ♘xh6 4.♖h1 ♖g8 (4...
♗h3 5.♖xh3+−) 5.♖xh6#

700 1.♕xf7 ♕a3+ (1...h4 2.♕g7+
♔h5 3.♕h7#) 2.♔f2 ♕b2+ (2...
♕a2+ 3.♔g3 h4+ 4.♔h3+−)
3.♔g3 h4+ (3...♕c3+ 4.♔h4

♕e1+ 5.g3+−) 4.♔h3 (4.♔xh4?
♕f2+ 5.♔h3 ♕xf4=) 4...♕c3+
5.g3+− (5.♔xh4 ♕e1+ 6.g3+−)

Chapter 26

701 1.g4+−

702 (Based on the game Zelcic
– Tseitlin, 1988) 1.♖h1 ♘f6
(1...♖b7 2.♖xb7+−; 1...♖h5
2.♖xh5+−) 2.♖h8+ ♘g8
3.♖xg8#

703 (Based on a position by Rinck)
1.d8=♘ g1=♕ 2.c4#

704 1.♖a1 ♖d4 (1...♖a8 2.♖xa8+−;
1...♖a7 2.♖xa7+−; 1...d2 2.♖a5#)
2.♖xd4 ♖xd4 3.♔xd4+−

705 1.♕xh6 (1.♗h7+? ♔h8 2.♕xh6
♘e5−+) 1...gxh6 (1...f5 2.♕h7#)
2.♗h7#

706 1.♕xf8+ ♔xf8 (1...♔h7
2.♕g7#; 1...♖xf8 2.♖xh6+−)
2.♖xh6+−

707 (Based on a position by Rinck)
1.d4 (1.d3? ♘xh3−+) 1...♖xd4
(1...♗xd4 2.♘d2#; 1...♖xh7
2.♘d2#; 1...♘xh3 2.♘e5#)
2.♘e5#

708 1.♕g6 ♗f5 (1...hxg5
2.♕h5#+−; 1...♘g3 2.♕h7#)
2.exf5 hxg5 (2...♗xf7 3.♕h7#)
3.♕h5#

709 1.♕f5 ♔g7 (1...♕xf6
2.♕xf6++−; 1...♗xf2+
2.♖xf2+−; 1...♖g8 2.♖xh7#)
2.♕g5+ (2.♘h5+?! ♔h6 3.♘f6
♖h8=) 2...♔h8 3.♕h6+−

710 (Based on a position by
Prokes) 1.♕f5+ ♔h4 (1...♕g5
2.♕xg5#+−) 2.♔g2+−

711 1.♖f8 (1.♕f8+?! ♔g6 2.♖e7

♕xd4 3.♔xf7+ ♔f5 4.♔e6+
♔g6 5.♕f7+ ♔f5=; 1.♘e6+?!
♔g6 2.♘f8+ ♔g7 3.♘e6+
♔g6=; 1.♘f5+? ♔g6−+) 1...
♕xd4 (1...♕b7+ 2.♕xb7+−;
1...♕b3 2.axb3+−; 1...♖g1+
2.♔xg1+−; 1...♕c6+ 2.♘xc6+−;
1...♕c7 2.♖xf7++−; 1...♗c7
2.♖xf7++−) 2.♕xf7#

712 (Based on the game Alekhine –
Brunner, 1932) 1.♖g6 (1.♘f5?!
♗xf5 2.♕xf5 ♕b6=) 1...fxg6 (1...
♗g5 2.hxg5 fxg6 3.♕xg6+−; 1...
♗g7 2.♖xg7+−) 2.♕xg6+− ♕e7
3.♕xh6+ ♕h7 4.♕xf6+

713 (Based on a position by
Kubbel) 1.♕d8+ ♔c6 2.a4 ♕f4+
(2...♕a5 3.♕xa5+−; 2...♗xf3
3.♕c7#) 3.e5+− ♕xf3

714 (Based on the game Krysztofiak
– Heymann, 1998) 1.dxc6
(1.♗xc6?! ♕xe1+ 2.♔g2
♕e4+=) 1...♕xe1+ 2.♗f1
(2.♔g2? ♕e4+ 3.♔g1 ♖d1+
4.♗f1 ♕xc6−+) 2...♕xf1+
3.♔xf1+−

715 1.♕xa6+ ♕a7 2.♖a5 (2.♕c4?!
♖b2=) 2...♕xa6 (2...♘c6
3.♕xc6+ ♖b7 4.♕xb7#; 2...♘c8
3.♕c6+ ♖b7 4.♕xb7#; 2...♖b7
3.♕xb7#) 3.♖xa6#

716 (Based on the game Csulits
– Bade, 1972) 1.♔h6 gxh4
(1...♕d7 2.♖xd7+−; 1...♖d7
2.♖xd7+−; 1...♖g8 2.♖xg8+
♔xg8 3.♕g7#) 2.♖xh7+ ♗xh7
3.♕g7#

717 (Based on the game Yarikov –
Shvedova, 2022) 1.♕d7 ♗xd4
(1...♖g6 2.♕xb5+−; 1...♕e5

2.♗xe5+−; 1...♖f6 2.♕xb5+−;
1...♗f7 2.♕xf7 ♗xd4 3.♕f8#; 1...
♗e5 2.♕xc6+−) 2.♕xd4+ ♕e5
(2...♖f6 3.♕xf6#) 3.♕xe5+ ♖f6
4.♕xf6#

718 1.♕d6+ (1.♕e7? ♘xb5 2.♕d8+
♔c6∓) 1...♔c8 2.♕e7+− ♔c7
3.♕d8#

719 (Based on the game Vatter –
Klundt, 1981) 1.♕d3 (1.♕g2?
g6−+; 1.♕c2? ♕xc2+ 2.♔xc2
g6−+) 1...♕xd3 (1...g6 2.♕xf5
gxf5 3.♖h3#; 1...g5 2.♕xf5++−;
1...♔h8 2.♕xf5+−) 2.♖h3#

720 1.f6 hxg5 (1...♗f5 2.♕xf5+−;
1...♕c5+ 2.d4+−; 1...g6
2.♕xg6+ ♔h8 3.♕h7#; 1...gxf6
2.♕h7#) 2.♕g6 ♕xd5 (2...♕xf6
3.♖xf6+−; 2...♖e6 3.♕xg7#; 2...
♕c5+ 3.d4+−) 3.♕xg7#

721 (Based on the game Gutop –
Roshal, 1963) 1.♕xd4 ♗xd4
(1...♕e5 2.♕xe5+−; 1...♕f6
2.♕xf6+−; 1...♗e5 2.♕xe5+−;
1...♗f6 2.♕xf6+−; 1...♕xe3+
2.dxe3+−) 2.♗xd4 ♗e6 (2...♕f6
3.♗xf6+−; 2...♕xe3+ 3.dxe3+−;
2...♗h3 3.♖xh3+−; 2...♕h4
3.♖xh4+−; 2...♕e5 3.♗xe5+−)
3.♖h8#

722 (Based on a position by
Wotawa) 1.♗d4 cxd4 (1...♖e8
2.♗c3#) 2.c5 ♖e8 3.♖c4#

723 (Based on the game Kahn –
Kohlweyer, 1987) 1.♖xg7 ♘xf5
(1...♕f4 2.♕g6+−; 1...♔xg7
2.♕g6+ ♔h8 3.♕xh6#) 2.♕g6
♘xg7 (2...♘g3+ 3.hxg3+−;
2...♕e1+ 3.♖xe1+−; 2...♕f1+
3.♖xf1+−; 2...♕g1+ 3.♔xg1+−;

2...♕xg2+ 3.♕xg2+−) 3.♕xh6#

724 1.♕h6 ♗xf6 (1...♕xf6
2.♖xf6+−; 1...♖e8 2.♕g7#)
2.♗d3 (2.♖xf6?! ♕xe2∓) 2...♗g7
(2...♕e4 3.♗xe4+−; 2...♕d4+
3.♘xd4+−; 2...♕e3+ 3.♕xe3+−;
2...♗f5 3.♗xf5+−) 3.♕xh7#

725 (Based on a position by Benko)
1.♔f3! (1.♔f2?! ♖g4=) 1...
♖h3+ (1...♔g1 2.♖e1#; 1...♖g4
2.♔xg4+−; 1...♖f4+ 2.♔xf4+−)
2.♔f2 ♖e3 (2...♖f3+ 3.♔xf3
♔g1 4.♖e1#; 2...♖g3 3.♔xg3
♔g1 4.♖e1#; 2...♖a3 3.♖e1#)
3.♔xe3+−

726 (Based on a position by Prokes)
1.♖c8+ ♔g8 2.♘f8 f3 (2...♖xf8
3.♖xf8#) 3.♘g6#

727 1.♖e5 ♖xe5 (1...b5 2.♖xc5+−;
1...♗e2 2.♖xc5+ bxc5 3.♗c7#)
2.♗xe5 b5 (2...♗d1 3.♗c3#)
3.♗c7#

728 1.♕d8 (1.♕f6?! ♕f8=) 1...
♗g8 (1...♕f8 2.♕xd5+−; 1...g5
2.♕h8+ ♔g6 3.♕f6++− ♔h5
4.♗e8+ ♔h4 5.♕xh6#; 1...♗f7
2.♕h8#; 1...♕c1+ 2.♔g2+−)
2.♕f6 ♕e7 (2...♕c1+ 3.♔g2+−;
2...♕xe5 3.♕xe5+−; 2...♕f8
3.♕h8#) 3.♕h8#

729 1.♕xh6 (1.♕xg3?! ♖xg3=)
1...♘e6 2.♕xg6 ♕xg6 (2...fxg6
3.f7#; 2...♖e2 3.♕h7+ ♔f8
4.♕xf7#) 3.♕xe3+−

730 (Based on a position by A.
Zhukov) 1.♕d8+ (1.b8=♕?!
♕f2+=) 1...♔xd8 (1...♔f7
2.♕d7+ ♔f8 (2...♔g8 3.b8=♕#)
3.b8=♕# (3.b8=♖#)) 2.♔e6
♕c3 3.b8=♕# (3.b8=♖#)

731 (Based on a position by Nunn) 1.♗xh7+ ♔xh7 (1...♔h8 2.♕h5+–) 2.♕h5+ ♔g8 3.♖h3+– (3.♖g3?! f6 4.♖xg7+ ♔xg7 5.♕g4+=)

732 1.♖a8+ (1.bxc7+? ♔xc7–+) 1...♔xa8 2.bxc7 ♕xf8 (2...♖xg2+ 3.♔xg2+–; 2...♔a7 3.cxd8=♕+–; 2...♘c6 3.cxd8=♕++–) 3.♖a1#

733 (Based on a position by Wotawa) 1.♘c2 (1.♘c4? ♗xc4–+) 1...bxc2 (1...f2 2.♘b4+ ♔a7 3.♖a5#) 2.b4 c1=♕ 3.♖a5#

734 1.♕h2 (1.♕g2?! ♖fe8 (1...♘d4=; 1...♘e5=) 2.♕h3 ♖e1+ 3.♗f1 f6=) 1...♗xh2+ (1...♗f2+ 2.♖xf2+–; 1...♗h4 2.♕xh4+–; 1...♕h5 2.♕xh5+–; 1...♕h6 2.gxh6+–) 2.♖cxh2 ♖fe8 (2...♕h6 3.gxh6+–; 2...♕h7 3.♖xh7+–; 2...♕h5 3.♖xh5+–; 2...♕b1+ 3.♘xb1+–; 2...♖d1+ 3.♘xd1+–) 3.♖h8#

735 1.♖b7 ♘xb7 (1...♔h5 2.♖h7+ ♔g4 3.♖xh1+–; 1...♘d7 2.g4+–; 1...♕xg2 2.♖h7#) 2.g4 ♘d6 (2...♕a1 3.♗xa1+–) 3.♗g7#

736 1.♕xa7 (1.♕b6? ♘xd5–+; 1.♘b6+? axb6 2.♕xb6 ♘d5! (2...♕e5 3.♗xe5 ♖xe5=) 3.♗xd5 ♕g4+ 4.♗g3 ♖e5∓) 1...♘xa7 (1...♕e5 2.♗xe5+–; 1...♕d6 2.♗xd6+–) 2.♖c1+ ♕c6 (2...♘c6 3.♘b6#; 2...♗c6 3.♘b6#) 3.♘b6#

737 1.♘g6+ (1.♕h5?! ♔g8=) 1...hxg6 2.♖f3 ♖xf7 (2...♕xc2 3.♖h3#) 3.exf7 ♔h7 (3...♕xc2 4.♖h3#) 4.♖h3#

738 1.♔g4 h5+ (1...♖xd3 2.f4+ ♔e4 3.♖e6#; 1...g5 2.f4+ gxf4 3.gxf4#; 1...c3 2.f4#) 2.♔g5 ♖xd3 (2...c3 3.f4#) 3.f4+ ♔e4 4.♖e6#

739 1.♘f5 ♖d3+ (1...♗e2+ 2.♔xe2+–; 1...♖xg4 2.hxg4+–; 1...♖f4+ 2.♔xf4+–) 2.♔f4 d4 (2...♖f3+ 3.♔xf3+–; 2...♖d4+ 3.♘xd4++–) 3.♔e4 ♖d2 (3...♖e3+ 4.fxe3+–) 4.♖e7#

740 (Based on a position by Nunn) 1.♕d5+ ♔h8 (1...♖f7 2.♖xe8#) 2.♕f7 ♖xf7 (2...♖xe7 3.♕xf8#; 2...♖g8 3.♖xe8+–; 2...♕b8 3.♕xg7#) 3.♖xe8+ ♖f8 4.♖xf8#

741 1.♔f4 ♔h3 (1...♘d4 2.♖h1#) 2.♘e1 ♔h2 3.♘f3+ ♔h3 4.♖g3#

742 (Based on the game Loskutov – Burmakin, 1996) 1.♖xg6 fxg6 (1...♖xd7 2.♖xg7+ ♔f8 (2...♔h8 3.♖h7+ ♔xh7 4.♕g7#) 3.♖g8+ ♔e7 4.♕g5+ ♔e6 (4...f6 5.♕xf6#) 5.♕f6#) 2.♕xg6 ♖xd7 (2...♕xd7 3.♖xd7+–; 2...♕e5!? 3.♘df6+ (3.♘hf6+ ♕xf6 4.♘xf6++–; 3.♘xe5? ♖xd1+) 3...♕xf6 (3...♗f8 4.♕xg7#; 3...♔h8 4.♕xg7#) 4.♘xf6++–) 3.♘f6+ (3.♖xd7?! ♕xd7 4.♘f6+ ♔f8 5.♘xd7+ ♗xd7=) 3...♔f8 (3...♔h8 4.♕xe8#) 4.♕xe8#

743 (Based on the game Tsharotshkin – Hanko, 1992) 1.♖h7 (1.♖ee3? ♖c7∓; 1.♖g3? ♖c7–+) 1...♖f7 (1...♖c7 2.♕h5+–; 1...♕e7 2.♕h5+–; 1...♕d7 2.♕h5+–; 1...♕c7 2.♕h5+–) 2.♕h5 ♔f8 (2...♕xh2+ 3.♔xh2+–; 2...g6 3.♕xg6+ ♔f8 (3...♖g7 4.♕xg7#)

4.♕xf7#) 3.♖h8+ ♔e7 4.♖xc8+−

744 (Based on the internet game Dugin_Sergey – iusegine, 2017) 1.♖dxg7+ (1.♖gxg7+? ♘xg7−+) 1...♘xg7 (1...♔f8 2.♖g8+ ♕xg8 3.♗xb4++−; 1...♔h8 2.♕d7+−) 2.♕xf6 ♖e1+ (2...♕f7 3.♖xg7+ ♕xg7 4.♕xg7#; 2...♕f1+ 3.♖xf1+−) 3.♗xe1 ♖xe1+ 4.♖xe1+−

745 1.♖d8+ ♔h7 2.♘f7 g5 (2...♖h1+ 3.♔xh1+−) 3.h5 g6 (3...♖h1+ 4.♔xh1+−) 4.h6+−

746 1.♘f6+ (1.♗c2? f5−+) 1...♗xf6 (1...♔g7 2.♕xh7+ ♔xf6 3.♘g4#; 1...♔h8 2.♕xh7#) 2.♗c2 ♖e8 (2...♗xe5 3.♕xh7#) 3.♕xh7+ ♔f8 4.♕xf7#

747 (Based on the game Meier – Muller, 1994) 1.♕c7 (1.♖e8+? ♕xe8 2.♖xe8+ ♖xe8−+) 1...♖d7 (1...♖xc7 2.♖e8+ ♕xe8 3.♖xe8#; 1...♕xc7 2.♖e8+ ♖xe8 3.♖xe8#) 2.♕xc8 ♗xc8 3.♖e8+ ♕xe8 4.♖xe8#

748 1.♖g7+ ♔h8 2.♖f7 (2.♖e7?! ♘d6=; 2.♖d7?! ♖d4=) 2...h6 (2...h5 3.fxg6 ♖g4 4.♖f8#; 2...♖a3 3.♖f8#; 2...♔g8 3.♖f8#) 3.fxg6 ♖g4 4.♖f8#

749 1.♘e6 ♗xe6 (1...♖f7 2.♕xf7+−; 1...♖f5 2.♕xh7+ ♔xh7 3.♖h3+ ♗h4 (3...♖h5 4.♖xh5#) 4.♖hxh4+ ♖h5 5.♖xh5#; 1...♖f6 2.♕xh7+ ♔xh7 3.♖h3+ ♖h6 4.♖xh6#; 1...♗h4 2.♖g7 ♗xf2+ 3.♔h1+−; 1...♕d8 2.♖g7+−) 2.♕xh7+ ♔xh7 3.♖h3+ ♗h4 4.♖hxh4#

750 1.♕xh7+ (1.♖f3? hxg6 2.fxg6 ♖c7−+) 1...♔xh7 2.♖f3 ♔g8 (2...♖c7 3.♖h3+ ♔g8 4.♖h8+ ♔f7 5.♖f8#; 2...♘d6 3.♖h3+ ♔g8 4.♖h8#) 3.♖h3 ♖c7 (3...♘d6 4.♖h8#) 4.♖h8+ ♔f7 5.♖f8#

751 1.♘f5+ (1.♘g6+? ♔h5−+; 1.♗g6? ♗xe7−+) 1...♔h5 2.♘g3+ ♔h4 3.♗g6 (3.♘f5+ ♔h5 4.♘g3+ ♔h4) 3...g4 (3...♖xb7 4.♘f5#) 4.f4 ♖xb7 5.♘f5#

752 1.♗f6 ♕f1+ (1...♘d7 2.♕e6+ ♔f8 3.♕e7+ ♔g8 4.♕g7#; 1...♕xf6 2.♕xf6+−; 1...h5 2.♕e8+ ♔h7 3.♕h8#; 1...♔f7 2.♕e7+ ♔g8 3.♕g7#) 2.♔h2 ♘d7 (2...♕xf6 3.♕xf6+−) 3.♕e6+ ♔f8 4.♕e7+ ♔g8 5.♕g7#

753 (Based on the game Roussel – Mikhalevski, 2005) 1.♖d8 ♕a3 (1...♔g8 2.♖xf8+ ♔xf8 3.♖d8#; 1...♖xd8 2.♖xd8#; 1...♔g8 2.♖xg8+ ♔xg8 3.♖d8#; 1...♖e8 2.♖xe8#) 2.♖1d6 ♖g8 (2...♔g8 3.♖xf8+ ♔xf8 4.♖d8#; 2...♖e8 3.♖xe8#; 2...♖xd8 3.♖xd8+ ♕f8 4.♖xf8#; 2...♕c1+ 3.♔h2+−; 2...♕a1+ 3.♔g2+−) 3.♖xg8+ ♔xg8 4.♖d8+ ♕f8 5.♖xf8++−

754 1.♘xh7+ ♔g8 2.♖xe8+ ♔xh7 3.♗f6 (3.♗xd4? ♘xd4−+) 3...g5 (3...♘d7 4.♖h8#) 4.h5 ♘d7 5.♖h8#

755 1.♕c7 ♖c8 (1...♖xa6 2.♕a7#; 1...♖xa6 2.♕xb7#) 2.♕b8+ ♖xb8 3.♘c7#

756 (Based on the game Richter – Reinhardt, 1937) 1.♖f5 ♔g8 (1...♘f4 2.♖xf4+−) 2.♖xh5

(2.♕xh5?! gxh5 3.♖fxh5 ♕g7=)
2...gxh5 (2...♕c5+ 3.♔h1 gxh5
4.♕xh5+−) 3.♕xh5+−

757 (Based on the game Capablanca
– Steiner, 1933) 1.♕xb7
(1.♕b3? b5−+; 1.♕c4+?! ♔b6
2.♕b4+ ♔a6 3.♕c4+ ♔b6=)
1...♕b6 (1...♕xf6 2.♕b4#; 1...
♖xg2+ 2.♔xg2+−) 2.♖xc6+
♕xc6 (2...♔b5+ 3.♖xb6++−)
3.♕b4#

758 1.♕h6 ♘xf6 (1...♖xc3 2.♕g7#;
1...♖g8 2.♕xh7+ ♔xh7 3.♖h3#)
2.♗c6 ♖xc6 (2...♔g8 3.♗xf6+−;
2...♗e7 3.♗xf6+ ♗xf6 (3...♔g8
4.♕g7#) 4.♕xf8#) 3.♗xf6+
♔g8 4.♕g7#

759 (Based on the internet game
zitelo – Istanbul1, 2014) 1.♘f6+
gxf6 (1...♔h8 2.♕xh7#) 2.exf6
♔h8 (2...♖fd8 3.♕h6+−; 2...♘d7
3.♕g5+ ♔h8 4.♕g7#) 3.♗e4
(3.♕h6? ♖g8 4.♗e4 ♖g6−+)
3...♘d5 (3...h6 4.♕xh6+ ♔g8
5.♕g7#) 4.♕xh7#

760 1.♕d8+ (1.♖dh1? ♔f8−+) 1...
♕e8 (1...♖xd8 2.♖xd8+ ♕e8
3.♖xe8#) 2.♖dh1 f5 (2...♕xd8
3.♖h8#; 2...♖xd8 3.♖h8#; 2...
f6 3.g6+−; 2...g6 3.♖h8+ ♔g7
4.♖1h7#; 2...♔f8 3.♖h8#) 3.g6
♕xd8 (3...♖xd8 4.♖h8#; 3...♔f8
4.♖h8#) 4.♖h8#

761 (Based on the game Ulfarsson
– Gausel, 1996) 1.♖g4 ♖xg4
(1...♘d7 2.♕xh7#; 1...♘g6
2.hxg6+−; 1...♗xd3 2.♖xg8+
♔xg8 3.♕g7#) 2.♗g6 ♖xg6 (2...
♘xg6 3.♕g7#; 2...fxg6 3.♕g7#)
3.hxg6 fxg6 (3...♘xg6 4.♕g7#;

3...♕xa2+ 4.♔xa2+−) 4.♕g7#

762 1.b6 a6 (1...♕e2+ 2.♔xe2+−;
1...♕d1+ 2.♔xd1+−; 1...a5
2.♕xa5#) 2.♖c7 (2.♕xa6+?
bxa6 3.♖c7 ♗b7−+) 2...♖h2
(2...♖g7 3.♖xg7+−; 2...♕d1+
3.♔xd1+−; 2...♕e2+ 3.♔xe2+−;
2...♖h7 3.♖xh7+−; 2...♔b8
3.♖e7++− ♔c8 4.♕c2+ ♗c6
(4...♗c4 5.♕xc4+ ♔d8 6.♕c7#;
4...♔d8 5.♕c7#) 5.♕xc6+!?
bxc6 6.b7+ ♔d8 7.b8=♕+ ♗c8
8.♕b6+ ♕c7 9.♕xc7#) 3.♕xa6+
bxa6 4.♖a7#

763 (Based on a position by
Wotawa) 1.♘e6 ♖f7 (1...d2
2.♘f4#; 1...♖e7 2.♗xe7+−)
2.♗f6 ♖xf6 (2...d2 3.♘f4#)
3.♘g7+ ♔g5 4.h4#

764 1.♘h5 (1.♖4e3?! ♗g5
2.♕xg5 f6=) 1...gxh5 (1...♖xe5
2.♖xe5+−; 1...♗f6 2.♘xf6+
♔h8 3.♕xh7#; 1...♖fe8 2.♕g7#)
2.♖1e3 (2.♖4e3? h4−+) 2...♔h8
(2...h4 3.♖g4+ ♗g5 (3...♔h8
4.♕g7#) 4.♖xg5+ ♔h8 5.♕g7#)
3.♖g3 ♖g8 (3...♗g5 4.♖xg5+−;
3...♕xe5 4.♖xe5+−) 4.♘xf7#

765 (Based on a position by A.
Zhukov) 1.♕f5+! ♗g5 (1...♕g5
2.♕h3+ ♕h4 3.♕xh4#) 2.g4+
(2.♕f3+? ♗g6+−+) 2...♔h4
3.♕f4! ♕g6 (3...♗h5 4.g5#; 3...
♖g6 4.g5+ ♔h5 5.gxh6+−; 3...
♖f5 4.♕xh6++−) 4.♕g3#

766 (Based on a position by
Wotawa) 1.♖d4 (1.b3+?
♔a3−+) 1...♖xd4 (1...♖h4
2.♖xh4+− ♖d4 (2...♖d6
3.♗xd6) 3.♖xd4; 1...g1=♕

2.♖xb4#) 2.c3 g1=♕ (2...♖d6
3.♗xd6+−; 2...♖h3 3.♖xh3+−;
2...♖d3 3.♖xd3+−) 3.♖a3+ bxa3
4.b3#

767 1.♕f6 (1.♘ef6+? ♔h8−+;
1.♘hf6+ ♔h8−+) 1...gxf6 (1...
♕xg3+ 2.fxg3 gxf6 3.♘exf6+
♔h8 4.♗h6+−; 1...♕e5 2.dxe5
gxf6 3.♘exf6+ ♔h8 4.♗h6+−;
1...♗xd2 2.♕xg7#) 2.♘exf6+
♔h8 3.♗h6 e5 (3...♕xg3+
4.fxg3+−) 4.♗g7#

768 1.♕d7+ (1.♕b7+?! ♔f6 2.f4
♘d4+ 3.♔b2 (3.♔c3? ♕a1+−+)
3...♔f5 (3...♘e6=) 4.♕d5+
♔xf4=; 1.♕c7+? ♔f6 2.f4
♘d4+ 3.♔b2 ♔f5 4.♕d7+ ♔xf4
5.♕xd6+ ♔g5∓) 1...♔f6 (1...
♔h8 2.♕e8+ ♔g7 3.♕f7+ ♔h8
4.♕g8#; 1...♔f8 2.♕f7#; 1...
♘e7 2.♕xe7+ ♔h8 3.♕f8#) 2.f4
♘d4+ (2...♕f2 3.♕f7#; 2...d5
3.♗xd5 ♘d4+ 4.♔b2+−) 3.♔b2
(3.♔c3? ♕a1+−+) 3...g5 (3...
♘e6 4.♕xe6+ ♔g7 5.♕f7+ ♔h8
6.♕g8#; 3...d5 4.♗xd5+−; 3...
♕c1+ 4.♔xc1+−) 4.♕f7#

769 1.♕h6 (1.♗f6?! ♖g8=; 1.♕f6?
♖g8−+) 1...♖g8 (1...gxh6
2.♗f6#; 1...g6 2.♗f6+ ♔g8
3.♕g7#; 1...g5 2.♕f6+ ♔g8
3.♖xg5#; 1...♕c5 2.♕xg7#)
2.♗f6 ♕f8 (2...gxf6 3.♕xf6+
♖g7 4.♕xg7#; 2...♕c5 3.♕xh7+
♔xh7 4.♖h1#) 3.♕xh7+ ♔xh7
4.♖h1#

770 1.f7 (1.♕g4?! ♘g6=) 1...♗g7
(1...♘g6 2.♕f6+ ♗g7 3.f8=♕+
♘xf8 4.♕xg7#; 1...exf5 2.♖g8#;
1...♕h2+ 2.♔xh2+−; 1...♕g2+

2.♖xg2+−) 2.♕f6 ♕xd4 (2...
♘g6 3.f8=♕+ ♘xf8 4.♕xg7#;
2...♕h2+ 3.♔xh2+−; 2...♕g2+
3.♖xg2+−) 3.♕xg7 ♕xf6 (3...
♕d1+ 4.♖g1#; 3...♕e4+ 4.♖g2#;
3...h6 4.♕xh6+ ♘h7 5.♕xh7#)
4.♖g8#

771 (Based on the game Fox
 – NN, 1901) 1.♕xg6 hxg6
(1...fxg6 2.♗xc4+ ♔f8 (2...
♕d5 3.♗xd5++−; 2...♗e6
3.♗xe6+−) 3.♘xg6+
(3.♖xh7+−) 3...hxg6 4.♖h8#; 1...
♘xe5 2.♕xh7+ ♔f8 3.♕h8#)
2.♘xg6 fxg6 (2...♕xd4+
3.cxd4+−; 2...f6 3.♗xc4+ ♕d5
(3...♗e6 4.♗xe6#) 4.♗xd5+
♗e6 5.♗xe6#; 2...f5 3.♗xc4+
♕d5 (3...♗e6 4.♗xe6#)
4.♗xd5+ ♗e6 5.♗xe6#; 2...♗xg4
3.♖h8#) 3.♗xc4+ ♗e6 (3...♕d5
4.♗xd5++−; 3...♔f8 4.♖h8#)
4.♗xe6+ ♔f8 5.♖h8#

772 (Based on the game Rakocevic
 – Masovic, 2008) 1.♕xh5 gxh5
(1...♖xd3 2.♕h8#) 2.♖dg3+
(2.♖xh5? ♖xd3−+) 2...♔f8
(2...♔h7 3.♖xh5#; 2...♔h8
3.♖xh5#) 3.♖xh5 ♖d1+ (3...
♕xf4 4.♖h8#) 4.♗xd1 ♕xf4
5.♖h8#

773 (Based on a position by Archer)
1.♗f6 gxf6 (1...♖g8 2.♕h4+
♔g6 3.♕g5+ ♔h7 4.♕h5#; 1...
g5 2.♕xg5+−; 1...g6 2.♕h4+
♔g8 3.♕h8#; 1...♗g4 2.♕h4+
♔g8 (2...♗h5 3.♕xh5++−)
3.♕g5 g6 (3...cxd6 4.♕xg7#)
4.♕h6+−) 2.♖d4 ♗g4 (2...♖g8
3.♖h4#) 3.♖xg4 ♕f5 (3...♕xg4

4.♕xg4+−; 3...♖g8 4.♖h4#)
4.♖h4+ ♕h5 5.♖xh5#

774 1.f3 (1.h4+?! ♔f5=) 1...fxg3 (1...
e4 2.g4+−; 1...♖ad8 2.h4+ ♔f5
3.g4#) 2.♔xg3 (2.h4+? ♔f4−+)
2...♘c5 (2...e4 3.fxe4+−; 2...♖ad8
3.h4+ ♔f5 4.e4#) 3.e4 ♖f4 (3...
♖xf3+ 4.♔xf3+−) 4.h4+ ♖xh4
5.♖xh4+−

775 (Based on the game Nikolov
– Vucinic, 2008) 1.♘xh6+
gxh6 (1...♔h8 2.♘f5+ ♔g8
3.♘e7#; 1...♔h7 2.♘f5+ ♔g8
3.♘e7#) 2.♕g6+ ♔h8 3.♖xh6+
(3.♖d3? ♖b7−+) 3...♔g8
4.♕g6+ (4.♖d3? ♔f7∓) 4...♔h8
5.♖d3+−

776 1.♖a7+ ♗d7 (1...♔g8 2.♖g7+
♔h8 3.♖xh7+ ♔g8 4.♘e7#; 1...
♔e8 2.♖e7#) 2.♖xd7+ ♔e6 (2...
♔e8 3.♖e7#; 2...♔g8 3.♖g7+
♔h8 4.♖xh7+ ♔g8 5.♘e7#)
3.♖e7+ ♔f5 4.♖e4 ♖xg2 5.♘e7#

777 (Based on the internet game
idiot445 – NEWGAME, 2008)
1.♕g6+ (1.♗xd5?! ♗xd5
2.♕g6+ ♔h8 3.♕xh6+ ♔g8
4.♕g6+=) 1...♔h8 2.♕xh6+
(2.♗xd5?! ♗xd5 3.♕xh6+ ♔g8
4.♕g6+=) 2...♔g8 3.♕g6+
(3.♗xd5?! ♗xd5 4.♕g6+
♔h8 5.♕h6+=) 3...♔h8 4.h4!
(4.♕h6+=) 4...♕e8 5.hxg5#

778 (Based on the internet game
knightstour – lazycast, 2009)
1.♖xg7+ ♔xg7 (1...♔h8
2.♕h6+−) 2.♕g5+ (2.♖g1+?!
♔h8 3.♕h6 ♖g8=) 2...♔h8
3.exf6 ♖g8 4.♕h6 ♖g6 (4...♗f8
5.♕xh7#) 5.♗xg6 fxg6 (5...♗f8

6.♕xh7#) 6.♕g7#

779 (Based on a position by Nunn)
1.♖xh7+ ♔xh7 2.♕xf7+ ♔h8
3.g6 ♕e7 (3...♖g8 4.♕h7#; 3...
♕f6 4.♕h7#; 3...♖e7 4.g7+ ♔h7
5.g8=♕+ ♔h6 6.♕gg6#) 4.g7+
♔h7 5.g8=♕+ ♔h6 6.♕gg6#

780 (Based on the game Van
Foreest – Giri, 2022) 1.d7
(1.gxh3?! ♕e2+=; 1.♔xh3?
♕h5+ 2.♔g3 g5−+) 1...♖f8
(1...♗xd7 2.♕b8+ ♗c8 (2...
♗e8 3.♕xe8+ ♖f8 4.♕xf8#; 2...
♖f8 3.♕xf8#) 3.♕xc8+ ♕d8
4.♕xd8+ ♖f8 5.♕xf8#; 1...♕xd7
2.♕b8+ ♕c8 (2...♕d8 3.♕xd8+
♖f8 4.♕xf8#; 2...♗e8 3.♕xe8+
♖f8 4.♕xf8#; 2...♖f8 3.♕xf8#)
3.♘xc8+−; 1...♖xe7 2.♕b8+ ♖e8
3.♕xe8#) 2.♘xg6+ (2.gxh3?!
♕e2+=; 2.♔xh3? ♕xd7+−+;
2.♕h6? ♕d6+!−+) 2...♔g8 (2...
hxg6 3.♕h6+ ♔g8 4.♕g7#)
3.♘xf8+− ♗xd7 4.♕g5+ ♔f8
5.♕g7+ ♔e8 6.♕e7#

781 1.♘g6+ (1.♖xf7?! ♖xf7 2.♘g6+
♔g8=) 1...♗xg6 (1...hxg6
2.hxg6+ ♖h2 3.♖xh2#) 2.hxg6
♖f1+ (2...dxc3 3.♖hxh7#)
3.♖xf1 dxc3 4.♖xh7+ ♔g8
5.♖g7+ ♔h8 6.♖h1#

782 1.♖e1+ ♔f6 2.♖ce7 g4 (2...♔g6
3.♖1e6+ ♔h5 4.♖h7#) 3.h4 g3+
(3...♔g6 4.♖1e6+ ♔h5 5.♖h7#)
4.♔h3 (4.♔g2?! ♔g6 5.♖1e6+
♔h5 6.♔h3 ♖h8=) 4...♔g6
5.♖1e6+ ♔h5 6.♖h7#

783 (Based on the game Bluebaum
– Jones, 2021) 1.♖h1+ (1.♔f3?!
♘e5+ 2.♔f4 ♔h3! 3.♖d2!=)

1...♗g5 2.♘f3 (2.♔g3? ♗d6+
3.♔f3 ♘e5+−+) 2...♘e5+ (2...
♖h8 3.♖xh8+−; 2...♗d6 3.♖h5#)
3.♔g3 ♘xg4 (3...♖h8 4.♖xh8+−;
3...♗d6 4.♖h5#) 4.♗xg4 ♗d6+
(4...♖h8 5.♖xh8+−) 5.♔f3 ♖e8
(5...♗h2 6.♖xh2+−; 5...♖h8
6.♖xh8+−) 6.♖h5#

784 1.♗g5 (1.♗f4? g6 2.♕xh7+
♔xh7 3.♖h3+ ♗h4 4.♖xh4+
♔g7 5.♗h6+ ♔f6−+; 1.♗xh7?
gxh6 2.♕xh6 ♖g7−+) 1...
g6 (1...h6 2.♗xh6 gxh6 (2...
g6 3.♗f8+ ♗h4 4.♕xh4#; 2...
♗h4 3.♕xh4+−) 3.♕xh6#; 1...
♗xg5 2.♕xh7#) 2.♕xh7+ ♔xh7
3.♖h3+ ♔g7 4.♗h6+ ♔h7 (4...
♔h8 5.♗f8+ ♗h4 6.♖xh4#)
5.♗f8+ ♗h4 6.♖xh4#

785 1.♖xg7+ ♔h8 (1...♔xg7
2.♕g5+ ♔h8 3.♕xf6+ (3.♗e5?!
♘cd5=) 3...♔g8 4.♗e5+−)
2.♖g8+ ♔xg8 (2...♖xg8 3.♕xf6+
♖g7 4.♕xd8+ ♘e8 (4...♖g8
5.♗e5+ f6 6.♗xf6#) 5.♕xe8+
♖g8 6.♗e5+ f6 7.♗xf6#)
3.♕g5+ ♔h8 4.♕xf6+ ♔g8
5.♗e5+−

786 (Based on the game Geller –
Grela, 2017) 1.♖fh1! (1.♕h3?
♗xg6−+; 1.♕h4? ♗xg6−+;
1.♕h2? ♗xg6−+; 1.♖xg8+?!
♔xg8 2.♖h1 fxe5! 3.♕g4 ♗g5+!
4.♕xg5 ♖xc3 5.bxc3 ♖d6=) 1...
♗b4 (1...♖xc3 2.♖xg8+ ♔xg8
3.♖h8+ ♔xh8 4.♕h4+ ♔g8
5.♕h7+ ♔f8 6.♕h8#; 1...♗xg6
2.♕xg6+−; 1...♖d1+ 2.♗xd1+−)
2.♖xg8+ ♔xg8 (2...♔e7
3.♖xg7+ ♔f8 4.exf6+−) 3.♖h8+

♔xh8 4.♕h4+ ♔g8 5.♕h7+
♔f8 6.♕h8+ ♔e7 7.♕xg7+ ♗f7
8.♕xf7#

787 (Based on the game Svidler
– Iordachescu, 1994) 1.♖d8
(1.♕c3? ♕xc3−+) 1...♖xd8
2.♕c3 (2.exd8=♕+ ♕xd8
3.♕c3 ♔h7−+) 2...♕xc3 (2...f6
3.♕xa5+−; 2...♔h7 3.♕xa5+−)
3.exd8=♕+ ♔h7 (3...♗f8
4.♗xc3+−) 4.♗xc3+−

788 1.♘h6+ (1.♘e7+? ♔h8−+)
1...gxh6 (1...♔h8 2.♘hxf7+
(2.♘exf7++−; 2.♕xf7+−) 2...
♖xf7 (2...♔g8 3.♘h6+ ♔h8
4.♕g8+ ♖xg8 5.♘ef7#) 3.♘xf7+
♔g8 4.♘d8+ ♔h8 (4...♔f8
5.♕f7#) 5.♕e8#) 2.♕f6 ♕h1
(2...♕b7 3.♕h8+ ♔xh8 4.♘xf7+
♔g8 5.♘xh6#; 2...♕d8 3.♕h8+
♔xh8 4.♘xf7+ ♔g8 5.♘xh6#;
2...♖g7 3.♘g4+−) 3.♕h8+
♔xh8 4.♘g6+ ♔g8 5.♘e7#

789 1.♕xh7+ (1.♖ee3? ♗g7∓;
1.♗xa6?! ♖xa6 2.f5=) 1...♔xh7
2.♖h3+ (2.♖ee3? ♗g7−+) 2...
♗h6 (2...♔g8 3.♖h8#) 3.♖ee3!
(3.♖xh6+? ♔xh6 4.♖e3
♔h5−+) 3...♗xd3 (3...♔g8
4.♖xh6+−) 4.♖xh6+ ♔xh6 (4...
♔g8 5.♖h8#) 5.♖h3#

790 1.♗d6! (1.♗c5? ♖d7−+;
1.♗b4? ♖c7−+; 1.♗a3? ♖b7−+)
1...♖f5 (1...♗xc2 2.♗e5#; 1...
♖e7 2.♗xe7+−) 2.♗b4! (2.♗a3?
♖b5−+) 2...♖f3 (2...♖b5
3.♗c3+ ♖b2 4.♗xb2#; 2...♖c5
3.♗xc5+−; 2...♖xc2 3.♗c3#)
3.♗c5! (3.♗d6 ♖f5) 3...♖f4
(3...♖d3 4.cxd3+−; 3...♗xc2

4.♗d4+ ♖c3 5.♗xc3#) 4.♗a3!
(4.♗d6 ♖f5) 4...♗xc2 (4...♖b4
5.♗xb4+−) 5.♗b2#

Chapter 27

791 (Based on the game Fikus
– Czarnota, 2004) 1.♕g2+−
(1.♘b6+? ♔c7∓)

792 1.♖f6++−

793 1.0–0–0+−

794 (Based on the game Schroeder
– Hodges, 1916) 1.♔g1 (1.fxg4?
f3+ 2.♔g1 f2+−+) 1...♕g3+
2.♕g2+−

795 (Based on a position by
V. Berezin) 1.♖a3 (1.♖g1?
♖xf2+−+) 1...♖g3+ (1...♗c6?
2.♖xh3+ ♔g8 3.f3+−; 1...♗e4?
2.♖xh3+ ♔g8 3.f3+−; 1...♗d5?
2.♖xh3+ ♔g8 3.f3+−; 1...♗b7?
2.♖xh3+ ♔g8 3.f3+−) 2.♖xf3
♖xf3=

796 (Based on the game Bellon
Lopes – Larsen, 1977) 1.♗g5
(1.♕a2+?! ♔h8 2.♗g5 ♕xg5
3.f4 ♗xf4 4.♘h3 ♕g3 5.♖xf4
♕xh3+ 6.♕h2 ♕xd3 7.♖g1=)
1...♖xg5 (1...♕xg5 2.♕e8#)
2.♕e8#

797 1.♖c2 (1.♖xc5?! ♗a2+
2.♔a1 ♗b3 3.♔b1=) 1...♕d1+
2.♔b2+−

798 1.♔h1 ♗xf2 (1...♕h4
2.♖f7!?+−) 2.♗xh3+−

799 1.♖b8+ ♔g7 2.♗b2+−

800 1.♕c3 f6 2.♘e2+− (2.♘b3?!
♗b6 3.♖d1 ♘g4=)

801 (Based on the internet game
jkriger – Panoramix81, 2007)
1.♕e3 (1.♕d5?! ♕xb3+=;

1.♕e2?! ♕xb3+=) 1...♕b1+ (1...
♕f1+ 2.♔c2+−) 2.♔e2+−

802 (Based on the internet game
osirisblk – Falcao, 2007) 1.f4
(1.g3? ♖f6! 2.♕xg7+ (2.gxh4
♖xg6#) 2...♔xg7 3.d5 ♕a4!−+)
1...♖f6 2.♕g3+−

803 1.♗f3 (1.h3? ♕xg3−+;
1.♖xf8+? ♖xf8 2.♗f3 ♗d4+−+)
1...♗d4+ (1...♖xf3 2.♖xf3+−)
2.♔h1+−

804 (Based on the game Geller
– Khalyavsky, 2006) 1.♔b1
(1.♖d5? ♕a1#; 1.♗a4? ♕xa4
2.♔b1 ♗e6−+) 1...♕a3
2.♕c1+−

805 1.♘f5+ (1.♖d7? ♘g2#) 1...exf5
2.♖h7+ ♔xh7=

806 1.axb5 c5+ (1...c6 2.bxc6+−)
2.bxc6+−

807 (Based on the game Saitta –
Schuh, 2012) 1.♔h3 (1.♖f7+?
♔g8 2.♖g7+ ♔f8 3.♔h3 ♖h1+
4.♗h2 ♔xg7−+) 1...♖h1+
2.♗h2=

808 1.♖h6+ (1.♖g1? ♕f3+ 2.♖g2
♕xg2#) 1...♔g7 (1...♔g8
2.♖g1+−) 2.♖g1+−

809 1.♘f5+ ♔g5 (1...♔h7
2.♘d4+−; 1...♔h5 2.♘d4+−; 1...
♔g6 2.♘h4++−) 2.♘d4+−

810 1.♘f2 (1.♗h2? ♕h4 2.♘xg3
♗xg3−+; 1.♘f6+? ♕xf6−+;
1.♘g5 ♕xg5−+; 1.♗e3? ♕h4+
2.♔g1 ♕h2#) 1...gxf2 (1...♕h4+
2.♘h3+−) 2.♗xf2+− ♕d6 3.g3

811 1.♘f7+ (1.♖xg8+? ♔xg8−+;
1.♘f5? h6+ 2.♔g6 ♕e4−+;
1.♕xa4? ♕h6#) 1...♖xf7
2.♖xg8+ ♔xg8 3.♕f8+ ♔xf8=

(3...♖xf8=)

812 1.♖e8+ ♔xe8 2.♕xg7+−

813 (Based on the game Kempinski – Gdanski, 2002) 1.♕d8+! (1.♖xd1? ♕xd1+ 2.♔g2 ♘d2−+; 1.a7? ♖xe1+ 2.♗xe1 ♕xe1+ 3.♔g2 ♘e3#) 1...♖xd8 (1...♔g7 2.♕xd1+−) 2.♖xe2+−

814 1.♗f6 (1.f3? ♗xf3+ 2.♔f1 ♘e3−+; 1.♗e5? ♘h4−+) 1...♕xf6 (1...♘h4 2.♗xh4+−; 1...♗f3+ 2.♕g5+−) 2.♔xg2+−

815 (Based on the game Penalver – Sanchez, 2007) 1.♖xg5+ (1.f3? ♗c4 2.g4+ (2.♖xg5+ ♔xg5 3.♗e3+ ♔h5−+) 2...fxg4+ 3.fxg4+ ♖xg4 4.♖f8 ♗e6−+) 1...♔xg5 (1...♔h6 2.b8=♕+−) 2.f4+ (2.f3? ♗c4−+; 2.♗e3+ ♔h5 3.f3 ♗c4−+) 2...♔h5 (2...exf4 3.♗xg1+−) 3.♗xg1+−

816 1.♕c6+ ♔f8 (1...♔d8 2.♘xf7#; 1...♗d7 2.♕a8+ ♗c8 3.♕xc8#) 2.♕xh6+ (2.♕a8+?! ♔g7 3.♕a1!=) 2...♖g7 (2...♔e8 3.♕xh2+−; 2...♕g7 3.♕xg7++−) 3.♕xh2+−

817 1.♕f5+ (1.♗g6+? ♔g8!−+) 1...exf5 (1...g6? 2.♕xg6#) 2.♗g6+ (2.♗g8+ ♔g6 3.♗f7+ ♔f6−+) 2...♔g8 (2...♔xg6=) 3.♗f7+ ♔h7 (3...♔xf7=) 4.♗g6+ ♔xg6=

818 (Based on the game Kuzmin – Andrienko, 1994) 1.♖a3 (1.♖h3? ♕f1#; 1.♖c1? ♖xe3+ 2.fxe3 (2.♕e2 ♕xe2#) 2...♕xe3+ 3.♕e2 ♕xe2#) 1...♗xa3 2.♘xc4 ♗b4+ 3.♘d2+−

819 1.♕xh4 (1.♗g1? ♕xg1−+;

1.♕d6+? ♔h5−+; 1.♔xh4? ♘h5+ 2.♕f2 ♕h1#) 1...♕h1+ 2.♔xg3 ♕e1+ 3.♗f2+−

820 (Based on the game Tal – Keres, 1959) 1.♕d6! (1.♘e6+? fxe6 2.♕b7+ ♘f7−+; 1.♕e4? ♕h6#; 1.♕xe5? ♕xe5−+) 1...♖xd6 2.♘f5+ ♔f6 (2...♔f8 3.♘xd6+−; 2...♔g8 3.♘xd6+−; 2...♔h8 3.♘xd6+−) 3.♘xd6+−

821 (Based on the game Arakhamia Grant – Ftacnik, 1991) 1.♗d6 (1.♖xf7? ♕h2+ 2.♔f1 ♕h1+ 3.♔e2 ♕xg2+ 4.♔d3 ♕e4+ 5.♔e2 (5.♔c3 ♕c4#) 5...♕xc2−+; 1.f3? ♕h2+ 2.♔f1 ♕h1+ 3.♔e2 ♕xg2+−+; 1.f2? exf2−+) 1...♕xd6 (1...cxd6 2.♕c8+ ♗e8 3.♕xe8#; 1...♖h1+ 2.♔xh1+−) 2.gxh3 ♕g3+ 3.♕g2+−

822 (Based on the game Lipinsky – Tischbierek, 2002) 1.♕xd7+! (1.hxg3?! ♖xg3+ 2.fxg3 ♕xg3+ 3.♔h1 ♕h3+ 4.♔g1 ♕g3+=; 1.fxg3?! ♖xg3+ 2.hxg3 ♕xg3+ 3.♔h1 ♕h3+ 4.♔g1 ♕g3+=) 1...♔xd7 2.♘e5+ ♔e6 (2...♔d6 3.♘xf3+−; 2...♔e7 3.♘xf3+−; 2...♔c7 3.♘xf3+−; 2...♔c8 3.♘xf3+−; 2...♔d8 3.♘xf3+−; 2...♔e8 3.♘xf3+−) 3.♘xf3+−

823 (Based on the game Malinin – Shnejder, 1978) 1.♖f2! (1.♕xe2? ♘xg3+ 2.♔g1 ♘e2+ 3.♖xe2 ♗c5+−+; 1.♖xe2? ♕xf1#) 1...♖xf2 (1...♖xe1+ 2.♗xe1+−) 2.♖e8+ ♗f8 3.♖xf8#

824 (Based on the internet game Gmmorenovic – malti, 2014)

1.♕xg4 (1.♘xg4? ♘f3+ 2.♔h1 h5!–+) 1...♘f3+ (1...♕xg4 2.♘xg4+–) 2.♕xf3 (2.♘xf3? ♕xg4–+) 2...♖xf3 3.♘xf3+–

825 (Based on the game Shirov – Topalov, 1999) 1.♕f8+ (1.fxg4? ♕h2#; 1.♔f2? ♖xe7–+) 1... ♔xf8 2.fxg4+ ♔g7 (2...♕f7 3.♖xf7++–; 2...♖f7 3.gxh5+–) 3.gxh5+–

826 1.e4 ♕xe4 (1...♕d7 2.♕e3++–; 1...♕f7 2.♕e3++–) 2.♕e3+ ♕xe3 (2...g5 3.♕xe4+–) 3.♘xe3+–

827 (Based on the game Karpov – Lautier, 1997) 1.♖f2 (1.♕xe2? ♖xe2–+; 1.♖d8+? ♗xd8 2.♕xd8+ ♖e8–+) 1...♗xf2 (1...♖xf2 2.♖d8+ ♗xd8 (2... ♖e8 3.♖xe8#) 3.♕xd8+ ♖e8 4.♕xe8#) 2.♕xe2 (2.♖d8+? ♖e8 3.♕xe2 ♖xd8–+) 2...♖xe2 (2...♗b6 3.♕f3+–) 3.♖d8+ ♖e8 4.♖xe8#

828 (Based on the game Smyslov – Vasiukov, 2012) 1.♖h5+ gxh5 (1...♔xh5 2.♕xg7 ♖aa2!=) 2.♕d6+ ♕g6 (2...♕f6? 3.♕xf6#) 3.♕f8+ ♕g7 4.♕d6+=

829 1.♕xf7+ (1.♕xg5? hxg5–+) 1...♔h8 2.♘f4! (2.♕f8+?! ♔h7 3.♕f7+ ♔h8=; 2.♘g3?!=; 2.g4?!=; 2.g3? ♕e5–+) 2...♗e4 3.♕e8+ (3.♕f8+ ♔h7 4.♕f7+ ♔h8) 3...♔h7 4.♕xe4+–

830 (Based on the game Bailet – Shirazi, 2018) 1.♕d5+ ♔h8 (1...♔g7 2.♕g5+–; 1...♔h7 2.♕g5+–; 1...♖f7 2.♕g5+–) 2.♕g5 ♕h3+ (2...

♕h2 3.♖xe4+–) 3.♔f2 ♕h2+ 4.♔e3+–

831 (Based on a position by V. Berezin) 1.♕xf7+ (1.g3?! ♕d7=; 1.♗f4?! ♗xf4=) 1... ♔xf7 (1...♕xf7 2.♖xc8+ ♕e8 (2...♕f8 3.♖xf8#) 3.♖xe8++–; 1...♔h8 2.♕xb7 ♖a1+ 3.♖b1+–) 2.♖xb7+ ♔f6 (2... ♖c7 3.♖bxc7++–; 2...♗c7 3.♖bxc7++–; 2...♔e8 3.♖xc8#; 2...♔g8 3.♖xc8#) 3.♖xc8 (3.♗g7++–) 3...♖a1+ 4.♖c1+–

832 1.♕a8+ (1.♕c8+?! ♔h7 2.♕h3+ ♔g8 3.♕c8+=) 1... ♔h7 2.♕e4+ ♔g6 (2...♔g8 3.♕xc2+–; 2...♔h8 3.♕xc2+–; 2...♕f5 3.♕xf5++–; 2...g6 3.♕xc2+–) 3.♕h4+ ♔g8 (3...♔h6 4.♗xh6+–; 3...♕h5 4.♕xh5++–) 4.♖d8+ ♗f8 5.♖xf8+ ♔xf8 6.♕d8#

833 1.♕d8+ ♔h7 2.e5+ g6 (2... f5? 3.exf6+ g6 4.♕e7+ ♔h8 (4...♔g8 5.♕g7#) 5.♕g7#) 3.♗xg6+ ♔xg6 (3...fxg6 4.♕e7+ (4.♕d7+=; 4.♕xc7+=) 4...♔g8 (4...♔h8 5.♕f8+ ♔h7 6.♕f7+ ♔h8 7.♕f8+=) 5.♕e8+ ♔g7 (5...♔h7 6.♕f7+ ♔h8 7.♕f8+ ♔h7 8.♕f7+=) 6.♕e7+ ♔h8 (6...♔g8 7.♕e8+=) 7.♕f8+ ♔h7 8.♕f7+ ♔h8 9.♕f8+=) 4.♕f6+ (4.♕g8+? ♔f5 5.♕xf7+ ♔xe5–+; 4.♕d3+? ♔g7–+) 4... ♔h7 (4...♔h5? 5.g4#) 5.♕xf7+ (5.♕f5+? ♔h8 6.♕f6+ ♔g8 7.♕d8+ ♔h7–+) 5...♔h8 6.♕f8+ (6.♕e8+=; 6.♕f6+=) 6...♔h7 7.♕f7+ (7.♕e7+=;

7.Wf5+=) 7...Kh8 8.Wf8+=

834 1.Wxd8+ (1.Bd2? Rxd2−+; 1.Nd2? Rxd2−+) 1...Bxd8 (1...Kh7 2.Wd2+−; 1...Kg7 2.Wd2+−) 2.Bd2+− (2.Nd2=)

835 (Based on a position by A. Zhukov) 1.Wf4! (1.Bc2? Wc3+ 2.Kb1 (2.Kd1 Wd2#) 2...Nd2+ 3.Ka2 Wb3+ 4.Ka1 Wa3#; 1.Ke2? Ng3+−+; 1.Kc1? Wd2+ (1...Wc3+−+) 2.Kb1 Nc3+ 3.Ka1 Wa2#) 1...Nc3+ (1... Nf2+ 2.Wxf2=) 2.Ke1! (2.Kc2? Wxf4−+; 2.Kc1? Wxf4+−+; 2.Kd2? Wxf4+−+) 2...Wxf4=

836 1.Ra8! (1.Ra7? Rxa7 2.Ra8 Rxa8 3.h8=W Rxh8+−; 1.Rc8? Ra1+ 2.Rc1 Rxc1#) 1...Rxa8 2.Ra7! (2.h8=W? Ra1#) 2... Rxa7 (2...Rb8 3.Ra3++−; 2...Rc8 3.Ra3++−; 2...Rd8 3.Ra3++−; 2...Rf8 3.Ra3++−) 3.h8=W+−

837 1.Wf4+ Kh5 (1...Nxf4 2.gxf4+ Kxf4= (2...Kh5=; 2...Kh4=)) 2.Wg4+ (2.g4+? Kh4 3.Wh2+ Kg5 4.f4+ Nxf4−+) 2...fxg4 3.fxg4+ Kxg4= (3...Kg5=)

838 (Based on the game Minic – Savic, 1989) 1.Rc3 Wxc3 (1... Wb4? 2.Rxe3 (2.b6+?!=) 2... Wh4+ 3.Kg1 Wh2+ 4.Kf1 Wh1+ 5.Ke2 Wxg2+ 6.Kd3+−; 1...Bf2 2.Rxg3 (2.b6+=; 2.Wc1=) 2...Bxg3 3.Wd4+ Kxd4 4.b6+ Kxb6=; 1...Bb6?! 2.Rxg3±) 2.Wd4+! (2.b6+? Bxb6) 2... Wxd4 (2...Bxd4 3.b6+ Bxb6=; 2...Ka8? 3.Wxc3+−) 3.b6+ Kxb6= (3...Ka8=; 3...Ka6=; 3... Kb8=; 3...Kxb6=)

839 (Based on the game Vidmar – Opochensky, 1932) 1.Kh1 (1.h4? Rxf1+−+; 1.h3? Rxf1+−+) 1... We2 2.Kg1 (2.h4? Rxf1+ 3.Rxf1 Wxf1+ 4.Kh2 We2−+; 2.h3? Rxf1+ 3.Rxf1 Wxf1+ 4.Kh2 We2−+) 2...We3 3.Kh1=

840 1.f4!! (1.dxe3? Bc5! 2.f4 (2.e4 Bd6+−+) 2...Bxe3 3.Nf3 Bxf4+ 4.g3 Bxg3#; 1.g3? hxg3#) 1... Bd6 (1...exd2 2.Nf3+−; 1...Bc5 2.Nf3+−) 2.dxe3 Bc5 (2...Kxe3 3.Nf3+−) 3.Nf3+−

841 1.f3 Wxf3 (1...Bxf3?! 2.Nf4 Wg3+ 3.Ng2+−) 2.Nf4 (2.Ng3? Wxg3+ 3.Kf1 Wh3+ 4.Kg1 Wh1+ 5.Kf2 Wg2#; 2.Nc3? Wh1+ 3.Kf2 Wg2#) 2...Wh1+ (2...g5? 3.Ng2+−; 2...Wg3+? 3.Ng2+−; 2...Wg4+? 3.Kh2 Wh4+ 4.Nh3+−; 2...Rac8? 3.Kh2+−) 3.Kf2 Wf3+ (3... Wh4+? 4.Kf1 Wh1+ 5.Bg1 Wf3+ 6.Wf2+−; 3...Wh2+? 4.Kf1 Wh1+ 5.Bg1 Wf3+ 6.Wf2+−) 4.Kg1 Wh1+=

842 (Based on a position by V. Berezin) 1.Rc7 (1.Rxh7+? Kxh7 2.Wd7+ Kh8−+) 1...Wxc7 (1... Rxd2+ 2.Bxd2 Wxc7 3.Wd3+−; 1...Wa1+ 2.Rc1+−) 2.Bxd4 Rxh3 (2...Rxd4 3.We3+−) 3.e6+!?+− (3.Bxh3+−; 3.Rxh3? Rxg2−+) 3...Kg7 4.Rxh3+−

843 (Based on the game Lukarelli – Karra, 1932) 1.Rd2! (1.Rh2? Rxh2 2.Rd2 Rxd2 3.d4 Wf1+ 4.Bc1 Bd6−+; 1.d4? We2−+; 1.Bxe5? Wxa2+ 2.Kc1 Wc2#) 1...Rxd2 2.d4 (2.Bxe5? Wxa2+

3.♗c1 ♕c2#) 2...♖f2 (2...♕e2
3.♗c1!+− (3.♗a1? ♖d1+ 4.♖xd1
♕xd1+=)) 3.f8=♕! (3.f8=♖+−;
3.dxe5?! ♕e2 4.♗d4=) 3...♖xf8
4.dxe5+−

844 1.♕e7+ (1.♔g1 ♗e3+ 2.♔h1
♗f4; 1.♕d7+?! ♔h6 2.♔g1
♗e3+ 3.♔h1 ♗f4=; 1.♕c7+?!
♔h6 2.♔g1 ♗e3+ 3.♔h1 ♗f4=)
1...♔h6 (1...♔g8 2.♖d8#; 1...
♔h8 2.♖d8#) 2.♕f8+ (2.♔g1
♗e3+ 3.♔h1 ♗f4) 2...♔h5 (2...
♔h7 3.♖d7#; 2...♔g5 3.♔g1
♗e3+ 4.♔f1+−) 3.♔g1 ♗e3+
(3...♕e3+ 4.♔f1+−) 4.♔f1+−

845 (Based on the game Vaganian
– Taimanov, 1974) 1.♖h2
(1.g4? fxg3+−; 1.♘e7+?!
♕xe7 2.♕xh5 ♖xg2+ 3.♔xg2
♕e2+=; 1.♘h6+? ♕xh6−+) 1...
♗xf3 2.♘e7+ ♕xe7 (2...♖8xe7
3.♕xg5+−; 2...♖2xe7 3.♕xg5−;
2...♔h8 3.♕xg5+−) 3.♕xe7
♖8xe7 (3...♖2xe7 4.gxf3+−)
4.gxf3+−

846 1.♕xa7+ ♔xa7 2.♗d4+ b6 (2...
♔a8 3.♖a1#; 2...♔a6 3.♖a1#)
3.♖a1+ (3.♖a2+? ♔b7−+) 3...
♔b7 4.hxg3+−

847 1.exf4 (1.gxf4? ♕g2#;
1.♕xd6+? ♔xd6−+; 1.g6? ♕h3+
2.♔g1 ♕g2#; 1.♕c4+? d5−+)
1...h4 (1...♗xf2 2.♖xf2+−)
2.f5+! (2.gxh4? ♖xh4#; 2.♔g1?
♕xg3+; 2.♕c4+? d5−+) 2...
♕xf5 (2...♔xf5 3.♕f7+ ♔g5
4.♕f6+ ♔h5 5.♕xh8++−; 2...
♔d5 3.♕xb7+ ♔c4 4.♖fc1+!?
♔b3 (4...♔d3 5.♕xa6+ ♔d2
6.♗c3+) 5.♕d5+ ♔a4 6.♕c6+

♔b3 7.♕c2#) 3.♗xh8 hxg3+
4.fxg3+−

848 (Based on the game Shirov –
Adams, 1996) 1.♕h1! (1.♘f1?
♕f2+ 2.♔h1 (2.♔h3 ♗f3+−+)
2...♖f3 3.♘h2 ♖e3−+; 1.♘xe4?
♕xe4−+) 1...♕f2+ (1...♔g6?
2.♕xe4+ ♕xe4 3.♘xe4+−;
1...♖f2+? 2.♔g1+ ♖h2+ (2...
♔g6 3.♖xh7+ ♔f6 4.♕f7#; 2...
♕h3 3.♕xh3++−) 3.♔xh2+−)
2.♕g2 (2.♔h3? e3−+) 2...e3 (2...
♖f4 3.♘xe4=; 2...♕h4+ 3.♔g1
♖f4 (3...♕e1+? 4.♘f1+−; 3...e3
4.♘e4=) 4.♘xe4 (4.♕h2=) 4...
♕e1+ 5.♔h2 ♕h4+=; 2...♔g6
3.♘xe4 ♕h4+ 4.♔g1 ♕e1+
5.♔h2 ♕h4+=) 3.♘e4 ♕h4+
4.♔g1 ♕e1+ 5.♔h2 ♕h4+=

849 (Based on the game Vidmar –
Adam, 1936) 1.♖e4+ (1.♕g7+?
♔d6 2.♕xf6+ (2.♘f5+ ♔c5−+)
2...♔c5 (2...♖8e6−+) 3.♖xd5+
♔xd5 4.♖g5+ ♖8e5−+) 1...
♗xe4 (1...♖xe4 2.♕xd5+−; 1...
♔f8 2.♕xf6+ ♗f7 3.♕xf7#;
1...♔d7 2.♕xd5++−) 2.♕g7+
♔e6 3.♖g4+ (3.♕f7+ ♔e5
4.f4+ ♔xf4 5.♕xf6+ ♗f5 (5...
♔e3 6.♘g4+) 6.♕xf5+ ♔e3
7.♘g4+) 3...f5 (3...♔e7 4.♖d7+
♔f8 5.♕g8#; 3...♔e5 4.f4#; 3...
♗f5 4.♕xe2+ ♔e4 5.♕xe4#)
4.♕g6+ ♔e7 (4...♔e5 5.♘f7+
♔f4 6.♕g3#) 5.♕f7#

850 (Based on the game Panchenko
– Beliavsky, 1971) 1.♕xc7+
(1.gxh3? gxh3+ 2.♗g5
(2.♗g4+ ♖xg4#) 2...♖xg5+
3.♗g4+ ♖xg4#; 1.f3? gxf3−+;

1.♗f3? gxf3−+; 1.♗xg4+?
♖xg4−+; 1.♖fc1? ♕xg2#) 1...
♔xc7 2.♖fc1+ ♔d7 (2...♔b8
3.gxh3+−; 2...♔d6 3.gxh3+−;
2...♗c6 3.gxh3+−; 2...♗c4
3.gxh3+−) 3.gxh3 gxh3+ 4.♔f1
♗g2+ 5.♔e1+−

851 1.♖a6 (1.♗xf7? ♕xh3 2.exf4
♕g4+ 3.♔h2 ♖h6+ 4.♗h5
♖xh5#) 1...♖xa6 (1...♕xh3
2.exf4 ♕g4+ (2...♖xe1 3.♖xe1
♕g4+=) 3.♔h2 ♕h4+=) 2.bxa6
♕xh3 (2...♖e5? 3.exf4+−; 2...
♖e6? 3.♗xe6+−) 3.exf4 ♕g4+
(3...♖xe1? 4.♖xe1 ♕g4+
5.♔f1+−) 4.♔h2 (4.♔h1 ♕h3+
5.♔g1 ♕g4+=) 4...♕h4+ 5.♔g2
(5.♔g1 ♕g4+=) 5...♕g4+=

852 (Based on the game Bakhtadze
– Petrosian, 2003) 1.♗xf4
(1.♖c1? ♕h2+ 2.♔f1 ♗h3+
3.♔e1 (3.♗g2 ♕h1#) 3...♕g1#;
1.♕a8+? ♔e7−+) 1...exf4 (1...
♗f3? 2.♗xf3+−) 2.♖c1!+−
(2.♕a8+? ♔e7−+) 2...♕h2+
3.♔f1 ♗h3+ 4.♔e1 ♕g1+
5.♔d2+−

853 (Based on the internet game
NawazAhmedToor – odioklop,
2014) 1.♖f8+ (1.♕e4? ♖g4−+;
1.♕f2? ♕h4#) 1...♔g7 (1...
♔h7? 2.♕e4+ ♔g7 3.♖af1+−)
2.♖f7+ (2.♕e4? ♔xf8−+;
2.♕f1? ♕h4+ 3.♕h3 ♖xh3#;
2.♖af1? ♕h4#) 2...♔g6 (2...
♔h8? 3.♕e4+−; 2...♔g8 3.♖f8+
♔xf8 (3...♔g7 4.♖f7+=; 3...
♔h7? 4.♕e4++−) 4.♕f2+ ♔e7
5.♕xg3 ♕d2+=; 2...♔xf7 3.♕f2+
♔e7 (3...♔e6 4.♕xg3 ♕d2+=)

4.♕xg3 ♕d2+=) 3.♖f6+ (3.♕f2?
♕h4#) 3...♔xf6 (3...♔g7
4.♖f7+=; 3...♔xf6? 4.♔xg3+−;
3...♔h7? 4.♕e4++−) 4.♕f2+
♔e7 (4...♔e6 5.♕xg3 ♕d2+=)
5.♕xg3 ♕d2+=

854 (Based on the game Capablanca
– Raubitschek 1906) 1.♕g8+
♔xg8 (1...♔g6? 2.♕e6+ ♔h7
(2...♔g5 3.d8=♕++−; 2...
♔h5 3.♕f7+!? g6 4.♕f3++−)
3.♕f5+ g6 (3...♔g8 4.d8=♕#;
3...♔h8 4.d8=♕#) 4.♕f7+ ♔h8
5.d8=♕#) 2.d8=♕+ ♔h7 (2...
♔f7? 3.♖f1+ ♔g6 4.♕d3++−)
3.♕d3+ (3.♕d5? ♖xb1+ 4.♖xb1
♖xb1+ 5.♔xb1 ♕b2#) 3...♔h8
(3...g6? 4.♕d7+ ♔h8 5.♕e8+
♔g7 6.♕e7+ ♔g8 7.♕e6+ ♔g7
8.♖bd1+−; 3...♔g8 4.♕d8+
(4.♕d5+=) 4...♔h7 5.♕d3+=)
4.♕d8+ ♔h7 5.♕d3+=

855 1.♖xf4+ ♔g8 (1...♔g7 2.♗f6+
♔g6 3.♗d4 ♖a1+ 4.♗g1+−;
1...♔e8 2.♖e4+ ♔f7 3.♖e1+−)
2.♖g4 ♖a1+ (2...♔f7 3.♖xg3+−)
3.♗c1+ ♔f7 (3...♔h7 4.♖xg3+−;
3...♔h8 4.♖xg3+−; 3...♔f8
4.♖xg3+−) 4.♖xg3 ♖xc1+
5.♔h2+−

856 1.♗d5 (1.f3? ♖g2+ 2.♔h1
♕d6−+) 1...♕xd5 (1...♕c8?
2.♗xb7 ♕xb7 3.♕e8+ ♔h7
4.♕h5+ ♔g8 5.♕xg4+−)
2.♕e8+ ♕g8 (2...♔h7 3.♕h5+
♔g8 4.♕e8+=) 3.♕h5+ ♕h7
4.♕e8+ ♕g8 5.♕h5+=

857 1.♖e3 (1.f3? ♗xf3+ 2.♔f2
♕g2+ 3.♔e3 ♗xd1!? (3...
♕g5+ 4.♔f2 ♕g2+=) 4.♗xd1

♕xh2∓; 1.♖e2? ♗f3+ 2.♔f1
♗xe2+−+; 1.♖xe4? ♗xe4+−+)
1...♗f3+ 2.♔f1 ♕g2+ (2...♗xd1
3.♘xd1+−) 3.♔e1 ♕g1+ 4.♔d2
♕xf2+ 5.♔c1+−

858 1.♖fe1! (1.♖fd1? ♕h4 2.♔f1
♕e7−+; 1.♖f3? ♕h4 2.♖xg3
♕xg3 3.♕d4! ♕h2+!∓) 1...
♖h1+ (1...♕h4 2.♖e8++−; 1...c6
2.♕d4!? (2.♕d1+−; 2.♕b4+−)
2...♕h4 3.♕e5+ (3.♔f1+−;
3.♕d6+ ♔a8 4.♔f1+−) 3...♔c8
(3...♔a8 4.♕e8++−) 4.♕xf5+
♔b8 5.♕h3+−) 2.♔xh1 ♕h4+
3.♔g1 ♕h2+ 4.♔f1 ♕h1+
5.♔e2+−

859 (Based on the game Moreno
– Dimitrijevic, 2004) 1.♕g8+
(1.a6? ♖g1#) 1...♔a7 (1...♗d8
2.♕xd8+ ♔a7 3.♕b6+ ♔b8
4.♖c7+−; 1...♔c8 2.♕xc8++−)
2.axb6+ ♔xb6 (2...♔a6 3.♕c4+
♔xb6 (3...♔a5 4.♕b5#)
4.♕b5+!? ♔a7 5.♖c7+−)
3.♕b3+ ♔a7 (3...♔a6 4.♕b5+
♔a7 5.♖c7+−) 4.♖c7+− ♘d6
5.♖xb7+!? ♘xb7 6.♔xg2+−

860 (Based on the game Geller
– Frolyanov, 2012) 1.♖f8+
(1.♘xg4? ♖e1+ 2.♔f1 ♖xf1#;
1.♕xg4? ♖e1+ 2.♖f1 ♖xf1#) 1...
♗xf8 (1...♖xf8? 2.♘f7+ ♖xf7
(2...♔g8 3.♕xh7#) 3.♕xh7#)
2.♘f7+ ♔g7 (2...♔g8?
3.♕xh7#) 3.♕h6+ (3.♕xh7+?
♔f6 4.♕h4+ ♔xg6 5.♘xd8
♖e4!?−+) 3...♔f6 (3...♔g8
4.♕xh7#) 4.♕g5+ (4.♕h4+?
♔xg6−+) 4...♔g7 5.♕h6+
(5.♗h5+? ♕xg5−+) 5...♔f6

6.♕g5+=

861 1.♗c1! (1.♗e6+?! ♔b7 2.♖a7+
♔b8 3.♗c1 ♕d4 4.♕xd4 exd4=;
1.♖a8+?! ♗xa8 2.♕xf5+=) 1...
♖xc1 (1...♕d4 2.♕xd4+−)
2.♗e6+ (2.♖a8+? ♗xa8
3.♕xf5+ ♔b8−+) 2...♔d8 (2...
♔b7 3.♕b6#; 2...♔c7 3.♕b6#;
2...♔b8 3.♕a7#) 3.♕h4+
(3.♕b6+? ♕c7−+; 3.♖d6+?
♔e7−+) 3...♔e8 (3...♔c7
4.♕e7+ ♔b8 5.♕a7#) 4.♕h8+
(4.♕h5++−) 4...♔e7 5.♕g7+
♔e8 (5...♔d8 6.♕d7#) 6.♕f7+
♔d8 7.♕d7#

862 1.♖a7 (1.♖g7+? ♔f3−+) 1...
♖b8 (1...♖xa7=; 1...♗xa7=; 1...
♖c8 2.♖c7=; 1...♖d8 2.♖d7=; 1...
♖e8 2.♖e7=; 1...♖f8 2.♖f7=; 1...
♖h8 2.♖h7=; 1...♔g8 2.♖g7+=)
2.♖b7 ♖c8 (2...♖xb7=; 2...
♖a8 3.♖a7=) 3.♖c7 ♖d8 (3...
♖b8 4.♖b7=; 3...♖xc7=; 3...
♖a8 4.♖a7=) 4.♖d7 ♖e8 (4...
♖c8 5.♖c7=; 4...♖xd7=; 4...♖b8
5.♖b7=) 5.♖e7 ♖f8 (5...♖xe7=;
5...♖d8 6.♖d7=; 5...♖c8 6.♖c7=;
5...♖b8 6.♖b7=; 5...♖a8 6.♖a7=)
6.♖f7 ♖h8 (6...♖xf7=; 6...♖e8
7.♖e7=; 6...♖d8 7.♖d7=; 6...
♖c8 7.♖c7=; 6...♖b8 7.♖b7=; 6...
♖a8 7.♖a7=) 7.♖h7 ♖g8 (7...
♖xh7=; 7...♖a8 8.♖a7=; 7...♖b8
8.♖b7=; 7...♖c8 8.♖c7=; 7...♖d8
8.♖d7=; 7...♖e8 8.♖e7=; 7...♖f8
8.♖f7=) 8.♖g7+ ♖xg7= (8...♔f3
9.♖xg8=; 8...♔h3 9.♖xg8=; 8...
♔f4 9.♖xg8=)

863 (Based on the internet game
ColdHeater – nostradamus45,

2014) 1.♕a8+ ♔d7 2.♕b7+ ♔e8 3.♕xb5+ ♖d7 (3... ♔e7 4.♕b4+ ♔e8 (4...♔d7 5.♕b7+=) 5.♕b5+=; 3...♔f8 4.♕b4+ ♔e8 5.♕b5+=) 4.♕b8+ ♔e7 (4...♖d8 5.♕b5+=; 4...♕c8? 5.♕xc8++−) 5.♕b4+ ♔d8 6.♕b8+ ♕c8 (6...♔e7 7.♕b4+=) 7.♗f6+ ♖e7 (7...♔e8? 8.♕xc8+ ♖d8 9.♕xd8#) 8.♕d6+ ♕d7 (8...♔e8? 9.♕xe7#) 9.♕b8+ ♕c8 10.♕d6+=

864 1.♖a8+ ♔h7 (1...♖c8? 2.♕xc8+ ♗d8 (2...♔h7 3.♕g8#) 3.♕xd8+ ♔h7 4.♕g8#; 1...♗d8 2.♖xd8+ (2.♕xf7+ ♕xf7 3.♘xf7 ♔xf7 4.♖xd8=) 2...♔h7 3.♕e4+ ♕xe4 4.fxe4=) 2.♖h8+ (2.♕e4+? ♕xe4 3.fxe4 ♗f4−+) 2... ♔xh8 3.♘g6+ fxg6 (3...♔h7? 4.♘xf4 ♗xf4 5.♕e4++−; 3... ♔g8 4.♕a8+!?+−) 4.♕xg7+ (4.♕b8+? ♕xb8−+; 4.♕c8+? ♖xc8−+; 4.♕a8+? ♗d8 5.♕xd8+ ♔h7−+) 4...♔xg7=

865 (Based on a position by V. Berezin) 1.♗xe6+ (1.♗e3? ♕xa1 2.♗xd4 ♕xa2−+) 1... ♗xe6 (1...♔h8 2.♗e3+−; 1... ♔g7 2.♗h6+ ♔xh6 3.♖xd1+−; 1...♖f7 2.♕xc8++−) 2.♕xf8+ ♔xf8 3.♗h6+ ♔g8 (3...♗f7 4.♖xd1+−; 3...♔g7 4.♗xg7+ ♔xg7 5.♖xd1+−; 3...♔e7 4.♖xd1+−; 3...♔e8 4.♖xd1+−) 4.♖xd1+−

866 (Based on the game Kudrin – Arnason, 1984) 1.♗g5 (1.g3?! ♕xd3 2.♕xe7=; 1.g4?! ♕xd3 2.♕xe7=; 1.♕g3?! ♕xd3

2.gxf3=) 1...♕xg5 (1...♕xd3 2.♕xe7+−; 1...♗xg5 2.♖xf3 ♖xf3 3.♕c8+ (3.♕b8++−) 3...♗d8 (3...♕e8 4.♕xe8+ ♖f8 5.♕xf8#; 3...♖f8 4.♕xf8#) 4.♕xd8+ ♕e8 (4...♖f8 5.♕xf8#) 5.♕xe8+ ♖f8 6.♕xf8#; 1...♗xg2 2.♕xe7+−) 2.♖xf3 ♖xf3 3.h4! (3.♕c8+? ♖f8−+) 3...♕xh4 (3...♕g6 4.♕xe7+−; 3...♕g4 4.♕xe7+−) 4.gxf3+−

867 1.♖b8+ ♔g7 2.♘e6+ (2.♖b7+? ♔h6−+) 2...♕xe6 (2...♘xe6 3.♕xd6+−) 3.♖b7+! (3.♕d2? ♕f6−+; 3.c4?! ♕h3 4.♗c3+ ♔h6 5.♕f1 ♕xf3=; 3.♗d2?! ♕d5!=) 3...♔h6 (3...♔h8 4.♕a1+−; 3...♔g8 4.♕a1+−; 3... ♔f8 4.♕a1+−) 4.♗d2!+−

868 (Based on the game Ljubojevic – Hodgson, 1986) 1.♗g4 (1.♖xf4? hxg2+ 2.♔xg2 ♕xf4−+; 1.gxh3? g2#; 1.♗xf6? hxg2#) 1...♕h4 (1...hxg2+ 2.♕xg2 ♕h4 3.♘xc5+ (3.♖xf4? ♕xh2+ 4.♕xh2 ♖xh2#) 3...♔b8 4.♖xf4!?+− ♕xh2+ 5.♕xh2 ♖xh2+ 6.♔g1+−; 1...♖xd7 2.♗xf6+−) 2.gxh3 (2.♘e5+?! ♔b8=; 2.♗xh3?! ♘xh3 3.gxh3 ♖hg8 4.♕g2 gxh2 5.♗f6 ♕h7 6.♕f3 ♖xd7±) 2...g2+ (2...♘xh3 3.♗xh3!? ♕xh3 4.♗xh8 ♖xh8 5.♘xc5+−) 3.♕xg2 ♘xg2 4.♘xc5+ ♔b8 5.♗xh8+−

869 1.♔b2! (1.axb4? ♕a1#; 1.cxb4? ♗xd4 2.c3 (2.♕xd4 ♕xc2#; 2.♖e1 ♕xa3+ 3.♔d1 ♗c3−+) 2...♗xf2!−+) 1...♗xd4 (1...♘d5 2.hxg5±) 2.cxd4 ♗xc2 (2...♘xc2

3.♕c3 ♘xa3 4.♕b3+−) 3.♕xb4!
(3.♕c3?! ♗xd1 4.axb4=) 3...
♗xd1 (3...♕xb4+ 4.axb4 ♗xd1
5.hxg5+−) 4.♕xa4+ ♗xa4
5.hxg5±

870 1.e7 fxe5 2.e8=♘! (2.e8=♕?
♖h7+ 3.♔g8 ♖ag7+ 4.♔f8
♖h8#; 2.♖xe5? ♖xe7 3.♖xe7
♖a8+ 4.♖e8 ♖xe8#) 2...♖h7+
(2...♔f7 3.♔g8 ♖xf3 4.♖xe5=; 2...
♖e7 3.♖xe5 ♖xe5 4.♘xe5=; 2...
♖a8 3.♖xe5=; 2...♖b8 3.♖xe5=)
3.♔g8 ♖ae7 (3...♖a8 4.♖xe5=)
4.♖xe5 ♖xe5 5.♘xe5=

871 (Based on a position by A.
Zhukov) 1.♗d5+! (1.♕g2?
♖b6+ 2.♗c6 ♖bxc6+ 3.♕xc6
♖xc6+−+) 1...♖xd5 (1...♔h8?
2.♕h1#; 1...♔f8 2.♕f2++−)
2.♕c5!! ♖g5+ (2...♖dxc5=; 2...
♖bxc5=) 3.♕xg5 ♖xg5+ 4.♔xg5
♔h7 (4...♔f7 5.♔f5!=) 5.♔h5!=

872 1.♘f6+ (1.♗xf7+? ♔h8−+)
1...gxf6 (1...♕xf6 2.e4!? ♕g6+
3.♕g3+−) 2.♗d5 (2.♗xf7+?
♖xf7−+) 2...♕xd5 3.e4 (3.f3?
♕g5+ 4.♔f2 ♕g2+ 5.♔e1
♘xf3+ 6.♖xf3 ♕xf3∓) 3...♕xe4
(3...♕g5+ 4.♕g3+−) 4.♕g3+
(4.f3? ♕g6+ 5.♔f2 ♕g2+ 6.♔e3
(6.♔e1 ♖e8+−+) 6...♖e8+
7.♔d3 (7.♔f4 ♕g5#) 7...♕e2#)
4...♔h8 5.f3+−

873 1.♖h1! (1.♖g2? ♖fxg2 (1...
♖hxg2?! 2.♕xa5=) 2.♕xa5
♖g1#; 1.♕xa5? ♖e2+ 2.♔f1
♖hf2#; 1.♗d3? ♗xd2+ 2.♖xd2
♖xd2−+) 1...♖e2+ (1...♗xd2+
2.♖xd2 ♖xd2 3.♖xh2=) 2.♔f1
♖hf2+ (2...♗xd2? 3.♖xh2+−)

3.♔g1 ♖g2+ (3...♗xd2? 4.♖h7+
♔f6 5.♗d3+−) 4.♔f1 ♖gf2+ (4...
♗xd2 5.♖xd2=) 5.♔g1 ♖g2+=

874 (Based on a position by A.
Zhukov) 1.♕d1+! (1.♕d3+?
♔e1!−+) 1...♔f2 2.♕d2+ ♔g3
(2...♔f1 3.♕d1+ ♔f2 4.♕d2+=)
3.♕g5+! (3.♕e3+? ♔h4−+)
3...g4 (3...♔f2 4.♕d2+ ♔g3
5.♕g5+=) 4.♕e3+ (4.♕e5+?
♖f4−+) 4...♔h4 (4...♔f3?
5.♕xf3++−) 5.♕f2+!! ♕xf2 (5...
♔g5? 6.♕xf8+−) 6.g3+! ♔xg3=
(6...♕xg3=; 6...♔xg3=)

875 (Based on a position by
Reinfield) 1.♖c8+ (1.♕b8+?!
♔h7 2.♕f4 ♖xf4 3.gxf4 ♕f1+
4.♔c2 ♕d3+=) 1...♔h7 (1...♔g7
2.♕f8+ ♔h7 3.♕g8#) 2.♖h8+
♔xh8 (2...♔g7 3.♕f8#) 3.♖c8+
(3.♕b8+? ♔h7−+) 3...♔h7
(3...♔g7 4.♕f8+ ♔h7 5.♕g8#)
4.♔c1 (4.♖h8+? ♔xh8−+) 4...
♖f1+ 5.♔b2 ♖b1+ (5...♕b1+
6.♔a3+−) 6.♔a3+−

876 1.♖xd6+ ♔g7 2.♖f7+
(2.♖g6+?! ♔f8 3.♖b8+ ♔e7
4.♖b7+ ♔f8=) 2...♗xf7 (2...
♔h8 3.♖d8#; 2...♔g8 3.♖h7+−)
3.♖d7+ ♔g8 (3...♔f6 4.♖h7+−)
4.♖h7 ♖xh7 5.♗xh7+ ♔xh7
6.a6+−

877 1.♔h2 (1.♗xg3? hxg3−+;
1.♕f3? ♖xf3−+) 1...♘f1+ (1...
♖f1 2.♗xg3 hxg3+ 3.♔xg3+−;
1...♗b3?! 2.♗xg3 hxg3+ 3.♔xg3
♗xa4±) 2.♔g1 (2.♗h1= ♘e3!?)
2...♘e3 (2...♘g3 3.♔h2=; 2...
♘d2 3.♗xb6=; 2...♘d3 3.♕xb6
♘g3 4.♔h2 ♘f1+ 5.♔g1=; 2...

♗d5?! 3.♕xb6 ♘d2 4.♕d4
♖f1+ 5.♔h2 ♘f3+ 6.gxf3 ♗xf3
7.♕g1 ♖xg1 8.♔xg1±) 3.♗xb6
(3.♔h2? ♗d5 4.♕xb6 ♖f2−+;
3.♕xb6?! ♖f1+ 4.♔h2 ♖e1
5.♗d8 ♔h7! 6.♕xf6 ♘f1+
7.♔g1 ♘g3+ 8.♔f2 ♖f1+ 9.♔e3
♖xf6 10.♗xf6∓) 3...g4 (3...♖f1+
4.♔h2 ♘f5 5.♗c7=) 4.hxg4
♘xg4 5.♔h1! ♖f1+ 6.♗g1=

878 1.♗f4 (1.♖xf1? ♗xf3−+;
1.♘xg4? ♕h2+ 2.♘xh2 ♘g3#;
1.fxg4? ♕h2#) 1...♕xf4 (1...exf4
2.♕a1+!? (2.♖xf1=; 2.♕b2+=)
2...♖g7 (2...♔h7 3.♕xf1 ♗f5±)
3.♕xf1 ♗f5=; 1...♗xf3 2.♗xg3
♘xg3+ 3.♔h2 ♘f1+ 4.♔h1=)
2.♖xf1 ♗xf3 (2...♗xh3?
3.♘xh3+−; 2...♗f5=) 3.♘g4
(3.♘d3? ♖xg2 4.♘xf4 ♖xa2+
5.♖xf3 exf4−+) 3...h5 4.♖xf3
♕c1+ 5.♔h2 hxg4 6.hxg4=

879 1.♖h6+ gxh6 (1...♕xh6
2.♕xh6++−; 1...♔g8 2.♖xh3+−)
2.♕d4+ (2.♕c3+? ♔g8−+;
2.♕b2+? ♔g8−+) 2...♔g8 (2...
♖f6? 3.♕xf6++−) 3.♕d5+ ♔h8
(3...♖f7 4.♖e8+ ♔g7 5.♕e5+
(5.♕d4++−) 5...♖f6 6.♖e7+
♔g6 7.♕e4+ ♖f5!? 8.♕c6+ ♖f6
9.♕e8++−; 3...♔h7 4.♖e7++−;
3...♔g7 4.♖e7++−) 4.♕e5+
♔h7 5.♕e7+ ♔g8 6.♕e6+ ♕xe6
7.♖xe6+−

880 (Based on the game Goh
Koon Jong – Saric, 2003)
1.♘f6+ (1.♖h1? ♕g2+!?
2.♔g4 h5+!? 3.♔xh5 ♕h3+−+;
1.♔g4? h5+!?−+) 1...♔h8 (1...
gxf6 2.♕g4+ ♔f8 (2...♔h7

3.♕f5+=; 2...♔h8 3.♕c8+!?
♔h7 4.♕f5+=) 3.♕c8+!? ♔g7
4.♕g4+=) 2.♕h4! (2.♖h1?
♕g2+ 3.♔h4 ♕xf3−+; 2.♔g4?
♕xh2−+; 2.♖g1? ♕xh2+
3.♔g4 gxf6−+; 2.♘h5? f5−+)
2...♕xf3 (2...gxf6? 3.♕xf6+
♔g8 4.♕xd6+−; 2...♕xh2+?
3.♔g4+−; 2...♗e5 3.♘d7=)
3.♖e1 (3.♖g1? ♖f2∓) 3...♕f5+
(3...♕xf6 4.♖e8+ ♔h7 5.♕xf6
gxf6 6.♖b6±) 4.♘g4!? (4.♕g4
♕xf6 5.♖f1 ♖f2 6.♖xf2 ♕xf2=)
4...♖f2!=

Chapter 28

881 (Based on the game Cermak
– Martinovsky, 2012) 1.♕d3!
(1.♕h3?! ♕c2+ 2.♔a1 ♕c1+
3.♔a2 ♕c2+=) 1...♕xe1 (1...
♔b8 2.♕g3++−; 1...♔a4 2.♕h7+
♔a6 3.♕b7#) 2.♕h7+ ♔b8 (2...
♕e7 3.♕xe7+ ♔b8 4.♕b7#)
3.♕b7#

882 1.♕xb2 (1.♖gh1? ♖b1+
2.♔c2 ♖6b2#) 1...♖xb2 2.♖gh1
(2.♔xb2? ♕e8−+) 2...♖c2+ (2...
♖b1+ 3.♔xb1+−) 3.♔xc2+−

883 1.♕e3 ♕xc2+ 2.♕xc2 ♖d1+
3.♕c1 (3.♖c1? ♗d3+−+) 3...
♖xc1+ 4.♔xc1+− (4.♖xc1
♗d3+−+)

884 1.♖xg7+ ♔h8 2.♖h1
(2.♖xh7+?! ♔xh7 3.♖h1+ ♔g8
4.♖g1+=) 2...♕c3+ (2...♕xf6
3.♖hxh7#) 3.♔d1 ♕a1+ (3...
♕xf6 4.♖hxh7#) 4.♗c1+−

885 1.♕e8+ ♔h7 2.♖d8 ♖f1+
(2...♕xd8 3.♕xd8+−; 2...
♕xb2+ 3.♔xb2+−; 2...♕f5

3.♕h8#) 3.♔a2 ♖a1+ (3...♕xd8 4.♕xd8+−; 3...♕xb2+ 4.♔xb2+−) 4.♔xa1 ♕f1+ (4...♕xd8 5.♕xd8+−) 5.♔a2+−

886 (Based on a position by P. Benko) 1.g5 d1=♕ (1...c1=♕ 2.♖h6+ gxh6 3.g6+ ♔h8 4.g7+ ♔h7 5.g8=♕#; 1...♔h8 2.♖xd2 c1=♕ 3.♖h2#; 1...g6 2.♖xd2 (2.♖xg6+−) 2...c1=♕ 3.♖h2#) 2.♖h6+ gxh6 3.g6+ ♔h8 4.g7+ ♔h7 5.g8=♕#

887 (Based on the game Foessmeier – Sauper, 1988) 1.♕xa6! fxe3+ (1...c5 2.♕a8++−) 2.♔xe2 (2.♔e1? ♖f1+ 3.♔xe2 ♕h5+−+; 2.♔g3? e1=♕+−+) 2...♖f2+ (2...c5 3.♕a8++−) 3.♔e1 ♖f1+ 4.♕xf1!+− (4.♔xf1? ♕f7+−+)

888 (Based on the internet game Joeelefant – 19john45, 2013) 1.♖b8+ ♔h7 2.♘f7 g5 (2...♖a8 3.♖xa8+−; 2...a1=♕ 3.♖h8#) 3.f5 g6 (3...a1=♕ 4.♖h8#; 3...♖a8 4.♖xa8+−) 4.f6 a1=♕ (4...♖a8 5.♖xa8+−) 5.♖h8#

889 1.♗c4 ♕xc4 (1...♖xc4 2.♖xf6+−) 2.♕g6+ (2.♕g5++−) 2...♔f8 (2...♔h8 3.♕xf6++−) 3.♖xf6+ ♔e7 4.♕g7+ ♕f7 (4...♔e8 5.♖f8#; 4...♔d8 5.♖f8#) 5.♕xf7++−

890 1.♖e5 ♖g1+ (1...♔g7 2.♖e8 ♖g1+ 3.♔f3+−) 2.♔f3 ♔g7 (2...♖f1+ 3.♔e4 ♔g7 4.♖e8+−; 2...a1=♕ 3.♖e8+ ♔g7 4.♖g8#; 2...♖g3+ 3.♔xg3+−) 3.♖e8 ♖f1+ 4.♔e4 a1=♕ (4...♖xf4+ 5.exf4+−) 5.♖g8#

891 1.♕h6 ♕d4+ (1...♖xg2+

2.♔xg2 ♖e2+ 3.♔g1; 1...♖e1+ 2.♖xe1 ♖xe1+ 3.♔f2) 2.♔f1! (2.♔h1? ♖e1+ 3.♖f1 ♖xf1+ 4.♖xf1 ♕xf6+−+) 2...♕c4 (2...♖e1+ 3.♖xe1 ♖xe1+ 4.♔xe1+−; 2...♕xf6 3.♖xf6+−) 3.♕g7#

892 (Based on the game Sir – Nunhert, 1973) 1.♕c7+ (1.♔xh2? ♘g4+ 2.♔g1 ♕h6−+; 1.♘xf3? exf3−+ 2.♔xh2 ♘g4+ 3.♔g1 (3.♔h3 ♘e5+!? 4.♔h2 ♕h6+ 5.♔g1 ♘g4−+) 3...♕h6 4.♕h8+ ♔c7 5.♕c3+ ♔d8 6.♕h8+ ♔e7−+) 1...♔xc7 (1...♔a8? 2.♕d8+ ♕c8 3.♕xc8#) 2.♘xe6+ fxe6 3.♔xh2=

893 1.h6 ♕a4+ (1...♕b4+ 2.♔h5+−) 2.d4 (2.♔h5? ♗e8−+; 2.♔g3? ♕f4−+; 2.♔h3? ♗d7+−+) 2...♕xd4+ (2...exd4 3.♕g7#) 3.♔h5+−

894 1.♘g4+ (1.♕g8?! g4=; 1.♕f6?! ♔h7=) 1...♕xg4 (1...♔h5 2.♘e3+− ♕d4 3.♕h7#) 2.♕g8+− (2.♕f6? ♕c8−+) 2...♕f5 (2...♕d7+ 3.♔xd7+−; 2...♕c8 3.♕xc8+−) 3.♕h8#

895 (Based on the internet game Altotemmi – namatsub, 2013) 1.♖h5 (1.♕xf6?! ♖xf3+=) 1...♖xf3+ (1...♕e1+ 2.♘xe1+−; 1...♖h1 2.♕xh1+−) 2.♔h2!+− (2.gxf3? ♕e1+−+; 2.♔xf3?! ♕f1+ 3.♔e3 ♕g1+=) 2...♖h3+ 3.♕xh3+−

896 (Based on a position by V. Berezin) 1.♕xc6! (1.♖xg2? ♖xg2+ 2.♔h3 ♖2g5−+; 1.♕b5? ♖h6+ 2.♗h5 ♖hxh5#) 1...♖xc6 (1...♖h6+ 2.♕xh6+−; 1...♖h5+

2.♗xh5+−; 1...bxc6 2.♗a6+ ♚b8 3.♖d8#) 2.♖xg2 ♖h6+ 3.♔g1+−

897 (Based on the game Bologan – Akopian, 2002) 1.♖e6 ♖4xe6 (1...♖f8 2.♕xe4+−; 1...♖e7 2.♖d8++−; 1...♖8xe6 2.♕f7+ ♔h8 3.♕h7#; 1...♕b2+ 2.♔g3+−) 2.♕f7+ ♔h8 3.♕h7#

898 (Based on the game Portisch – Gulko, 1976) 1.♖d8! (1.♖d7? ♖f2+ 2.♔g1 (2.♔h3 ♖h2#; 2.♔h1 ♕c1+ 3.♕e1 ♕xe1#) 2...♕c1+ 3.♕e1 ♕xe1#; 1.♕c4?! ♕d2+ 2.♔h3 (2.♔g1? ♕h2#; 2.♔h1? ♕h2#) 2...♕h2+ (2...♘f4+ 3.♗xf4 ♕h2+ 4.♔g4 ♕e2+=) 3.♔g4 ♕e2+ 4.♔h4 (4.♔h3 ♕h2+ 5.♔g4 ♕e2+=) 4...♕h2+ 5.♔g4 ♕e2+=; 1.♖c5?! ♕d2+ (1...♘f4+ 2.♗xf4 ♕xf4=; 1...♘f6=) 2.♔h3 ♘f4+ 3.♗xf4 ♕xf4=) 1...♕d2+ (1...♖xd8 2.♕c4+ ♖d5 (2...♔f8 3.♕f7#) 3.♕xd5+ ♔f8 4.♕f7#; 1...♘f4+ 2.♗xf4 ♕xd8 3.♕e6+ ♔g7 4.♗e5++−; 1...♕xd8 2.♕c4+ ♕d5+ (2...♖f7 3.♕xf7#) 3.♕xd5+ ♖f7 4.♕xf7#) 2.♔h3 ♕h2+ 3.♔g4+−

899 1.♖h5 ♗xh5 (1...♖c8 2.♘c6+−; 1...♖g8 2.♘c6+−; 1...♖b8 2.♘c6+−) 2.♘c6 ♗f3 (2...♖h7 3.♖d8#; 2...♖e1+ 3.♔xe1+−; 2...♖f2+ 3.♔xf2+−) 3.♖xa7#

900 (Based on the game Marolleau – Karafiath, 1967) 1.♖d4 (1.♕h7+? ♔xh7 2.♖xd7+ ♖c2−+; 1.g3?! ♖h4+ (1...♖xg5=; 1...♗c6+ 2.♔h2 ♖h4+ 3.gxh4 ♕c7+=) 2.gxh4 ♗c6+ 3.♔h2

♕c7+ 4.♔h3 ♕c8+ 5.♔g3 ♕c7+=) 1...cxd4 (1...♖h4+ 2.♕xh4+−; 1...♖c2 2.♗xc2 bxc2 3.♗xe3+−) 2.♕h7+ (2.♗h7+ ♔f8 3.♗e4+−) 2...♔f8 3.♕h8#

901 1.♗e8! (1.a3?! ♘b3+ 2.♔a2 ♕xc4=; 1.♗g6? ♘b3+ 2.axb3 axb3+ 3.♘a2 (3.♘a4 ♖xa4#) 3...♖xa2#) 1...♘b3+ (1...♗f5 2.♖xf5+−) 2.axb3 axb3+ 3.♗a4+−

902 (Based on the game Costa – Froewis, 2018) 1.♕f6 (1.♕h6?! g6 2.♘xe6 (2.h5 ♕a1=; 2.♖xg6+ fxg6 3.♕xg6+ ♔h8=) 2...♖h1+! 3.♔xh1 ♕a1+ 4.♔h2 ♕xe5−+) 1...g6 2.♘xe6 (2.h5? ♘d7−+; 2.♖xg6+?! fxg6 3.♕xg6+ ♔h8=; 2.♖f3?! ♕d1 3.♕xf7+ ♔h8=) 2...♖h1+ 3.♔xh1 ♕a1+ 4.♔h2+−

903 1.♖a3 (1.♔c1? ♕a1+ 2.♔d2 ♕xb2−+) 1...bxa3 (1...♕xa3 2.bxa3+−) 2.♗d7! ♗xd7 (2...♖xd7 3.♖xh7+ ♔xh7 4.♕h5#; 2...♕xd7 3.♖xh7+ ♔xh7 4.♕h5#; 2...♖g5 3.♗xa4+−; 2...a2+ 3.♔a1+−) 3.♖xh7+ ♔xh7 4.♕h5#

904 (Based on a position by V. Berezin) 1.♕g2 (1.f8=♘+? ♔g8−+; 1.f8=♕? ♖h1#) 1...♘xg2 (1...♕b4 2.♕xc6+−; 1...♕e7 2.♕xc6+−; 1...♕xg2+ 2.♖xg2+−) 2.f8=♕+− ♖h1+ 3.♔xh1 ♘h4+ 4.♔h2+−

905 (Based on a position by Wotawa) 1.♖e7 (1.♖xb6?! ♕f1+ 2.♔b1 ♕xb1+ 3.♔xb1=; 1.♗c1+?! ♔b4=; 1.c3? ♕f1+ 2.♗c1+ (2.♗e1 ♕xe1#) 2...

♕xc1#) 1...♕xe7 (1...♕f1+
2.♖e1+−; 1...♕f2 2.♖e3+ ♕xe3
3.♗xe3+−; 1...♕h8+ 2.c3 ♕h1+
3.♖e1+−) 2.c3 ♕e2 (2...♕e1+
3.♗xe1+−; 2...♕e5 3.♗c1#)
3.♗c1+ ♕b2+ 4.♗xb2#

906 (Based on the game Kozyrev
– Scherbakov, 2001) 1.♗h5!
(1.♘f7+?! ♖xf7 2.♕c5!?=; 1.h4?
♕e3−+) 1...♖xc2 (1...♕xh5
2.♕xf2+−; 1...cxd6 2.♕xf2+−;
1...♖ef8 2.♖xe5!? (2.♕xf2 ♖xf2
3.♖xe5+−) 2...♖xc2 3.♘f7++−)
2.♘f7+ ♔g8 (2...♘xf7 3.♖xe8#)
3.♘xh6+ gxh6 4.♗xe5+−

907 (Based on a position by
Wotawa) 1.♖a5 ♗f5 (1...♗f4
2.♗xf4+−; 1...♗e5+ 2.♖xe5+−)
2.♖a7! ♗xa7 (2...♗e5+
3.dxe5+−; 2...♗d7 3.♖xd7+−; 2...
♗c7 3.♖xc7+−) 3.f4 ♗b6 (3...
♗xd4+ 4.cxd4+−) 4.fxg5#

908 1.♗b5 (1.♕g5+? ♔d7−+)
1...♕b6 (1...fxg6 2.♕g5+ ♔f7
3.♖h7+ ♔g8 4.♕xg6#; 1...♘f4
2.♕g5+ f6 3.♖h7+ ♖f7 4.♖xf7#;
1...f6 2.♕h7+ ♖f7 3.♕xf7#)
2.♕g5+ f6 3.♖h7+ (3.exf6+?
♖xf6 4.♖h7+ ♔d6−+) 3...♔d8
(3...♔f7 4.♕xf6+ ♔f8 5.♕xf7#)
4.g7!? (4.♕xg2+−) 4...♖g8
5.♕xf6++−

909 1.♘xh4 (1.♕xh4? ♗xf3
2.♕xg4+ ♗xg4 3.f3 ♗h5∓; 1.g3?
♘xf3+−+; 1.♘e1? ♕xe2−+) 1...
♕xe2 (1...♕g5 2.♕xg5+ hxg5
3.♘f3+−) 2.♘g6! (2.♕xh6?!
♕g4=) 2...fxg6 (2...♕g4 3.♕h8#;
2...♔h7 3.♖d7+−) 3.♕xg6+
(3.♕xe6+ ♖f7 4.♖d7+−) 3...

♔h8 4.♖d7 (4.♕xh6+ ♔g8
5.♕g6+ ♔h8 6.♖d7+−) 4...♕g4
5.♕h7#

910 (Based on the game Svidler
– Andreikin, 2018) 1.♕xh7+
(1.g6? hxg6 (1...fxg6? 2.♖xg6+
♔f8 3.♖g8++−) 2.♖xg6+
♔f8−+) 1...♔xh7 (1...♔f8
2.♗f6+−) 2.♖xh5+ ♔g6 (2...
♔g8 3.♖h8#) 3.♖h6+ ♔f5
4.♖f6+ (4.♖g3? ♕g2+ 5.♖xg2
♗xg2−+) 4...♔e4 5.♖g3+−

911 1.♖xg7+ ♔xg7 2.♖g1+ ♔h8
(2...♔h6 3.♘g4+ (3.♘xf7+
♖xf7 4.♖g6+ hxg6 5.♕xg6#;
3.♕f4++−) 3...♔g7 4.♘f6+ ♔h8
(4...♔h6 5.♕xh7#) 5.♕xh7#; 2...
♗g5+ 3.♕xg5+ ♔h8 4.♕g7#)
3.♕xf7 (3.♘xf7+?! ♖xf7 4.♕xf7
♖g8 5.♖xg8+ ♔xg8 6.♕xe7=)
3...♗f6 (3...♖g8 4.♕xg8+ ♖xg8
5.♘f7#; 3...♕g4 4.♖xg4+−; 3...
♖xf7 4.♘xf7#; 3...♗g5+ 4.♖xg5
♖d7!? 5.♕xd7+−) 4.♕g8+ ♖xg8
5.♘f7#

912 1.♖c8+ (1.♕e5?! ♖xg2+
2.♔f4 ♖bc2=) 1...♔h7 (1...♖d8
2.♖xd8++−; 1...♔g7 2.♕e5+ f6
3.♕c7+ ♔h6 4.♖h8#) 2.♕e5
♖xg2+ (2...f6 3.♕c7+ ♔h6
4.♖h8#; 2...g5 3.♕h8+ ♔g6
4.♖g8#; 2...♖d8 3.♖xd8+−)
3.♔f4 g5+ (3...♖g4+ 4.fxg4+−;
3...f6 4.♕c7+ ♔h6 5.♖h8#; 3...
♖b4+ 4.♔e3+−) 4.hxg5 ♖b4+
(4...♖g4+ 5.fxg4+−) 5.♔e3+−

913 1.♘e7+ (1.gxh4? ♘e3+ (1...
♘f6+−+) 2.♔h2 (2.♔h1
♖xh4#) 2...♖xh4#; 1.♔g2?
♘h2!−+ 2.♘e7+ ♔d8 3.♘xg8

♕h3+ 4.♔g1 ♘f3#; 1.♘b6+?
♔d8–+) 1...♕xe7 (1...♔d8
2.gxh4 ♘e3+ 3.♘xg8+–; 1...♔c7
2.gxh4+–; 1...♔b8 2.gxh4+–;
1...♔b7 2.gxh4+–) 2.♖xa7+–
(2.♕a2? ♕h4! 3.♕a6+ ♔d8
4.♕a5+ ♔e7!–+) 2...♕h4
3.♖a8+! ♔c7 4.gxh4 ♘e3+
5.♖xg8+–

914 (Based on a position by
Wotawa) 1.♕g2! (1.♖b5?
♖xf8–+) 1...♗xf3 (1...♖xf8
2.♕g4#) 2.♖b5+ ♗c5 (2...♗d5
3.♕f3+ ♔h4 4.♘g6#; 2...♕d5
3.♕xf3+ (3.♖xd5+? ♗xd5–+)
3...♔h4 4.♘g6#) 3.♖xc5+ ♕xc5
(3...♗d5 4.♕f3+ ♔h4 5.♘g6#;
3...e5 4.♖xe5+ ♔h4 5.♘g6#; 3...
♔h4 4.♘g6#; 3...♕d5 4.♕xf3+
♔h4 5.♘g6#) 4.♕xf3+ ♔h4
5.♘g6#

915 (Based on a position by
Troitzky) 1.♘d7+ ♔g7 2.f6+
♔h7 3.dxe7 (3.fxe7?! ♔g7=)
3...♖d8 (3...♖a8 4.♘f8+ ♖xf8
5.exf8=♘#; 3...♖b8 4.♘f8+
♖xf8 5.exf8=♘#; 3...♖c8
4.♘f8+ ♖xf8 5.exf8=♘#; 3...
♖f8 4.♘xf8#; 3...♖xe7 4.♘f8#)
4.♘f8+ (4.exd8=♕?!=) 4...♖xf8
5.exf8=♘# (5.exf8=♕?!=)

916 (Based on the game Korobov –
Volokitin, 2001) 1.♗h2 (1.♕e6?
♖f5–+) 1...♕h4 (1...gxh2
2.c5+–; 1...♖xd6 2.♕xd6+–
♕h4?! 3.♕xf8#; 1...♕g5!?
2.♖xd8 ♖xd8 3.f4!?+–) 2.♕xe5+
♔g8 3.♖xg6+ (3.♕e6+?! ♔g7
4.♕h3 ♕xh3 5.gxh3 ♖xd6
6.♖xd6 gxh2±) 3...hxg6 (3...♔f7

4.♖g7#) 4.♖xg6+ ♔f7 5.♖g7#

917 (A. Mouterde, 1921) 1.♘g4+
♔d5 2.♘f6+ (2.♔f4? c3–+) 2...
♔e5 3.♘d7+ (3.♘g4+ ♔d5)
3...♔d5 4.♔f4! (4.♘b6+ ♔e5
5.♘d7+ ♔d5; 4.♘f6+ ♔e5)
4...e5+ (4...c3 5.♘b6#; 4...e3
5.♘f6#; 4...d2 5.♘f6#) 5.♔f5 c3
(5...e3 6.♘f6#; 5...d2 6.♘f6#)
6.♘b6#

918 1.♖g8+ (1.♖xe2? ♗c5+–+;
1.♘e6+? ♔h6–+) 1...♔h6
2.f8=♕+ (2.f8=♗+? ♔h5–+) 2...
♗xf8 (2...♔h5 3.♕f7+ ♔h4 (3...
♔h6 4.♕xh7#; 3...♔g4 4.♘f3#)
4.♕xh7+ ♔g4 5.♕h3#) 3.♘f7+
♔h5 4.♖g5+ ♔h4 5.g3+ ♔h3
6.♖h5+ ♔g4 7.♖h4# (7.♖g5+
♔h3 8.♖h5+ ♔g4)

919 1.♘f5+! exf5 (1...♔f8 2.♖xc6!?
♖xc6 3.♖d8#; 1...♔e8 2.♖d8#)
2.exf6+ ♔f8 (2...♔e8 3.♖d8#)
3.♖xc6! (3.♖d8+?! ♗e8 4.♖1d7
(4.♖e1 ♖e5–+) 4...♖c7! 5.♖d1!
♖c5 6.♖1d7 ♖c7=) 3...♖xc6 (3...
♔e8 4.♖xc5+–) 4.♖d8#

920 (Based on the game Zverev –
Lu Miaoyi, 2021) 1.♖f5 ♔g8
(1...♗xf6 2.♖xf6+–; 1...♗f4
2.♖xf4+–) 2.♖xh5 (2.♖ef1?!
♖fe8 3.♖xh5 ♗xf6=; 2.♕g5?!
♖fe8=) 2...♗xf6 (2...gxh5
3.♕g5+ ♔h8 (3...♔h7 4.♕g7#)
4.♕g7#) 3.♕xf6 gxh5 (3...♕h2+
4.♔xh2+–; 3...♖fe8 4.♖h8#)
4.♘f5+–

921 (Based on the game Topalov
– Tukmakov, 1994) 1.♖xh5
♘xh1 (1...gxh5 2.♖g8#) 2.♖xg6!
(2.♘xg6+? fxg6 3.f7+ ♗g7–+)

2...fxg6 (2...♗h6 3.♖gxh6+−;
2...♗xe7 3.fxe7+ ♖d4 (3...f6
4.♗xf6#) 4.♗xd4+ f6 5.♗xf6#;
2...♖xe7 3.fxe7+ f6 (3...♗g7
4.exd8=♕#; 3...♖d4 4.exf8=♕#)
4.♗xf6+ ♗g7 5.exd8=♕#; 2...
♖d1+ 3.♔c2 ♖g1 (3...♗b4+
4.♔xd1+−) 4.♖xg1+−) 3.f7+
♗g7 (3...♖d4 4.♗xd4+ ♗g7
5.♘xg6#) 4.♘xg6#

922 (Based on the game Geller –
Rodshtein, 2019) 1.♖xg7 ♕xe3
(1...♔xg7 2.♕h6+ ♔g8 (2...
♔h8 3.♕xf8++−) 3.♘f6+ ♖xf6
(3...♔f7 4.♕xh7#; 3...♔h8
4.♕xh7#) 4.♖d8+ ♔f7 (4...♖f8
5.♖xf8#) 5.♕f8+ ♔e6 6.♕xf6#;
1...a2 2.♖xh7+ ♔xh7 3.♕h6+
♔g8 4.♖xg6+ ♔f7 5.♖g7+ ♔e8
6.♕c6+ ♔d8 7.♕d7#) 2.♖dd7!
(2.fxe3? ♕xg7−+; 2.♘xe3?
♔xg7−+) 2...♕g5 (2...♕xe5
3.♖xh7+ ♔g8 4.♘h6#; 2...fxf2
3.♘xe3!?+−; 2...♖f7 3.♖gxf7+−)
3.♖xh7+ ♔g8 4.♖dg7#

923 (Based on a position by A.
Zhukov) 1.♕f4+! ♔a8 (1...♖c7
2.♕xc7+ ♔a8 3.♕xb7#; 1...
♔c8 2.♕f8#) 2.♕f3!! (2.♖e3?
♕xe3+−+) 2...♕xf3 (2...♖xf3
3.♖e8+ ♕c8 4.♖xc8#; 2...♕h8
3.♕xb7#; 2...♕h6+ 3.♔xc3+−)
3.♖e8+ ♖c8 4.♖xc8#

924 (Based on the game Kramnik
- Ivanchuk, 1996) 1.♗g3
(1.♗f1? ♕e1−+; 1.bxa5? ♕e1+
2.♗f1 ♕xf1#) 1...♕c1+ (1...
h5? 2.♗h2±; 1...♕e1+ 2.♔h2
♗g4 3.♘d4! exd4 4.♕b5 ♕xb4
5.♕d5=) 2.♔h2 ♗g4!? (2...

♕xc4 3.♔xh3±) 3.♘d4! ♕xc4
(3...exd4? 4.♕b5+−; 3...♘xd4?!
4.♗xe5+ ♔f8 5.♗xd4 ♕xc4
6.♕xa5±) 4.♘xc6 bxc6=

925 (A. Akerblom, 1952) 1.♖g8+
(1.c6? ♖h1 2.b6 (2.♖g8+
♔a7 3.♖g7+ ♔b8 4.♖g8+
♔c7−+) 2...♖b1+ 3.♔c5
(3.♔a5 ♖a1+ 4.♔b5 g1=♕−+)
3...♖c1+ 4.♔d6 g1=♕−+;
1.♔a5? ♖h1−+; 1.b6? ♖h1
2.c6 ♖b1+−+) 1...♔b7 (1...
♔a7 2.b6+! (2.♖g7+? ♔b8
3.♖g8+ ♔c7−+) 2...♔a6
(2...♔b7 3.♔b5+−) 3.♖g7
(3.♖a8++−) 3...g1=♕ 4.♖a7#)
2.c6+! (2.♖g7+? ♔c8−+) 2...
♔c7 (2...♔a7 3.♔a5+−; 2...
♔b6 3.♖g7+−) 3.♔c5 (3.♖g7+?
♔d6−+) 3...♖h1 4.b6#

926 1.♕g3 (1.♕h4?! bxc3+ 2.♔e3
d4+ 3.♔f3 ♕d5+ 4.♔f2 ♕d8
5.♕xd8+! ♖xd8 6.♔e2=) 1...
bxc3+ (1...♕xc2+ 2.♔xc2+−;
1...b3 2.♕g7#) 2.♔e3 (2.♔d1?
♕b1+−+; 2.♔c1? ♕a1#; 2.♔e1?
♕b1+−+; 2.♔e2? ♕xc2+−+;
2.♔d3? ♕c4+−+) 2...d4+ (2...
♕xc2 3.♕g7#) 3.♔f3 (3.♔xd4?!
♕d5+=) 3...♕d5+ (3...♕xc2
4.♕g7#) 4.♔f2 (4.♔e2?! ♕e4+
5.♔d1 (5.♔f1 ♕h7) 5...♕h7=)
4...♕xe5 (4...♕e4 5.♕g7#)
5.fxe5+−

927 1.♖e8+ (1.♕g6? ♗xg6
2.♘xg6+ ♔g8−+) 1...♗xe8 (1...
♗g8 2.♘g6#) 2.♕g6 ♗xg6
(2...♕d8 3.♕xh7#; 2...♖xh4
3.♕xe8#) 3.♘xg6+ ♔g8 4.♗c4+
♕d5 5.♗xd5#

928 1.♗d3+ (1.♕f5+? ♖g6
2.♕xg6+ ♔xg6 3.gxh3 ♕g5+
4.♔h1 ♕d2∓; 1.♕h8+? ♔g6−+;
1.♕g8+? ♔g6−+) 1...♖xd3 (1...
g6 2.♕h8#; 1...f5 2.♕xf5++−)
2.♕f5+ ♖g6 (2...g6 3.♕xf7#)
3.♕xd3 ♘f4 (3...♖g4 4.g3+−)
4.♖ee8! (4.♕e4? ♘h3+−+;
4.♕f3? ♖xg2+? 5.♕xg2 ♘xg2
6.♔xg2−+; 4.g3? ♘xd3−+) 4...
♘xg2 (4...♕xf2+ 5.♗xf2 ♘xd3+
6.♔f3+−; 4...♘h3+ 5.♕xh3+−)
5.♖h8#

929 (Based on a position by
Stamma) 1.♘d7+ ♖xd7 (1...
♗xd7 2.♕c7+ (2.♕e5+ ♕xe5
3.♖xa7+−) 2...♘xc7 3.bxa7+
♔c8 (3...♔a8 4.♘xc7#)
4.a8=♕+ ♘xa8 5.♖xa8#;
1...♔a8 2.♖xa7#) 2.♕e5+!
(2.bxa7+? ♔a8−+; 2.♕c7+?
♘xc7−+) 2...♕xe5 (2...♘c7
3.♕xc7+ ♖xc7 (3...♗a8
4.♖xa7#) 4.bxc7+ ♔a8 5.♖xa7#;
2...♔a8 3.♖xa7#; 2...♖d6
3.♕xd6++−; 2...♖c7 3.bxc7+
♔a8 (3...♘xc7 4.♕xc7+ ♔a8
5.♖xa7#) 4.♖xa7#) 3.♖xa7+−
♖h1+ (3...♕a1+ 4.♖xa1+−; 3...
♘c7 4.bxc7+ ♖xc7 5.♖a8#; 3...
♕xg3+ 4.fxg3 f2+ 5.♔xf2+−)
4.♔xh1 ♕h5+ 5.♔g1+−

930 (V. Kuzmichev, 1986) 1.♗d7!
(1.♗e6? ♖d8!−+; 1.♗h3?
♖g8−+) 1...♖f6 2.♗c8!
(2.♗g4?! ♗d2=) 2...♖b6 (2...
♖f7 3.♗e6+−) 3.♗f5! (3.♗g4?!
♖b3=) 3...♖b4 4.♗h3! ♖g4
5.♗xg4+−

931 (Kubbel, 1911) 1.♘c4+ ♔b3

2.♘a5+ ♔a3 3.♗f2!+− ♖e5
(3...♔b4 4.♘xc6++−; 3...c5
4.♗xc5#; 3...♖e1+ 4.♗xe1+−)
4.♘c4+ ♔b3 (4...♔b4
5.♘xe5+−) 5.♘xe5+−

932 (Based on a position by
Wotawa) 1.♘f6 (1.♗e4?
♖f2+!−+) 1...gxf6 (1...♗a5
2.♖axa5+−; 1...♖a3 2.♖xa3+−;
1...♖f2 2.♖a8#) 2.♗e4 (2.♔g6?
♖g3+−+; 2.♖a8+?! ♔h7=) 2...
dxe4 (2...♗a5 3.♖axa5+−; 2...
♖a3 3.♖xa3+−) 3.♗g5 (3.♔g6?
♖g3+−+; 3.♖a8+? ♔h7−+)
3...fxg5 (3...♗xg5 4.♔g6+−)
4.♔g6 ♔g8 (4...♗a5 5.♖xa5
♖a3 6.♖xa3 ♖a2 7.♖xa2+−; 4...
♖a3 5.♖xa3 ♗a5 6.♖xa5 ♖a2
7.♖xa2+−) 5.♖a8#

933 1.♕b6 (1.♖xa7?! ♖h8 2.♗g1
♖fh7=) 1...♕xh2+!? (1...
♕c1+ 2.♖xc1 axb6 3.♖a1#; 1...
♕f1+ 2.♖xf1 axb6 3.♖a1#; 1...
axb6 2.♖a1#) 2.♔xh2 ♖h8+
(2...♖h7+ 3.♔g1+−) 3.♔g1
(3.♔g3?! axb6 4.♗d6 f4+! 5.♔f3
♖h5= 6.♖a1+? ♖a5−+) 3...axb6
(3...♔b8 4.♕xa7++−; 3...♖h1+
4.♔xh1+−) 4.♗d6 (4.♗d4?!
♖c8= 5.♗e5? ♖c5−+) 4...♖fh7
(4...♖h1+ 5.♔xh1+−; 4...♖c7
5.♗xc7+−) 5.♖a1#

934 (Based on the game Hammpe
– Meitner, 1872) 1.c3+!
(1.♗d2+ ♔c5 2.♗e3+ ♔b4) 1...
♔xb3 (1...♔a5 2.b4#) 2.♔d2!
(2.♔e2?! ♘bc6!? (2...♔c4
3.♘a3+ ♔xc3=; 2...♘ec6=)
3.dxc6 (3.♖hb1+ ♔c4 4.♘a3+
♔xc3 5.♖c1+ ♔b3=) 3...♘xc6

4.Rhb1+ ♔c4 5.Na3+ ♔xc3
6.Rc1+ ♔b3=) 2...Bc5 (2...
axb5 3.Rhb1+ ♔c4 4.Rb4#; 2...
Qh4 3.Rhb1+ ♔c4 4.Na3#; 2...
Bxe3+ 3.♔d3 axb5 (3...Bg1
4.Rhxg1+−; 3...Bc1 4.Rhxc1
Qh3+ 5.gxh3+−) 4.Rhb1#; 2...
Bd4 3.Rhb1+ ♔c4 4.Rb4+ ♔c5
5.Bxd4#; 2...a5 3.Rhb1+ ♔c4
4.Na3#) 3.♔d3! (3.Rab1+?
♔c4−+; 3.Rxc5? ♔c4−+)
3...Ba3 (3...axb5 4.Rhb1#)
4.Rhb1+ Bb2 (4...♔xa4
5.Rxa3#) 5.Nd4#

935 (Based on the internet game
Ailiendonkykong – filkin, 2014)
1.Qd7 Ne6 (1...Bd8 2.Qa4+−;
1...Nb5 2.cxb5+−) 2.Qa4 (2.h4?!
Bd8 3.Qa4 Nc7 4.Qa5+ ♔c6
5.Qa4+ ♔b6=; 2.Qxe7?! Nf4+
3.gxf4 Rg8+ 4.♔f3 Qd1+=) 2...
Nf4+ 3.gxf4 Rg8+ 4.♔f3 Qh1+
(4...Qd1+ 5.Qxd1+−; 4...Rg3+
5.hxg3+−) 5.♔e2+−

936 1.Bg5 Rxh1+ (1...Qf7 2.Bf6+
Qxf6 (2...Qg7 3.Qxh7#)
3.Qxh7#) 2.♔d2 Rh7 (2...Rd1+
3.Rxd1+−; 2...Qg7 3.Qe8+ ♔h7
4.Rxh1++−; 2...Rxa1 3.Bf6+
Qg7 4.Qxg7#; 2...e3+ 3.fxe3+−)
3.Rh1! Rxh1 (3...e3+ 4.fxe3;
3...Ne6 4.Bf6+ Ng7 (4...Qg7
5.Qxh7#) 5.Qxh7#) 4.Bf6+
Qg7 5.Qxg7#

937 1.Be6 (1.Qxf8+? ♔xf8 2.Be6
Qe4+−+; 1.Rc8? Qxc8−+) 1...
Qe4+ (1...Qxe6 2.Rxe6+−;
1...Rxe8 2.fxe8=Q+−; 1...
Qd3 2.Qxf8+ ♔xf8 3.Rc8+
♔g7 (3...Qd8 4.Rxd8+ ♔g7

5.f8=Q#) 4.f8=Q#) 2.♔h3
(2.♔f2? Bd4+−+; 2.♔g1
Bd4+−+; 2.♔f1? Qf3+ 3.♔e1
(3.♔g1 Bd4#) 3...Qc3+
4.Rxc3 Qxc3+−+) 2...h5 (2...
Qxc6 3.Qxc6+−; 2...Rxe8
3.fxe8=Q+−) 3.Qxf8+ ♔xf8
4.Rc8+ ♔g7 5.f8=Q++−

938 1.Qb3+ (1.Rb4+? ♔c8−+;
1.Qa3? Bxe2−+) 1...♔c8 (1...
♔a7 2.Ra4#; 1...♔a8 2.Ra4#)
2.Qa4 (2.Ra4? Qe8!−+; 2.Rb4
Qe8!−+) 2...Qh3 (2...Qe8
3.dxc6 Qxc6 4.Qxc6+−; 2...
Qe7 3.dxc6+−) 3.dxc6 Qe3+
(3...♔b8 4.Rb4+ ♔c8 5.Qa8#)
4.♔b1 (4.♔d1? Qxe2+−+) 4...
Nd2+ 5.♔a1+−

939 (Based on a position by Prokes)
1.g4 (1.Rf4? Rh1−+; 1.f7?
Rxg2−+; 1.d6? Rxg2−+) 1...
hxg3 (1...Rxg4 2.Rh5+ ♔xh5
3.Rxh7#; 1...c5 2.Rh5#) 2.♔f7
(2.Rd6? Rb7−+) 2...Rb7 (2...
c5 3.Rd6#; 2...e3 3.Rd6+ Be6
4.Rxe6#) 3.Rxb7+− g2 4.Rd7
Re1 5.Rd6+ Re6 6.Rxe6#

940 (Based on a position by Prokes)
1.Bd6 (1.Bb4?! Rd8=; 1.Bg7+?
♔g8−+; 1.Rb8? Qg8 2.♔g6
Bd3+ 3.♔xf6 Rf5+−+) 1...Rg5
(1...♔g8 2.Rg7+ ♔h8 3.Rf7
Rg5 4.Be7! Bd3 5.Rf8+ Rg8
6.Bxf6#; 1...Nxd6 2.Rb8+ Nc8
(2...Ne8 3.Rxe8#) 3.Rxc8+ Rd8
4.Rxd8#; 1...Rxd6 2.Rb8+ Rd8
3.Rxd8#) 2.Rb8+ Rg8 3.Bf8
Rg6+ (3...Rxf8 4.Rxf8#; 3...Bd3
4.Bg7#) 4.♔xg6 Bd3+ 5.♔xf6
(5.♔h6?! ♔g8=; 5.♔f7+−) 5...

♔h7 6.♗g7+−

941 1.♘g6+ (1.♕xf3? c4−+) 1...
♔h7 2.♘f8+ ♔h8 (2...♖xf8
3.♕xg7#) 3.♕g6 (3.♘g6+ ♔h7
4.♘f8+ ♔h8) 3...♗f5 (3...♖xf8
4.♕xg7#; 3...♘3g5 4.♕h7+
♘xh7 5.♘g6#; 3...♘7g5 4.♕h7+
♘xh7 5.♘g6#) 4.exf5 ♘3g5 (4...
♘7g5 5.♕h7+ ♘xh7 6.♘g6#)
5.♕h7+ ♘xh7 6.♘g6#

942 (Based on the game Lutz
– Gelfand, 2002) 1.♖xg7+!
(1.dxc4? ♕a1#; 1.♖xe8+? ♖xe8
2.dxc4 (2.♖xg7+ ♕xg7−+) 2...
♕a1+ 3.♔d2 ♕xg1−+) 1...
♕xg7 (1...♔h8? 2.♖xh7+
♔xh7 3.♗f5++−; 1...♖xg7?
2.♘e4+ (2.♘e2++−) 2...♔h8
3.♘xc3+−) 2.♘e4 (2.♖xe8+?
♖xe8−+) 2...♖xe4! (2...
♕xg1? 3.♖xg1++−; 2...♘xa3?
3.♘f6++−) 3.♕xg7+! (3.dxe4?
♘xa3∓) 3...♔xg7 4.♗b2+!?
(4.♖xe4? ♘xa3∓; 4.♖g1+? ♔h6
5.♗xc5 ♖e5∓) 4...♘xb2 5.♖xe4
♘xd3+! 6.cxd3 ♖xd3=

943 1.♗xe4 (1.♘f5? ♖xg3−+;
1.♖h3? ♕g5−+) 1...dxe4 (1...f5
2.♗xf5+− ♕e7 3.♗xh7 ♕xh7
4.♕f6+ ♔g7 5.♘f5+−; 1...♔g6
2.♘xg6+ fxg6 3.♗xg6+−) 2.♘f5
♖xg3 (2...♖g5 3.♖xg5+−; 2...♕f8
3.♕f6+ ♖g7 4.♖xg7+−) 3.fxg3
♕f8 (3...♕g5 4.♕xg5+−; 3...♕g8
4.♕f6+ ♕g7 5.♕xg7#; 3...♕d4+
4.cxd4+−; 3...♔g8 4.♕g7#)
4.♕f6+ ♔g8 (4...♕g7 5.♕xg7#)
5.♘h6+ ♕xh6 6.♕xh6+−

944 1.♕h5+ ♔g8 2.♖xg7+ ♔xg7
(2...♔f8 3.♕h8+ ♘g8 4.♗c5+

♕d6 (4...♖e7 5.♖xg8#; 4...
♕e7 5.♖xg8#) 5.♗xd6+ ♖e7
6.♖xg8#) 3.♗h6+ (3.♕h6+?!
♔g8 4.♗d4 f6 5.♕xf6 ♘f5=) 3...
♔h7 (3...♔h8 4.♕e5+ f6 (4...
♔g8 5.♕g7#; 4...♔h7 5.♕g7#)
5.♕xf6+ ♔g8 6.♕g7#; 3...♔g8
4.♕g5+ ♘g6 (4...♔h8 5.♕g7#;
4...♔h7 5.♕g7#) 5.♕f6+−; 3...
♔f6 4.♕g5#) 4.♗g5+ ♔g8 (4...
♔g7 5.♕h6+ ♔g8 6.♗f6+−)
5.♗f6 ♘g6 6.♕h6+−

945 (Based on the game Green –
Hilton, 2008) 1.♖h8+ (1.♖h7?!
♕xg5 2.gh1 ♖ad8=) 1...♔g7
(1...♔xh8 2.♕h4+ ♔g7 (2...
♔g8 3.♖h1+−) 3.♕h6+ (3.♖h1?
♖h8−+) 3...♔g8 4.♖h1+−)
2.♖h7+ (2.♕h4? ♖xh8−+;
2.gh1? ♖xh8−+) 2...♔xh7
(2...♔g8 3.♕h4 ♕e5 4.♖h1+−)
3.♕h4+ (3.♖h1+? ♔g7 4.♕h4
♖h8−+) 3...♔g7 (3...♔g8
4.♖h1+−) 4.♕h6+ (4.♖h1?
♖h8−+) 4...♔g8 5.♖h1 ♕e5
(5...♕xc2+ 6.♔xc2+−; 5...♕h3
6.♖xh3+−) 6.♕h7#

946 1.♕xg7+ ♔xg7 2.♖g3+ ♔h8
3.♗b2+ f6 (3...♗c3 4.♗xc3++−;
3...♖e5 4.♗xe5++−) 4.♖xf6
♕c5+ (4...♖xf6 5.♗xf6#; 4...
h6 5.♖xh6#; 4...♕b4 5.♖xf8#)
5.♖f2+ (5.♔h2 ♕h5+ 6.♔g1
♕c5+; 5.♔h1 ♕h5+ 6.♔g1
♕c5+) 5...♖e5 6.♗xe5+ ♕xe5
7.♖xf8#

947 (Based on the game Geller –
Bocharov, 2006) 1.♕h6 ♖g8
(1...♘xf6 2.♖xf6+−; 1...♕g4
2.♖xg4+−; 1...♗xf6 2.♕xf8#)

2.♕xh7+! (2.♖h4?! ♕f5 3.♖h5 d4!∓) 2...♔xh7 3.♖h4+ ♔g6 4.♖h6+ ♔f5 5.♘ed4+ (5.♘bd4+ ♗xd4 6.♘xd4++−) 5...♗xd4 6.♘xd4+ ♔e5 (6...♔g4 7.h3#) 7.f4#

948 1.♕d4 (1.♖xf8+? ♘xf8−+) 1...f6 (1...♕b1+ 2.♔h2+−; 1...♕a1+ 2.♕xa1+−; 1...♕b2 2.♕xb2+−; 1...♕e2 2.♕xg7#) 2.♕d5+ (2.♖xf8+? ♔xf8−+) 2...♔h8 3.♖xf8+ (3.♕f7? ♕a1+ 4.♔h2 ♕e5+ 5.♘g3 ♕d6−+; 3.♖e8?! ♕xf2 4.♕f7 ♕h4+ 5.♔g1 ♕d4+ 6.♔h2 ♕h4+=; 3.f4? ♕a3−+) 3...♘xf8 4.♕f7 ♕a1+ (4...♕b1+ 5.♔h2+−; 4...♕a3 5.♕xg7#) 5.♔h2 ♕e5+ (5...♘e6 6.♕e8+ ♘f8 7.♕xf8#) 6.f4 ♕xh5+ 7.♕xh5+−

949 1.♖h3 (1.♖h7+? ♔g8 2.♖g7+ (2.♖xh6 ♖g5−+) 2...♔f8 3.♖h7 ♖g5−+) 1...♖a1+ (1...h5 2.♖h7+ ♔g8 3.♖g3+ ♖g5 (3...♔f8 4.♖h8#) 4.♖xg5+ ♔f8 5.♖h8#; 1...h5 2.♖xh5 ♖a1+ 3.♔d2+−) 2.♔d2 ♕xd3+!? (2...♖d1+ 3.♔xd1 ♖a1+ 4.♔d2+−; 2...♗e4 3.♖xh6+ ♗h7 4.♖hxh7#) 3.cxd3! (3.♔xd3? ♗b5+−+) 3...♖8a2+ (3...♖d1+ 4.♔xd1+−; 3...♖1a2+ 4.♔e3+−) 4.♔e3 ♖e1+ (4...♖e2+ 5.♔xe2+−) 5.♔d4 ♖a4+ (5...♖e4+ 6.dxe4+−; 5...e5+ 6.♔c5 ♖a5+ 7.♔b6 ♖b5+ 8.♔c7+−) 6.♔c3 (6.♔c5? ♖e5+ 7.♔b6 h5−+) 6...♖a3+ (6...♖c1+ 7.♔b2+−; 6...♖c4+ 7.dxc4+−; 6...♖h4 7.♖xh4+−) 7.♔b2+−

950 (Based on a position by Prokes)

1.♘d5 b4 (1...cxd5 2.♖a3+ ♔b4 3.♗e7+ ♔c4 4.♖c3+ ♔d4 5.♗f6+ ♔e4 6.♖e3+ ♔f4 7.♗e5+ ♔g5 (7...♔g4 8.♖g3#) 8.♖g3+ ♔h6 9.♗g7#) 2.♖xb4+ ♔a5 3.♗d8+ ♔a6 4.♖b6+ (4.♘e7+−) 4...♔a7 (4...♔a5 5.♖b8+ ♔a6 6.♘b4+ ♔a7 7.♘xc6+ ♔a6 8.♖b6#) 5.♘e7 f4 (5...♖h6 6.♘c8+ ♔a8 7.♗c7+−; 5...♖g8+ 6.♔a3+−) 6.♘xc6+ ♔a8 7.♖b8#

951 1.♖d4 (1.♖e7?! ♗f7 (1...♖d8 2.♖e8!?=) 2.♖xf7 ♘d6=) 1...♖e4 (1...♖e2+ 2.♗g2+ ♖e5 3.♗xe5#; 1...♖d8 2.♖d7#) 2.♗c3 (2.♗f6 ♖f4 3.♗c3 ♖c4) 2...♖c4 (2...♖e2+ 3.♗g2+ ♖e5 4.♗xe5#) 3.♗b2 (3.♗e5 ♖e4 4.♗c3 ♖c4; 3.♗f6 ♖f4 4.♗c3 ♖c4) 3...♖b4 (3...♖c2+ 4.♘xc2+−) 4.♘b3! (4.♗f6 ♖f4; 4.♗e5 ♖e4; 4.♗c3 ♖c4) 4...♖xb3 5.♗e5 (5.♗d4?! ♖b4=; 5.♗f6?! ♖b6=) 5...♖b6 (5...♖b5 6.axb5+−) 6.♖g2+ ♖f6 7.♗xf6#

952 (Based on the game Antipov – Krishna, 2018) 1.♕d7 (1.♖c2? ♕e7−+) 1...♕xa2+ (1...♖g8 2.♖c8+−; 1...♕e7 2.♕xe7+−) 2.♖c2 (2.♔d3? ♕xb3+−+; 2.♔e1?! ♕f2+=) 2...♖f2+ (2...♕xc2 3.♗xc2+−; 2...♖g8 3.♖xa2+−) 3.♔e1 ♖f1+ (3...♕xc2 4.♕g7#; 3...♖xc2 4.♕g7#; 3...♖e2+ 4.♖xe2+−; 3...♕b1+ 4.♔xf2 ♕xc2+ 5.♔g3 ♕d3+ 6.♔h2+−) 4.♔xf1 ♕b1+ 5.♗f2 ♕xc2+ 6.♔g3 ♕d3+ 7.♔h2+−

953 (Based on the game Debayan

– Shetty, 2009) 1.Qf5+ (1.e5?! Qc8=) 1...Kh8 2.e5 (2.Rg6? Qc7+ 3.f4 fxg6 4.Qxf8+ Kh7 5.hxg6+ Kxg6 6.Qg8+ Kf6 7.Qf8+ Qf7∓) 2...f6 (2... Qc6 3.Qg4+−; 2...Qxe5+ 3.Qxe5++−; 2...Bxf2 3.Qf6+ Kh7 4.Qg7#) 3.Qg6 (3.Rg3?! Qd4=) 3...Qxe5+ (3...Qc7 4.Qxh6+ Qh7 5.Qxf8+ Qg8 6.Qxg8#) 4.Rg3 Qe7 (4... Qxg3+ 5.fxg3+−; 4...Qg5 5.Rxg5+−) 5.Qxh6+ Qh7 6.Qxf8+ Qg8 7.Rxg8#

954 (Based on the game Somborski – Brkic, 2010) 1.Nd6+ (1.Qxf4? Qxf4−+) 1...Kb8 (1...Kd8 2.Nf7+ Kc7 (2...Kc8? 3.Qxc6+ Kb8 4.Re8+ Rxe8 5.Rxe8#; 2... Kd7? 3.Re7+ Kc8 4.Qxc6+ Kb8 5.Qb7#) 3.Re7+ Kb8 (3...Kb6? 4.a5++−; 3...Kc8? 4.Qxc6+ Kb8 5.Qb7#) 4.Re8+ Rxe8 (4...Kb7? 5.R1e7++−; 4... Kc7? 5.R1e7++−) 5.Rxe8+ Kc7 (5...Kb7? 6.Nd6+ Kc7 7.Rc8+ Kxd6 8.Qxc6++−) 6.Rc8+!? (6.Ke1=; 6.Re7+=) 6...Kxc8 7.Qxc6+=; 1...Kc7 2.Re7+=; 1...Kd7 2.Re7+ Kxd6 3.Qxf4+=) 2.Re8+ Kc7 3.R8e7+ (3.R1e7+? Kxd6−+) 3...Kxd6 (3...Kb8 4.Re8+ Kc7 5.R8e7+=) 4.Qxf4+ Qxf4 5.R1e6+ Kd5 6.c4+ Qxc4 (6... Kd4 7.Rd7+ Qd6 8.Rdxd6#) 7.dxc4+ Kxc4=

955 1.Qd7 Qxe1+ (1...Rc7 2.Qe6++−) 2.Kh2 Bh8 (2... Rxe8 3.Qxe8+ Bf8 (3...Kh7

4.Bxg6#) 4.Qxg6+ Bg7 (4... Kh8 5.Qh7#) 5.Qe6+ Kh8 (5... Kf8 6.Bg6+−) 6.Qe8+ Bf8 7.Qxf8#; 2...Bf8 3.Bxg6+−; 2...Bf8 3.Nf6+ Kh8 4.Qh7#; 2...Rc7 3.Qxc7+−) 3.Bxg6 (3.Qe6+?! Kf8=) 3...Qxf2 4.Qh7+ Kf8 5.Qxh8+ Ke7 6.Qxe5+ Kd7 (6...Kd8 7.Qd6#; 6...Kf8 7.Qg7#) 7.Qd6#

956 1.Qd4+! (1.Qe8+?! Kh7=; 1.Qd8+?! Kh7=; 1.Qc8+?! Kh7 2.Qb7+!=; 1.Rf3?!=) 1... Kh7 (1...Kg8 2.Ra1+−; 1... Nf6 2.Qxf6++−; 1...Ne5 2.Qxe5++−) 2.Ra1!+ (2.Rf2?! Nxf2=; 2.Rb1?! Qh2+ 3.Kf1 Qh1+ 4.Qg1 Qf3+ 5.Ke1 Qxd3=; 2.Qa7+?! Kh6=) 2... Qh2+ 3.Kf1 Qh1+ (3...Qh3+ 4.Ke2 Qg2+ 5.Kd1+−; 3...Qxh4 4.Ra7+ Kh6 (4...Kg8 5.Qg7#) 5.Qh8#) 4.Ke2 (4.Qg1?! Qf3+=) 4...Qg2+ 5.Kd1 Qf1+ 6.Kd2 Qg2+ 7.Kc3 Qc6+ 8.Qc4+−

957 1.Qxa7+ (1.Rb2? Bxc4−+) 1...Kxa7 2.Ra2+ Kb8 3.Ra8+ Kxa8 4.Nb6+ Kb8 (4...Ka7 5.Ra1+ Ba2 (5...Ka4 6.Rxa4+ Kb8 7.Ra8#; 5...Kb8 6.Ra8#) 6.Rxa2+ Qa4 (6...Kb8 7.Ra8#) 7.Rxa4+ Kb8 8.Ra8#; 4...cxb6 5.Ra1+ Ba2 (5...Qa4 6.Rxa4#) 6.Rxa2+ Qa4 7.Rxa4#) 5.Nd7+ Ka7 (5...Ka8 6.Ra1+ Ba2 (6... Qa4 7.Rxa4#) 7.Rxa2+ Qa4 8.Rxa4#) 6.Ra1+ Ba2 (6...Qa4 7.Rxa4#) 7.Rxa2+ Qa4 8.Rxa4#

958 (Based on the game Thandalos

– Petch, 2007) 1.♖d8+ (1.♕f1?
♖xf1+−+) 1...♔f7 (1...♖f8
2.♖xf8+=) 2.e6+ (2.♖d7+?
♔e8−+; 2.♕f1? ♖xf1+−+)
2...♔e7 (2...♔f6? 3.♖f8+
♔g5 4.♖xf2+−; 2...♔xe6?
3.♕xc6++−) 3.♖e8+ ♔xe8 (3...
♔f6? 4.♖f8+ ♔g5 5.♖xf2+−;
3...♔d6? 4.♕c5++−) 4.♕xc6+
♔f8 (4...♔d8? 5.♕d7#; 4...
♔e7 5.♕d7+ ♔f6 (5...♔f8
6.♕d8#) 6.♕f7+ (6.♕d8+?
♔xe6 7.♕e8+ ♔f5 8.♕f7+ ♔g5
9.♕xf2 ♕xf2+ 10.♔xf2 ♔h4−+)
6...♔g5 7.♕xf2 ♕xf2+ 8.♔xf2
♔f6=) 5.♕c8+ ♔e7 6.♕d7+
♔f6 (6...♔f8? 7.♕d8#) 7.♕f7+
(7.♕d8+? ♔xe6 8.♕e8+ ♔f5
9.♕f7+ ♔g5 10.♕xf2 ♕xf2+
11.♔xf2 ♔h4−+) 7...♔g5
8.♕xf2 ♕xf2+ 9.♔xf2 ♔f6=

959 (Based on the game Walbordt
– Mieses, 1894) 1.♘f5+
(1.bxc3? ♕a1#) 1...♔g8 (1...
♔h8 2.g7+ ♔g8 3.♘h6#)
2.♕h6!+− (2.♘e7+ ♔g7 3.♘f5+
♔g8; 2.♘h6+ ♔g7 3.♘f5+
♔g8; 2.gxh7+? ♔h8−+) 2...
♕a7 3.gxh7+ (3.bxc3+−;
3.♔d2+−) 3...♔h8 4.♖g8+ ♖xg8
5.hxg8=♕+ ♔xg8 6.♕g6++−
♔h8 (6...♔f8 7.♕xf6+ ♔e8
(7...♔g8 8.♕xd8++−) 8.♕h8+
♔d7 9.♕g7+ ♔c6 10.♕xa7+−)
7.♕xf6+ ♔h7 (7...♔g8
8.♕xd8++−) 8.♕h4+ ♔g6 (8...
♔g8 9.♕xd8++−) 9.♕h6+ ♔f7
10.♕g7+ ♔e8 11.♕xa7+−

960 1.♕h1 ♕xg5!? (1...♖f6 2.♕h7+
♔f8 3.♕h8+ ♔e7 4.♕xg7+ ♔e8

5.♖h1+−) 2.fxg5 ♗xg3 (2...f4+
3.♔f2+−) 3.♘c4! (3.♘xe4?!
fxe4=; 3.♖f1? f4+ 4.♖xf4
♗xf4+−+; 3.g6? f4#) 3...f4+ (3...
dxc4 4.g6+−; 3...♖xc4 4.g6+−)
4.♔d2+−

961 (Based on a position by
Wotawa) 1.♗d5 (1.♘d4?
♕xg2−+) 1...exd5 (1...♕xg2
2.♖a8#) 2.♘d4 exd4 (2...♕xg2
3.♘c6+ ♔a6 4.♖a8#; 2...♔a6
3.♖a8#) 3.♗d6 exd6 (3...♕xg2
4.♗c5+ ♔a6 5.♖a8#) 4.♖e1
fxe1=♕ (4...♕xg2 5.♖a1#)
5.♖a2#

962 1.♘h4 (1.♘f4?! ♗c2=) 1...♗c2
(1...♗f7 2.♖xf7+−; 1...a1=♕
2.♘g6#) 2.♖a5 (2.♘g6+?!
♗xg6 3.♖xa4=) 2...♗d1 (2...
♗g6 3.♘xg6+ ♔h7 4.♘f4+−;
2...a1=♕ 3.♖h5+ ♗h7 4.♘g6#)
3.♖a6 (3.♖a7?! ♗h5=) 3...♔h7
(3...♗c2 4.♖h6+ ♗h7 5.♘g6#)
4.♘f5 a1=♕ 5.♖h6#

963 1.♕a8+ ♘xa8 2.♖a3 ♘ac7
(2...a1=♕+ 3.♖xa1+−; 2...♘b6
3.♗a6#; 2...♘xc5 3.bxc5+−; 2...
♘ec7 3.♖xa8+ ♔b7 (3...♘xa8
4.♗a6#) 4.♗f3+ ♘d5 5.♗xd5#;
2...♔b7 3.♗f3+ ♘c8 4.♖xa8#)
3.♖a8+ ♔b7 (3...♘xa8 4.♗a6#)
4.♗f3+ ♘d5 5.♗xd5#

964 1.♖h1 ♕d5 (1...♖fe8 2.♖h8+
♔xh8 3.♕h5+ ♔g8 4.♕h7#;
1...♕xb4 2.♖h8+ ♔xh8
3.♕h5+ ♔g8 4.♕h7#) 2.♕g1!
(2.♕e1? ♕g2+−+; 2.♕f1? ♖b5!
3.♖h8+ (3.♕h3 ♕xb3+ 4.♔a1
♕xh3−+) 3...♔xh8 4.♕h3+
♕h5−+; 2.♖h8+? ♔xh8 3.♕h1+

(3.Qh5+ Qxh5–+) 3...Qxh1–+)
2...Rb5 (2...Qxb3+ 3.Ka1+–;
2...Qd2+ 3.Bxd2+–) 3.Qh2
(3.f5+–) 3...Qh5 4.Qxh5 Rxh5
5.Rxh5+–

965 (Based on the game Helmers
– Harestad, 1976) 1.Qh3
(1.Qh4?! Bf6!=) 1...Bxd4 (1...
Be5 2.Bf5+ Kg7 3.Qh7+ Kf6
4.Qh4+ Kg7 5.Qg5+ Kh8
6.Qh6+ Kg8 7.Qh7#; 1...Re6
2.Bg6+ Kg8 (2...Rh6 3.Qxh6+
Kg8 4.Qh7#) 3.Qh7#; 1...Bf6
2.Bf5+ Bh4+ (2...Kg7 3.Qh7#;
2...Kg8 3.Qh7#) 3.Qxh4+ Kg7
4.Qg5+ Kh8 5.Qh6+ Kg8
6.Qh7#) 2.g5! (2.Bf5+?! Kg7
3.Qh7+ Kf6 4.Qh4+ Be5=) 2...
Kg7 3.Qh6+ Kh8 4.Bf5+ Kg8
5.Qh7#

966 (Based on the game Geller –
Kozlov, 2006) 1.Qd8+ (1.Nf6+?
Bxf6 2.Qxf6 Rxg3 3.Qf8+
Kh7 4.Bxg3 Qxg2+! 5.Kxg2
Bb7+–; 1.Qxh6?! Bb7=;
1.Rxg7+?! Bxg7 2.Qd8+ Kh7
3.Qe7 Bb7 4.Be5 Rg8 5.Qf7
Qxe4!=; 1.d4?! Bxd4 2.Qd8+
Kh7 3.Nf6+ Bxf6 4.Qxf6 Rxg3
5.Bxg3 Qe4=) 1...Kh7 (1...Kf7
2.Qf8#) 2.Nf6+ (2.Rxg7+?!
Bxg7 3.Qe7 Bb7 4.Be5 Rg8
5.Qf7 Qxe4!=; 2.d4?! Bxd4
3.Nf6+ Bxf6 4.Qxf6 Rxg3
5.Bxg3 Qe4=; 2.Ng5+?! hxg5
(2...Rxg5=) 3.Qe8 (3.Rh3+
Kg6 4.Qe8+ Rf7 5.Qg8+ Rg7
6.Qe8+ Rf7) 3...g4 4.Qh5+ Kg8
5.Qe8+ Kh7=) 2...Bxf6 3.Qxf6
Rxg3 (3...Qxg2+ 4.Rxg2+–;

3...Rg5 4.Qf7+ Kh8 (4...Rg7
5.Qg7#) 5.Be5+ Rxe5 (5...
Rg7 6.Qxg7#) 6.Qg7#; 3...Rg4
4.Qf7+ Kh8 (4...Rg7 5.Qxg7#)
5.Be5+ Rg7 6.Qxg7#) 4.Bxg3
(4.fxg3? Qxd6–+) 4...d6 (4...
Qxg2+ 5.Kxg2+–; 4...Qd5
5.Qf7+ Kh8 6.Bh4+–; 4...Kg8
5.Be5+–; 4...Bb7 5.Qf7+ Kh8
6.Be5#) 5.Qf7+ Kh8 6.Bh4+–

967 (Based on a position by
Wotawa) 1.Nd2! (1.Nxa3?!
Nb6! (1...Rc7? 2.Nc4+! Rxc4
3.Bg7#) 2.Rxa7 (2.bxb6
Rg8+–+) 2...Rg8+ 3.Bg7+
Rxg7+ 4.Rxg7 d3=; 1.Nxc3?
Bc1+!) 1...cxd2 (1...d3 2.Ra4
Rf7 (2...Bb4 3.axb4+–) 3.f4+
Rxf4 4.Bg7+ Rf6 5.Bxf6#; 1...
Rxa6 2.Bg7#; 1...h1=Q 2.f4#)
2.Re3! dxe3 (2...d3 3.Ra4+–;
2...Rf7 3.f4+ Rxf4 4.Bg7+ Rf6
5.Bxf6#) 3.Ra4 Rf7 (3...Bb4
4.Rxb4 Rf7 5.f4+ Rxf4 6.Bg7+
Rf6 7.Bxf6#) 4.f4+! Rxf4
5.Bg7+ Rf6 6.Bxf6#

968 1.Bxh7+! (1.f4?! Kh8 2.Bxh7
Rg8 3.Rf3 Rg4 4.Rh3 Be8∓) 1...
Kh8 (1...Kf7 2.Qg6#) 2.Bg7+!
(2.f4?! Rg8 3.Rf3 Rg4 4.Rh3
Be8∓) 2...Kxg7 3.Qg6+ Kh8
4.Bg8! (4.Qh6? Bg5–+) 4...
Nf6 (4...Bg5 5.Qh7#; 4...Rxg8
5.Qh6#) 5.exf6 Bxf6 (5...Rxg8
6.Qh6#) 6.Qh7#

969 1.Qxg5+ Kxg5 2.Be7+ Kf4
(2...Kg6 3.Bg5#) 3.Bd6+ Ke4
4.Re5+ Kd4 (4...Kf4 5.Nd3#)
5.c3+ Kxc3 6.Be4+–

970 (Based on the game Milenkovic

– Ujhazi, 1992) 1.♖d8+ ♖f8
(1...♗f8 2.♗d4+ e5 (2...♖g7
3.♖xf8#; 2...♖f6 3.♗xf6#)
3.♕xe5+ ♖f6 (3...♖g7 4.♖xf8#)
4.♕xf6#) 2.♖xf8+ ♗xf8 3.♗d4+
♗g7 (3...e5 4.♕xe5+ ♗g7
5.♕xg7#) 4.♕e5 (4.♗xg7+?!
♔xg7 5.♕e5+ ♔f7=) 4...♖xe7
(4...♗xe5 5.♗xe5#; 4...♕xb2+
5.♗xb2+−) 5.♕b8+ ♖e8
6.♕xe8#

971 (Based on a position by F.
Aitov) 1.♘d5 (1.♘e4? ♕f8+
2.♔xf8 ♔g6−+; 1.♘xe2?! ♕f7+
2.♔xf7=) 1...♕f8+ (1...e1=♕
2.♘df6+ ♕xf6 3.♘xf6#)
2.♔xf8 e1=♕ (2...♔g6 3.♘e7+
♔h7 (3...♔h5 4.♘f6#) 4.♘f6+
♔h8 5.♘g6#) 3.♔f7! (3.♔g7?!
♕e7+ 4.♘xe7=) 3...♕xg3 (3...
♕xe8+ 4.♔xe8+−) 4.♘g7+
♔h4 5.♘f5+ ♔h3 6.hxg3+−

972 1.♖xd3 ♖xd3 (1...♕h1+
2.♔e2+−) 2.♕xd3 ♕h1+
3.♔e2 ♕xc1 4.♕d8+ (4.♗d5?
♗g4+−+) 4...♗g8 5.♗d5 ♕c2+
(5...♕xc4+ 6.♗xc4+−) 6.♗d2
(6.♔f3? ♕d1+ 7.♔g3 ♕g4#) 6...
♕xc4+ 7.♗xc4 ♖xc4+−

973 1.♖xg7+ ♔xg7 2.♖g1+ ♔h6
(2...♔h8 3.♕h3+ ♘h7 (3...♔h5
4.♕xh5#) 4.♕xh7#; 2...♘g4
3.♖xg4+ ♔h8 (3...♔h6 4.♕h3#)
4.♕h3#) 3.♗e2 (3.♕h3+? ♘h5
4.♗e2 ♘df4−+) 3...♕a3 (3...
♘h5 4.♕xh5#; 3...♘f4 4.♕xf4+
♔h7 5.♕h4+ ♘h5 6.♕xh5#; 3...
♕b3 4.cxb3+−) 4.♕xa3 (4.c3?
♖xc3−+) 4...♖g8 (4...♘h5
5.♕xf8+ ♔h7 6.♕g8+ ♔h6

7.♕h8#; 4...♘f4 5.♕xf8+ ♔h7
6.♕g7#) 5.♕h3+ ♘h5 6.♕xh5#

974 1.♕f5+ g6 (1...♔g8 2.♕e8#; 1...
♔h8 2.♕e8#) 2.♕e7+ ♗g7 (2...
♔g8 3.♕f7+ ♔h8 4.♕h7#; 2...
♔h8 3.♕f8#) 3.♕f6 (3.♕f7?
♕a1+−+; 3.♕e5? ♕b1+ 4.♔h2
♕a1 5.♖xg7+ ♔h8−+) 3...♖b1+
(3...♕a1 4.♕xa1+−) 4.♔h2
♖h1+!? (4...♕c7+ 5.♖xc7+−;
4...♕c3 5.♖xg7+ ♔h8 6.♕f8#;
4...♕a1 5.♖xg7+ ♔h8 6.♕f8#)
5.♔xh1 ♕e1+ 6.♔h2! (6.♖xe1?
♗xf6∓) 6...♕xe7 (6...♕e5+
7.♕xe5+−) 7.♕xe7+−

975 (Based on the game Geller –
Popov, 2004) 1.♕xe6 ♖xd4 (1...
♖d5 2.♕f7+ ♔d7 3.♕xd5++−;
1...♕b6 2.♕g8+ ♗f8 3.♕xf8#)
2.♘d6+ ♖xd6 (2...♘xd6
3.♖f8+ ♔xf8 4.♕g8#; 2...♕xd6
3.exd6+−) 3.exd6 ♕b6+ (3...
♘xd6 4.♖f8+ ♔xf8 5.♕g8#; 3...
♕xd6 4.♕xc8++−) 4.♔g2 ♕c6+
(4...♕xd6 5.♕xc8++−; 4...♘e3+
5.♔h3+−) 5.♔h3 (5.♗f3+−)
5...♘xd6 (5...♕d7 6.♖f8+ ♔xf8
7.♕xd7+−) 6.♖f8+ (6.♗d5+−)
6...♔xf8 7.♕g8#

976 1.♖g3+ ♔f4 (1...♔h4 2.♖g7
(2.♘xh5+−) 2...♗g1 (2...
♗xc4 3.♖h1#) 3.♖dxg1+−
♗xc4 4.♖h1#) 2.♘xh5+ ♔xe4
3.♖f1! (3.d3+?! ♔f5 4.♘g7+
♔f4 5.♘h5+ ♔f5=; 3.♖e1+?!
♔f5 4.♖f3+ (4.♘g7+ ♔f4
5.♘h5+ ♔f5=) 4...♔g4 5.♖g3+
♔f5=) 3...♗f2! (3...♗xc4 4.d3+
(4.♖g4+?! ♔d5 5.♘f4+ ♔e4=)
4...♗xd3 (4...♔d5 5.♘f4#)

5.cxd3+ ♔d5 6.♘f4#; 3...♗d4
4.d3+ ♔e5 5.♖e3#; 3...♘ce5
4.♖f4#) 4.♗e3+! (4.♖xf2? ♗xc4
5.d3+ ♔d5 6.♘f4+ ♔c5–+;
4.♖e1+?! ♗xe1 5.d3+ ♔f5
6.♘g7+ ♔f4 7.♘h5+ ♔f5=;
4.d3+ ♔f5 5.♘g7+ (5.♖xf2+?
♔e6–+) 5...♔f4 6.♘h5+ ♔f5=)
4...♔f5 (4...♗xe3 5.♘g3#)
5.♖xf2+ ♔g6 (5...♔g5 6.♖g3+
♔h5 (6...♔h4 7.♖h2#) 7.♖h2#;
5...♔g4 6.♖g3+ ♔h5 (6...♔h4
7.♖h2#) 7.♖h2#) 6.♖g3+ ♔h5
(6...♔h7 7.♖g7#) 7.♖h2#

977 1.♗b2 ♕xb2 (1...♗f6+
2.♗xe5+–) 2.♖e1 ♕g7 (2...
♕e2+ 3.♖xe2+–; 2...♗e7
3.♖exe7+–; 2...♕e5 3.♖xe5+–)
3.♖xg7 (3.♖e8+?! ♔xh7
4.♖xg7+ ♔xg7 5.♔g4=) 3...
♔xg7 4.h8=♕+ (4.h8=♖ ♔xh8
5.♔g6; 4.h8=♗+ ♔xh8 5.♔g6)
4...♔xh8 (4...♔f7 5.♕e8++–)
5.♔g6 ♗h6 (5...♗e7 6.♖xe7+–;
5...♔g8 6.♖e8#) 6.♖e8+ ♗f8
7.♖xf8#

978 (Based on the game Fridshtein
– Antoshin, 1953) 1.♖xf8+
(1.♖f1? ♘xe3–+; 1.♖d2?
♘xe3–+; 1.♕d2? ♘xe3–+;
1.♖c2? ♘xe3–+; 1.♕c2?
♘xe3–+) 1...♔xf8 (1...♔g7?
2.♖f1+–) 2.♗xe7+ (2.♕d2?
♘xe3–+; 2.♖f1? ♘xe3–+;
2.♖d2? ♘xe3–+; 2.♕c2?
♘xe3–+; 2.♕c8+? ♔g7–+) 2...
♔xe7 (2...♔g7? 3.♕d2+–; 2...
♔e8 3.♕c8+ ♔xe7 4.♕c7+=;
2...♔g8? 3.♕c8+ ♔g7 4.♕f8#)
3.♕c7+ ♔e6 (3...♔f6? 4.♕d6+

♔f5 (4...♔g5 5.♕f4++–) 5.e4+
♔g5 6.♕f4+ ♕xf4 7.gxf4+ ♔xf4
8.♖xd4; 3...♔e8 4.♕c8+ ♔e7
5.♕c7+=) 4.♕c8+ (4.♕c4+
♔e7 5.♕c7+=) 4...♔f6 (4...
♔e7 5.♕c7+=) 5.♕d8+ ♔e6
(5...♔g7? 6.♕xd4++–; 5...
♔f5? 6.e4+ ♔xe4 7.♕xd4+–;
5...♔e5? 6.♕xd4++–) 6.♕e8+
(6.♕c8+=) 6...♔f6 7.♕d8+=

979 1.♖xh4! (1.♕f8+?! ♖xf8
2.♖xh4 ♕xh4 3.♖h1 ♕xh1+
4.♔xh1=) 1...♕xh4 2.♖g1!
(2.♕f8+?! ♖xf8 3.♖h1 ♕xh1+
4.♔xh1=; 2.♖e1?! ♕h2+ (2...
♕h3+ 3.♔f2 ♕h2+=) 3.♔f1
♕c2!?=) 2...♕h2+ (2...♕h3+
3.♔f2 ♕h2+ 4.♖g2 (4.♔f1
♕h3+ 5.♔f2 ♕h2+) 4...♕h4+
5.♔e2 ♕h1 6.♖f2+–) 3.♔f1
♕h3+ (3...♕c2 4.♕c3!? ♕d1+
5.♕e1+–) 4.♔f2 ♕h2+ 5.♖g2!
(5.♔f1 ♕h3+ 6.♔f2 ♕h2+) 5...
♕h4+ 6.♔e2 ♕h1 7.♖f2+–

980 1.♗xc6+ ♔c7 (1...dxc6 2.♖e7+
♔c8 (2...♔b8 3.♕d8#; 2...
♘d7 3.♕xd7+ ♔b8 4.♘xc6#)
3.♕a6+ ♔d8 (3...♔b8 4.♘xc6#)
4.♘xc6#) 2.♘a6+ ♔xc6
3.♕e4+ d5 (3...♔b5 4.♕a4#;
3...♔d6 4.♕e5+ ♔c6 5.♘b4+
(5.♕c7+ ♔b5 6.♕c4+ ♔a5
7.♕a4#) 5...♔b7 6.♕d5+ ♔c7
7.♘a6#) 4.♘b4+ (4.♖e6+?!
♘xe6 5.♕xe6+ ♔b7 6.♕d7+
♔xa6 7.♕a4+ ♔b7 8.♕d7+=)
4...♔b5 (4...♔c7 5.♕e5+ ♔b7
(5...♔d7 6.♕e7#) 6.♕e7+ ♘d7
7.♕xd7#; 4...♔b7 5.♕e7+ ♘d7
6.♕xd7#; 4...♔c5 5.♕xd5#; 4...

♔d6 5.♕e7#; 4...♔d7 5.♕e7#)
5.♕xd5+ ♕c5 6.♖e5! ♖xc3 (6...
♕xd5 7.♖xd5#; 6...♖h4 7.♕c6+
♔a5 8.♕a4#; 6...♔a5 7.♕c4+−;
6...♖c8 7.♕c4+ ♔a5 8.♕a6#; 6...
♖h1+ 7.♕xh1+− ♕xe5 8.♕c6+
♔a5 9.♕a4#) 7.♕c6+ ♔xb4 (7...
♔a5 8.♕a4#) 8.♕a4#

981 1.♕g4+! (1.f4? hxg3−+;
1.cxb7+? ♔xb7−+; 1.f3?
hxg3−+) 1...♔b8 (1...♕xg4
2.bxa7 bxc6 3.a8=♕+ ♔d7
4.♕xc6+ ♔e7 (4...♔c8
5.♖a1!?+−) 5.♔xg2!?+−)
2.bxa7! (2.♕xh3?! ♗xh3
3.bxa7+ ♔a8=; 2.bxc7+?! ♔xc7
(2...♖xc7=) 3.cxb7+ ♔xb7=) 2...
♔xa7 (2...♔a8? 3.cxb7+ ♔xb7
(3...♔xa7 4.♖a1++−) 4.a8=♕+
♔xa8 (4...♖xa8 5.♖b1++−)
5.♖a1+ ♔b7 6.♖fb1+ ♔c6
7.♖a6++−) 3.♖a1+ (3.♕xh3
♗xh3 4.♖a1+ ♔b6!? (4...
♔b8 5.♖fb1+−) 5.♖fc1!+−)
3...♔b8 (3...♔b6 4.♗e3++−)
4.♕xh3 ♗xh3 5.♖fb1! ♗c8 (5...
b6 6.♖a3!?+−) 6.♗e3 b6 7.♖a3
(7.♖b3+−) 7...hxg3 8.♖ba1+−

982 1.♗f6 ♗xf6 (1...♘xd3 2.♕g7#)
2.e5 ♗f5 (2...♘e4 3.♗xe4+−)
3.♗xf5 (3.exf6? ♗xd3+ 4.♔c1
♘e6−+) 3...♖fe8 (3...♖fd8
4.exf6+−) 4.♗xh7+ (4.exf6?
♖xe1+−+) 4...♔h8 5.♗e4+!
(5.♗g6+ ♔g8 6.♗h7+ ♔h8;
5.♗f5+ ♔g8 6.♗h7+ ♔h8;
5.♗d3+ ♔g8 6.♗h7+ ♔h8;
5.♗c2+ ♔g8 6.♗h7+ ♔h8)
5...♔g8 6.exf6 (6.♕h7+ ♔f8
7.exf6+−; 6.♗h7+ ♔h8) 6...♘e6

(6...♘xe4 7.♕g7#) 7.♕h7+ ♔f8
8.♕h8#

983 (Based on the game Blatny –
Kavalek, 1959) 1.♕f3! ♕h4+!
(1...♖h5+? 2.♕xh5 gxh5
3.♖g1+−; 1...♕xf3+? 2.♘xf3+−)
2.♔g2 (2.♔g1? ♕xd4+−+) 2...
♕g5+ (2...♖g5+? 3.♔f1+−; 2...
♖xd4? 3.♕f7+ ♔h8 4.♕f8#)
3.♔h3 (3.♔h2 ♕h6+ 4.♔g2=)
3...♕h6+ 4.♔g2 ♕d2+ (4...♖g5+
5.♔f1 ♖f5 6.♘xf5 ♕c1+=; 4...
♖xd4 5.♕f7+ ♔h8 6.♕e8+ ♔g7
7.♕f7+ ♔h8=; 4...♕g5+ 5.♔h3
♕h6+ 6.♔g2=) 5.♘e2 ♖g5+
(5...♖f5? 6.e7±) 6.♔h2 (6.♔h1
♖h5+=) 6...♖h5+ (6...♖f5?
7.e7±) 7.♔g1 (7.♔g2 ♖g5+=)
7...♖g5+ 8.♔h2=

984 (Based on a position by Rinck)
1.♗e5 ♔b1 (1...♖c1+ 2.♔d2+
♔b1 (2...♖c3 3.♗xc3+ ♔b1
4.♗xe4#) 3.♗xe4+ ♖c2+
4.♗xc2#; 1...♖b1 2.♔c2+ ♖b2+
3.♗xb2#; 1...h1=♕ 2.♔c2#)
2.♗xe4+ ♔c1 (2...♔a1 3.♔c2#)
3.♗f4+ ♔d1 4.♗f3+ ♔e1
5.♗g3+ ♔f1 6.♔d2 (6.♔d3 ♖h1
7.♗e2+ ♔g1 8.♔e3+−) 6...♖h1
(6...h1=♕ 7.♗e2#) 7.♗e2+ ♔g1
8.♔e3 a1=♕ 9.♗f2#

985 (Based on the game
Montgomery – Nedev, 1999)
1.♔xg4 ♕f2 2.♖d8+! (2.♖6d2?!
♕xe3=) 2...♗f8 (2...♖xd8
3.♖xd8+ ♗f8 (3...♔f7 4.♕xa7+
♔e6 5.♖e8++−; 3...♕f8
4.♖xf8++−) 4.♖xf8+ (4.♕xc6
♕g2+ 5.♔h4 ♕f2+ 6.♔h3
♕f1+) ; 2...♔f7 3.♖1d7+ ♔e6

(3...♔f6 4.♕xc6#) 4.♕xc6#)
3.♖xa8 (3.♕xc6?! ♕g2+ (3...
h5+=) 4.♔h4 ♔g7!? 5.♖1d7+
♔h6=; 3.♕h3?!=; 3.♖1d2?!=)
3...♕g2+ (3...h5+ 4.♔h3!
(4.♔g5?! ♕xe3+=) 4...♕f3+
5.♔h2 (5.♔h4? ♕g4#) 5...♕f2+
6.♔h1 ♕f3+ 7.♔g1 ♕g3+ 8.♔f1
♕f3+ 9.♔e1 ♕xe3+ 10.♘e2+−)
4.♔h4 ♔g7!? (4...♕h2+ 5.♔g5
♕g3+ 6.♔f6 ♕h4+ 7.♔xe5+−;
4...g5+ 5.♔h5 ♕h3+ 6.♔xg5
♕xe3+ 7.♔g4! ♕f4+ 8.♔h3
♕f3+ 9.♔h2 ♕f2+ 10.♔h1
♕f3+ 11.♔g1 ♕g3+ 12.♔f1
♕f3+ 13.♔e1 ♕e3+ 14.♘e2+−)
5.♖d7+ ♔h6 6.♖xh7+ ♔xh7
7.♖xf8 ♕h2+ (7...g5+ 8.♔h5
♕h3+ 9.♔xg5+−) 8.♔g5 ♕g3+
9.♔f6+−

986 (Based on the game Brooks
– Kumaran, 1990) 1.♕d8+
(1.♖e2?!=) 1...♔h7 2.♖h3+
(2.♕d3+? g6∓) 2...♔g6 3.♕d3+
(3.♖xe6+?! fxe6 4.♕e8+=)
3...♔f6 (3...f5 4.♖xe6+ ♔f7
5.♕xf5+ ♔g8 6.♖e8#; 3...♗e4
4.♕xe4+ ♔f6 (4...f5 5.♕xe6#)
5.♕xg2+−) 4.♖f3+ (4.♕c3+?!
♔f5 5.♕d3+ ♔g4!?=; 4.♕d8+?!
♔f5 5.♕d3+ ♔g4!?=) 4...
♔e7 (4...♗xf3 5.♕xf3+ ♔g6
6.♕xg2+−) 5.♖xf7+ ♔xf7 (5...
♔e8 6.♕d7#) 6.♕d7+ ♔f8 (6...
♔g8 7.♕xe6+ ♔h7 (7...♔f8
8.♕e8#; 7...♔h8 8.♕e8+ ♔h7
9.♕h5+ ♔g8 10.♖e8#) 8.♕h3+
♔g6 (8...♔g8 9.♖e8+ ♔f7
10.♕e6#) 9.♖e6+ ♔f7 10.♕f5+
♔g8 11.♖e8#; 6...♔f6 7.♕xe6#;

6...♔g6 7.♕xe6+ ♔h7 (7...
♔h5 8.♕h3+ ♔g6 9.♖e6+ ♔f7
10.♕f5+ ♔g8 11.♖e8#) 8.♕h3+
♔g8 (8...♔g6 9.♖e6+ ♔f7
10.♕f5+ ♔g8 11.♖e8#) 9.♖e8+
♔f7 10.♕e6+) 7.♕d6+ ♔g8
(7...♔e8 8.♕xe6+ ♔d8 (8...♔f8
9.♕e8#) 9.♕d6+ ♔c8 10.♖e8#;
7...♔f7 8.♕xe6+ ♔f8 9.♕e8#)
8.♕xe6+ ♔h7 (8...♔h8 9.♕e8+
♔h7 10.♕h5+ ♔g8 11.♖e8#; 8...
♔f8 9.♕e8#) 9.♕h3+ ♔g6 (9...
♔g8 10.♖e8+ ♔f7 11.♕e6#)
10.♖e6+ ♔f7 11.♕f5+ ♔g8
12.♖e8#

987 (Based on the game Costa –
Froewis, 2018) 1.g3 ♘xe3!?
(1...♖xg3+ 2.fxg3 ♕xg3+
3.♔h1=; 1...h4 2.♕d8 (2.♕a8=;
2.♖h8+=) 2...♖xg3+ 3.fxg3
♕xg3+ 4.♔h1=) 2.♖h8+!
(2.fxe3? ♕xg3+ 3.♔f1 (3.♔h1
♕h3#) 3...♕g1+ 4.♔e2 ♖g2#)
2...♔xh8 3.♕a8+ (3.♕d8+?
♔h7−+) 3...♔h7 4.♕xe4
h4!? (4...♘c4? 5.♘c3+−; 4...
♘g4 5.♕g2 ♘xf2!?=) 5.fxe3
(5.♕xe3? hxg3−+) 5...♕xg3+
(5...hxg3? 6.♕h1+−) 6.♔f1
(6.♔h1? ♕h3#; 6.♕g2? ♕xg2#)
6...♕g1+ (6...h3? 7.♕e2+−)
7.♔e2 ♕xc1 8.♕xh4+ (8.♘d2?
♕c6∓) 8...♖h6 (8...♔g8 9.♕d8+
♔f7 10.♕d7+=) 9.♕e4+ g6 (9...
♔h8 10.♕e8+ ♔h7 11.♕e4+=;
9...♖g6 10.♕h4+=; 9...♔g8
10.♕e8+ ♔h7 11.♕e4+=)
10.♕e7+ ♔g8 11.♕e8+ ♔g7
12.♕e7+=

988 (Based on a position by

Wotawa) 1.b3 (1.♔b6? ♖xb2
2.♖xb2 ♖b1–+) 1...cxb3 (1...
e4 2.♖e7+–; 1...a1=♕ 2.bxc4#)
2.♖f7! (2.♖c4? ♖h7!–+;
2.♖e7? ♖c2!–+) 2...♖d1 (2...
♖e2 3.♖d4+ exd4 4.♖xf5+ ♗e5
5.c4#; 2...♖f2 3.♖c4! a1=♕ (3...
♖h6 4.♖xd7+– a1=♕ 5.♖c5#;
3...e4 4.♖e7+–; 3...♖h7 4.♖xh7
e4 5.♖e7+–) 4.♖c5+ dxc5
5.♖xd7#; 2...a1=♕ 3.♖d4+ exd4
4.♖xf5#; 2...♖d2 3.♖c4+–)
3.♖c4! ♖h6 (3...a1=♕ 4.♖c5+
dxc5 5.♖xd7#) 4.♖xd7+– a1=♕
5.♖c5#

989 1.♕e7 (1.g3? ♕h3 2.f4 ♗xg3+
3.♔g1 ♗xe1–+) 1...f6 (1...g5
2.♕d8+ ♔g7 3.♖e1+–; 1...♕h5
2.♕d8+ ♔h7 3.♖e1+–; 1...♕h6
2.♕d8+ ♔h7 3.♖e1+–) 2.♕d8+
(2.♖e1? ♗xd6+ 3.♔g1 ♗xe7–+;
2.g3 ♗xg3+ 3.♔g2 ♕h2+ 4.♔f3
♕h5+ 5.♔g2 ♕h2+=) 2...♔h7
3.♖e1! (3.♖d1?! ♗xd6+ (3...
♕h5=; 3...♗e6=) 4.♔g1 ♕h2+
5.♔f1 ♗e6=; 3.♖fb1?! ♗xd6+
4.♔g1 ♕h2+ 5.♔f1 ♕h1+
6.♔e2 ♕h5+ 7.f3 ♕h2=; 3.g3?!
♗xg3+ 4.♔g2 ♕h2+ 5.♔f3
♕h5+!? 6.♔g2 ♕h2+=) 3...
♗xd6+ 4.♔g1 ♕h2+ 5.♔f1+–

990 1.♕xh6+ ♔xh6 (1...♔g8
2.♖h3+– ♗e8 (2...♗h5
3.♕xh5+–) 3.♕h8+ ♔f7
4.♗h5+ ♔e7 5.♕xg7++–)
2.♖h3+ ♔g5 (2...♗h5 3.♖xh5#)
3.♔h2! (3.♖g3+ ♔h6 4.♖h3+
♔g5; 3.f4+?! ♔xf4 4.♖f3+
(4.♖h4+ ♔g3 5.♖h3+ ♔f4=)
4...♔g5 5.♖g3+ ♔h6 6.♖h3+

♔g5=; 3.♘f3+? ♔f4 4.♘h2
(4.♖h4+ ♖g4–+; 4.♘e1 ♖g4–+)
4...♖g4!–+) 3...♕b1 (3...♖h8
4.♖xh8+–; 3...♖h7 4.♖xh7+–;
3...♗h5 4.♖xh5+ ♔f4 5.♘h3#)
4.f4+ (4.♖g3+ ♔h6 5.♖h3+
♔g5) 4...♗xf4 (4...exf4 5.♘f3+
♔g4 6.♖h4#) 5.♖h4+ ♔g5 (5...
♖g4 6.♖xg4#) 6.♘f3#

991 (Based on a position by
Troitzky) 1.♔c7 ♗e6 (1...
♖xh7 2.♖a2#) 2.♔b8 (2.♖d3?
♖xh7+–+; 2.♖d1? ♖xh7+–+)
2...♗d5 (2...♖d5 3.♖xd5 ♗xd5
4.h8=♕+–; 2...♖xh7 3.♖d6#)
3.♖xd5 ♖xd5 (3...♖xh7 4.♖d6#;
3...♖h6 4.♖d8!? ♖xh7 5.♖d6#)
4.h8=♖ (4.h8=♕? ♖d8+
5.♕xd8=) 4...♖d6 (4...♔b6
5.♖h6+ ♖d6 6.♖xd6#; 4...♖d8+
5.♖xd8+–) 5.♔c7 ♖g6 (5...♔a7
6.♔xd6+–) 6.♖a8#

992 (Based on a position by
Kubbel) 1.♗c4! ♘f5+ (1...
♕e1 2.♕a2+ ♔b4 3.♕a3#; 1...
♕xb2+ 2.♕xb2+–) 2.♔g6!
(2.♔g8?! ♕b8+=; 2.♔h8?!
♕b8+=; 2.♔f7?! ♕b7+=;
2.♔f8? d5+–+; 2.♔h7?! ♕b7+=;
2.♔f6?! ♗d8+=) 2...♘h4+
(2...♘e7+ 3.♔f7+–; 2...♕xb2
3.♕xb2+–; 2...♕e1 3.♕a2+
♔b4 4.♕a3#) 3.♔h6! (3.♔g7?!
♕b7+=; 3.♔f7?! ♕b7+=;
3.♔h7?! ♕b7+=; 3.♔f6?!
♗d8+=; 3.♔g5? ♗d8+–+;
3.♔h5?! ♕c5+=) 3...♕d2+
(3...♘f5+ 4.♔h5 ♘g3+ (4...
♘g7+ 5.♔g4+–) 5.♔g4+–) 5.♔g4+–)
4.♔h7! (4.♔g7?!=; 4.♔h5?!

We2+=) 4...♛b4 (4...♛xb2
5.♕xb2+−; 4...♛e1 5.♕a2+
♚b4 6.♕a3#) 5.♕a2! ♚c5 (5...
♛xd3+ 6.♗xd3+−) 6.b4+!
♗xb4 (6...♛xb4 7.♕f2#; 6...
♚xb4 7.♕xd2++−; 6...♚b6
7.♕xd2+−) 7.♕a7#

993 1.♕h4+ (1.♖xa2? ♘xf5−+)
1...♚g7 (1...gxh4 2.♖xh4#)
2.♕xg5+ ♚f8 (2...♚h8 3.♕h6#;
2...♚h7 3.♕h5#) 3.♕xg8+
(3.♕h6+? ♚e7−+) 3...♚e7 4.f6+
(4.♖e2+? ♚f6 5.♖xe8 ♛c1+
6.♚e2 ♘c3+ 7.♚f2 ♛xd2+
8.♚g1 ♘xe8−+; 4.♕g5+? f6−+)
4...♚d8 (4...♚xf6 5.♕g5+ ♚e6
6.♖e2++−; 4...♚e6 5.♕g4++−;
4...♛xf6 5.♖e2+ ♚d8 6.♖xe8+
♘xe8 7.♖xa2+−) 5.♖xa2 ♖xg8
6.♖xg8+ ♘e8 7.♖xa7+− (7.d4?!
d5=)

994 (Based on a position by P.
Benko) 1.♖h8+! (1.♖xc5?!
♘xe1=) 1...♚xh8 (1...♖xh8
2.♕g3+ ♚f8 (2...♚h7 3.♕g7#;
2...♛g5+ 3.♕xg5++−) 3.♕b8+
♛c8 4.♕xc8#) 2.♕a1! ♛f8+
(2...♚h7 3.♕b1+ ♚h8 (3...
♚g8 4.♕g6+ ♚f8 5.♕f7#)
4.♕b8+ ♚h7 5.♕b7+ ♚h8
6.♕g7#) 3.♚g6+ ♚g8 (3...♛f6+
4.♕xf6++−; 3...♕g7+ 4.♕xg7#)
4.♕a2+ ♚h8 (4...♛f7+ 5.♕xf7+
♚h8 6.♕h7+) 5.♕b2+ ♚g8
6.♕b3+ ♚h8 7.♕c3+ ♚g8
8.♕c4+ ♚h8 9.♕d4+ ♚g8
10.♕d5+ ♚h8 11.♕e5+ ♚g8
12.♕e6+ ♚h8 13.♕xh3+ ♘h4+
(13...♚g8 14.♕h7#; 13...♛h6+
14.♕xh6+ ♚g8 15.♕g7#)

14.♕xh4+ ♛h6+ (14...♚g8
15.♕h7#) 15.♕xh6+ ♚g8
16.♕g7#

995 1.♘e5 (1.♗f5?! ♕xf5 2.♚g2=;
1.♕g3?! ♕xg3 2.hxg3 ♗xf1
3.♚xf1∓) 1...♛g5 (1...♗f3+
2.♘xg4+−) 2.h4! (2.♘f7 ♛g4
3.♘e5 ♛g5; 2.♕f7+?! ♚h8
3.♕e8+ ♖xe8 4.♘f7+ ♚g8
5.♘xg5 ♗xf1 6.♗b3+ ♚f8
7.♘xh7+ ♚e7 8.♚xf1∓; 2.♘d3?!
♗xf1+ 3.♚xf1 ♛d2∓) 2...♛g3
(2...♛xh4 3.♕f7+!? (3.♚xg2?!
♛g5+ 4.♚f3 ♛h5+ 5.♚e4
♛e2+ 6.♚d5±) 3...♚h8 4.♕xg2
♛g5+ 5.♚f3 ♖xe5 6.♖h1+−)
3.♕xa7 (3.♕f7+? ♚h8 4.♕xa7
♛h4−+) 3...♛xe5 (3...♛xh4
4.♕f7+!? (4.♗b3++−) 4...♚h8
5.♚xg2+−) 4.♗b3+ (4.♚xg2?
♖xa7−+) 4...♚h8 5.♖d1!
(5.♚xg2? ♖xa7−+) 5...♗f3 (5...
g6 6.♕d4+−) 6.♕xa8+ ♗xa8
7.♖d8+ ♛e8 8.♖xe8#

996 1.♕xf7+ (1.♖g8+? ♘xg8−+)
1...♚xf7 (1...♚h6 2.♖xh7#)
2.♖xh7+ ♛xh7 (2...♚g6
3.♖xh3+−) 3.♘g5+ ♚g7 (3...
♚e8 4.♘xh7 ♖h6 5.♘f6+!
♗xf6 (5...♖xf6 6.♖xb4+−)
6.♖xb4 ♗e5 7.♖xg4 ♗xh2+
8.♚f1+−; 3...♚g6 4.♘xh7 ♚xh7
5.♖xb4+−; 3...♚g8 4.♘xh7
♚xh7 (4...♖h6 5.♘f6++−)
5.♖xb4+−; 3...♚f8 4.♘xh7++−;
3...♚f6 4.♘xh7++−) 4.♘xh7
♖h6!? (4...♚xh7 5.♖xb4+−)
5.h3! ♖xh3 (5...♚xh7 6.♖xb4+−;
5...♖xh7 6.♖xb4+−) 6.♘g5
(6.♖xb4?! ♗h2+ 7.♚f1 ♗f4=)

6...Bh2+ (6...Rh5 7.Ne6+!? Kf6 8.Nf4+−) 7.Kf1+− (7.Kh1?! Rh5=) 7...Rh5 8.Nxf3!? (8.Bxb4+−) 8...gxf3 9.Bxb4 Be5 10.Ke1+−

997 (Based on a position by Troitzky) 1.Ra3+ Na4+ 2.Rxa4+ Kxa4 3.Bd1+ Ka5 4.b4+ Ka6 5.Kc6+− Re7 (5...f3 6.Bxf3 Re7 7.Bd5 Rc7+ 8.Kxc7+−; 5...Rg7 6.Be2#; 5...Rc7+ 6.Kxc7 Kb5 7.Kd6 Kxb4 8.Ke5 Kc5 9.h5!?+−) 6.Bg4 Re8 (6...Rc7+ 7.Kxc7 Kb5 8.Bd6+−) 7.Bh3 f3 8.Bf1 (8.h5+−) 8...Re2 9.h5 f2 10.Bxe2#

998 (G. Afanasjev, 1959) 1.Kg3 f4+ (1...a1=Q 2.Nf2#) 2.Kg4 f5+ (2...a1=Q 3.Nf2#) 3.Kg5 Bf6+ (3...h6+ 4.Kg6+−; 3...Bh6+ 4.Kxh6+−) 4.Kxf6 Rf7+ (4...a1=Q 5.Nf2#) 5.Kxe6 Rfe7+ (5...Rbe7+ 6.Kd6 Nxc8+ 7.Kc5+−; 5...Rf6+ 6.Kxf6 Rf7+ 7.Kxf7+−; 5...a1=Q 6.Nf2#) 6.Kd6 Nxc8+ (6...Re6+ 7.Bxe6+−; 6...Rbd7+ 7.Bxd7 Rxd7+ 8.Kxd7+−; 6...Red7+ 7.Bxd7 Rxd7+ 8.Kxd7+−; 6...Nb5+ 7.Kc5+−) 7.Kc5 Rb5+ (7...a1=Q 8.Nf2#) 8.Kc4 Nd6+ (8...Rb6+ 9.Kc3 Rc5+ 10.Kd2 Nc4+ 11.Ke2+−; 8...Rb4+ 9.Kxb4 Rb7+ 10.Kc3+−; 8...Rc5+ 9.Kxc5+−; 8...a1=Q 9.Nf2#) 9.Kc3 (9.Rxd6? a1=Q−+) 9...Rc5+ (9...a1=Q 10.Nf2#) 10.Kd2 Rxc2+ (10...Nc4+ 11.Ke2+−; 10...a1=Q 11.Nf2#) 11.Rxc2 Rg7 (11...

bxc2 12.Nf2#) 12.Nf2#

999 (V. Kuzmichev, 1995) 1.Rh8+! Kg1 (1...Qh4 2.Rxh4++−; 1...Nh5 2.Rxh5+ Kg1 (2...Qh4 3.Rxh4++−) 3.Rh1+! (3.Rg5+ Kf1 4.Rf8+−) 3...Kxh1 4.Rh8+ Kg1 5.Rh1+ Kxh1 6.a8=Q+−) 2.Rh1+! Kxh1 3.Rh8+! Kg1 (3...Nh5 4.Rxh5+ Kg1 (4...Qh4 5.Rxh4++−) 5.Rh1+! Kxh1 6.a8=Q+−) 4.Rh1+! Kxh1 5.a8=Q! Kg1 (5...Qf1+ 6.Kg3+! Kg1 7.Qa7+! Kh1 8.Qb7+ Kg1 9.Qb6+ Kh1 10.Qh6+ Kg1 11.Qh2#; 5...Nf5 6.Kf2+ Kh2 (6...Qd5 7.Qxd5+ Kh2 8.Qg2#; 6...Qe4 7.Qxe4+ Kh2 8.Qg2#; 6...Qc6 7.Qxc6+ Kh2 8.Qg2#) 7.Qg2#; 5...Nh5 6.Kf2+ Kh2 7.Qg2#; 5...Kh2 6.Qh8+ Nh5 (6...Kg1 7.Qxg7++−) 7.Qxh5+ Kg1 8.Qg6+−) 6.a7+! (6.Qa1+?! Qf1+ 7.Qxf1+ Kxf1=) 6...Kh1 (6...Qd4 7.Qxd4++−; 6...Kf1 7.Qf2#; 6...Kh2 7.Qf2+ Kh1 (7...Kh3 8.Qg3#) 8.Qg2#; 6...Qc5 7.Qxc5++−) 7.Qa1+ (7.Qa8 Kg1 8.Qa7+ Kh1) 7...Kh2 (7...Kc1 8.Qxc1++−; 7...Qf1+ 8.Qxf1+ Kh2 9.Qg2#) 8.Qe5+ Kh1 (8...Kh3 9.Qg3#; 8...Kg1 9.Qg3+ Kh1 (9...Kf1 10.Qf2#) 10.Qg2#; 8...Qf4+ 9.Qxf4++−) 9.Qe1+ Kh2 (9...Qf1+ 10.Qxf1+ Kh2 11.Qg2#) 10.Qg3+ (10.Qf2++−) 10...Kh1 11.Qg2#

1000 1.Rxd7+! (1.Bc3?! dxc3−+) 1...Kf8!? (1...Ke8 2.Nf6+

♔f8 3.♘xg4+−; 1...♔xd7
2.♘f6+ ♔d8 3.♘xg4+−)
2.♖d8+ (2.♗c3?! dxc3−+) 2...
♔e7 (2...♔f7 3.♘g5+!+−; 2...
♔g7 3.♖g8+! ♔xg8 (3...♔f7
4.♖xg4+−; 3...♔h7 4.♖xg4+−;
3...♔h6 4.♖xg4+−) 4.♘f6+ ♔f7
5.♘xg4+−) 3.♖e8+! (3.♖d7+
♔f8 4.♖d8+ ♔e7) 3...♔f7 (3...
♔xe8 4.♘f6+ ♔f7 5.♘xg4+−;
3...♔d7 4.♘f6+ ♔d6 5.♘xg4+−)
4.♘g5+! (4.♘d6+?! ♔g7=) 4...
♘xg5 (4...♔xe8 5.♘xf3+−)
5.♖c8! (5.♖xe5? ♘f3−+) 5...
♘f3 6.♖c7+!! (6.♖c1?! ♘g1+=
7.♔d2 (7.♖xg1? ♖xg1−+) 7...
♘f3+ 8.♔c2 (8.♔e2 ♘g1+=) 8...
♖xc1+ 9.♗xc1 (9.♔xc1? g3−+)
9...g3 10.fxg3 fxg3=) 6...♔e8 (6...
♔f8 7.♖c1+−; 6...♔g8 7.♖c1+−;
6...♔f6 7.♖xb6+ ♔f5 8.♖c1+−;
6...♔g6 7.♖xb6+ ♔f5 8.♖c1+−)
7.♖c1 (7.♖c8+?! ♔d7=) 7...
♘g1+ 8.♔d2 ♘f3+ 9.♔c2
♖xc1+ 10.♗xc1 g3 11.fxg3
fxg3 12.♖xb6 g2 13.♖g6 g1=♕
14.♖xg1 ♘xg1+−

www.ingramcontent.com/pod-product-compliance
Lightning Source LLC
Chambersburg PA
CBHW071714120626
46550CB00001B/229